Recruitment, Selection and Deployment of Human Resources

A Canadian Perspective

PH SERIES IN HUMAN RESOURCES MANAGEMENT

HARI DAS

ANDREW TEMPLER, SERIES EDITOR

PEARSON
Prentice
Hall

Toronto

Dedicated to:

My parents who taught me to select the good from the bad,
my teachers who taught me the psychometrics in selection,
my students who inspired me to ask questions about selection, and
my wife who selected me for the good and the bad.

Library and Archives Canada Cataloguing in Publication

Das, Hari, 1948–
Recruitment, selection and deployment of human resources: a Canadian
perspective/Hari Das.

(PH series in human resources management)
ISBN 0-13-127178-4

1. Employees—Recruiting—Textbooks.   2. Employee selection—Textbooks.   I. Title.   II. Series.

HF5549.5.R44D38 2007   658.3'11   C2005-906793-4

ISBN 0-13-127178-4

Vice President, Editorial Director: Michael J. Young
Editor-in-Chief: Gary Bennett
Acquisitions Editor: Karen Elliott
Executive Marketing Manager: Cas Shields
Developmental Editor: Rema Celio
Production Editor: Laura Price
Copy Editor: Nancy Mucklow
Proofreader: Nicole Mellow
Production Coordinator: Deborah Starks
Formatting: Laserwords
Permissions Research: Lynn McIntyre
Art Director: Julia Hall
Cover Design: Julia Hall
Interior Design: Gail Ferreira Ng-A-Kien
Cover Image: Photodisc

21 22 23 CP 15 14 13
Printed and bound in Canada.

PEARSON

Prentice
Hall

Contents

FOREWORD

Human Resources in a Changing World

The world in which HR professionals operate is changing as never before, particularly in the shift towards a knowledge society. Where in the past we used to measure success through production, the basis for success in the new HR reality is knowledge: what we know and how we use it.[1] Changing demographics and the growth in knowledge work mean that the assumptions many HR professionals hold about the nature of the workforce no longer hold. In the foreseeable future, most workers will not be full-time employees, and knowledge workers will dominate the total workforce. Yesterday's reality was characterized by stability, growth, monopolistic markets, and predictable technology: tomorrow's world will be a knowledge society characterized by "borderlessness," increased opportunity, and instability.

Adjusting to this change is not easy. Productivity growth is slowing, our manufacturing sector is under significant competitive stress, and HR expenditures in the public sector are under scrutiny. The impact of globalization, while much debated, has hardly begun to be truly appreciated in Canada. I think the entry of China into the WTO will turn out to be a pivotal event, as world power and benchmarking reference points shift inevitably away from the USA towards Asia.

As the importance of a world of global knowledge and its application to organizational innovation increases, HR professionals are in a position as never before: a position to play a vital role in organizational effectiveness, especially in the battle for corporate talent. However, playing a key organizational role requires qualified professionals. Across Canada, the HR field is demonstrating this need by increasingly requiring the national Certified Human Resources Professional (CHRP) designation, which is characterized by a mix of HR knowledge and applied professional competencies. Students of HRM seeking the knowledge and application base necessary for achieving this designation, and thereby success in the profession, will find the new Prentice Hall Series in Human Resources Management an essential tool for helping them achieve this goal.

The Prentice Hall HRM Series

The Prentice Hall HRM series is designed for today's HR students, instructors, and professionals, who need access to HR knowledge reflecting current realities, rather than yesterday's traditions, and who need it in a usable, applied format that considers their time pressures. Some of the key characteristics of the series are:

- An emphasis on practicality and applicability to daily HR situations
- Ease of use and flexibility
- Incorporation of the CCHRA Required Professional Capabilities for Entry Level Practitioners and Experienced Professionals
- Guidelines for fostering leadership and strategic vision
- Guidelines for evaluating your organization's effectiveness
- A focus on innovations in HRM

The HRM series intends to match all the key knowledge requirements of professional certification with an eye to the evolving nature of these requirements. While in

---

[1]P. F. Drucker. (2001, November). "The Next Society." *The Economist*, 3, pp. 1-20.

transition to a knowledge economy, a qualified workforce equipped with the necessary skills for present and future endeavours remains a critical source of organizational growth and prosperity in Canada. In this context of change and ever increasing competency demands, I am delighted to introduce this new training and development text, which clearly addresses the fundamental contribution of a qualified and skilled workforce to organization effectiveness.

Recruitment, Selection and Deployment

Recruitment, Selection and Deployment: A Canadian Perspective, by Hari Das, presents a carefully reasoned and comprehensive analysis of HR methods, especially recruitment, selection, and placement of talented employees. The author's preface emphasizes the impact of the new knowledge economy and the competitive edge that having the right employees in the right place at the right time can provide. I particularly endorse his emphasis on the need to be lean and flexible in a world of global competition and accountability.

This text is organized in a way that ensures students find useful information quickly and easily. It recognizes the changing reality of knowledge work and competencies in Canada today and hence the need for students to question and think about what they read. Hari Das uses strategic models to introduce each stage of the staffing process: establishing HR plans, setting criteria, recruiting, selecting, deploying, and sometimes, regrettably, terminating. Particularly valuable is Das's emphasis on strategies and audits: a guiding strategic framework must form the basis for all HR plans from the beginning of the staffing process to the end, and an audit must complete, assess, and renew the effectiveness of the process.

A Winning Match between Theory and Practice

The author has specifically incorporated into the text all of the key *Entry Level* Required Professional Capabilities (RPCs) for Staffing as outlined by the Canadian Council of Human Resources Associations (CCHRA), as well as the majority of the *Experienced Professional Level* RPCs. A key strength of *Recruitment, Selection, and Deployment of Human Resources* is the way the author demonstrates a thorough grasp of the essential foundational, social, and psychological principles of HR learning, yet at the same time provides practical applications those principles. Hari Das has combined in-depth coverage of theory with numerous practical applications. These applications include scenarios that demonstrate staffing in action, real-world examples, and guidelines for small businesses. Finally, each chapter has substantial end-of-chapter material, including case studies, critical thinking questions, implications for practice, and web research exercises that will appeal to students and HR professionals alike.

Dr. Andrew Templer
Odette School of Business Administration
University of Windsor
2005

PREFACE

We are at the threshold of a major revolution in the way humans live and work, making this a very exciting era. Consider these facts:

- Vast amounts of information can be stored on tiny media and accessed whenever and wherever we choose.

- The human species is making preparations for possible settlement in space.

- We can travel to any part of the world in mere hours rather than the months or years it took in the not-too-distant past

- Exploring undersea is no longer just a fantasy. Indeed, in the near future, we may even have human settlements underwater.

- Decoding human genes costs just a few hundred dollars today, compared to costs in the millions of dollars in the recent past.

- Billions of dollars of capital move across national borders each hour, something unthinkable to our forefathers.

- Whether you live in downtown Toronto, a remote village in Africa, or a small island close to the Antarctic, you can tune in to your favourite music or news program at your convenience.

These developments have changed the way we think, work, and live. Already, a large number of people don't have to travel to their workplaces to perform their duties—a major shift from the lifestyle we inherited from the Industrial Revolution of the eighteenth century. Moreover, many organizations have made their employees part owners, challenging traditional assumptions about the employer–employee relationship. With high levels of education, today's workers do not want to be led by others: in many settings, they can and want to design, execute, and evaluate plans on their own. Hence, traditional notions of leader–follower relations have become irrelevant. What does this mean for hiring employees?

To succeed, today's organization has to be agile: thinking, performing, and changing continuously. To survive, it must meet the ever-changing needs of the market and constituents. Therefore, its employees must be:

- *focused*—knowing market requirements well and responding to them quickly;

- *fastidious*—aiming for perfection and precision, continuously improving quality;

- *flexible*—always changing their practices to meet emerging challenges and priorities; and

- *fast*—responding faster than competition, maintaining high productivity levels, and processing orders quickly.

To survive and prosper, an organization must have employees of the highest calibre, regardless of whether it is a profit-seeking, private, nonprofit, or governmental organization. Lethargy and inefficiency guarantee failure and possible extinction.

Recruitment, Selection, and Deployment of Human Resources: A Canadian Perspective has been written to help you manage the staffing function effectively. While this book is primarily written for business students at universities and colleges, many managers, owners, and employees will find valuable information that will help improve employee or organizational performance.

1. The book takes a *practical approach* to defining, planning, and executing staffing decisions. While all major theories are covered, they are always discussed from the viewpoint of a practitioner, rather than an arm-chair theorist.

2. The book contains *actual case studies* of real organizations as well as incidents based on real-life events. The book describes how organizations successfully and unsuccessfully made employment-related decisions.

3. The book contains a *large number of forms and "how to" lists* which will facilitate implementation of the recruitment, selection, and deployment strategies discussed.

4. The book has *many figures and diagrams* which aid understanding of the links between concepts.

5. The book deals with the *latest developments* in selection, including measurement of the "g" factor, changes in employment law, and new ideas on test validation.

6. The book *raises ethical issues* critical for successful and long-term performance enhancement.

FOR THE STUDENT

This book has been written with your needs in mind. Whether you are a novice in the area of recruitment and selection or are coming to this field with experience and prior studies, you are likely to find ideas to challenge and help develop your thinking. In particular, the following features will make the learning process easier, as well as more interesting and exciting:

*   A thought-provoking *opening quotation* in each chapter introduces you to the topic and stimulates your interest in the material.

*   The *chapter objectives* inform you of the learning outcomes for each chapter.

*   Most chapters begin with a description of an *experience from a real organization* relevant to the chapter topic. Other chapters provide incidents based on real organizations to highlight the importance of the subject matter.

*   *Easy-to-read, jargon-free language* is used throughout the book.

*   Over 50 *examples or incidents based on actual events* are used to illustrate the concepts.

*   All key concepts are shown in bold letters and their *definitions* provided in the margins for easy reference. A list of key terms with page numbers is also provided at the end of each chapter.

*   Over 100 *figures and charts* are used to illustrate various ideas and concepts.

*   *Focus on Ethics* features help you explore difficult ethical dilemmas facing employment managers.

*   *Critical thinking questions* challenge you to expand on what you have learned by discussing broader, real-life relationships.

*   *Chapter exercises* help you put chapter material into practice by solving realistic problems.

*   *Weblinks* in each chapter help you conduct further research.

FOR THE INSTRUCTOR

Recruitment, Selection and Deployment of Human Resources: A Canadian Perspective includes a variety of features to help instructors prepare and present material:

*   *PowerPoint® slides* are available to help you present the chapter material in class.

*   *Discussion questions* at the end of each chapter help you test students' understanding of the chapter material and suggest topics for class or group discussions.

*   The text contains the *latest information on important concepts*, such as Canadian competitiveness, global trade challenges, and testing.

- *Web research questions* at the end of each chapter help you assign outside-class projects, which can add value and currency to class discussions.

- The *exercises* at the end of each chapter provide material for lively class discussions, while the *case studies* help you test students' ability to synthesize and integrate the material learned.

- The *Focus on Ethics* features provide material for lively class discussions on important ethical issues.

- The *easy-to-read language* used in the text, combined with the large number of *real-life examples*, facilitate student comprehension and heighten student interest in conducting further research

- A *comprehensive Instructor's Manual* containing answers to discussion questions and multiple-choice questions accompanies this text.

FOR THE PRACTITONER AND TRAINER

Whether you are using this book for personal development or to train or advise others, you should find several features of this book very attractive:

- *Over 100 examples and incidents based on real-life events* help you relate performance management concepts to practical work settings.

- The *implications for practice* sections in each chapter help you apply key concepts to real-life settings.

- *Sample forms* help you readily collect and store employment-related information.

- A *"how-to" approach* is emphasized, making it easier to apply the concepts discussed.

- The book emphasizes *generating practical results*. Practical ideas, such as job and task analysis, test validation, exit surveys, and orientation programs, can be implemented to add value and bring about immediate improvements.

FOR THE ASPIRING CERTIFIED HUMAN RESOURCES PROFESSIONAL (CHRP) DESIGNATE

Recruitment, Selection and Deployment of Human Resources: A Canadian Perspective meets all major Required Professional Capabilities (RPCs) listed by the Human Resources Professionals Association of Ontario (HRPAO), other provincial human resource certification bodies, and the Canadian Council of Human Resources Associations (CHRA). Moreover, it focuses on developing the following competencies:

Entry-Level RPCs

- Maintains an inventory of HR talent for the use of the organization.

- Identifies potential sources of qualified candidates, implements and monitors processes for attracting qualified applicants, and evaluates recruitment effectiveness.

- Analyzes position requirements to establish selection criteria.

- Establishes screening and assessment procedures.

- Establishes appointment and deployment procedures.

- Ensures legality and smooth administration of required medical testing.

Experienced-Level RPCs

- Directs the organization in ethical HR practices in staffing.

- Collects data and analyzes and reviews existing HR programs to ensure that they are consistent with business activities.

- Monitors HR activities of the organization and evaluates the effectiveness of employment strategies.
- Identifies legislative challenges and constraints, including issues related to foreign workers and expatriate employees.
- Responds to formal or informal complaints or appeals related to alleged human rights violations.
- Identifies the organization's HR needs and develops systems and processes that link employee career plans and skills with organizational needs.
- Selects candidates and negotiates terms and conditions of employment and, where necessary, develops employment contracts.
- Evaluates screening, selection, and orientation processes and their outcomes.

ACKNOWLEDGEMENTS

The writing of any book requires the cooperation and support of many people and *Recruitment, Selection and Deployment of Human Resources: A Canadian Perspective* is no exception. I am deeply indebted to my reviewers who commented on the manuscript and provided valuable and constructive suggestions. The book is much stronger because of their input:

Wenlu Feng, Centennial College

Carol Ann Samhaber, Algonquin College

Deri Latimer, University of Winnipeg

Barbara Lipton, Seneca College of Applied Arts and Technology

Gordon Hollis, University of Alberta

Don Schepens, Grant MacEwan College

Christine Coulter-Whittaker, George Brown College

I am also thankful to the professional colleagues who helped me produce and improve the manuscript, especially Hermann Schwind, Professor Emeritus at Saint Mary's University. In addition, several of my students were "guinea pigs" for class-testing of the cases and incidents included in the text. I would like to thank all of them for their patience and helpful suggestions in improving the material.

A very special thank you goes to the editorial staff of Pearson Education Canada. Karen Elliott, Acquisitions Editor, shepherded the text along, was a strong believer in the book, and made several constructive suggestions which enhanced its quality. I am also thankful to Rema Celio, Developmental Editor, and Laura Price, Production Editor. Finally, I would like to mention my special thanks to James Bosma, who initiated the project. If not for James' persistence, this book would have never emerged.

Last but not least, I want to express my gratitude to my wife Mallika. During the preparation of the manuscript, Mallika not only took care of my home duties but also critiqued several parts of the book, reviewed cases and incidents, and introduced me to new sources of information. There were times when I also had to seek the help of my daughter Nitya to supply me with the right word for an occasion. My heartfelt thanks to both of them.

Finally, as you, the reader, go through the book, ideas for its improvement are bound to strike you. I would appreciate hearing your comments, whether they are about a topic or chapter that you found particularly informative or one that needed additional details. I can be reached at *hari.das@smu.ca*.

I thank you in anticipation,

Hari Das, Halifax, Nova Scotia

DR. HARI DAS

Dr. Das received his M.Sc. and Ph.D from the University of British Columbia. Currently, he is a Full Professor in the Department of Management teaching graduate and doctoral level courses in human resource management, research methodology, performance management, international management, and organizational change. Dr. Das has served as the Director of the MBA Program and Chair of the Department of Management in Saint Mary's University and has received a teaching excellence award for his work in the EMBA program.

Dr. Das has written over 100 articles and papers in areas such as organizational control, performance appraisal, power and influence, managerial pay, training, and research methodology. He wrote *Organizational Theory with Canadian Applications*, the first Canadian text in organizational theory, and has contributed chapters to *Retail Environments in Developing Countries and Canadian Human Resource Management*. His co-authored work, *Canadian Human Resource Management: A Strategic Approach* is the market leader in the field. His other work, *Strategic Organization Design: For Canadian Firms in a Global Economy*, examines the challenge of preparing Canadian firms to face today's global economy. His last work, *Performance Management*, is the very first university text on the subject.

Dr. Das has served as a consultant to a number of organizations in both private and public sector in Canada and abroad. In addition to being a member of the Academy of Management and the Administrative Sciences Association of Canada, he has served as academic reviewer for professional meetings, journals and granting agencies and as an external examiner for a number of doctoral programs. He can be reached at *hari.das@smu.ca*.

FORMULATION OF HUMAN RESOURCE STRATEGY

In today's global business environment, attracting and retaining competent employees has become a precondition for business success. Organizations—small and large, public and private, profit and nonprofit—recognize the importance of human capital in ensuring survival and success. Indeed, in most instances, the development of human capital is the most critical factor in success, even more than other factors of production such as capital or technology. The first part of this book identifies the steps in formulating a human resource strategy, especially with respect to hiring qualified employees.

1 ESTABLISHING A HUMAN RESOURCE STRATEGY

"The better the fit between the requirements of a job and competencies of the jobholder, the higher the performance and job satisfaction will be."[1]

Lyle Spencer and Signe Spencer

CHAPTER OBJECTIVES

After studying this chapter, you should be able to:

- Discuss the steps in formulating a human resource strategy, especially relating to the employment function

- Discuss the steps in staffing in organizations

- Explain the key competencies of a staffing manager

Tim Campbell was hired into a design team at Canada Software Developers, mainly based on his resume and good references provided by a previous employer. It was only after his probation period that it became obvious that Campbell was not suited for teamwork. Initially, it was thought that his communication and attitude problems were caused by a lack of familiarity with the organization's culture and work procedures, but eventually it was recognized that his rigid and confrontational personality interfered with communication with his co-workers. Because of Campbell, a major project was delayed, a crucial deadline missed, and the project was eventually lost. He had been counselled, warned, and reprimanded, but despite these efforts, there were no visible improvements in his performance. It took the management of Canada Software Developers more than a year and a lot of paperwork before the company was able to dismiss him legally for cause. Meanwhile, the delays in design had cost the company two major projects.

Hiring Tim Campbell was a costly mistake for Canada Software. Not only did the organization lose market opportunities during his tenure, but it also had to expend additional resources to replace him. Unfortunately, Canada Software is not alone in making such mistakes. The lack of aptitude, skills, or motivation on the part of new hires has caused problems for many employers. Past research studies indicate that the cost of such poor decisions is also high. One estimate suggests that the cost of poor performance can be as much as 40% of the employee's annual salary for each year of the employee's tenure with the company![2] Others say that this estimate is too low,[3] especially when the cost of lost opportunities should be included. Other costs include additional training expenses, the cost of recruiting new hires, and potential litigation expenses. There are also the costs involved in lost time, the inefficiency of new recruits (until they reach optimal performance), the inferior performance of their work teams or units, and lost customers due to inferior service or product quality. In contrast, the presence of qualified and motivated employees can generate superior organizational and team performance, high morale, superior customer satisfaction, and better organizational agility to meet future challenges.

This book is about how to attract, hire, and deploy human resources. In this book, you will learn about important concepts related to formulating and implementing a human resource strategy that will attract and retain highly qualified and motivated employees. This chapter will introduce you to the meaning of human resource strategy and the key steps involved in attracting and hiring employees. But before we proceed further, it is important to define human resource strategy and the steps in formulating it.

FORMULATING A HUMAN RESOURCE STRATEGY

A strategy can be compared to a "game plan" for a football or volleyball game. Before a team enters the playing field, the coach looks at the team's strengths and weaknesses and those of its competitors. The coach carefully studies the two teams' past successes, failures, and performances on the field. The objective is to win the game with minimal risk and injuries to the players, and the coach may not use all of the team's best players (the coach may keep some players in reserve for future games or to maintain an element of surprise). Also, the coach might modify the game plan to recognize new realities (perhaps, for example, the opponent will come out playing more aggressively than in the past).

However, a strategy is much more than a game plan. A game plan covers only one game and one opponent, whereas a strategy deals with a number of basic issues (such as technological advancements, changes in customer preferences, and new government regulations) and is oriented towards the many elements of an organization's environments (such as competitors, governments, and employees). A **strategy**, then, is a comprehensive and integrated plan with relatively long-term implications designed to achieve the basic objectives of an organization.

Strategy: a comprehensive, integrated plan with relatively long-term implications designed to achieve the basic objectives of an organization

Examples of strategies include decisions to compete in specific product-market segments, to diversify, to expand, or to close down specific operations.

> Granville Island Brewing of Vancouver, voted best BC microbrewery in 2004, doubled its equity to $3.4 million, achieved sales of 80 000 dozen bottles of beer a year, and acquired beer concessions in major trade fairs within two years of its inception. The strategy responsible for this success—in an industry characterized by fierce competition and slow market growth—was simple: the firm made beer following the Bavarian Purity Laws of 1516, which allow no artificial ingredients. In particular, the company's beer appealed to health conscious, upwardly mobile, young Canadians. The company's Kitsilano Maple Cream Ale was chosen as the best BC beer in 2004.[4]

In the case of Haley Industries Limited, cost control, improved customer relations, and the use of technology led to a successful turnaround.

Haley Industries Limited, Ontario, formerly known as Light Alloys Limited, is one of the world's leading light-alloy aerospace foundries today. However, when Bob Turnbull took his first look at Light Alloys Ltd. in 1967, it had only one positive feature: an attractive price. The federal government was trying to sell the entire assets of the foundry for $1. The company had a loss of $500 000 on sales of $1 million, and was being kept alive only through massive financial aid from the government. Turnbull's turnaround strategy was multi-dimensional: he reduced staff by over 25%; he automated the plant, thus reducing the cost of production; and he emphasized personal relationships with customers. The company also successfully linked itself with winners such as Beech Aircraft, de Havilland, and Cessna. The combination of these strategies paid off, and also opened foreign markets to the company.[5]

Whatever an organization's overall strategy may be, developing human resources is critical to strategic success. **Strategic human resource management (HRM)** links human resource management practices to the strategic needs of an organization and aims to provide it with an effective workforce while meeting the needs of its members and other constituents of the society. Even the best-laid strategies may fail if sound human resource programs and procedures do not accompany them. Strategic HRM is important for organizations in order for them to differentiate themselves from their competitors and achieve a sustainable advantage. Although human resource strategies must be formulated on the basis of organizational strategy, the HR function must play a key role in formulating organizational strategy if the strategy is to succeed.[6] More recently, others have proposed an even more proactive and influential role for the HR function in formulating strategy. Today, it is recognized that HR, like other critical functions such as finance, production, and marketing, should have a clear role in identifying corporate or divisional opportunities and threats, as well as a role in the review of possible strategic options.[7] While "the overall business strategy still provides the foundation on which the HR strategy would be formulated, the business strategy adopted in this manner would be more likely to take into account the constraints and concerns of HR systems."[8] When an organization's human resource strategy and tactics accurately reflect an organization's priorities, the results can be very positive, as Camco's experience illustrates:

> Camco Inc. is the largest Canadian manufacturer and exporter of home appliances including such popular names as GE, Hotpoint, and Moffat. Much of this success is owed to the company's human resource management system that enhances employees' involvement. In the past, Camco's management implemented structural changes that gave additional importance to its human resources. More specifically, it decided to break its organizational chain of command and listen to its workers. The organization's structure became "flat" when every employee was encouraged to talk to everyone else. The results went beyond the most optimistic expectations. Employees made several recommendations that at first seemed unworkable, but because of the commitment of the employees to their ideas, these recommendations became viable. For example, in the production of glass microwave shelves, the employees made a suggestion that was at first considered impractical, but when this suggestion was implemented, it saved Camco $25 000 annually. Productivity improvement in just one year after the change was 25%, while absenteeism went down by 30%.[9]

To be effective, a human resource strategy should be formulated on the basis of an organization's environment, mission, and objectives and its strategic posture and internal strengths and weaknesses, including its culture. Typically, formulating a human resource strategy consists of several steps, as outlined below (see also Figure 1-1).

Strategic human resource management (HRM): links human resource management practices to the strategic needs of an organization and aims to provide it with an effective workforce, while meeting the needs of its members and other constituents of the society

ENVIRONMENTAL ANALYSIS

Through the continuous monitoring of economic, legal, social, and labour-market trends, a human resource manager can identify environmental threats and opportunities, which

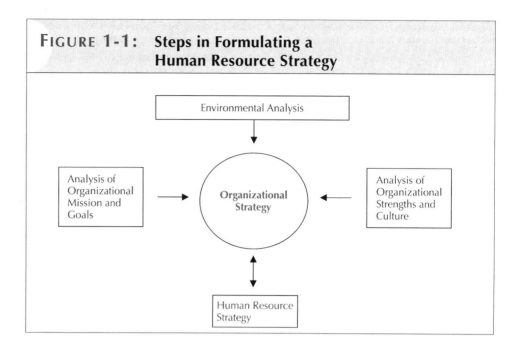

FIGURE 1-1: Steps in Formulating a Human Resource Strategy

will help formulate new strategies and tactics. We will briefly discuss some important environmental trends with implications for the human resource function.

Environmental trend 1: Globalization and the push for productivity

International trade has always been critical to Canada's prosperity. With more than 200 trading partners, on a per capita basis, Canada exports much more than either the United States or Japan.[10] However, what is different today is the extent of Canada's dependence on foreign markets. Today, about one in four jobs depends on exports, which explains the importance of international trade for this country.

> Canada's $418 billion worth of exports amount to more than 40% of gross domestic product (GDP). Imports of $363 billion amount to approximately 35% of GDP, which means that, more than ever before, Canadian economic prosperity is linked to global trade.[11]

The bad news is that compared to other nations, such as China, Canada's share of world trade has been dropping. For example, China has gone from having less than 1% of world trade in 1979 to more than 5% in 2003; Canada's share is about 3% and falling. Canada, which at one time sold more goods and services to the U.S. than any other country in the world, is only third place in the world today, after the European Union and China.[12]

This trend can be partly explained by the emergence of several low-cost trading nations such as Korea, Thailand, China, and India which took away Canada's market shares in traditional strongholds such as pulp and paper, cotton yarn, and steel manufacturing. At the same time, Canada's traditional exports have been adversely affected by the slow growth of our productivity compared to that of the U.S. Unless Canadian firms are able to add value to products or reduce costs, they may not be able to survive in the new marketplace, which asks for continuous improvements in quality, service, and value.[13]

Productivity improvement is one solution for meeting the challenges posed by global competition. **Productivity**, a ratio of an organization's outputs (goods and services) to its inputs (people, capital, materials, and energy), increases as an organization finds new ways to use fewer resources to produce its output. Through gains in productivity, managers can reduce costs, save scarce resources, and enhance profits.

Information on Canada's foreign trade:
www.dfait-maeci.gc.ca/ tna-nac/local_benefits-esn.asp

Productivity: a ratio of an organization's outputs (goods and services) to its inputs (people, capital, materials, and energy)

In 2004, Canada's productivity growth (measured in terms of annual growth rate of GDP per hour worked) was 0%! For our biggest trading partner, the United States, the figure was 3.2%. Indeed, in an OECD study, Canada had the lowest productivity growth rate in 2004 among most of the developed nations, far below the rates for Britain, France, Euro15 (excluding Denmark, Sweden, and the UK) and Germany.[14] Canadian productivity grew at a cumulative rate of 4.2% from 1996 to 1999; the comparable figure for the U.S. was 11.5%.[15] Similarly, comparing Canada's global economic competitiveness (a combination of economic measures) to those of other nations shows that Canada's ranking is slipping, from third place in 2001 to eighth in 2002.[16]

Articles about productivity measurement:
www.policyalternatives.ca
www3.sympatico.ca/
dylan.reid/productivity.htm

In 2005, Canada was ranked 13th in business competitiveness and 14th in growth competitiveness, according to the World Economic Forum. This ranking is far below Canada's potential.[17] A growth competitiveness index, developed by Professor Michael Porter of the Harvard Business School, also suggests that Canada has fallen behind other developed nations in business and growth competitiveness. Professor Porter's index draws on economic data and surveys of nearly 11 000 business leaders in 117 economies around the world to develop microeconomic indicators that measure the set of institutions, market structures, and economic policies supportive of high national prosperity. This index consists of two sub-indices: first, the quality of the business environments, which include a country's financial markets, the impact of competitive pressure, and support in the economy as well as public administrative effectiveness. In this sub-index, Canada held at 13th. In the second sub-index, which measures the sophistication of companies' operations and strategies, Canada fell from 16th to 18th. In 1998, Canada stood 6th in the overall Porter index and by 2004, Canada had fallen to 15th. Among the larger economies, that is, those with half of Canada's population or more, Canada fell from 5th to 7th in one year, and Japan showed the most improvement over the last seven years, moving from 18th to 8th.[18]

Indeed, Canada is last among the Group of Eight (G8) industrialized countries in terms of competitiveness, according to another report:

> According to a study by the Canadian Manufacturers and Exporters, Canada's competitiveness earned 62 points out of a possible 100, compared to 94 points for the U.S. (which was in the first place). Japan was second with 82 points, while the European members of the G8 ranked in the 70s. Canada was last, at a full 10 points behind sixth- place France. It is the second year in a row that Canada has placed last.[19]

If the gap in overall productivity growth between the U.S. and Canada were to persist, this factor alone would reduce Canadian living standards from 61% of U.S. levels in 1999 to 52% in 2010.[20] As one writer put it bluntly, "Productivity . . . it's Canada's most important long-term challenge."[21]

The importance of productivity means that human resource strategy should focus on improving organizational and employee productivity. Canadian competitiveness depends, in part, on developing human resources. As one writer pointed out, "There is no longer such a thing as an unskilled job. The workers of today and tomorrow need to know how to learn so that they can continuously improve their skills after they leave school."[22] Implementing the various tools, systems, and practices discussed in this book can directly contribute to productivity improvement by helping an organization to attract, deploy, develop, and keep human resources. By better matching employees with job demands, an organization can improve the quality of work life, which can indirectly raise productivity levels.

Environmental trend 2: Importance of human capital Human capital is now firmly acknowledged as a strategic source of value creation. Indeed, human capital is a company's most valued asset in today's knowledge-based economy. Most progressive employers realize that the depth and breadth of their employees' talents, education,

experience, knowledge, and skills are the most important assets of the organization. Employers not only have elaborate systems to attract and retain highly competent and motivated employees, but they also continually invest in human capital through training and development activities.

While the development of human capital is critical for all organizations, its impact on organizational performance is most vivid in the case of knowledge workers. Since almost all employees use information to some extent, the ability to process information is key to superior performance, especially in knowledge-based jobs. Knowledge workers, such as scientists, programmers, and consultants, are required to develop ideas and expert opinions.[23] The demand for knowledge workers has exceeded the demand for any other type of worker in the Canadian labour force in the last two decades or so. This demand is expected to be even higher in the foreseeable future.

> While total employment was growing at an average rate of 2.1% per year in the past two decades, the employment of knowledge workers grew at a rate of 5.2% per year. This is twice the hiring rate of service workers, the second fastest-growing group of workers over the same period. Today, information workers constitute over 54% of the labour force. The proportion of the labour force employed in blue-collar and unskilled jobs simultaneously reflects a decrease. In the foreseeable future, the demand for knowledge workers is likely to grow even faster than ever before.[24]

To preserve their valuable asset of human capital, some organizations take extraordinary measures:

> Siemens Canada has introduced an official practice that helps preserve knowledge. A Knowledge Manager is in charge of classifying employees whose knowledge is significant and exceptional, and of high value to the organization. Siemens makes special efforts to maintain that knowledge through employee training, which enables knowledge transfer to other employees. Knowledge workers are also continuously sought after by the firm.[25]

Developing human capital takes time and concerted effort. Organizations may need to make significant additional investments in recruitment and selection systems and to continually develop employees. Such investments, however, provide high return to the employer, as the Watson-Wyatt's study found:

> Watson-Wyatt (WW), a management consulting firm, developed the Human Capital Index[26] (HCI), a measure which links investments in human capital to shareholder values. The HCI measures the relationship between human resource practices and shareholder value, on a scale from 1 to 100, where 1 represents the poorest HC management and 100 represents the ideal relationship. The results of a study involving over 400 publicly traded companies showed that improvement in 30 key HR practices was associated with a nearly 30% increase in the market value of the firm (see Figure 1-2). The HCI is highly predictive of financial success as well. Watson-Wyatt categorized companies in the sample as high-, medium-, and low-HCI, and found that there was a relationship between HCI and the five-year total return to shareholders (TRS). The higher the company's HCI score, the higher the TRS.

As the results of the Watson-Wyatt study reflect, investments in improving human capital pay off in higher returns. Such investments begin with sound hiring and employee-development activities. Despite such research evidence, both American and Canadian organizations have emphasized controlling costs over developing human capital.

> A global survey of 320 organizations, including interviews with 106 corporate heads of HR, found a clear association between increased business profitability and the use of performance measures, management development, and workforce planning. Latin American organizations had the highest number of learning days and more management development and succession planning for middle-level managers. Japanese organizations paid considerable attention to the attraction and retention of key staff. Asian organizations also had the greatest flexibility in staffing. In contrast, North American organizations focused on

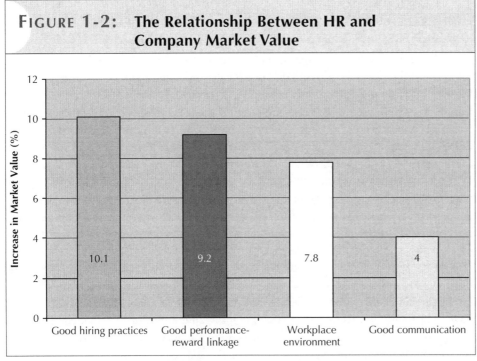

FIGURE 1-2:   **The Relationship Between HR and Company Market Value**

Source: Chart prepared by the author based on Watson-Wyatt study results reported at **http://www.socialfunds.com/news/article.cgi/article493.html,** visited on March 3, 2006 and **http://www.watsonwyatt.com/surveys/hci,** visited on March 13, 2005.

individual learning, and succession plans in the American and Canadian organizations were limited to senior executives. Few organizations surveyed held their executives accountable for improving and retaining human capital.[27]

Environmental trend 3: Shifting demographic characteristics and workforce diversity
Five major developments in Canada's demography and population are significant when formulating HR strategy:

1. Increasing participation by women The rate of women participating in the labour force has been steadily increasing. An estimated 82% of Canadian women aged 25 to 44 years are currently in the labour force. It is interesting to note that compared to the rates of several other industrialized nations, the participation rate of Canadian women is high. Today, compared to a decade ago, fewer women work in non-professional occupations (such as clerical and sales), and proportionately more work in management, law, engineering, and medicine. The fact that women accounted for 70% of the total employment growth in Canada in the last two decades has highlighted the need for adequate childcare, counselling for two-career families, and employment equity.[28] Furthermore, while the percentage of women in the workforce has been increasing rapidly, most CEOs, board members, and senior executives are still men. The sexual segregation of occupations and organizations continues to haunt the Canadian economy, as does pay inequity between men and women.

2. Coexistence of highly skilled and semi-literate employees While an increasing number of organizations require highly skilled and knowledgeable workers, the proportion of people with low literacy levels in the Canadian population continues to be unacceptably high, compared to the populations of other developed nations:

In a survey of 20 countries conducted by the Organization for Economic Cooperation and Development, Canada ranked behind several countries such as Sweden, Finland, Norway,

Information on essential skills:
*www.ppforum.com/
skills_symposium/
backgrounder_e.pdf*

Information on workplace
literacy:
*www.conferenceboard.ca/
workplaceliteracy*

and Denmark. Literacy was defined as the ability of adults to use written information to function in society, to achieve their goals, and to develop their knowledge and potential. Close to 50% of Canadians were found to be unable to work well with words and numbers.[29]

While formal educational attainment among workforce entrants is at an all-time high, the skills of these individuals are not well matched to organizational needs.[30] Further, an estimated 20% of Canadians aged 16 or over (or approximately 5 million Canadians) fall in the lowest level of literacy and have difficulty understanding printed materials and most likely experience problems reading any written words.[31] These individuals are unable to complete a cheque or fill out a job application form.[32] The mathematical skills of many Canadian students compared to those of Asian and European students are quite poor. In 2004, nearly three-quarters of Ontario Grade 9 students failed to meet provincial standards in mathematics, forcing the provincial government to make major alterations to the mathematics curriculum.[33] Statistics such as these pose great challenges to human resource managers, especially when hiring and placing employees. In the absence of rigorous and valid selection procedures, job applicants with high expectations but without basic skills might enter the organization. On the other hand, recruits who lack basic verbal and quantitative skills may not understand sophisticated selection tests or other assessment devices. Selection tools have to be continually refined to match the individual applicant's characteristics. Some progressive employers, such as Syncrude Canada, have also taken proactive measures to develop their employees:

> Syncrude Canada's trend-setting program Effective Reading in Context (ERIC) was initiated in 1988 to tackle the issue of workplace illiteracy. Since then, this program has been expanded to include a wide range of courses, including a math upgrade program called Working in Numeracy, a workplace writing fundamentals course, advanced math for engineers, and applied mechanics and physics courses. ERIC has since been adapted for use by other businesses such as Schuller International Canada, Alberta Power, and Imperial Oil.[34]

3. *Workforce diversity*

The coexistence of anglophones and francophones along with dozens of other national, racial, and ethnic groups, each with its unique cultural and social background, makes Canadian society a cultural mosaic.[35] In addition to contributing to canada's cultural diversity, immigrants can also encourage economic growth.

> The number of visible minorities in Canada is expected to double by 2017 and form more than half the population in greater Toronto and Vancouver. If current demographic trends hold, one in every five faces in this country will be non-white in twelve years.[36] Currently, only 47% of the total immigrants originate from Britain or other European countries.[37] Today, almost 5 million Canadians are referred to as allophones, which literally means "other-speaking." That is a 15% increase since 1991, with Chinese surpassing Italian for the first time as the most common non-official language.[38]

Canadian organizations need to alter their hiring practices to respond to this societal change, as the Toronto Police recognized recently:

> Toronto police departments must "outreach like crazy" to recruit more people from visible minority groups according to Jay Hope, superintendent of the Ontario Provincial Police. There are very few black police officers in Canada, he said: just 350 in Ontario, and 660 in law-enforcement occupations across the country. Diversity must be pursued at all ranks to better reflect the communities they serve and to create more role models for visible minorities.[39]

By and large, Canada has done well in assimilating and fostering different cultures. However, there are many instances when new immigrants face obstacles such as the prevalence of culturally biased selection tools and the unwillingness of employers to recognize foreign credentials. The Canadian government's Internationally Trained Worker Initiative has an entire program dedicated to simplifying the recognition of foreign

Information on diversity
management:
www.gendertraining.com

credentials, but until professional bodies and private employers change their practices, these obstacles will remain a major employment hurdle to new arrivals.[40]

> Professional bodies, such as the Canadian Council of Professional Engineers, have begun to make efforts to simplify the recognition of foreign qualifications. However, the number of highly skilled immigrants working in low-skilled and low-paid jobs in Canada is at an unacceptable level. There are doctors driving taxicabs, engineers and accountants working as cleaners, and veterinarians employed as security guards.[41]

Ignorance about other cultures fosters stereotypes about immigrants. Roughly 4 million Canadians, that is, one in six adults, have been victims of racism, according to a 2005 national survey.[42] A majority of the respondents in the survey felt that racism in their communities had not diminished in the last five years; instead, according to 17% of the respondents, racism had been on the increase. Muslims and Arabs topped the list as targets of racism, while aboriginals, blacks, East Indians, and Jews were not far behind. As one immigrant from Pakistan pointed out:

"There's still racism in Canada. There are obstacles many of us face because our skin may not be as fair as those of some others, or because our ways seem odd. ... I remember one interview at a pharmaceutical company. On the phone, the interviewer was more than enthusiastic about me and my credentials. As soon as I got there, he saw my hijab and his jaw literally dropped. ... it was clear that I was not getting the job."[43]

Selection procedures that are valid for the mainstream white community may not be valid for members of minority groups. In meeting potential new employees, the members of an organization might have to alter their prevailing assumptions about appropriate behaviour:

> Many Canadian employers believe that a firm handshake reflects character and that looking someone in the eye indicates trustworthiness. However, for many Asians, looking someone in the eye is a mark of disrespect and is to be avoided at all costs. People originating from several cultures do not greet others by shaking hands. Indeed, touching someone, especially of the opposite gender, may be taboo in some cultures.

4. An Aging and declining population
Several industrialized, western nations currently experience declining population growth. Canada is no exception.

Statistics Canada website: *www.statcan.ca*

> For the first time in its history, Canada is facing a population decline. Even to keep the population at its current level, Canada will require more immigrants because Canada's fertility rate is 1.5 (the average number of children a woman will have over her lifetime), well below the rate of 2.1 children per woman needed to sustain the population.[44] Between 1994 and 2004, the Canadian population grew by approximately 1%, but the natural increase in population during this time was only 0.39%, and it was the arrival of large numbers of immigrants that helped the country maintain its required growth.[45] In years to come, the immigration figures may have to rise even faster if we are to combat a shrinking workforce caused by an aging population and declining births. By 2010, the 65-and-over age group will form approximately 14% of the Canadian population. The average age of the population will then approach 41 years. But the workforces in several other countries such as India and Mexico will be much younger: the average age will be under 30 years.[46] By 2015, our domestic labour force will actually begin to shrink, which means that all of the net growth will need to come from new Canadians.[47]

In 1993, the ratio of Canadians aged 15 to 24 to those aged 55 to 64 was 2:1. By 2015, the same ratio will flip to 1:2.[48] Tight labour markets will result in employers competing more aggressively to find the needed labour to make their operations successful. This, in turn, will necessitate more innovative recruiting practices and more attractive rewards, making the future years "the decade of the employee."[49]

5. Changing priorities of employees The expectations and work attitudes of employees can vary markedly, depending on their age, family status, and other socio-economic and demographic variables. For example, "boomers" (born between 1940 and 1960) are significantly different in their values and behaviours than are "X-ers" (born between 1960 and 1980) or the Generation Y segment of the population. Generation Y, also known as the "echo boomers" and the "millennium generation", refers to the approximately 6.9 million Canadians born between the years 1977 and 1994 (i.e., the children of baby boomers). Members of Generation Y are often described as pragmatic, savvy, socially and environmentally aware, and open to new experiences.

> Some people claim that X-ers think of work as a "job," while boomers are in the middle of a "career." Generation X-ers are unfazed by power and authority; boomers are impressed and attracted by it. X-ers see scarcity; boomers see abundance. X-ers mistrust most business practices; boomers instituted many of them and defend them. X-ers are more self-reliant; while boomers are team-oriented.[50] Generation Y workers fear boredom and continuously develop opportunities. If they do not find them at the workplace, they are more likely to walk out the door in disillusionment.[51] Generation Y employees have grown up in a media-saturated environment, tend to be aware of "marketing hype,"[52] and are cynical of the claims made by organizations. Unlike boomers, they are more Internet savvy and, compared to their parents, they are less likely to read newspapers. They also do not trust many of the organizations their parents deal with.[53] The newest generation of Canadians may also be somewhat disengaged from their surroundings.[54]

To meet the needs of the Generation X and Y workforce, employers may need to radically alter work practices and systems. Generation Y employees have been found to be completely unresponsive to "or else" motivational tactics and are likely to leave the employer much faster than their parents or grandparents would have.[55] They are also more likely to bluntly tell their superiors and other employees exactly what they think of a situation. When boomers were growing up, work was harder to come by, and job hunters were taught to show respect and enthusiasm. This is not the situation with Generation Y employees. They are easily turned off with inflexible hours, nasty bosses, and a work atmosphere that is not fun.[56] Fundamental changes in work-related attitudes,[57] including notions of fairness and equity at the workplace, must change to attract and keep the new generation of workers.

Environmental trend 4: Computerization and changing work requirements As in most other developed countries, computers have become an integral part of Canadian life, changing the way we work and play.

> Currently, half of Canadian households have at least one person who regularly accesses the Internet. Over 40% of Canadian adults have access to the Internet, making us one of the most wired nations in the world.[58]

The arrival of computers and the Internet has helped us break temporal and geographic barriers. At the click of a mouse, an organization's manager located in Guelph can compare the performance, pay, absenteeism, and safety records of the organization's workforce in Victoria and Halifax, and transfer large data files to India or Brazil. Often, decisions that took weeks to make in the past can now be made in minutes, giving the information the important property of timeliness. For many jobs, computers permit employees to telecommute: that is, to work without ever leaving their homes by using the Internet, fax, telephones, and other communication devices. While **telecommuting** cuts employee stress, boosts productivity, and reduces operating costs,[59] it also requires changes in human resource practices. Computerization has also accelerated the trend towards the automation of all routine operations, which has changed the workforce profile in many organizations. Well-planned human resource management systems help to mesh new and existing technologies and help to avoid employee stress

Telecommuting: employees work at home using the Internet, fax, telephone, and other communication devices

and turnover. Thorough job analysis and careful identification of needed competencies can be invaluable to an organization's efforts to take full advantage of emerging technology.

Environmental trend 5: Ever-increasing legal requirements Today's employment manager must abide by an increasing array of federal and provincial laws and city and municipal regulations. The most applicable ones in this situation are the *Canadian Charter of Rights and Freedoms*, the *Canadian Human Rights Act*, the *Canada Labour Code*, the *Hazardous Products Act*, the Canada Pension Plan, provincial minimum wages acts, and the provincial workers' compensation acts. However, a large number of other acts, regulations, and court decisions regulate and direct the activities of employers and managers:

> For example, the law requires that an applicant's characteristics such as gender, race, and physical characteristics (e.g., height) cannot be used for selection purposes unless the employer can prove that these characteristics are related to performance. Even where a particular attribute (e.g., height) or behaviour (e.g., not working on a specific day of the week because the day is a religious holiday) is job-relevant, past court decisions indicate that the onus is on the employer to show that with reasonable accommodation, persons who score low on that attribute or behaviour cannot perform satisfactorily.

The specific implications of such legal requirements for employment practices will be discussed in detail in Chapter 3 of this book. In all instances, the employer should clearly define and accurately measure performance requirements in order to avoid possible litigation.[60] The following case illustrates this point.

> The owner of Hamilton Tools, a small engineering firm, terminated a supervisor in charge of 18 employees. The supervisor had been employed in the firm for over 20 years. The owner claimed that the supervisor's performance had gradually deteriorated, although he did not produce any evidence supporting this claim. In an out-of-court settlement, the owner had to pay over $100 000 to the supervisor for wrongful dismissal.

ANALYSIS OF ORGANIZATIONAL MISSION AND GOALS

Even similar organizations often pursue different goals. A thorough organizational analysis, involving a close look at the organization's overall mission and goals, is another integral aspect of identifying human resource strategies.

All organizations exist to accomplish something in their larger environments. The mission—the purpose of an organization's existence—should guide strategic thinking. In identifying the mission, the organization's members should ask some fundamental questions, such as: What is our business? Who is the customer? What represents value to the customer? What will our business be? What should our business be?[61]

A **mission statement** specifies the activities the organization intends to pursue and its future course. The mission statement is a concise statement of "who we are, what we do, and where we are headed" and gives an organization its own special identity, character, and path of development.

> For example, two similar electronic manufacturers have varying missions. One manufacturer's mission is "to be a successful organization in the entertainment business," while the other's is "to occupy a technological leadership position in the industry." The associated strategies showed significant differences. Apart from manufacturing electronic goods for home entertainment, the former firm acquired video and film production firms and got into the music industry (e.g., produce CDs); while the focus of the second firm was to develop innovative electronic products through research. The associated human resource strategies also

Information on computers and productivity: *www.csls.ca/events/ceal1998/ revpaper.asp*

Information on employers' legal obligations: *www.employers.gc.ca*

Mission statement: specifies the activities the organization intends to pursue and its future course

showed variation. For example, achieving excellence in customer service was a guiding principle in the former firm's employment strategy, but hiring high-calibre technical personnel who could design innovative products was a priority of the latter organization.

ANALYSIS OF ORGANIZATIONAL STRENGTHS AND CULTURE

Before formulating a human resource strategy, the organization should carefully examine its strengths, weaknesses, opportunities, and threats. An organization should avoid goals that cannot be attained within its human resource capabilities (unless the organization has adequate resources to remove such deficiencies). Consider this example:

> Calgary Electronics, which employs twelve salespeople and seven service and repair personnel, was concerned about the growing competition in the electronics equipment market. Historically, the firm had sold and repaired all makes of electronic and electrical equipment (ranging from blenders to large-screen TVs and complex security alarm systems). To meet the competition, the firm initially decided to implement an aggressive advertising and personal-selling strategy. However, a detailed investigation into the company's past performance indicated that the strength of the firm lay in its prompt and cheap repair service. A review of the employee skills and training also indicated that several of the salespeople did not have any formal training in selling. Based on the results of the internal analysis, Calgary Electronics decided to focus on repairs and after-sales service in its advertising campaigns.

Organizational culture: the patterns of behaviour, underlying values, beliefs, meanings, and knowledge shared by the members of an organization, as shaped by all of the organization's features (employees, objectives, technology, size, age, unions, policies, and views on successes and failures)

Every organization is unique. Organizations can be similar, but each organization has a unique character. **Organizational culture** refers to the distinctive patterns of behaviour and the underlying values, beliefs, meanings, and knowledge shared by the members of an organization.[62] The culture is shaped by all of the organization's features: employees, objectives, policies, technology, size, age, unions, and views on successes and failures.[63] Some organizations have a very strong culture, which acts as a driving force behind most of the organization's actions. Consider the example of the Sierra Systems Group:

> Sierra Systems Group Inc, established in 1966, is perhaps Canada's oldest information technology consulting firm and one of the most successful, with nearly 1000 employees working in fifteen locations and annual sales exceeding $120 million.[64] When Sierra went public in 1998, the firm created the positions of a chief executive officer, a chief financial officer, and several vice presidents to satisfy securities regulators. Beyond these three management positions, there are only three other job categories in the firm: partners who manage the branches across the country, principals who are in charge of projects, and the consultants who work under the principals. Sierra Systems is a flat organization, and the "flat" principle extends to more than just the job titles. All employees are expected to take courses continuously to upgrade their skills. Every one participates in the profit-sharing plan, and every one is encouraged to constantly think about change and suggest ways of successfully meeting it. Needless to say, the type of employees who are attracted to the organization and the firm's hiring procedures reflect Sierra System's differences from other firms operating in the same field.[65]

Equifinality: the idea that there are usually many paths to any given objective

Human resource specialists should be familiar with and adjust to the character of the organization. For example, it is sometimes overlooked that objectives can be achieved in several acceptable ways. This idea, called **equifinality**, means there are usually many paths to any given objective. The key to success is picking the path that best fits the organization's character:

> Human resource manager Clayton Johnson feared that his request to hire a training assistant would be turned down. So instead of asking for funds to hire someone, Clayton expressed concern that poor supervisory skills were contributing to employee complaints and

turnover. He observed at the weekly management meeting that unskilled replacements could lead to rising labour costs. Knowing that top management was concerned that the company remain a low-cost producer, Clayton was not surprised when the plant manager suggested hiring "someone to do training around here." Clayton got a budget increase for training. By adjusting to the organization's character, he achieved his objective.

ANALYSIS OF ORGANIZATIONAL STRATEGY

Organizational and human resource strategies are intricately intertwined. Many believe that HR strategy must be formulated on the basis of organizational strategy. However, more firms are recognizing that organizational strategy should take into account the firm's HR strategy and constraints.[66]

The members of each organization represent a unique set of skills and capabilities. Organizational **core competencies** are the skills or capabilities in value-creating activities—such as manufacturing, marketing, or research and development—that allow an organization to achieve superior quality, product innovation, low cost, or better customer responsiveness, and thus to outperform its competitors. Core competencies permit an organization to enter new market segments faster than its rivals through strategies that capitalize on those strengths.

> Gillette applied its superior marketing competence in selling razor blades to selling other products such as toiletries.

The quality of core competencies depends on specialized resources and organizational ability. Specialized resources include the technical skills of the organization's employees, the skills of top managers, the vision of the CEO, and access to valuable and scarce resources. Organizational ability refers to the firm's ability to manage these resources to create maximal value, through the creation of an appropriate internal structure and culture. Other factors related to organizational ability are internal communication systems and the control systems for motivating and coordinating member behaviour.

Even though each organization is unique, organizations can be similar. However, organizations with similar goals and operating in the same industry show remarkable differences in their strategies to achieve those goals. There are at least three major generic strategies that a firm may pursue: cost leadership, differentiation, or focus.[67]

An organization that pursues a **cost leadership strategy** aims to gain a competitive advantage through lower costs. It aggressively seeks efficiencies in production and uses tight controls (especially in managing costs) to gain an advantage over its competitors.

> Wal-Mart is a good example of a firm that successfully competes in the retail business by offering "everyday low prices." Similar cost leadership strategies are seen in the case of Timex (watches), ABC Detergent (detergents), and Federal Express (overnight package delivery).

Product differentiation strategy focuses on creating a distinctive or even a unique product that is unsurpassed in quality, innovative design, or other feature, which may be accomplished through product design, unique technology, or through carefully planned advertising and promotion. The firm that employs this strategy may even be able to charge a higher than average price for its product.

> Bose (speakers), iPod (Apple), Nikon (cameras), and Calvin Klein (fashion apparel) employ a differentiation strategy and by doing so command a premium price for their products.

Under the **focus strategy**, a firm concentrates on a segment of the market and attempts to satisfy that niche market with a highly distinctive product. The niche market may be defined by geographical boundaries or special consumer needs.

> Topol (toothpaste), Nuvo (magazine), and Listel (boutique hotel) are examples of products that are aimed at very specific niche markets.

Core competencies: skills and capabilities in value-creating activities (such as manufacturing, marketing, or research and development) that allow an organization to achieve superior quality, product innovation, low cost, or better customer responsiveness, and thus to outperform competitors

Cost leadership strategy: gaining a competitive advantage through lower costs

Product differentiation strategy: creating a distinctive/unique product unsurpassed by competitors in quality, innovative design, or other feature

Focus strategy: focusing on one segment of the market and satisfying that niche market with a highly distinctive product

FORMULATION OF THE HUMAN RESOURCE STRATEGY

Depending on the overall strategies employed by organizations, the priorities of human resource department strategies will vary substantially. Figure 1-3 outlines key differences in HR priorities under three different corporate strategies.

Whatever the specific HR strategy of an organization may be, it must be closely aligned with the organization's priorities and be implemented in a timely fashion as the following example of Canada Power Corporation illustrates:

> Canada Power Corporation, a large electric utility, decided to reduce coal burning and shift to hydro power. This decision in turn necessitated the replacement of its plant and equipment as well as the development of new employee skills. The changeover from existing HR systems (e.g., compensation, appraisal, and training) had to be smooth and cause as little disruption to the work as possible. A strategy based on considerable in-house and external training was drawn up and implemented. By the time Canada Power switched to hydro power, it had the necessary supply of skilled labour.[68]

Popular human resource strategies Identifying the HR strategy of an organization is often a complex task. It is not unusual to see the same organization adopting somewhat different employment practices for different employee groups or in different regions.[69] "Although in any given organization, there tends to be a *dominant* HR strategy or HR system architecture, on a more operational level multiple bundles of HR practices unique to particular organizational subgroups are likely to develop."[70] Recent research studies[71] have identified four archetypical HR strategies: commitment, paternalistic, compliance, and collaborative.

Commitment strategy: forging a common interest between the organization (often symbolized by the management) and its employees

Commitment strategy A **commitment strategy** attempts to forge a common interest between the organization (often symbolized by the management) and its employees. To develop that common interest, the organization emphasizes employee training and development, internal staffing, and career development, and formulates compensation levels on the basis of internal equity norms rather than market rates.[72]

Compliance strategy: focusing on achieving labour efficiencies through control over labour costs, temporary or contingent workers, and control over processes

Compliance strategy In a **compliance strategy**, the focus is achieving labour efficiencies through controlling labour costs, employing temporary or contingent workers, and maximizing control over processes and using this control as a key competitive weapon. Jobs are designed to be simple to ensure a constant and stable supply of

FIGURE 1-3: Variations in HR Priorities Under Different Strategies

	Cost Leadership	Focus	Differentiation
Employee skills	Narrow	Moderate	Broad
Employee flexibility	Low	Moderate	High
Focus on quantity of production	High	Moderate	Moderate
Employee behaviours	Predictable, repetitive	Moderately creative, yet predictable	Creative, nonrepetitive

Source: Adapted from Hari Das, *Performance Management*, 2003, p.13. Toronto: Pearson Education. Reprinted with permission from Pearson Education Canada.

employees and to reduce training costs. To ensure uninterrupted production and eliminate all uncertainties, employees are expected to behave in a prescribed manner. Their work is closely monitored by their supervisors.[73] In many instances, the employer may also seek efficiency by shifting production infrastructures to areas in which trade unions and government regulations pose fewer constraints on management. At times, the employer may woo new immigrants or people who have temporary work visas in order to reduce costs.

Paternalistic strategy Under a **paternalistic strategy**, an organization can achieve flexibility in staffing and maintain workforce stability through training and job rotation. Management typically provides some employment guarantees as well as a system of internal staffing, typically based on seniority.[74] The employer also offers adequate rewards to maintain the stability of the workforce. The organization does achieve a limited degree of learning capability that is not available in a compliance strategy.

Paternalistic strategy: achieving flexibility in staffing and maintaining workforce stability and competency through training, job rotation, and employment guarantees

Collaborative strategy Under the **collaborative strategy**, an organization relies on highly skilled contract workers to supply the needed specialized work by hiring them "as needed" or retaining them on an "on-call" basis. These highly skilled and specialized "crafts" people[75] are, most often, solely evaluated on the basis of their performance outcomes. "Because they are employed to provide certain outputs or 'deliverables' but engage in processes that are often well beyond the ability of the employer to comprehend, contingent pay (rather than in-house socialization or employee development) is often used to align their interests with those of their employer and to ensure that organizational objectives are met."[76] Often, "virtual organizations" choose this strategy.[77]

Collaborative strategy: relying on highly skilled contract workers to supply the needed specialized work by hiring them "as needed" or retaining them on an "on-call" basis

An organization may employ several strategies at different stages of its life cycle or in dealing with different labour markets. However, this schema can help us understand some key correlates of HR strategies (see Figure 1-4). However, given the nascent nature of HR strategy research, conclusions based on this research should be cautiously adopted.

FIGURE 1-4: Some Correlates of HR Strategies

Dimension	Type of HR Strategy			
	Commitment	*Compliance*	*Paternalistic*	*Collaborative*
Primary HR-related objective	Maximize employee involvement; Retain employee knowledge and human capital	Low labour cost; Remove uncertainties in production process; ensure continuous supply of cheap labour	Ensure continuous production, and ensure employees have the requisite capabilities to meet new challenges	Maintain high efficiency by routinizing the process and subcontracting work to qualified professionals
Type of input-output conversion processes and technology used	Complex; Management lacks complete understanding of the transformation process	Simple; Management is fully aware of the transformation process; Jobs are simple	Relatively simple; Management is mostly aware of the transformation process	Complex; Management has very limited knowledge of the transformation process

FIGURE 1-4: *(Continued)*

Dimension	Type of HR Strategy			
	Commitment	*Compliance*	*Paternalistic*	*Collaborative*
Degree of employee behaviour monitoring	Low; Employees are controlled through shared values	High; Employees closely monitored for their behaviours and outputs	Fairly high, though lower than compliance model	Low; Employees are professionals hired to do specific jobs and evaluated on their outcomes only
Focus on employee training and development	High	Minimal	Some level of training is offered so employees have the minimal capabilities to meet new challenges	No training is offered
Focus on maintaining internal equity in rewards	High	Moderate (only to the level to maintain undisrupted production)	Fairly high; Seniority is often used as a norm to maintain equity	Reward system is based on external market norms
Assumptions about the nature of employer-employee relations	Focus on mutual interests and establishing long-term relationships	Employer continually searching for low-labour cost alternatives; Relationship focuses on short to medium term	Medium-to long-term relationship; Management offers certain employment guarantees to ensure uninterrupted production	Employees are contract workers who, when needed, will be rehired if proven competent

Source: This table was prepared by the author. The data are based on findings reported in a number of research studies including the following: J. Arthur. (1994). "Effects of Human Resource Systems on Manufacturing Performance and Turnover," *Academy of Management Journal, 37* : 670–87; Peter Bamberger and Ilan Meshoulam. (2000). *Human Resource Strategy* (Thousand Oaks, California: Sage Publications); D.P. Lepak and S.A. Snell. (1999). "The Strategic Management of Human Capital: Determinants and Implications of Different Relationships." *Academy of Management Review, 24,* 1, pp. 1–18; J.P. MacDuffie. (1995). "Human Resource Bundles and Manufacturing Performance: Organizational Logic and Flexible Production Systems in the World of Auto Industry." *Industrial and Labor Relations Review 48,* pp. 197–221; L. Dyer and G.W. Holder. (1988). "A Strategic Perspective of Human Resources Management." In L. Dyer and G.W. Holder (eds). *Human Resources Management: Evolving Roles and Responsibilities.* (Washington, D.C.: American Society for Personnel Administration) pp. 1–45; D. Organ. (1988). *Organizational Citizenship Behaviour* (Lexington: MA, D.C. Heath); P. Osterman. (1987). "Choice of Employment Systems in Internal Labour Markets." *Industrial Relations 26,* 1 pp. 48–63; P. Osterman. (1995). "Work/Family Programs and the Employment Relationship." *Administrative Science Quarterly 40,* pp. 681–700; P.M. Swiercz. (1995). "Research Update: Strategic HRM." *Human Resource Planning 18,* 3, pp. 53–62.

In summary, HR strategies vary depending on the organization's strategic posture and size, nature of its environment, and technology. Of these, the factor of strategic posture is particularly important, since it reflects the role that a firm has carved out for itself in the marketplace. Is the organization a leader or a follower in the marketplace? Is the organization a *defender*,[78] that is, a conservative business unit that prefers to maintain a secure position in relatively stable product or service areas instead of expanding into unchartered territories? Or, is it a *prospector* which emphasizes growth, entrepreneurship, and an eagerness to be the first player in a new market or to be selling a new product? Defender organizations are more likely to focus on control, to emphasize predictability in operations, and to foster long-term employee attachment to the firm. In contrast, prospector organizations focus on creating flexible, decentralized structures that encourage creativity and reward risk taking. The role and overall philosophies of human resource departments also reflect marked differences even in organizations competing in the same industry.

STEPS IN STAFFING

Once an organization has established an overall HR strategy, it is important that the organization implement the strategy in an effective and timely fashion. To achieve implementation, the HR department establishes and administers various systems and practices including those related to hiring, training, compensation, performance evaluation, safety and health, and communication with employees. Given the theme of this book, our primary concern will be with the hiring and deployment of human resources although it should be clearly understood that these activities are influenced by, and in turn influence, all other HR systems and activities. Figure 1-5 illustrates the relationship between corporate strategy and the employment function, or staffing.

Once the organization identifies the broad HR strategy, the next step is to identify the required employee competencies before any hiring can take place. A **competency** is a knowledge, skill, ability, or characteristic associated with high performance on a job, such as problem solving, analytical thinking, or leadership.[79] Competencies can also denote an "attribute bundle," consisting of task competencies; and knowledge, skill, behaviour, and attitude competencies.[80] The objective of identifying competencies in almost all instances is to identify characteristics that are associated with superior job performance. The employer can identify competencies after careful analysis of the work of effective employees through observation, by noting critical behaviours or work incidents, through interviews, by reading employee logs, or otherwise. More on identifying competencies will be discussed in Chapter 2.

Staffing can be defined as a matching process between an organization and an individual to form an employment relationship that facilitates high organizational and employee performance and fosters employee morale and a desired organizational culture. This definition underscores several important attributes of the staffing process such as the following:

- Staffing is a planned, ongoing process consisting of a number of steps such as recruitment, selection, hiring, and deployment.

- It is integral to the organization's overall plan to compete and succeed in the marketplace.

Competency: a knowledge, skill, ability, or characteristic associated with high performance on a job, such as problem solving, analytical thinking, or leadership

Staffing: a matching process between an organization and an individual to form an employment relationship that facilitates high organizational and employee performance and fosters employee morale and a desired organizational culture

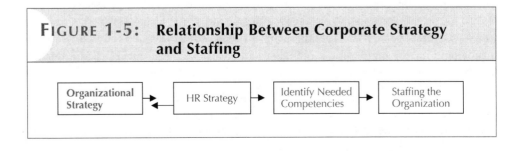

FIGURE 1-5: **Relationship Between Corporate Strategy and Staffing**

Organizational Strategy → HR Strategy → Identify Needed Competencies → Staffing the Organization

- Staffing is not an end onto itself. It is a process to attain and enhance organizational success and effectiveness and to be consistent with an organization's resources and overall strategy.

- Through an effective staffing system, the employer does not stop at simply hiring competent people but goes beyond this goal to deploy the hired employees in positions which best make use of their talents and offer opportunities to develop them.

- Also through an effective staffing system, the employer may respond to and foster the culture of the organization.

The last point about culture requires further elaboration. Today, the critical link between the organization's culture and its success is clearly recognized. Technology, capital, land, and other factors of production are available to all organizations; what often separates successful organizations from the mediocre is the quality of their employees. In turn, these employees create a work culture that has a strong beneficial impact on the organizational and individual performance.

> Organizations such as Southwest Airlines, 3M, Disney, Dofasco, Scotiabank, and Marriott are known for their cultures, which have a strong impact on employee attitudes and performance. On joining these organizations, new hires are socialized into the organization's culture and way of dealing with the organization's customers and its public.

The flow of people into and within the organization is managed through the various activities that form part of the staffing function. Ideally the goal of these staffing activities should be to ensure a perfect fit between a candidate's expectations and his or her personality with what the organization is able to offer. When an organization oversells a job, it creates expectations in the mind of the applicant that may be difficult or impossible to meet. The result can be employee alienation or even possible turnover, as one company learned:

> When Frederic Schmidt graduated from the university of Toronto as a mechanical engineer, he was interviewed by Star Detergents, a large U.S. detergent manufacturer. During the hiring process, the interviewers emphasized the attractive salary, almost unlimited career growth potential, and several employee benefits. Later, star Detergents made a job offer to Schmidt, who accepted the position and entered the organization with great expectations. Only during an orientation program was it revealed that this company had a policy that each management candidate had to start at the lowest job level, that is, working at the "freezing tower" for at least six months. The salary would be at a manager's level, but the job would entail mainly servicing the tower equipment. This organizational reality, though probably an effective one for learning the production processes, was so contrary to Frederic's expectations that he left the organization within two months of arriving.

The manufacturer could have avoided this expensive mistake by including a realistic job preview (discussed in Chapter 9) as part of the selection process. Through a good staffing system, an employer should always attempt to provide accurate information to job applicants that help them form a realistic image of the life within the organization.

Proactive: anticipating and responding to challenges before they happen

Finally, to be most effective, employment decisions should be **proactive**, that is, employment managers should anticipate and respond to challenges before they become realities. By recognizing the human resource needs well in advance and taking appropriate actions, the employment manager can ensure strategic success. Consider the example of Jim Crawford:

> When Jim Crawford, the founder of Scotia Ecological Consultants in Nova Scotia, planned the expansion of his firm's services into China, he first opened a branch in British Columbia. Part of his strategic plan was to utilize the abundance of skilled Chinese immigrants or

descendants of Canadian-Chinese parents, trained at the University of British Columbia, Simon Fraser University, and local colleges. He could reach potential candidates easily via the campus newspapers, the Internet, and professional organizations. By the time he opened his branch in China ten months later, he had already hired a large pool of Chinese-speaking engineers and technicians who were ready to execute his plans.

KEY STEPS IN STAFFING

As shown in Figure 1-6, the staffing process consists of five steps: human resource planning, recruitment, selection and hiring, deployment, and termination and outplacement. Each of these components should be mutually consistent in scope and demands. For example, poor recruitment can make selection and deployment harder, just as poor deployment practices can adversely affect the success of future recruitment efforts. The following example of a flawed recruitment and hiring attempt highlights the need for this seamless integration among the various staffing functions:

> A large Canadian consulting company in the field of compensation had advertised the position of consulting trainee in Hamilton, Ontario. However, the ad for the position did not specify qualifications. A few weeks later, when the local principal of the company was asked about the outcome of the advertisement, his answer was, "After I read through the first 400 applications, I gave up." He had received over 700 applications for this one job. Clearly, the firm's recruitment approach did not help him achieve his objectives.

Human resource planning Staffing begins with **human resource planning** (HRP), or the systematic forecasting of the organization's future demand and supply of employees and their skills and competencies. The organization should accurately identify both the number and quality of employees needed and currently available, since this data will form the basis of all later actions. The HR manager can predict the number of required employees through, for example, expert forecasts, budgets, trend projection forecasts, and labour market surveys. In large organizations, the HR manager may use more complex tools such as simulation. The HR manager can identify job specifications and the required competencies through job analysis. **Job analysis** involves the systematic collection, analysis, and interpretation of job information. This information is the basis for describing jobs, hiring suitable candidates for various jobs, and setting performance standards.

Human resource planning (HRP): systematically forecasting the organization's future demand and supplying appropriate employees, skills, and competencies

Job analysis: systematically collecting, analyzing, and interpreting job information

Recruitment Recruitment is the process of attracting suitable candidates for actual or planned job vacancies. It involves more than placing an ad in a newspaper and getting

Recruitment: attracting suitable candidates for actual or planned job vacancies

FIGURE 1-6: Key Steps in Staffing

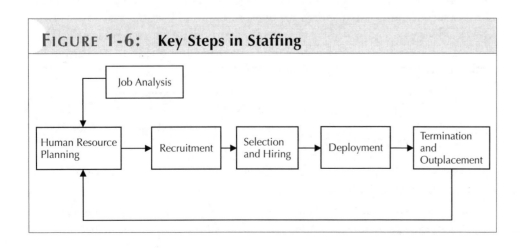

a few responses, because both the number and quality of job applicants define the success of recruitment. Will the ad attract a sufficient number of candidates in order to have a realistic choice? Will the candidates be the "right" ones? The time taken to recruit the required number of applicants as well the costs of recruitment are important indicators of recruitment effectiveness.

Selection and hiring

Selection: identifying applicants from the pool of recruits who best meet the organization's needs and are expected to perform well on the job in future

Predictors: application forms, tests, and interviews, and other tools for predicting future performance and potential of job applicants

Criteria: desired organizational outcomes, such as the quantity or quality of production, low absenteeism, and few accidents

Selection is the process of identifying individuals from the pool of recruits who best meet the organizational needs and are expected to perform well on the job in the future. A variety of **predictors** (for example, completed application forms, tests, and interviews) can help to predict future performance and the potential of job applicants. A predictor is based on a set of **criteria**, that is, a set of desired organizational outcomes such as the quantity or quality of production, low absenteeism, few accidents, and so on. Once the best candidate is selected, then the terms of employment are negotiated with the successful candidate and the employment contract is drawn up.

Deployment

Deployment: all activities aimed at placing newly hired employees in their job positions and helping them become proficient

Deployment includes all the activities aimed at placing the newly hired employee in his or her job position and helping the employee get up to speed in executing his or her job responsibilities. Orientation to the position and the organization, socialization to familiarize the employee to the firm and its culture, and classification and placement of the new employees (in the case of multiple hires) to available positions are other relevant activities at this stage.

Termination and outplacement

Termination: permanent separation of the employee from the organization (also referred to as being fired, discharged, separated, or dismissed)

Wrongful dismissal: dismissal without just cause or reasonable notice of termination

Outplacement: helping terminated employees find new jobs in other firms

Termination and outplacement Despite the best-laid plans, sometimes organizations have to reduce their workforce. In other instances, poor job performance or other just cause may necessitate employee dismissal. **Termination**, or the permanent separation of the employee from the organization (also referred to as being fired, discharged, separated, or dismissed), has to be done as humanely as possible and only as a last resort. Human resource managers often provide advice to line managers on alternatives to termination, and in those instances where termination is unavoidable, HR managers also develop appropriate security measures to protect corporate assets while preserving the dignity of the terminated employee. In all instances, care should be taken to avoid **wrongful dismissal**, that is, dismissal without just cause or reasonable notice of termination. Increasingly, many progressive employers offer **outplacement** services which help terminated employees find new jobs in other firms. These efforts may include providing office space, secretarial service, photocopying machines, long-distance phone calls, counselling, and referral services.

Many successful organizations have realized the strategic importance of staffing and made it an integral part of their overall corporate strategy. In such instances, various human resource functions, such as training, employee development, career counselling, compensation management, etc., are well-integrated with the staffing strategy. Organizations which have invested heavily in employee development have benefited both in terms of corporate success and employee morale and retention. Maritime Life Assurance is a good example of such an organization:

> Maritime Life Assurance Company of Halifax, now Manulife Financial, has been consistently rated in the past as a progressive employer in this country. This firm provides each of its 1900 employees with a Career Investment Account, which is an annual stipend that employees can use to purchase career development materials ranging from business journals to home Internet accounts. Employees can also use the funds to pay tuition for university courses. Maritime Life focuses on constantly upgrading employee skills so that they are able to anticipate and meet emerging challenges and take on higher responsibilities.[81]

Figure 1-7 lists some of the benefits of an effective staffing system. Implementing effective staffing procedures is vital for all organizations—large and small, public and

---

FIGURE 1-7: Some Benefits of an Effective Staffing System

Individual Employee Level

- Improved job satisfaction because of better job–employee match
- Clearer performance standards
- Improved awareness of the link between performance and reward
- Focused career development
- Clearer understanding of competencies needed for career growth

Organizational Level

- Higher employee productivity and efficiency
- Improved employee creativity
- Reduced risk of lawsuits from unsuccessful job applicants
- Reduced need for training and counselling
- Improved alignment of organizational strategy and individual performance
- Reduced employee turnover and absenteeism
- Improved competitive advantage based on employee competencies and work culture

---

private, profit and nonprofit. Improving organizational and individual employee productivity has become so important today that all but the smallest firms have some formal staffing procedures.[82] But even in the case of small businesses, effective recruitment and selection procedures are vital for success and even survival.

KEY COMPETENCIES OF AN EMPLOYMENT MANAGER

To be effective, staffing or employment managers need to possess a number of competencies.[83] Figure 1-8 shows the required professional competencies (RPCs) demanded of Canadian Human Resource Professionals (CHRP) in staffing. Past studies have indicated that a variety of competencies and personality characteristics are needed to successfully carry out the duties specified in Figure 1-8. These competencies and characteristics are outlined in Figure 1-9. Because of rising expectations, human resource specialists have become increasingly involved in the management of their respective organizations. As a result, in most large organizations, the HR function is represented at the highest level: the VP of Human Resources. Even some presidents and CEOs are now chosen from the HR field, when historically such positions were typically filled by candidates from marketing or finance.

Information on human resource management competencies: *www.chrpcanada.com*

GOALS FOR THE EMPLOYMENT MANAGER

To be effective, an employment manager needs to balance three sets of goals: those of the organization, the employee, and society.

Organizational goals Staffing practices are a means to an end, the end being the achievement of the organization's goals. The existing staffing practices should facilitate the successful implementation of organizational strategy and achieve excellence.

FIGURE 1-8:   **Required Professional Competencies Demanded of Canadian Human Resource Professionals in Staffing**

- Identifies the organization's HR needs.
- Identifies potential sources of qualified applicants.
- Implements and monitors processes for attracting qualified candidates.
- Evaluates recruitment effectiveness.
- Analyzes position requirements to establish selection criteria.
- Establishes screening and assessment procedures and evaluates their effectiveness.
- Establishes appointment procedures and develops employment contracts.
- Selects candidates, and negotiates terms and conditions of employment.
- Develops orientation policies and procedures for new employees and evaluates their effectiveness.
- Develops deployment procedures (e.g., transfers and reassignments).
- Implements deployment procedures, ensuring that necessary compensation and benefit changes and education plans are addressed.
- Advises other managers on matters of substandard performance, discipline, and ultimately termination.
- Advises managers on alternatives to terminations.
- Develops procedures for the defensible termination of employees.
- Develops appropriate security strategies to protect corporate assets, while preserving the dignity of the terminated employee.
- Participates in termination meetings by preparing termination notices, conducting exit interviews, and arranging outplacement services.

Source: Adapted and summarized from the RPCs listed in **www.hrpao.org** and **www.cchra-ccarh.ca/en3/chrp_designation.asp**. Reproduced with the permission of the Canadian Council of Human Resources Associations.

FIGURE 1-9:   **Required Competencies and Personality Characteristics of Employment Managers**

Studies have indicated that certain skills and competencies are critical for a successful employment manager. The more important ones are listed here.

- **Business mastery**: A sound knowledge of the business and strategic focus of the firm, including financial and marketing realities.
- **HR mastery and technology**: State-of-the-art knowledge in all areas of human resource management, with particular emphasis on job analysis, human resource planning, performance management, and organizational change.
- **Communication and leadership skills**: Effective verbal, nonverbal, written and oral communication, and interpersonal and leadership skills, including the ability to listen, show support, empathize, and inspire.
- **Legal knowledge**: Awareness of provisions of all relevant employment laws, especially human rights legislation, the *Canadian Charter of Rights and Freedoms*, the *Canada Labour Code*, and provincial legislation relating to work hours, compensation, safety, and discipline.
- **Statistical proficiency**: Knowledge of statistical tools such as correlation, regression, and profile analysis.
- **Personal credibility**: Trustworthiness, high ethical standards, and social responsiveness.

Sources: Hari Das. (2003). *Performance Management.* Toronto: Pearson Education; David Brown. (2004, Nov. 22). "Cream of the HR Crop Rise Beyond Traditional Skills." *Canadian HR Reporter,* p. 9; Diana Winstanley and Kate Stuart-Smith. (1996). "Policing Performance: The Ethics of Performance Management." *Personnel Review 25,* 6: 66–84.

For example, an organization that is moving away from a low-cost strategy to a strategy based on superior customer service will need to hire employees with vastly different skill sets. It will also need to make changes in deployment and employee development practices to support such a strategy.

Staffing practices should work within organizational restrictions, including the limited availability of resources. In the case of a very small organization, an elaborate staffing department may not be cost effective. However, even in the case of small organizations, the staffing process must deliver results in a timely and effective fashion.

Employee goals All progressive employers recognize the importance of helping employees achieve career and developmental goals that are in line with the organization's mission and goals. Careful planning that focuses on employee development will help employers attain this goal, while internal transfers and promotions expose the employees to new challenges and skill sets.

Societal goals An organization's staffing procedures should also be consistent with the larger society's priorities and demands.

For example, diversity management initiatives are becoming increasingly important in Canada to reflect this country's commitment to a multicultural society.

Poorly conceived staffing practices, on the other hand, can reduce the quality of life of an entire community, as the following example illustrates:

In 2003, Pearson International Airport in Toronto, Canada's largest airport, came under fire for its shoddy selection practices when several part-time security personnel were charged with offences connected to drug smuggling at the airport. One part-time inspector was alleged to have helped former school friends try to spirit multi-kilo loads of drugs into the country. Another charge involved a former senior manager who used his authority to funnel hundreds of thousands of dollars to cocaine suppliers in Florida. These arrests were traced to the sloppy hiring practices at the airport. The normal hiring process for security personnel until 2003 consisted solely of a fingerprint check and, in limited cases, an inquiry directed to the Canadian Security Intelligence Service. It is noteworthy that anyone seeking a job at a bank in this country must go through a thorough background screening including personal and job history, face-to-face interviews, character references, and a hard look at the applicant's finances.[84]

Organizational, employee, and societal goals need not always converge. Often, trade-offs become necessary.

Staffing practices should also be ethical (see the Focus on Ethics box on page 24). Staffing is an activity that is full of situations that lead to ethical dilemmas. This book will introduce you to a number of ethical challenges related to the topics under discussion in each chapter.

THE SERVICE ROLE OF THE STAFFING DEPARTMENT

Staffing departments are service departments. They exist to assist others and the larger organization. Their managers do not have the authority to order other managers in other departments to accept their ideas. Instead, the department has only **staff authority**, which is the authority to advise, not direct, managers in other departments. In contrast, **line authority**, possessed by managers of operating departments, allows them to make decisions about hiring, placement, and task assignment, and evaluate the performance of employees. It is the operating managers who are normally responsible for job assignments, promotions, and other employee-related decisions. Staffing specialists merely advise line managers, who are ultimately responsible for hiring and managing employees.

In highly technical or extremely routine situations, the staffing specialist may be given functional authority. **Functional authority** gives the functionary or the department

Staff authority: the authority to advise but not direct managers in other departments

Line authority: the authority to make decisions about hiring, placement, task assignment, and the performance evaluation of employees

Functional authority: gives the functionary or the department the authority to make decisions usually made by line managers or top management

the right to make decisions usually made by line managers or top management. For example, some of the decisions about hiring procedures and tools are technically complex; similarly, selection procedures to deal with minority members in the community may be necessary from an equity point of view, so the top manager may give the staffing department the functional authority to decide on the procedures or tools. If each department manager made separate decisions about employment equity, promotion, or disciplinary procedures, there might be excessive costs and inequities. For this reason, in many organizations, the staffing department is entrusted with the responsibility for developing procedures for the defensible termination of employees. During terminations, the staffing department is also responsible for developing appropriate security strategies to protect corporate assets, while preserving the dignity of the terminated employee.

Ethics: moral principles that guide human behaviours, based on a society's cultural values, norms, customs, and beliefs

Focus on Ethics

What is the "right" behaviour?

Ethics are moral principles that guide human behaviours and are often based on a society's cultural values, norms, customs, and beliefs. Ethics also describe correct or right conduct, or a system of moral values.

Standards of behaviour vary widely across different cultures. But even within the same society, ethical standards can vary among individuals and within groups, making judgments of "right" and "wrong" extremely difficult. Several past thinkers have responded to this by offering different guidelines of "good" behaviour.

1. **The Universalist Approach:** Moral standards are universally applicable. In other words, regardless of the society or place, a bad act (such as killing or stealing) is bad. There are no exceptions to moral "rights" and "wrongs."

2. **The Exceptionist Approach:** This approach suggests that morals are only guidelines. While they are to be followed on most occasions, an individual may have to make exceptions when the circumstances of a particular situation justify them.

3. **The Situational Approach:** What is good or bad depends essentially on the situation or culture surrounding the individual. While telling the truth is desirable in some societies, there may be other cultures that do not give the same importance to truth. Similarly, while killing is bad, there may be situations that justify this act. It all depends on the situation in which the decision maker finds himself or herself.

4. **The Individual Subjectivist Approach:** There is no absolute right or wrong, good or bad, in any social situation. The individual decision maker facing a situation should determine what is right and wrong after considering all aspects of the situation. Moral decisions should be based on personal values and preferences.

Staffing is full of situations with hard choices between good and bad, right and wrong, desirable and undesirable. The **Focus on Ethics** feature in each chapter in this book will introduce you to an ethical challenge. For each Focus, read the paragraph describing the challenge and decide how you would respond to the challenge. Then compare your response to the responses provided by others. Discuss the rationale behind each person's response. Try to categorize the responses under the four approaches listed here to gain new insights into the ways people look at ethical situations.

Instructions: Consider the following situation and decide how you will respond. Note your response and describe the rationale behind your response on a separate sheet of paper. Compare your response with the responses of others.

You work as a customer service representative in Next Age Electronics, a firm that specializes in consumer electronics with 15 stores in Ontario. The present situation relates to the downtown store managed by the owner himself. The store employs 26 sales, clerical, and other employees. In addition, the store has a Sales Manager and an Employment Manager. Recently, the Employment Manager abruptly resigned, and Pat Hoskins, one of your co-workers, was promoted to the position. Until the promotion, Pat was a very popular employee and maintained good relations with everyone, which is part of the reason why Pat was promoted in the first place. However, you have begun to notice a disturbing trend recently: Pat, when faced with a problem employee, does not deal with the issue or confront the person. Instead, when faced with a problem such as absenteeism, tardiness, or poor performance, Pat simply goes to the owner and complains about the employee without first raising the issue with the person concerned. Often, the owner calls the employee to his office and reprimands the employee. In other instances, the owner fired some of these employees on other pretexts. You believe that this situation has demoralized the workforce in the store. What should you do now?

Finally, staffing focuses on the management of people, which means that the function should be carried professionally and humanely.[85] Improving the productive contribution of the people is a major aim of any organization. However, this aim cannot be achieved without also improving the overall quality of work life, indeed, the quality of life, of the employees involved if the firm is to grow and prosper.

THE FRAMEWORK OF THIS BOOK

This text is divided into four parts (see Figure 1-10).

Part 1: Formulation of human resource strategy This part sets the stage for a discussion of all the staffing activities that follow. The chapter discusses the steps in formulating a consistent HR strategy and examines the environmental challenges facing the employment manager. It also discusses the competencies that the employment specialist needs to effectively carry out the HR function.

Part 2: Preparation for hiring The next three chapters detail the various actions that precede staffing. Chapter 2 deals with the key steps in identifying human resource plans and performance standards. In the same chapter, we also outline the steps in

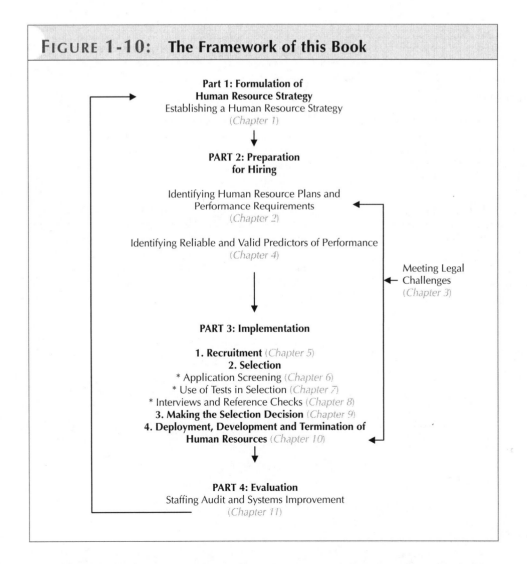

FIGURE 1-10: The Framework of this Book

Part 1: Formulation of
Human Resource Strategy
Establishing a Human Resource Strategy
(Chapter 1)

PART 2: Preparation
for Hiring

Identifying Human Resource Plans and
Performance Requirements
(Chapter 2)

Identifying Reliable and Valid Predictors of Performance
(Chapter 4)

Meeting Legal
Challenges
(Chapter 3)

PART 3: Implementation

1. Recruitment (Chapter 5)
2. Selection
* Application Screening (Chapter 6)
* Use of Tests in Selection (Chapter 7)
* Interviews and Reference Checks (Chapter 8)
3. Making the Selection Decision (Chapter 9)
4. Deployment, Development and Termination of
Human Resources (Chapter 10)

PART 4: Evaluation
Staffing Audit and Systems Improvement
(Chapter 11)

analyzing the requirements of a job and its associated tasks and in establishing performance standards. Chapter 3 outlines federal legislation, provincial laws, and other regulations that affect a staffing department's actions. Finally, Chapter 4 discusses the important properties of predictors and criteria used in staffing.

Part 3: Implementation In this part, we discuss the various steps in staffing, from the identification of a job vacancy through to employee termination. Chapter 5 discusses alternative approaches to recruiting job candidates, highlighting both the traditional and emerging approaches in this area. Chapter 6 looks at the importance of job application forms and biographical "blanks" in screening job applicants. Chapter 7 describes performance, knowledge, personality, and medical and drug tests currently permitted in Canada, with detail about their merits and limitations. Chapter 8 elaborates on the use of reference letters and interviews in the staffing context. Chapter 9 discusses alternative ways to combine pieces of information about the employee to form a final employment decision. The last chapter in this section, chapter 10, discusses the deployment of staff and examines the special challenges faced by firms when terminating employees.

Part 4: Evaluation of the staffing function Chapter 11 discusses evaluation. This chapter looks at the important task of reviewing and enhancing the staffing department's effectiveness and reviewing internal procedures to sustain high levels of performance and client satisfaction.

The next chapter discusses the very first step in hiring: namely, preparing for hiring. It focuses on the process of identifying the number and quality of employees to be hired and the tools employment managers can use for that purpose.

Implications for Practice

1. To be effective and to add value, human resource management practices should be closely aligned to the strategic needs of an organization and provide the organization with an effective workforce, while meeting the needs of its members and other constituents of the society.

2. To be effective, staffing should be an ongoing process that is integrated with other organizational systems. It should be focused on achieving the organizational, employee, and the larger society's goals.

3. All staffing-related activities, namely, job analysis, human resource planning, recruitment, selection,

deployment, termination, and outplacement, should be executed systematically and professionally. These activities should also be well-integrated with one another.

4. Staffing managers should recognize and adapt to the culture of the organization. In some instances, staffing managers should also be entrusted with the responsibility of altering or shaping the same. To play their roles effectively, staffing managers should possess a number of competencies and carry out the various activities listed in this chapter on a timely basis.

Key Terms for Review

Collaborative strategy, *p. 15*

Commitment strategy, *p. 14*

Competency, *p. 17*

Compliance strategy, *p. 14*

Core competencies, *p. 13*

Cost leadership strategy, *p. 13*

Criteria, *p. 20*

Deployment, *p. 20*

Equifinality, *p. 12*

Ethics, *p. 24*

Discussion Questions

1. What are the steps in formulating a human resource strategy for a grocery chain? For a small, owner-operated grocery store?

2. What are the various steps in staffing? Select two organizations in an industry with which you are familiar. Do you see any differences in the way the organizations do staffing? Explain.

3. If you were entrusted with the task of hiring a staffing manager for your firm, what attributes or skills would you focus on?

Critical Thinking Questions

1. You are the person in charge of all employee-related matters (e.g., compensation, recruitment of temporary workers) in a small business that employs 20 people. The firm is expected to grow substantially in the near future, and the owner plans to hire over 50 full-time and 60 part-time employees. Recently, the owner asked you for your advice on implementing a formal staffing system for the business. What would your response be? Why?

2. The dean of your community college or university has invited you to serve on a committee which has been entrusted with the responsibility of improving student recruitment at your institution. While the overall number of applications to your institution has shown some growth, other similar institutions have done much better both in terms of the number of applications and the quality of recruits. The committee asked you to provide information on environmental changes with bearing on the issue. What factors would you consider?

3. After years of operating a self-serve coffee-and-donut shop that made mediocre profits, the owners decided to close the shop (which is situated near a suburban mall and high school) and open a new shop in the downtown core. The new shop will only sell gourmet coffee and higher-priced pastries and provide a sit-down service facility. What changes in recruitment and selection of employees are necessary for it to become successful in the new location?

Web Research

Visit the websites of four major firms in any two industries. Collect the relevant information on their staffing philosophy and systems. Did you find any differences? Are these differences simply attributable to size or profitability? Are there differences between the industries? Are any of the differences attributable to the firms' cultures?

CASE INCIDENT

Ontario Electronics Limited: Performance of Plant C

Ontario Electronics Company Limited (OECL) manufactures electronic, communication, aerospace, and audio equipment. The company currently employs over 500 workers, a large proportion of whom are professionals. The company's head office and major plant are located near Scarborough, Ontario, and its plants and sales offices are located in four other Canadian provinces and in major U.S. cities. While in the recent past the company has faired well financially, the top management is unhappy about the productivity levels in various plants. The management was particularly displeased with the performance of employees in Plant C, and has decided to focus on this plant to improve work procedures and productivity.

Tim Hutton, who was recently hired as a staffing analyst, reviewed the records and studied the situation for over one month. He also surveyed a representative sample of all workers in Plant C. Here is a brief summary of Hutton's findings:

1. In 72 of the 80 appraisal records that Tim Hutton examined, the employee's performance showed little change from the previous year. Poor performers rated poorly year in and year out. Most of the employees had excellent academic credentials, but did not seem to perform well on the job once they were hired.

2. Approximately 50% of the employees whom Hutton informally interviewed complained about the lack of detailed information about company projects and priorities and how the current project related to the overall business strategy.

3. Of the 25% of employees who were considered to be superior performers (based on the company's performance evaluation records), over 60% commented that their impression of the company that they formed during job interviews was very different from the impression that developed once they started working for the company. The work conditions they faced on arrival at the company after they were hired were markedly different from what they were told during job interviews and from what was reported in company brochures and annual reports.

4. Fourteen employees who had resigned recently completed exit surveys. Ten of the fourteen commented that their interests and job demands did not match. While they were happy overall about the rewards offered by the firm, they felt that their talents could be utilized better elsewhere.

Questions

1. *What is the central problem in Plant C?*
2. *What should Hutton do now?*

CASE

Kanata Food Distributors*

In 1963, six independent grocery retailers in Ontario decided to form a buying group that would enable them to purchase food products at significantly lower costs because of economies of scale and enhanced bargaining power. The result was the formation of the Ontario Grocers' Association (OGA), which expanded to represent 13 independent grocers in less than three years. OGA's original charter set out the organization's mission as "the wholesale and retail of grocer-butcher-dairy products, brokerage in food and affiliated activities" and mainly focused on acquiring grocery products and meat at cheaper rates that the members could sell at reasonable prices and still make handsome profits.

Over the years, dozens of other grocers joined the association. In the early 1970s, the management decided to supply nonmember grocers as well. In less than 15 years since its inception, the association had over $12 million in sales. The leadership and tenacity of OGA helped it make fast inroads into the Ontario grocery market, often by acquiring new units or offering new services. What began with an authorized capital of $60 000, consisting of 600 shares of $100 each, soon grew into a large chain of food stores. Today, OGA, renamed Kanata Food Distributors in 1978, is the third largest grocer in Ontario with nearly 300 stores spanning Ontario and Quebec and is an acknowledged leader in the food industry in the region. Besides the food outlets, the firm also has ninety 24-hour convenience stores and 26 pastry and prepared-food stores in the two provinces.

*Case written by Professor Hari Das of Saint Mary's University, Halifax. All rights retained by the author, © 2005.

Kanata's growth can be traced in three distinct phases: 1963 to 1977, when growth was primarily through the opening of new stores and offer of new products; 1978 to 1994, when the firm rapidly grew through the acquisition of other grocery stores and offering new products; and 1995 to the present, when the firm primarily focused on new large, discount-store concept stores, known as Super-K stores; the introduction of a large number of convenience shops, known as 24-7; and bakery, pastry, and prepared-food stores, known as Temptations. Throughout the company's history, management focused on continuously renovating the stores to make them competitive with the pleasant shopping settings and village-fair atmosphere offered by several large retailers such as Loblaws, Sobey's, and Metro.

The financial figures of the company present a conservative management approach, which consistently focused on growth while minimizing investment risk. The result has been steady returns on investment over the years. Currently, the return on shareholders' equity is approximately 22%, exceeding the 20% management target for the sixth consecutive year and positioning Kanata as one of the most profitable Canadian public companies. In 2002, the company split its shares on a two-for-one basis. The share price of the company is currently about $17. It is worth noting that during the worldwide stock-market decline in 2001 and 2002, the company's share price declined by less than 6%. The details of the company's financial performance are given in Table 1. Figure 1 shows the change in share price over the last several years.

ORGANIZATION OF THE COMPANY

Kanata is organized into three semi-autonomous units: the Grocery Business, the Super K Division, and the Convenience and Pastry Stores group. (Employees in the firm refer to them as "Grocery," "Super K," and "24-7.") While most management functions are independently planned and executed, Kanata continues to purchase most materials centrally to reap economies of scale. Frequent formal meetings among division heads and operating managers ensure consistency in policies and practices. The organization attempts to implement uniform human resource practices, although the salary rates in Super K and 24-7 are somewhat lower than those in

the Grocery division. While all units employ large numbers of part-time employees, the proportion is perhaps the highest in the 24-7 stores. An approximate organization chart of the organization is shown in Figure 2. The three divisions have their own internal structures that are hybrids of the geographic and functional structures. For example, the 24-7 shops have a regional head office in Montreal that coordinates the activities of all the shops located in the metro region, but the functions such as marketing or human resources report to their parent divisions located in Ontario. The Super K and Grocery lines have similar arrangements. In general, Kanata has attempted to maintain a lean structure that facilitates quick decision making and delegation to lower levels, while at the same time maintaining high standards of performance at all levels.

GROCERY STORES

Kanata currently owns 256 grocery stores in Ontario and Quebec. While the stores in both provinces carry all groceries and popular brands, the average size of the stores in Quebec is somewhat smaller (see Table 2 for physical details about the stores). The newer stores in both provinces are larger than the older ones. Stores in both provinces also have other facilities such as pharmacies, newsstands, and photo-developing units. The newer stores also have other facilities (e.g., laundry, video stores, post office) adjacent to the stores, although these are owned and operated by independent businesspeople. In return for location, they pay a licensing fee to Kanata along with a monthly rent that is linked to their sales revenues. Nearly 40% of total revenues for the firm emerge from the grocery business.

Fierce competition and a price war prompted Kanata to introduce its own house brands for many products. Kanata Club products offer high quality at economical prices, while Royal Kanata is a premium brand for many products aimed at the upper-income segment of the market.

SUPER-K STORES

Compared to other grocery stores, Super-K stores offer a limited range of products in family sizes at discount prices. They are relatively newer (they were introduced as a competitive

TABLE 1:   Kanata's Financial Performance

Item	This year	Last year	Change over a 3-year period (% of base year)
Total Revenue (thousands of dollars)	$4 374 780	$4 138 565	+8.53
Earnings before Interest and Tax (thousands of dollars)	$190 825	$160 820	+22.53
Profit/Loss (thousands of dollars)	$122 145	$104 380	+24.33
Earnings per share	$1.44	$1.23	+23.09
Total assets (thousands of dollars)	$1 12 97 35	$1 008 100	+10.20
Dividends per share	$0.23	$0.18	+3
Return on common equity	22.3%	24.08%	+6
Number of employees	21 950	21 100	+5.3

FIGURE 1:   Kanata's Stock Price and Industry Trends

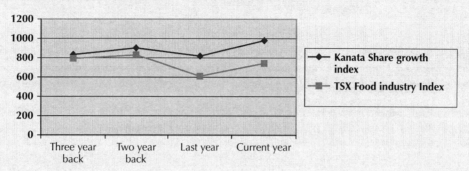

weapon against the inroads made by large grocery ware-houses such as Costco, Loblaws, and Metro). Many of the newer superstores use automated scanning systems so that their customers can avoid long lineups at the checkout point. Approximately 30% of Kanata's total revenues have emerged from this line of business.

CONVENIENCE AND PASTRY STORES

About eight years ago, Kanata entered this lucrative segment of the food industry by offering major brand-name grocery items, baked products, prepared foods, and, more recently, premium-quality meals. Today, over 25% of the total revenues

for the firm have emerged from this line of business. Within this group, about 60% of revenues has been generated by 90 convenience stores (under the logo of "24-7 Stores") and the balance from 26 pastry food outlets ("Temptations"). Many of the convenience stores were located adjacent to major traffic areas (e.g., gas stations) or residential areas; and the pastry stores were strategically located in shopping malls, near high traffic areas such as bus and rail stations, educational institutions, and hospitals. Increasingly, the pastry shops also offer light meals. Kanata has made a conscious decision to hire experienced bakers and cooks to offer high-quality meals and fresh pastries—a critical factor, especially in Quebec.

FIGURE 2:   An Approximate Organization Chart of Kanata Food Distributors

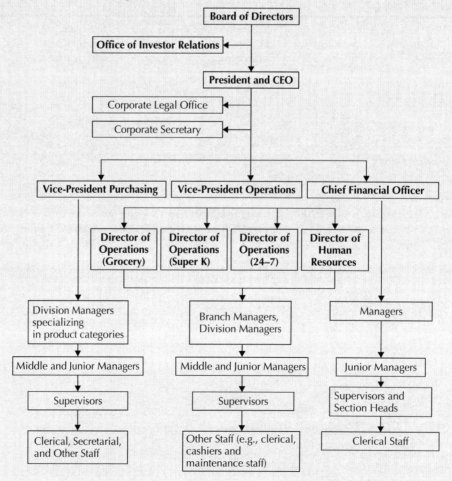

TABLE 2: Some Background Information on Kanata Stores

Details of units	This year	Last year
GROCERY STORES (Ontario)		
Number of stores	220	205
Average floor area (m^2)	24 200	24 000
Total floor area (m^2)	5 324 000	4 920 000
Number of employees	15 957	15 659
GROCERY STORES (Quebec)		
Number of stores	36	32
Average floor area (m^2)	22 000	21 000
Total floor area (m^2)	792 000	672 000
Number of employees	3 132	2 816
SUPER-K STORES		
Number of stores	43	35
Average floor area (m^2)	46 000	43 000
Total floor area (m^2)	1 978 000	1 505 000
Number of employees	2 408	2 065
24-7 CONVENIENCE STORES		
Number of stores	90	72
Average floor area (m^2)	5 200	4 980
Total floor area (m^2)	468 000	358 560
Number of employees	360	298
TEMPTATIONS		
Number of stores	26	21
Average floor area (m^2)	6 700	6 500
Total floor area (m^2)	174 200	136 500
Number of employees	182	152

Note: The number of employees does not include head office management staff.

The grocery industry is highly competitive. With the arrival of foreign competitors like Wal-Mart (which introduced large retail warehouses called "Sam's Clubs") and a host of Internet-based grocery chains, the traditional-style grocery chains have found it hard to maintain their competitive positions. Kanata is no exception. To meet the increasing competition in the food sector in Ontario and Quebec, the firm's top management is currently looking at various alternatives. One possibility is to expand into western Canada where the level of competition is somewhat lower, though existing large chains such as Safeway are major forces to be reckoned with. Many new competitors have also been primarily targeting urban areas. By expanding into rural and suburban markets, the firm may be able to capture a niche that is not currently sought after by large chains. A second possibility is to expand overseas, especially into quickly developing countries such as China and India, where large, modern grocery chains are still a rarity. (The management feels that more familiar foreign markets in the U.S. and U.K. are as crowded as in this country, if not even more so.) Internet marketing and the prepared-food markets have also been looked at as possible new growth areas. However, each of these alternatives is also fraught with fresh challenges. For example, the population shifts from rural to urban areas may make many rural stores not viable in the longer term. Entering foreign markets can bring major new challenges including cultural adaptation.

Whatever the new focus, it is bound to have a major impact on the company's human resource policies and practices and its nearly 22 000 employees. The firm has been considered to be a good employer and, despite several attempts by local and international unions, the labour force has remained non-union. However, the signs that the company may have its first union are increasing. Major support for unionization has emerged from part-time workers and women. To control costs, Kanata, like many other employers, has been increasing the number of its part-time workers, a practice to which full-time employees object. Lori Klean, the Director of Human Resources, along with all of her colleagues, considers the emergence of a powerful union as a major challenge to the management's ability to respond to changes quickly. Besides this challenge, the firm is also trying to identify solutions to a host of other issues related to human resource management at this time. Here are some examples:

Hiring large numbers of new immigrants has caused resentment and occasional interpersonal conflicts. Many of the problems occur between white employees and visible minority employees.

The average age of key managers in the firm is currently 58. Several managers have been talking about "leaving the rat race" and retiring. Even if only 10% of the present managers retire in the near future, this will create a major managerial shortage in the organization.

In the past, Kanata has made a major effort to recruit minority employees into managerial positions. Despite this effort, the proportion of Asians, black, and other visible minorities in the management cadre has been marginal. While the firm receives a large number of applications from such groups, most applicants have not been successful in the employment process. Klean is beginning to wonder whether the selection process is as unfair as it is touted to be.

Many employees, especially women, have been advocating for more flexible work arrangements. Klean is aware that many of the employees have to look after children as well as aging parents. This has resulted in a number of employees being frequently absent from work or arriving late for work. Klean realizes that major changes in work arrangements may be necessary, especially if unionization is to be avoided.

Kanata is considering entering the Internet market in a big way. If this becomes a reality, required employee skills may vastly change.

If Kanata plans to enter foreign markets like China or India, this expansion can be a major challenge. More than 90% of the firm's managers have not visited any foreign countries other than the U.S. and the U.K. Klean, who studied international management while she was taking her MBA. at Saint Mary's University in Halifax, realizes that foreign cultures can be vastly different.

The firm's top management team is planning to discuss the various options at a meeting scheduled for next week. John Kiuru, President and CEO, has indicated to Klean that three strategies are likely to be seriously considered at the meeting, namely: Internet marketing, expanding abroad, and the expansion of the convenience stores and pastry division. Klean knows that the Board will be expecting her to provide an elaborate paper on the strategic and economic implications of each of these three alternatives in the context of human resources. Of course, she should be ready to answer questions related to other alternatives and challenges facing Kanata as well.

Questions

1. *Assume that you are Klean. What are the current specific challenges facing Kanata as they relate to the human resource function?*

2. *Evaluate the firm's current human resource practices.*

3. *What changes in human resource priorities and practices may be needed for each of the strategic alternatives currently being considered?*

PART 2

PREPARATION FOR HIRING

Once an organization has identified a basic human resource strategy, it has to implement that strategy by establishing systems and procedures, assigning responsibilities for various decisions, and allocating the necessary resources. Together, these tasks can be called the "preparation stage." The following three chapters deal with various activities involved in this stage. Attracting qualified individuals to the organization begins with identifying the organization's human resource needs and performance requirements (Chapter 2) within the existing legal provisions. An employer must also anticipate changes in society and social attitudes and introduce progressive employment practices. Chapter 3 discusses ways to meet legal challenges. Chapter 4 elaborates on the steps in identifying reliable and valid predictors of job success. Such predictors form the foundation of the entire selection process.

2 IDENTIFYING HUMAN RESOURCE PLANS AND PERFORMANCE REQUIREMENTS

"The driving force behind a 21st century organization will be its people... . Twenty-first century organizations will utilize a measurement called ROT (Return on Talent). ROT measures the payback from investment in people. It shows if managers are hiring the right people and how effectively they use them to achieve business success. Effective knowledge generated means high ROT. It leads to creative workforces, innovations, smooth processes, continuous product improvements, and proper communications." [1]

Subhir Chowdhury

CHAPTER OBJECTIVES

After studying this chapter, you should be able to:

- Determine performance criteria in the light of an organization's mission and goals

- Discuss the steps in analyzing a job and identifying the specifications and required competencies for a job

- List the steps in identifying performance standards

- Discuss key approaches to planning human resource needs

A want ad reads something like this: "A rare opportunity for an outgoing, self-driven person to work in an administrative capacity in a small but dynamic consulting firm. This western Canadian firm, which has several well-known clients, is making fast inroads into the Atlantic region and is now looking for a person who will be part of a highly results-oriented team. We are also looking for a person who will enjoy being part of a busy and exciting work environment and who will be able to help the consultants with organizing presentations. The ideal candidate will be strong in client relations, highly self-confident, and outgoing. Past experience in a consulting organization is highly desirable. Apply with full details of qualifications and past work experience to _____."

The above recruitment ad will likely attract dozens, possibly hundreds, of applications. Ironically, its ability to attract a large number of applications is due to its glaring limitation: namely, its imprecise job specifications. Almost everyone who reads the advertisement is likely to feel qualified for the position. After all, how many of us would like to admit that we are *not* self-driven or *not* self-confident? Don't we all see ourselves as outgoing? What does "help with organizing presentations" mean? Does this phrase refer to merely booking halls and arranging for refreshments, or does the task involve researching topics and preparing presentation material? What kind of consulting is this firm engaged in? Is it management, engineering, real-estate development, lawn care, psychiatric, or something else? What does being part of a "busy and exciting work environment" entail? Does this phrase mean that the employee will have to work long hours? Or does it mean that there will be a lot of pressure to attend to multiple tasks simultaneously?

Precisely identifying job responsibilities and requirements is one of the first steps in any hiring process. However, this is a complex task consisting of several steps. As Figure 2-1 shows, identifying the number and nature of jobs to be filled begins with a clear specification of performance criteria. After a thorough job and task analysis, performance standards and competencies must be established for each of the criteria identified. The final step is to combine this information with the firm's human resource plans to arrive at the number and type of job vacancies to be filled at any particular time.

This chapter begins with a discussion of the steps in determining performance criteria. A discussion of the steps in job and task analysis follows, which will help an organization determine job specifications. The following section describes steps in establishing performance standards. The chapter ends with a brief overview of the steps in identifying human resource needs through human resource planning (or HRP, as it is commonly referred to).

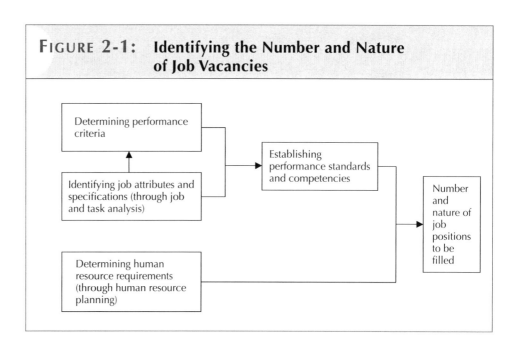

FIGURE 2-1:   **Identifying the Number and Nature of Job Vacancies**

DETERMINING PERFORMANCE CRITERIA

A **criterion** is an evaluative standard used to measure an employee's performance, attitude, or both.[2] An organization attempts to maximize or minimize criteria through proper hiring procedures. Typical criteria include quantity and quality of production, service quality, absenteeism and turnover, promotability, and the ability to work as part of a team. Criteria may be behaviours, outcomes, or attitudes. They may be objectively (e.g., number of units sold) or subjectively (e.g., supervisory ratings) measured. An employer may want to maximize (e.g., productivity) or minimize (e.g., number of workplace accidents) specific criteria. Despite such differences, all criteria are standards of excellence. The employer must also carefully identify all criteria before any hiring can begin.

> **Criterion:** an evaluative standard used to measure an employee's performance, attitude, or both

Determining performance criteria for employees has two interrelated steps: (1) identifying performance criteria for departments and individual employees relative to larger organizational goals and linking them to organizational strategies; and (2) ensuring that the criteria identified are robust and reliable.

1. LINKING PERFORMANCE CRITERIA TO ORGANIZATIONAL GOALS AND STRATEGIES

As discussed in Chapter 1, human resource strategies are intricately linked to the organizational mission, goals, and strategies. An organization's mission is a vision of what the organizational future course should be. A **mission statement** specifies the activities the organization intends to pursue and the course charted for the future. It is a concise statement of the organization's identity, that is, a statement of "who we are, what we do, and where we are headed." An organization's mission and strategies define the firm's customer, the directions taken by the firm to meet the customer's needs, and the level of performance the firm expects to achieve in the foreseeable future. Typically, once an organization defines its mission and strategies, it then identifies specific goals for its departments and employees (see Figure 2-2). However, an organization's strategies might need to be refined whenever organizational objectives change. The bidirectional nature of influence between goals and strategies is captured in Figure 2-2.

> **Mission statement:** the activities the organization intends to pursue and the course charted for the future

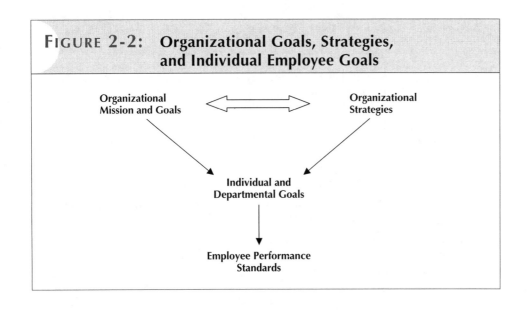

FIGURE 2-2: Organizational Goals, Strategies, and Individual Employee Goals

Organizational Mission and Goals ⟺ Organizational Strategies

→ Individual and Departmental Goals

→ Employee Performance Standards

Stakeholders: persons or groups who have a stake in the organization's continued operations and well-being

Typically, an organization has multiple goals that are designed to meet the needs of different **stakeholders**: persons or groups who have a stake in the organization's continued operations and well-being. Furthermore, even organizations operating in the same industry may show remarkable differences in their strategies and goals.

Compare the goals and strategies of two successful hockey teams: one team may have set its current year's goal as winning the Stanley Cup, while another may have decided to treat this year as a rebuilding year. A rebuilding team seeks to develop new players and allow rookies (inexperienced players with potential) to gain experience, often sacrificing winning in the process. It trades proven veterans who are close to retirement for high-potential new players. The team's objective is to win next year.

Even similar organizations are often different in the relative importance they assign to specific goals, while different organizations may have vastly different priorities. For example, one firm may attempt to maximize its immediate profits, while another may be willing to forgo short-term profits for a greater market share in the future. Figure 2-3 lists some sample organizational goals, along with measures to assess achievement. Apart from formal goals, most organizations also have unwritten, informal goals that direct its members' behaviour and are related to the firm's overall mission:

Federal Express, Scotiabank, and McDonald's are examples of organizations that have communicated the importance of customer service to their employees. Some of these organizations value customer service to such an extent that it is no longer a mere goal, but rather part of their overall basic business philosophy.

Clear goals provide standards for evaluating the performances of an organization and its employees. Criteria such as profits, sales volume, percentage of market share, and the number of customer complaints all provide measurable goals against which actual performance can be evaluated. Not all goals need to be market- or profit-related;

FIGURE 2-3:   Sample Organizational Goals

Goals	Meaning	Sample Measures of Goal Achievement
1. **Profitability**	Revenue remaining after all costs and obligations are met	Return on investment
2. **Growth**	Increase in such variables as plant capacity, workforce size, and market share	Growth in workforce size
3. **Innovation**	Introduction of new products, processes, or ways of looking at phenomena with significant practical implications	Number of new patents
4. **Productivity improvement**	Ratio of organization's outputs (goods and services) to its inputs (people, capital, materials, resources, and energy)	Labour productivity indices
5. **Employee satisfaction**	Extent to which an organization meets the needs of its employees	Attitudinal survey measures
6. **Social responsibility**	Extent to which an organization meets societal concerns and contributes to the society	Contributions to social projects

however, in some organizations, such as Dofasco, good employee relations are identified as a key goal:

> Dofasco, one of the largest steel manufacturers in Canada, has always emphasized good
> employee relations as a goal. Since 1938, when it introduced its profit-sharing plan, Dofasco
> has maintained economic efficiency in a highly competitive industry. Part of achieving this
> efficiency is attributable to high employee motivation levels and a healthy cooperative rela-
> tionship between labour and management.[3]

Articles on performance goals:
http://humanresources.about.
com/library/weekly

Once broad organizational goals are identified, they need to be translated into every-day performance goals for departments (or divisions) and individual employees and into criteria on which performance can be assessed.[4] Figure 2-4 shows how the mission of an organization can be translated into operative goals for divisions and individual employees in two sample areas. For example, measures of customer satisfaction, overall sales volume (and market share), and repeat purchases reflect the organization's success in providing value to its customers. To be useful, the mission (or vision) and strategies should be translated in terms of factors that are highly relevant to the stakeholder group concerned.

To provide direction, goals should not only delineate the desired outcomes but also be well-integrated with each other and well-understood by all the organization's members. This means that the goals and performance requirements must be linked horizontally across various job positions as well as linked vertically across various management levels to ensure consistency. To be useful, such goals should be specific, measurable, cost-bound, time-bound, and realistic.[5]

> At Canadian Electronic and Computer Manufacturers Ltd., the new sales goal was to sell
> 200 000 personal computers in the fiscal year 2008. This meant that the four geographical
> divisions in western, prairie, central, and eastern Canada had to achieve sales of 70 000,
> 10 000, 90 000, and 30 000 units, respectively. Given this overall goal, each regional office,
> sales office, and sales manager of the company calculated the sales goals for the year and
> for various months. The company also ensured that the needs of the production, materials,
> human resource, and finance divisions were met to achieve these goals. Revised procedures
> and systems were initiated where necessary in order to meet the overall goal.

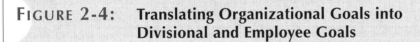

FIGURE 2-4:   Translating Organizational Goals into Divisional and Employee Goals

MISSION:

"To be among the top six organizations in the field known for product quality and progressive employment practices."

SAMPLE MEASURES OF GOAL ACHIEVEMENT:

1. Product Quality
Customer satisfaction measures on delivery, quality, and service quality
Sales volume
Repeat purchases
Continuous improvement in product quality
Awards for product quality
Customer complaints totalled over time and compared to the industry's average

2. Progressive Employment Practices
Employee satisfaction with working conditions
Work challenge offered and employee involvement
Employee satisfaction with rewards
Tenure of employees
Turnover and absenteeism figures compared to the industry's averages

The process of identifying specific performance standards for individual employees is detailed in a later section in this chapter.

2. Choosing Robust Criteria

Defining performance criteria for employees is, in many instances, a complex task requiring thoughtful consideration of the answers to a number of questions, such as the following:

Ultimate or actual criteria? Should an organization look at the more obvious performance outcomes of an employee's job, or the less visible, but often more important dimensions? The term **ultimate criterion** describes the full domain of performance and includes everything that ultimately defines success on the job.[6]

> For example, in the case of a salesperson, the more visible criteria include sales volume, customer satisfaction, and display of merchandise. However, ultimately, the salesperson's performance must be judged with other criteria, such as the number of new accounts, level of customer loyalty, and impact on co-workers and the larger organization. Timely paperwork, effectiveness in handling customer calls and complaints (even those related to other aspects of the organization), and an increase in total sales during the person's tenure in the firm are also important.

Ultimate criterion embodies the notions of "total," "true," or "ultimate worth," with a focus on the long term:

> For example, for an investment firm, the ultimate goals include investor confidence, profitability, growth of investments, a large market share, a reputation for integrity, highly competent investment planners, and total customer satisfaction.

Recently, constructs such as "organizational citizenship" (see Chapter 7) have been used to indicate such commitment on the part of the employee and indicators of employee contribution to the ultimate goals of the organization. Despite such efforts, validly assessing the ultimate criterion remains an ideal, since several longer-term goals by their very nature cannot be measured in the short term, and often the individual employee's impact on them is indirect. Despite such challenges, the notion of ultimate criterion is important since it recognizes the fact that individual performance should be ultimately congruent with, and relevant to, the major goals of the organization.[7]

For practical reasons, other criteria, referred to as actual criteria, are employed for organizational purposes. However, these criteria may be "deficient" or "contaminated." **Criterion deficiency** refers to those aspects of performance that should have been measured but were not. If a firm continuously measures only some aspects of the ultimate criterion, there may be a tendency to overlook important aspects of the organizational mission and goals.

> For example, if a salesperson's performance is assessed solely by the number of units sold or sales calls made, important aspects of the ultimate criterion, such as training new sales personnel, displaying merchandise, and serving customers, would be ignored to the detriment of the firm.

Criterion deficiency is more likely to emerge when the job has multiple performance dimensions and for practical reasons only a few are assessed. In some instances, some of the performance dimensions may not even be visible to the untrained observer. Consider these situations:

> Studies indicate that even a familiar job such as selling has a number of relatively independent skills, some of which are not obvious to the observer.[8] Similarly, a pilot's flying performance has at least six component abilities,[9] many of which are not visible to the untrained observer.

Ultimate criterion: the full range of performance criteria and includes everything that ultimately defines success on the job

Criterion deficiency: aspects of performance that should have been measured but were not

A physician's performance dimensions include psychological (e.g., skill in human relationships with patients), physical (e.g., physiological activities such as standing, sitting, working on a computer), economic (e.g., number of patients diagnosed), and ecological (e.g., the doctor's performance in different working conditions).

Often, a single criterion (e.g. economic) is used for human resource management purposes which can result in significant criterion deficiency.

Criterion contamination occurs when a firm measures aspects of performance that are not linked to the ultimate criterion for the firm. Continued criterion contamination can result in confusion and poor morale since employees may not see a direct link between the assessment criteria and the ultimate goals of the firm.

Criterion contamination: measuring aspects of performance that are not linked to the ultimate criterion

In the above example involving a salesperson, if the salesperson is assessed on problem-solving skills which are unrelated to selling or to the performance of people not under the individual's control, criterion contamination occurs since these criteria are not directly related to the individual's performance or job requirements.

Figure 2-5 shows how ultimate and actual criteria are related in each case.

What is the best time to assess an employee's performance? What is
the best time frame for assessing a person's performance? Different results may emerge, depending on when the employee's performance for a set of criteria is assessed. Further, for the same job position, different performance yardsticks may be appropriate for different times. As the employee "learns the ropes," dimensions of performance that seemed appropriate at the beginning of his or her employment become less important, and newer dimensions assume greater importance as the employee gains experience over time. Thus, criteria can be "dynamic," changing in importance over time.[10]

For example, the performance of a new hire in an accounting firm may be mainly gauged by the individual's proficiency in accounting procedures and the ability to carry out assigned tasks accurately and on a timely basis. However, as time passes, interpersonal skills and the ability to generate new business may become more important than technical expertise.

The optimum time for evaluating an employee's performance varies from situation to situation and job to job in the same organization.

FIGURE 2-5: Criterion Deficiency and Criterion Contamination

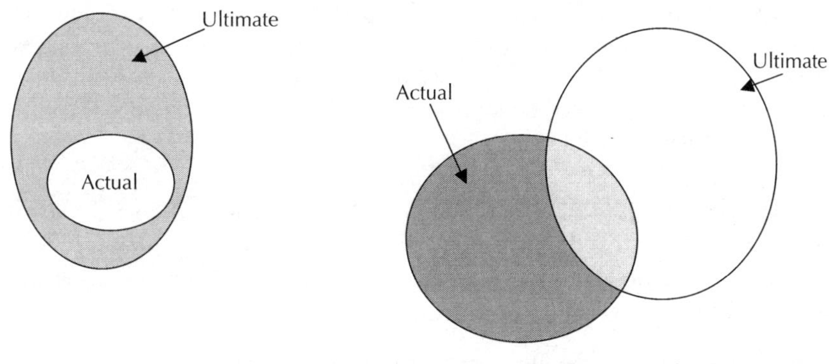

Criterion Deficiency
(Shaded area indicates deficient area)

Criterion Contamination
(Shaded area indicates irrelevant aspects of the performance measured)

The time frame for evaluating a production worker's performance will be significantly different from that for evaluating a research scientist's work in the same organization. For a production worker, daily performance indicators (e.g., volume of production, number of defects) may be appropriate, while for the scientist, his or her performance should be evaluated over a much longer time, and evaluating research productivity (e.g., number of innovative ideas) may be in order.

Which performance dimensions are more important than others? For those jobs for which multiple performance dimensions are assessed, the relative importance or weight of each dimension has to be first determined. Individuals performing identical jobs may score differently on various dimensions, making their contributions to the larger organization also quite different.

Some managers are effective primarily due to their ability to plan well; in the case of other managers, their success may be linked primarily to their ability to inspire others and make them strive towards a goal. Other managers are successful due to their ability to coordinate various activities and solve problems proactively. While all these attributes are important, effectiveness in a specific setting may be linked to just one dimension.[11] For example, some managerial abilities may be more important during organizational downsizing than during growth periods.

How stable should criteria be? Organizational goals and strategies have to continually adapt to the emerging realities around them. A criterion that is desirable at one time may become irrelevant or even undesirable at another time. Consider this situation:

During the sixties and early seventies, any land developer in eastern Canada who owned many acres of expensive real estate was considered "rich" and "astute in management." However, during the late seventies, interest rates soared, making the developer's mortgage payments burdensome. Liquidity became critical; and continued ownership of land became difficult, especially as the demand for new homes declined. The same managers who were earlier praised for their performance were then criticized for "lacking foresight."

This situation raises an interesting question: What is an appropriate time frame for assessing performance? Should the organization focus on short-term goals or on longer-term goals? Should the organization try to maximize short-run productivity and profits or should it maximize the probability of long-term growth, even if this longer-term growth results in some short-run losses? Ford Motor's experience indicates that short-term and long-term goals need not necessarily converge:

The Ford Motor Company, having introduced its Model A in the 1920s, became extremely successful in the late 1920s and early 1930s. To maximize efficiency, Ford did not change any of the major features of the car for several years. (Fords were said to be available "in any colour, so long as it's black.") The company's attempt to maximize production efficiency almost resulted in financial ruin, because Ford's competitors had branched out, offering different models and colours.

How to measure criteria? Finally, some criteria such as sales growth and market share can be directly measured, but others are harder to measure (e.g., adaptiveness or organizational citizenship). For some non-profit and service organizations, measuring less tangible criteria is difficult. Consider the following example:

How does one evaluate the effectiveness of a drug control and rehabilitation agency? Should one criterion be the number of persons treated and cured of drug addiction? Obviously, this criterion would be an oversimplification since some addicts are chronic users of drugs, while others are in earlier stages of drug use. Further, how does one define "cured"? Is it abstinence for a period of time or total freedom from all drugs for the remainder of the drug user's life? If total freedom from drugs is the criterion, how does one know for sure that even a single drug user has been truly cured? Should the effectiveness of the agency be evaluated instead by the increase in the number of cases referred to it? Or perhaps the agency should be seen as more effective when there are fewer new cases?

In the same way, evaluating the "performance" of service agencies or projects, such as driver education programs, consumer education classes, and neighbourhood and block parent units, may be difficult.

The challenges in choosing robust criteria underscore the importance of defining performance criteria carefully and exhaustively. For some guidelines for establishing useful performance criteria are listed in Figure 2-6 and discussed below.

Select relevant criteria
Relevance of a criterion refers to the correspondence between the criterion's measure and the organization's ultimate criterion or criteria. While relevance is intuitively appealing, ensuring the relevance of chosen criteria is no simple task. Even organizations operating in the same industry in the same region can be markedly different in their philosophies and internal practices, necessitating different performance criteria and measurement practices.

Relevance: the correspondence between a criterion's measure and the organization's ultimate criterion or criteria

> Two researchers collected data from 1282 managers in 50 life insurance companies to identify common performance criteria across different organizations in the same industry. The researchers developed a set of six behavioural job functions for the agency manager's position, based on five variables traditionally associated with the insurance industry: length of time the agency has been in existence, the type of agency (independent versus company-controlled), the number of agents employed, the number of supervisors, and the tenure of the individual company's manager. However, detailed data analysis indicated that these five variables together accounted for only 8.6% of the variance in managerial functions. Thus, over 90% of the differences in managerial activities could be explained by firm-specific variables including a firm's goals, strategy, and internal processes.[12]

Research findings such as the above underscore the importance of identifying performance criteria that are unique to a specific organization.

Select reliable criteria
Reliability refers to consistency in measurement and the degree to which measurements are free from random measurement errors. In turn, consistency is reflected in two dimensions of measurement: *stability* and *internal consistency*. The notion of reliability is discussed in detail in Chapter 4.

Reliability: consistency in measurement and freedom from random errors

If multiple measurements of a criterion taken within a short period produce different results, the criterion is not reliable. It is susceptible to considerable measurement error. Thus, ideally, repeated measurements of the same criterion over a relatively short period should show a high degree of robustness. This measure, usually referred to as test-retest reliability, indicates the *stability* in a criterion's measurement.

> For example, assume that a student who took an exam in human resource management today received a score of 70%. If the same student retakes the exam within a short period (without any additional preparation), we would expect the new test score to be similar to

---

FIGURE 2-6:   Attributes of Useful Criteria

1. Relevance
2. Reliability
3. Controllability
4. Practicality
5. Discriminability

the original score. If the new score turns out to be either 20% or 95%, we would consider the exam to be unreliable (or not equivalent to the one written today). If the exam were reliable, the student's score would show considerable similarity, assuming the testing conditions were identical.

Reliability is also reflected by the *internal consistency* of the measure. If the same criterion is measured by multiple indices, we would expect the results to point in the same direction, that is, to be internally consistent.

For example, suppose we measure a supervisor's leadership ability by giving a questionnaire to all of her subordinates. The questionnaire has six questions. If all six questions relate to the criterion of leadership, we would expect the total score for the answers to questions 1, 3, and 5 to show a significant and positive relation to the total score for questions 2, 4, and 6 in the questionnaire. This correlation, which is a measure of reliability, focuses on the internal consistency of the measure.

The notion of stability is related to the time frame used. As seen earlier, the "ultimate criterion" itself may shift in response to environmental changes; this means that long-term stability beyond a certain point may not be possible or even desirable. However, in the short term, performance criteria should reflect a high level of stability to facilitate measurement and comparison.

Select criteria that can be controlled by the employee Controllability

refers to the extent to which a performance criteria can be influenced, monitored, and changed by the individual or unit whose performance is being evaluated. If a performance cannot be controlled by the individual or unit concerned, then the measure does not validly reflect performance.

If a bank branch manager's performance is solely judged by the profits generated by the branch, the principle of controllability is violated because the manager cannot control this criterion. In many banks, the lending interest rates are set by regional or head offices. In addition, bank policy dictates that loans above specific limits must be approved by regional or head offices. Economic conditions, unemployment rates, regional income disparities, and industry trends are some factors that can affect the profits generated by a bank's branch, most of which are beyond the control of an individual manager.

Select practical, cost-effective criteria Do the costs of measuring a crite-

rion and comparing the resulting data justify using that criterion? Are the logistics of gathering performance data feasible given the organization's resources? If the answer to each question is "no," then the criterion is not practical. **Practicality** refers to the feasibility of using a criterion given the expected costs and logistics of gathering data. Note that a reliable and relevant criterion may still be impractical.

Most firms consider sales volume and customer service quality to be important dimensions of a salesperson's performance. Sales volume is relatively easy to measure. However, collecting valid information about the quality of the salesperson's customer service is a lot more difficult. To collect valid information, someone has to choose a random sample of each salesperson's customers, contact these customers, and collect and compare their responses to questions about the salesperson's quality of customer service. In some instances, in-depth interviews with customers may be necessary to identify the salesperson's performance with respect to dimensions that are not readily apparent. In many instances, such detailed data collection is impractical, given the time and resources that would have to be invested into such an undertaking. Many firms look at simpler measures such as the number of customer complaints. However, such measures can be inadequate, since there need not be a consistent relationship between poor service and customer complaints. (In other words, a number of dissatisfied customers may never complain.) Also, positive customer service measures are never collected.

Controllability: a performance criterion that is under the control of the individual or unit whose performance is being judged

Practicality: the feasibility of using a criterion given the expected the costs and logistics of gathering data and an organization's resources

Select criteria that discriminate between good and poor performance

For management decision-making purposes, a criterion is useless if it cannot help management to discriminate good and poor performers. If there is no variance in the measure, the criterion cannot help management make important human resource decisions. **Discriminability** refers to the sensitivity of the measure to help management discriminate between superior and poor performance.

Discriminability: the sensitivity of the measure to discriminate between superior and poor performance

> Consider an organization that has a highly automated manufacturing process. Most employees work with automated robots which produce at a predetermined rate. Production volume will be an improper measure in this instance since every employee will produce the same volume of similar products. The individual's performance is better gauged by other measures such as the number of errors made, the amount of scrap and waste produced, the amount of work that has to be redone to repair items, absenteeism, and machine downtime (if maintenance of machinery was part of the performance requirement).

Criterion variance and criterion relevance need not necessarily be positively correlated. A criterion (e.g., the number of accidents) may have low variance (e.g., the number of accidents may have increased from five to six), but even such a seemingly small change may have a significant impact on the organization. Nor is the lack of variance always caused by the inherent weakness of the criterion. It may be more attributable to an imprecise measurement process. Consider the following:

> For example, in one Canadian accounting firm, when the supervisors were asked to rate the service quality of their subordinates on a five-point rating scale (with anchors, "poor," "fair," "good," "very good," and "excellent"), several supervisors tended to pick good or very good for all employees. The problem here was not with "service quality" as a criterion but with the measurement tool. With a more sophisticated measurement tool or better training for supervisors, "service quality" could have been a valid criterion.

The solution, in part, lies in training supervisors to make proper assessments (see **Focus on Ethics**). Redesigning the appraisal forms can also significantly enhance the quality of measurements in such instances.

In summary, criteria have to be identified carefully and methodically. Figure 2-7 lists some popular performance criteria. Where practical, the quality of an employee's performance should be defined by multiple criteria to ensure that there is no criterion deficiency. Criteria should also be identified only after a good review of the job and all

Focus on Ethics

Consider the following situations. Suggest a solution for each case.

1. A supervisor allocates overtime (which pays double wages) to employees on the basis of personal preferences. She ignores some employees who want to work overtime, while she allocates overtime to employees she likes. When confronted, the supervisor justifies her actions on the basis of her faith in the employees who she believes will get the job done on time.

2. The employees in Division A of an organization believe that their jobs and competencies are very similar to those of employees in Division K, although the salaries for Division K employees are approximately 30% more and the working conditions are better. If anything, Division A employees believe they should be paid more because they have to work in unclean and dusty working conditions.

FIGURE 2-7:   Popular Performance Criteria

Production

- Number of units produced
- Number of documents word-processed
- Number of projects completed (e.g., for construction firms)
- Time taken to complete a project
- Average number of calls made each day (for call centre operations)
- Speed of production

Sales

- Number of items sold
- Commission earned
- Dollar volume of sales
- Average size of orders
- Rate of sales growth

Quality Measures

- Number of rejects per period
- Cost of reworking
- Cost of spoiled or rejected work
- Number of errors detected
- Number of customer complaints
- Number of cancelled contracts

Other Outcome Measures (for Systems)

- Number of job applicants attracted (for recruitment programs)
- Number of grants received (for fund-raising activities)
- Number of readers for a print ad
- Number of viewers for a TV commercial
- Number of grievances
- Number of accidents
- Number of safety violations
- Average time to locate and repair variation (in inspection, quality control, or maintenance jobs)
- Rate of employee turnover
- Number of transfers due to unsatisfactory performance

Employee Behaviours and Performance

- Number of days absent
- Number of times tardy
- Frequency of unauthorized work stoppages
- Length of unauthorized work stoppages
- Time taken to reach standard performance
- Level of performance reached in a predetermined period
- Number of promotions received
- Number of times considered for promotion
- Length of time in job
- Rate of salary increase
- Period between promotions
- Supervisor's ratings of performance
- Supervisor's ratings of personality traits or attitudes
- Peer ratings of behaviours or attitudes

of its components lest criterion contamination may result. Further, specific performance standards on these criteria have to be determined only after a thorough job and task analysis. The steps in job and task analysis are detailed in the following section.

IDENTIFYING JOB SPECIFICATIONS AND COMPETENCIES THROUGH JOB ANALYSIS

A **job** is a group of related activities and duties. A job may be held by a single employee or several employees. A job should be distinguished from a position and a task (see Figure 2-8). A **job specification** describes the job demands of the employees who do the job, and it is a profile of the human characteristics required by the job. These requirements include experience, training, education, physical demands, and mental demands. The determination of job specifications, performance criteria, and performance standards can only take place after a thorough job analysis. This section briefly discusses the steps in job analysis.

Job analysis involves the systematic collection, analysis, and interpretation of information about a specific job, which is used for describing the job, hiring suitable candidates, and setting performance standards. **Task analysis** involves analyzing the various tasks that constitute a job and looking for interdependencies and overlaps. The immediate outcome of job and task analyses is a **task inventory,** which is a list of all of the tasks that form a job and the competencies required to perform them. Without accurate information about jobs and tasks, it is virtually impossible to specify hiring requirements, provide fair compensation to employees, assess their performance, and counsel them when they face difficulties. Efforts to improve employee productivity levels and to eliminate unnecessary job requirements that can cause discrimination in employment should be based on the careful study of jobs.

Job: a group of related activities and duties, which can be held by a single employee or several employees

Job specification: the job demands and the profile of human characteristics required to perform the job

Job analysis: systematically collecting, analyzing, and interpreting job information

Task analysis: analyzing tasks that constitute a job and looking for interdependencies and overlaps

Task inventory: a list of all the tasks that form a job and the competencies required to perform them

---

FIGURE 2-8: Performance-Related Terms

Job: A group of related activities and duties. A job may be held by a single employee or by several people.

Position: The collection of activities, duties, and responsibilities performed by an individual employee.

Task: Each job has a number of tasks or identifiable and normally related activities.

Example: In a service department with one supervisor, three clerks, and twelve service personnel, there are sixteen positions but only three jobs. Each job requires the job incumbent to do a number of tasks.

Performance Criteria: The outcomes or behaviours associated with a job or position that are used to measure the employee's effectiveness. Performance criteria may include "quantity and quality of production" and "promotability," which an organization wants to maximize, as well as "wastage" or "number of accidents," which the organization wants to minimize. Other typical performance criteria include "response time in minutes," "punctuality," "tenure," and "attendance" (see also Figure 2-7).

Performance Standard: The level of performance expected or achieved for each performance assessment criterion. Usually, a performance standard is measurable, specific, and bound by time. "Achieve 93% customer satisfaction rate by the end of the first quarter" or "Reduce wastage by 2% by the end of February" are examples of performance standards.

Position: the collection of activities, duties, and responsibilities performed by an individual employee

Tasks: related activities associated with a job

Performance criteria: outcomes or behaviours associated with a job that are used to measure an employee's effectiveness

Performance standard: the level of performance expected or achieved for each performance assessment criterion

With hundreds (or even thousands) of jobs, it is nearly impossible for a large organization to know the details of every job. It is, however, unnecessary to collect information about identical jobs separately. Consider this example:

> One grocery chain has 390 cashiers. Each job is the same. Therefore, job analysis requires only a random sample of these positions, and the data collected from the analysis of this random sample generate an accurate information base for all 390 positions.

STEPS IN JOB ANALYSIS

Job analysis is a complex activity with six interrelated steps.[13]

Step 1: Identify the objectives of job analysis
The specific details collected during job analysis are influenced by the objectives of the study, so an organization must identify these objectives before performing job analysis. While the most common goals of job analysis are to establish performance standards, identify criteria for selection of employees, determine training needs, and design performance appraisal and compensation systems,[14] job analysis may also help to eliminate discrimination against specific employee groups, redesign a job, or even identify career paths for employees. The objectives also determine which jobs are to be analyzed and in what sequence. While almost all jobs could benefit from an in-depth analysis, resource and time constraints often prevent such analysis. Likely targets of job analysis are jobs that are critical to the success of an organization, jobs that are difficult to learn or perform (since this determines the extent of training), jobs for which the organization continuously hires new employees (since identifying clear job requirements is very important in this case), or jobs that preclude minority members, women, and the physically challenged. Jobs should also be analyzed if the introduction of new technology or an anticipated change in the work environment will affect the way a job is performed.

> One job analysis study[15] found that the skills, knowledge, and abilities essential for performance in secretarial and clerical positions were very similar to those needed in entry-level management positions. Employers can apply this finding to save money and time. For example, an employer could, after appropriate training, transfer employees in administrative and clerical jobs to managerial positions when these positions become available, rather than hiring outside of the organization. Employees can also apply this finding to develop future career paths based on their work experience and training. This finding may also encourage employees to look at their work experience and training in a new way.

Articles on job analysis:
www.hr-guide.com

Articles on relating employee practices to strategy:
www.chrs.net

Step 2: Become familiar with the organization and its jobs
Job analysis should be based on an awareness of an organization's objectives, strategies, structure, and culture and on information about the industry. Government reports, professional magazines and newspapers, and other documents are also a source of information about jobs.

Step 3: Determine the sources of job data
Although the most direct source of information about a job is the job incumbent, there are many other sources to consider. If a job has been analyzed before, previous records may be very helpful, although the analyst should take into account changes in technology and the work environment. Existing job descriptions, process specifications, machinery design blueprints, maintenance manuals, and other reports may also help in establishing the nature of a specific job. Professional magazines and publications, such as the *National Occupational Classification* (NOC) in Canada and the U.S. Department of Labor's

Handbook for Analyzing Jobs, also provide information on various jobs. Some other sources include the following:

- Job incumbents

- Supervisors, subordinates, colleagues, union officials

- Customers, other outside experts

- Company records, including existing job descriptions, organizational charts, and mission statements

- Equipment design blueprints, maintenance and safety manuals, and training videos for operating machines

- Professional publications

- The Internet

Step 4: Design an instrument for collecting data

To study jobs, analysts most often develop checklists or questionnaires with the goal of collecting uniform data about duties, responsibilities, human abilities, and performance standards. Such questionnaires are particularly important when collecting information from people (although using common checklists can help enhance the collection of information from other sources as well, such as company records). Always use the same questionnaire or survey instrument when collecting data about similar jobs. Analysts want differences in information about jobs to reflect differences in the jobs, not differences in the questions asked. Uniformity in data collection is especially hard to maintain in large organizations where many jobs have to be studied; only uniform questionnaires can generate valid data. Some of the more important items on which questions should be based in typical job analysis questionnaires are summarized in Figure 2-9.

FIGURE 2-9:   Sample Items to Be Addressed in a Job Analysis Questionnaire

1. Date of job analysis
2. Person conducting the job analysis
3. Job identification number, job title, and the department where the job is located
4. Nature of primary duties (managerial, mechanical, professional, clerical, blue collar, other)
5. List of duties and proportion of time spent in each task and activity
6. Performance criteria for evaluating success
7. Training needed to perform the various tasks and the job well
8. Responsibilities associated with the job (for tools, equipment, safety, material usage, other)
9. Physical attributes necessary to perform the job (e.g., vision, hearing, strength, height)
10. Mental attributes necessary to perform the job (e.g., mathematical skills, verbal skills)
11. Education required. Unusual psychological or physical demands required of the job holder (e.g., hot working area, abusive clients)
12. Level of prior work experience needed to perform the job
13. Safety or other health hazards associated with the job
14. Performance standards for the various activities

A sample job analysis tool: *http://mime1.marc.gatech.edu/ mm_tools/jcat.html*

There are a number of standardized forms currently available for job analysis. Two of the more popular ones are the Functional Job Analysis form and the Position Analysis Questionnaire.

Functional Job Analysis[16] rates a job on responsibilities pertaining to data, people, and things, in addition to a number of other dimensions, such as reasoning, judgment, mathematical ability, and the verbal skills needed to do the job. This approach to job analysis is more quantitative, and it can help produce a summary of the training requirements and performance standards associated with a job.[17]

Information on job analysis approaches: *http://harvey.psyc.vt.edu/*

The *Position Analysis Questionnaire* (PAQ)[18] can be applied to all types of jobs and can help produce a highly quantitative and finely tuned description of a job. On the basis of a five-point scale, the PAQ aims to determine the degree to which 194 different task "elements" are involved in the performance of a particular job (the five-point scale measures each task element on a continuum of "nominal or very infrequent" at the lowest level to "very substantial" at the highest). The PAQ groups job elements in a logical and quantitative manner, and the number of job elements covered under various categories are large (e.g., there are 36 different elements that measure "relationships with other people"). PAQ, in turn, is supposed to make job comparison easy. However, research has indicated that PAQ works best with lower-level jobs.[19]

Step 5: Choose a data collection method
There is no single best way to collect job analysis information. A job analyst must evaluate the trade-offs between time, cost, and accuracy associated with each method of collecting data.[20] Once an analyst decides which trade-offs are most important, he or she can collect data by conducting interviews, distributing questionnaires, observing, reading employee logbooks, or some combination of these techniques.

Interviews Face-to-face interviews are an effective way to collect job information. Analysts can refer to a questionnaire as a guide during the interview, but they can ask other questions. The advantage of an interview method is flexibility. Thus, although the process is slow and expensive, an interview allows the interviewer to explain questions that may not be clear to the interviewee and probe uncertain answers through follow-up questions.

Questionnaires A fast and less costly option is to survey employees through questionnaires. Questionnaires can be distributed using inter-office mail (or e-mail), the regular mail system, or even the Internet. This approach allows many jobs to be studied at once and at little cost. However, it is less accurate, because the recipient may misunderstand questions, give incomplete responses, or fail to return the questionnaire.

Observation Some researchers have argued that "the most effective way to determine what effective job incumbents do is to observe their behaviour."[21] However, this argument is open to debate. While observation does allow the analyst to come into direct contact with the employee and get a first-hand feel for his or her duties, it is also slow, costly, and potentially less accurate than other methods. The process may be inaccurate because the analysts may miss irregularly occurring activities that take place while the employee is actually working. The presence of an observer may also change the behaviour of the employee. Observing unobtrusively may be a possible solution; but it also raises a host of ethical questions. However, the analyst may prefer to observe when he or she questions the validity of data collected using other methods, or when language barriers exist with temporary foreign workers or new immigrants. Direct observation is most useful when the job involves easily observable activities.

> Thus, jobs involving auto repair and landscaping are more amenable to observation than jobs involving writing or fashion apparel design. The steps involved in the latter jobs are often invisible to an observer.

Employee log Reading an employee's log or diary is another option for collecting data about a job. Some workers periodically summarize their tasks and activities in a log. If a worker makes entries over the entire job cycle, the diary can prove to be quite accurate. By asking employees to monitor their own performance, the analyst can overcome the key limitations of observation. Collecting data from employee logbooks is a cheaper method than observation, and it is suitable for settings where the presence of an outside observer may be dangerous or inconvenient. Self-monitoring can also provide information on unobservable cognitive or mental processes related to job performance. But keeping a logbook is not popular, since doing so can be time-consuming. Managers and workers often see recording information in a logbook as a nuisance and resist the introduction of logbooks. Moreover, after the novelty wears off, accuracy tends to decline and entries become less frequent. Self-reporting may also tend to inflate the importance and time requirements of various tasks in some instances.

Combining data collection methods Since each method has its faults, analysts often use two or more techniques concurrently. Combinations can ensure high accuracy, and are also particularly attractive when all the employees of an organization are at the same location.

Step 6: Use job analysis information to make human resource decisions
Once the analyst has collected information about various jobs, the analyst can create job descriptions, job specifications, and job performance standards. A **job description** is a written statement that explains the duties, working conditions, and other aspects of a specified job. In contrast, a job specification focuses on the human characteristics such as work experience and training, and the educational, physical, and mental demands posed by the job. The difference between a job description and a job specification is one of perspective. A job description defines what the job does; it is a profile of the job, and specifications are usually a part of the description, so they are often combined into one document. The combination is simply called a job description. Figure 2-10 illustrates a job description that includes job specifications.

Job description: a written statement that explains the duties, working conditions, and other aspects of a specific job

---

FIGURE 2-10:   A Sample Job Description that Includes Specifications

Office Supplies Depot Limited
Job Description for Customer Service Representative

JOB IDENTIFICATION DETAILS

Job Title: Customer Service Representative	**Job Code**: CS 078
Date: May 13, 2006	**Author**: Kim Chan
Job Location: Downtown Toronto Store	**Job Grade**: 6
Report to: Natasha Shah, Manager	**Status**: Not exempt from overtime

JOB SUMMARY
Interacts with customers on a daily basis, promptly responding to all inquiries in person or over the telephone in a courteous and efficient manner. Encourages the sale of company products at every opportunity and applies exemplary customer-relationship skills. Provides information to customers about product features and substitutes. Helps customers when they are faced with problems or need information.

DUTIES AND RESPONSIBILITIES
1. Responds to customer inquiries on product features, prices, services, and delivery terms.
2. Takes customer orders for products and communicates these orders accurately to supply and servicing personnel in the company.

FIGURE 2-10: *(Continued)*

3. Accepts returns of merchandise by customers and gives them credit.

4. Displays and stocks merchandise on shelves.

5. Accurately prices items based on instructions received from the supervisor.

6. Prepares the necessary documents and transmits and files copies to the relevant offices within the company.

7. Responds to other miscellaneous inquiries, especially those related to warranties, delivery terms, and servicing frequencies (in the case of equipment).

8. Undertakes other tasks assigned by the supervisor.

WORKING CONDITIONS
Works in a well-ventilated office.
Must be able to work shifts.

SKILLS, EFFORT, COMPETENCIES, AND OTHER SPECIFICATIONS

Education:	Ten years of general education or equivalent. Familiarity with popular computer programs highly desirable.
Experience:	Prior selling experience in an office products industry is desirable. Familiarity with computers, scanners, and printers highly desirable.
Communication:	Strong interpersonal skills a must. Should have strong oral communication skills. Knowledge of French highly desirable.
Physical Demands:	Long periods of standing may be required. Should be able to lift a product weighing 10 kilograms or less. Finger dexterity for operating a computer keyboard and cash register is essential. Should not be allergic to solvents used in printer ribbons or printer cartridges or other chemicals normally used in an office setting.
Mental Demands:	Ability to respond to customer inquiries regarding prices, service terms, etc., a must. This ability requires good short-term memory. Ability to learn and remember product codes of popular items.
Other competencies:	Ability to empathize with the customer a must. Ingenuity and ability to solve problems in a creative manner is associated with superior performance on the job.

The above information is correct, as approved by:

(Signed) _____   (Signed)_____
       Customer Service Representative   Manager

Sample government job descriptions:
www.spb.ca.gov/employment

The key parts of a job description are: job identity, job summary, working conditions, and skills and competencies. All job descriptions also usually identify the author, the work supervisor, and the date on which the job description was prepared.

Job identity The section on job identity typically includes the job title, job location, job code, job grade, and its status (e.g., whether exempted from overtime laws or not). A job code is a combination of numbers and/or letters that can provide a quick summary of the job to the trained observer. These codes are useful for comparing jobs.

Job summary and duties A job summary is a written narrative that concisely summarizes the job in a few sentences. The summary tells what the job is, how it is done, and why. Most authorities recommend that job summaries specify the primary actions involved. Job duties can be simply listed in the job description.

Working conditions A job description also explains working conditions. This explanation may go beyond a description of the physical environment to include hours of work, safety and health hazards, travel requirements, and other features of the job.

Skills, effort, and competencies A job specification should include the individual requirements of the job, that is, requirements in terms of specific tools, actions, experiences, education, competencies, and training. For example, it should describe "physical effort" in terms of the special actions demanded by the job. "Will be expected to lift 15-kilogram boxes" is better than "Will be expected to lift heavy weights." Clear statements about expected behaviour give a better picture than vague generalities.[22] When preparing specifications, the analyst must not include needless job requirements since they not only exclude potentially qualified individuals from consideration but will also expose the organization to possible litigation from unsuccessful job applicants who feel they were unfairly discriminated against.

> Human Resources and Social Development website lists generic work skills such as reading text, numerical skills, thinking, problem solving, and oral communication, which can be customized and adapted to a specific job and an organization's unique conditions.[23]

Human Resources and Social Development website: *www.hrsdc.gc.ca/en/ home.shtml*

Approvals Since job descriptions affect most work-related decisions, selected employees and their supervisors should review them, and then supervisors can approve the descriptions. This approval serves as a further test of the accuracy of the job description and a further check on the validity of the job analysis information.

A job description is a broad-brush picture of the job on an analyst's canvas; a task inventory can be thought of as a painting with a finer brush.[24] In conducting task analysis and preparing a task inventory, the analyst lists each task that is an integral part of the larger job and also lists the specific competencies, skills, and personal resources needed to do the job effectively. Often, simple job descriptions cannot point to the differences in job responsibilities and duties between two firms or even two divisions in the same firm.

> For example, the job descriptions of a human resource manager in two different firms may look somewhat similar, although in one firm, the HR manager may be in charge of a large department which has a $3 million budget and supervises a team of professionals, while in the other firm, the HR manager may oversee all human resource functions under severe budgetary constraints and a skeleton team. In both firms, the HR manager must carry out all essential human resource functions, although under qualitatively different conditions.

Figure 2-11 shows parts of a task inventory for a shipper in Office Supplies Depot Limited. It shows that a task inventory is not a substitute for a job description; rather, a task inventory elaborates and explains items that cannot be described in detail in a job description.

In summary, job analysis enables an organization to identify unique job demands, working conditions, and other demands associated with the job. It is the starting point for establishing competencies to be used in hiring decisions. More on developing competencies is discussed in the next section.

DEVELOPING PERFORMANCE COMPETENCIES

A **competency** is a knowledge, skill, ability, or characteristic associated with high performance on a job, such as problem solving, analytical thinking, or leadership.[25] Others have defined the concept as "an attribute bundle," consisting of competencies in completing tasks, in achieving results, and in knowledge, skills, behaviours, and attitude,

Competency: a knowledge, skill, ability, or characteristic associated with high performance on a job, such as problem solving, analytical thinking, or leadership

FIGURE 2-11:   Parts of a Task Inventory for a Shipper

Office Supplies Depot Limited
Task Inventory for Shipper

JOB IDENTIFICATION DETAILS

Job Title: Shipper   **Job Code**: CS 083
Date: May 18, 2006   **Author**: Kim Chan
Job Location: Downtown Toronto Store   **Job Grade**: 3
Report to: Joan Hardy, Supervisor   **Status**: Not exempt from overtime

JOB SUMMARY

Receives delivery orders from customer service department, arranges them in sequence based on established criteria, packs products, addresses packages, and attaches invoice in standard containers as per procedures detailed in the company's operating manual, and delivers packages to the delivery counter for pick-up. The shipper is responsible for the safety of the products at the delivery point and during transit, to the extent that all packages and procedures meet the safety standards specified in the operating manual. The shipper is also responsible for lifting packages properly and for safely operating lift-trucks and carts.

PERFORMANCE STANDARD

100% accuracy in address labelling and 95% accuracy in shipping the correct products. At least 90% of the orders should be shipped out within two days after the shipper receives the delivery orders from the customer service department.

TASKS	STANDARDS		
	Time (Minutes)	*Accuracy* (%)	*Skills* (Primary only)
1. Review delivery order tickets			
A) Note quantity	$\frac{1}{2}$	98	C
B) Note brand/style/grade	$\frac{1}{2}$	98	C
C) Note delivery speed desired	$\frac{1}{2}$	97	C
D) Note prepaid or to be billed	$\frac{1}{2}$	95	C
E) Note address of destination	$\frac{1}{2}$	99	C
2. Obtain supplies and equipment needed to process order			
A) Obtain shipping containers	2	95	C, P
B) Obtain flatbed cart to transport containers	3	90	P
C) Use forklift where necessary	4	90	P
D) Retain order ticket and mark items collected in the boxes provided	-	90	C

....
....
....

Skills: C = *Cognitive*; P = *Psycho-motor*; A = *Affective*

The above information should be interpreted in conjunction with the *Operating Manual* and *Safety Instructions*. In the event of any discrepancy between the above information and instructions contained in the *Operating Manual* or *Safety Instructions*, the latter will prevail. The Management reserves the right to assign other duties so long as they are not beyond the capabilities of the employee concerned and not in contravention of the current *Collective Agreement*.

The above information is correct as approved by:

(Signed) _____   (Signed)_____
                Shipper   Supervisor

including work-related values and beliefs.[26] The objective of competency modelling is to identify characteristics that are associated with superior job performance. Figure 2-12 lists illustrative competencies for a supervisory position. In the case of this position, interpersonal and planning skills are the most important competencies.

Competencies are identified after a careful analysis of the work of high performers. This may be done through various job analytical approaches such as observation, listings of critical behaviours or incidents at work, interviews, employee logs, or otherwise. The job analysis information combined with the information on an organization's goals and strategies form the basis of identifying competencies and their relative importance to the position under consideration.

A **competency model** describes the output from analyses that differentiate high performers from average and low performers. Competency models are different depending on the method used to collect the data, the customers' requirements, and the focus of the person who develops the model. Some competency models identify specific competencies, provide a behavioural description for each competency, order the competencies by criticality, and establish a proficiency level for each competency. Competencies might include values, such as "integrity" and "tenacity." Such

Competency model: a model of various skills, abilities, behaviours, and other characteristics that differentiate high performers from average and low performers

---

FIGURE 2-12: Illustrative Competencies for a Supervisor in a Textile Firm

The weights attached to the competencies listed in this table are specific to a particular firm and may have to be changed to meet the needs of other firms. Each weight is based on the relative frequency with which the competency distinguished superior supervisors from average supervisors in this firm.

Competency	Meaning	Weight
1. **Professional expertise**	Knowledge of all relevant professional practices, including a sound awareness of situational factors considered in decision making	8
2. **Interpersonal skills**	Ability to communicate, negotiate, lead, and effectively resolve conflicts with others in the desired time frame	14
3. **Initiative**	Tendency to initiate actions before being asked	9
4. **Planning**	Consistency in making realistic production plans. Ability to anticipate production-related challenges and take action	12
5. **Customer service focus**	Focus on consistently providing the highest quality service to internal and external customers	11
6. **Flexibility**	Ability to alter plans, practices, and behaviours in light of emerging challenges and to respond to emergencies	7
7. **Analytical thinking**	Ability to analyze situations thoroughly and to see valid interdependencies among events and variables. Capacity to form valid conclusions and action plans	5
8. **Directiveness**	Ability to form clear plans, design structure and logistics; focus on achievement; tendency to lead (rather than follow)	8

competency models are helpful not only for placing employees into the correct positions and performance planning but also for hiring, training, and career planning for employees.

> A survey of 219 Canadian organizations by the Conference Board of Canada found that 45% of the responding firms implemented/applied a competency framework for training and development activities. A large number of the respondents had also used it for hiring, compensation, and performance management. According to 85% of the respondents, the adoption of a competency framework had enabled their training programs to become more strategic, while facilitating decision making, because a competency framework allowed employees to quickly identify the success factors in their organizational and personal work.[27]

Competencies must be carefully established and continually evaluated for their relevance to organizational **strategy** and processes. Employees must also be encouraged to acquire new competencies by relating competency building to internal reward systems. To be effective, employees should also have opportunities to use their newly acquired skills.

Trait and ability inventories are related to, but different from, competencies. Indeed, the notion of competencies is latent in the worker trait and ability inventories developed by researchers. **Trait inventories** focus on observable traits or characteristics that distinguish one employee from another. For example, the Threshold Traits Analysis System[28] focuses on 33 observable characteristics such as stamina, perception, adaptability to pressure, and tolerance, that distinguish one employee from another. In a similar vein, the Fleishman Job Analysis System[29] suggests that all jobs can be classified according to ability requirements including multi-limb coordination and oral communication. Other approaches such as the Job Element Method[30] also separate superior and poor performers on the basis of job-related abilities such as accuracy in perception. Most of such methods require the involvement of experts and work supervisors who can rate various job elements and traits on their relative importance to a particular situation.

Whatever the approach, the ultimate goal of competency modelling is to identify characteristics of superior employees in an effort to duplicate them in future hiring and training decisions. In some instances, performance standards are also identified on the basis of such benchmarks. The process of establishing performance standards is, however, complex and this process will be the focus of the next section.

ESTABLISHING PERFORMANCE STANDARDS

For a number of jobs, there are clear and visible performance *outcomes* associated with the position. Thus, salespersons are expected to sell, painters are expected to paint surfaces, and tax accountants are expected to complete tax returns. However, for several other jobs, such clear performance outcomes may not be readily apparent. There are also jobs where the employee only provides part of the total input, holding the person responsible for the entire outcome in such instances may not be appropriate or even fair.

> A college instructor may be extremely knowledgeable and enthusiastic about the course that she teaches (where teaching is the input), but her students' learning (the outcome) is affected by a number of factors beyond her control.

In other instances, simply focusing on outputs may detract the job incumbent from important non-quantitative aspects of the job. *Behaviours* and *attitudes* of the job

Information on psychology journals containing articles on competency modelling: *www.tulsa.oklahoma.net/ ~jnichols/ejournals.html*

Strategy: a comprehensive, integrated plan with long-term implications for achieving the organization's mission and objectives

Trait inventories: observable traits or characteristics that distinguish one employee from another

incumbent may be used as indicators of performance in such instances. Most organizations, in fact, use multiple measures of job performance:

> Salespersons are not only expected to sell a certain volume (an outcome) but also to be punctual, cleanly dressed, and courteous to customers (behaviours), and also to be willing to work extra hours when needed (an attitude).

Performance standards are obtained either from job analysis information or from alternative sources. For example, industry standards may be used as benchmarks for performance in certain jobs (especially service functions like accounting).[31] Job analysis information is usually sufficient to set performance standards for jobs that have the following features:

- the performance can be quantified;
- the performance can be easily measured;
- performance standards are understood by workers and supervisors; and
- the performance requires little interpretation.

Performance standards should be established after a careful evaluation of all job demands and working conditions. Sometimes the challenges facing the job holder may not be apparent, and working conditions have to be carefully investigated to avoid dysfunctional consequences as illustrated in the following study:

> A 2005 study of 40 000 Canadian nurses found that nurses work very long hours, have a large number of work tasks, and work many casual shifts. In turn, this work environment adversely affects their physical and mental health and results in higher absenteeism, emotional exhaustion, and higher injury claim rates than for workers in other professions. Attempt to bring in new immigrants to fill the shortage of nurses has created a new set of challenges. Another survey of 62 Canadian nurses found that systemic racism persists in the workplace, which negatively affects the performance of the respondents. The respondents, only five of whom were Caucasian, reported that race and ethnicity affect relations with patients, nurse recruitment, and job assignments. A number of nurses belonging to visible minority groups had decided to leave the profession.[32]

For jobs with short work cycles, such as assembly-line jobs, questions on the job analysis checklist or questionnaire may generate specific, quantitative answers. When supervisors confirm the accuracy of this information, these answers become job performance standards. In the case of some service jobs, quantifiable "outputs" may not be readily available; in these situations, performance is typically appraised by looking at employee behaviour. The process of setting standards for quantifiable outcomes is discussed in the following section. A later section looks at the process of setting performance standards for jobs with nonquantifiable outcomes.

SETTING QUANTITATIVE PERFORMANCE STANDARDS

Although job analysis does not always provide a source of performance standards, it is necessary even if analysts use other means to develop reasonable standards. The most common alternative sources of job standards are work measurement and participative goal setting.

Work measurement

Work measurement techniques estimate the normal performance of average workers; the results dictate job performance standards. Such techniques are applied to non-managerial jobs and involve examining company records, conducting time studies, and work sampling.

Company records Historical data from company records can supply information about necessary performance standards.

Work measurement: techniques that estimate the normal performance of average workers, the results of which create job performance standards

For example, based on information about past sales, production volume, and inventory, one large Canadian furniture manufacturer first decides on the number of beds, sofas, tables, and chairs that need to be produced each quarter. This in turn helps the manufacturer to identify the number of table legs, sofa cushions, drawers, table tops, etc., that should be made or assembled by each employee.

One weakness of collecting historical data is that it assumes past performance is average performance. Another weakness is that historical data are useless for analyzing performance of workers in "new" jobs, such as high-tech workers. However, if the analyst develops performance standards by reviewing production records for information about long-standing jobs, these historically based standards may be more accurate than the standards an analyst draws from a job analysis checklist. For analyzing the performance of job holders who are affected by rapid changes in production technology, this approach is unlikely to lead to satisfactory results.

Time study: setting performance standards by systematically observing and timing a job holder's various tasks and determining a standard time for each task after making allowances for rest breaks and fatigue

Time study A **time study** produces standards where the work of the job holder can be observed and timed. For a time study, each element within a job is identified. Then, while an average worker using the standard method of doing the job works, each element is timed. The work is timed repeatedly. The average times for each element of the job are summed up to yield the "rated job time." Allowances for rest breaks, fatigue, or equipment delays are added to produce a standard time. On the basis of standard times, the organization computes performance standards:

> After several observations, the human resource staff of Universal Painters found that a painter could paint 10 square metres of wall in an average of 4 minutes. Allowances for moving ladders, changing drop sheets, taking rest breaks, etc., were added to this rated job time of 4 minutes. The result was a standard time of 5 minutes. This result can be translated into a painter's standard of performance: a painter should be able to paint an average of 10 square metres for every five minutes, or 120 square metres each hour.

Work sampling By taking a random sample of work done by different job holders over a representative period, the analyst can determine how much time should be added for making allowances in the above instance. Allowances are, thus, usually set through *work sampling*.

> By making 200 observations of different painters at different times during the day over a two-week period, for example, the human resource analyst at Universal Painters discovered that the painters were actually painting four-fifths of the time. The rest of the time was spent on other activities including preparatory work. It was observed that 4 minutes of uninterrupted painting was required to paint 10 square metres. The standard time was computed by dividing the rated time of 4 minutes by the fraction of time spent working, or four-fifths in this example. The result was a standard time of 5 minutes.

Mathematically, the computation is:

$$\frac{\text{Rated Time}}{\text{Observed Time Spent Working}} = \text{Standard Time}$$

Standards for some jobs cannot be determined through either job analysis or work measurement. In service or managerial jobs, output may reflect changing trade-offs.

> For example, the length of a doctor's appointment cannot be accurately determined as this time depends on the seriousness of the patient's illness.

But standards are still useful, even though they are difficult to set. In some cases, mutual agreement about standards between the job incumbent and others in the organization (typically the boss) is more likely to be effective.

Participative goal setting When a job lacks obvious standards, managers may develop them by talking to their subordinates about the purpose of the job, the employee's role in relation to others, the organization's requirements, and the employee's needs. Through participation, the employee may gain insight into what is expected. Implicit or explicit promises of future rewards may also result. From these discussions, the manager and the employee should reach some jointly shared objectives and standards. The process may even lead to greater employee commitment, morale, satisfaction, and motivation.

Performance standards sometimes are set in the same way with union leaders. Labour leaders understand the important role of job analysis, and they may insist on negotiating performance standards for jobs. Negotiated agreements are usually written into legally enforceable contracts:

> In one paper products company, management decided to increase production rates by 5% to meet customer demand. Management decided to implement this increase without consulting first with the union. After the increase was implemented, the union threatened legal action because the new standards conflicted with those in the labour contract. Management was forced to retain the old standard.

DEVELOPING STANDARDS FOR OTHER JOBS

Objective criteria such as the quantity of production or the number of letters word processed, etc., are feasible for some jobs, mainly lower-level and production jobs. However, as an employee moves further and further away from actual production or sales work, objective measures of performance become increasingly scarce. Higher-level jobs in administration or project team management typically involve performance dimensions that are not easily measured in objective terms.

> For example, how does one measure the ability of a team leader to inspire her teammates to complete a project successfully? How does one measure the work of a volunteer fundraiser whose painstaking work may have inspired long-term donor loyalty even if it did not generate immediate contributions? How does one rate the leadership ability of a new manager who changed the work culture of his unit?

Assessing the performance of individual employees simply on the basis of their performance outcomes may be difficult for a variety of reasons such as the following:

- performance outcomes may depend on a number of external factors over which the employee has no control,
- because of the element of chance in results, especially when their outcomes are dependent on other people or external events, employees would want to be compensated for bearing that risk,[33]
- due to high task interdependence, it is hard to assign individual responsibility to outcomes, and
- the results of employee actions is known only after considerable delay, as in the case of the work of a research scientist.

In such instances, the performance of an employee is rated by other relevant people (e.g., superiors, clients, peers).[34] Whether an employee or team meets the performance standards is typically evaluated by using a rating scale, checklist, or other instrument.

Reliability of ratings As already noted, reliability refers to the consistency in measurement. If the same person who is rating an employee's performance, or rater, gives two different ratings for the same performance, then the assessment will be unreliable.

Reliability, thus, is the degree to which measurement is free from random error. The reliability of an assessment depends, among other things, on the assessment procedure and the type of measure used.

Direct assessment: the rater witnesses the actual performance or behaviour

Indirect assessment: the rater evaluates substitutes for actual performance or behaviour

Direct assessment occurs when the rater actually sees the performance or behaviour. **Indirect assessment** occurs when the rater can evaluate only substitutes for actual performance.

> For example, a supervisor's monitoring of an operator's calls is direct observation; giving a written test on company procedures for handling emergency calls is indirect observation.

Indirect observation usually yields less accurate results, because it allows only for the evaluation of substitutes, referred to as *constructs*, for actual performance. Since constructs are not exactly the same as actual performance, indirect observation is usually affected by error.

> For example, in the above instance, the call operator may know how to correctly handle emergency calls, but may not actually exhibit this required behaviour when his performance is evaluated. It is also possible that fast readers would score better in a written test even if their on-the-job behaviour is no different from that of slower readers.

Verifiable performance measures: indicators of job performance that can be observed and checked by others

Non-verifiable performance measures: ratings that cannot be seen or checked by others

The reliability of assessment also depends on the verifiability of the measure used. **Verifiable performance measures** are indicators of job performance that can be observed and checked by others.

> For example, if two supervisors monitor an operator's calls, they can count the number of wrongly dialled ones. The results are more objective since each supervisor should count the same number of calls.

Usually, verifiable measures are quantitative. They typically include items such as units produced, scrap rates, number of computational errors, number of customer complaints, and so on. These kind of items were discussed in the previous section. **Non-verifiable performance measures** are those ratings that cannot be seen or checked by others. Usually, such measures represent the rater's personal opinions, and therefore these measures are more susceptible to bias and inaccurate measurement (see Figure 2-13). By using verifiable and direct measurements, the rater can enhance the reliability of ratings.

Articles on performance management:
www.p-management.com
www.work911.com
www.hr-guide.com

In part, low reliability is also due to the personal bias of the rater and errors committed by this person. Raters should be skilled in observation and categorization and be trained to avoid rating errors (see Figure 2-14).

Individual ratings: ratings of individual employees, comparing the person's performance with an expected standard or past performance levels

Comparative evaluation methods: methods that compare one employee's performance with that of co-workers or an entire workgroup

A variety of ratings scales, checklists, and other assessment tools and techniques are currently available. Ratings may be conducted individually or on a comparative basis. **Individual ratings** focus on a single employee by comparing the person's performance with an expected standard or with past performance levels. **Comparative evaluation methods** involve comparing one person's performance with the performance of co-workers or of an entire workgroup. The more popular rating approaches are briefly discussed below.

Individual Ratings

Rating scale: uses a scale from high to low to subjectively evaluate an employee's performance on a number of job-related dimensions

Rating scale Perhaps the most widely used form of performance appraisal is the **rating scale**, which requires the rater to provide a subjective evaluation of an employee's

FIGURE 2-13:   Type and Reliability of Performance Measures

	Direct	Indirect
Verifiable	High reliability	Moderate reliability
Non-verifiable	Moderate reliability	Poor reliability

FIGURE 2-14: Appraisal Errors and Biases

Leniency error is the tendency to give very generous ratings to every employee. This error is most likely to occur when performance standards are very vague and the organization has a highly political climate (because the supervisor wants his or her people to advance in the organization).

Severity or strictness error is the opposite of leniency error and occurs when the rater is too harsh on the employee being evaluated. This error is common when performance standards are vague. The tendency to rate others harshly is often linked to the type of ratings the rater has received from others; thus, a supervisor who has received a poor rating is more likely to rate others more harshly.

Halo error is the tendency of the rater to carry over his or her overall favourable or unfavourable opinion about the job incumbent from one dimension of performance to other dimensions. For example, a rater who rates an employee as high-producing might also automatically rate the same employee as analytical; or the rater might rate an employee who is tardy as uncooperative without justification. The halo error is likely to emerge when the rater is using indirect and non-verifiable measures, or when the rater has been asked to evaluate friends.

Central tendency or **range restriction error** is a predisposition to cluster ratees in the middle of a rating scale. For example, when a five-point rating scale is used ("1" indicating poor, "3" meaning average, and "5" indicating outstanding), the rater will give a rating between 3 and 4 on most dimensions to all job incumbents. This type of error is most likely to occur when the rater has to justify extreme ratings (such as a 1 or 5) to the human resource department, the union, or the employee.

Recency error occurs when the ratings are unduly biased by the ratee's most recent actions. This type of error is most likely to occur when the appraisal occurs annually or infrequently. To reduce this bias, raters should keep a log of all critical behaviours and achievements of the employee and make frequent assessments.

Stereotypes are the rater's prejudices against specific groups who share one or more common attributes (e.g., "accountants are not outgoing people" or "women cannot be good in technical jobs"), which unduly bias their ratings of members of such groups.

Attribution errors occur because of the tendency to attribute favourable outcomes to personal effort and unfavourable outcomes to external forces or working conditions. For example, an individual may attribute successful job performance to his or her own traits (e.g., "I am intelligent") or work habits (e.g, "I am a hard worker") and assign poor performance to external conditions ("The equipment is obsolete"). When raters are evaluating the achievements of others, many assign reverse attribution: that is, another person's success is usually attributed to luck or working conditions, and failure is attributed to the person's incompetence.

Personal prejudice is the rater's personal like or dislike of an employee, which influences his or her assessment of that person's performance. Often the rater is not even aware of this subconscious prejudice, which further complicates the picture. The rater's generalized assumptions about a job also bias the ratings in some instances (for example, when evaluating a woman holding a job traditionally held by a man).

Self-serving errors are biases that encourage raters to inflate ratings to make themselves look good. For example, a supervisor who is responsible for training or mentoring another employee may inflate the ratings assigned to that person to improve his or her status as a trainer or mentor.

Leniency error: tendency of raters to give very generous ratings to everyone

Severity or **strictness error:** tendency of raters to rate employees too harshly

Halo error: tendency of raters to carry over favourable or unfavourable assessments of one dimension of performance to other dimensions

Central tendency or **range restriction error:** predisposition to cluster most job incumbents in the middle point of a rating scale

Recency error: the ratings are unduly biased by the most recent actions of the ratee

Stereotypes: rater prejudices against groups or individuals who share one or more common attributes

Attribution errors: tendency to attribute favourable outcomes to our own efforts and unfavourable outcomes to external forces or working conditions

Personal prejudice: rater's personal like or dislike of the employee, which influences the assessment of that person's performance

Self-serving errors: rater tendency to inflate ratings to make themselves look good

Information on ten managerial errors in conducting performance appraisals: *www.work911.com/ performance/particles/ stupman.htm*

performance on a number of job-related dimensions on a scale from low to high. A rating scale can be easily constructed and understood, and it is also one of the oldest approaches to assessing employee performance. As Figure 2-15 indicates, the evaluation is based solely on the opinions of the rater. In many cases, the criteria are not directly related to job performance. Although subordinates or peers may rate the employee, the immediate supervisor is usually the appraiser.

FIGURE 2-15:   A Sample Rating Scale

Ontario Leather Products
Performance Rating Scale

Instructions: For the following performance factors, please indicate on the rating scale your evaluation of the named employee.

Employee's Name: *Department:*
Appraiser: *Date:*

	Excellent	Good	Acceptable	Fair	Poor
	5	4	3	2	1
1. Quantity of production					
2. Quality of production					
3. Initiative					
4. Dependability					
5. Concern for safety					
6. Cooperation					

.....
.....
.....

12. Resourcefulness

Total Score for this employee: _____

The rating scale in Figure 2-15 is completed by checking the most appropriate response for each performance factor. Responses may have numerical values so that an average score can be computed and compared for each employee. The rating scale is inexpensive to develop and administer, and raters need little training or time to complete the form. For this reason, it is widely used. Because of its simplicity, the rating scale can be applied to a large number of employees whose total scores can be compared for the purpose of making placement and compensation decisions.

The disadvantages of the rating scale, however, are numerous. Some of these scales provide only very general and ambiguous anchors to the rater without specifying what "good" or "satisfactory" means (see Figure 2-16). This ambiguity can result in different raters assigning varying meanings to an anchor, thus reducing the usefulness of the total scores for comparing different employees. A rater's biases are likely to be very high in these circumstances. Further, raters and ratees may interpret the anchors (i.e., the points on the scales) differently, thus reducing the developmental value of the feedback.

Checklist: statements and/or adjectives describing an employee's job-related behaviours or performance, from which the rater makes selections

Checklists The **checklist** requires the rater to select statements and/or adjectives describing an employee's job-related behaviours and performance or other characteristics. Again, the rater is usually the immediate supervisor. Figure 2-17 shows a portion of a checklist, including a brief list of desirable behaviours and traits. If the rater

---

FIGURE 2-16:   Ambiguous Rating Scale Anchors

Safety: High |_____|_____|_____|_____| Low

Safety: *Outstanding* ▫ *Very good* ▫ *Good* ▫ *Satisfactory* ▫ *Marginal* ▫ *Unsatisfactory* ▫

Safety: *Outstanding* ▫   ▫   ▫   ▫   *Poor* ▫

FIGURE 2-17: Parts of a Weighted Checklist for Office Products Depot Limited

Instructions: Check ALL items that apply to the employee.

Employee's Name: _____   *Department:* _____
Appraiser: _____   *Date:* _____

Weights		
(6.2)	☐	Greets customers in a friendly manner and smiles
(4.0)	☐	Keeps work station or desk well organized
(3.9)	☐	Is cooperative
(4.3)	☐	Employee plans actions before beginning job
(6.0)	☐	Utilizes suggestive selling
(4.0)	☐	Works overtime when asked
(7.0)	☐	Serves customers promptly
(5.5)	☐	Is conscientious

....
....

(0.2)	☐	Employee listens to others' advice, but seldom follows it.

Total Score: _____
(Computed by the Human Resource Department)

Note: The weights are unknown to the rater and not shown in the form.

---

believes the employee has exhibited a particular behaviour or trait, then the rater checks off the item. If the rater perceives that the employee does not possess a behaviour or trait, then he leaves this item unchecked. The number of check marks represents the employee's score.

Figure 2-17 also shows weights, which are assigned to different items on the checklist to reflect their relative importance. These weights do not appear on the actual checklist that the rater uses and the weights are unknown to the rater. The items with the higher weights are deemed to be either more predictive of success or more critical for the success of the organization's strategy. When weights are used, the human resource department computes the total score for the individual employee, after taking into account the values of the weights. If a checklist contains enough items, it may provide an accurate picture of employee performance.

The advantages of a checklist are economy, ease of administration, minimal training required of the rater, and standardization. Although the checklist method is practical and standardized, the use of general statements reduces its job-relatedness. When the weights are unknown to the rater, the evaluation is less open to bias; however, when the items refer to personality traits or are subjective, it can still result in many of the deficiencies of the rating scale. Other disadvantages include susceptibility to rater bias (especially the halo effect), misinterpretation of checklist items, and use of incorrect or invalid weights by the human resource department. Moreover, the rating scale does not allow the rater to give relative ratings. For example, in the above form, employees who gladly work overtime would get the same score as those who work overtime unwillingly. Since the disadvantages outweigh the advantages, organizations choose more objective and behaviourally based measures.

Canadian Paper and Pulp Products Corporation had historically used a checklist for the performance evaluation of all types and levels of employees. But Pat Sullivan, the new human resource manager, realized that the performance criteria for different jobs were vastly different. In consultation with the relevant groups, she created three new formats: one for the managers and supervisors, another for clerical and sales staff, and a third one for operating personnel in the factory and field. She also replaced personality-based items (such as dependability and resourcefulness) with more behavioural and work-oriented measures. The result was better feedback to job incumbents and more task-relevant training programs for poor performers.

Critical incident method: the rater records statements that describe extremely good or bad employee behaviour related to performance

Critical incident method The **critical incident method** requires the rater to record statements that describe extremely good or bad employee behaviour related to performance. These statements are called critical incidents. Critical behaviour is that which differentiates between successful and unsuccessful performance in a particular work situation. Critical incidents are recorded for each employee very soon after they occur. The records should also briefly explain what took place when the incident occurred. Several typical entries for a water works employee appear in Figure 2-18. As shown in the figure, both positive and negative incidents are recorded. Incidents are classified (either as they occur or later by the human resource department) into categories such as safety, quality control, and employee development.

The critical incident method is extremely useful for giving employees job-related feedback. It is also less open to the recency bias. This method is also useful for performance appraisal interviews since a supervisor can focus on the actual job behaviour of the person concerned rather than on vague personality traits or general characteristics.[35] When a large number of critical incidents are collected and analyzed, the results can provide valid indications of employee training needs and organizational improvement efforts.

A year after she joined the company, Pat Sullivan, of Canadian Paper and Pulp Products Corporation, embarked on a project to develop a behaviourally anchored rating scale for the clerical and sales staff. She collected information on 670 critical incidents from the employees for this purpose. These incidents helped Sullivan identify seven major dimensions of performance and associated behaviours. During the development of the scale, she also identified a number of areas that needed further improvement. Among these were: training the supervisors in communication and diversity management, training salespersons in handling difficult customers, and time-planning skills for project heads.

Of course, the practical drawback of the critical incident method is the difficulty of getting supervisors to record incidents as they occur because recording incidents on

---

FIGURE 2-18:   Critical Incidents Related to a Performance Dimension of a Water Utility Employee

Town Waterworks

Instructions: In each category below, record specific incidents of extremely good or poor employee behaviour.

Employee's Name _____
Appraiser:_____   **Period: *January 1, 2006, to December 31, 2006***

Date	*Behaviours/Incidents*
Safety	
Positive	
2/1	Put out small trash fire in the storeroom promptly
2/5	Reported broken rung on utility ladder promptly
Negative	
12/3	Left leaky hose in front of storeroom, causing wet and slippery floor
4/6	Smoked a cigarette in the chemical supply room
3/8	Smelled of alcohol after lunch
4/9	Poured acid into plastic container, ruining countertop

a daily or even weekly basis can be time-consuming and burdensome. Many supervisors start out recording incidents as they occur faithfully, but then lose interest. But they may, just before the evaluation period ends, add new entries. When this happens, the recency bias may be exaggerated and employees may feel that supervisors are building a case to support their subjective opinions. Even when a supervisor records critical incidents over the entire rating period regularly or as needed, employees may feel that the supervisor is unwilling to forget negative incidents that occurred months before. The incidents, in their narrative form, do not lend themselves to quantification, which means that individual or group comparisons of performance are impossible. To overcome this problem, two suggestions have been made in the past. First, commonly occurring behaviours (or incidents) can be converted into a checklist or rating scale. Alternatively, the incident can be modified into a behaviourally anchored rating scale, which is discussed below.

Behaviourally anchored rating scale (BARS) The focus of evaluation instruments may be the frequency of specific behaviours or their value to the organization. A **behaviourally anchored rating scale (BARS)** attempts to reduce the biases inherent in subjective performance measures by focusing on specific and critical work behaviours rather than traits or personality characteristics. Figure 2-19 shows an example of a BARS. The specific examples of behaviours listed on the right are a result of an expert collecting descriptions of good and bad critical incidents or behaviours from incumbents, peers, and supervisors and then grouping them into performance-related categories such as employee knowledge, customer relations, and the like. These behaviours are rated from 1 to 7.

The various behaviours for a department store sales supervisor for the performance dimension "employee supervision" are illustrated on the rating scale shown in Figure 2-19. Since specific, job-related behaviours are listed, an objective evaluation is

Behaviourally anchored rating scale (BARS): a performance assessment approach that reduces subjectivity and bias in performance measures by focusing on specific and critical work behaviours, rather than on traits and personality characteristics

---

FIGURE 2-19: BARS for a Sample Performance Dimension of a Department Store Supervisor

Maple Leaf Department Stores

Store Supervisor: <u>Performance Dimension: "Employee Supervision"</u>

Outstanding performance	7 – Can be expected to conduct a workshop for new salespeople, providing them with adequate skills to be among the top 10% of the sales force in the department
Very good performance	6 – Can be expected to publicly praise an employee for a job well done and constructively criticize in private those employees who did not perform to expectations, offering guidance for the future
Good performance	5 – Can be expected to provide great confidence to his or her salespeople by delegating important tasks to them
Satisfactory performance	4 – Can be expected to keep timely, accurate human resource records and conduct salary reviews on time
Marginal performance	3 – Can be expected to remind salespeople about their duties and ask them to come to work, even if they are ill
Poor performance	2 – Can be expected not to honour promises on transfer or compensation
Extremely poor performance	1 – Can be expected to blame the salespeople for his or her own mistakes

more likely. This type of scale also provides specific performance feedback to employees. If the rater collects specific incidents during the rating period, the evaluation is apt to be more accurate besides being a more effective counselling tool. A BARS is job-related, practical, and can be standardized for similar jobs. But the rater's personal bias may still result in a rating that is too high or too low. Unlike rating scales which use vague anchors like "poor" and "excellent," a BARS's anchors are more concrete, thus making them more legally defensible.

One serious limitation of a BARS is that the number of performance categories, such as "customer relations" or "employee supervision," is limited. Also, each category has only a limited number of specific behaviours. While the anchors (or points on the scales) are clear and behavioural in their description, they are only examples of behaviour an employee may exhibit. The fact that some of the employees may never exhibit specific behaviours that are listed on the scale can potentially cause confusion to the raters. As with the critical incident method, most supervisors are reluctant to maintain records of critical incidents during the rating period, which reduces the effectiveness of this approach. Many supervisors also find the behavioural focus to be unnatural if they are more familiar with trait-based rating scales. Supervisors may simply translate their impressions of an employee's traits into behavioural ratings, thus reducing the overall accuracy of this approach.[36] Nor is the BARS appropriate for all jobs as one HR manager found:

> Encouraged by her success at developing a behaviourally anchored ratings scale for the clerical and sales staff, Pat Sullivan of Canadian Paper and Pulp Products Corporation considered the same format for the manufacturing and field staff. But soon she gave up the idea. For one thing, the supervisors did not actually see several of the behaviours exhibited by their subordinates on a regular basis. Further, there was often not a close correspondence between an employee's behaviours and the performance outcomes. For many of the jobs, the employees preferred a more objective measure of their performance, especially since the top management was planning to introduce a performance-linked pay system in the near future.

Comparative evaluation methods

One or several supervisors or raters may conduct a comparative evaluation, where the supervisor compares an employee's performance with the performance of the employee's co-workers. Typically, the supervisor rates each employee in a group, resulting in a ranking of employees from best to worst. To reduce bias and improve acceptance, some organizations use a more elaborate group evaluation method where several raters may evaluate an employee's performance. When the raters get an opportunity to compare their ratings of an employee, the result can be more valid future evaluations. Usually, the comparative ratings themselves are not shared with the employees, fearing that this knowledge might result in loss of cooperation among employees. The most common forms of comparative evaluations are the ranking method and forced distribution.

Ranking: the evaluator ranks employees from best to worst

Ranking Ranking requires the evaluator to rank employees from best to worst. Ranking has the advantage of forcing the rater to differentiate among employees. When rankings are not mandatory, a supervisor may have the tendency to rate every one the same, thus reducing the system's usefulness for reward and placement purposes. However, ranks do not provide any information about the performance or the difference between employees who hold different ranks. All that an evaluator can say is that certain employees are better than others. Ranks can be particularly confusing when the performance of two work teams are compared, as shown in Figure 2-20.

FIGURE 2-20: Ranks and Performance Levels in Two Workgroups

Performance Level (10 = highest)	Work Team 1	Work Team 2
	(Ranks of employees in parentheses)	
10	Ann (1)	
9		Francois (1)
8		Kevin (2)
7		Rajesh (3)
6	Mark (2)	
5	Su-Yin (3)	Sonia (4)
4	Mohammed (4)	
3	Tom (5)	Matt (5)
2		
1		

In Figure 2-20, although both Ann and Francois hold the first ranks in their respective teams, Ann's performance is superior to Francois's. Further, Kevin and Mark, both of whom hold second rank, not only have different performance levels but are also different distances from the first rank holder. Indeed, the third rank holder in work team 2 has a higher absolute performance level than the second rank holder in work team 1.

Ranking is also susceptible to halo and recency effects, although the rankings given by two or more raters can be averaged to help reduce bias. The advantages of ranking are that it is easy to administer and explain to ratees.

Forced distributions Forced distributions require raters to sort employees into each of several classifications or categories based on their performance. For example, a certain portion of employees must be categorized as either "outstanding" or "poor," and so on. Figure 2-21 illustrates how a rater might classify ten subordinates on overall performance. Raters may also be asked to classify their subordinates on a variety of other criteria such as reliability, service quality, safety, and so on.

Forced distributions: raters sort employees into several classifications or categories such as "outstanding" or "fair" based on their performance

As with the ranking method, raters do not know the relative differences among employees, but this method overcomes the biases of central tendency, leniency, and strictness. Some workers and supervisors strongly dislike this method because employees are often rated lower than expected. However, the use of a forced distribution requires some employees to be rated low.

FIGURE 2-21: The Forced Distribution of the Performance of Ten Employees

Pilkington Foundry
Forced Distribution Rating of the Overall Performance of Employees

Outstanding (Top 10%):	Mildred Knox
Very Good (Next 20%):	Mallika Dhawan, Mohammed Aboubacker
Good (Middle 40%):	Ted Miner, Jack Gale, Terry Summers, Russ Mills
Fair (Next 20%):	Yuan Chan, Cathy Rider
Poor (Bottom 10%):	Pat Cromier

In summary, wherever feasible, objective measures of performance should be used. When subjective measures such as ratings are the only option, efforts should be made to enhance the reliability of ratings through the careful design of the rating instrument and the rater's training.

Once the performance criteria and performance standards are identified, the human resource needs have to be identified through human resource planning, which is discussed in the next section.

DETERMINING HUMAN RESOURCE NEEDS

Human resource planning (HRP): systematically forecasting of an organization's future demand for and supply of human resources and matching supply with demand

The hiring process cannot begin until the employment manager has a clear idea of the number and type of job vacancies in the organization. **Human resource planning (HRP)**—or employment planning, as it is also called—involves the systematic forecasting of an organization's future demand for and supply of human resources and attempts to match supply with demand.[37] (See Figure 2-22 for steps in HRP.) As the figure shows, a number of forecasting techniques can be employed to predict human resource needs. Today, several sophisticated statistical and mathematical tools may help a firm plan its human resources. Given the primary focus of this book, only the more popular tools are discussed here. For a more detailed discussion of various human resource planning systems and tools, the reader is directed to the various publications cited in the following pages.

As Figure 2-22 shows, forecasting techniques range from the informal to the sophisticated and help the organization predict its human resource needs. The objective in all instances is to match supply of human resources with demand. Even the most sophisticated methods are not perfectly accurate; instead, they are best viewed as approximations. Most organizations make only casual estimates about the immediate future. As they gain experience with forecasting human resource needs, they may use more sophisticated techniques (especially if they can afford specialized staff).

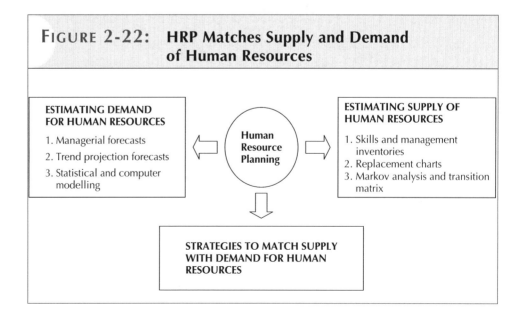

FIGURE 2-22: HRP Matches Supply and Demand of Human Resources

ESTIMATING DEMAND FOR HUMAN RESOURCES

1. Managerial forecasts
2. Trend projection forecasts
3. Statistical and computer modelling

Human Resource Planning

ESTIMATING SUPPLY OF HUMAN RESOURCES

1. Skills and management inventories
2. Replacement charts
3. Markov analysis and transition matrix

STRATEGIES TO MATCH SUPPLY WITH DEMAND FOR HUMAN RESOURCES

ESTIMATING DEMAND FOR HUMAN RESOURCES

Three major approaches for predicting future human resource needs are managerial forecasts, trend projection forecasts, and statistical and computer modelling. These are briefly discussed below.

Managerial forecasts

Managerial forecasts—sometimes referred to as "expert forecasts"—rely on knowledgeable managers to estimate future human resource needs. In many small business organizations, it is the owner or manager who identifies the need for full-time or part-time help. Even in larger organizations, a perceived need for additional human resources begins at the operational level. Consider this conversation between the supervisor and a billing clerk in a home heating oil company:

Supervisor: *Why haven't the monthly bills gone out yet?*

Billing Clerk: *I am sorry, but after Debbie switched to part-time last month, things have been quite hectic here. The new computer system does not help either. Right now, the old and new billing systems are not compatible. I have been working overtime on this, but nothing helps.*

Supervisor: *Yes, I talked to Jack in the IT department about the incompatible systems. It seems it will take at least another four months for the new system to be fully operational. Meanwhile, I'll ask the HR department to get us another temporary person. The cost of hiring a temporary will be much less than what we lose in overtime costs and lost interest in unpaid accounts.*

Such informal and instant human resource plans are not uncommon. However, more progressive employers do not wait for a situation such as this to arise before taking corrective actions. A better approach is to survey knowledgeable managers about their future employment needs and take action.

An approach such as the *nominal group technique* (NGT) takes a more focused approach to conducting such a survey. In the NGT, a group of experts are asked to identify the factors that will have an impact on an organization's future staffing needs (typically, a year or two ahead). Each of the five to fifteen participants in a group meeting lists as many answers as possible. The group shares these ideas in round-table fashion until all of the ideas have been recorded. The group then discusses the ideas and ranks them. The organization chooses the top three or four ideas for implementation.[38]

In situations where it is difficult to bring the experts face to face, a variation of the above, called the *Delphi technique*, is employed. The Delphi technique involves the following: the employment specialist in an organization's human resource department solicits estimates from a group of experts, usually managers. The employment specialist in the HR department also acts as an intermediary by summarizing their findings and sending this summary back to the experts. The experts are surveyed again after they have gone through the findings. These steps are repeated until the experts' opinions begin to converge on future human resource needs and developments. Normally, three to five surveys are adequate.

Trend projection forecasts

In many situations, especially for organizations operating in relatively stable environments, projecting past trends into the future is an easy and fast approach to predicting future human resource needs. The two popular tools for projecting trends are extrapolation and indexation.

Extrapolation involves linearly extending past rates of human resource changes into the future.

For example, for Maple Leaf Auto Dealers, a national auto dealer, if an average of 12 salespeople left the firm for other opportunities each quarter, then the organization can predict that 48 new positions will have to be filled in a year.

Extrapolation: linearly extending past rates of human resource changes into the future

Indexation approach: estimating future employment needs by matching employment growth with a specific index

The indexation approach involves estimating future employment needs by matching employment growth with a specific index. A common index is the ratio of number of employees to sales.

> For example, for Maple Leaf Auto Dealers, the management finds that for each $1 million increase in sales, six new salespeople are needed. Then, if the firm has plans to increase its sales by $2 million next year, it will need to hire twelve new salespeople.

Both the extrapolation and indexation approaches are based on the assumption that the past is a good predictor of the future and that past relationships between variables, with the appropriate modifications, will apply to the future. Extrapolation and indexation, thus, are crude, short-run approximations because they assume that the causes of demand—external, organizational, and workforce factors—remain constant, which is seldom the case. While these approaches permit adjustments for changes in labour productivity, technological improvements, etc., the fundamental relationship among variables is expected to hold true over the predicted period. It should, however, be noted that growth or decline in the labour force may change over time (typically, the management tier grows at a somewhat faster pace than it is compressed). When using indexation, this factor must be recognized.

The limitations of the above methods render them inappropriate for making long-range human resource projections. The more sophisticated statistical analyses make allowances for changes in the underlying causes of demand.

Statistical and computer modelling

Statistical and computer modelling A variety of statistical and management science tools, including multiple regression, linear programming, waiting line theory, and queuing theory, are available for producing more sophisticated models of future human resource needs.

> For example, using queuing theory, the manager of a fast-food restaurant can identify the precise number of service staff needed to ensure a maximum customer waiting time of two minutes. The model can also identify the queue length given the number of customers and the average time, per customer, that existing service staff take to serve customers.

Computer models: mathematical formulas that simultaneously use extrapolation, indexation, survey results, and estimates of workforce changes in simulated settings to compute future human resource needs

The most sophisticated forecasting approaches involve computers. **Computer models** are series of mathematical formulas that simultaneously use extrapolation, indexation, survey results, and estimates of workforce changes through the use of simulated settings to compute future human resource needs. Computer models may simulate and then forecast changes in demand for human resources given various internal and external organizational factors. Over time, actual changes in human resource demand are used to refine the computer's formulas.

ESTIMATING THE SUPPLY OF HUMAN RESOURCES

There are two sources of supply: internal and external. The internal supply consists of the number of currrent employees who can be promoted, transferred, or demoted to meet anticipated needs. Until this number is determined, external recruitment cannot begin. The recruiting function and sources of external recruits are discussed in Chapter 5. The focus here is on the approaches to estimating internal supply of human resources.

Estimating the internal supply involves identifying the number of employees and their capabilities. Job analysis and employee records provide the needed information to planners, who can, based on the information, identify openings that can be filled by present employees. Planners use three major tools, namely, skills and management inventories, replacement charts, and Markov analysis with a transition probability matrix to estimate the supply of human resources.

Skills and management inventories

Human resource audits summarize the various skills available in the firm. A **skills inventory** is a comprehensive catalogue of the capabilities of the organization's workforce listed in a uniform manner or style. Typically, a skills inventory has four major parts:

- **Part I** identifies each employee's job title, experience, age, and previous jobs. Typically, the human resource department collects the data from employee records.

- **Part II** lists information about the skills, duties, responsibilities, and education of each employee. The human resource department may collect the data from job specifications, or from phone or face-to-face interviews, or more recently, from the organization's intranet and Human Resource Information System (HRIS) where present.

- **Part III** provides the supervisor's evaluation of each employee's performance and potential. Details about actual work performance (both volume and quality), readiness for promotion, and any deficiencies are noted here. The supervisor's signature helps to ensure that the evaluation has been done by someone who knows the employee better than the human resource specialists.

- **Part IV** includes recent employee evaluations, which give more insight into past performance and function as a check for completeness.

Managerial inventories are similar in nature and provide comprehensive reports of available management capabilities in the organization. Some organizations use the same form to collect information for managers and non-managerial employees. Where these forms differ, the management inventory also includes additional information about management activities, such as the number of employees supervised, the type of employees supervised, the type of management training programs attended, the total budget managed, any previous experience in management (including a listing of management duties), and the duties of the manager's subordinates.

To be useful, skills and management inventories must be updated periodically. Updating inventories every two years is sufficient for most organizations if their employees are encouraged to report major changes to the human resource department as they occur. Major changes include acquiring new skills, completing a degree or a certificate, changes in job duties, and the like. Failure to update skills inventories can lead to employees being overlooked for job openings within the organization.

Replacement charts

A **replacement chart** is a visual representation of who will replace whom in the event of a job opening. The chart, which is much like an organization chart, depicts the various jobs in the organization and shows the status of likely candidates. Typically, the replacement *status* of an individual consists of two variables: present performance of the individual and promotability. Present performance is determined largely from supervisory evaluations. Opinions of others (e.g., peers, subordinates, customers) may also be included in appraising present performance. Future promotability is based primarily on present performance and the estimates, made by immediate superiors, of future success in a new job. Sometimes assessment centre reports are also used to rate managerial potential (Chapter 7 discusses assessment centres). The human resource department also contributes to these estimates by providing the results of tests and interviews.

Human resource and management decision makers find that these charts provide a quick reference. However, often, the charts do not contain enough information about the individual involved.[39] This deficiency is addressed through the preparation of *replacement summaries*. Replacement summaries list likely replacements and their relative strengths and weaknesses for each job.

More recently, in many large organizations, replacement charts and summaries are no longer the norm. Instead, the best fit for various openings are identified using

Skills inventory: a comprehensive catalogue of the capabilities of the organization's workforce, listed in a uniform manner or style

Managerial inventories: comprehensive reports of available management capabilities in the organization

Replacement chart: a visual representation of who will replace whom in the event of a job opening

computers and electronic matching of applicant profiles with job demands. When human resource records, job analysis information, and skills inventories are computerized, the best candidate for a job position can be identified in minutes as the following example shows:

> Canada Paper and Office Products, a company with operations in five countries, has a computerized human resource information system (HRIS). All the key information about every employee, including training and performance details, is fed into a central HRIS. When a new position is to be filled, first a search is made for internal candidates on the basis of key skills required. A separate program helps produce career-development plans, pinpointing weaknesses and suggesting solutions. For example, in the case of some managers who did not possess any cross-cultural experience, these individuals were sent on temporary assignments abroad to help develop the required experience. When a new position falls vacant, potential replacements can be found in minutes through a computerized search.

Markov analysis and the transition probability matrix The Markov analysis reflects the pattern of past movements of employees from one job (or rank) to another within the same organization. This type of analysis is particularly useful in organizations where employees move from one job (or rank) to another on a regular basis and when jobs or human resource movements do not fluctuate rapidly due to external (e.g., technological) or internal (e.g., strategic) change.

A Markov model, also referred to as a probabilistic or a stochastic model, determines the pattern of employee movements across jobs or divisions and helps project the patterns into the future.[40] A **transition probability matrix** describes the probabilities of an incumbent staying in his or her present job for the forecast time period (usually one year), moving to another position in the organization, or leaving the organization. When the forecaster multiplies the number of employees in each type of job by the matrix coefficients at the beginning of a year, the forecaster can easily identify the number of people who will be working in the same jobs at the end of the year. Markov analysis is a fairly simple method of predicting the internal supply of human resources in the future as the following example shows:

> Figure 2-23 shows a sample transition matrix. Based on past records, Canada Grocers has identified the probabilities of employee movements across three major job categories. The table shows that 80% (or 0.8) of the incumbents in Job 1 are expected to be in their present positions at the end of the year, 10% (or 0.1) are expected to move to Job 2, 5% (or 0.05) to move to Job 3, and 5% (or 0.05) are expected to leave the organization (through resignations or otherwise). When these probabilities are multiplied by the number of persons in Job Category 1 at the beginning of the year (namely, 200), we can estimate that 160 of them will remain in their present position, 20 of them will move to Job Category 2, 10 of them will move to

Transition probability matrix: the probabilities of an incumbent either staying in his or her present job for the forecast time period (usually one year), moving to another job position in the organization, or leaving the organization

FIGURE 2-23:   Transition Probability Matrix for Canada Grocers

Jobs	Job Category 1	Job Category 2	Job Category 3	Exit from Firm
Job Category 1 (=200)	0.80	0.10	0.05	0.05
Job Category 2 (=100)	—	0.70	0.10	0.20
Job Category 3 (=80)	0.05	—	0.90	0.05

Job Category 3, and the remaining 10 will leave the organization. If similar calculations are performed for all the jobs (in the case of this firm, for Job Categories 1, 2, and 3), the firm may predict the approximate number of employees who will remain in each job position and the recruitment needs. For example, in the case of Job Category 1, it may lose 40 employees to other jobs or employers, but gain 4 employees from Job Category 3. This means that 36 new employees will have to be recruited to maintain the current staff strength.

Many firms use the previous year's transition rates for predicting next year's movements. However, if the previous year was atypical, the predictions may be erroneous.[41] Markov analysis is popular because it's easy to use. However, it is only as good as the transition probabilities used. The probabilities will not be very reliable if there are only a few job incumbents in each job. Generally, Markov analysis works best if there are at least 50 employees in each job position,[42] which makes this analysis more appropriate for medium and large organizations. Markov analysis can also be used to assess the potential impact of possible changes. Thus, "What if?" analyses can be undertaken to understand the impact of possible future scenarios (e.g., "What if a major change in technology results in the loss of 15% of jobs in Category 1 or doubles the movement from Job Category 1 to Job Category 2 next year?"). Markov analysis is a useful tool for human resource forecasting, especially in the context of strategic planning.

> A leading lumber firm used a sophisticated Markov-type model to plan its human resources. The model analyzed the flow of human resources, the demand for various types of employees, and the transition rates across jobs, thus helping the management to balance supply and demand for human resources. For instance, under the assumptions of varying transition rates, the company could forecast the workforce supply and demand for different levels and different periods. Thus, the Markov-type model enabled the policy makers of the company to analyze the impact of different policies on human resource supply and demand.[43]

Today's sophisticated computers permit increasingly complex modelling for human resources, such as *holonic modelling,* which portrays interactions with dynamic environments and reflect the impact of strategic decisions on the supply of human resources at different organizational levels.[44] The benefits of holonic modelling include a better design and greater flexibility, which can contribute to a better understanding of the pattern of human resource movements.

MATCHING SUPPLY WITH DEMAND

Rarely does the employment manager find a perfect match between the supply of and demand for human resources. More often than not, either supply will be higher than demand, or vice versa. Matching supply with demand requires careful planning, since careers may be affected or even lost.

When there is an oversupply of human resources, the employment manager can turn to these typical strategies:

- **Hiring freeze:** as a first step, most organizations do not permit any new hiring from outside of the company, in the hope that, over time, natural attrition (e.g., through retirement, voluntary separations, death) would bring supply in line with demand.

- **Early retirements:** when a hiring freeze alone does not bring the required reduction in human resource supply, many organizations offer early retirement to, or ask for voluntary retirement from, its workforce. Sometimes, phased retirements, which allow individual employees to work gradually shortened workweeks, are introduced.

- **Job sharing:** Job sharing, or job splitting, involves dividing the duties of a single job among two or more workers, thus essentially eliminating the need for some employees to work on a full-time basis.

- **Internal transfers:** At times, reducing the number of employees in some divisions may be accomplished by transferring them to other sections or job categories. This may entail additional training in several instances. It is also likely that employees will resist being transferred to geographically distant areas.

- **Part-time workers:** Sometimes the organization may convert full-time positions into part-time or contract positions.

- **Leave without pay:** Some organizations offer a leave of absence to some employees without pay. When the conditions facing the organization change, these employees are welcomed back into their regular jobs.

- **Layoffs:** In some instances, laying off, or the temporary withdrawal of employment from, some workers may be the only viable option. While unpleasant to both employees and their supervisors, layoffs may be warranted under poor economic conditions or scarce organizational resources.

An organization responds to a shortage of employees using the following approaches:

- **Overtime:** Many organizations begin by asking employees to work beyond their normal hours, helping the organization avoid incurring fixed expenses that are typical of many new positions and save on expensive employee benefits.

- **Temporary employment agencies:** Temporary employment agencies are a source of short-term help, which is particularly popular for filling secretarial, janitorial, and clerical jobs. More recently, temporary agencies are also a source of scientific and professional workers.

- **Part-time and contract workers:** Increasingly, many organizations attempt to meet a shortage by hiring part-time workers. In other instances, individuals are hired as independent contractors who can carry out a job at a location outside of the organization, saving the employer overhead costs and employee benefits.

- **Transfers:** In several instances, positions are filled internally through transfers. It should be noted that transferring employees may not solve a shortage, since a new vacancy (i.e., the position of the transferred employee) is now created.

- **Employee leasing:** Increasingly, several companies lease employees to organizations in a variety of areas such as payroll, taxation, accounting, and legal services.

- **Promotions:** As in the case of internal transfers, existing employees can be promoted to higher positions as they become vacant.

- **Hiring full-time employees:** For several positions where internal transfer or promotion may not be feasible or even desirable, new employees are hired from outside of the organization.

In summary, both internal and external staffing strategies can be employed to match supply and demand for human resources. Regardless of strategy, the new employee's knowledge, skills, and capabilities have to match the needs of the job. For assessing the match between employee capabilities and job criteria, the employer uses a number of indicators (called "predictors"), which include items such as educational qualifications, work experience, test and interview scores, and references. The indicators must be reliable and valid for selection purposes. The characteristics of such measures are discussed in Chapter 4. All predictors should also be legally defensible and should not unfairly discriminate against any protected group. The following chapter elaborates on the legal considerations in the context of hiring.

Implications for Practice

1. Performance criteria should be systematically related to the organizational goals and mission, and they should be exhaustive. Criterion deficiency and criterion contamination result when important performance dimensions are disregarded, and they expose the organization to possible legal challenges.

2. In general, the total performance of an employee cannot be evaluated solely on the basis of any one single criterion. Hence, an effort should be made to identify the total performance domain of a job before hiring decisions are made. The selected criteria should be relevant, reliable, sensitive, and controllable.

3. Systematic job and task analysis should precede the identification of job requirements and performance standards.

4. Developing criteria for job evaluation without objective measures is beset with a number of challenges. While a number of rating and ranking procedures are available, it should be recognized that none of these totally overcome bias or other deficiencies associated with subjective measures. When a rater or evaluator uses subjective measures, his or her training in appropriately using such measures is critical.

5. Hiring decisions should be made only after a thorough analysis of the existing supply and anticipated demand for human resources. Where feasible, more sophisticated human resource planning tools should be used to make such predictions.

Key Terms for Review

Attribution errors, *p. 59*

Behaviourally anchored rating scale (BARS), *p. 63*

Central tendency, *p. 59*

Checklist, *p. 60*

Comparative evaluation methods, *p. 58*

Competency, *p. 51*

Competency model, *p. 53*

Computer models, *p. 68*

Controllability, *p. 42*

Criterion, *p. 35*

Criterion contamination, *p. 39*

Criterion deficiency, *p. 38*

Critical incident method, *p. 62*

Direct assessment, *p. 58*

Discriminability, *p. 43*

Extrapolation, *p. 67*

Forced distributions, *p. 65*

Halo error, *p. 59*

Human resource planning (HRP), *p. 66*

Indexation approach, *p. 68*

Indirect assessment, *p. 58*

Individual ratings, *p. 58*

Job, *p. 45*

Job analysis, *p. 45*

Job description, *p. 49*

Job specification, *p. 45*

Leniency error, *p. 59*

Managerial inventories, *p. 69*

Mission statement, *p. 35*

Non-verifiable performance measures, *p. 58*

Performance criteria, *p. 45*

Performance standard, *p. 45*

Personal prejudice, *p. 59*

Position, *p. 45*

Practicality, *p. 42*

Range restriction error, *p. 59*

Ranking, *p. 64*

Rating scale, *p. 58*

Recency error, *p. 59*

Relevance, *p. 41*

Reliability, *p. 41*

Replacement chart, *p. 69*

Self-serving errors, *p. 59*

Severity or strictness error, *p. 59*

Skills inventory, *p. 69*

Stakeholders, *p. 36*

Stereotypes, *p. 59*

Strategy, *p. 54*

Task analysis, *p. 45*

Task inventory, *p. 45*

Tasks, *p. 45*

Time study, *p. 56*

Discussion Questions

1. What are the desired attributes of performance criteria? Would the performance criteria for employees working at two different banks that are operating in the same region be different? Why?

2. What steps would you take to analyze the jobs of 300 assembly-line workers in a garment unit? Would your approach be different if most of the workers are new immigrants?

3. How would you develop criteria for jobs for which no objective performance standards exist?

4. What are the major tools for planning human resource needs?

Critical Thinking Questions

1. If you were part of a team that had been asked to look into the quality of training offered in your college or university, what criteria would you employ to evaluate the quality of the training?

2. Assume that you are asked to conduct a job and task analysis of the instructor for this course. How will you go about it?

3. Would there be differences in the human resource planning approaches for a large bank and for a local police department or division? Why?

4. Consider the organizations in the chart below. What differences are likely to exist in setting performance standards for the two organizations?

	Organization A	Organization B
Number of employees	4200	22
Region of operation	All of western Canada	Whitby, Ontario
Type of business engaged in	Grocery business	Legal services
Size (by industry standards)	Medium	Small

Web Research

Conduct a web search and identify ten recruitment ads for human resource managers. Ideally, you should focus on two different industries and also different job ranks, such as VP Human Resources, Director of Human Resources, and Manager of Human Resources. List the required competencies in each advertisement. Write a report summarizing your findings and highlighting the differences across different organizations and job levels.

CASE INCIDENT

Kempt Road Auto Limited

Kempt Road Auto Limited is a medium-size distributor of popular American and Japanese cars. The company sells both new and used cars in the same location. It has an auto service unit, adjacent to the sales office, which provides routine and emergency maintenance to cars. Aggressive marketing and the introduction of a performance-based compensation system has resulted in fast sales growth. In just two years, the company's sales have increased by 180%.

The customers were, however, beginning to note delays in auto service. Consequently, despite the impressive sales growth of the unit, the service arm of the company grew only by a meager 14%. Informal conversations with some of the

---

FIGURE A: Kempt Road Auto Limited
Customer Satisfaction Survey

KEMPT ROAD AUTO LIMITED
Customer Satisfaction Survey

At Kempt Road Auto, customer service comes above everything. We are delighted that you chose us for your auto service needs. To make our service even better in the future, may we ask if you could spend a few minutes to fill out this form? Please drop it in the box at the customer service counter when you are finished filling it out. Thank You!

Today's Date:_____   Time:_____

Name of the Attending Technician:_____
(FILLED BY THE OFFICE BASED ON ORDER NUMBER AND COMPANY RECORDS)

                      Excellent (5)   Good (4)   Satisfactory (3)   Fair (2)   Poor (1)

Did the staff who attended to you
1. *explain everything properly?*
2. *appear professional?*
3. *appear polite?*

Was your repair
4. *done with speed?*
5. *done properly?*

Your overall evaluation of
this service call:

Comments:
....
....

This part of the form to be filled out by the customer service representative:

Details of the problem/service job: _____

Time arrived:_____   Time departed:_____

customers indicated that many felt the service to be expensive and time-consuming. Often, there were delays in delivery and the final service charges presented to the customer were significantly higher than the initial estimates provided to them at the time of order.

In an effort to turn things around, Kempt Road Auto introduced a new form to measure service excellence. At the end of each service call, each customer was requested to complete a form evaluating the service they received (over 85% routinely obliged). The relevant portions of the form are shown in Figure A. The ratings on the various questions were added together to get a total score. The staff whose ratings were above the unit average for the month were given a bonus ranging anywhere from 1% to 8% of their monthly salary. The customer service person and the maintenance technicians were given a straight monthly

salary plus a bonus, based on their overall performance as rated by the clients.

The company monitored the results for a period of six months. While 90% of the service personnel had earned the extra commission in one time period or another, the overall unit had not shown any significant growth during the period. The number of service orders had increased by 16% (and the total revenue of the unit by 18%). During the same period, the car sales division had grown by over 60%.

Questions

1. What is your assessment of Kempt Auto's new performance assessment approach?

2. What improvements would you recommend to the company?

CASE

Kanata Food Distributors*

Note: This case continues the case in Chapter 1: Kanata Food Distributors. Review the case background in Chapter 1 before examining this case.

The three divisions of Kanata Food Distributors have their own internal structures, which are hybrids of geographic and functional structures. For example, the 24-7 shops have a regional head office in Montreal, which coordinates the activities of all the shops located in the metro region; but the functions such as marketing or human resources report to their parent divisions located in Ontario. Similar arrangements can be seen in the Super K and Grocery lines. In general, Kanata has attempted to maintain a lean structure that facilitates quick decision-making and delegation to lower levels, while at the same time maintaining high standards of performance at all levels (See case background in Chapter 1 for more details).

The 24-7 shops had no formal appraisal procedures for their staff in the past. Given that these stores use a large number of part-timers (whose turnover was high), management felt that these stores needed some degree of standardization in performance appraisal. In the past, individual store managers simply used whatever appraisal system they favoured. Some of the stores had informal systems. The supervisors kept track of critical incidents and communicated the events annually, or in rare instances, semi-annually. In other stores, the supervisors used short performance rating forms for all employees. The form's four-point scale allowed supervisors to rate workers as

poor, average, good, or very good on five dimensions (performance, attitude, cooperation, initiative, and absenteeism). The manager then calculated the total score for each employee and gave raises to those with a total of 15 points or more each year. In general, stores which used such rating forms gave 70% of the staff raises.

Everyone agrees that a prime focus of the new evaluation procedure should be customer service. One suggestion was to slightly modify the existing rating form to include "customer service focus" as a sixth dimension. However, there was no universal support for this idea. In the end, the company decided to hire a consultant to look into the current situation and suggest a course of action.

Questions

1. If you were the consultant, what steps would you take?

2. Is it adequate to modify the current rating form used in some of the stores? Why?

3. Elaborate on the various performance dimensions and measurement criteria that you would recommend to the company management.

*Case written by Professor Hari Das of Saint Mary's University, Halifax. All rights retained by the author, © 2005.

CHAPTER

3 MEETING LEGAL CHALLENGES

"Employers today face a complicated environment affecting the recruiting and hiring process. This environment has been brought about by ever-increasing, overlapping legislation and government regulations, complex case law decisions, and some large arbitration awards. ... Managers and human resource professionals must be aware of acceptable and unacceptable hiring practices, because even a hiring practice that appears neutral on the surface can lead to a discrimination claim if it has an adverse impact on individuals in a class protected by human rights legislation. Managers need to understand the risks involved in hiring the wrong person and the potential to end up involved in a painful wrongful dismissal human rights case."

Fiorella Callocchia and Joan Bolland[1]

CHAPTER OBJECTIVES

After studying this chapter, you should be able to:

- Discuss the impact of the Canadian Constitution and the *Canadian Charter of Rights and Freedoms* on hiring practices

- Describe the major implications of human rights legislation for staffing managers

- List key provisions of other legislation that affect hiring

- Discuss actions to foster bias-free hiring and a culture that values diversity

A partially hearing-impaired person who applied to the Canadian Coast Guard College was rejected on the basis of a low score in a test developed at a cost of $100 000. The applicant filed a complaint with Canadian Human Rights Commission, claiming that the test did not validly measure his ability to perform the required duties and hence discriminated against persons like him who suffered from a degree of hearing impairment. During tribunal hearings, expert witnesses criticized the test on various grounds including incomplete technical development, lack of reliability and validity, and test administration under non-standardized conditions. The test designer also did not provide norms against which an applicant's score could be validly compared and interpreted. The tribunal concluded that the test was discriminatory and granted monetary compensation to the complainant.[2]

Welcome to the complex and ever-changing world of staffing! Several federal, provincial, and municipal laws and regulations routinely have an impact on staffing policies and procedures. Factors such as shifting demographics, economic fluctuations, international events, and changes in cultural values result in new legislation which, in turn, adds to the complexity of human resource selection practices.

> For example, in 2005, Ontario removed the mandatory retirement requirement at the age of 65. While this change benefits Ontario employers by increasing the size of their organizations' pool of human resources, it also has implications for various human resource activities such as job design, training, compensation, and succession planning. Older employees may require less training, but they need different ergonomics in the workplace. Pension plans may have to be changed to accommodate the generally longer tenure of employees. Internal managerial and career succession plans may require modifications since employee movements may become less frequent in some instances.

Unless a human resource department is able to recognize and respond to these realities on a timely basis, its policies and practices will become outdated, resulting not only in possible legal violations but also a waste of resources, lost productivity, and employee dissatisfaction. While legal challenges are better known and easier to predict than other challenges such as technological advances or international developments, their implications are seldom clear. The impact on human resource planning of the *Canadian Human Rights Act*, passed more than 20 years ago, is still somewhat unclear. Major judicial verdicts, changes in employment laws including minimum wages, federal and provincial government regulations, and so on have all had great implications for any organization's staffing department. Although many large firms have established employment equity programs, almost every day, new court decisions underscore the need for changes in employment practices. Even the judicial system itself is not immune to these changes, as the following example shows:

> In the recent past, an independent committee recommended to the Department of Justice in Nova Scotia that law firms in the province must hire a certain percentage (some members recommending 20%) of lawyers from visible minorities in the future. Such a decision can have profound implications for law firms operating in the province.[3]

Where the organization's workforce does not reflect the larger society's workforce profile, the organization may have to formulate new policies, as in the case of the police organization in the following example:

> Metro Police never pursued hiring policies that intentionally discriminated against any group. But over the years, new hires had been mostly white males who lived in a 30-kilometre radius of the city. In the recent past, the force had initiated a voluntary diversity management program that focused on bringing more women and minorities into its patrol. To fulfill the intent of the diversity management program, Percy, who headed the staffing department, decided to recruit from distant educational institutions that had higher numbers of minority students. He also put several recruitment ads in churches, transit stations, and other community centres frequented by minorities.

To meet new social priorities and emerging legislation, some organizations take proactive measures. Proactive employers, such as Pizza Hut, use innovative recruitment programs to tap the skills of an external diverse workforce:

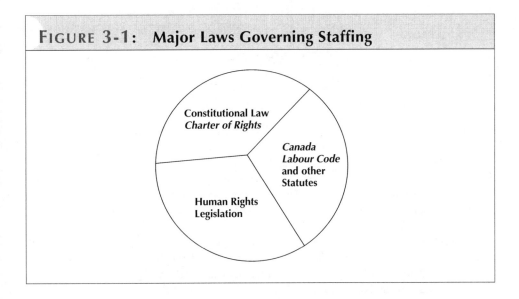

FIGURE 3-1: Major Laws Governing Staffing

Realizing that there are thousands of physically challenged individuals who want to work but are without jobs, Pizza Hut actively started to seek entry-level personnel among this group, and later included those with mental disabilities as well.[4]

This chapter discusses the major legislation affecting the employment function. For the purpose of our present discussion, these laws are discussed under the three headings shown in Figure 3-1. The remaining sections of this chapter will focus on these three areas, concluding with some suggestions for bias-free hiring practices.

THE CONSTITUTION AND THE CHARTER OF RIGHTS

The *Constitution Act, 1982* (the Constitution) replaces the acts and orders contained in the *British North America Act, 1867*, and today is the "supreme law" of this country. Section 52(1) of the Constitution proclaims that:

> 52. (1) The Constitution of Canada is the supreme law of Canada, and any law that is inconsistent with the provisions of the Constitution is, to the extent of the inconsistency, of no force or effect.

Sections 1 to 34 of Part 1 of the Constitution are collectively called the *Canadian Charter of Rights and Freedoms*. The Charter of Rights provides these fundamental rights to every Canadian (Section 2):

1. freedom of conscience and religion;
2. freedom of thought, belief, opinion, and expression, including freedom of the press and other media of communication;
3. freedom of peaceful assembly; and
4. freedom of association.

The Charter of Rights provides protection to every Canadian in the following areas:

1. fundamental freedoms;
2. democratic rights;
3. the right to live and seek employment anywhere in Canada;
4. legal rights: the right to life, liberty, and personal security;

Information and documents relating to government issues: *www.communication.gc.ca/index_e.html*

5. equality rights for all individuals;

6. officially recognized languages of Canada;

7. minority language educational rights;

8. Canada's multicultural heritage; and

9. aboriginal peoples' rights.

A section of the Constitution often cited in the context of employment is Section 15 of the Charter of Rights, which says:

> 15 (1) Every individual is equal before and under the law and has the right to equal protection and equal benefit of the law without discrimination and, in particular, without discrimination based on race, national or ethnic origin, colour, religion, sex, age or mental or physical disability.
>
> (2) Subsection (1) does not preclude any law, program or activity that has as its object the amelioration of conditions of disadvantaged individuals or groups including those that are disadvantaged because of race, national or ethnic origin, colour, religion, sex, age or mental or physical disability.

Subsection (2) above paves the way for employment equity actions on the part of employers to correct past imbalances or injustices in an employment situation. This will be discussed in greater detail in the next section on human rights legislation.

The constitutional law affects many of the routine activities of staffing departments. The constitutional law sets the limits and conditions on what the various levels of government (federal, provincial, and municipal) can do to influence employment practices. Section 1 of the Charter of Rights guarantees rights and freedoms "subject only to such reasonable limits prescribed by law as can be demonstrably justified in a free and democratic society." Of course, such adjectives as "reasonable" and "demonstrably justified" will lead to different interpretations by different judges, which is one of the reasons why many cases are winding their way through the judicial system up to the Supreme Court of Canada in order to get a final opinion. Every time someone invokes one of the rights or freedoms, a court must determine if the infringement upon the right or freedom is justified. Courts have the delicate task of balancing individual and collective rights.

Website of the Government of Canada; information on all matters related to human rights and the Charter of Rights issues:
http://canada.gc.ca

HUMAN RIGHTS LEGISLATION

"All human beings are born free and equal in dignity and rights," proclaimed Article 1, in the Universal Declaration of Human Rights by the General Assembly of the United Nations on December 10, 1948. In a similar spirit, Section 2 of the *Canadian Human Rights Act* states, "(A)ll individuals should have an equal opportunity ... to make for themselves the lives that they are able and wish to have ... consistent with their duties and obligations as members of society, without being hindered in or prevented from doing so by discriminatory practices based on race, national or ethnic origin, colour, religion, age, sex, sexual orientation, marital status, family status, disability or conviction for an offence for which a pardon has been granted."

Today, the federal government and all of the provinces and territories have human rights legislation which prohibit discrimination within their respective jurisdictions. Section 7 of the *Canadian Human Rights Act* says:

Information on human rights legislation:
www.canada.justice.gc.ca

Information on the Canadian Human Rights Act:
laws.justice.gc.ca/en/H-6

Canadian Human Rights Commission website:
www.chrc-ccdp.ca

> 7. It is a discriminatory practice, directly or indirectly,
>> (a) to refuse to employ or continue to employ any individual, or
>> (b) in the course of employment, to differentiate adversely in relation to an employee, on a prohibited ground of discrimination.

While the Charter of Rights guarantees equality before the law for every Canadian, the *Canadian Human Rights Act* seeks to provide equal employment opportunities without regard to race, national or ethnic origin, colour, religion, age, sex, sexual orientation, marital status, family status, disability, or conviction for an offence for which a pardon has been granted. Common sense dictates such a policy, but Canadian human rights legislation requires every employer to ensure that equal opportunities are, in fact, a reality and that there is no discrimination either intentional or unintentional. No other law—perhaps no other single external development—rival the impact that human rights legislation has had on human resource management. The effects are not limited to a single human resource activity.[5] Instead, human rights legislation touches nearly every human resource function: human resource planning, recruiting, selection, training, performance appraisal, compensation, and labour relations.

Human rights legislation is a family of federal and provincial acts, with the common objective to provide equal employment opportunity for members of protected groups. Human rights legislation permits employers to reward outstanding performers and penalize insufficient productivity. Its only requirement is that the basis for rewards and punishments be work-related, not based on a person's race, sex, age, or other prohibited criteria. Discrimination between workers on the basis of their effort, performance, or other work-related criteria remains both permissible and advisable:

> Mary Caplan complained to her provincial human rights commission, charging her former employer with discrimination. When questioned, she insisted to the commission that the real reason for her discharge as a welder was that the company discriminated against women who were working in jobs traditionally held by men. Mary's case was dismissed when the company showed the commission her records of excessive absenteeism and poor productivity.

The *Canadian Human Rights Act* applies to all federal government departments and agencies, Crown corporations, and businesses and industries under federal jurisdiction, such as banks, airlines, railways, and interprovincial communication companies (e.g., radio and television), in their dealings with the public and in their employment policies. In areas not under federal jurisdiction, protection is given by provincial human rights laws. All Canadian provinces have their own anti-discrimination laws, which are broadly similar to the federal law. The chart in Figure 3-2 compares federal and individual provincial human rights legislation with respect to the prohibited grounds of discrimination.

> Despite positive efforts on the part of various governments, the representation of minorities in various sectors continues to be below target. For example, only 7.8% of the employees of the Federal Public Service are from visible minority groups, well below its goal of 10.4%, and the 15% share of the total population. Less than 5% of visible minorities were promoted to executive or middle management.[6]

The responsibility for the enforcement of the *Canadian Human Rights Act* lies in the hands of the specially created Canadian Human Rights Commission (the Commission). It consists of a chief commissioner, a deputy chief commissioner, and from three to six other members, all appointed by the governor-in-council. The chief commissioner and his or her deputy are full-time members. The Commission deals with complaints it receives concerning discriminatory practices covered by this Act. The Commission may also act on its own when it perceives a possible infraction. It also has the power to issue guidelines interpreting the Act. If warranted, the Commission can ask the president of the Canadian Human Rights Tribunal Panel to appoint a tribunal, which may order cessation of the discriminatory practice and the adoption of measures to ensure that it will not recur, as well as compensation being paid to the individual affected.

Any individual or group may file a complaint with the Commission, given that the individual (or group) has reasonable grounds to believe he, she, or they have been discriminated against. The Commission may refuse to accept the complaint if it is submitted by someone other than the person who allegedly has been discriminated against, unless the

FIGURE 3-2:   Prohibited Grounds of Discrimination in Employment*

Prohibited Grounds	Federal	British Columbia	Alberta	Saskatchewan	Manitoba	Ontario	Quebec	New Brunswick	Prince Edward Island	Nova Scotia	Newfoundland	Northwest Territories	Yukon
Race or colour	•	•	•	•	•	•	•	•	•	•	•	•	•
Religion or creed	•	•	•	•	•	•	•	•	•	•	•	•	•
Age	•	• (19–65)	• (18+)	• (18–64)	•	• (18–65)	•	•	•	•	• (19–65)	•	•
Sex (incl. pregnancy or childbirth)	•	•	•	•	•[1]	•[2]	•	•	•[3]	•	•[3]	•	•
Marital status	•	•	•	•	•	•	•[4]	•	•	•	•	•	•
Physical/mental handicap or disability	•	•	•	•	•	•	•	•	•	•	•	•	•
Sexual orientation	•	•		•	•	•	•	•		•	•[3]	•	•
National or ethnic origin (incl. linguistic background)	•			•[5]	•	•[6]	•	•	•	•	•	•[5]	•
Family status	•	•	•	•[7]	•	•	•[4]		•	•		•	•
Dependence on alcohol or drug	•	•[3]	•[3]	•[3]	•[3]	•[3]		•[3,8]	•[3]	•[8]			
Ancestry or place of origin		•	•	•	•	•		•				•	•
Political belief		•			•		•	•	•	•	•	•	•
Based on association				•	•			•	•	•	•	•	•
Pardoned conviction	•											•	•
Record of criminal conviction							•						•
Source of income			•	•[9]	•	•				•	•		
Assignment, attachment, or seizure of pay											•		
Social condition/origin							•	•			•	•	
Language							•[3]	•					•

Harassment on any of the prohibited grounds is considered a form of discrimination.

* Any limitations, exclusion, denial or preference may be permitted if a bona fide occupational requirement can be demonstrated.
1) includes gender-determined characteristics
2) Ontario accepts complaints based on a policy related to female genital mutilation in all social areas on the grounds of sex, place of origin, and/or handicap
3) complaints accepted based on policy
4) Quebec uses the term "civil status"
5) defined as nationality
6) Ontario's Code includes only "citizenship"
7) defined as being in a parent–child relationship
8) previous dependence only
9) defined as "receipt of public assistance"

Threatening, intimidating, or discriminating against someone who has filed a complaint, or hampering a complaint investigation, is a violation of provincial human rights codes, and at the federal level is a criminal offence.

Source: Canadian Human Rights Commission. "Prohibited Grounds of Discrimination in Canada." **http://www.chrc-ccdp.ca/pdf/ ProhibitedGrounds_en.pdf.** Reprinted with the permission of the Minister of Public Works and Government Services Canada, 2006.

alleged victim permits the investigation of the claim. It may also refuse to deal with complaints if other procedures seem more appropriate, if the complaint seems trivial or it seems to have been made in bad faith, or if too much time (one year) has elapsed since the alleged discrimination took place. The Commission itself may initiate a complaint if it has reasonable grounds to assume that a party is engaging in a discriminatory practice.

DIRECT VERSUS INDIRECT (SYSTEMIC) DISCRIMINATION

Discrimination is not defined in the Charter of Rights, nor in any federal or provincial human rights legislation, with the exception of Quebec. Section 10 of the Quebec Charter states:

> Every person has a right to full and equal recognition and exercise of his human rights and freedoms, without distinction, exclusion or preference based on race, colour, sex, pregnancy, sexual orientation, civil status, age except as provided by law, religion, political convictions, language, ethnic or national origin, social condition, a handicap or the use of any means to palliate a handicap.
>
> Discrimination exists where such a distinction, exclusion or preference has the effect of nullifying or impairing such right.

The dictionary definition of discrimination, namely, "a showing of partiality or prejudice in treatment; specific action or policies directed against the welfare of minority groups," would meet the needs of most other situations.

Normally, intentional **direct discrimination,** or the differential treatment of people contrary to the grounds specified in the human rights legislation, is illegal. However, under certain circumstances, intentional direct discrimination is acceptable.

> A fashion store catering to women will be allowed to advertise for female models, and schools controlled by religious groups are permitted to limit their hiring to members of a specific faith.

This legal discrimination, or a justified business reason for discriminating against a member of a protected class is called **bona fide occupational requirement (BFOR).** More on BFOQ will be discussed in the next section.

Systemic or **indirect discrimination** takes place if there is no intention to discriminate, but the system, arrangements, or policies create discrimination. Such employment

Information on the *Canadian Human Rights Act* with respect to discriminatory practices:
http://laws.justice.gc.ca
Information on bona fide occupational requirement (BFOR):
www.chrc-ccdp.ca

Direct discrimination: illegal differential treatment of people contrary to the grounds specified in human rights legislation

Bona fide occupational requirement (BFOR): a justified business reason for discriminating against a member of a protected class

Systemic or **indirect discrimination:** there is no intention to discriminate, but the system, arrangements, or policies create discrimination

Focus on Ethics

An advertising and public relations firm is about to hire a new accounts manager, who will have to deal with several influential clients, many of whom hold conservative values. Of the three people who reached the final stages of the interview process, Bob Turnbull was clearly ahead of the other two candidates, although Peter Thompson was the second choice of many who interviewed him. Kathy Wright, the staffing manager, has recently come to understand that Turnbull's wife had posed nude for men's magazines and had acted in blue movies. Most of the clients of the about-to-be-hired accounts manager will be highly influential people who may be offended by being served by a person whose wife had such a past career. Wright knows that the general manager will not hire Turnbull if she becomes aware of the alleged past conduct of Turnbull's wife; on the other hand, Wright feels that Turnbull's wife's past is not relevant to his effective functioning as an accounts manager. Or is it?

practices may appear neutral and may be implemented impartially, but they still exclude specific groups of people for reasons that are not job-related.

> An example of an indirect (systemic) violation based on ethnic origin occurred when the hiring requirements for a certain job specified that the candidate had to be 5'8" (173 cm). But reflection reveals that such a standard disproportionately discriminates against Asian Canadians, who tend to be shorter than descendants of immigrants from European countries. Because of this, although the height rule may not intend to discriminate, the result is discriminatory.

In the context of staffing, here are some other situations that illustrate systemic discrimination:

- minimum height and weight requirements for employment with police forces, which make it more difficult for women and Canadians of Asian origin to be hired
- the requirement for minimum scores on employment tests, which discriminates against distinct groups (e.g., culturally biased intelligence tests tend to screen out a disproportionate number of minorities)
- internal hiring policies, word-of-mouth hiring, or the requirement to submit a photograph with an application form
- limited accessibility of buildings and facilities, which often makes it impossible for persons with disabilities to work at such places
- organizational culture where minority groups feel unwelcome and uneasy, resulting in a disproportionate turnover rate for such groups
- lack of explicit anti-harassment guidelines, which allows an atmosphere of abuse to develop in the workplace.

Sometimes, invisible and subtle barriers prevent members of minority groups from gaining employment or advancing in their careers:

> Canadian managers call it "lack of fit;" visible minority members call it prejudice. Often "fit" or suitability for a job comes down to the chemistry between the hiring manager and the job candidate. Members of visible minority communities who are unable to create a rapport with hiring managers because of their cultural differences do not get job offers. Often "lack of fit" is an indication of the preference for status quo and underlying racism within an organization.[7]

While the Canadian Human Rights Commission has been active in detecting the causes and sources of systemic discrimination, it should be emphasized that such indirect discrimination is more difficult to detect and fight because it is often hidden. Figure 3-3 shows the number of signed complaints citing direct and indirect discrimination in 2004. As in the past, most of the discrimination charges are related to disability, sex, nationality and ethnicity, and race: 45% of all complaints emerged in the public sector, while the private sector and individuals accounted for 37% and 10% of the complaints, respectively.[8] The remaining cases emerged from unions, reserves, and bands, etc. In most provinces, the picture remains somewhat similar. For example, an analysis[9] of the complaints before the Ontario Human Rights Commission in 2005 indicated the following top issues:

- Failure to accommodate physical disability
- Failure to accommodate mental disability
- Discrimination on the basis of age
- Harassment on the basis of sex and race
- Systemic barriers based on race-related grounds

Of course, these issues deserve the particular attention of managers and human resource departments when managing employees. Some proactive steps in this context are listed in Figure 3-4.

FIGURE 3-3: Grounds of Discrimination Cited in Complaints to the Canadian Human Rights Commission

Ground of Discrimination	Number of Signed Complaints	Percent of Total Complaints
Disability	389	39%
Sex	165	17%
National or ethnic origin	109	11%
Race	105	11%
Family status	61	6%
Age	60	6%
Religion	34	3%
Colour	26	3%
Sexual orientation	21	2%
Marital status	14	2%
Pardoned convicts	5	-

Source: Canadian Human Rights Commission, "CHRC 2004 Annual Report."
http://www.chrc-ccdp.ca/pdf/AR_2004_RA_en.pdf. Reproduced with the permission of the Minister of Public Works and Government Services Canada, 2006.

FIGURE 3-4: Proactive Steps to Avoid Workplace Discrimination

To avoid racial discrimination:

- Establish a zero tolerance policy on racial jokes, slurs, and innuendo.
- Emphasize the organization's commitment to a harassment-free environment from the day each employee joins the organization, through internal communication devices such as "in-house" magazines and bulletins.
- Train supervisors and managers about the issue of racial discrimination regularly.
- Do not insist that an applicant have "Canadian experience" if the applicant has acquired equivalent experience in other countries. Focus on the applicant's skills, not on where they were acquired. Skilled immigrants have had to take low-paying, low-status jobs[*] because employers do not recognize skills and work experience acquired outside of this country.
- Do not turn down foreign-born applicants by citing they have "too much experience" or are "overqualified."

To prevent sex discrimination and sexual harassment:

- Establish a zero tolerance policy on sexual harassment, jokes (innuendo), and sex discrimination.
- Emphasize the firm's commitment to a harassment-free work environment whenever the opportunity to do so arises.
- Train supervisors and managers about the issue of sex discrimination and sexual harassment regularly.
- Assign mentors to female employees and encourage participation in women's networks. In some instances, active discrimination may not prevent women from reaching the top positions so much as the lack of role models and visibility.[#] Progressive employers recognize this deficit and take corrective actions.

FIGURE 3-4:   (Continued)

- Change the *language* used and the *existing rules* to make the organization more friendly to women. The language of many business organizations is masculine in tone (e.g., "businessman" or "manpower").

To better meet the needs of employees with disabilities:

- Redesign office spaces, recognizing the importance of accessibility. Remove all physical barriers, which prevent employees with disabilities from participating on an equal and full basis.
- Help employees recognize and change stereotypes and misconceptions about mental disabilities through communication and education.
- Change the nature and/or frequency of performance evaluations to meet the special needs of an employee with a disability.
- Organize counselling and other support and training programs.
- Initiate organization-wide employee assistance programs.

To avoid age discrimination:

- Help employees recognize and change stereotypes and misconceptions about older workers through organizational communication and training. Emphasize the fact that older workers may be more productive, more creative, less accident prone, and keener to do the job than many younger workers.
- Treat older workers in the same way as their younger counterparts without any signs of condescension. Apply similar performance standards and criteria to older workers.
- Offer the same training, promotional, and other opportunities to the older workers as offered to younger employees.
- Do not assume a relationship between age and absenteeism, performance, information-processing abilities, and safety at work.
- Offer flexible work arrangements such as job sharing and a reduced workweek to help older employees transition from full-time to part-time employment.

---

[*] David Brown. (2005, Jan.31). "Ottawa Asks Why Skilled Immigrants Drive Cabs," *Canadian HR Reporter*, p. 1.
[#] Uyen Vu. (2005, May 9)."Tapping into Women Networks to Reach the Top," *Canadian HR Reporter*, p. 1.

BONA FIDE OCCUPATIONAL REQUIREMENT

Human rights legislation allows an employer to follow a discriminatory practice if it is a bona fide occupational requirement. Section 15(a) of the Act states that "it is not a discriminatory practice if (a) any refusal, exclusion, suspension, limitation, specification or preference in relation to any employment is established by an employer to be based on a bona fide occupational requirement." For example, even if an employment test would adversely affect a protected group (such as a visible minority), the test would still be allowed if the employer can show it is a sufficiently valid predictor of job performance. In practice, many past court decisions have interpreted a bona fide occupational requirement to be a "requirement ... imposed honestly, in good faith and in the sincerely held belief that such limitation is imposed in the interests of adequate performance of the work involved with all reasonable dispatch, safety and economy and not for ulterior or extraneous reasons aimed at objectives which could defeat the purpose of the Code. In addition, it must be related in an objective sense to the performance of the employment concerned, in that it is reasonably necessary to assure the efficient and economical performance of the job without endangering the employee, his fellow employees and the general public."[10]

According to this definition, the BFOR has two important elements:

- *objective evidence*, such as validation data, which demonstrates that such a requirement is an important predictor of job performance, and

- *a subjective element*, which is a consideration of the employer's state of mind in connection with the setting of the requirement or policy. That is, the requirement which restricts a member of a minority group should be imposed in good faith, without any intention to discriminate.

A recent and far-reaching Supreme Court decision pushed the above requirement even further.

> In 1994, Ms. Meiorin, who was employed in an elite fire fighting unit in B.C., failed one of the new fitness tests introduced by the agency, namely, a 2.5 km run to be completed in 11 minutes. She lost her job as a result. In a subsequent grievance launched by her and her union, the Supreme Court decided in favour of Ms. Meiorin since the employer had failed to provide credible evidence that her inability to meet the standard created a safety risk.[11]

The Supreme Court decided in favour of Ms. Meiorin, agreeing with an earlier arbitrator's ruling that the government had failed to justify the test as a BFOR by failing to provide credible evidence that her inability to meet the standard created a safety risk.[12] The Supreme Court established three new criteria to assess the appropriateness of a BFOR:

1. Is the standard rationally connected to the performance of the job?

2. Was the standard established in an honest belief that it was necessary to accomplish the purpose identified in stage one?

3. Is the standard reasonably necessary to accomplish its purpose?

These new and stricter criteria put a considerable onus on staffing managers to defend BFORs. Several past court decisions illustrate the onus of the staffing manager to prove that every requirement imposed on potential applicants is actually a BFOR:

> A Canadian citizen originally from Haiti was refused entrance into the Armed Forces because he was not eligible for security clearance until he had lived in Canada for at least ten years. At the time, he had been in this country for six years, and he was unusually highly qualified in every other respect. During investigations of his complaint, the Armed Forces agreed to invoke a rule already in place which allowed for the ten-year residency requirement to be waived for exceptional candidates. The Armed Forces granted him security clearance and offered enrollment as an officer cadet.
>
> A bank in a small town advertised a position, specifying that the applicant should have a pleasing appearance and that a recent photograph be submitted along with an application. The bank personnel were all Caucasian. A black community leader filed a discrimination complaint, which was settled when the bank agreed to include human rights training in its courses on interviewing, human resource selection, and counselling.

Many employers consider that the requirement of a minimum, or a maximum, age for a certain job is justified, although in several instances such a restriction on age may not be a BFOR since a person's age is not an accurate indication of that person's ability to perform a given type of work. As mentioned earlier, the law makes an exception for a mandatory retirement age. Where mandatory retirement age has not been abolished, it is not considered a discriminatory practice if a person's employment is terminated because that person has reached the normal age of retirement for employees working in similar positions.

> The General Pilotage Regulations, under the Pilotage Act, require that a pilot be removed from the eligibility list after reaching the age of 50. A special human rights tribunal found

that such a regulation was invalid and ordered that pilots affected by this rule be restored to their former positions. An appeal court set aside the tribunal's decision on the basis that the removal of the pilots from the eligibility list because of age was not a discriminatory practice. The Commission appealed to the Supreme Court of Canada, but the appeal was denied.

However, it should be noted that the picture on mandatory retirement is quickly changing. Manitoba banned mandatory retirement in 1982; Quebec and the Canadian federal service did so in 1983. In August 2004, the Ontario government announced it would legislate a ban on mandatory retirement,[13] and in June 2005, New Brunswick tabled Bill 62, which would amend the provincial legislation on retirement. The abolition of mandatory retirement will bring additional challenges to human resource managers in a variety of areas, including performance assessment and the making of succession plans.[14]

Sufficient risk The notion of "sufficient risk" underlies the courts' decisions on BFOR. A "sufficient risk of employee failure" will warrant the retention of an otherwise discriminatory employment qualification or requirement. In other words, whether an occupational requirement is reasonably necessary will depend, at least in part, on whether the members of the group alleging discrimination pose a sufficient risk of harm to themselves or others in the event of employee failure.

> Thus, when a security firm asked a male Sikh employee to remove his beard (which his religion required), the court did not consider this requirement to be a BFOR for the job. However, in another instance, when a male member of the same religion refused to remove his turban and wear a safety helmet when working in the maintenance yard of a major railway, the court decided that this employee's refusal posed sufficient risk and that the requirement of wearing a safety helmet should be treated as a BFOR. In this instance, the employee was asked to remove his turban in favour of the safety helmet.

In general, the court considers factors such as the following when assessing the risk factor in a case:

- the nature of employment (e.g., a professor versus a miner in the case of a physical disability),
- whether the risk of employee failure is restricted to health and safety,
- the probability of employee failure stated in empirical rather than speculative terms, and the seriousness of the harm arising from employee failure.

Reasonable alternative: places the burden on an employer to show that no reasonable substitute exists for an employment practice that discriminates against a group

Reasonable alternative The concept of **reasonable alternative** is closely related to BFOR. Under the burden of reasonable alternative, an employer must show that no reasonable substitute exists for an employment practice that discriminates against a group.

> For example, if a particular employment test adversely affects a group (say, Asians), the onus is on the employer to show that no other reasonable test or selection practice is available which will achieve the same results in predicting job performance.

Principle of reasonable accommodation: an employer should take reasonable steps to accommodate groups protected under human rights legislation, as long as the policy or practice does not unduly interfere in the operation of the business or create an unsupportable expense to the employer

PRINCIPLE OF "REASONABLE ACCOMMODATION"

The **principle of reasonable accommodation** posits that an employer should take reasonable steps to accommodate an individual or group protected under human rights legislation so long as the policy or practice does not unduly interfere in the operation of the business or create an unsupportable expense for the employer. This principle means that an employer can be expected to take reasonable steps to make a suitable job available to a person with a physical handicap if doing so does not impose undue hardships on the organization. The phrase "undue hardship" is not well-defined; however, relevant considerations would include financial cost, the disruption of an existing collective agreement, lower morale of other employees, the interchangeability of workforce and facilities, and the magnitude of potential risk for employees, customers, and the general public if safety might be compromised.

No person should be denied employment solely for the reason that he or she is disabled. Of course, there are exceptions. A blind person cannot be a truck driver, or a totally deaf person cannot be a telephone operator. However, the principle of "reasonable accommodation" still applies. Section 5 of the *Employment Equity Act* provides that "every employer shall implement employment equity by," among other measures, "making such reasonable accommodations as will ensure that persons in designated groups achieve a degree of representation" commensurate with their representation in the Canadian workforce and their availability to meet reasonable occupational requirements. Section 10 of this act specifies that "the employer shall prepare an employment equity plan" that provides for "reasonable accommodations ... to correct ... underrepresentation."

> Examples of "reasonable accommodation" would be providing a sign language interpreter for a job interview with a deaf applicant, providing telephone or computer equipment for people who are hard of hearing or who are blind, providing a barrier-free work site for wheelchair-bound employees, allowing religious minorities to alter their work schedules to accommodate religious obligations, or altering dress or grooming codes to allow for cultural or religious customs.

The following case illustrates this concept:

> A man was refused a technician's job because he failed a hearing test. However, he had been tested when he was not wearing his hearing aid; he asserted that he could perform the job using a hearing device. Medical advisers for the company claimed that the job required perfectly normal hearing. After conciliation, the company agreed that if the man wore his hearing aid, he would be able to do the job. The complaint was settled with the complainant being hired as a technician, and he was awarded damages of $750.

Even after an employee is hired, an employer is expected to make accommodations in the workplace to meet individual employee needs. **Workplace accommodation**[15] refers to removing workplace barriers that negatively affect job performance and adjusting the workplace to respond to the needs of individual employees or applicants. "Needs" arise from disability (physical or psychological), family status, ethnic or national origin, and religious beliefs.

> After becoming a member of the Worldwide Church of God, an employee of a milk-processing plant requested unpaid leave for a particular Monday in order to observe a holy day of his church. The request was refused because Mondays were especially busy days at the plant. When the employee did not report for work on that Monday, he was fired. The Court ruled that the company had discriminated on the basis of religion. Although the company had not done so directly, the refusal had an adverse effect on the complainant due to his religion. Notably, the Court stated that the employer must meet the "duty to accommodate" up to the point of "undue hardship."[16]
>
> A Muslim employee of a communications company lost his job over his request to take time off each week to attend prayers at his mosque. After conciliation, a settlement was reached which did not impose undue hardship on the employer. The employee was allowed to take 1.5 hours per week of leave without pay. He was reinstated with the company, with retroactive pay and benefits.

Accommodation may include, but is not restricted to, the following:

- Technical aids (e.g., specialized software, optical scanners, magnifiers, or other equipment)

Workplace accommodation: removing workplace barriers that negatively affect job performance and adjusting the workplace to respond to the needs of individual employees or applicants

Information on workplace accommodation: *www.hrsdc.gc.ca/en/on/epb/ disabilities/onworking.shtml*

- Leave for religious or cultural observances
- Provision of workspace and furnishings that are appropriate to the nature of the disability
- Information in alternative, accessible formats
- Flexible working arrangements
- Temporary or long-term accommodation due to recuperation from injury, illness, or changing family responsibilities

Information on employment equity:
www.chrc-ccdp.ca

EMPLOYMENT EQUITY

Consider these facts:

- In the near future, nearly 85% of women between 18 and 64 years old will be in the labour force. But only a tiny proportion of them will be in senior managerial positions or on the board of directors of major organizations. In the foreseeable future, women will continue to earn less than 80 cents for each dollar that men earn, unless corrective actions are taken.
- Over 6% of working Canadians have some disability, but very few of them make it into managerial or executive ranks.
- Canadians of Asian and African origins have more education than other ethnic groups, yet less than 1% of top executives in this country belong to these ethnic groups.[17]

"Employment equity" is how the Honourable Madam Rosalie Silberman Abella, the Commissioner of the Royal Commission on Equality in Employment (1984), described a distinct Canadian process for achieving equality in all aspects of employment.[18] In the report submitted by the Royal Commission on Equality in Employment (1985), Madam Justice Abella wrote:

"It is not that individuals in the designated groups are inherently unable to achieve equality on their own, it is that the obstacles in their way are so formidable and self-perpetuating that they cannot be overcome without intervention. It is both intolerable and insensitive if we simply wait and hope that the barriers will disappear with time. Equality in employment will not happen unless we make it happen."[19]

The term "employment equity" was meant to distinguish this process from the primarily American "affirmative action" model as well as to imply a need to move beyond the "equal opportunity" measures available in Canada at that time. Recognizing that "systemic discrimination" was responsible for most of the inequality found in employment, the Commission outlined a systemic response and chose the term "employment equity" to describe this process. The major difference between the Canadian "employment equity" process and American "affirmative action" programs is that the first is based on the principle of equitable access in all employment systems, while the second is based on the principle of "righting past wrongs."[20] Employment equity is an ongoing planning process through which an employer endeavours to do the following:[21]

- identify and eliminate barriers in the organization's employment procedures and policies;
- put into place positive policies and practices to eliminate the effects of systemic barriers; and
- ensure appropriate representation of "designated group" members throughout the organization's workforce.

The goals of Employment Equity are among the following:[22]

- eliminate employment barriers for the four designated groups identified in the *Employment Equity Act*, i.e., women, persons with disabilities, Aboriginal people, members of visible minorities;

- remedy past discrimination in employment opportunities and prevent future barriers;

- improve access and distribution throughout all occupations and at all levels for members of the four designated groups; and

- foster a climate of equity in the organization.

The federal government proclaimed the *Employment Equity Act* in August 1987. The act requires each employer with 100 or more employees under federal jurisdiction to develop annual human resource plans setting out goals and timetables and to maintain these plans for three years. The act requires further that each employer submit annual reports describing the progress in attaining the goals set out in the above-mentioned plans. The *Employment Equity Act* was amended in 1995. The act has been in operation for nearly 20 years. Despite this length of time, many employers and employees do not clearly understand the intent or provisions of the act. Figure 3-5 lists some of the popular myths and realities about employment equity. It is the responsibility of the human resource department to ensure that managers and employees have a true understanding of the legal implications of employment equity.

The amended act also established the Commission as a monitoring agency, which would carry out compliance audits for federally regulated public and private sector employers. The *Employment Equity Act* also gives the Commission great latitude in pursuing the enforcement of the act. One way for the Commission to comply with the intent of the act, which is to improve equal employment opportunities for special groups, is to encourage the development of **employment equity programs**, the purpose of which is to help undo past employment discrimination or to ensure equal employment opportunity in the future. Section 15(1) of the *Employment Equity Act* specifies that special programs are a legitimate mechanism for improving the opportunities of a group through the elimination, reduction, or prevention of discrimination. This section usually implies that an organization must self-evaluate its own hiring, promotion, and compensation policies. If it finds discrepancies, it would be good human resource practice to check the criteria used for different decisions, adjust them if necessary, and ensure that they are consistently applied. Notably, mandated employment equity programs take place mainly at the federal level, i.e., in organizations and industries under federal jurisdiction. At the provincial level, such programs are implemented almost exclusively on a voluntary basis, when organizations see an advantage in doing so.

Employment equity programs: in-house programs to undo past employment discrimination and to ensure equal employment opportunity in the future

> The law school at Dalhousie University in Halifax developed an Indigenous Black and Mi'kmaq Program to train more black and Mi'kmaq lawyers. The law school appointed a director and began a publication campaign aimed at these groups by advertising in local newspapers and association publications. The program director visits high schools and universities and holds information sessions at reserves and community centres.[23]

Under the federal *Employment Equity Act*, employers are obliged to correct past imbalances and inequity in employment. Major corrective actions that employers may take in this regard are listed in Figure 3-6. Assessing a current workforce profile to ascertain representation of the designated groups and reviewing employment procedures to eliminate barriers are critical steps at the hiring stage. Employers must eliminate employment practices that adversely affect the employment prospects of designated groups even if these practices are invisible or indirect. Some progressive employers have taken proactive steps. Consider these examples:

FIGURE 3-5:   Myths and Realities about Employment Equity (EE)

Myth	Reality
1. Employment equity (EE) means treating everyone the same.	EE means treating everyone with fairness, taking into account people's differences. Sometimes EE requires treating people the same despite their differences; at other times, EE means treating them as equals by accommodating their differences.
2. EE is all about quotas.	Quotas are explicitly prohibited by the *Employment Equity Act*. EE is about goals: flexible, rational targets that employers set. In contrast, quotas are rigid. But employers can set their own goals and realistic timetables to achieve quotas.
3. EE means hiring unqualified people.	EE means providing all qualified and qualifiable people with equal employment opportunities—not just a select few. EE is not about putting someone in a job solely because he or she is a member of a designated group. EE encourages the selection, hiring, training, promotion, and retention of qualified and qualifiable people.
4. EE means lowering job standards.	EE implies that the employer should examine the organization's job standards to ensure that job criteria are realistic and job-related. A sound EE program guarantees that people are not denied jobs for reasons unrelated to their skills or abilities. EE frees the workplace from outdated job requirements and traditions that screen out valuable human resources.
5. EE results in reverse discrimination.	EE means that everyone has equal employment opportunities, not just a select group. EE does not mean that all employees hired or promoted will be members of designated groups. EE is about eliminating barriers faced by some groups in the society that historically discriminated against them.
6. EE threatens the seniority principle.	EE and the seniority principle share a common goal: to make sure that employment opportunities are fair, without favouritism or discrimination. Seniority rights are protected under the 1995 *Employment Equity Act*. This act states that seniority provisions are not employment barriers. Only if a seniority provision in a collective agreement has an adverse impact on designated group members is an adjustment warranted. EE encourages company-wide seniority (as opposed to seniority in a particular job), since this opens opportunities to employees who have only worked in low-paying jobs in a company

Source: Human Resources and Skills Development Canada, "Myths and Realities about Employment Equity," 2004. **http://www.hrsdc.gc.ca/en/lp/lo/lswe/we/publications/mr/myths_realities.shtml.**
Reproduced with the permission of the Minister of Public Works and Government Services Canada, 2006.

FIGURE 3-6: Employer Actions to Achieve Employment Equity

1. Analyze existing systems and procedures:

Inequity occurs in two major forms: *Under-representation* (also referred to as *under-utilization*) of members of designated groups (e.g., women, minorities) in high-paying, high-status jobs, and *concentration* of the same people in low-paying, dead-end jobs.

- Analyze the profile of the current workforce to determine the representation of designated groups. Compare existing workforce representation against that of the labour market to identify the extent of under-representation and concentration.
- Review existing employment policies and practices (including predictors of job performance and cut-off scores) to identify and eliminate barriers against designated groups.

2. Plan and set achievable targets:

- Establish numerical employment targets for designated groups.
- Combine these targets with qualitative goals and plans to achieve targets (e.g., training of specific employee groups to help them move up the hierarchy).
- Identify specific actions with a clear timetable to remove under-representation and concentration.

3. Implement plans:

- Implement plans with haste and efficiency.
- Provide for reasonable accommodation to attract members of under-represented groups.

4. Monitor progress and take timely corrective actions:

- Ensure the existence of clear, measurable criteria for monitoring the progress of the initiative.
- Collect data to compare targets with actual and take corrective actions as soon as discrepancies are observed.

5. Communicate widely:

- Establish and maintain employment equity records covering all aspects of the program.
- Communicate to all employees and their representatives about the employment equity programs.

Some organizations have found it helpful to appoint an employment equity officer who directly reports to the CEO. An employment equity officer communicates the firm's commitment to employment equity to the outside world. In any case, for an employment equity initiative to succeed, it needs the full support and open endorsement of the organization's top management.

The Law Society of Upper Canada, which has over 400 employees, has a number of EE initiatives. Its CEO is fully committed to such initiatives. All of the Law Society's staff, as well as the members of the Board of Directors, have received equity and human rights training. Ongoing educational programs, survey feedback efforts, outreach recruitment, and the establishment of an equity advisory group are part of the organization's operational strategy with respect to employment equity.[24]

Compass Group, the world's largest food service company, employing over 117 000 people, has a vibrant EE program covering everything from training to advisory groups to mentorship programs. Compass Group has made the integration of diversity into its business practices a priority. Diversity is a topic at every board meeting, and the company reviews workforce data periodically. In addition, diversity goals are a part of the performance scorecards of all managers.[25]

In summary, human rights legislation requires employers to abstain from any direct or indirect discrimination during the hiring process that is not justified by the job requirements. The legislation asks employers to respect the dignity of all people and to make equal employment opportunities for everyone irrespective of their race, colour, gender, ethnicity, sexual orientation, disability, and so on. While employers may discriminate on the basis of a bona fide occupational requirement (BFOR), the duty of the employer is to accommodate employees and take reasonable actions to make the workplace inclusive. To establish a BFOR, the onus is on the employer to show that the requirement was established in good faith and compelling evidence exists to show that the requirement is reasonable and necessary for the organization. The exact requirements from the employers will vary somewhat, depending on the province or territory; however, the federal law requires that employers file annual reports on or before June 1 of each year with Human Resources and Social Development.

THE CANADA LABOUR CODE AND OTHER LEGISLATION GOVERNING STAFFING

A variety of other laws regulate the employment function. The employer-employee relationship began with what was formerly called the master-servant relationship, where the master rewarded the servant with wages for a "honest day's work" and loyalty. An early test that is still used to determine the existence of an employment relationship is called the "four-fold test"[26] and is based on the following factors:

- who owns the tools used,
- who has control over the relationship,
- who has the chance of making profits, and
- who has the risk of loss.

Contract workers: employees who have a direct contractual relationship with an organization

In several settings, the distinction between an employee and a contract worker may not be very clear. **Contract workers** (also called consultants and freelancers) are employees who have a direct contractual working relationship with a firm. Many professionals with specialized skills are hired as contract workers.

> Universities hire part-time instructors; publishers hire editors on a project-by-project basis; hospitals hire emergency-room physicians on a contractual basis; construction firms hire architects and other skilled persons on a contractual basis.

In many cases, former executives, who either left voluntarily, were laid off, took early retirement, or left the company to start their own businesses are hired back as consultants.[27] These arrangements are often closely linked to particular tasks—for example, a market analysis, overseeing a new project or arranging a merger, and so on.[28] From the organization's point of view, employing contract labour has several typical advantages including lower costs (since many employee benefits are not available to contract workers), lower overhead (since work is usually done "off-site"), and greater flexibility in hiring. For these reasons, the use of contract labour has shown a marked increase in this country recently.

> More than one-third of the Canadian workforce is now engaged in non-standard, temporary, or contract work. Since the eligibility for most labour rights, benefits, and protections are available only in standard full-time, permanent employment, today a large segment of the

workforce has virtually no access to several benefits and may be "stuck in high stress, low-reward, and even harmful work situations that can be difficult to escape."[29]

Sometimes questions arise about whether the individual is, in fact, an employee or a contractor. In doubtful cases, the Canada Revenue Agency (CRA) can be asked to make a ruling. To establish an employee's status, the CRA reviews certain activities that generally indicate whether individuals are employees:

- Did they have a set number of working hours each day?
- Did they have to account for their time?
- Were they given specific job instructions?
- Were they members of the company's benefit plans?
- Did they use the company's computer equipment and office supplies on a regular basis?
- Did the company supply them with offices?
- Did the company give them specific titles and business cards showing the company's logo and address?

To be considered independent contractors, workers must agree to do specific jobs with no commitment to working a set number of hours. They also must work on their own without supervision. They have to bill the employer directly and receive cheques for the completed work. They must keep their own financial books and records of accounting. In addition, they must not receive any company benefits. Independent contractors operate from their own offices with their own equipment; they should go to the employers' place of business only for meetings. They also must provide services to more than one organization. The CRA has developed four tests (see Figure 3-7) to check the authenticity of a worker's contract status.

Information on the *Canada Labour Code:*
http://laws.justice.gc.ca/en/L-2/index.html

FIGURE 3-7:   The CRA's Tests for Contract Labour

The Canada Revenue Agency has developed four tests, which may assist human resource managers in deciding whether a person working for the organization is an employee or an independent contractor:

1. **Control Test.** This test determines whether the employee is restricted under a "master-servant" relationship. Usually an employer has more control over an employee than over an independent contractor. For example, in a master-servant relationship, the "master" can order not only what is to be done, but also how and when. Independent contractors are usually free to choose how they will perform their services.

2. **Ownership of Tools Test.** What tools or materials are needed for the work to be done? Who owns them? If the business owns them, the relationship resembles an employer-employee relationship.

3. **Risk of Loss and Chance of Profit Test.** Who bears the financial risk or gain in the event of a loss or a profit? Who controls the pricing of the work? If there is little financial risk for the employee, then again the relationship looks more like one of dependency.

4. **Integration Test.** This test answers the question whether the work performed by an employee under an employment contract is done as an integral part of the business. If a worker were under contract for services, his or her work would be classified as "necessary" to the business but not an integral part of the company. The more "critical" the work is for the business, the less likely it is done by an independent contractor.

Sources: Tim Cestnick. (2000, Oct. 7). "How to Check If You're Really Self-employed." *Globe and Mail* [Toronto], p. N5. See also Daphne Kelgard. (1997, Sept. 8). "Beware of the Legal Pitfalls of Contract Workers." *Canadian HR Reporter*, p. 18-19. A more comprehensive discussion of the legal and tax issues involved can be found in Joanne Magee. (1997). "Whose Business Is It? Employees Versus Independent Contractors." *Canadian Tax Journal* Vol. 45, No. 3.

CANADA LABOUR CODE

The *Canada Labour Code* (the Code), enacted in 1971, regulates union certification, the right to organize, union prosecution, and mediation and arbitration procedures. In organizations which are unionized, the employer's actions are guided by the provisions in this act. The Code also sets the standard workday at eight hours and the standard workweek at 40 hours, and overtime pay at one and one-half times the regular pay. The Code specifies that employees must be given at least one full day of rest during the week, preferably on Sunday. The Code also requires every employer in those industries falling under federal jurisdiction to furnish information relating to wages of employees, their hours of work, general holidays, annual vacation, and conditions of employment whenever the Ministry of Labour demands this information. Similar provisions also exist in provincial legislation.

EMPLOYMENT STANDARDS LEGISLATION

All provinces have employment standards legislation which specify the minimum age for employment, hours of work, minimum wages, statutory holidays, parental and bereavement leave, termination notice, overtime pay, and so on. Employment standards legislation now goes much further than specifying, for example, the minimum standards of non-unionized employees. These laws apply to all contracts of employment, which means that minimum standards apply to all employment relationships whether they are

- verbal or written,
- express or implied,
- full-time, part-time, or contractual, and
- where the employment of a person is for work or services to be performed within the jurisdiction of the legislation.

The minimum wage legislation in all provinces applies to most classes of workers, other than farm labourers and domestic servants. In each province, a board periodically sets minimum wage rates, which are imposed through minimum wage orders. The general minimum wage rates for adult workers in various provinces are shown in Figure 3-8. For young workers, the rates are lower.

An employee can claim damages if he or she can prove that employment standards have been violated, irrespective of whether the employment contract was in writing or not. These claims are usually resolved through an audit of the employer's payroll and other records. Most employment standards laws prohibit waiving or contracting out the minimum standards they prescribe. This prohibition applies to groups of employers and employees as well. For example, a union cannot come to an agreement with an employer if the agreement would violate employment standards legislation. Similarly, if an employer initially offers employment terms that are better than minimum standards, these cannot be arbitrarily lowered once the employee is hired.

> A painting company in Atlantic Canada, which routinely uses college students in the summer, offers each student $9 per hour. When a new manager took over the operation, he suggested reducing this rate to the minimum wage levels for all temporary employees in an effort to save costs. The human resource manager of the company intervened and warned him of the possible legal violation in pursuing this reduction. Since the company had already entered into an employment contract at the higher rate, it could not arbitrarily lower the wages.

FIGURE 3-8: Minimum Wages for Adult Workers in 2005	
Alberta	$7.00
British Columbia	$8.00
Manitoba	$7.25
New Brunswick	$6.30
Newfoundland	$6.25
Northwest Territories	$8.25
Nova Scotia	$6.80
Nunavut	$8.50
Ontario	$7.45
Prince Edward Island	$6.80
Quebec	$7.60
Saskatchewan	$7.05
Yukon	$7.20

Source: Human Resources and Skills Development Canada, "Minimum Wages for Adult Workers in 2005." **http://www110.hrdc-drhc.gc.ca/psait_spila/lmnec_eslc/eslc_salaire_minwage/report2/report2d_e.cfm.** Reproduced with the permission of the Minister of Public Works and Government Services Canada, 2006.

OTHER LEGISLATION

A variety of other legislation on safety, compensation (e.g., pay equity), and union-management relations also affect staffing activities, although not to the same extent as the above-mentioned provisions, including the provincial occupational health and safety acts, provincial labour relations acts, provincial workers' safety and insurance acts, and the federal *Privacy Act.* The federal government requires that all federally regulated organizations comply with pay equity. All provinces have legislation dealing with equal pay for work of equal value, although this principle is enshrined in different enactments, depending on the province.

> For example, Manitoba, New Brunswick, Nova Scotia, Ontario, Prince Edward Island, and Quebec have a pay equity act. In the Northwest Territories, the act that deals with pay equity is called the *Fair Practices Act.* In Alberta, it is called the *Human Rights, Citizenship and Multiculturalism Act.* British Columbia and Newfoundland deal with pay equity under their employment and labour standards legislation.

Other laws affect the employment function as well. For example, the *Transportation of Dangerous Goods Act, 1992* gives considerable powers to Transport Canada to regulate and oversee all activities related to the transportation of dangerous materials. The *Hazardous Products Act* requires employers to provide training to employees so that they will recognize hazard symbols under the Workplace Hazardous Material Information System (WHMIS). A variety of other acts including the *Occupational Safety and Health Act* (Ontario), the *Steam Boiler and Pressure Vessel Act* (Nova Scotia), the *Elevators and Lifts Act* (Nova Scotia), the *Coal Mines Regulation Act* (Nova Scotia), etc., enforce additional restrictions on specific activities and industries and ensure uniform work standards. In addition, in some instances, the common law applies.

For example, according to common law, every employee has a contract with his or her employer, even if there is nothing in writing. An employee or employer can terminate an employment relationship by giving reasonable notice. An immediate dismissal is possible if an employee is compensated through appropriate severance pay.

Employers must also take care to accurately portray the job for which they are hiring. If an employer misrepresents the conditions of work or misleads an employee (as during a job interview) about employment prospects that resulted in the employee accepting the job, the employer may be held liable to the employee when the job does not work out because of the way in which it was represented. Even where the representation of the job duties and rewards have been accurate, employees who have been enticed to accept a position may be entitled to extra notice of dismissal if they are dismissed without cause in the initial periods of employment.[30]

Finally, the actions of human resource managers should also conform to the principles of natural justice. To assure that a decision-making process is fair, the concept of natural justice has been accepted internationally as non-legal guidelines for arbitrators or mediators, and also by the courts in their decision-making process. The rules of natural justice address minimum standards of fairness and imply obligations for decision makers. Some of the rules are:

1. The right to a fair hearing.
2. The rule against bias (e.g., a person adjudicating a dispute should have no personal interests in the outcome of the proceedings).
3. Hearing the other side.
4. The right of legal representation.
5. The right of timely notice of a hearing.
6. Timeliness of process (according to the principle "justice delayed is justice denied").

Courts have decreed that natural justice rules supersede organizational policies and regulations, which means that human resource managers must ensure that organizational procedures follow the above rules.

The notion of negligent hiring

Negligent hiring: employers can be held responsible for injuries caused by their employees if the employer failed to make reasonable inquiries into the employee's background and suitability for the position

Negligent hiring is a legal theory under which employers can be held responsible for injuries caused by their employees if it can be shown that they failed to make reasonable inquiries into the employee's background and suitability for the position.[31] The doctrine of negligent hiring is not recognized by every province, and standards for determining liability vary. Although there is no list of jobs for which thorough background checks are required, as a general rule, the greater the interface between the employee and his or her co-workers and between the employee and the general public, the greater the obligation of the employer to conduct appropriate background checks. Most negligent hiring lawsuits rest on the employer's failure to conduct reasonable and appropriate research, such as reference checks and an investigation of criminal records that would have disclosed the employee's past misconduct. Under the theory of negligent hiring, even though the employer may not have actually known of the risk presented by the employee, an employer will be held liable if it should have known about the risk.

> For example, employers have been found liable for negligent hiring in situations where an employee with a history of criminal violence attacked a co-worker or client. Employers who have been found negligent in the hiring process have been subjected to substantial financial penalties, which can include both actual and punitive damages.[32]

BIAS-FREE HIRING AND THE DEVELOPMENT OF A CULTURE THAT VALUES DIVERSITY

Fairness is a social rather than a statistical or psychometric concept. Whether an employment tool or practice is considered *fair* depends on a variety of things, including the validity and transparency of the procedures used in implementing the tool or practice, the segment of the workforce and population affected, the historical factors surrounding the event, and the prevailing social values.

THE NOTION OF "FAIRNESS"

"Fairness" is more complex than "bias" although, to some, a selection procedure cannot be fair unless it is also unbiased. Thus, in the past, the following alternative interpretations of fairness have been used to assess the fairness of a test (or other selection tools such as interviews and assessment centre reports).

- **As equal treatment:** All respondents should be treated in the same way throughout the testing process, experiencing identical or comparable procedures in the testing, scoring, and the application of test scores.

- **As lack of bias:** The test or testing procedure does not produce any systematic effects that are related to a person's age, sex, race, etc.

- **As equality of outcomes:** The success rates of different groups (based on age, sex, or race) in the test are comparable, that is, the same percentage of scores from each group of applicants are above the cut-off score (i.e., deemed "successful") for the predictor score.

- **As opportunity to learn:** All examinees should have had equal exposure to and opportunity to learn the material on which the test is based. This is particularly critical for achievement testing, since some people of lower socio-economic status and inner-city residents may face different realities when preparing for such a test.

- **As predictive ability of scores:** To be considered fair, the same test score should predict the same performance level for members of all groups. If the average test scores for different groups differ, but show similar correlation with performance, the test will be perceived as unfair. This means that to achieve the same performance level, members of different groups may require different levels of performance in the test.

Two of the above interpretations of fairness, namely "equality of outcomes" and "predictive ability of scores" are two of the more common interpretations of fairness cited in the selection context. For equality of outcomes, a measure of adverse impact of selection on a particular group of applicants can be calculated. **Adverse impact** occurs when the selection rate for a particular group (based on characteristics such as sex, age, race, etc.) is lower than that for a relevant comparison group. Adverse impact can be proved by providing statistical evidence showing that proportionately fewer of a group's members are successful in the case of a particular predictor of job performance (e.g., test, interview) or the entire selection system taken as a whole. Figure 3-9 illustrates the concept of adverse impact. In the figure, out of the 24 women who applied for a position, only two were finally selected, while for men, the selection rate

Adverse impact: the selection rate for a demographic or cultural group is lower than that of a relevant comparison group

FIGURE 3-9:   An Illustration of Adverse Impact

	Number of Applicants (A)	Number of Applicants Who Were Hired (B)	Selection Ratio (B/A)
Women	24	2	0.083
Men	100	18	0.180

Minimum selection rate for women according to the four-fifths rule must be: $4/5 \times 0.18 = 0.14$. Because the selection ratio for women (0.083) is less than the selection rate under the four-fifths rule (0.14), we conclude that the selection procedure has an adverse impact on female applicants.

was much higher. While establishing adverse impact in selection is a complex activity requiring professional assistance, one rule of thumb for establishing adverse impact in selection is the four-fifths rule.[33] According to this rule, adverse impact is established when the selection rate for the protected group is less than four-fifths of the selection rate of the comparison group.

BIAS-FREE EMPLOYMENT PRACTICES

Given the complex nature of "fairness" in hiring, no single set of actions is likely to achieve results in all instances. However, taking a number of the following actions is likely to reduce bias in hiring in many if not most settings.

1. Set clear goals An organization's human resource plans should reflect the organization's employment equity goals. Constant monitoring of the workforce profile will help the organization to understand where over-concentration and underutilization of. The firm's replacement chart and summary (see Chapter 2) would also help identify possible future job openings which can be used to implement these human resource plans.

2. Use only relevant job requirements Predictors and performance criteria should arise from valid job analyses. Job descriptions must not contain unneeded requirements that would exclude members of protected classes.

3. Employ open recruitment practices When an organization is recruiting new employees, it must ensure that all types of applicants are sought without discriminating among applicants. In some instances, special recruitment efforts may have to be initiated to attract protected groups. More specifically, organizations should do the following when recruiting:

- Post objective information about job vacancies in employment agencies and conspicuous spots where members of protected groups gather for formal or informal meetings.
- Advertise job openings in media that are widely read or listened to by all members of the community including members of protected groups. Place special recruitment advertisements in publications catering to protected groups.
- Include role models from protected groups in employment advertisements.

- Establish networks with various community groups and ethnic associations.
- Train recruiters to reach out to the larger community.

4. Use only reliable and valid selection tools Selection tools should be continuously monitored for reliability and validity.

- Screening devices for selecting applicants should be job-relevant and non-discriminatory. Screening criteria such as appearance and dress may be misleading and should be avoided.
- Selection criteria should be strictly based on bona fide job requirements.
- The success rates of various applicant groups for each predictor should be continuously monitored so that if necessary the selection tools can be adjusted or replaced.
- The employer should attempt to validate predictors for various subgroups and take corrective actions (such as application of differential cut-off scores if relevant) should be taken. More on subgroup validation will be discussed in Chapter 4.
- If a selection tool (e.g., a test) has an adverse impact on a group, the employer should be able to show that no reasonable or practical alternative to this tool exists. In all other instances, the employer should substitute a predictor with no adverse impact or one with a very small adverse impact.

5. Recognize the duty for reasonable accommodation In all situations, the employer has the burden of reasonable accommodation.

- Educate managers about their human rights responsibilities. Every person should have the opportunity to compete for a job position on an equal basis. Only objective, job-relevant criteria should guide an employment decision.
- Accommodate the individual when necessary (e.g., providing a large print test to a visually impaired applicant) at the employer's cost.
- Make training and developmental opportunities available to all employees, without discrimination. Some employees with special needs may need alternative times or training procedures.

DEVELOPING A CULTURE THAT VALUES DIVERSITY

Managing workforce diversity has emerged as a major managerial challenge, and is likely to become even more critical in the foreseeable future. Indeed, few trends have received as much publicity or gained as much attention in managerial circles recently. The proliferation of cultural backgrounds at work results in widely varying values, work ethics, and norms of behaviour. Organizations that cannot adapt to the cultures of these diverse groups are unlikely to maintain effectiveness in the long run. Managers who do not recognize these differences are likely to face problems emerging from poor communication, insensitivity, and reduced motivation. The diverse workforce also brings *in* new approaches, new insights, and new solutions to the workplace, enabling an organization to bring *out* new products and services, reduce costs, improve efficiency, or to compete in foreign markets more effectively. Homogeneity in the workforce may expedite some decision processes, but such convenience may be at the expense of the creativity that is triggered by differences in values, opinions, and approach. Differences among employees, if ignored or handled poorly, can reduce workplace effectiveness, but if managed well, can be a competitive advantage.

This means that today, firms must recognize individual differences and respect them. Canada has always opted for a "mosaic" cultural model in which immigrants are encouraged to preserve their native cultures (in the United States, a "melting pot" model has traditionally been more popular, with immigrants being expected to learn the "American" way of living). In reality, until the recent past, most immigrants to Canada were whites who had originated from Europe. This is no longer true. In recent years, half of Canada's immigrants originated from Asia and Africa. These new immigrants hold very different values and life styles compared to the early immigrants to this country. "Assimilation" into an overall Canadian way of life may simply be impossible or unacceptable to new immigrants.

Managing diversity: proactive, long-term, organization-wide efforts to bridge the connection between employees and organizational goals and practices by promoting individual and organizational change

Managing diversity is an active recognition and appreciation of the increasingly multicultural nature of contemporary organizations. **Managing diversity** involves a proactive, organization-wide effort with a long-term focus that bridges the connection between employees and organizational goals and practices by promoting individual and organizational change. The focus of managing diversity is ensuring that the variety of talents and perspectives that already exist within an organization are used to benefit the organization and its stakeholders. Managing diversity has three essential dimensions:

1. A strategic, proactive approach

2. The creation of connections between individual aspirations and culture with organizational goals

3. A focus on individual and organizational change

To be effective, diversity management must be *strategic*. Taking a long-term perspective, the management of the organization should ask: "Where is the organization now?" and "Where does it want to go?" The strategic approach often requires a fundamental shift in managerial thinking. Management should be proactive to achieve the organizational mission.

> For example, an organization that requires a dress code that is resented by a segment of the workgroup might begin by asking questions such as "What is the purpose of our dress code?", "Is this purpose still relevant for today's setting?" and "Can we achieve the same objective in alternative ways?" Depending on the answers, the organization may decide to abolish the dress code or alter it to make the work setting more comfortable for all employees.

Because through diversity management, the organization attempts to address the concerns and gain the participation of the entire workforce, management should address problem areas before they manifest in a serious way, that is, before they result in legal or government intervention. Management should also ensure it does not limit itself to the concerns of only a section of the employees (e.g., white women).

Effective diversity management results in the recognition of the uniqueness and complexity of individuals and attempts to empower them to contribute to the organizational mission. It tries to *match organizational goals with individual aspirations, values, and priorities.*

> In one U.S. firm, it was a long-standing policy that English was the chosen language for conducting all business and dealing with other employees. This worked quite well until the firm expanded its operations into areas where large numbers of Hispanics lived. After the expansion, a large segment of the workforce was much more comfortable speaking in Spanish than in English. Finding that its policy was causing unnecessary inconvenience to the workforce, the firm abolished its old rule. Employees could talk to each other and to customers in Spanish if they so desired, but more formal communications to the head office were still to be in English; however, not all employees would need to be fluent in English to work for the company.

Diversity management requires *making a link between the assumptions about the organizational culture and the personal cultures of the organization's employees.* Such efforts are based on the recognition that all employees play multiple roles in their lives.

Organizational demands in conflict with other role demands need to be identified and, where feasible, modified. Research into an organization's practices and open discussions can reveal different perspectives, and contradictions, and may also lead to their resolution.

> For example, recruitment ads for organizations that would like to attract more women and minorities often call for applications "from qualified women and minorities." However, this very phrase suggests a lesser expectation about this candidate pool since rarely, if ever, do recruiters talk about "qualified male candidates." Such hidden biases or negative portrayals can be eliminated through in-depth research and open discussion.

Finally, diversity management also *requires a focus on critical systems and organizational processes and changing them where necessary*. For example, in many organizations, performance appraisal, training, rewards, and communication systems are biased against specific groups like women, African-Canadians, the physically challenged, and older workers. A key component of diversity management is to change outmoded assumptions and practices by training the organization's members to recognize the new realities and revise their own behaviour and assumptions to meet these new realities.

Creating an organizational culture that values diversity is not easy. Even some of the more progressive organizations have found changing their existing practices and culture difficult. Simple changes in an individual's behaviour may not necessarily indicate a change in this person's fundamental values. Individuals may appear to behave differently to others, but they may also inwardly cling to old beliefs and values. Thus, changes in culture can either precede or succeed behavioural changes, which explains why a change in an organizational chart may not produce the desired changes in core values. Sometimes the culture of an organization may be so deeply ingrained that any initiative for change is hard to accomplish.

> The top managers of a consumer food company were among the most successful in their industries before joining the firm. In their previous positions in other firms, they had created major strategic initiatives which led to the firm's growth and robust financial health for their employers. However, the new organization's prevailing culture was so strong that, despite their experience, it took them more than 15 years and two generations of top management to change the firm's culture and successfully reposition the firm.

Figure 3-10 shows some strategies for achieving cultural change.

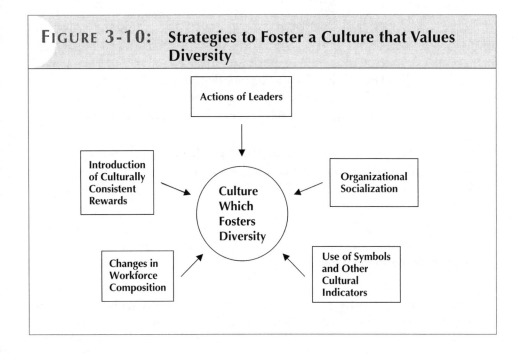

FIGURE 3-10:   **Strategies to Foster a Culture that Values Diversity**

1. Actions of leaders

One of the strongest influences on an organization's culture are the values and actions of its leaders. They are the ones to establish, from the very beginning, the firm's purpose and its basic philosophy.

> Frank Stronach of Magna International, Isadore Sharp of Four Seasons Hotels and Resorts, Ross Perot of EDS, and Anita Roddick of The Body Shop are all part of the long list of powerful founders who have had a major influence on the culture of their organizations.

Strong leaders can change cultural values by communicating a sense of new direction and required organizational values. Top management should "walk the talk" of commitment to diversity through their own actions and behaviours. They should show respect for members of different cultures and employees who lead non-traditional lifestyles. Often "cues" may come from the personal actions of the leaders themselves. Managers have to act as role models.

2. Organizational socialization

Socialization is a process that starts before the first day of employment and continues throughout one's career within an organization. Images of an organization are created in the minds of new recruits long before they join the firm. The organization communicates to the larger society through its dress code, the way in which the organization treats its customers and employees, and the stories and folklore about the organization that are circulated outside of the organization. The orientation and training programs within the organization may further reinforce some of these images. New recruits receive some objective information about their pay and work duties during hiring; however, much of the other "soft" information comes from their new colleagues. Organizational socialization can deeply change the individual's perceptions about the organization's work norms and required work behaviours.

3. Use of symbols and other cultural indicators

Symbols, physical structures, and other artifacts significantly impact the culture of an organization and are often used by leaders to convey and to change culture:

> One entrepreneur, who developed the world's largest dairy store with annual sales of $130 million, created a strong culture that focused on customer service. He had that policy chiselled into stone where the store's 100 000 weekly customers could read it: "Rule 1: The customer is always right. Rule 2: If the customer is wrong, re-read Rule 1."

Every organization relies on its "tribal storytellers" to keep its history and culture alive. The organization should use all opportunities to visually present the multicultural nature of the firm's workforce. Employment advertisements, public relations brochures, posters, and so on, should reflect the fact that the organization values diverse lifestyles and cultures. Executives who effectively transmit their values to others employ a variety of tools such as speeches, written messages, gestures, stories, symbols, and ceremonies.

4. Change the workforce composition

By hiring individuals who have beliefs and values that are consistent with an organization's culture, an organization can further reinforce this culture, leading to improved employee satisfaction and commitment to the organization.

> Companies like Shell Canada and Toyota Canada carefully select people with a deeply ingrained team orientation to ensure that a team-based culture is perpetuated at their new plants. For example, in one year, Toyota Canada processed 11 000 applications for 1200 jobs.

5. Introduce culturally consistent rewards

Reward systems can strengthen or change corporate culture. Federal Express Canada is one example of an organization that has made diversity management a key component of managerial performance:

FedEx Canada does not approach the question of diversity through the lens of compliance, according to the president of the company. Visible minorities make up 23% of its workforce, whereas the national proportion is 11%. Diversity policies at FedEx Canada are focused largely on communicating respect and fostering awareness of the importance of diversity to business. Managers are held accountable for counting the number of personnel from each of the four designated groups (namely, women, aboriginal peoples, people with disability, and visible minority) in their departments. Managers also monitor a variety of factors including promotion, wage gap, and clustering in specific jobs. "Putting people first is part of FedEx DNA, and unless one fundamentally believes that's the case, any policies, procedures, rules and regulations will ultimately not work. One has to fundamentally believe in an organization's employees and that has to come straight from the top and not delegated to HR," FedEx Canada's president has said.[34]

In summary, creating a culture that values and fosters diversity, while beneficial, is also a complex task requiring conscious effort. While creating such a culture should be a long-term goal, in the short run, the employer, when involved in the selection process, should recognize cultural differences and adapt to them in order to meet the new challenges posed by a multicultural workforce. This is particularly relevant when the employer is choosing selection tools, such as interviews, where members of different cultural groups may exhibit widely different behavioural patterns, as the following example illustrates:

> In North America, maintaining eye contact is the sign of a good communicator; in the Middle East, it is an integral part of successful communication; but to many Chinese and Japanese, it may indicate distrust. Greeting gestures in different cultures also differ. North Americans shake hands, the Japanese bow, and Middle Easterners of the same sex kiss on the cheek. "Personal space" also varies significantly across cultures. South Americans and Middle Easterners tend to stand or sit close to each other, while North Americans like to have greater personal space around them.[35]

Chapter 8 discusses different approaches to refining interviews to enhance their reliability and validity. Chapter 7 and Chapter 9 discuss the implications for other selection tools such as testing and cut-off scores during selection decisions.

In the foreseeable future, some significant changes in employment law are expected. A wide range of regulations relating to working conditions, leave, and the nature of employment contracts are under consideration at this time:

> For example, Part 3 of the *Canada Labour Code* is currently under review. This far-reaching review of labour standards for federally regulated industries is expected to raise new questions and changes in policy. For instance, recognition that minimum work conditions and rest periods should be job-specific (e.g., the demands on a long-haul truck driver are significantly different from those on bank employees) has increased. Other issues such as job protection for employees on sabbaticals and the definition of temporary and part-time workers are also being deliberated.[36] According to the Law Commission of Canada, Canada's labour laws are failing a growing number of workers and are in need of fundamental reform. The world of work has changed drastically in recent years, with the result that more than one-third of the Canadian workforce is engaged in non-standard temporary or contract work. But eligibility for most labour rights, benefits, and protections are available only in standard, full-time, permanent employment.[37]

As discussed in this chapter, virtually every aspect of the staffing function is affected by legal requirements. If there is a basic rule in human resource management, it has to be "Obey the law."[38] This chapter provides an overview of the various laws governing the employment function. It is the responsibility of the human resource manager to ensure that all policies and rules take legal aspects into account The next chapter will deal with the topic of predictors, namely, tools such as application blanks, tests, job interviews, which help predict future job performance of a job applicant.

Implications for Practice

1. Human resource selection should begin by recognizing the constraints imposed by the local, provincial, and national legal requirements. In the case of organizations operating in foreign locations, a good awareness of the relevant laws of the host country is also critical.

2. Human resource plans must reflect the organization's employment equity goals.

3. Job descriptions must not contain unneeded requirements that exclude members of protected classes.

4. Recruiting must ensure that all types of applicants are sought without any intended or unintended discrimination.

5. The screening tools for selection must be job-relevant and non-discriminatory. If a selection device (e.g., a test)

has an adverse impact on a group, the employer has the burden to show that no reasonable or practical alternative exists to the discriminatory practice.

6. In all instances, the employer has the burden of reasonable accommodation.

7. Training and developmental opportunities must be made available for workers without discrimination.

8. Introducing bias-free employment practices not only helps the employer attract recruits from unconventional sources but also helps avoid potential legal challenges.

9. Fostering a culture that values and fosters diversity is beneficial to the organization; however, this requires a conscious, strategic effort.

Key Terms for Review

Adverse impact,   *p. 99*

Bona fide occupational requirement (BFOR),   *p. 83*

Contract workers,   *p. 94*

Direct discrimination,   *p. 83*

Employment equity programs,   *p. 91*

Managing diversity,   *p. 102*

Negligent hiring,   *p. 98*

Principle of reasonable accommodation,   *p. 88*

Reasonable alternative,   *p. 88*

Systemic or indirect discrimination,   *p. 83*

Workplace accommodation,   *p. 89*

Discussion Questions

1. What are the key implications of the Charter of Rights for employment practices?

2. Discuss the major implications of human rights legislation for employment managers.

3. What are the implications of the *Canada Labour Code* and employment standards legislation for employment managers?

4. Discuss the necessary actions to ensure bias-free hiring practices.

Critical Thinking Questions

1. If an employee refuses to work from 12:00 P.M. to 1:00 P.M. for religious reasons, can the supervisor reprimand the employee? Why?

2. You are an employer with a job opening for a warehouse helper, a position that requires the employee to lift heavy packages, up to 30 kilograms. A woman, originally from an Asian country, applied for the job and claims that she is able to do the work. She looks rather petite and you are afraid that she may hurt herself. When you deny her the job, she threatens to complain to the human rights commission in your province. How would you respond to this applicant?

3. The manufacturing facility of your employer, which has sales offices in several locations in

Atlantic Canada, is located in a remote town in the region. You work at this facility and you moved to this town several years ago. You were attracted to this town because of provincial tax rebates and subsidies. Recently, labour competition from countries where people work for much lower wages have cut your employer's market share significantly. At a recent meeting at the head office, one of your colleagues suggested hiring some of the locals "off-the-record" at wage rates lower than the provincial minimum wage rates. Given the high unemployment rate in the town, you are convinced that a large number of applicants would be willing to work at this lower rate. What should you do? Why?

4. You work as the human resource manager in a police force. Over the last four years, you have found that members of Group X rarely score well in interviews, even though they tend to score equal to or better then other applicants on the selection test. The result is that while this group's share in the local labour market is almost 12%, their representation in your workforce is barely 3%. What actions would you take to correct this imbalance in this instance?

Web Research

Visit the Human Rights Commission website. Find and summarize three cases decided last year in favour of employers and three cases decided in favour of employees. What conclusions do you form from these cases? Which of the principles discussed in this chapter seem to underlie these decisions?

CASE INCIDENT

Can-Mart Department Stores

The workforce of Can-Mart, a large department store with branches all over Western Canada, is composed of several groups, as listed in Table A:

Questions

1. *From the information provided, what can you conclude?*
2. *Suggest strategies for appropriate future staffing activities.*

TABLE A:

Job Classes	Male	Female	White	Black	Asian	Native Peoples
Executive	38	2	36	0	2	0
Management	189	23	180	4	5	0
Junior Management	321	150	191	60	50	20
Salaried/Commission	430	310	274	86	30	40
Hourly Paid	624	464	268	216	50	90

The results of an analysis of the local labour force from which Can-Mart draws its employees is provided in Table B:

TABLE B:

Male	Female	White	Black	Asian	Native Peoples
52%	48%	79%	10%	6%	5%

CASE

Kanata Food Distributors—Legal Challenges*

Note: This case continues from Chapter 2: Kanata Food Distributors. Review the case background in Chapters 1 and 2 before examining this case.

About eight years back, Kanata Food Distributors started offering major brand-name grocery items, baked products, prepared foods and, more recently, premium quality meals. Today, approximately 30% of the total revenues for the firm come from this line of business. About 50% comes from 90 24-7 stores. The other 50% of the revenues emerged from 26 Temptations pastry food outlets. Many of the convenience stores are located adjacent to major traffic areas (e.g., gas stations) or residential areas. The pastry stores are strategically located in shopping malls, near high traffic areas such as bus and rail stations, educational institutions, and hospitals. Increasingly, the pastry shops are also offering light meals and snacks. Kanata had made a conscious decision to hire experienced bakers and cooks to offer high-quality meals and fresh pastries—a critical factor, especially in Quebec.

The firm believes that a number of changes are taking place that will have a major impact on future operations and the firm's employment policy. These changes consist of the following:

- Qualified chefs and bakers have been hard to find, especially for stores that are located in suburban areas or smaller towns. Many of the present chefs are 55 years old or older and likely to retire in the next five years or so. (Many have indicated a desire to take early retirement.)

- Kanata is considering the purchase of a chain of pastry shops located in eastern Ontario and western Quebec. These shops were owned by a Lebanese entrepreneur who is planning to sell his controlling interests and move to join his son who lives in the United States. Most of the employees in these stores are of Lebanese or Greek origin.

- The inclusion of large numbers of new immigrants into the workforce has caused resentment and occasional interpersonal conflicts in Kanata's various units. The pastry shops have not been immune to these as well. Many of the problems occur between white employees and employees who belong to visible minorities. Many visible minority members have made occasional remarks that the company's performance management systems are biased against them. In the past, Kanata had made a major effort to recruit minority employees into managerial positions. Despite this, the proportion of Asians, African-Canadians, and other visible minorities in the management cadre has been marginal.

- While the firm receives a large number of applications from visible minorities, over 75% of the applicants belonging to these groups fail the standardized written test Kanata uses to select people for a personal interview. The success rate for white employees for the same test is about 73%.

- Many women employees hold cashier, clerical, or other low-paying positions. Only about 8% of the managerial personnel in these shops are women. A few vocal women have been demanding changes which will help them move up in rank. Currently, 60% of managerial positions are filled internally through promotions.

In recent months, a number of other incidents with potential legal implications have occured:

- Kanata has always enforced a dress code where all service staff are expected to wear business attire, including ties for male employees. The only exception was Fridays, when employees were permitted to wear casual clothing. Recently, a number of employees had approached the human resource manager with a request for wearing casual clothes each working day during the summer months of June through September. The management has yet to to respond to their request. Management, however, had to deal with three employees who dressed inappropriately during the last month. In one case, one employee had come to the office wearing torn jeans, another wore bike shorts, and a woman employee had come to work wearing a tight T-shirt.

- An aboriginal employee, Kevin Swan, had complained to the human resource department about negative comments made by his colleagues about "Indians." They included references to drunken Indians and comments such as "Indians aren't so bright, eh, Swan?" Mr. Swan alleged that he encountered racial comments, jokes, and slurs repeatedly since he joined the firm five months ago. When the human resource manager investigated the matter, Mr. Swan's colleagues mentioned that they all "horsed around" and "teased each other in good humour." For example, one of the other employees who had teased Swan was partially deaf and other employees called him "dumb, deaf, Defoe."

- Two African-Canadian customers had complained to the manager of a downtown store about the poor treatment they received from the service personnel. Apparently one of the security guards followed the couple as they walked through the store. While no one accused them directly of shoplifting or other fraudulent acts, the demeanour of the personnel who attended them at the store appeared racially motivated. For example, they noticed that one cashier checked their credit cards more closely than he checked the credit cards of white or Asian customers who were standing in front of them in the same line.

The firm's top management is planning to discuss the above items at its next meeting. Jane Petruchino, the Assistant Human Resource Manager (in the absence of the Human Resource Manager who was on a month's leave), was asked to identify an action plan that would adequately respond to these issues.

Questions

1. *Imagine yourself in Jane's position. What is your assessment of the situation?*

2. *What recommendations would you make to the management at the next meeting?*

---

*Case written by Professor Hari Das of Saint Mary's University, Halifax. All rights retained by the author, © 2005.

CHAPTER

"The more important concerns of HRM professionals, courts, unions, and the government include the reliability of the evaluations—ratings should not change dramatically if they were redone by the same rater shortly thereafter or by other raters from the same organization (assuming no dramatic events intervened)—and their validity, meaning that they are relevant to job performance."

James Baron and David Kreps[1]

CHAPTER OBJECTIVES

After studying this chapter, you should be able to:

- Define reliability and validity in the context of selecting human resources

- Discuss various approaches to establishing the reliability of a measure

- Discuss the steps in validating a selection tool

- Decide the number of predictors to be used in making staffing decisions

- Discuss the importance of validating a test for different employee groups

A man who had recently immigrated to Canada from Pakistan worked as a technician in a nuclear-related company on a three-month contract. At the end of the contract, he asked his employer about the possibility of becoming a full-time employee. When the employer refused to offer it to him, the man alleged that his ethnicity was the only reason. The employer then told him that a new policy forbade the hiring of people from countries that posed a security threat or a nuclear threat to Canada. Since Pakistan had not signed the Nuclear Non-Proliferation Treaty, which was ratified in 1970, his continued employment was considered a security threat to Canada. Because the claimant had been in Canada for only 20 months, the employer pointed out that it would be impossible for him to get enhanced security clearance. Consequently, he was let go, even though two co-workers, both Canadian citizens hired at the same time as the claimant, were offered permanent positions. In his appeal, the claimant maintained that (1) having done similar work in Pakistan, he was well suited for the position, and (2) had he been a security risk, he would not have been allowed to immigrate to Canada. Further investigation by the Canadian Human Rights Commission showed that the claimant had performed his job well and that the employer did not have any valid basis for asserting that the claimant posed a security risk. In a conciliated settlement, the claimant was rehired for an 18-month term position, but his duties were restricted and supervised until sufficient information about him became available in order to obtain the necessary security clearance. If he satisfied the requirements for enhanced clearance, he would be offered a permanent position.[2]

Today, it is illegal to enforce a requirement that is not job-relevant or to use biographical or background information unrelated to job performance in hiring employees. The onus is on the employer to show that the selection tools and decision criteria used in employee selection are consistent and related to job performance. As in the opening vignette, the fact that the employer *felt* that the continued employment of someone poses a security threat is insufficient; *facts* to corroborate such assumptions must exist. In turn, this means that the selection tools and processes should have the important property of validity: namely, a valid relationship to actual job performance or other factors affecting such performance (e.g., safety). Validity in turn requires that measurements are reliable or consistent. A tool that cannot measure something consistently over time also cannot measure it with validity.

This chapter elaborates on the concepts of reliability and validity, and discusses popular approaches to assessing reliability and validity and actions managers take to enhance these properties in employee selection procedures. Reliability and validity assessment requires an understanding of some statistical tools which are discussed in the Appendix to this chapter.

THE MEANING OF RELIABILITY AND VALIDITY

As discussed in Chapter 1, the selection process aims to match the characteristics of the job applicant with performance requirements. Predictors such as application blanks, tests, and interviews predict performance based on criteria, such as quantity and quality of job performance, absenteeism, the number of accidents, and the potential to assume more responsibility. To be useful, both the predictors and criteria must have reliability and validity.

RELIABILITY

In the context of selection, **reliability** refers to the consistency or stability of a measure or instrument. Reliability is often determined by the degree of consistency between two sets of scores on a measure (or instrument) or its stability over time.

> For example, assume that Jack weighed himself at 7:00 A.M. one day and found that he weighed 65 kg. At 7:01 A.M., he climbed on the scale again, but found that the scale showed a weight of 71 kg. Intrigued, he tried a third time a few seconds later, and found that this time, the scale showed his weight as 57 kg. Jack concludes that the scale is unreliable, since within such a short time, Jack's weight could not have increased or decreased significantly.

Information on testing and validation:
Canadian Association
www.cpa.ca
American Psychological Association
www.apa.org/science/testing.html

Reliability: the consistency or stability of a measure or instrument, usually determined by the degree of consistency between two sets of scores or its stability over time

In the context of human resource selection, reliability means that tests must yield *consistent* results.

> For example, a test of manual dexterity for assembly workers should give a similar score each time the same person takes the test. If the results vary widely with each retest because good scores depend on luck, then the test is not reliable.

Reliability also applies to measurement errors. **Measurement error** is the difference between the true score (or measurement) of a phenomenon or trait and its observed score. It refers to those factors affecting the observed (or actual) score in a test, unrelated to what is being measured by the test.[3]

Measurement error: the difference between the true measurement of a phenomenon and its observed score

> In the above example, assume that Jack's correct weight is 68 kg. The measurement errors on the three attempts were 3 kg, 3 kg, and 11 kg, respectively.

Figure 4-1 shows how the true scores and error scores affect reliability. Calculating measurement error is useful in the context of human resource selection, since it helps us to calculate indexes of reliability for specific situations.

In almost all testing situations, the score obtained by a person will be different from the true score for the same individual. The true score is an ideal conception and is achieved very rarely (if at all!) in real life. The true score is an individual's score if all external and internal factors could be perfectly controlled. For example, room temperature and noise level could affect test results. The individual's mood and physical health on the day of the test may also contaminate the outcomes. Moreover, the questions asked in the test may not be fully representative of all the possible questions that could be asked about the topic. In other words, depending on which questions are asked, the individual's score could vary if he or she is more or less knowledgeable about certain aspects of the topic.

When an individual takes the same test several times, the scores will show slight variation, although, if the test is well developed, the scores should be similar and converging. For practical purposes, the differences in scores on these multiple attempts are treated as errors of measurement. The score on any single occasion of testing can thus be expressed as:[4]

SCORE OBTAINED = TRUE SCORE + ERROR

Note that the error can be either positive or negative:

> Thus, the same student may do well or badly, depending on whether the instructor designed an easy or difficult test.

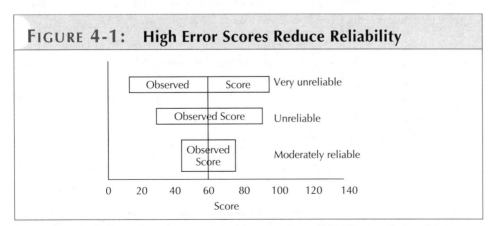

FIGURE 4-1: High Error Scores Reduce Reliability

Assume the individual's true score on a test is 60. When a test is unreliable, the spread around the true score is very high, as in the above case. A reliable test or measure would result in a score closer to 60.

True score is only an ideal construct,[5] since all extraneous variables cannot be controlled and all possible questions about a subject area cannot be covered. The true score is the individual's score if he or she had correctly answered the same proportion of test problems as he or she would have in an ideal test.

> For example, assume that 4000 questions constitute the entire universe of problems that can be formed on a topic. But due to practical constraints, only 40 sample questions are included in the actual test. Further assume that an individual answers 30 of the 40 sample questions correctly. If the test is accurate, then for the universe of 4000 questions, this proportion should remain the same: namely, the individual should get 3000 correct answers.

To get a true score, test-takers should have correctly answered only the questions for which they actually knew the answers, without being influenced by external factors such as temperature, noise, health problems, or even guesswork.

> Thus, if a person taking a test was sick on the day of the test, her or his ill health could adversely affect on the score. The true score in this instance is likely to be higher than the observed score.

Perfect conditions are hard to obtain in real life; hence, true scores are unattainable in many testing situations. Despite this shortcoming, the concept helps explain the notion of measurement error and, in turn, reliability.

Measurement error can be either systematic or random. **Systematic errors** occur in a predictable, consistent fashion, while **random errors** are unpredictable and do not follow any pattern. Systematic errors (or constant errors, as they are sometimes referred to) occur consistently in repeated measurements, while random errors influence different measurements to different degrees.

> A clock that is always 5 minutes slow is an example of systematic measurement error, since the difference between the true time and the observed time is knowable. A test for which a minority group always score 20 points lower than the mainstream population also is an example of systematic error.

In the human resource selection context, there are three important sources of systematic errors:

- errors attributable to the *measuring instrument,* also referred to as *instrumentation errors* (e.g., scoring a test with an incorrect answer key or using culturally loaded questions);

- errors attributable to the *measuring situation* relate to contextual factors that reduce reliability (e.g., noise or distractions that affect *all* of the applicants and reduce their scores);

- *individual factors,* including all personal characteristics unrelated to the construct being measured but that affect the person's performance in the test (e.g., an individual's test anxiety might lower his or her score by 20 points).

Knowing which types of errors are present is important, since they will impact the test outcomes. For example, most errors attributable to a measuring instrument do not affect the relative rank of the performances of the people taking the test, since everyone is exposed to the same test; yet individual factors, such as anxiety, affect the relative changes in the rank of performance.

> For example, a weighing scale that exaggerates an object's true weight by 5 kilograms, though inaccurate, does not change the relative ranks of the weights of everyone who uses that scale. Similarly, a clock that is always 5 minutes fast is consistent, though not accurate.

Of course, some instrumentation errors affect individual outcomes differently.

> A test using terminology which is understood by members of the mainstream community but not by other ethnic groups will discriminate against members of those groups. This can result in unintentional systemic discrimination.

Systematic errors: errors that occur in a predictable, consistent fashion

Random errors: unpredictable errors that do not follow any pattern

Random errors, by definition, are unpredictable. The underlying characteristic of a random error is that it influences different measurements to different degrees.

> The following are two examples of random errors: a few copies of a test contain printing errors, which creates confusion among the test takers; and a sudden noise during one of six test administrations negatively impacts on the results of some test takers.

In human resource selection, both predictors and criteria must have high reliability. An unreliable predictor can discriminate against a specific applicant or applicant groups, while poorly measured criteria make it difficult to identify valid predictors.

> For example, when the criterion of job performance is measured by supervisory ratings, those ratings must be free from bias or influence of other situational contingencies (e.g., time pressure); otherwise, they become unreliable. Unreliable criterion ratings in one instance can cast doubts on other more valid selection tools.

Reliability can be calculated in several different ways. Theoretically, the **reliability coefficient** shows the squared correlation between true scores and observed (or obtained) scores and is also called the *coefficient of determination*. A reliability coefficient of 0.90 means that 90% of the obtained variance in a measure is the true variance, and only 10% is attributable to error. A variety of symbols are used to indicate reliability, but popular one are r_{xx} and r_{yy}.

Reliability coefficient: shows the squared correlation between true and obtained scores and is interpreted as the coefficient of determination

$$r_{xx} = r^2_{tx}$$

Where

r_{xx} is the reliability coefficient (or coefficient of determination),

r^2_{tx} is the squared correlation between the true and obtained scores,

x is the obtained or observed scores, and

t is the true scores

The reliability coefficient is the estimated proportion of total variance due to systematic sources of variance. If such a correlation were perfect (that is, the reliability coefficient is equal to 1.00), then all variance actually obtained in a set of measures could be attributed to systematic sources. If the reliability coefficient is less than 1.00, then a part of the variance is due to errors in measurement. For example, if the reliability coefficient (or coefficient of determination) for a test on sales aptitude equals 0.89, then 89% of the differences in scores among people who took the aptitude test is due to true variance, and only 11% is due to error. The correlation between the true scores and the observed scores, in this instance, would be the square root of 0.89.

Consider another example:

> Assume that five people weigh 55 kg, 45 kg, 50 kg, 60 kg, and 65 kg, respectively. Now, let us suppose that the weighing scale used was not accurate and showed their weights as 59 kg, 41 kg, 54 kg, 55 kg, and 71 kg, respectively. The square of the correlation between the true and observed weights is 0.8019, indicating that the variability in observed weights that can be attributed to true differences is only 80%.

But the reliability coefficient is an abstract theoretical notion (or construct), and in many instances, the true scores may be unknown or unavailable. Hence, the index of reliability can never be computed directly.[6] This is particularly so for personality or attitude tests, where the true scores are unknown. For practical purposes, other approaches to estimate reliability have been devised. These approaches are discussed in later in this chapter.

To conclude, reliability indicates the consistency or stability of a measure. Without reliability, neither a predictor nor a criterion can be useful to the human resource practitioner. The factors reducing reliability include personal characteristics (such as health or, test anxiety), lack of standardization in the measuring instrument (such as different interviewers asking qualitatively different questions), and random factors. In practice, many predictors employed today by Canadian managers are only moderately reliable.

A *Canadian HR Reporter* online survey found that many managers are not trained to interview properly and rely on gut instinct. Many managers end up looking for people in their own image. Many respondents also had difficulty getting accurate and adequate information through background checks. Several respondents did not appreciate the usefulness of psychometric testing. Some line managers also found it hard to follow a standardized process during hiring.[7]

Even if a predictor is reliable, it does not ensure validity. Lack of reliability significantly reduces validity. The next section looks at validity in greater detail.

VALIDITY

Validity: the predictor scores measure what they are supposed to measure and are significantly related to a relevant criterion

Information on reliability and validity:
http://seamonkey.ed.asu.edu/~alex/teaching/assessment/reliability.html

Validity requires that the predictor scores measure what they are supposed to measure and are significantly related to job performance or some other relevant criterion. Thus, an intelligence test should measure intelligence, not a person's ability to read quickly. In the context of human resource selection, simply measuring attitudes or personality traits is not enough: the test must measure factors related to actual job performance. For example, the results of a sales aptitude test should help an organization predict the future sales performance of its hires. The stronger the relationship between test results and performance, the more effective the test is as a selection tool. When scores and performance are unrelated, the test is invalid and should not be used for selection:

> An Ontario trucking company used to give all its applicants an extensive reading test. However, because the job involved oral instructions and maps, the reading test had no relationship to job performance; it did not distinguish good drivers from bad ones. It only distinguished between those who could read English well and those who could not.

When an invalid test rejects people of a particular race, sex, religion, or national origin, it violates the *Canadian Human Rights Act* or related provincial legislation. Too often, tests fail to predict job performance.[8] A Toronto-based industrial psychologist[9] has estimated that "only 3% of firms use properly validated selection tests." If this estimate is correct, then HR professionals need to scrutinize testing to avoid discrimination.

To ensure that tests are valid, human resource departments should conduct validation studies. There are several approaches to test validation, the more popular of which are discussed in this chapter. Regardless which approach is used, validation studies for subgroups, such as women and minorities, will help avoid unintended discrimination. Otherwise, an organization may face discrimination charges and enter costly legal battles, as one U.S. firm discovered:

> The Albemarle Paper Company gave several black job applicants a battery of tests that had not been validated. The applicants sued Albemarle, so the company then implemented a validation study. But the study had several weaknesses, and the Court ruled the tests as invalid and discriminatory. The problem was that Albemarle used tests that had been validated for advanced-level jobs, not for the entry-level positions for which the applicants had applied. Such validation did not prove the tests were valid for entry-level jobs. Furthermore, the company had validated the test on a group of white workers and then applied the test to the black applicants, which was considered invalid.[10]

THE RELATIONSHIP BETWEEN RELIABILITY AND VALIDITY

As already noted, even the most reliable test may not necessarily be valid. Reliability only ensures consistency or precision of measurement, not the selection tool's ability to predict job performance. However, a selection tool cannot validly predict performance unless it is reliable. Reliability is then a basic minimum requirement for a selection tool: without reliability, a selection tool can never be valid.

The reliability of a selection tool, however, establishes the "upper limit" of its validity. The reliability of the predictor and the reliability of the criterion jointly define the upper bound for validity as follows:[11]

$$r_{xy} = \sqrt{r_{xx} \times r_{yy}}$$

where

r_{xy} is the maximum possible correlation between predictor x and criterion y (or the validity coefficient),

r_{xx} is the reliability coefficient of predictor x, and

r_{yy} is the reliability coefficient of criterion y

For example, if the reliability of a sales aptitude test (x) is 0.81, and the reliability of the criterion (namely, supervisory evaluation of performance) is 0.64, then the maximum possible validity of the sales aptitude test is 0.72.

This formula shows that if the reliability of either the predictor or criterion decreases, it affects the overall validity of the selection tool. If the value of either the predictor or the criterion approaches zero, which means the predictor or the criterion is completely unreliable, the value of the validity also approaches zero. Herein lies the importance of ensuring high reliability for the predictors and criteria. The next section will elaborate on various approaches to assess reliability.

Factors which can affect the validity of a measure: *http://psych.athabascau.ca/ html/validity/concept.shtml*

ESTABLISHING RELIABILITY

As already noted, true scores are rarely known. For this reason, the reliability coefficient is usually a mere theoretical construct. For practical purposes, reliability is estimated by examining the relationship between two sets of measures measuring the same phenomenon, trait, or construct. When the two sets of measures yield similar scores, the reliability is considered high. When the two sets of scores are dissimilar, reliability is assumed to be low. Most of the time, the *Pearson product-moment correlation coefficient* (see Appendix 4A following this chapter) is used as an index of reliability where 0.00 and 1.00 are the lower and upper bounds of its value. The higher the coefficient, the lower the measurement error, and the higher the estimated reliability.

ESTIMATING RELIABILITY

In this general approach, several methods of estimating reliability exist, with four being more popular. These are the test-retest method, the parallel or equivalent form approach, the internal consistency measure, and the inter-rater reliability coefficient. The critical difference among these procedures is what each method considers to be errors of measurement. Thus, the same factor may be treated as an error or a systematic variance in different methods. For example, systematic error (e.g., the watch that is consistently five minutes fast) may not affect reliability when it is defined as "consistency." However, the same watch would be considered unreliable if reliability means "precision."

Test-retest method Test-retest reliability assessment involves the administration of the same test at two different times and correlating the two resulting sets of scores using the Pearson product-moment correlation coefficient. The respondents and the test

Test-retest reliability: administering the same test at two different times and correlating the two sets of scores using the Pearson product-moment correlation coefficient

(or measure) are the same both times. The resulting correlation reflects the stability of the measure. Test-retest reliability (or the coefficient of stability) can define error only after an appreciable interval of time; immediate test-retest is hence not recommended.[12]

Consider Figure 4-2. It shows the test scores of six individuals for a test (first trial) and a retest (second trial). The figure also shows retest scores for two different scenarios. In both instances, the retest is administered after the expiry of an identical time period. However, the results are quite different under the two scenarios. In Scenario 1, there is some fluctuation in the test scores, but none significant. The scores of some of the applicants (e.g., Jackson, Menon, Chan, and Smith) have increased the second time, while the scores of Mantely and Mohammed have decreased the second time. The overall correlation between the two sets of scores is still very high at 0.99. The situation represents a high test-retest reliability.

Scenario 2 shows markedly different results. The correlation between the first test score and second test score is very low at 0.45. The relative ranks of the different applicants have also changed dramatically. Jackson, who ranked first in the first trial, is now only fourth, while Menon, who ranked third in the first trial, now ranks first. Significant error in measurement has reduced the reliability coefficient to a very low level. Thus, using an instrument such as this one for selection purposes would reduce the effectiveness of the selection procedure and expose the firm to legal challenges.

Needless to state, an organization needs many more than six applicants to test the reliability of an instrument. While the exact number it needs depends on several factors, including test complexity and contextual factors, it should ask a minimum of 30–40 people to undergo testing. It must also administer the test under the exact same conditions to minimize the impact of extraneous factors.

One problem with test-retest reliability coefficients is the effect of memory on retest scores. If all respondents on a test remember most of their answers from the first test, this will artificially increase the reliability coefficient. Hence, memory tends to exaggerate the reliability coefficient and cause overestimates.[13] However, learning confounds the results in the opposite direction. If respondents learn new information between tests such that they change their responses the second time, this will decrease the reliability coefficient.

> For example, assume that a group of employees took a sales aptitude test two weeks ago. Last week, their employer arranged for a sales training workshop, which most employees attended.

FIGURE 4-2: Results of a Sales Aptitude Test on a Group of Six Applicants on Two Different Occasions

Job Applicant	Test Score (First Trial)	Test Score (Second Trial) SCENARIO 1	Test Score (Second Trial) SCENARIO 2
K. Jackson	93 (Rank = 1)	95 (Rank = 1)	74 (Rank = 4)
M. Mantely	87 (Rank = 2)	85 (Rank = 2)	77 (Rank = 3)
T. Menon	82 (Rank = 3)	83 (Rank = 3)	89 (Rank = 1)
R. Mohammed	74 (Rank = 4)	71 (Rank = 4)	86 (Rank = 2)
W. Chan	63 (Rank = 5)	66 (Rank = 5)	57 (Rank = 6)
J. Smith	52 (Rank = 6)	55 (Rank = 6) Correlation between first and second test scores= 0.987	71 (Rank = 5) Correlation between first and second test scores =0.452

If the group of employees were to re-take the same aptitude test, the reliability coefficient would have been adversely affected by the information they learned during the workshop.

The above example raises an important question. What is the ideal time interval between two successive administrations of the test to minimize the effects of memory and learning? Keeping the interval too short significantly increases the impact of memory; but too long a period almost invariably results in new learning by respondents. Moreover, many attitudes, interests, and even personality traits of individuals are not static but in a state of constant change. Given these concerns, how relevant is the test-retest method?

While there are no hard and fast rules, the following guidelines for conducting test-retest have been offered by researchers:

- Test-retest is appropriate for measures involving sensory discrimination and psychomotor abilities,[14] since the effects of memory and learning are low for such measures. This approach is also appropriate for situations where memory may have minimal effects, such as a test containing complex shapes or detailed drawings and questions.

- Some researchers[15] recommend tests of knowledge which include an entire range of information on a restricted topic and a time interval of months between test and retest.

- Normally, a six- to eight-week interval minimizes the impact of memory, although the possibility of learning during the period should be considered.

- When there is reason to believe that no event has occurred to affect the retest responses, the test-retest approach is appropriate.

- The administrator is interested in measuring the *stability* component of reliability (as opposed to the *precision* component)

- Because of the large number of items in a test, memory and new learning will only affect a few of them, which will not significantly bias the retest scores.

In summary, when estimating test-retest reliability, always consider the effects of two types of factors: learning factors that cause scores within a test group to change differentially over time, thus reducing reliability, and memory factors that cause the scores to remain the same over time, thus exaggerating the estimate. Identifying the appropriate interval before the retest requires a trade-off between these two sets of factors.

Equivalent form approach

Equivalent form approach One strategy for avoiding the effect of memory over retest response is to avoid using the same test twice. The **equivalent form approach** uses two equivalent but different versions of a test to estimate reliability. The index of reliability calculated using this approach is typically referred to as *coefficient of equivalence*.

Figure 4-3 illustrates a test assessing single-digit mathematical computational ability with two equivalent forms. All the test questions in both equivalent forms come from the same content domain and are of an equal level of difficulty. The scores of the same group of test-takers in the two equivalent form tests are correlated. The correlation, referred to as parallel or equivalent form reliability, is an estimate of the reliability. The **coefficient of equivalence** is the correlation between scores on two parallel tests. Note that this coefficient of reliability is qualitatively different from the coefficient of stability calculated in the test-retest method. This is because parallel forms, despite our best efforts, are never precisely the same.[16] In the test-retest method, the test does not change. Thus, the test-retest method examines the stability of the measure or phenomenon under consideration. The true variance is the stable

Equivalent form approach: two equivalent but different versions of a test used to estimate reliability in the test-retest method

Coefficient of equivalence: the correlation between scores on two equivalent form or parallel tests

FIGURE 4-3: An Illustration of Equivalent Form Reliability Estimate for a Mathematical Computational Ability Test

Universe (or Content Domain) of Elementary Mathematical Operations

$1 \times 2 = ?$	$1 \div 2 = ?$	$1 + 2 = ?$	$1 - 2 = ?$
$2 \times 2 = ?$	$2 \div 2 = ?$	$2 + 2 = ?$	$2 - 2 = ?$
$3 \times 2 = ?$	$3 \div 2 = ?$	$3 + 2 = ?$	$3 - 2 = ?$
$4 \times 2 = ?$	$4 \div 2 = ?$	$4 + 2 = ?$	$4 - 2 = ?$
....	....	....	....
$7 \times 6 = ?$	$7 \div 6 = ?$	$7 + 6 = ?$	$7 - 6 = ?$
$8 \times 6 = ?$	$8 \div 6 = ?$	$8 + 6 = ?$	$8 - 6 = ?$
....	....	....	....
$9 \times 8 = ?$	$9 \div 8 = ?$	$9 + 8 = ?$	$9 - 8 = ?$
$9 \times 9 = ?$	$9 \div 9 = ?$	$9 + 9 = ?$	$9 - 9 = ?$

Test A
(6 randomly picked items from Content Domain)

$1 \times 2 = ?$
$2 \div 8 = ?$
$1 \div 3 = ?$
$3 + 4 = ?$
$7 - 5 = ?$
$8 \div 3 = ?$

Test B
(6 randomly picked items from Content Domain)

$1 \times 9 = ?$
$4 \div 2 = ?$
$2 + 5 = ?$
$8 - 3 = ?$
$4 + 3 = ?$
$6 \div 2 = ?$

The two test forms A and B are equivalent if
1. each has the same number and type of questions;
2. each test has the same level of difficulty; and
3. the average score and standard deviation on each test for test groups are the same.

variance. When using parallel tests, keep the time interval constant, but use different tests. The assumption here is that the true variance is the equivalent component. Then treat both non-equivalent and random components as errors.

While there are no firm rules, the following guidelines can improve the use of equivalent form reliability:

- For simple tests in vocabulary, mathematical skills, and spelling, create equivalent tests.

- Avoid trying to create equivalent tests for personality traits, which requires considerable skills and resources, including time; moreover, equivalence in these tests is difficult to attain in practice.

- Use equivalent test forms for ability measures, since they prevent learning from affecting the results.

- Use equivalent test forms to prevent transmission of test content from one applicant to the next.

- Be aware that because equivalent forms of the same test are never completely equal in all respects, the reliability coefficient computed using this approach is more conservative than test-retest reliability coefficient.[17] High equivalent form reliability suggests that the participants' test scores would have been very similar if they had taken an equivalent test on a different occasion.

Note that using equivalent forms to estimate reliability requires allocating additional time and resources for test design and administration.[18] If you are creating an objective test of 120 items, you will need 240 for two forms, 360 for three forms, etc. In addition, persuading the same respondents to take the test twice is also challenging. In real-life situations, organizations lose several respondents between administrations of the same test, which in turn affects the accuracy of the conclusions. To avoid some of these difficulties, some organizations use internal consistency measures of reliability.

Internal consistency measure Researchers[19] have argued reliability means that the parts of a total measure (or questions in a complete test) should be interrelated such that they can be interpreted as measuring the same construct or phenomenon.

> Thus, all items in a leadership aptitude test should measure leadership aptitude, just as the scores on questions in a sales aptitude test should show convergence.

As a result, many organizations compute an **internal consistency measure of reliability,** which is the extent to which all parts of a measure (or all items or questions in a test) assess similar qualities.

> **Internal consistency measure of reliability:** measures the extent to which all parts of a measure (or all questions on a test) assess similar qualities

The procedure for computing internal consistency is quite simple. Suppose that a sales aptitude test has 20 questions, all of equal importance in the same format. Add the scores of respondents on all ten odd-numbered questions (namely 1, 3, 5 . . . . 19) and correlate them against the total score on all even numbered questions (2, 4, 6 . . . . 20). If the entire test has been measuring the same construct (e.g., sales aptitude), then this correlation should be high. A low correlation indicates that the items do not contribute equally to the construct being measured. A coefficient calculated in this fashion is referred to as *split half reliability*, since it involves splitting the scale or measure into two equal halves.[20]

However, like parallel test reliability, internal consistency measures the equivalence of two subsets of items or questions, not the stability of the measure over time. Furthermore, the obtained reliability coefficient is developed on only half of the test items. Other things being equal, reliability increases with the increasing length of a measure. Thus, the split half reliability underestimates the reliability. Recognizing this problem, researchers have suggested several modifications to internal consistency measurement. While a detailed discussion of these is beyond the scope of this book, the key suggestions and modifications are listed below:

Spearman-Brown correction The Spearman-Brown correction[21] for split half reliability coefficients uses the formula given below:

$$r_{sb} = \frac{nr_{12}}{1 + (n-1)\, r_{12}}$$

where

r_{sb} is the corrected Spearman-Brown split half reliability,

n   is the number of times the test or measure is increased in length (for odd-even consistency measure, this will be equal to 2), and

r_{12} is the correlation between two Parts 1 and 2 of the measure or test

> Thus, if the sales aptitude test containing 20 questions were split into two parts containing 10 items each, and a split half reliability of 0.80 was found between the total scores on two parts, the corrected reliability will be 2 (.80)/ 1+(2-1).80 or 0.888.

Kuder-Richardson reliability estimate Apart from the odd-even split, there are several other ways to divide the test into two equal halves. What is best way to divide a test into two equal halves? This challenge is greater when the test is long.

The Kuder-Richardson reliability estimate[22] solves the problem by taking the average of the reliability coefficients that would result from all possible ways of subdividing a measure or instrument. There are several alternate formulae to calculate the Kuder-Richardson estimates, but the most popular one is the K-R 20 (the twentieth formula in their series). K-R estimate of reliability computes reliability by aggregating scores on the correct responses and incorrect responses. For example, questions on a test that are scored as "right" are given a score of 1 and "wrong" a score of 0. Most statistical programs calculate the K-R 20 and popular variations of the measure. But because the K-R estimate represents an average of all possible splits, these reliability estimates are usually lower than simple split-half estimates.

Cronbach's alpha As noted above, K-R 20 is suitable when the items on the test are scored in dichotomous categories of "correct" and "incorrect." But some tests use a range of responses.

> For example, an employee's performance may be evaluated using four statements, each of which is rated on a five-point scale. The total score for the employee may be computed by adding the scores on the four statements.

For these tests, Cronbach's alpha[23] is preferable to K-R 20 to determine how well the combined statements measure the same construct (in this instance, employee performance). In other words, Cronbach's alpha helps answer the question: "How well do the items in this instrument or measure hang together?"

Figure 4-4 illustrates the usefulness of Cronbach's alpha. In Scenario A, the responses to the four questions for the respondents converge. The alpha will be quite large (0.97) in this instance. But in Scenario B, the alpha is very small because the same respondent's response to one question is qualitatively different from his or her response to the other three questions. In this instance, the alpha approaches 0. An unacceptably-low alpha indicates that the instrument or scale is measuring more than one underlying construct and hence is multidimensional. Thus, the results of the survey in Situation B indicate that multiple factors or dimensions are being measured, since the responses don't hang together. However, the opposite conclusion is not justified: a very high alpha does not necessarily mean that the instrument is unidimensional or homogenous. Several dimensions could be latently present in the single dimension. For example, in Situation A, all that the results indicate is that one construct is being measured. In turn, this construct could contain additional latent dimensions, such as pay satisfaction, satisfaction with supervisor, and satisfaction with working conditions. Further analyses are needed to establish the unidimensionality of the instrument.

Coefficient alpha and K-R 20 are two of the most popular reliability coefficients. These are also among the easiest ones to compute, especially with the availability of statistical softwares. As a minimum, always check all predictors and criterion measures for their internal consistency. While no single number of reliability is acceptable in all situations or measures, internal consistency reliability (odd-even split, Kuder-Richardson, Cronbach's alpha) should be 0.85 or higher.[24] Of course, not all researchers agree on this number.

Inter-rater reliability coefficient Several constructs used in the context of selection can be objectively measured. An **objective measure** can be directly coded and entered into analysis without the analyst or manager applying judgment in the stages of data collection and data entry. Variables such as age, gender, number of days absent, and quantity of production are all objective measures requiring little discretionary judgment on the part of the analyst or manager. In contrast,

Objective measures: can be directly coded and entered into analysis without the analyst or manager using his or her own judgments in the data collection or entering stages

---

FIGURE 4-4:   An Example of Cronbach's Alpha in a Survey Setting

Assume that six respondents (A through F) answered a survey instrument supposedly measuring job satisfaction. The survey instrument contained four items, which were measured using a scale of *1=Not at all, 2= Somewhat, 3=Much,* and *4=Very Much.*

SCENARIO A: Responses to the four questions show convergence.

Scale item	A	B	C	D	E	F
1. I am happy with my coworkers	2	3	4	3	2	4
2. I like my job	2	3	4	3	2	4
3. My supervisor is considerate towards me	2	3	4	4	2	4
4. I believe that the working conditions here are safe	2	3	3	3	1	4

Total score on the four-item scale: 8   12   15   13   7   16
Cronbach's alpha (calculations not shown here): 0.97

SCENARIO B: Responses to the four questions are divergent.

Scale item	A	B	C	D	E	F
1. I am happy with my coworkers	1	2	2	4	1	1
2. I like my job	2	1	1	3	2	4
3. My supervisor is considerate towards me	3	4	1	1	4	1
4. I believe that the working conditions here are safe	4	3	4	1	3	4

Total score on the four-item scale: 10   10   8   9   10   10
Cronbach's alpha (calculations not shown): 0

---

subjective measures require judgments on the part of the analyst or rater. For example, assessing a job candidate's performance during a job interview or enthusiasm for the job involves a subjective rating.

To minimize biases in subjective measures, many organizations use multiple raters during interviews or performance appraisals. However, this in turn generates differences in ratings. Differences among raters may result from a variety of reasons:

- Raters may interpret the rating rules or procedures differently.
- Raters may interpret the meaning of construct differently.
- Raters may interpret the same information or behaviour as indicative of different traits.
- Raters may have unconscious or conscious biases that affect their ratings.

Thus, an index of inter-rater reliability has to be calculated. There are various approaches, the three most popular indices being Kendall's *coefficient of concordance,*[25] Cohen's *Kappa,*[26] and percentage of rater agreement. Popular statistics programs can calculate the former two statistics, while the third can be calculated with a simple calculator. For this reason, the percentage of rater agreement is perhaps the most popular approach of the three. The minimum acceptable rate of agreement for a new measure (or procedure) should be 80%; and for an established procedure (such as an on-going interview), it should be 90%.[27] When two raters are making judgments using rating scales, you can also calculate correlation

Subjective measures: require judgments on the part of the analyst or rater

between these ratings. Again, the correlation should be 0.90 or higher to ensure inter-rater reliability.

Difficulties with reliability assessment At times, reliability assessment faces challenges, three of which are briefly discussed below.

1. Homogeneity of the group under consideration The size of a reliability estimate varies with the range of individual differences in the group. As the variability of the individual scores increases, the correlation between them also increases.[28] On the other hand, if most individuals have very similar scores, the correlation also decreases.

> A good example is using only current employees for checking the reliability of a performance measurement instrument. Employees who have been with a firm for an extended period of time are likely to have similar performance levels, since the outstanding employees would have been promoted or transferred to other positions or would have left the organization for other opportunities. In the same way, very poor performers would have left the firm or been dismissed. This means that the variability in performance of the group will be low.

2. Very easy or very difficult items in the instrument If the measurement instrument contains extremely easy or extremely difficult items, once again, a limited range in test performance will result.

3. Sampling error While the sample size and reliability coefficient are not necessarily systematically related, a reliability estimate based on a large number of observations will have a smaller sampling error than one computed with a small sample. In other words, a larger sample provides a more dependable estimate.[29]

IMPROVING RELIABILITY OF MEASURES

How high should a reliability coefficient be? Unfortunately, no single agreed-upon value applies to all settings. Obviously, you want the reliability coefficient to be as high as possible. Whether a low coefficient is acceptable in a particular setting depends on the purpose for which the measure is being used, as well as the unique situational challenges you face. In general, the more critical the decision to be made, the greater the precision should be.[30] Nunnally[31] suggested that in applied settings when important hiring and promotion decisions are made on the basis of test scores, a reliability coefficient of 0.90 is the absolute minimum that should be accepted. Others have suggested a minimum reliability of 0.85 or higher. One researcher recommended that for instruments assessing an employee's individual performance, a reliability coefficient of 0.94 is mandatory.[32] For internal consistency reliability measures, such as Kuder-Richardson or Coefficient Alpha, reliability coefficients of 0.85 or higher are usually recommended.[33] For parallel or equivalent measures, 0.80 is considered acceptable by some.

Several factors affect the reliability of a measure. The more important ones are briefly discussed below.

The method used You will obtain different reliability estimates, depending on which procedure you use to calculate the estimate. For example, some methods, such as test-retest or split-half, provide liberal estimates, whereas parallel form reliability is more stringent.[34]

The length of the instrument or measure If the length of an instrument increases, in general the reliability also increases.[35] One formula to determine how much a measure must be lengthened to obtain desired reliability level is as follows:[36]

$$n = \frac{r_2 (1 - r_1)}{r_1 (1 - r_2)}$$

where

   r_1 is the reliability attained before the test is lengthened,

   r_2 is the reliability attained after the test is lengthened, and

   n is the number of times a test must be lengthened

For example, if the current reliability for a 10-item test is 0.80, and you want to extend it to 0.90, then substitute the numbers in the above formula:

$$n = \frac{.9 (1 - .8)}{.8 (1 - .9)} = 2.25$$

Thus, the new test should have 25 items.

The number of response categories Up to a point, you can enhance the reliability of the measure by increasing the number of response categories. Research indicates that using five to nine response categories (rather than a simple yes/no dichotomous category) improves reliability, since the ratee has greater flexibility to make fine distinctions in responses.

Difficulty of test questions If the test questions are too difficult or too easy, the total score is likely to be less reliable than if test questions are moderately difficult.

Homogeneity of items If the test questions measure the same factors, then the scores will make sense together, and hence the internal consistency will be higher.

Control over extraneous or confounding factors The lower the influence of extraneous factors, such as ill health or noise, on test performance, the greater the reliability of the scores.

> For example, you can remove error in speed tests by utilizing precise timing devices, which automatically signal starting and stopping time, rather than depending upon reading a watch. You can also ensure uniform lighting in the test room and train raters to interpret responses the same way to further increase the reliability of the scores.[37]

Thus, to enhance reliability, you should also focus on the test items (their difficulty level and homogeneity), test length, test format, the response categories, and control over extraneous factors, all of which affect a person's performance in a test. To enhance inter-rater reliability in interviews, standardize the questions. Rater training enhances reliability by forcing the raters to focus on the same criteria and interpret them with identical definitions and standards.

ESTABLISHING VALIDITY

When selecting new employees, the validity of a measure ensures that it is measuring what it purports to measure so that it predicts future job performance.

> For example, if you use a sales aptitude test to hire salespersons, then during validation procedures, you will ask these questions: How do we know that this test in fact measures sales aptitude? Is a high score on this test related to superior sales performance? Can the test score predict future sales performance of the hire?

It is convenient to think of validity as a correlation between the predictor and "something else,"[38] whether that something else is a construct, job performance or simply a behaviour. But to be useful, high scores on the predictor should predict superior job performance in the future or some other criterion measure (e.g., performance rating and concern for safety).

There are several types of validity, depending on the number of inferences you want to make.[39] The more popular validation methods can be classified in two groups: empirical approaches and rational approaches (see Figure 4-5). **Empirical or criterion-related validation approaches** attempt to relate test scores with a job-related criterion, usually performance. If the test actually measures a job-related criterion, the test and the criterion exhibit a positive correlation between 0 and 1.0. The higher the correlation, the better the match. **Rational approaches,** on the other hand, focus on the contents and design of the test itself and ask the question: Does this test measure what it purports to measure? Thus, an intelligence test should contain only test items that measure intelligence; a sales aptitude test must measure an individual's aptitude for selling (rather than extraversion or sociability). Rational approaches are useful when the number of subjects is too low to have a reasonable sample for testing criterion-related validity.

Empirical or criterion-related validation approaches: relate test scores with a job-related criterion, usually performance (the higher the correlation, the better the match)

Rational approaches to validation: focus on the contents and design of the test itself and ask the question: "Does this test measure what it purports to measure?"

EMPIRICAL OR CRITERION-RELATED VALIDITY

The criterion-related validation approach has four requirements:

- A reliable criterion free from contamination is available. Even apparently reliable criterion may on closer examination prove to be unreliable or influenced by factors other than employee performance.

- The job is fairly stable and not undergoing major changes during validation.

- Predictor and criterion scores are available for a large enough number of employees.

- The sample of employees and jobs used for validation are identical or very similar to the jobs to which the findings will be generalized.

FIGURE 4-5:   Major Approaches to Validation of Predictors

1. Empirical or Criterion-Related Approaches

Predictive validity is determined by giving a test to a group of applicants. After these applicants have been hired and have mastered the job reasonably well, their performance is measured. This measurement and the test score are then correlated.

Concurrent validity is determined by testing current employees and correlating these scores with measures of their performance. This approach does not require a delay between hiring and mastery of the job.

Synthetic validity is a systematic, logical process of inferring test validity for components of a job. The organization assembles a battery of predictors and infers its validity from predetermined validities of individual predictors for specific components of the total job.

2. Rational Approaches

Content validity is assumed to exist when the test includes representative samples of the skills, competencies, or behaviours needed to successfully perform the job. A keyboarding test for an applicant being hired simply to do keying is an example of a test with content validity.

Construct validity is the relationship between performance on the test and psychological or other attributes assumed to be necessary for successful test performance. For example, an honesty test should in fact measure a person's honesty and not mastery over vocabulary; items in an anxiety test should show greater correlation with anxiety than, say, with depression, which is different from anxiety.

If these conditions change, criterion validity may decay or even become irrelevant over time. For example, if the skills of new employees change, earlier validation coefficients may not be relevant. Keep in mind that almost all jobs change over time, and in some industries and jobs, the rate of change is rapid.

Predictive validity
As the term denotes, predictive validity reflects the predictive power of a test or other selection measure to predict future job performance. **Predictive validation** measures predictors at one point in time and correlates them with criterion scores assessed later. For example, scores on a job interview are correlated with subsequent performance scores.

There are several variations in predictive validation methods.[40] Here are the steps for one popular approach:

Predictive validation: measures predictors at one point in time and correlates them with criterion scores assessed later

1. Perform the job analysis
Perform a thorough job analysis to identify the knowledge, skills and abilities (KSA) needed for the job.

2. Identify a new predictor
Next, identify the new predictor (e.g., a new test), based on available evidence and link it to one or more of the KSAs. Normally, use only tests with reliability coefficients of 0.85 for a similar workforce.

> Assume that a sewing factory is attempting to improve its selection procedures. Currently, the selection procedure uses application blanks and supervisory interviews to hire entry-level workers. On recommendation from a consultant, the factory is considering implementing a performance test as well. One of the first steps will be to assess the reliability of the test, because in the absence of acceptable reliability, the test is also likely to be invalid.

3. Identify a reliable criterion or set of criteria
Next, identify reliable and realistic benchmarks of performance. For example, quantity of production and number of days absent can be more objectively measured than job commitment and enthusiasm. When using ratings as criteria, make every effort to assess their reliability and maintain that reliability at a high level. The standards or benchmarks established should also be realistic for the technology and working conditions.

> For example, in the case of the sewing factory, "number of metres of cloth stitched" may be a valid criterion. However, the performance standard itself should be established only after a thorough job/industry analysis. Consider the current state of technology, working conditions, results of work sampling studies, and the competency levels of the average employee. Group employees who meet or exceed this standard as "successes," and those below as "failures."

4. Administer the new test along with all currently used predictors
Administer the new test to all job applicants under standardized conditions, and use procedures suggested by the test developers.

> In the sewing factory example, assume that the firm receives 300 applications for 60 entry-level jobs. All 300 applicants must submit application blanks and appear for a job interview, as in the past. However, now they will also be required to take the new performance test.

5. Hire using normal predictors
Hire the new employees using only normal predictors. Simply score the new performance tests and file them away for later use.

> In the case of the sewing factory, you would hire the new 60 employees based on their application blanks and interview scores. You would not consider the results of the new test at this point.

6. Assess performance on the criterion after a reasonable period
After a lapse of reasonable period (typically, 6 months to a year), when the new employees

should have mastered their jobs and familiarized themselves with the new work settings, assess their performance based on the chosen criterion.

> For example, in the sewing factory, six months after hiring, you would record the number of metres of cloth that the employees could stitch in the given time period.

7. *Correlate the test scores with their criterion scores* Correlate the original performance test scores of the employees against the recent performance criterion scores. If the correlation is not high, this means that the test has no predictive validity for this criterion. Discard the test and look for a new predictor.

8. *Identify cut-off scores* If the correlation is uniformly high for all employee groups, then establish cut-off scores to maximize future "successes" on the criterion measure. Check whether validity coefficients and cut-off scores are equal for all relevant human groups (e.g., groups formed on the basis of age, gender, ethnic, racial, or socio-economic background). If satisfactory, proceed to the next step. If not, conduct further statistical analysis and identify new relevant cut-off scores for different groups.

> In the sewing factory example, if it is found that all "successful employees" (that is, those who meet minimum performance standards) received 70% or more in the test, this will be the cut-off score, subject to confirmation in cross-validation studies.

9. *Cross-validate the findings* When developing correlations or regression equations showing a relationship between performance predictors and performance criterion, an existing group of employees is normally used. However, when applying these regression equations to new employees, the predictive accuracy is almost always lower[41]—a phenomenon called *shrinkage* in predictive accuracy. The new group of employees will almost always differ in some respects from the current employees, which will impact the relation between predictor and criterion. To avoid this problem, use **cross validation,** which investigates whether a predictor-criterion relationship in one group of employees (current employees) can be generalized to a different sample of employees (new employees). After determining the expected criterion levels for the new employees, the actual levels are compared to the expected. This correlation will almost always be lower for the new group, due to shrinkage.

Cross validation: investigates whether a predictor-criterion relationship in one group of employees can be generalized to a different sample of employees

Ideally, cross validation should be performed over a period of time using different samples of employees. Here are the key steps involved in cross validation, which recognize the practical realities facing many organizations:

1. Divide the total sample of employees for whom predictor and criterion scores are available into two groups *randomly.* For discussion purposes they are referred to as Group A and Group B.

2. Develop a regression equation for Group A that shows the relationship between predictor and criterion.

3. Use the equation developed from Group A to predict the criterion for Group B.

4. In Group B, correlate the predicted and actual criterion scores. A high correlation indicates that the regression equation is useful for predicting performance of employees other than those with whom the equation was developed.

> For example, in the case of the sewing factory, the 60 new hires would be randomly divided into two groups. One group would be the validation sample (Group A) and the other one would be used for cross validation purposes (Group B). A regression equation will be formulated based on the test scores and performance records of Group A. Using this predictive equation, the performance of employees belonging to Group B can be estimated. If

the estimated and actual performance scores of members of the Group B are highly correlated with those of Group A, then the preliminary findings are generalizable. Needless to say, further ongoing validation is needed, especially if job duties or other factors affecting performance fluctuate.

Though the above approach is systematic, it still has weaknesses. The validity coefficient relates only to those applicants who were hired and remained with the organization for a relatively long period. Do these conclusions formed on the basis of the study apply to all applicants (those hired and those not hired)? Only if the applicants were selected randomly (rather than using existing predictors) can the findings be generalized to all applicants. However, in real-life organizations such a strategy is not practically feasible. To overcome this dilemma, researchers have developed a number of statistical formulas[42] for estimating shrinkage in validity without going through an empirical cross validation.

Whatever approach is used, cross-validation is critical before using regression equations to predict future performance. Cross-validation should be continued even after identifying the predictors, because performance criteria fluctuate over time and are never fully reliable. As a result, the correlation between predictors and the criteria also fluctuates. Predictive validation studies require that the job being examined is stable and not in a period of change or transition.[43] Anytime this assumption is violated, the validity of the predictor also suffers.

How large should the pool of employees for a validation study? There is no single number that meets the needs of all occasions. Ideally, large samples (several hundred) are required to identify a predictor-criterion relationship.[44] But for practical purposes, numbers much lower than 60 are considered inappropriate, since normality of score distribution cannot be assumed (see Appendix 4A). Indeed, in a multicultural society such as Canada, to do a thorough validation of certain predictors, hundreds of new hires would be required. This is a challenge to most Canadian organizations, since they do not hire that many employees even on an annual basis.

Note that the time lapsed between gathering predictor and criterion data can have a significant impact on the observed validity coefficient. Research studies indicate that predictive validity for some measures decays rapidly over time.[45] Further, a variable that will predict early proficiency, such as performance in the first month, may fail entirely for long-term performance, and vice versa.[46] Similarly, the stage of the selection process at which the test is used can also have significant impact on the outcomes. For example, a test that "screens out" applicants in the earliest selection stage can have a validity coefficient that is significantly different from that of the same test if it is used as a "final hurdle" in employment.[47]

Concurrent validity
Ideally, predictive validation requires a relatively large number of new hires. But concurrent validation allows smaller organizations to overcome this challenge. **Concurrent validation** is the collection of predictor and criterion scores at roughly the same time from a group of existing employees and correlating them to establish validity for the predictor. If the measures are significantly correlated, that correlation indicates the validity of the predictor.

Concurrent validation: collecting predictor and criterion scores at roughly the same time from a group of existing employees and correlating them to establish validity for the predictor

Maple Leaf Furniture (MLF) currently employs sixty skilled employees and seven supervisors. Records indicate that on average, the organization has to hire four to six new employees to replace those who retire, quit, or move away. MLF is also on a growth track, with new contracts coming from the U.S. and Europe, all of which require the hiring of two or three additional new workers. However, faced with a shortage of skilled trades people, hiring high-quality employees has been a major challenge for the organization. Recently, the human resource staff discovered a new performance test with proven reliability and validity for trades people in the industry. MLF's president wanted to test the validity of the new test on his current employees first. Realizing the difficulties associated with predictive validation, he opted for a concurrent validation strategy. He asked all fifty-seven experienced employees to take the test (three of the sixty employees were relatively new to their job, so he felt that their inclusion would bias the results). He correlated the test scores with performance ratings by supervisors and found that high scores in the test did predict superior performance. The correlation in this instance was 0.85, which he considered acceptable.

Like in the case of predictive validation, concurrent validation also starts with job analysis. To perform a concurrent validation of a predictor, follow these specific steps:

1. Identify the relevant knowledge, skills, and abilities (KSA) for the job.
2. Identify the new predictor and link it to specific KSAs.
3. Ensure that the new predictor is reliable.
4. Identify clear, measurable, and reliable criteria of job success.
5. Administer the new predictor to current employees.
6. Collect criterion data.
7. Correlate predictor and criterion scores to determine validity.
8. Do subgroup analyses among employee groups to see whether any differences in patterns exist among different subgroups.
9. Do the above steps for all new predictors covering all KSA.

While in many ways easier than predictive validation, concurrent validation has some significant limitations:

- Concurrent validation assumes that the present employees are typical of future employees, which in a country like Canada may not be true. The composition of the new workforce may be qualitatively different from that of the current workforce.

- The motivation levels of the new hires undergoing testing will also be significantly different from those of current employees, who already have a secure job.[48] Moreover, some employees may not want to participate in a study which does not directly benefit them. Hence the scores they receive may under-represent their true abilities, thereby adversely affecting the validity coefficient.

- Outstanding employees in the workforce may have been promoted or may have left the firm for better jobs, and the poor performers may have been demoted, transferred, or replaced. This means that in any particular job position, the typical employee is the one with average abilities.

- Differences in job tenure or length of employment between the two groups raises questions about the generalizability of the findings. Employees with several years of experience typically outperform new hires; thus, the validity coefficient identified may be exaggerated.

The last point, namely the impact of job experience on performance, casts doubt on the results of several concurrent validation studies. Information learned on the job and events that happened in the workplace can significantly influence the person's test responses. The influence may be positive or negative. In some jobs, experience may help one employee work better, while for someone else, the same experience could reduce performance.

> Almost every instructor has come across superior students who read too much into multiple-choice questions, which adversely affects their performance. This happens because such students see implications to the items that go well beyond the level of learning for which the test was designed.[49]

In summary, concurrent validation is qualitatively different from predictive validation. Because of the limitations listed above, predictive validation is generally considered to be superior to concurrent validation. However, research findings have not supported this belief. A review of 99 published validation studies showed that a majority of them in fact used concurrent validation.[50] Moreover, minimal differences were found between results of predictive and concurrent validation. This is particularly so for ability tests, where a concurrent validation strategy may be as defensible as a predictive one. On the other hand, for several other predictors (such as personality and integrity measures), predictive validity may be preferable.[51] Forming conclusions based on concurrent validation data alone may not be advisable in such instances.

Synthetic validity While predictive and concurrent validation are very useful, they also assume that the sample size is moderate to large. Empirical validation strategies are less feasible for an organization which employs only five or six employees and hires one or two replacements each year. The question then is: how can small businesses ensure validity of their predictors? There are at least three options:

First, they can employ an approach known as synthetic validity. **Synthetic validity** is the systematic, logical process of inferring test validity for components of a job. Synthetic validity studies assemble a battery of predictors and infer the validity from predetermined validities for specific components of the total job.[52] They collapse the jobs into components or work activities and validate them together. In this sense, the validity is synthetic, since we are not creating validity but only creating a setting where it is possible to estimate validity.

Synthetic validity: a systematic, logical process of inferring test validity for components of a job by assembling a battery of predictors and inferring validity from predetermined validities for specific components of the total job

For instance, job analysis can identify components of jobs. Table 4-1, below, lists four kinds of jobs in an organization: cashiers, accountants, clerks, and sales persons. All four jobs have at least one of the three performance components, namely, the ability to use computers, communication skills, and skills in dealing with the public. The X's indicate that a job requires meaningfully high scores on a particular component. None of the jobs by itself has enough employees to do a meaningful validation study. However, for any single *job component*, there are enough employees for a validation study. For example, for the Computer Aptitude test, there are 40 employees. There are 45 for the Communication Test, and 35 for the Test in Dealing with the Public. Either commercially available tests with proven validity for the specific job components or tests created in-house with acceptable reliability and content validity can be used to assess these competencies. Some of the tests in the example (e.g., computer aptitude and dealing with the public) only relate to one of the job dimensions in each case; however, communication skills may be related to multiple performance components as shown in Table 4-2.

Second, a small organization can also employ content validation approaches discussed below. Content validation does not require a large number of workers or jobs. Even an organization with ten employees and four different jobs can benefit from such an approach.

A final option is to use information gathered through validity generalization (discussed later in this chapter). But care must be taken to ensure that the measure used in

TABLE 4-1: Job Types and their Components

Job	Number of Employees	Sample Job Performance Components		
		Using Computers	Communication	Deal with Public
Cashiers	20	X	X	X
Accountants	10	X	X	
Clerks	10	X		
Sales Persons	15		X	X

TABLE 4-2: Tests for Job Performance Components

Job	Sample Job Performance Components		
	Using Computers	Communication	Deal with Public
Computer Aptitude Test	X		
Test of Communication Skills		X	X
Test in Dealing with the Public			X

selection assesses the same constructs as a measure used in the other studies. Jobs within the organization should also be similar to the jobs used in prior validity generalization studies.

RATIONAL APPROACHES

Test validation appears on a continuum from practical to conceptual validity.[53] On the practical end, it focuses on the criterion, which has practical relevance to the organization. On the conceptual end, it focuses on the test itself: its content, meaning, and relationship to other similar and dissimilar constructs. Rational logical arguments and information about the predictor can establish validity. Content and construct validity are the two most popular rational approaches to validation.

Content validity: established by showing that its contents sample all concepts and situations relevant to the construct that the predictor measures

Content validity
The **content validity** of a predictor is established by showing that its contents sample all concepts and situations relevant to the construct that the predictor measures. Content validity differs from criterion-related validity because it focuses on the construction of a new predictor.

> For example, the content validity of an achievement test for salespersons is established by showing that the test includes representative samples of the skills, competencies, or behaviours associated with achievement. The criterion validation of the same test examines whether and to what extent the scores in the test relate to sales performance.

Content validation primarily uses expert judgment, rather than correlation coefficients, to establish validity of a measure. Unlike criterion-related validity, content validation focuses on description (of the predictor) rather than prediction (of the criterion). As one researcher noted, content validity is essential to the basic, intrinsic meaning of any measure.[54] This means that both predictors and criterion measures need content validity.

Establishing content validity for a new test in a work setting is a complex and time-consuming task requiring experts. The key steps are listed below:

1. Conduct a comprehensive job analysis While job analysis is the heart of any validation study, it is particularly critical in content validation, since the entire basis of the validation rests on how accurately and comprehensively you identify the KSAs.

2. List the tasks and associated KSAs for the job Specify the operational definition of each KSA and the level of mastery expected.

> For example, for the position of a cashier in a grocery store, "ability to read" will be a poor description of reading ability. Instead, it should be specified more precisely as "ability to read at a Grade 10 level at a speed of 120 words in a minute with no errors in understanding."

3. Select experts carefully Choose current employees, supervisors, and other knowledgeable individuals as experts to review the relevance of the new test's content to job duties. To avoid bias, select experts using random sampling techniques from a larger pool. Typically, their participation in the validation exercise is voluntary, although in some instances they may be nominated. When using current job incumbents and supervisors, their motivation and interest in participating in the validation exercise should be high. Sometimes a "carelessness index"[55] is used to screen people. A carelessness index is a set of tasks that are known *not* to be performed by the employees. The tasks are placed randomly amongst the items describing the job. Those respondents who indicate that they do perform these tasks (when, in fact, they do not) are eliminated from the pool of potential experts. Studies indicate that 45% to 50% of respondents report performing tasks that were not part of their job or not performed at all.[56]

4. *Conduct domain sampling*

Domain sampling involves choosing the items and questions in the new predictor that match the KSAs. Ensure that the content you choose for the sample is in proportion to the relative importance of the KSAs for job performance.

> For example, if knowledge of the names of vegetables is considered twice as important for a cashier as the names of spices, a relevant knowledge test would have twice as many questions on vegetable names as it would spice names.

Determining the final number of items in the test depends on the judgments of the experts. Sample questions asked during this phase are shown in Figure 4-6. In addition, standardized forms, such as Content Validation Form II, help assess the appropriateness of selection measure content during this phase.[57]

When a predictor measures observable job behaviours, establishing content validity is relatively easy, since the inferential leap between what a selection device measures and the what the job entails is likely to be small. However, the more abstract the nature or content of the job, the harder matching KSAs with predictors will be.

> Consider the job of a senior executive, which has several non-observable KSAs, such as leadership, emotional stability, and innovation. Establishing content validity for tests to measure such hidden dimensions is a major challenge.

The **psychological fidelity** of a predictor[58] is the congruence between the psychological requirements of the job and the psychological requirements imposed by the predictor when it is measured. Psychological fidelity is particularly important for some jobs, such as police officers,[59] prison wardens, and hospital staff, who have to deal with emotional and violent clients.

> For example, a nurse in a psychiatric ward has to respond to angry, irritated and hostile patients. The psychological demands made on the nurse who faces such a situation are far different from the ones imposed by a written test or statement about handling emotions in such a situation. A written test is unlikely to have much psychological fidelity. On the

Domain sampling: choosing the items and questions in the new predictor that match the required KSAs

Psychological fidelity of a predictor: the congruence between the psychological requirements of the job and the psychological requirements imposed by the predictor when it is measured

---

FIGURE 4-6:   Sample Questions in Assessing Content Validity of a New Test

- What are the key tasks in this job?
- Are all relevant KSAs for the job and its tasks listed here?
- How important is each KSA for successful job performance?
- Can there be tradeoffs among KSAs while maintaining job performance level?
- Are there implications for safety or efficiency if a particular KSA is deficient?
- Are the language and mathematics requirements of this test consistent with job requirements?
- Would persons with weak test-taking skills be able to do well on this test?

other hand, a role play in which the applicant is asked to interact with an actor playing an angry patient may have greater psychological fidelity.

Psychological fidelity deals with both the manner in which a test measures a KSA and the level it measures. Thus, when a test measures KSAs not required by a job, psychological fidelity suffers. This is particularly true for multiple-choice tests.

> Often candidates being considered for promotion are expected to remember voluminous materials about procedures and systems, which are tested using multiple-choice knowledge tests. However, once on the job, they rarely rely on their memory when making decisions and have access to manuals for all relevant information.[60]

With weak psychological fidelity, the content validity suffers.

Face validity: a predictor "looks as if" it ought to be related to subsequent job performance

Sometimes, the term **face validity** is used to describe how a predictor "looks as if" it ought to be related to subsequent job performance. The notion of "content validity comes uncomfortably close to the idea of face validity unless judges are especially precise in their judgments."[61] Face validity, like content validity, is not an adequate substitute for empirically determining the predictive power.[62] Face validity is, however, important for establishing credibility in the minds of the applicants and the community. A predictor with no face validity may do serious public relations damage.[63]

In summary, to establish content validity, the predictor must contain the same KSAs that are seen in the actual job and must measure them using processes similar to those employees would encounter on the job.

Construct validity: establishes a definite relationship between predictor scores and psychological or other attributes measured by the predictor

Information on personality tests: *www.2h.com/ personalitytests.html*

Construct validity
Construct validity seeks to establish a definite relationship between predictor scores and psychological or other attributes measured by the predictor. For example, an anxiety test should in fact measure anxiety and not something else.

Establishing construct validity is an arduous job and is typically beyond the competency of many human resource managers. To establish construct validity for a test, it must at the very least be shown that the test scores converge with other measures of the construct and diverge from scores on constructs negatively related to it.

> For example, if a test to measure the construct called 'anxiety' is being designed, the test scores should converge with scores on other existing measures of anxiety (see Figure 4-7). Anxiety itself is not observable (since it is an abstract construct); but body language and oral reports of being worried are associated with it. For example, galvanic skin responses can be used to check whether the high scores are indicative of anxiety or something else. The new test score should also show variation across situations that are high and low in anxiety. That is, when an individual is not facing anxiety, his or her scores should be low; and on other occasions when the individual is anxious, the score should be high. Test scores should also show low correlation with test scores on constructs considered opposite to the state of anxiety (e.g., a peaceful mental state).

Information on intelligence testing: *http://www.apa.org/monitor/ feb03/intelligent.html*

Thus, establishing construct validity is difficult and time consuming. The matter is complicated by the fact that many constructs (such as leadership, intelligence, creativity) are not easily observable: there is no way to be sure that what is observed is indicative only of the construct in question and nothing else. For the reasons described, establishing construct validity remains outside the capabilities of many human resource managers.[64]

However, more and more organizations are requiring that their human resource managers defend the tests they use, especially those assessing aptitudes and personality traits. This means that they should only use tests that have some degree of established construct validity.

FIGURE 4-7: Conditions to Establish Construct Validity For a New Test on Anxiety

Scores on new test of anxiety

Highly and positively correlate with scores on other anxiety tests

Highly and positively correlate with observable measures of anxiety

Highly and negatively correlate with scores on tests which measure states-of-mind opposite to anxiety

Highly and negatively correlate with other observable indicators of states-of-mind opposite to anxiety

Scores show no correlation with constructs which are not related to anxiety

Scores on the test should vary (that is, become high or low) depending on the degree of anxiety faced by an individual

---

Focus on Ethics

Selection activities are full of ethically challenging situations. Consider these two situations, and describe how you would respond to each and why.

1. You are the Human Resource Manager in a food processing plant employing 210 people. You report to the VP Human Resources. Your firm is growing quickly and is in the process of hiring six new work supervisors and twenty employees to start a new work shift. While the organization's management is unenlightened and paternalistic, over the last seven years you have been successful in implementing a number of HR systems that have been well accepted by the employees and management. You know that you have a reputation for your professionalism and candor. Recently, your boss bought a new personality test that is supposed to predict leadership potential and, more specifically, emotional intelligence. It was supplied to him by one of his close friends, a management consultant who convinced your boss of its validity. Your boss wants you to begin using the test immediately to identify employees who can be promoted to the supervisory rank. However, you have never heard of this test before. The consultant who supplied the test to your boss is currently away on a cruise and will not be available for the next several months. Your boss wants action now.

2. You are the HR manager of an owner-managed grocery chain that has three stores and employs 180 people. In recent years, the media has been carrying many news stories about employee theft. Your boss is convinced that several employees are also helping themselves to groceries and other small but valuable items. Recently he asked you to administer a paper-and-pencil honesty test to all employees. The test was supplied by a reputed testing agency and seemed to have had validity of 0.7 and above in past administrations in the manufacturing sector.

You administer the test according to the instructions. Based on the test results, a number of employees end up categorized as "risks," including Mrs. Jones, your neighbour, who has been with the company for the last four years. You have always been impressed by Mrs. Jones's conscientious and helpful nature. Impressed by her work, you were about to promote her to the supervisory rank. But now, your boss wants you to "get rid of all those crooks" using any pretext (such as poor job performance or downsizing plans). You strongly believe that Mrs. Jones as well as several others have been misclassified by the test, but your boss seems determined. Meanwhile, many employees, including Mrs. Jones, are visibly upset by the new test, which included questions such as " Have you stolen any item from this store in the last week?"

VALIDITY GENERALIZATION

Validity generalization: suggests that validity information collected on a predictor in studies can be applied to a new setting involving same or similar jobs

Validity generalization focuses on evidence that shows that validity information collected on a predictor in studies can be applied to a new setting involving same or similar jobs. Validity generalization applies a procedure known as *meta-analysis*, which combines validity coefficients for similar predictor and criterion scores reported in studies to arrive at an overall validity for the predictor concerned.

> For example, if forty-five past studies have validated job interviews against sales performance, the meta-analysis will combine these forty-five studies to produce a single validity coefficient for interview scores in predicting sales performance.

Meta-analysis has been used to validate predictors since the mid-1970s. While statistically complex, meta-analysis rests on the basic principle of separating true and error variance in validity coefficients. Thus, errors caused by differences in criterion and predictor stability across studies are separated to arrive at the *true* validity of a predictor. Meta-analysis also weights the results from each study to reflect its sample size, since validation studies involving small samples are less accurate. By using predictors that have shown considerable validity across studies and time, an organization can have confidence in their tests and procedures. This in turn enhances the perceived fairness of the selection procedure.

HOW MANY PREDICTORS TO USE?

The number of predictors to be used in a specific selection situation depends on several factors, including the nature of the job, the reliability and validity of the predictors, and the cost of collecting predictor information compared to the cost of making an erroneous selection decision.

> While all jobs add value, there are still differences in the error tolerance between jobs. In some jobs, even a small error can be extremely costly in monetary and human terms (e.g., airline pilots, surgeons), whereas in other jobs (e.g., janitor, front receptionist), the consequences of an error are usually not severe.

Inter-correlations among predictors also guide action in some instances. If two predictors are highly correlated, predictive power may be incrementally raised by using both predictors, but this increase may not be significant enough to warrant the additional costs, as the following example shows:

> In the past, a major telephone company used three predictors for their entering clerical staff: a paper-and-pencil knowledge test, education level, and interview scores. On further analysis, the organization found that the education levels and test scores of applicants were correlated at 0.92. This was true for all groups of employees and for different time periods. While the two predictors had almost identical criterion validity, collecting information about education cost the firm virtually nothing, since only the cost of printing the application form was involved. However, each knowledge test cost the firm $40 plus administrative expenses. After the study, the firm decided to discard the test as a predictor. Follow-up studies indicated that the overall predictive accuracy had not declined significantly.

The example shows that both the written test score and education level were highly correlated and measured the same construct. By including both of them, the employer did not learn anything new about the applicant.

The number of predictors to use also depends on situational contingencies, especially the validity of the predictor for specific employee groups. A predictor that is valid for one group of employees may not be valid for another group, even if the latter work under identical conditions. Three important constructs expand this idea and shed additional light on the use of predictors: differential validity, moderator variables, and suppressor variables.

DIFFERENTIAL VALIDITY

Differential validity refers to the possibility that a predictor validly measures a particular criterion for some people in some situations, but has no (or different) validity for different groups of people or different situations. In other words, if a third variable is added to the test situation, it may affect the relationship of the two variables of interest.[65]

> For example, ability may be unrelated to performance when employees perceive a pay inequity.[66] Even valid measures of ability may not show significant correlation to later measures of performance.
>
> Several other organizational and working conditions affect the relationship between predictor and criterion scores. Leadership style, reward and control systems, and socio-emotional support offered at the workplace all affect the relation between predictor and criterion.
>
> Thus, peer pressure and support can contaminate the relationship between ability and performance. In addition, lack of role clarity can cause a competent, newly hired employee not to perform to the best of his or her ability. Peer support and cultural unfamiliarity (resulting in lack of role clarity) may be especially important in the case of new immigrants, thus affecting validity measures.

Differential validity: the possibility that a predictor validly measures a criterion for certain people in certain situations but has no (or different) validity for different groups of people and in different situations

MODERATOR VARIABLES

Closely related to the notion of differential validity is the construct of moderator variables. A **moderator variable** distinguishes between two employee groups, one with high validity for the predictor, and another with relatively low validity. In a sense, it helps organizations predict the predictability of a measure. In Figure 4-8, the correlation between predictor and criterion for employee Group A is high and indicated by an ellipse, while the shape for Group B is close to zero, since it is indicated by a large circle with no consistent pattern between predictor and criterion scores. In

Moderator variable: distinguishes between two employee groups, one with high validity for the predictor and another with relatively low validity to assess the predictability of a predictor

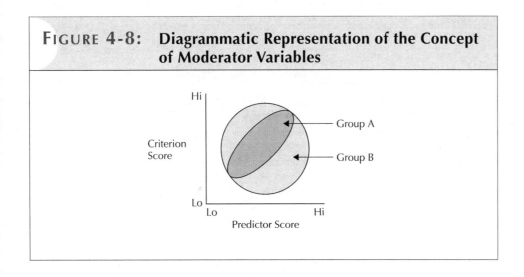

FIGURE 4-8: **Diagrammatic Representation of the Concept of Moderator Variables**

other words, for Group B, a high score on predictor can be associated with high or low criterion scores (almost with equal probability). Both groups may have the same average score on both predictor and criteria.

One study showed that achievement scores of college students who had high anxiety levels had a correlation of 0.63 with grades, while the same scores did not predict the performance of low-anxiety students well (0.19).[67] Anxiety level was a moderator variable that helped improve the predictability of achievement score since by combining the two variables, the investigator could significantly enhance the predictive power.

The same predictor cannot always predict job performance for different groups. Researchers have found that several moderators, including age, education, race, years of experience, and attitudinal and personality variables, moderate the relationship between predictors and criteria.

In Manitoba Metal Fabricators, the correlation between a performance test and job performance was found to be 0.74 for a group of 400 employees. However, when the employees were categorized on the basis of age and education, a different set of results emerged. For the younger and less educated employees, the validity coefficient was only 0.64, while for the older and more educated employees, the validity exceeded 0.82.

Moderators can be identified in several ways. One popular approach is quadrant analysis: classifying the predicted and actual criterion scores of all sample respondents into two categories, high and low (successful and unsuccessful). The categories are formed by the splitting the distributions at their median (see Appendix A for a definition of median). The results will look along the lines of Figure 4-9.

In Figure 4-9, applicants in quadrants 2 and 3 are in the predicted range. For those in quadrant 2, the criterion score was predicted to be high and actually turned out to be high. For those in quadrant 3, once again, the predicted and actual values were low. These two quadrants contain "hits," while the remaining two quadrants are "misses" (since their criterion scores were either over or under predicted). Examining the profiles of the employees in these pairs of quadrants can reveal commonalities. By studying these commonalities and performing further data analysis, you can identify moderator variables, which in turn help improve the predictive power of the new predictor.

SUPPRESSOR VARIABLES

Occasionally, a variable correlating nearly 0 with a criterion may still be useful when employed with a predictor with which it is highly correlated. Such variables, referred

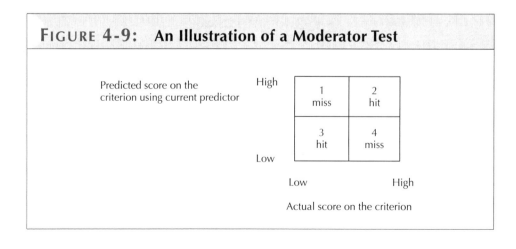

FIGURE 4-9:   An Illustration of a Moderator Test

to as **suppressor variables,** are helpful in multiple regression for predicting criterion scores. Though this appears to be paradoxical, it happens because the suppressor variable is able to remove influences of factors which affect the predictor but which are irrelevant for the purpose of predicting the criterion. Only the remaining, relevant variance of the predictor is included in the multiple regression, which in turn, increases the predictive power of the model.

> Consider the example of a group of students who wrote a college entrance test (the predictor) that was used to estimate their later academic performance (the criterion). Several factors such as the hassles they faced travelling to the test centre, their personal or family situations on that day, and their health or mental framework, could have affected their test scores but bear little theoretical relation to the criterion. By including such suppressor variables into the regression model, you can remove the error variance of the predictor scores and thus increase the overall validity.

Thus, if the correlation between[68]

- a predictor and criterion is 0.40,

- a suppressor variable and predictor is 0.70, and

- the suppressor variable and criterion is 0.00, then, by including the suppressor variable into the regression model, the overall predictive power can be increased from the present 0.40 to 0.56.

The circumstances in which suppressor variables occur are not many; yet the potential of such variables for increasing the predictive power is substantial in some instances.

In summary, the usefulness of any predictor depends on its reliability and validity. While reliability is a critical attribute, it does not guarantee validity. Before employing any predictor for hiring purposes, the human resource manager should ensure its reliability and validity.

The quality of selection decision also depends on the number of qualified applicants available. Naturally, the firm is in an advantageous position if there are twenty applicants, rather than two. In the latter case, despite having the best predictors, the overall quality of selection decision will suffer. While the firm's salary and benefit package, working conditions, and work culture affect the success of attracting qualified applicants, the firm's recruitment strategy has perhaps the greatest influence on the size of applicant pool. The next chapter looks at this important activity.

Suppressor variable: correlates nearly zero with a criterion; yet when employed with a predictor with which it is highly correlated, can significantly enhance the validity coefficient by removing the error or unwanted variance of the predictor

Implications for Practice

1. Only reliable and valid predictors should be used for selection purposes.

2. Ideally, the criterion related validity of all selection tools for all major employee groups should be established before using them. If this is not possible, other rational approaches to validity must be established as a minimum.

3. In small organizations and situations where predictive validation is impossible, synthetic validity and information from validity generalization studies should be assembled before predictors are chosen for selection purposes.

4. Managers and relevant employees should be encouraged to participate in the data collection process and designing the selection system. This will not only enhance commitment but also reduce future errors.

5. In several instances, the use of moderator and suppressor variables can enhance the predictor's ability to forecast criterion scores.

6. Care should be taken to assess differential validity of predictors for various groups and situations. Just because a predictor is currently valid does not mean that it will be valid in the future for the same group of employees. Continuous cross validation of predictors is necessary in situations characterized by dynamism and change.

Key Terms for Review

Coefficient of equivalence, *p. 117*

Concurrent validation, *p. 127*

Construct validity, *p. 132*

Content validity, *p. 130*

Cross validation, *p. 126*

Differential validity, *p. 135*

Domain sampling, *p. 131*

Empirical or criterion-related validation approaches, *p. 124*

Equivalent form approach, *p. 117*

Face validity, *p. 132*

Internal consistency measure of reliability, *p. 119*

Measurement error, *p. 111*

Moderator variable, *p. 135*

Objective measures, *p. 120*

Predictive validation, *p. 125*

Psychological fidelity of a predictor, *p. 131*

Random errors, *p. 112*

Rational approaches to validation, *p. 124*

Reliability, *p. 110*

Reliability coefficient, *p. 113*

Subjective measures, *p. 121*

Suppressor variable, *p. 137*

Synthetic validity, *p. 129*

Systematic errors, *p. 112*

Test-retest reliability, *p. 115*

Validity, *p. 114*

Validity generalization, *p. 134*

Discussion Questions

1. Why should a selection test be reliable? Can it be reliable but not valid, and vice versa?

2. Would your approach to testing the reliability of a written test be different from your approach for a selection interview?

3. If you were asked to validate a new mathematical aptitude test for hiring insurance adjusters, what steps would you take?

4. What factors would you consider when deciding on the number of predictors to use in staffing decisions?

5. What is meant by *differential validity*? Why is it important?

Critical Thinking Questions

1. You are working as the human resource manager in a large insurance firm. A human resource consultant whom you met at a national conference claims that with her new mathematical aptitude test, you can improve the quality and productivity of insurance adjusters in your firm. What questions would you ask her initially? What actions would you take immediately after deciding to use the test in your firm in the future?

2. You are the new human resource manager in a furniture assembly unit employing 120 persons and 16 supervisory-managerial personnel. For hiring supervisors, the firm has historically used job interviews along with a review of application forms. Employees have been hired using a combination of application forms, interviews and performance tests conducted in the factory. The quality of supervisors (as measured by employee satisfaction, performance targets, and supervisory evaluation) hired in the recent past has been mediocre at best, and you have identified this as an area needing immediate attention. What actions would you take and why?

3. If you were validating a new entrance test for a small art design institute that accepts only 6–8 students each year, how would you do it? Would your answer be different if you were in charge of a large training institute for computer design that admits 120–130 students every six months? (Assume that each training program lasts only six months.)

4. Would the number of predictors you use for hiring clerical employees in a library be the same as for hiring police officials? Why?

5. Select a job position. Identify the usual predictors for hiring people into this position. Now suggest a moderator and suppressor variable that may be relevant.

CASE INCIDENT

Preparing to Hire at Pemberton Lake View Estates

Pemberton Lake View Estates is a 200-resident facility for seniors situated on the banks of a picturesque lake about 60 km east of Halifax, Nova Scotia. The majority of seniors who live in the facility are healthy and require virtually no assistance, but 15% require wheelchair assistance, and another 5% require acute care. About 75% of the residents are women. The organization employs qualified medical staff, nurses, and assistants. Currently, it is in the process of hiring a supervisor who will be in charge of nine female assistants. The job of an assistant is relatively simple and does not require medical knowledge. Most of the assistants are youths who don't look at the job as a career. Typically, each year, the organization loses about a third of its assistants who move into the city seeking better pay and careers and greater social interaction. The last supervisor left the organization abruptly when one of the assistants complained about sexual harassment. In the absence of a supervisor, the organization has been experiencing difficulties in planning and scheduling the work and is urgently looking for someone to fill the position. The nurses have their own nursing supervisor, one of whom is currently looking after this position in addition to her own.

In response to the advertisement in the local papers, the organization received 28 applications, out of which only 12 seemed to fit the present requirements. Through successive selection steps, this pool was reduced to three final candidates. The relevant information on the three candidates is shown in Table A. Although not asked for by the facility, the candidates supplied some personal information, which is also shown in the table.

In the past, the clerical test administered to applicants had shown a validity of 0.7 in other settings. However, a quick look at the organization's records indicated only a weak relationship between scores and job performance ratings.

TABLE A:

	Applicants		
	Jane Powell	**Peter Christie**	**Anne Melon**
Years of experience in similar setting	4	2	1
Education	B.A. degree	Completed one year university	B.A., B.Ed
Test score	77%	71%	81%
Age	26 years	49 Years	30 Years
Medical evaluation	OK	OK	OK
Performance evaluation in last job	Very Good	Excellent	Good
Work history	Limited data	Stable	Stable
Past supervisory experience	Yes	Yes	No
Ranking during Interview:			
Interviewer 1	1	2	3
Interviewer 2	3	2	1
Apparent eagerness	Moderate	High	Weak
Availability	4 weeks	2 Weeks	Immediate

Questions

1. Which of the above predictors would you consider irrelevant in the present instance?

2. Which candidate would you hire? Why?

3. What changes in the hiring procedures would you recommend?

CASE

Kanata Food Distributors: A Validation Exercise*

Note: This case continues from Chapter 3: Kanata Food Distributors. Review the case background in Chapters 1, 2, and 3 before examining this case.

Until last year, Kanata Food Distributors hired its cashiers using three predictors: educational and related achievements, past work experience, and interview scores. Last year, a consultant suggested using a new Mental Ability Test for hiring cashiers. He felt that the new predictor would allow the company to hire cashiers capable of pursuing a longer-term career within the firm. Currently, many cashiers stay with the company for three years or less; the annual employee turnover in some grocery stores is as high as 35%. The consultant pointed out that hiring cashiers who can be promoted or transferred to other more challenging jobs within the grocery operations or other divisions would lead to greater employee satisfaction, as well as cost savings.

The human resource manager sought more details of the test and found that its internal consistency was 0.76. The test had a reported test-retest reliability coefficient of 0.7, though in a different setting. Because it was a new test, validation data was not available in quantity. Prior validation using blue-collar workers and auto assembly employees had indicated validity coefficients ranging anywhere from 0.54 to 0.73. The test is scored on a 1 to 500 scale although scores below 100 and above 480 are rare.

Given the limited information about the test, the HR Manager decided to administer it to only one group of applicants at four of the company's stores. All applicants were asked to take the new test, but the scores were not used for hiring purposes. Instead, the usual predictors were used to hire eighty cashiers, 27 of these in Store A, 13 in Store B, 18 in Store C, and 22 in Store D. All stores were more or less similar in the type of clientele they served. The data in the table shows the information on the candidates hired.

Six months after the employees were hired, the immediate supervisor evaluated their performance on a five-point scale. The HR department also calculated the internal consistency of the new measure to be 0.84, although this was smaller for minority employees (0.63).

Detailed results of the validation exercise are shown in Table 1.

TABLE 1:

MINDTEST	EDUCN	EXPRCE	PERFRATE	GRPMBR	INTVW1	INTVW2	INTVSCOR
150	1	1	1	1.00	4.00	2.00	6.00
225	1	2	3	2.00	5.00	1.00	6.00
250	1	2	2	1.00	5.00	2.00	7.00
175	1	1	2	1.00	4.00	2.00	6.00
250	1	2	2	1.00	4.00	2.00	6.00
300	1	3	2	1.00	5.00	2.00	7.00
190	1	1	1	1.00	4.00	1.00	5.00
240	1	2	4	2.00	5.00	4.00	9.00
300	1	2	3	1.00	4.00	3.00	7.00
400	1	5	4	1.00	3.00	4.00	7.00
300	2	2	3	1.00	4.00	3.00	7.00
325	2	2	4	2.00	3.00	3.00	6.00
250	2	1	2	1.00	4.00	2.00	6.00
250	2	2	3	1.00	4.00	3.00	7.00
300	2	3	3	1.00	5.00	4.00	9.00
400	2	3	5	2.00	4.00	5.00	9.00
400	2	3	3	1.00	3.00	4.00	7.00
200	2	2	1	1.00	4.00	1.00	5.00
300	3	1	3	1.00	4.00	2.00	6.00
450	3	2	4	2.00	5.00	3.00	8.00
320	3	2	3	1.00	2.00	4.00	6.00
400	3	2	5	2.00	5.00	4.00	9.00
300	3	2	3	1.00	4.00	3.00	7.00
400	3	4	5	2.00	5.00	4.00	9.00
350	3	3	3	1.00	3.00	3.00	6.00
420	3	4	4	1.00	3.00	4.00	7.00
300	3	3	2	1.00	4.00	2.00	6.00
300	3	2	2	1.00	4.00	2.00	6.00
300	3	2	4	2.00	3.00	4.00	7.00
320	3	2	3	1.00	3.00	3.00	6.00
400	4	2	4	1.00	3.00	4.00	7.00
420	4	3	3	1.00	3.00	3.00	6.00

TABLE 1: (Continued)

450	4	3	4	1.00	4.00	4.00	8.00
480	4	4	4	1.00	3.00	4.00	7.00
480	4	5	5	1.00	3.00	5.00	8.00
500	4	5	5	1.00	3.00	5.00	8.00
490	4	4	5	2.00	5.00	4.00	9.00
500	4	4	3	1.00	4.00	3.00	7.00
400	4	3	5	2.00	3.00	4.00	7.00
300	4	2	3	1.00	4.00	3.00	7.00
240	1	3	2	1.00	3.00	2.00	5.00
150	1	1	1	1.00	5.00	1.00	6.00
225	1	3	4	2.00	4.00	2.00	6.00
250	1	2	2	1.00	3.00	3.00	6.00
175	1	1	4	2.00	5.00	3.00	8.00
250	1	2	2	1.00	4.00	3.00	7.00
300	1	3	2	1.00	4.00	2.00	6.00
190	1	2	1	1.00	5.00	2.00	7.00
240	1	2	2	1.00	4.00	2.00	6.00
300	1	3	3	2.00	4.00	3.00	7.00
400	1	4	3	1.00	5.00	2.00	7.00
300	2	3	3	1.00	5.00	1.00	6.00
325	2	2	3	1.00	4.00	2.00	6.00
250	2	3	2	1.00	5.00	2.00	7.00
250	2	3	2	1.00	5.00	1.00	6.00
300	2	3	3	1.00	5.00	3.00	8.00
400	2	4	4	1.00	5.00	2.00	7.00
400	2	3	4	2.00	4.00	4.00	8.00
200	2	4	5	2.00	4.00	2.00	6.00
300	3	2	5	1.00	4.00	3.00	7.00
450	3	3	4	1.00	4.00	2.00	6.00
320	3	3	4	1.00	4.00	3.00	7.00
400	3	3	3	2.00	4.00	2.00	6.00
300	3	2	4	1.00	3.00	3.00	6.00
400	3	3	3	1.00	4.00	2.00	6.00
350	3	2	3	1.00	3.00	3.00	6.00
420	3	3	3	1.00	3.00	3.00	6.00
300	3	3	4	2.00	2.00	4.00	6.00
300	3	3	4	1.00	2.00	4.00	6.00
300	3	2	3	1.00	4.00	3.00	7.00
320	3	2	3	1.00	4.00	2.00	6.00
400	4	3	3	1.00	4.00	2.00	6.00
420	4	4	4	2.00	4.00	2.00	6.00
450	4	5	4	1.00	3.00	3.00	6.00
480	4	4	4	1.00	4.00	2.00	6.00
480	4	5	5	1.00	4.00	3.00	7.00
500	4	5	4	1.00	4.00	2.00	6.00
490	4	2	5	2.00	4.00	2.00	6.00
500	4	4	4	1.00	3.00	3.00	6.00
400	4	3	5	1.00	3.00	4.00	7.00

Codes Used: MINDTEST = Scores received by the employee in the Mental Ability Test EDUCN = Education level (1 = High school or less, 2 = Diploma/Certificate after school, 3 = Some University Education, and 4 = University Degree) EXPRCE = Experience in number of years (1 = 1 year, 2 = 2 years, 3 = 3 years, 4 = 4 years, 5 = 5 years or more) GRPMBR = Whether the applicant is a member of protected minority group or not (1 = Majority group; 2 = Minority group) INTVW1 = Score received by the applicant in an interview with the Branch Manager (on a five point scale) INTVW2 = Score received by the applicant in an interview with the immediate Work Supervisor (on a five point scale) INTVSCOR = Sum total of INTVW1 and INTVW2 scores. A Candidate has to receive at least a score of 5 to be hired into Kanata's stores.

Questions

1. What is your evaluation of the HR manager's approach to introducing the new Mental Ability Test?

2. What recommendations would you make to the company's management about using the test?

3. What other conclusions can you form about the selection process in this company?

Appendix 4A   Fundamentals of Statistics for Human Resource Selection[1]

Human resource selection is rooted in the notion of *measurement*. Skills, abilities, knowledge, attitudes, potential, and performance must be measured and compared to select the best employees. In some instances, we are also interested in comparing the demographic or other background information of potential candidates (e.g., age), which also requires measurement.

Measurement can take place at four levels:

1. Nominal level measurement Here, people are assigned numbers simply to classify them into groups. For example, numbers 1 and 2 may be used to denote male and female. These numbers have no mathematical significance, and might be compared to numbers to on a sports jersey or on a hotel room door. Such numbers are simply indicators of a basic property and nothing more.

2. Ordinal level measurement The ordinal level of measurement refers to an order or ranking system among the items measured. For example, as shown in Figure 4A-1, let us assume that a work supervisor rated the quality of work of five of his employees as follows (assume that a rank of 1 means the best quality).

Here, the numbers do mean something: they reflect the relative position of each employee on the dimension of "work quality." Thus, Bernice's work is of a higher quality than Andrew's, whose work is, in turn, better than that of Eddy, Denise, or Chan. But beyond this, few other conclusions can be formed. For example, it cannot be said that the difference in the quality of work between Andrew and Bernice (2 − 1 = 1) is half of that of the difference between the quality of work of Chan and Eddy (5 − 3 = 2). The ranks do not provide any information about the magnitude of the differences between the rankings.

3. Interval level measurement With interval level measurement, the numbers take on meaning. Consider Figure 4A-1 that ranks the quality of work. Using interval level measurement, a rating scale is used to compare the performance of employees,

FIGURE 4A-1:   Ranking of the Work Quality of Five Employees

Employee's Name	Ranking
Andrew	2
Bernice	1
Chan	5
Denise	4
Eddy	3

rather than the ranking scheme, above. The rating scale might look like the example in Figure 4A-2.

Now, assume that five employees were rated as shown in Figure 4A-3.

The order, differences, and magnitude of the differences in the data can now be identified. For practical purposes, the magnitude of difference between rating points will be assumed to be equal. For instance, the difference between Andrew and Eddy (4 minus 3) will be considered to be equal to the difference between Eddy and Denise (3 minus 2).

Interval scales do not have an absolute zero point. Most of the tests employed in the human resource management field do not have a *real* zero score. The zero score on a test, when it does exist, is arbitrary. For example, someone who responded to a 20-question math aptitude test and did not have a single correct answer might still have mathematical ability, even if their test score is zero. Unless the test covered all possible types of mathematical ability, it cannot have conclusively established that a participant has no knowledge in the subject. The test was only a *sample* of the innumerable possible questions that could measure a person's knowledge of mathematics.

Because there is no absolute zero on an interval scale, it cannot be said that a person who got 20 points in our test has twice as much ability as someone who scored 10. However, despite this limitation, interval level measurement allows us to subject the data to various statistical tests and procedures. And despite its limitations, the interval level scale is a truly quantitative scale and the information yielded may, in most instances, be treated with common arithmetic operations of addition, subtraction, and multiplication.[2]

4. Ratio level measurement Ratio level measurement allows for absolute zero scores, and provides the greatest level of measurement. This ratio level measurement is widely seen in physics and other pure sciences (e.g., weight, velocity) but less so in the human resource management area. Some of the ratio level measures that relate to selection include number of days absent, number of items produced, number of promotions received, and amount of pay. Demographic characteristics such as age, height, weight, etc., are also measured using ratios.

FIGURE 4A-2: Sample Rating Scale

1	2	3	4	5
Almost never meets quality standards	Quite often does not meet quality standards	Always meets quality standards	Quite often exceeds quality standards	Almost always exceeds quality standards

---

FIGURE 4A-3: Performance Rating of Five Employees on the Dimension "Work Quality"

Employee's Name	Rating
Andrew	4
Bernice	5
Chan	1
Denise	2
Eddy	3

Numerical values on a ratio scale can be subjected to various mathematical operations (addition, subtraction, multiplication, and division) while preserving their integrity. The presence of an absolute zero point permits us to make statements about the ratio of one employee's performance to that of another. For example, if one employee sells 60 computers while the other sells only 30, we can say that the second employee sold only half as much as the first.

Understanding the differences in levels of measurement is an important skill for human resource managers, especially when they are involved in the selection function of HR. This is because the same activity can generate different types of measures as illustrated below:

> Consider a sales aptitude test with 100 questions and each question has a value of 1. Two participants, Joe and Ann, have answered 40 and 80 questions correctly, respectively. If only the number of correct questions for each participant is being considered, we would measure them on a ratio scale. It could then confidently be said that Ann's test performance is twice that of Joe's. However, the underlying concept, sales aptitude, is not being measured at ratio level. It cannot be claimed that a zero on this test, which contains only a sample of 100 questions, reflects the participants' knowledge of the entire domain of sales aptitude. Recognizing this difference is critical when interpreting test results and making selection decisions.

In summary, interval level measurements help to identify differences among employees and job applicants, order or rank them, and compare the magnitude of the differences. Ratio scales go even further because the precision of the scales permits complex statistical analysis to be performed on the data. Nominal level measurements are useful only for identifying differences between two or more groups, while ordinal measures help such differences to be ranked.

MEASURES OF CENTRAL TENDENCY

There are a variety of ways to present measurements that have been gathered on a particular subject. For example, if 1000 Canadians were surveyed on their attitude towards the privatization of health care and their responses presented as in Figure 4A-4, below, it would form a *qualitative frequency distribution*.

The problem in a survey such as this rests with the definition of each category. Do the categories in the figure above give us sufficient information? Are there degrees of favourable responses to the question? How are people who disagree with privatization but would consider a tiered health-care system classified? Are these people the same as those who gave "no opinion"? Unless very precise definitions of each category are available, it is hard to make sense of the data collected.

FIGURE 4A-4:	Qualitative Distribution of Survey Results on the Privatization of Health Care

Categories	Frequency
Oppose	423
Favour	520
No opinion	57
Total	**N = 1000**

FIGURE 4A-5:   Cumulative Frequency Distribution of Mental Ability Test Results

Test score range	Frequency	Cumulative Frequency	Cumulative Percentage
0–20	5	5	5
21–40	15	20	25
41–60	10	30	37.5
61–80	40	70	87.5
81–100	10	80	100
Total	**N = 80**		

A *cumulative frequency distribution* may provide greater insights into the data and also offer an opportunity to make finer distinctions among respondents and their observations. For example, if 80 job applicants took an aptitude test in which scores could range from 0 to 100, their test performance could be shown as in Figure 4A-5 above.

The cumulative percentage is found by dividing the value in the cumulative frequency column by the total number of cases (N) and multiplying by 100. A table such as this offers much more insight into the test results, since finer differences (or variances) in performance among those taking the test can be calculated. It also permits calculation of measures of central tendency.

Measures of central tendency provide important information about the data collected. They also permit a mass of data to be reduced to a single numerical value that, in some respects, represents the character of the entire distribution. A **measure of central tendency**, then, is an index of central location that is used to define the data. The three most important measures of central tendency are the mode, the median, and the mean.

Measure of central tendency: an index of central location that is used to define the data. The most common are the mode, the median, and the mean

MODE

The **mode** is the most frequent item or measurement class in a given set of data. In Figure 4A-5, for example, the modal class is 61–80 since this class has the highest frequency (40) compared to the rest of the classes. It is possible to have more than one modal class if the frequencies are identical (hence it is possible to have a *bi-modal* or *tri-modal* distribution if there are two or three modal classes). Consider the data set shown in Figure 4A-6.

In the case of the data set in Figure 4A-6, the mode can be 64 or 67. Such cases can create confusion when interpreting the data. The mode can also be very sensitive to the size of the class interval.

Mode: the most frequent item or measurement class in a given set of data

FIGURE 4A-6:   Raw Scores of Nine Job Applicants in a Mental Ability Test

61, 64, 64, 64, 65, 67, 67, 67, 83

MEDIAN

The **median** is the middle item in a distribution. For raw scores such as those shown in Figure 4A-6, it is usually calculated using the formula $(N+1)/2$ where N is the number of items. In Figure 4A-6, the median is $(9+1)/2 = 5$. This means that the fifth number in the data set is the median. Thus, the median in Figure 4A-6 is 65.

For data that is organized into classes, locate the class interval within which the median is contained. This is done using the formula:

$$Median = L + [(N/2 - C)/f\,]i$$

where

C is the cumulative frequency at the class interval before 50th percentile

L is the lower limit of the class interval which contains the 50th percentile

N is the number of observations

f is the number of cases for the class interval of the 50th percentile

i is class interval

Here is an example of the formula using the data from figure 4A-5:

$$Median = 60 + [(80/2 - 30)/40]20$$

$$= 65$$

A slight adjustment in the above calculation is in order. The class intervals are shown as 31–40, 41–60, 61–80, and so on, not including values between 40 and 41, 60 and 61, etc. To adjust for the gap between the classes, the lower limit of the class interval in the above formula should be changed to 60.5 instead of 60. Thus, the calculated median is:

$$Median = 60.5 + [(80/2 - 30)/40]20$$

$$= 65.5$$

The advantage of using the median is that it is not affected by extreme scores since it looks at only the middle item in a distribution. This makes it particularly helpful when dealing with data like income, age, etc., where the data may range a great deal.

MEAN (OR AVERAGE)

The **mean,** or **arithmetic average**, is the most popular of the central tendency measures, and is equal to the sum of the values of all items in a data set, divided by the total number of items. In the case of the data in Figure 4A-6, the mean is $(61 + 64 + \ldots\ldots67 + 83)/9 = 66.89$. For grouped data, such as that in Figure 4A-5, the middle point of each class interval is multiplied with its associated frequency. Then the products are added together and divided by the total number of observations. In the case of Figure 4A-6, the mean is:

$$Mean = [(10 \times 5) + (30 \times 15) + (50 \times 10) + (70 \times 40) + (90 \times 10)]/80$$

$$= 58.13$$

In the case of ungrouped data the mean, unlike the mode or median, need not be a number from the data set. For example, in Figure 4A-6, 66.89 does not appear in

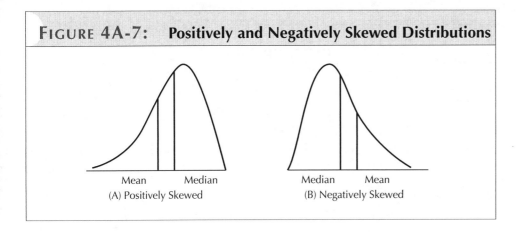

FIGURE 4A-7:   Positively and Negatively Skewed Distributions

| Mean   Median | Median   Mean |
| (A) Positively Skewed | (B) Negatively Skewed |

the data. Even in the case of grouped data, the mean is often hidden amongst the figures. For instance, the number 58.13 is not readily seen as a representative of the data presented in Figure 4A-5.

Unlike the median, the mean is affected by the presence of extreme figures. For example, if we have a data set containing three figures—30, 30, and 90—the mean will be 50. Here, the mean is much higher than the median, which is equal to 30 (See Figure 4A-7a above). This type of situation is referred to as a positively skewed distribution. On the other hand, if the data set were 30, 60, and 60, the mean would be lower than median. This is referred to as negatively skewed distribution (Figure 4A-7b). Clearly, when such conditions prevail, the median is a much better measure of central tendency than mean because the median is less affected by extreme values.

The mean can also be an artificial, even misleading, index in some instances. For example, the average of 1 and 99 is 50, which does not accurately represent either number. Thus, when a data set includes items that vary greatly from the rest of the items in the set, the mean becomes less accurate, and less useful. Despite this, averages continue to be popular because they are relatively easy to calculate.

VARIANCE

Above, it was shown that representing an entire data set with a single representative value such as the mean or median can create problems. This is particularly evident when the values in a distribution differ greatly from each other. Consider the test scores of seven job applicants on the three tests shown in Figure 4A-8. All of the tests have average and median scores of 50, yet all of the test scores are qualitatively different. In Test A, the scores of the seven candidates are very similar. In Test B, the test scores vary among the candidates, and finally in Test C, the differences between the scores are so great that the mean and median do not reflect the true values in the distribution.

In many such instances, measures of central tendency alone are insufficient to describe the data and additional measures of dispersion used to interpret the data. It is the variation of a characteristic within a group of people that is of interest to researchers[3] and practitioners like human resource managers. Such characteristics (e.g., mathematical aptitude) are identified and their variation measured. We then attempted to link these variations to job performance. The three popular measures of dispersion are range, variance, and standard deviation.

FIGURE 4A-8:   Scores of Seven Applicants on Three Different Tests

Test A

49, 49, 50, 50, 50, 51, 51   mean = 50; median = 50

Test B

40, 45, 50, 50, 50, 55, 60   mean = 50; median = 50

Test C

10, 20, 30, 50, 70, 80, 90   mean = 50; median = 50

RANGE

Range: the distance between the highest and lowest score in a distribution

Range is the distance between the highest and lowest score in a distribution. For example, the range of the scores in Test A in Figure 4A-8 is 2 (51 − 49 = 2), while for Tests B and C the range is 20 and 80 respectively.

STANDARD DEVIATION

Standard deviation: the square root of the sum of the squared deviations about the mean, divided by the number of deviations

Standard deviation is defined as the square root of the sum of the squared deviations about the mean, divided by the number of deviations. The square of the standard deviation is referred to as the *variance*. Figure 4A-9 illustrates the calculation of the standard deviation for scores on Test C (in Figure 4A-7). To calculate the variance, we first find out the average score (50). We now deduct the average score from each observation to find the deviations from the average. We square the deviations, and add them all together. The sum of the squared deviations (5800) is then divided by the

FIGURE 4A-9:   Calculating Variance and Standard Deviation

Job Applicant	Test Score (x)	$x - \bar{x}$	$(x - \bar{x})^2$
A	10	−40	1600
B	20	−30	900
C	30	−20	400
D	50	0	0
E	70	20	400
F	80	30	900
G	90	40	1600
			TOTAL: 5800

Average of test scores = $\bar{x}$ = 350/7 = 50
Number of observations = N = 7

Variance = $\dfrac{\Sigma (x - \bar{x})^2}{N}$ = 5800/7 = 828.57

Standard deviation = square root of variance = $\sqrt{\dfrac{\Sigma (x - \bar{x})^2}{N}}$ = $\sqrt{5800/7}$ = 28.78

number of observations (7) to get the variance (828.57). The standard deviation is the square root of this figure (28.78).

If data is scattered widely around the mean, the standard deviation will be larger. If all values in a data set are the same, the deviation around the mean will be zero, making the standard deviation (and the variance) zero. The standard deviation and the variance are the two most useful tools in the context of selection. In part, this is because of their ability to accurately reflect—and even predict—the relative positioning of observations in data that is shaped like a normal distribution.

NORMAL DISTRIBUTION

Distributions of data are somewhat like individuals in that they come in many shapes. We can see the shape of a data set when it is plotted in a graph. Figure 4A-10 shows some of the common shapes of distributions. One particular format, the normal distribution, is of particular interest to us since it can be used to approximate the distribution of many physical phenomena.

The normal curve, which assumes the shape of a bell, has some unique statistical properties which makes it extremely useful in statistical analysis and prediction. Some of the statistical properties of normal curves are:

1. *Continuous*: the values of the variable are infinitely divisible and infinite in number
2. *Symmetrical*: the mean, median, and mode of a normal distribution are identical
3. *Unimodal*: there is only one mode for the distribution
4. *Asymptotic*: the left and right hand tails of the distribution approach the abscissa (or horizontal axis) but reach it only at infinity. They also approach it in the same pattern and at the same rate.

In a normal distribution, one can also determine the percentage of observations that are of any particular value. As shown in Figure 4A-11, 68.26 % of all observations will fall within the mean plus-or-minus one standard deviation value. Similarly, 95.54% and 99.72% of all observations will fall within the mean plus-or-minus two and three standard deviations respectively. This makes predictions easier to make.

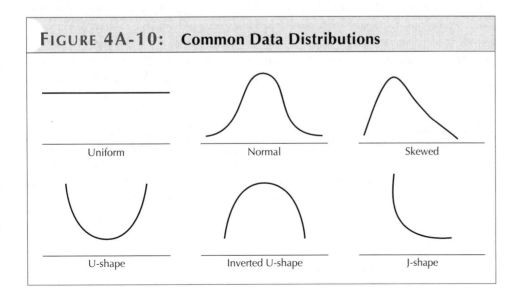

FIGURE 4A-10:   Common Data Distributions

Uniform   Normal   Skewed

U-shape   Inverted U-shape   J-shape

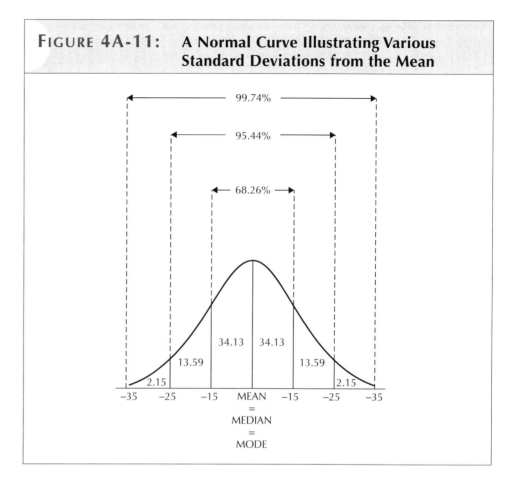

FIGURE 4A-11:   A Normal Curve Illustrating Various Standard Deviations from the Mean

STANDARD NORMAL DISTRIBUTION

Standard normal distribution: a normal distribution of data that has a mean of zero and a standard deviation of one

Depending on the values of the mean and standard deviation (SD), there can be an infinite number of normal curves. For example, we can have normal curves with mean = 10, SD = 1; another one with mean = 25, SD = 1; and a third with mean = 25, SD = 2, all possessing various attributes of a normal distribution. However, a normal distribution with a particular value of mean and SD is of special interest to us. A **standard normal distribution** is a *normal distribution of data which has a mean of zero and a standard deviation of one*. When a variable has a mean of zero and a variance of one, it is called a standardized normal random variable.[4] The standard normal distribution, also called a *Z-distribution*, facilitates comparison and prediction since standard tables are available to calculate the area under the curve for any specific value of *x* (see Figure 4A-12).

For example, using the data in figure 4A-12 we can conclude that when Z = 1, the area under the curve (or the probability of an event occurring) is .3413 or 34.13%. When Z = 1.54, the probability increases to 43.82%, and so on. Individuals can be compared by converting their raw test scores into what are called "Z-scores." A person's Z-scores is computed by deducting the mean from the raw score and dividing the balance by the standard deviation for the data set. In algebraic format, Z is thus defined as:

$$Z = (x - \bar{x})/SD$$

Where

　　x is an individual's raw score

　　$\bar{x}$ is the mean

　　SD is the standard deviation

FIGURE 4A-12: Area Under the Curve for a Standard Normal (or Z) Distribution

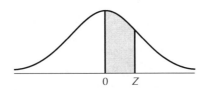

z	.00	.01	.02	.03	.04	.05	.06	.07	.08	.09
0.0	.0000	.0040	.0080	.0120	.0160	.0199	.0239	.0279	.0319	.0359
0.1	.0398	.0438	.0478	.0517	.0557	.0596	.0636	.0675	.0714	.0753
0.2	.0793	.0832	.0871	.0910	.0948	.0987	.1026	.1064	.1103	.1141
0.3	.1179	.1217	.1255	.1293	.1331	.1368	.1406	.1443	.1480	.1517
0.4	.1554	.1591	.1628	.1664	.1700	.1736	.1772	.1808	.1844	.1879
0.5	.1915	.1950	.1985	.2019	.2054	.2088	.2123	.2157	.2190	.2224
0.6	.2257	.2291	.2324	.2357	.2389	.2422	.2454	.2486	.2518	.2549
0.7	.2580	.2612	.2642	.2673	.2704	.2734	.2764	.2794	.2823	.2852
0.8	.2881	.2910	.2939	.2967	.2995	.3023	.3051	.3078	.3106	.3133
0.9	.3159	.3186	.3212	.3238	.3264	.3289	.3315	.3340	.3365	.3389
1.0	.3413	.3438	.3461	.3485	.3508	.3531	.3554	.3577	.3599	.3621
1.1	.3643	.3665	.3686	.3708	.3729	.3749	.3770	.3790	.3810	.3830
1.2	.3849	.3869	.3888	.3907	.3925	.3944	.3962	.3980	.3997	.4015
1.3	.4032	.4049	.4066	.4082	.4099	.4115	.4131	.4147	.4162	.4177
1.4	.4192	.4207	.4222	.4236	.4251	.4265	.4279	.4292	.4306	.4319
1.5	.4332	.4345	.4357	.4370	.4382	.4394	.4406	.4418	.4429	.4441
1.6	.4452	.4463	.4474	.4484	.4495	.4505	.4515	.4525	.4535	.4545
1.7	.4554	.4564	.4573	.4582	.4591	.4599	.4608	.4616	.4625	.4633
1.8	.4641	.4649	.4656	.4664	.4671	.4678	.4686	.4693	.4699	.4706
1.9	.4713	.4719	.4726	.4732	.4738	.4744	.4750	.4756	.4761	.4767
2.0	.4772	.4778	.4783	.4788	.4793	.4798	.4803	.4808	.4812	.4817
2.1	.4821	.4826	.4830	.4834	.4838	.4842	.4846	.4850	.4854	.4857
2.2	.4861	.4864	.4868	.4871	.4875	.4878	.4881	.4884	.4887	.4890
2.3	.4893	.4896	.4898	.4901	.4904	.4906	.4909	.4911	.4913	.4916
2.4	.4918	.4920	.4922	.4925	.4927	.4929	.4931	.4932	.4934	.4936
2.5	.4938	.4940	.4941	.4943	.4945	.4946	.4948	.4949	.4951	.4952
2.6	.4953	.4955	.4956	.4957	.4959	.4960	.4961	.4962	.4963	.4964
2.7	.4965	.4966	.4967	.4968	.4969	.4970	.4971	.4972	.4973	.4974
2.8	.4974	.4975	.4976	.4977	.4977	.4978	.4979	.4979	.4980	.4981
2.9	.4981	.4982	.4982	.4983	.4984	.4984	.4985	.4985	.4986	.4986
3.0	.49865	.4987	.4987	.4988	.4988	.4989	.4989	.4989	.4990	.4990
4.0	.49997									

Source: From *Business Research Methods (with Web Surveyor Certificate and InfoTrac)*, 7th edition, by ZIKMUND. © 2003. Reprinted with permission of South-Western, a division of Thomson Learning: **www.thomsonrights.com.** Fax 800 730-2215.

An example will make this clearer:

A mental ability test has been administered to thousands of job applicants. Based on this large sample, the average score on the test was calculated as 15 with a standard deviation of 4. With this information we can answer a variety of questions. Two illustrations are shown below.

1. *What is the percentage of people who have taken the test who are likely to be between the scores 15 and 19?*

   As shown in Figure 4A-13, here we are interested in the shaded area between the mean value of 15 and the score of 19. To get the Z value, we substitute the appropriate figures into the equation from above.

$$Z = (x - \bar{x})/\text{SD}$$

$$Z = (19 - 15)/4$$

$$= 1$$

   For Z = 1, the table value is .3413. We conclude that 34.13% of all applicants would have fallen into this interval.

2. *What percentage of applicants would have a score higher than 21?*

   The area that we are interested in predicting is shaded in Figure 4A-14. We know that the entire right area under the curve constitutes 50%, or 0.50, of the total area (since the area to the left of the mean has the remaining 50%). This means that the area beyond 21 is equal to 0.50 minus the area between 15 and 21.

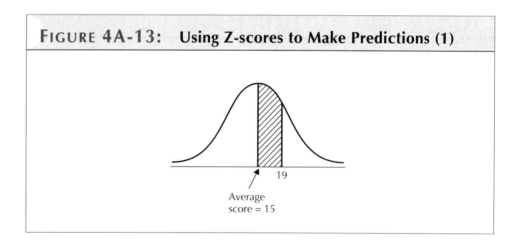

FIGURE 4A-13:   Using Z-scores to Make Predictions (1)

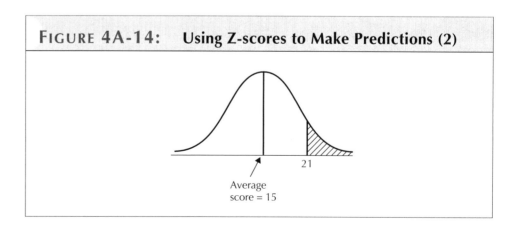

FIGURE 4A-14:   Using Z-scores to Make Predictions (2)

To determine the area between 15 and 21, we once again employ the formula for determining Z:

$$Z = (21 - 15)/4$$
$$= 1.5$$

For Z = 1.5, the area under the curve (from the table in Figure 4A-12) is equal to 0.4332. By subtracting this from 0.5, we find that the proportion of applicants with a score higher than 21 is .0668 or 6.68%.

Needless to point out, such information enables a staffing specialist to make valid comparisons among applicants and make better selection decisions.

STANDARD ERROR OF MEASUREMENT

In the context of testing, the **standard error of measurement (SEM)** indicates the amount of error to expect in an individual's score and is given by the formula:

$$\sigma_{meas} = \sigma_x \sqrt{1 - r_{xx}}$$

where

σ_{meas} is the standard error of measurement

σ_x is the standard deviation of test scores

r_{xx} is the reliability of test score

Standard error of measurement (SEM): indicates the amount of error to expect in an individual's score

The SEM is a very useful statistic because it helps us to identify an individual's true and error scores.

For example, assume that the standard deviation of the test scores for a particular group of people is 8. Further assume that the test's reliability is found to be 0.8. The SEM would be calculated as:

$$SEM = 8 \times \sqrt{1 - 0.8}$$
$$= 3.58$$

Thus, if a particular applicant's test score is 70, we can be 95% confident that on re-testing, the individual's score will be within 7.01 of this score (7.01 = 1.96 × 3.58; 1.96 is the Z value for 95% confidence level). Or in other words, the applicant is 95% likely to receive a score between 70 plus-or-minus 7.01 (i.e. between 62.99 and 77.01). This means that when the person received a score of 70 in the test, his or her true score was anywhere between 62.99 and 77.01.

The SEM also helps us determine true differences in test scores among different people. The above calculations, for example, would indicate that there is really no difference between a person who got a score of 63 and 77.

CORRELATION

Are an applicant's test scores and job performance related? Is there a link between stress during interviews and interview performance? Are the number of hours devoted to interviewer training related to greater reliability in interviews?

A **correlation** is the relationship between two variables. If the grades that job applicants receive in their courses are consistently related to job performance, we can conclude that academic performance and job performance are correlated. That is, someone who earns good grades is likely to do well on the job. In the same way, when we say that interviewer training and interview reliability are correlated, we imply that well trained interviewers, in general, are more reliable in their evaluations.

Correlation: the relationship between two variables, typically expressed on a scale of 0 to 1

There are a number of ways to denote the strength of a relationship between two variables. Only one measure is discussed here—a measure proposed by a statistician and biologist named Karl Pearson (1857–1936). The **Pearson r**, as it is called, is the most popular measure of the strength of a relationship between two variables.

Before getting into the formula for computing Pearson r, one point must be noted. A correlation can be either negative or positive. All the examples given above illustrate positive correlation; that is to say, the increase in the value or intensity of one variable is associated with an increase in the value of the second variable. However, with a negative correlation, an increase in the value of one variable is associated with a decrease in the value of the second variable. The more a person smokes, for example, the less healthy they are likely to be. Or, an increase in policing might result in a decrease in crime.

There can also be instances in which two variables are not related in a consistent fashion at all. In these scenarios, an increase in the value of one variable might increase *or* decrease the value of the second variable with no particular pattern. For example, the number of schools in an area is not likely to be consistently related to number of birds seen in a nearby park (unless there are some confounding factors such school children habitually feeding the birds during breaks!). In the same way, the number of trees in one city is unlikely to be related to the rainfall in another geographically separated city. In these cases, we say that the variables are uncorrelated. The three possible scenarios (positive, negative, and no correlation) are shown in Figure 4A-15. X and y denote the two variables in each instance.

To indicate the strength of relationship, Karl Pearson suggested using a scale of 0 to 1. A "0" means that there is no correlation between two variables. A "1" means that the two variables are perfectly correlated. A + or a – sign is used to indicate the positive or negative nature of the correlation. Thus, a perfectly correlated case can be denoted either by –1 or +1 depending on the type of relationship. Of course, a correlation can also lie anywhere between 0 and 1. For example, a weakly correlated scenario might be indicated by 0.2, while a strongly (but not perfectly) correlated scenario might be indicated by 0.8 or even 0.9. It is extremely rare to find a perfect relationship between psychological variables,[5] however, there are many instances where moderate relationships do exist and are useful for making practical decisions.

COMPUTING PEARSON *r*

Consider the data shown in Figure 4A-16 collected from ten job applicants. The x indicates the score on a safety test and y indicates the number of minor accidents by the same employee. Is there a correlation?

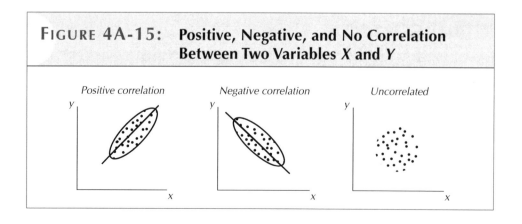

FIGURE 4A-15:   Positive, Negative, and No Correlation Between Two Variables *X* and *Y*

FIGURE 4A-16: Scores on a Safety Knowledge Test and Number of Minor Work Accidents by Ten Employees

Employee	Score on Safety Knowledge Test	Number of Minor Accidents in a Time Period
	(x)	(y)
1	60	3
2	65	2
3	70	1
4	62	4
5	60	4
6	55	8
7	58	7
8	40	12
9	80	0
10	48	9

FIGURE 4A-17: Calculating Linear Correlation Between Scores on a Safety Knowledge Test and Number of Minor Work Accidents

Employee	Test Score	Number of Accidents	$x-\bar{x}$	$(x-\bar{x})^2$	$y-\bar{y}$	$(y-\bar{y})^2$	$(x-\bar{x})(y-\bar{y})$
	(x)	(y)					
1	60	3	0	0	−2	4	0
2	65	2	5	25	−3	9	−15
3	70	1	10	100	−4	16	−40
4	62	4	2	4	−1	1	−2
5	60	4	0	0	−1	1	0
6	55	8	−5	25	3	9	−15
7	58	7	−2	4	2	4	−4
8	42	12	−18	324	7	49	−126
9	80	0	20	400	−5	25	−100
10	48	9	−12	144	4	16	−48
TOTAL	$\Sigma x = 600$	$\Sigma y = 50$		**1026**		**134**	**−350**

$$\bar{x} = \frac{600}{10} \qquad \bar{y} = \frac{50}{10}$$

$$= 60 \qquad = 5$$

Pearson $r = \dfrac{\dfrac{\Sigma(x - \bar{x})(y - \bar{y})}{N}}{\sqrt{\dfrac{\Sigma(x - \bar{x})^2}{N}} \sqrt{\dfrac{\Sigma(y - \bar{y})^2}{N}}}$ Simplified as: $\dfrac{\Sigma(x - \bar{x})(y - \bar{y})}{\left(\sqrt{\Sigma(x - \bar{x})^2}\right)\left(\sqrt{\Sigma(y - \bar{y})^2}\right)}$

$$= \frac{-350}{(\sqrt{1026})(\sqrt{134})} = -0.944$$

Hence an employee's test score is negatively correlated to their number of accidents.

We use the following steps to compute Pearson r:

1. As a first step, compute the sums of the x and y values.

2. Calculate the cross product (x multiplied by y), and determine x^2 and y^2 for each employee. These are shown in Figure 4A-17, on next page.

3. Once these figures are available, calculate the sum of all the x^2's, the sum of all the y^2's, and the sum of all the xy's. The necessary formulae are shown in Figure 4A-17.

4. Substitute the appropriate values into the equation shown in Figure 4A-17 to calculate the Pearsonian correlation between x and y.

It should be noted that r does not have a unit of measurement associated with it such as dollars, minutes, percentages, or degrees. It always has a value between −1 and +1 regardless of the unit of measurement used in the situation.

It should also be emphasized that a high correlation does *not* imply causality. If a large correlation is observed, it is *incorrect* to assume that x causes y, or vice versa. Rather, the only valid conclusion that can be drawn is that a linear trend may exist between x and y, and that the two variables may co-vary.

REGRESSION

Regression: predicting the value of a dependent variable given the value of one or more independent variables

Correlation measures the strength of association between two variables. While this information is helpful, often, we might want to go beyond this and find out whether we can *predict* the value of one variable if we know the value of the other variable. For example, while we may know that number of police officers on duty and the crime rate are related, we may want to use this information to predict the crime rates when certain numbers of police officers are on duty. **Regression** is a technique that helps us to predict the value of a dependent variable given the value of one or more independent variables.

Regression dates back to the work of Sir Francis Galton in 1886. Galton was a biologist and cousin of Charles Darwin. Regression is a very useful tool for staffing managers who want to predict the future job performance of applicants based on their scores on various predictors. Given the strategic role of today's human resource managers, a thorough understanding of this tool is absolutely essential.

STEPS IN FORMULATING A REGRESSION EQUATION

Consider the data shown in Figure 4A-16. The steps involved in regressing y against x are listed below and shown in Figure 4A-19.

1. For simplicity, we assume that in this example there is a straight-line relationship between x and y (that is, the relationship between them is linear in nature). A *linear* relationship indicates that for any change in the value of x (or y), the value of the other variable (y or x) will change in a constant fashion throughout the range of data. There are also other types of relationships that can exist between two variables (such as a curvilinear relationship). Here, the relationship pattern between x and y changes within the range of data available to us. Figure 4A-18 shows examples of linear and curvilinear relationships between two variables. Linear relationships are generally easier to understand and to estimate. Most statistical software packages (such as SPSS or SYSTAT) have provisions for fitting non-linear trend lines between variables.

2. To estimate y (given x), we will express the former as a function of the latter. A straight-line relationship between two variables is typically indicated by the equation:

$$y = a + bx$$

'A' is the value y would take when $x = 0$, and is usually referred to as the *y-intercept*. The second term, 'b', is the *slope of the line*. It is the ratio between the y values and

FIGURE 4A-18:   Linear and Curvilinear Regression

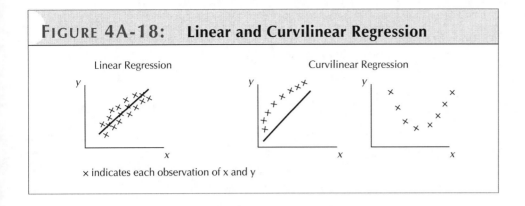

Linear Regression   Curvilinear Regression

x indicates each observation of x and y

the x values, or the rate of change in y divided by the rate of change of in x. The slope is related to the correlation between x and y but is also related to the variance (or spread) observed in the distributions of x and y. Because of these relationships, the approach taken to calculate 'b' closely follows the approach taken in calculating Pearson r earlier. The calculations are shown below and in Figure 4A-19.

FIGURE 4A-19:   Estimating a Linear Regression Equation between Test Score and Number of Work Accidents

Employee	Score on Test	Number of Accidents			
	(x)	(y)	x^2	y^2	xy
1	60	3	3600	9	180
2	65	2	4225	4	130
3	70	1	4900	1	70
4	62	4	3844	16	248
5	60	4	3600	16	240
6	55	8	3025	64	440
7	58	7	3364	49	406
8	42	12	1764	144	504
9	80	0	6400	0	0
10	48	9	2304	81	432
	$\Sigma x = 600$	$\Sigma y = 50$	$\Sigma x^2 = 37026$	$\Sigma y^2 = 384$	$\Sigma xy = 2650$

$\bar{x} = 60$
$\bar{y} = 50$
$N = 10$

The basic regression equation is: $a + bx$

b is calculated as follows:

$$b = \frac{\Sigma xy - \dfrac{\Sigma x\, \Sigma y}{N}}{\Sigma x^2 - \dfrac{(\Sigma x)^2}{N}} = \frac{2650 - [(600)(50)]}{37026 - \dfrac{360000}{10}} = -0.34$$

Since $y = a + bx$, this is also true for the average values of x and y.

Hence: $\bar{y} = a + b\bar{x}$ or
          $5 = a + [(-0.34)60]$

Simplifying, we get: $a = 25.5$

The linear regression equation between score in the test and number of accidents is:
   $y = 25.4 - 0.34x$
This means that the higher the test score, the lower the number of accidents.

Using the above regression equation, we can predict the number of accidents that are likely, based on a person's score in the safety knowledge test. For example, for a score of 40, the number of likely accidents is:

$$y = 24.76 + [(-.330)x]$$

$$= 11.56 \text{ (which can be rounded-off to 12)}$$

It is important to note that predictions will almost always have a degree of error. To illustrate this, let us substitute the value of $x = 55$ into the equation above. Now, y is predicted as 6.61. But we know from the information provided to us that y's value is in fact 8. The lower the error, as intuition will tell us, the better the predictive power of the regression equation.

CONCLUDING OBSERVATIONS

Applying the statistical concepts outlined in this appendix can help human resource managers to find valuable insight into current and potential employees when the appropriate data is available. Further study of statistical analysis and statistical programs such as the Statistical Program for Social Sciences (SPSS) is strongly recommended for those who are likely to be involved in the testing and validation of predictors.

Key Terms for Review

Arithmetic average,   *p. 146*

Correlation,   *p. 153*

Mean,   *p. 146*

Measure of central tendency,   *p. 145*

Median,   *p. 146*

Mode,   *p. 145*

Pearson *r*,   *p. 154*

Range,   *p. 148*

Regression,   *p. 156*

Standard deviation,   *p. 148*

Standard error of measurement (SEM),   *p. 153*

Standard normal distribution,   *p. 150*

PART 3

IMPLEMENTATION

Hiring and deploying human resources is a step-by-step process. Chapter 5 discusses the steps needed to recruit employees, beginning with preparing the request to hire a new employee. Chapter 5 also describes recruiting methods and ways to assess their effectiveness. Chapter 6 discusses the importance of job application forms and biographical blanks in screening job applicants. Chapter 7 describes performance, knowledge, personality, and medical and drug tests that are currently used in Canada, with a detailed discussion on their strengths and weaknesses. Chapter 8 explains how to use reference letters and interviews for best results. Chapter 9 discusses ways to synthesize applicant information to form a final employment decision. Finally, Chapter 10 discusses ways to deploy new staff and looks at special challenges, such as hiring for international positions and terminating employees.

5 RECRUITMENT

"The old employment system of secure, lifetime jobs with predictable advancement and stable pay is dead... While employers have quiet clearly broken the old deal and its long-term commitments, they do not control the new deal, which is fundamentally an agreement negotiated between employer and employee. It is an open-ended relationship that is continually being re-drafted. Which side gains and loses depends on bargaining power, which in turn stems from the state of the labour market."

Peter Cappelli[1]

CHAPTER OBJECTIVES

After studying this chapter, you should be able to:

- Explain the link between recruitment strategy and overall organizational human resource strategy and activities

- Describe the job search process used by potential recruits

- Discuss methods of recruitment and the steps involved

- Discuss ways to evaluate the effectiveness of recruitment programs

Charlene Thwaites was a senior programmer in Ontario Electronics when she quit to work for a competitor. Her resignation created a problem for the head of the Programming Division, Brad McLellan. As he expressed it, "She was an important member of the team designing a new program for planning mechanical tolerances. Her contribution was mainly theoretical, quite different from all others in the team, and it's something that no one else can offer at this time. In less than three months, we have to deliver the new program to our client who will not give us an extension. We must find a bright programmer to complete the work—and today! I sincerely hope that HR will be successful in recruiting someone soon."

McLellan's situation is not unusual in the current labour market. The employment relationship that characterized the industrial world for past several decades—the long-term employment contract between employer and employee—no longer applies. Increased competition, rapid information exchange, new management tools such as profit centres and benchmarking, and an almost exclusive focus on shareholder interests have made it very difficult for firms to retain long-term relationships with employees.[2] Moreover, the planning horizon for firms is now much shorter than can be accommodated by an individual employee's career. This shorter horizon, in turn, has created changes in employee behaviours, altering fundamentally the relationship between employer and employee. Today, turnover of key employees is a major problem for many employers; and in tight labour markets, such as information technology industry, retaining employees has become a persistent challenge.

Finding new employees for the organization is a continuing challenge for most human resource departments. Sometimes the need for new workers is known well in advance because of detailed human resource plans (see Chapter 2). At other times, such as the opening example, the human resource department is faced with urgent requests for replacements that it must fill as quickly as possible. In either case, finding qualified applicants is a key activity. **Recruitment** is the process of attracting suitable candidates for actual or planned job vacancies. It involves more than placing an ad in a newspaper and getting a few responses. Recruitment focuses on getting the "right" candidates precisely when they are needed. Will there be a sufficient number of applicants to offer a realistic choice? How much will the recruitment effort cost? Balancing the number and quality of job applicants with the cost of recruiting and the timeliness of the process determines the success of the recruitment plan.

This chapter discusses the recruitment methods used in Canadian industry today. It also explains the motivations of job seekers, which can aid you in your recruitment efforts. But first, you need to understand the link between recruitment and a firm's overall HR strategy.

Recruitment: the process of attracting suitable candidates for actual or planned job vacancies

Government of Canada Recruitment tools: *http://youth.gc.ca*

LINKING RECRUITMENT TO OVERALL HUMAN RESOURCE STRATEGY

In a global and technologically demanding business environment, sourcing and retaining talent is a competitive battleground.[3] Just as sports teams recruit aggressively for the best athletes, business organizations compete aggressively for the best talent. Successful firms are those most adept at attracting and retaining individuals with the skills and attitudes they need to achieve their corporate goals. That is, an effective recruitment strategy reflects and harmonizes with organizational and human resource strategies. It identifies knowledge, skills, and other job competencies based on the technological, cultural, and strategic requirements of the organization.

> Wal-Mart's strategy of low cost operations coupled with superior customer service made it imperative that the firm attract and train recruits as high involvement "associates" rather than "employees." Asea-Brown Boveri's strategy of creating a participative, team-oriented workplace meant that its recruitment efforts focused on hiring "team leaders" rather than "foremen."

As discussed in Chapter 1, firms pursue a wide variety of human resource strategies. Some seek long-term employees, while others depend on contingent labour. With every change in an organization's strategy, the firm must also revise its skill-mix. In addition, the work environments (and more specifically, the labour market) may also undergo major changes requiring adaptive strategies. Whatever the case, with every change in an organization's strategy and human resource strategy, an employer must review its recruitment practices for continued relevance.[4] Several studies[5] have demonstrated the strong relationship between HR practices and corporate productivity, profits, and shareholder value. In particular, the type of recruitment strategy adopted by a firm has profound impact on the quality of its human capital, productivity, and culture. To aim for the right impact, HR must make four important decisions about recruiting employees:

1. How Much Importance Should We Assign to Human Capital?

Chapter 1 discussed the strategic importance of human capital. Successful firms recognize that human capital spells the difference between success and failure. Indeed, despite state-of-the-art technology and access to capital, poorly qualified or motivated recruits can cause decay and death of an organization. For example, a study of 1000 companies found that investors place a much higher value on companies that improve their bottom lines through revenue growth rather than through simple cost cutting. This study found virtually no correlation between company size and revenue growth rate; nor was there any relationship between industry growth rate and the growth rates of companies within each industry.[6]

This means that organizations that look at labour primarily as a cost that needs to be controlled may not be contributing to company growth. These companies maintain only the smallest workforce consistent with short-term operational requirements, rather than long-term goals. Investments into training and development are also minimal. Thus, the focus in recruitment is on finding candidates who already have requisite skills so as to minimize out-of-pocket costs. In the short term, these strategies offer some cost savings; but in the long-term, they fail to contribute to revenue growth.

However, these decisions depend on the nature of environments, technology, and challenges faced by the organization. Past studies indicated that organizations facing simple, predictable environments and driven by a high-volume, low-cost operational philosophy are more likely to have a **low-commitment strategy**: hiring employees on an as-needed basis, allocating them to tasks which need little training, and terminating when those tasks are no longer needed. Thus, the employment relationship in these organizations is focused on the short term and is governed by rules, rather than shared values. In contrast, a **high-commitment human resource strategy** (where the employer seeks a close relationship with employees who become psychologically and emotionally involved with the enterprise, and where opportunities for personal and career development are built into employment practices) is used most effectively in organizations facing considerable environmental and technological uncertainty.[7] In general, HR must determine its short-term and long-term needs when assessing the relative importance of its human capital.

Today, many progressive employers recognize that cost cutting and downsizing alone do not provide a sustainable advantage over any significant period of time.[8] They also recognize that the *relative* costs—and not absolute costs—should be the primary focus. Further, a cost model does not fully recognize the value-adding potential and innovative contributions of employees. Progressive companies recognize the importance of consistent implementation of good ideas for success[9] and the role of highly competent and committed employees in this context.

Low-commitment strategy: hiring employees on an as-needed basis, allocating them to tasks which need little training, and terminating when those tasks are no longer needed

High-commitment strategy: establishing a close, long-term relationship with employees who become psychologically and emotionally involved with the enterprise, with opportunities for personal and career development built into employment practices

2. HOW MUCH DIVERSITY SHOULD WE AIM FOR?

Monolithic organizations:
organizations that predominantly employ people who hold similar beliefs, values, and orientations

While several Canadian firms recognize the vitality and competitive advantage offered by a diverse workforce, many employers still recruit only from traditional sources. These **monolithic organizations** employ predominantly the same type of people; and people who look and hold different values from the majority often work only in a limited number of positions or departments. Members of the majority culture in such organizations are unlikely to adopt minority-culture norms to any extent.[10] In addition, the organization does not value or recognize the accomplishments and credentials of minority employees.

> A Statistics Canada study found that 70% of the 164 000 immigrants who settled in Canada in 2000 and 2001 had trouble entering the labour force—60% them forced to take jobs outside their areas of training.[11] A later study of 829 immigrant engineers in Ontario found that 55% were unable to find jobs, and 29% were working in fields other than engineering, not commensurate with their skills.[12] Many employers seem to discount overseas training and experience. But at the same time, Canada faces a skilled trades shortage, while white-collar immigrant workers are forced to take jobs sweeping floors and delivering flyers. It is not uncommon to see foreign doctors working as bricklayers and nurses slinging coffee at fast food restaurants because their qualifications and skills were not recognized.

Multicultural organizations:
organizations that employ people who hold diverse values and lifestyles

In contrast, **multicultural organizations** value diversity and pluralism where both majority and minority group members adopt some of the norms of the others. In a multicultural organization, members of different groups hold positions throughout the organization and participate fully in informal activities.[13] Little prejudice or discrimination is visible, all employees identify equally with the organization, and conflicts between groups are minimal. Managers in these organizations recognize that hiring from a larger, diverse pool of candidates offers greater choice of job applicants to the firm as well as larger pools of talent. They believe that a diverse workforce offers greater flexibility and additional capabilities in many instances.

3. HOW MUCH RESOURCE SHOULD WE ALLOCATE TO RECRUITMENT?

The size of the recruitment budget affects the quality of recruits and the overall effectiveness of recruitment activity. Naturally, small businesses have a much smaller budget for recruitment. But many large, established firms do not assign great importance to recruiting—often relying on traditional recruitment practices, without trying to understand the psychology and aspirations of job candidates or incorporating these ideas into their recruitment strategies. A small pool of recruits can reduce the overall effectiveness of selection practices (discussed in the next three chapters); and poor-quality recruits, even if they bring about short-term cost savings, can adversely affect product and service quality and public image of an organization.

It is important to note that the costs of recruitment are not simply the hiring costs (such as the costs of advertisement, recruiter's travel, and so on). The costs of recruitment must also include the indirect costs of a bad hire. Often, the costs of a bad hire are not translatable into monetary terms, since there is no accurate way of measuring the number of lost customers and resources due to delays and inefficient handling of a situation.[14] Furthermore, bad hires often end up leaving the organization, causing significant additional costs to hire and train replacements. Some organizations have recognized the importance of the recruitment function and identified innovative ways to identify recruits without incurring high recruitment costs:

> A large American electronics firm maintains its competitive edge by hiring employees at the entry level, training them, and promoting them from within. Its recruitment program uses

standardized procedures to recruit the best university students for entry-level positions. The firm rates universities and colleges on a four-point scale ("1" being the best). For students from category 1 schools, those with a GPA of 3.2 or higher would be contacted for interviews; for those from category 4 schools, only students with a GPA of 3.4 or better would be considered by the recruiter. Such formalized screening procedures have allowed the firm to secure high-quality recruits while minimizing recruitment costs.

In a global knowledge economy, highly skilled and motivated workers are a real competitive advantage. Most progressive HR departments recognize that the costs of attracting and keeping them are less than the benefits they bring to the company.

4. HOW MUCH SHOULD WE INVEST IN EMPLOYEE DEVELOPMENT?

Organizations differ in their policies related to employee development. Many organizations invest significant resources in training and development, while other organizations regard training as a frill. The latter firms just leave the responsibility for training and career development to the individual employee.

> Japanese automobile assembly units provide an average of 364 hours of training to new workers in the first six months of employment. The corresponding figures for European and North American auto manufacturers are 178 and 42 hours respectively. In contrast, emerging economic powers such as Korea, Taiwan, and Brazil provided 260 hours of training.[15] But even within the same industry and same country, there can be significant differences in focus on employee development. The amount of training in flexible or lean manufacturing auto assembly units is significantly higher than in mass production systems.[16] Similarly, the amount of training provided in steel mills, which primarily focuses on generating employee commitment is substantially higher than in units which primarily focus on controlling labour costs and improving efficiency by enforcing employee compliance with rules and procedures.[17]

When recruiting, especially for middle- and upper-level jobs, a firm has to choose between developing and promoting internal candidates or hiring from the outside. The strategic choice of internal versus external recruitment has profound implications for an organization and affects the way it manages employee training and development. Current employees, especially in smaller organizations, know a lot more about the organization, its strategy, and its culture than do new recruits. Moreover, employees who are transferred internally or promoted to more challenging jobs do not have to go through the same learning process as do new recruits. In addition, a well-designed employee development plan also acts as a strong motivator for many employees to learn and improve their skills, thereby earning promotions. For these reasons, many employers incorporate substantial employee development programs into their overall HR strategy, which has benefited them, as the following example of a paper mill shows:

> A longitudinal study of a unionized paper mill showed that by instituting high commitment work practices, such as extensive training, reduction in job classifications (which enriched jobs), guarantees of employment security, and increases in wages, combined with simplification of compensation system, the company substantially increased its production and reduced its non-labour costs. The result was the tripling of the mill's profitability.[18]

In summary, recruitment is closely related to the success of HR and larger corporate strategy. In the same way, an organization's overall strategy drives recruitment requiring the recruiter to identify critical human competencies and attract them to the firm.

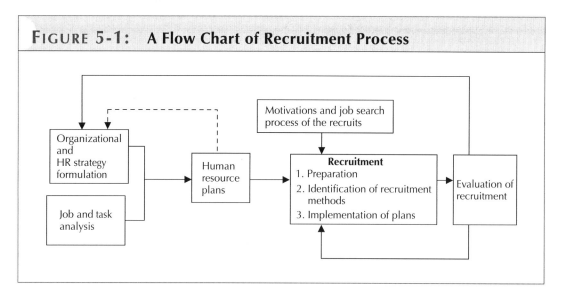

FIGURE 5-1:   A Flow Chart of Recruitment Process

Whatever the overall philosophy and human resource strategy of an organization, recruitment of human resources involves a number of steps. The ideal sequence of activities is presented in Figure 5-1 above. Recruitment cannot take place until the recruiter has a clear idea about the number and type of employees needed. This means that the recruiter begins by examining the overall HR strategy and operational and human resource plans (see Chapter 1). HR prepares job requisitions to match these long-term plans, identifying the number and type of vacancies. These documents act as the focal point in recruitment. The organization then selects the most appropriate recruitment methods (or channels, as they are sometimes called), based on assessments of the motivations and job search methods of the applicants. Finally, HR assesses the effectiveness of the recruitment strategy to bring about timely changes in an organization's recruitment practices. At times, fundamental changes in the HR strategy or its components (e.g., pay) may have to be made to enhance recruitment effectiveness.

The various steps in recruitment will be discussed in the remainder of this chapter. But before going any further, it is important to learn about the motivations and job search process of recruits, since these issues affect the success of all recruitment actions.

UNDERSTANDING THE JOB SEARCH PROCESS AND MOTIVATIONS OF JOB SEEKERS

Kanika Singh does not remember the precise event that triggered her desire to aspire for an executive career in a large multinational firm. Probably, it was the day she accompanied her father, a real estate sales agent, to the mansion owned by a senior executive of a large multinational corporation (MNC) in Vancouver. She was very impressed by the opulence all around and the aura of importance around the manager who was constantly at his laptop, a relatively new product at that time. Later on, when she chose to study business at University of British Columbia, she had an opportunity to listen to a number of guest lectures by senior executives in banks and other international organizations. During their lectures, the speakers had narrated their experiences in various MNCs and offered helpful hints for prospective applicants to such organizations. Armed with this information, Kanika selected courses that exposed her to international management during the remainder of her program. Over the summer break, she worked for a bank with international operations, and in the evening, she volunteered in a local branch of an international development agency.

Having excelled in her studies, Kanika had little difficulty in getting admission to the MBA program at McGill University, where she continued to learn about other cultures and specialize in international marketing and management. Besides doing her major paper on cross-cultural issues in marketing communication, she also helped two professors with their research projects in international management. One of the professors considered her contributions worthy of a second authorship in a paper. At the end of the program, when the campus interviews were taking place, she chose employers who were planning to expand their operations to Asia or the far east. Given her academic training, cultural background, and competencies in cross-cultural issues, she had little trouble impressing the recruiter of a multinational firm planning to expand to Bangalore, India. Kanika was offered a position as a management trainee.

She was sent to New York for initial training for nine months, after which she was posted to the Bangalore office. She worked there for nearly three years, during which time she always met or exceeded targets. Then she moved to another large multinational organization whose head office was in Norway. Today, six years after her MBA, Kanika is the regional manager for the firm's Asia operations and lives in Bangkok. At 29, she is one of the youngest executives in the firm.

Mary Richardson had a very different approach to her career. In fact, she had not thought about a career until she was 39 years old. She had always lived in Grand Pre in rural Nova Scotia, where her life had revolved around her home, her farm, and her family. She married a worker at the local fish processing plant immediately after high school, and for the next sixteen years, she took care of her family. It was only when she and her husband separated four years ago that she suddenly felt the need for a paid career.

By then, her youngest child was nine years old, which meant that she had a lot more free time. Initially, she began working in the local Sobey's grocery store as a part-time cashier. A year later, she moved to a bank since she felt that the job in the bank held greater career potential. In any case, the bank offered higher salary and benefits, which was important for her family's needs. But joining the bank exposed her to new career possibilities. She enrolled in the commerce degree program in Acadia University in Wolfville and began taking courses in finance and HR on a part-time basis. During her stay at the bank, she had the opportunity to interact with a variety of clients, including the owner of a major hardware store. Impressed by Mary's efficiency and pleasant demeanor, the owner hired her as an assistant in the firm's HR department. Now, six years later, Mary is close to finishing her undergraduate degree in commerce with a major in human resource management and is already planning to get her CHRP designation. There are indications that her supervisor is about to move to Alberta. If that happens, she will likely be appointed as the human resource manager of the company.

The career patterns of Kanika and Mary are starkly different. Environmental and person-related factors have had significant impact on their career choice and progress. Even these brief vignettes show remarkable differences between their sources of motivation, their motivation levels, their family circumstances, their available job opportunities, and their constraints.

However, the two narratives also show a commonality. Both women were pursuing specific career goals through their actions. A **career** (also called a **vocation**) is a sequence of positions or a chain of interrelated occupations held by a person over a relatively long period of time. An **occupation** is a set of similar working tasks. Both Mary and Kanika identified the career they wanted and constantly adapted their behaviours to meet the demands of these careers. Indeed, many people actively choose and direct their careers, although the degree of involvement shows considerable variation. Available research evidence indicates that choices of careers and even specific occupations within those careers depend on personality types.

Unless organizational recruiters understand the variables that affect career and organizational choice, as outlined in Figure 5-2 , they will not be able to adapt their HR strategies to meet the needs of the recruits. As a result, they will be unable to attract the right type of applicants to the organization in time to fill the organization's needs.

Career or **vocation:** a sequence of positions or a chain of interrelated occupations over a relatively long period of time

Occupation: a set of similar working tasks

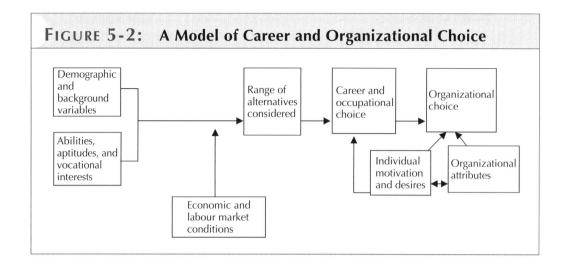

FIGURE 5-2:   A Model of Career and Organizational Choice

DEMOGRAPHIC AND BACKGROUND VARIABLES

While Canada has been actively trying to remove social and income barriers to career options, demographic and socioeconomic variables continue interfere with career choices, especially for young people. As two researchers have noted, "parental socioeconomic level is the starting point of the career pattern and one of its major determinants."[19] Available research studies confirm that parental income and status significantly influence choice of careers. For example, people belonging to higher socioeconomic groups are more likely to choose medicine, law, or business management than they are to choose clerical or salaried professions.[20] Family and community environment, race, gender, education, and locality of residence (rural versus urban) all influence an individual's career choice.[21] Although "different racial groups assign the same preferences to various occupations, different proportions of people from different racial groups choose to enter certain occupations."[22] In the same way, residents of inner cities tend to have different career preferences from those who live in the suburbs or rural areas.[23] Television, the Internet, and other mass communication devices have significantly reduced the information gap between urban and rural dwellers; however, limited educational opportunities and a lack of adequate role models prevent rural residents from considering certain career alternatives. As two past researchers[24] pointed out, the "local occupational structure" may impact on and constrain an individual's perception of career alternatives.

ABILITIES, APTITUDES, AND VOCATIONAL INTERESTS

Measuring a candidate's verbal ability, numerical ability, spatial reasoning, form perception, motor coordination, finger dexterity, and manual dexterity can help a recruitment team learn more about the individual's innate abilities, aptitudes, and interests. For example, studies have shown a consistent relationship between cognitive ability (intelligence) and occupation,[25] although such abilities alone cannot determine the potential for success or failure within an occupation. "What seems always to be true is that a certain level of general ability is required for particular occupations."[26] Figure 5-3 lists some of the more popular interest and aptitude inventories.

Holland's classification of vocational interests One popular classification of vocational interests was developed by John Holland. He contended that people tend to resemble and can be classified as one of six basic personality types. The more a person

> # FIGURE 5-3: Popular Interest Inventories
>
> Strong Interest Inventory
> Canadian Occupational Interest Inventory
> General Occupational Interest Inventory
> Kuder Preference Record
> Vocational Preference Inventory
> Sixteen Personality Factor Questionnaire
> Self-Directed Search
> Minnesota Importance Questionnaire.

resembles any given type, the more likely he or she is to engage in behaviours associated with that type. The personality characteristics associated with each type include both likes and dislikes. Here are Holland's six types, often described with the acronym RIASEC.

Realistic The realistic individual prefers activities requiring motor coordination, skill, and physical strength, and tasks involving the systematic manipulation of tools, machinery, or animals. A machinist is a typical realistic occupation. Such people may lack social skills and avoid tasks involving interpersonal and verbal skills.

Investigative The investigative person tends to be analytical, curious, methodical, and precise. A research scientist is a typical investigative occupation. Investigative people, however, often lack leadership skills.

Artistic Artistic individuals tend to be expressive, nonconforming, introspective, and original. Musicians and interior decorators are artistic types. These individuals may lack clerical skills.

Social Social people enjoy working with and helping others but tend to avoid systematic and ordered activities involving tools and machinery. Counsellors and bartenders are social types. Such people may lack mechanical and scientific ability.

Enterprising Enterprising individuals enjoy activities that result in attainment of economic gain or organizational goals, but generally avoid symbolic or systematic activities. Lawyers and salespersons are typical of this group.

Conventional Finally, conventional types enjoy systematically manipulating data, symbols, or other information and reproducing material. This type is characterized by a great concern for rules and regulations, self-control, and strong identification with power and status.[27] File clerks, bookkeepers, and tax accountants are typical of this group. They tend to avoid artistic activities.

Aptitude tests on the web:
www.careerkey.org

Holland noted that whereas one type usually predominates, individuals are typically an amalgam of multiple interests. Thus, individuals may primarily belong to one group with apparent influence of a second or third type contributing to their overall response to any specific situation.

Holland developed three devices to assess an individual's career preferences: the Vocational Preference Inventory, the Self-Directed Search (SDS), and the Vocational Exploration and Insight Kit. His model for the delivery of vocational guidance services and the Holland Occupational Classification represent other extensions of his theory. Past research has shown considerable support for Holland's model. Available evidence indicates that his model is applicable to people without regard to race, gender, or age.[28] While his SDS has come under attack for reinforcing gender stereotypes,[29] the overwhelming evidence is to the contrary. Today, there is general agreement that "Holland's occupational classification system works."[30]

ECONOMIC AND LABOUR MARKET CONDITIONS

Prevailing economic and labour market conditions act as major constraints in an individual's search for a specific career. Some jobs are simply not available in certain locations, while for other jobs, supply and demand cycles fluctuate wildly. At any point, unless job applicants are willing to travel to the locations where jobs are available, they may not be able to market their own skills and competencies effectively, no matter how intrinsically valuable they are.

> Every year, a number of B.Comm and MBA graduates from Atlantic universities move to Ontario, Alberta, or B.C. in search of jobs in their specialties. Given the larger than national unemployment rates and limited managerial opportunities in Atlantic Canada, many graduates feel that they can achieve their career goals faster by relocating. For the same reason, many commerce students at these universities attempt to improve their chances of securing a good job nearby by specializing in more than one subject. Thus, faced with an uncertain future labour market, students in Atlantic Canada have to develop strategies to overcome job market shortcomings.

At the same time, municipalities have embarked on new initiatives to reduce labour market imbalances due to the anticipated shortage and competition for skilled workers:

> In 2004, Hamilton, Calgary, and Edmonton each launched initiatives to improve and showcase the competitiveness of their labour forces and to reduce inefficiencies in the local labour market. Hamilton has worked to convince small and medium businesses to make better use of the pool of highly qualified immigrants who were holding jobs far below their skill levels. Looming skills shortages prompted the Calgary Chamber of Commerce to form a Talent Pool Development Society to encourage businesses to attract recruits from non-traditional sources. Edmonton has been promoting its "Edmonton Edge" in talents and resources hoping to attract highly skilled employees to the city's new ventures in nanotechnology and high-tech research.[31]

RANGE OF ALTERNATIVES CONSIDERED

An individual's background, interests, and perceptions of relevant labour market conditions combine to influence a person's consideration of a finite number of vocational alternatives. In a sense, an individual's eventual career choice may be heavily constrained and influenced by the pre-existing conditions in the person's larger environment. As two researchers have pointed out, "indeed, one may speak realistically of these choices as being, in many cases, the result of a series of externally imposed compromises."[32] The fewer the alternatives offered by the surrounding environments, the more the choice is directed by what is available rather than what the individual prefers.[33] These individuals have fewer opportunities to test the world and discover their true capabilities. A person's **vocational maturity**, or the ability to synthesize career-relevant knowledge with self-knowledge, determines the way the individual processes the available information. While people do develop and change during their life time and may change their careers, many are limited by career-relevant knowledge as well as self knowledge.[34]

Today, many progressive employers help their staff to identify various career paths and options, which they might not consider without guidance and encouragement. TD Bank is one good example:

> TD Bank created a Career Advisor website to offer a comprehensive career management tool to its employees. Through a combination of interactive diagnostic instruments, personal reports, advice, tools, and action planning exercises, the Career Advisor site is a comprehensive career management tool that helps the employees to figure out how best to develop their potential and

Vocational maturity: the ability to synthesize career-relevant knowledge with self-knowledge

Information on career choice: *www.careermag.com*

their career, overcome career challenges, and diagnose the root causes of career burnout and work-life imbalances. After going through the exercise, the employees are better able to match their needs and job requirements. For example, the site helps them understand whether they work best in a fast-paced multi-tasking environment or in a setting where they have time to do what they enjoy. Some employees may decide to leave the bank to work elsewhere; but in the end, this results in better outcome for all concerned.[35]

CAREER AND OCCUPATIONAL CHOICE

Choice of a career and specific occupations within those careers is the next step in career choice sequence. As already noted, the family environment, the larger community, and demographic variables have significant impact on an individual's choice of career and specific occupation within the career.

For example, a research study found that over a four-year period at college, students' career choices tended to become more like those of the "typical" student in the college. This was especially true of educational institutions specializing in a discipline like business or engineering.[36]

But in general, individual motivations, desires, and personality influence career, occupational, and organizational choices. Figure 5-4 shows how Holland's six personality types match with particular careers and occupation choices.

FIGURE 5-4: Sample Careers and Occupations		
Interest	**Preferred Careers**	**Sample Occupations**
Realistic (prefers activities requiring motor coordination and tasks involving systematic manipulation of tools and machinery)	Engineering Farming Forestry	Architect Farmer Civil engineer Metal worker
Investigative (tends to be analytical, curious, methodical, and precise)	Research Scientific occupations	Biologist R & D scientist Medical technologist Oceanographer
Social (enjoys working with and helping others but like to avoid systematic and ordered activities)	Social work Counselling	Field interviewer Social worker Career counsellor Clergy
Enterprising (enjoys activities that result in attainment of economic gain or organizational goals)	Sales Law Business management	Stock broker Estate law practitioner Sales manager
Artistic (tends to be expressive, nonconforming, introspective, and original)	Music Drama Literature	Music composer Television producer Photographer Guitar player Sketch artist
Conventional (enjoys systematic manipulation of data and symbols)	Clerical occupations Accounting Finance	Bank manager Accountant

ORGANIZATIONAL CHOICE

Once individuals have decided on careers that match their ability and interests, they must then choose an organization to work for, assuming their location offers choices. What motivates an individual to choose one organization over another? What makes people move from one employer to another, even when they continue to work in same occupation? Unfortunately, there are no simple answers. Two major factors are believed to influence these choices: the person's motivation and desires, and his or her perceptions of the organization's attributes.

Individual motivation and desires What motivates people? A number of theories have been formulated to explain individual motivation. An elaborate discussion of these theories is beyond the scope of this book. What is attempted below is a brief overview of the more popular models of motivation as they relate to career and organizational choice.

Popular motivation theories can be classified into two major groups: content theories and process theories. Content theories of motivation focus on the "what" of decisions, identifying the personal needs and gains that cause people to expend effort in specific activities. Process theories, in contrast, focus on the "how" of decisions, the development of the reasons that cause an individual to believe that one situation is better than another.

Content theories There are three popular content theories of motivation.

MASLOW'S HIERARCHY OF NEEDS MODEL. Maslow's hierarchy of needs is perhaps the most popular content theory of motivation. Abraham Maslow, an American psychologist, theorized that human needs can be arranged in a hierarchical order, and that an individual would try to satisfy one level of needs before pursuing the next level. Maslow's five levels are (1) physiological needs (basic requirements for survival such as food, sleep, sex drive), (2) safety and security needs (shelter and protection from danger), (3) affiliation needs (affection, friendship, belonging), (4) esteem needs (need for respect, status, recognition), and (5) self-actualization needs (need to develop one's full potential). The physiological needs are the lowest in the hierarchy, and the self-actualization at the highest, with the other needs in between. Therefore, a job seeker will need to satisfy his or her physiological needs (food) and safety needs (a roof over his or her head) before looking for deeper career fulfillment.

TWO FACTOR MODEL OF MOTIVATION. Building on Maslow's notions, Frederick Herzberg later developed a two factor model of employee motivation. Herzberg suggested that two factors, which he called hygiene and motivation, have differential effects on motivation especially relevant to job seekers. The **hygiene factors**, also called extrinsic or contextual factors, are factors outside the work itself that influence employee motivation. These include company policy and administration, supervision, relationship with supervisor and co-workers, work conditions, and salary. Herzberg asserted that these factors are associated with dissatisfaction at work. If these factors are absent or unsatisfactory, the employee will feel dissatisfied; but when fulfilled, these factors can only bring a person to a neutral state of satisfaction. What really satisfies and motivates an employee are **motivation factors**. Also called intrinsic or content factors, motivation factors are aspects of the work itself, including achievement, recognition, interest, autonomy, advancement, and growth. Herzberg maintains that to motivate workers, organizations should enrich jobs with these motivation factors. It is worth noting that Herzberg's

Hygiene factors: factors outside the work itself that influence employee satisfaction

Motivation factors: aspects of the work itself, such as achievement, autonomy, etc., that influence employee motivation to work

hygiene factors correspond to the lower level needs in Maslow's hierarchy, while the motivational factors correspond to the higher levels: esteem and self-actualization needs.

NEED FOR ACHIEVEMENT. David McClelland offered yet another theory of employee motivation. He suggested that there are three major needs in the workplace: need for power, need for affiliation, and need for achievement. **Need for power** is the concern for reputation, responsibility, influence, impact, and control over others. People with high needs in this area prefer leadership positions. But people with high **need for affiliation** want to establish and maintain social relationships and prefer cooperative rather than competitive situations. A third group of people have a high **need for achievement,** which according to McClelland is a desire to establish and maintain high levels of performance quality while taking personal responsibility for success or failure. These people take calculated (moderate) risks and like to receive immediate, concrete feedback on their performance. Individuals with high need for achievement are often dynamic entrepreneurs but may not make good managers because the achievement of others is not their primary concern.

Process theories Like content theories, several process theories of motivation have been developed. But only the three most popular models are outlined here.

REINFORCEMENT THEORY. The premise of B.F. Skinner's **reinforcement** or **learning theory** is that the environment determines people's behaviour. If individuals receive reinforcement or reward for what they do, they are likely to repeat it. But if no one acknowledges the behaviour, a person may stop doing it. Moreover, when people receive a negative outcome or punishment for their behaviour, they usually stop doing it, at least for the moment. Punishment, however, rarely extinguishes undesirable behaviour forever. The ideas of reinforcement theory are simple, and research supports the model in many settings. However, it should be noted that what is a "reward" to one person may not hold the same value for another person.

EXPECTANCY THEORY. Expectancy theory is built on four premises: (1) behaviour is a result of both personal and environmental factors; (2) decisions about whether to belong to an organization or to expend effort in jobs influence behaviour; (3) people seek different rewards from organizations because of different needs; and (4) people decide how to behave based on what they believe leads to the most desirable outcomes. Briefly put, this model suggests that a job candidate's decision to join an organization is based on the belief about the likelihood that a job will bring to him or her some valued outcomes. The process of calculating the individual's expectations is as follows.

First, a person considers whether making an effort could lead to successful performance. This is called E→P Expectancy, or effort leading to performance expectancy. Second, the person evaluates the likelihood that successful performance will result in the receipt of a reward. This is called the P→O Expectancy, or performance leading to outcome expectancy. Associated with each outcome is a **valence,** which is the value of the reward to the individual receiving it. If the person considers the reward valuable, he or she will increase effort to attain that reward. But if the person sees no connection between performance and outcome or does not value the reward, he or she is unlikely to exert further efforts. Finally, the person also considers **instrumentality,** the likelihood that a first level outcome will lead to a second level outcome. For example, would the fact that a supervisor praised good performance (a first-level outcome) result in a higher raise next year (a second-level outcome)? If no relationship is perceived, then, once again, no effort will be exerted.

Need for power: a concern for influence, impact, and control over others

Need for affiliation: a desire to establish and maintain social relationships and prefer cooperative rather than competitive situations

Need for achievement: a desire to establish and maintain high levels of performance quality while taking personal responsibility for success or failure

Reinforcement or **learning theory:** environment, more specifically, external reinforcements or punishments, determines people's behaviour

E→P Expectancy: a person's consideration of whether making an effort could lead to successful performance

P→O Expectancy: a person's consideration of whether a successful performance will result in the outcome

Valence: the value of a reward to the individual receiving it

Instrumentality: the likelihood that a first level outcome will lead to a second level outcome

Equity theory: people attempt to balance how much they work in relation to relevant others

EQUITY THEORY. Another content model is the **equity theory**, which posits that people attempt to balance their inputs and outputs in relation to those of relevant others. Motivation results through the process of comparing one's perceived outcomes-to-inputs ratio with the perceived ratio of relevant others, such as co-workers. In mathematical terms, equity exists when

$$\frac{\text{Outcomes}_{\text{self}}}{\text{Inputs}_{\text{self}}} = \frac{\text{Outcomes}_{\text{Other}}}{\text{Inputs}_{\text{Other}}}$$

When people perceive inequity, they experience tension or discomfort and use strategies to maintain equity, including distorting their own perceptions of the situation, changing inputs or outputs (where possible), or leaving the organization.

How do these six theories of motivation help us understand an individual's decision to join an organization? First, they tell us that different people value different rewards; hence they are likely to choose organizations that offer them the rewards they value. Some may value the security that money brings; others may value the prestige of being part of a well-known firm; yet others may desire the feeling of self-actualizing and achievement that comes from an interesting and difficult job. Second, people desire to be treated equitably. HR managers need to ensure that jobs are adequately rewarded relative to other jobs. Third, in choosing employers, people are likely to be guided by their perceptions of their ability to perform satisfactorily and obtain valued rewards. They ask questions such as: What do I desire? What do I have to do to obtain what I desire? Can I do what I have to do in order to get what I desire?[37] Figure 5-5 provides an illustration of expectancy notions in the context of organizational choice.

FIGURE 5-5:   An Illustration of Expectancy Model in Organizational Choice

Ann is about to graduate from her MBA and is looking for a position in marketing. She interviewed in a number of places and has finally received two job offers (Job A and Job B). Both are for management trainee positions with very similar initial salaries (considering the cost of living in the locations). But during the interviews, she had the impression that one of them (Job A) is more likely to offer her a better salary in a year's time, although she did not pursue the topic during the interview. But Job B offers some possibility of overseas work. Ann's family lives in eastern British Columbia, and she would like to be in easy commuting distance to her family for the next 2–3 years. At the same time, she realizes that in today's global economy, gaining some experience abroad is valuable in her field.

Last term, during a career-planning session, she was asked to rate various "rewards" associated with jobs. These were her ratings (all on a five point scale; 5 means the maximum):

1. Opportunity for career growth = 5
2. Salary after training period = 3
3. Location = 4
4. Possibility of getting a foreign posting in five year's time = 4

Job A is in British Columbia (though not in the eastern part of the province), and Job B is in Alberta. In her mind, these are the probabilities (on a 0 to 1 scale) of the two jobs meeting the above goals:

	Job A	Job B
Opportunity for career growth	0.5	0.8
Good salary after training period	0.7	0.4
Possibility of foreign posting	0.3	0.7
Stay close to family	0.8	0.2

FIGURE 5-5: (Continued)

The ratings she gives to these rewards resemble valence in expectancy theory, and the probabilities she has calculated are somewhat like expectancies. Multiplying each expectancy with its valence, she can calculate the total desirability of the two jobs:

Job A's overall value to Ann= [$(5 \times 0.5) + (3 \times 0.7) + (4 \times 0.3) + (4 \times 0.3)$] = 7.0
Job B's overall value to Ann= [$(5 \times 0.8) + (3 \times 0.4) + (4 \times 0.2) + (4 \times 0.7)$] = 8.8

Thus, considering Ann's goals and desires, she is most likely to choose the job in Alberta, even though it takes her away from her family and is not as likely to offer her a higher salary after the training period, as the job in British Columbia might have. This is because on the items that are really important to her (namely, opportunity for career growth and the possibility of a foreign posting), Job B offers more.

In making organizational choice, people measure their own interests and motivations with the attributes of the organization. They are more likely to apply to and accept offers from organizations that have attributes consistent with their personal needs.

For example, individuals with a high need for autonomy may find an organization with a flat structure, a delegated method of decision making, and few rules more appealing than a traditional, top-down bureaucracy. Similarly, a "conventional" person may be uncomfortable working in a loosely organized firm devoid of clear policies and procedural manuals, while an "investigative" type (e.g., a research scientist) may value the freedom and opportunity to experiment without being constrained by many rules and procedures.

Organizational attributes

Many attributes of the organization itself influence a job applicant's choices:

- *Organization's prestige*: Research indicates that for many people, being employed in a prestigious industry, occupation, and organization implies social status.[38] Since work is an important part of modern life in the industrialized world, a person's identity often comes from the prestige associated with his or her employment. While work is only a part of the human life, it often interacts with and becomes part of the larger life of the person.

- *Organization's core values*: An organization's values, such as its commitment to the larger society and the environment, are often important drawing (or repelling) factors because people seek to work in organizations with values similar to their own. Organizations which engage in socially beneficial activities (e.g., welfare work) find it easier to attract socially-oriented recruits, just as organizations which openly value diversity are able to attract minorities. In choosing among jobs, job candidates go through the process of **image matching**, in which they compare their own self-image with the image of an organization and select the one whose perceived image matches their own.[39] If an organization's perceived image is at odds with the recruit's self-image, the recruit is unlikely to accept a job there. For example, an applicant who considers herself an entrepreneurial person is unlikely to accept a job in a highly bureaucratic or autocratic organization. While the idea of image matching has not been widely tested, available research evidence indicates some support for these ideas.[40]

- *Organization's management style*: Perceived management and supervisory styles strongly influence a candidate's decision to accept a job. The perceived management style (supportive and people-oriented vs. task-oriented; or democratic and delegated vs. authoritarian and bureaucratic) draws candidates who agree with or feel comfortable under the style of management. Note that often the perceived management style may not be the real management style, as many recruits learn once

Image matching: the process where job candidates compare their own self image with the images of organizations and select the organization whose perceived image matches their own

they enter the firm. This results in dissatisfaction and possibly eventually the recruit's resignation to take a more suitable job elsewhere.

- *Overall organizational culture*: Finally, the overall culture and personality of the organization can have significant influence on recruiting success. Some organizations emphasize personal, face-to-face relationships despite a hierarchical structure, thus creating a *family organizational culture*. In contrast, an *Eiffel Tower culture* is a classic bureaucratic structure emphasizing division of labour and coordination of activities through a hierarchy. Another model is the *guided missile culture*, which is egalitarian, impersonal, task-oriented, and focused on technical expertise and team-work. An *incubator culture* is radically different from the others, because it attempts to minimize organizational structure and culture and maximize individual employee's creativity, self-expression, and self-fulfillment.[41]

In summary, people consciously or unconsciously ask a number of questions before they decide to join an organization:

- What do I like to do?
- What can I do?
- What do I value? Am I likely to get it here?
- How do I see myself? What kind of an organization will I best fit in?
- Where am I going? Where can I use my abilities?

The amount of effort they expend answering these questions varies. For example, people differ in their persistence of search, number of employers contacted, number of sources of information used, and number of hours spent per week looking for work.[42] However, most applicants consider a mix of alternatives in making their decisions, not just one alternative in isolation from all other possibilities.[43] Research evidence also indicates that persons with higher educational qualifications tend to use more methods to find a job than those with lower educational levels.[44]

But just as the job candidate assesses an organization, the employer also assesses the job candidates for their compatibility with organizational needs and culture. If the wrong people are recruited, despite best selection tools, the new hires may not last. If the recruit's expectations do not match organizational reality, dissatisfaction and turnover are the outcomes. The employer must take steps to ensure that the applicant's expectations are realistic. Here are a few useful strategies to adopt:

1. Present relevant and accurate information Presenting accurate information about the job based on proper job analysis reduces misunderstanding. Ensure that information about the organization, its mission and core values in annual reports, want ads, public relations documents, and other media events are always accurate, so that only recruits with compatible values and goals apply. The information offered should be

- *specific*: details on the job requirements, responsibilities, and working conditions, so that the candidate can make an informed decision;
- *accurate*: positive and negative aspects the job, work setting, and the organization; and
- *comprehensive*: information on all relevant variables including career growth potential, intrinsic and extrinsic rewards, organizational climate and values.

2. Use specific recruitment methods and media Recruitment methods and media differ in their effectiveness and ability to convey accurate information. Applicants recruited through referrals from present employees tend to stay longer than

those recruited through want ads. The strengths and weaknesses of different recruitment methods will be discussed later in this chapter.

3. Advertise your organization's image
Image advertising aims to raise the positive profile of the organization to attract job seekers.[45] By exhibiting an image that appeals to the target market, the organization increases the likelihood of getting the right applicants. For example, a software company aiming to attract young, creative programmers advertised themselves as a "fun place to work," focusing on teamwork, flexible work settings and hours, and informal work atmosphere.

4. Include a realistic job preview
A realistic job preview (RJP) involves showing the candidate the type of work, equipment, and working conditions involved in the job before the hiring decision is finalized. RJP attempts to prevent job dissatisfaction by giving the newcomer a realistic view of the job. RJP gives the applicant a small dose of "organizational reality," RJP helps prepare the recruit to deal with the realities of the job.[46] RJP is discussed in more detail in Chapter 9.

Realistic job preview (RJP): showing a candidate the type of work, equipment, and working conditions involved in the job before the hiring decision is finalized

5. Include a comprehensive orientation
When new employees start their jobs, progressive employers go through a thorough orientation with them, providing information that will help the person form accurate expectations and adapt to the new role. Research suggests that including material aimed at lowering expectations in orientation sessions results in lower dissatisfaction and turnover in certain organizational settings.[47] Chapter 9 discusses orientation procedures.

> In 2004, Vancity Credit Union, located in British Columbia and employing about 2000 people, was named the best employer in the country by *Maclean's* magazine. During its orientation, Vancity communicates its strong commitment to employee welfare and the larger society. It offers above-average salary and advancement opportunities to its employees. But what it also conveys during its orientation is a can-do attitude that is shaped by its social conscience. Its 48-page book, *Things Grow Here,* narrates several stories about how its employees responded to social needs—a tool that is effectively used during orientation. In return, creating such a culture has also helped the firm in its recruitment efforts. The organization receives about 800 unsolicited resumes a month, and according to the management, the quality of the applicants is "unbelievable."[48]

STEPS IN RECRUITING

There are three major steps or stages in recruiting: preparation, choice of recruitment methods, and implementation.

PREPARATION

Recruitment begins by carefully identifying the number of new employees and the types of competencies needed, along with clarifying the recruitment objectives. Chapter 2 discussed popular approaches to identifying staffing requirements. These estimates form the basis of all recruitment activities.

In order to make sound recruitment decisions, the HR department has to state the recruitment objectives in clear terms. Recruitment objectives are closely related to the overall HR strategy, philosophy, and tactics (e.g., emphasis on internal versus external recruiting). Therefore, recruitment objectives for each job or organization are different and can be any of the following: filling the position quickly, incurring the least recruitment costs, hiring candidates who will stay with the firm for a long period, hiring exceptionally qualified persons who will need little training and who will bring about major changes in the current practices and culture, hiring persons who have wide experience, or hiring persons who are promotable to a higher position in the near future. Although disagreements on recruitment objectives is sometimes unavoidable, the questions about recruitment objectives must be addressed before the recruitment begins.

> *A Canadian HR Reporter* online poll conducted in 2005 found that too few qualified candidates are being pursued by too many recruiting organizations. Often managers are not clear about what they really want in a candidate. Also, while there is a lot of interest in job analysis, the predictors of job performance were themselves often unclear. The same survey also found that there was a need for more specialized recruitment tactics and greater involvement by departmental managers.[49]

Requisition: a standardized form that identifies all key information about an open job position

Operationally, a requisition triggers the recruitment process. A **requisition** is a standardized form used across the organization that identifies all key information about an open job position and is completed by the hiring manager to whom the new job incumbent will report. A job requisition should contain all relevant job details, including required competencies and skills, knowledge of use of specific equipment or machinery, knowledge of languages, nature of the job (e.g., full time or part time), and "nice-to-have" skills. Typically, a requisition is accompanied by a detailed description of the job and job specifications. If this is not the case, then the requisition form itself should include a space for all job relevant information. Figure 5-6 lists information included in a typical job requisition.

Many companies have differing levels of authority for approving new or replaced positions. The level of approval needed is always indicated on the Requisition Form.

> For example, in a large engineering company, the plant manager is authorized to replace any vacant existing hourly or clerical position without higher approval. But the plant manager must get approval when creating a new hourly or clerical role. The same manager also needs higher approval when replacing a junior management employee.

In unionized workplaces, when new bargaining unit positions are created or when old positions are substantively changed, there may be the need to bargain a new rate or classification.[50] Where a new and different position is replacing an old one, senior HR may want to check whether any affected employees are being constructively dismissed as a result. In some provinces, this is a major concern:

> For example, in Nova Scotia, it is important to determine if the old job is really gone versus being only slightly changed, because the *Labour Standards Code* creates obstacles to the termination of employees with more than 10 years of service, except where the former position is eliminated.

In addition, the required qualifications have to be stated in precise terms since the newly defined position might trigger the recall of a qualified laid-off employee according to a termination agreement. Typically, recall clauses are "threshold" or "sufficient ability" clauses, meaning that the employee who wishes to exercise recall rights needs only to establish that he or she has the minimum requirements for the position. If this level is unacceptable to the company, then the HR staff must carefully design the new position to have a higher "minimum" requirement before the opening is announced.

Note that in many governmental agencies, a special situation exists for approving new hires. The approval process sometimes involves the notion of "complement control," a term possibly carried over from the military (in the post-war years, many senior civil servants were ex-military personnel). *Complement control* requires that the hiring process

---

FIGURE 5-6:   Sample Requisition Form

Ontario Engineering Works
Employee Requisition Form

POSITION TITLE: _____   DEPARTMENT: _____
JOB CODE: ____   REQUISITION NO:___
LOCATION: _____   MANAGER IN CHARGE:_____

CHECK ONE BELOW:
    □ New Position   □ Replacement for_____

If this position is a replacement, state why the employee is being replaced. If it is a new position, please attach detailed justification. [ATTACH EXTRA SHEETS IF NECESSARY]

_____

THIS POSITION REPORTS TO: _____ [Job Title and Name of Current Incumbent]

TYPE OF POSITION: □ Full-time □ Part-time □ Regular □Temporary □On call
            □ Hourly   □ Salaried

Work hours and weeks:_____   Require travel?   □ Yes   □ No   Details:_____
Shift____   Require relocation? □ Yes   □ No   Details:_____

This form MUST be accompanied by a CURRENT job description (Form 52 or 57, depending on the type of position). List below ALL required skills, education, experience, and special needs that do not form part of current job description.

SPECIAL REQUIREMENTS: Indicate any special training, skills (including language skills), driving skills, or other competencies needed. Attach extra sheet if necessary.

Date needed _____
SALARY LEVEL: Grade __ Step__ Justification:_____

Suggested recruitment activities (if any):

REQUESTED BY _____   DATE:
APPROVED BY _____   _____ DATE:
          Name   Designation

HUMAN RESOURCE DEPARTMENT APPROVAL: _____   DATE:_____

BELOW: HR DEPARTMENT USE ONLY

Person hired: _____   Budget Code:
Offer date: _____
Start date: _____

---

fully meets all regulations affecting the permitted complement (or total number of employees) of a department. In the military, complement control makes sense, as generals need to know that the term "battalion" consistently denotes a unit of 840 soldiers with certain specific subunits and certain defined capabilities. In a military context, interchangeability of units is the aim. But in public sector HR, complement control means that despite the need for a person, the availability of right candidate, and the budget to pay the person, hiring cannot begin unless there is an approved vacancy on the organization chart.

After identifying openings, the recruiter reviews the information about the job opening, particularly the job descriptions and specifications (normally attached to the requisition). In some organizations, recruiters must also review additional details relating to the job (e.g., travel requirements) and compensation (e.g., special benefits). If the recruiter notes any outdated or superficial information in the job description, they need to talk to the requesting manager and other relevant personnel before advertising the position.

Once the requisition is approved, the recruiter, in consultation with the hiring manager, identifies a recruitment strategy and action plan. In planning the recruitment strategy, successful recruiters consider additional information, such as nature of organizational environments and its mission, strategy, and culture (see Chapter 1). The recruiter is also constrained by existing employment equity programs (see Chapter 3).

Organizational recruitment policies
Existing human resource policies can constrain the recruiter in the preparation stage. Thus, the recruiter must consider all policies that dealing with uniformity, economies, public relations benefits, and other objectives unrelated to recruiting before making a recruitment plan. Four policies that have implications for recruitment are highlighted below.

Promote-from-within policies: policies that give present employees the first opportunity to apply for job openings in order to facilitate their career growth

1. Promote-from-within policies
Promote-from-within policies are formulated to give present employees the first opportunity to apply for job openings in order to facilitate their career growth. These policies are common, since they are found to improve employee morale, attract recruits looking for jobs with a future, and retain present employees (see Figure 5-7). Although these policies reduce the flow of new people and ideas into the organization, the alternative is to pass over employees in favour of outsiders. Bypassing current employees can lead to employee dissatisfaction and turnover, whereas promoting current employees facilitates the emergence of a positive organizational culture, which, in turn, encourages people to join and stay with a firm.[51]

Paule Chamard, head of the maintenance department in Ontario Waterworks, requested that the human resource department find two new junior engineers. Tom Barrister, a recruiter, reviewed the job's requirements and discovered that it required applicants to have a basic understanding of mechanical engineering concepts but did not require any significant experience. Barrister decided to seek applicants from among the graduating class of a local university. Cathy Thwaites, a technician currently working at Ontario Waterworks who was

FIGURE 5-7: Pros and Cons of Promoting from Within

Pros	Cons
Employees are familiar with the organization and its culture.	No "new blood" is brought into the organization; creative solutions to problems may not emerge.
Recruitment costs are lower.	May perpetuate an existing culture.
Workforce morale and loyalty improves.	Poor morale and possible turnover of employees who were not promoted may result.
Employee is "known" to the management and is unlikely to create major surprises.	Organization may not currently possess some of the competencies needed; simply promoting an existing employee may not add to the total capabilities of the firm.
Less time is needed to "fit into" the job and surroundings.	An employee who is effective at one level may not perform well at the next level. This is especially true when the higher level job requires greater leadership and visionary skills.

studying engineering through an evening program, was disheartened to hear about the external search. She expressed her unhappiness to the HR manager. Barrister was then instructed to search for internal talents before going outside.

2. Employment status policies Some organizations have policies restricting the hiring of part-time and temporary employees. In many unionized settings, existing contractual agreements may limit the use of part-time workers. Although there is a growing managerial interest in hiring part-time and contingent workers, the possibility of poor employee morale and loyalty have acted as a deterrent in some settings (see Figure 5-8). Similarly, existing HR policies against "moonlighting" (i.e., having a second job in spare time) may constrain recruiters. Prohibitions against holding extra jobs are intended to ensure that the full-time workforce is well rested and prevent actions that could lead to a conflict of interest. However, it becomes a deterrent for part-time applicants.

3. Compensation policies Existing compensation policies have to be fully recognized before embarking on recruitment efforts. Organizations with human resource departments usually establish pay ranges for different jobs. Recruiters seldom have the authority to exceed stated pay ranges:

> If Tom Barrister decides to recruit externally, the pay range will influence the job seeker's desire to become a serious applicant. For example, when the market rate for junior engineers is $4000 to $4500 per month, satisfactory applicants will be few if Barrister can offer only $3500 to $3700 per month.

Sometimes, organizations attempt to overcome limitations imposed by their compensation policy by focusing on non-monetary or even intangible rewards.

> A department of an Atlantic Canadian university takes all its potential faculty recruits on a day's car tour of the local scenic areas in an effort to "sell" the location (and through that, the institution). Faced with severe constraints on the compensation package it can offer, the department decided to use its "intangible" assets to assist in its recruitment and selection process.

FIGURE 5-8: Pros and Cons of Using Part-time and Contingent Workers

Pros	Cons
Wage and benefit costs are reduced, since contingent and part-time employees are not typically eligible for benefits.	Part-timers and contract labour typically receive lower salaries and benefits and therefore have lower job satisfaction.
Overhead costs are reduced, especially if the work is done on the contract worker's premises.	Part-time workers may possess fewer skills.
Absenteeism for personal reasons is reduced.	Part-time employees may have less training and work experience.
Part-time employees achieve better work-family balance.	Organizational loyalty is hard to create.
Need for work supervision is reduced, especially for contract labour. Work is evaluated by quality and timeliness of outcomes.	Strong organizational culture is hard to create.

Flextime and high quality of life can be potential selling points for a firm. More recently, several employers have been using non-traditional benefits to attract and retain their employees:

> Some of the newer benefits offered by organizations include fitness centre subsidies, reimbursement of professional membership fees and course fees, on-site vaccination programs, employee mental health insurance, retiree health-care benefits, financial planning assistance, and on-site parking.[52]

Even corporate culture and company values may become major drawing cards in some instances. An organization's ethical standards and values relating to social responsibility may significantly influence the employment decisions of several job applicants. Many job seekers believe that the work they do should not only offer financial rewards but also an opportunity to make a difference.[53] Conveying the organizational initiatives to further societal goals can prove to be a valuable recruiting advantage.

4. International hiring policies For overseas job openings, many countries, including Canada, require that job openings be staffed by local citizens, referred to as **host country nationals (HCN)**. The use of HCN reduces relocation expenses, lessens the likelihood of nationalization, and, if senior-level jobs are held by local citizens, minimizes charges of economic exploitation. Moreover, unlike relocated employees, host-country nationals are more apt to be involved in the local community and understand local customs and business practices.

However, many organizations prefer to staff their foreign operations with **parent company nationals (PCN)** (also referred to as **expatriates**) to ensure that the employee's nationality is the same as the organization's. Such a strategy is often employed to ensure better communication and tighter control over the subsidiary. But there are also organizations which hire **third country nationals (TCN)** where the employee's nationality is neither that of the organization nor that of the location of the subsidiary. For example, a Canadian working for a French company in Zambia would be a TCN. The benefits of different strategies are shown in Figure 5-9.

Organizations differ in their approaches to managing and staffing foreign operations. In an **ethnocentric organization**, the home country approach prevails. Headquarters makes key decisions, and employees from the home country (PCNs) hold important jobs. On the other hand, in a **polycentric organization**, the foreign

Host country nationals (HCN): local citizens

Parent company nationals (PCN) or **expatriates:** employees of the same nationality as the parent organization

Third country nationals (TCN): employees of a nationality that is neither that of the organization nor that of the location of the subsidiary

Ethnocentric organization: company headquarters makes key decisions and employees from the home country hold important jobs

FIGURE 5-9:   Benefits of Alternate Recruiting Sources for Global Operations

Expatriates (PCNs)	Host Country Nationals (HCNs)	Third Country Nationals (TCNs)
Greater control over human resource movements and planning	Knowledge of local customs and language	May know a number of languages and cultures
Familiarity with company culture and practices	Typically far less expensive than expatriates	Most likely to have an international outlook
Provides valuable overseas experience to the workforce	Preferred by host country governments	Can help the firm to enter other foreign markets
Can be an integral part of career development for employees	Helps generate positive public image in the host country	May blend more easily with host country culture
Can take advantage of overseas learning for future occasions	Avoids problems of transfers of personnel	Typically less expensive than expatriates but more expensive than HCNs
	Eliminates some administrative hassles, such as visa applications and immigration clearance	

subsidiary is allowed to manage on a local basis, and typically, a local employee (HCN) heads the operation, while PCNs generally manage headquarters operations. Despite their cultural differences, almost all foreign operations have to adapt their recruitment and selection procedures to suit the local culture:

> In international manufacturing and processing facilities in Mexico, known as *maquiladoras*, companies recruit with a sign announcing job openings outside the facility or by employees introducing family members who are seeking employment.[54]

Polycentric organization: foreign subsidiaries manage on a local basis and a local employee (HCN) often heads the operation

Recruiter habits

Recruiter habits A recruiter's past success can lead to habits, which can positively or adversely affect later recruitment processes. Admittedly, habits can eliminate time-consuming deliberations that reach the same answers. However, recruiter habits may also perpetuate past mistakes or obscure more effective alternatives. So although recruiters need positive and negative feedback, they must guard against self-imposed constraints.

> Consider again the recruitment of the junior engineer at Ontario Waterworks. Suppose that the engineering department has expressed satisfaction with recruits from the nearby university. Such positive feedback encourages Barrister to make a habit of using this source for beginning engineers. But since all these engineers have a similar curriculum, they may also share the same strengths and weaknesses. As a result, the engineering department may suffer because of the educational uniformity of new recruits.

CHOICE OF RECRUITMENT METHODS

Organizations must first decide who will do the recruiting. Since large organizations recruit almost continuously, their human resource departments use specialists called recruiters. In smaller organizations, HR staff and managers take responsibility for recruitment activity on a need-to basis.

The job's requirements influence the recruiter's methods of finding satisfactory applicants. Typically, recruiters use more than one recruitment method to find suitable candidates for vacant job positions. While the typical recruitment methods include campus visits, advertisements, and contacts with professional and government agencies, sometimes, to attract high-quality applicants, a recruiter may have to use unconventional procedures, as the following example shows:

> To increase the number of staff from visible minorities, one Canadian hospital first used traditional recruiting methods, including advertising in the newspapers and local magazines, visiting campuses of educational institutions, and offering rewards to present employees for referrals. But despite spending a large sum of money, the organization was not able to attract many applicants from minority communities. Finally, on the advice of a professor of human resource management, the recruiter put ads in buses in areas where most of the new immigrants and visible minorities lived. They also rented booths at events organized by minority groups. Within three months, the number of applications from visible minorities had increased by a whopping 700%! The cost of new recruitment methods? A small fraction of the money earlier spent on advertisements and campus recruitment efforts!

Or consider the following strategy used by Ottawa Police Service:

> Faced with the reality that 100% of its senior ranks officers would retire in the next ten years, Ottawa Police Service (OPS) had to devise a recruitment strategy to fill those vacancies. To complicate matters, 65% of the sworn officers had less than five years' experience. This meant that a large pool of qualified and experienced officers was needed at the lower levels to fill the gaps in senior ranks as they emerged. Rather than ramping up a recruitment drive to draw police candidates from across the country, the OPS opted for an unusual, almost counter-intuitive solution: recruit from immigrant communities which had traditionally

shown little interest in policing. To reach out to these groups, the OPS had to examine how it is perceived as an employer and launched a process of community consultation. Nine focus groups of officers and civilian staff including women, visible minorities, gay, lesbian, bisexual and transgender people were conducted to identify possible obstacles to recruiting from the community so that they could be elimintated.[55]

Recruitment is far more than just getting people to apply for jobs, and success in recruitment is not simply measured by the number of applications received. The right type of applicants is far more important than the number of applicants. This means that the recruitment method has to be chosen after great care. Popular recruitment methods are briefly discussed below.

Job posting

Job posting refers to the practice of an organization advertising job openings internally through newsletters, bulletin boards, or computer systems. Job posting is particularly appropriate and common for blue-collar and clerical positions.[56] It helps employees further their own careers by applying for lateral transfers and promotions. Moreover, it helps the organization discover hidden talent. Current employees may also pass on the information to their own friends and relatives, thus increasing the size of recruit pool.

Job posting is the least expensive recruiting approach because no additional investments in advertising or equipment are needed. But despite these advantages, this approach is not suitable for many jobs, especially highly technical or senior managerial jobs, where the organization may want to go beyond existing resources.

Relying on job postings has several disadvantages. First, hiring from within perpetuates the existing culture. Second, unsuccessful applicants may become demoralized or resentful, creating new problems for the organization. In addition, job posting can also set off a chain reaction of personnel moves within an organization, creating uncertainty, considerable paperwork, and an ongoing need for recruitment. For these reasons, some employers require employees to have worked in a position for at least six months before they become eligible to apply for a new position. Some researchers[57] have also recommended that only employees with at least a satisfactory rating level in their most recent performance appraisal should be allowed to apply.

Walk-ins and write-ins

Walk-ins are job seekers who arrive at the human resource department in search of a job. **Write-ins** are those who send a written inquiry about possible job openings. With the emergence of the Internet, applicants often research companies using websites and apply online. Indeed, many human resource managers prefer to receive resumes by email because of the ease of storage and retrieval.[58] Whatever the format used, in most cases, the applicant is asked to complete an application form describing his or her training, experience, interests, and skills. Suitable applications are kept in an active file until an appropriate opening occurs or until the application is too old to be considered valid—usually six months. Larger firms transfer this information to their overall human resource information systems. Using scanners, recruiters can store résumés on databases for fast, easy access using a few key words:

> Many large employers, like MCI Telecommunications and Disneyland Resorts, use computer scanning to take advantage of the large number of applications they receive. Resumes are scanned into a computer database and later searched using key words or criteria. If the number of resumes retrieved is too large or too small, the recruiter can change the required qualifications. Once the program finds a manageable number of applicants, the recruiter begins to review the resumes.[59]

A sample resume is shown in Figure 5-10.

Job posting: advertising job openings internally through newsletters, bulletin boards, or computer systems

Walk-ins: job seekers who arrive at the human resource department in search of a job

Write-ins: job seekers who send a written inquiry about possible job openings

FIGURE 5-10: A Sample Resume by a Job Applicant

Daniel Hiller

2657 Pine Ave.
Ottawa, ON K0A 2T4
(Home) 613-555-5555 (Other) 613-666-6666
Email: danielhiller@domain.com
URL: www.danielhiller.com

Career Objective

To use my artistic and interpersonal skills to create inspired designs that will exceed each client's expectation.

Education

Multimedia Certificate Northwest College of Art Ottawa, Ontario, Canada	**March 2001**
Bachelor's Degree - Applied Art Diploma Northwest College of Art Toronto, Ontario, Canada	**June 1996**

Work Experience

The Children's Safe Environment Council	**2001–Present**

- Assisted in maintenance of website
- Updated the program's student placement contact list
- Produced showcase "Victims of Violence"
- Designed, illustrated, wrote colouring book "12 Basic Rules of Safety for Children"

Film, Television, and Theatre	**1991–1995**

Created, developed, improvised, and performed a variety of roles in numerous productions.

Professional Qualifications

I am registered with the Ontario Board of Registered Web Designers.

Skills

- Quark XPress 3.31, 3.32, and 4
- Adobe Illustrator 6.0 and 7.0
- Adobe Photoshop 4.0.1 and 5.0
- Microsoft Word
- Director 6.5
- Acrobat Reader

Interests

- Acting and producing plays
- Participating in a hockey league
- Reading science fiction

Achievements

Best Supporting Role - 1994
The Impostor - from Joel Smith.

References

Upon request.

Source: Human Resources and Skills Development Canada. **https://www.jobsetc.ca/toolbox/resume_builder/normal/layout.sjsp?parentUserDatumId=1&lang=e.** Reproduced with the permission of Her Majesty the Queen in Right of Canada 2006.

Employee referrals

A popular recruiting method is employee referrals. In **employee referrals,** current employees refer job seekers to the human resource department. Although employee referral programs can take different forms, they are generally seen as an inexpensive way to get high quality, long-tenure employees. Employee referrals have several unique advantages. First, employees with hard-to-find job skills may know others who do the same work.

> For example, faced with an acute shortage of information technologists in some geographical areas, several high-tech firms requested their present employees to recommend professional colleagues and classmates for job openings in the firm. Similar strategies have been popular to attract potential employees in other fields, such as nursing, university teaching, and medical technology.

Second, new recruits already know something about the organization from those employees who referred them. Thus, referred applicants may be more strongly attracted to the organization than other recruits. Third, this approach brings the vacancy to the attention of individuals who are not necessarily actively looking for a job. Finally, employees tend to refer friends they identified through personal networking. These people are likely to have similar work habits and work attitudes. Even if work values are different, these candidates may have a strong desire to work hard so that they do not let down the person who recommended them:

> In the past, at some locations, McDonald's paid a referral bonus to current employees who recommended qualified candidates.[60]

While employee referrals have several strengths, recruiters must be careful that this method does not intentionally or unintentionally discriminate. The major problem with this recruiting method is that it tends to maintain the demographic characteristics (especially, racial, religious, gender profiles) of the organization's workforce, because people tend to befriend and recommend people who resemble them.

Job fairs

Job fairs have been used to recruit specialized and scarce talents. They allow for a two-way exchange of information between the recruiter and the recruit. Typically, **job fairs** are held at a large hotel or convention centre in a major metropolitan area and involve the participation of several employers. The company rents a recruiting booth to meet with and offer job information to potential recruits. Recently, many successful job fairs have been held in Ontario and other provinces:

> The Job Fair organized by the University of Waterloo, Wilfrid Laurier University, Conestoga College, and University of Guelph has tripled in size of attendees since it was first organized in 1994. In recent years, the event attracted some 200 companies and 2500 to 3000 students, making it the largest job fair in Canada. Over 10 000 visitors were estimated to have attended the event.[61]

Job fairs are more expensive than other recruitment methods. However, attending job fairs can pay rich dividends to recruiters who need to hire specialized talent or a large number of new employees.

Open houses

During an **open house,** potential employees living in the community are invited to visit the organization and talk about potential job openings and careers. Typically, light refreshments are served. In some cases, visitors may also be given a tour of the work place and offered an opportunity to meet with several employees.

For an open house to be successful, an organization must make sure that its target audience is aware of the event and is motivated to attend. Because of the speed of information technology, many recruits prefer to get preliminary information from the company website, rather than taking the time to go and visit an employer in person. However, for some organizations and jobs, an open house may be a potential solution:

> A fire department regularly holds open houses to attract new full-time employees and volunteer firefighters. In preparation for the event, the organization widely publicizes the open house to a number of community organizations, as well as making announcements in radio and local television channels.

Temporary-help agencies Most cities have temporary-help agencies that can respond quickly to an employer's need. Temporary agencies, as the name indicates, do not provide recruits; rather, they are a source of supplemental workers. The temporary workers actually work for the agency and are only "on loan" to the requesting employer. For temporary jobs—during vacations, peak seasons, and illnesses—these agencies can be a better alternative than recruiting new workers for short periods of employment. These agencies can often provide clerical and secretarial talent on short notice. Since the "temps" work for the agency and not the employer, when the need no longer exists, there is no need to lay them off.[62] But occasionally, an organization recruits temps as permanent employees.

Private employment agencies A private employment agency takes an employer's request for recruits and then matches it with its pool of job seekers, identified usually through advertising or walk-ins. Candidates are then told to report to the employer's human resource department to apply for the job. Some placement services carefully screen applicants for their client; others simply provide a stream of applicants and let the client's human resource department do most of the screening.

Private employment agencies may be particularly useful when an employer needs only a few new hires, especially if it's on a temporary or irregular basis. Also, when the employer has a critical need to fill a position quickly, employment agencies can be very useful. Private employment agencies can identify part-time workers more cost-effectively, especially if the employer is new to the local labour market.

The fees for this service commonly equal either 10% of the first year's salary or one month's wages. This fee can vary, depending on the volume of business from that organization. Most employment agency fees are paid by the employers. In many provinces, it is either illegal for private employment agencies to charge applicants a fee for placement, or the fees charged are regulated.

Private employment agency: takes an employer's request for recruits and then matches it with its pool of job seekers

Professional search firms Professional search firms are much more specialized than private employment agencies and usually recruit only specific types of human resources for a fee paid by the employer. For example, some search firms specialize in recruiting executives, while others focus on technical and scientific personnel. Also, while employment agencies hope to attract applicants through advertising, search firms actively seek out recruits from among the employees of other companies. Although they may advertise, the telephone is their primary tool for locating and attracting prospective recruits:

Professional search firms: specialized firms that recruit specific types of human resources for a fee

> Ontario Engineering Company needed a research scientist for its development division. After three months of unsuccessful recruiting efforts, the human resource manager hired a search firm. The search firm reviewed the in-house phone directories of competing firms and telephoned a junior scientist currently working in a similar firm in Vancouver. During the phone call, the scientist was encouraged to send in an application. Within three weeks, Ontario Engineering Company had a new hire.

Search firms have an in-depth recruiting experience that many human resource departments lack. Search firms are also willing to undertake actions that an employer would not do, such as calling a competitor. For this reason, they are sometimes referred to as "headhunters."[63] In the past few years, the number of executive recruiting firms in Canada has grown rapidly. While most of them are located in large metropolitan cities such as Toronto, Montreal, or Vancouver, an increasing number of these firms are making an appearance in smaller cities and towns.

When choosing a search firm, HR managers must take care to test the "fit" between the firm and the client organization. Some search firms, especially the smaller ones, are often highly specialized and may not be able to meet your organization's needs. Consequently, checking the recruiting record of the firm and its reputation is very important. In addition, check the fees. Larger firms can be quite expensive, often charging 30% of the candidate's gross starting salary as fees (not inclusive of other expenses).[64]

Despite the expense, many human resource departments view executive search firms as a regular part of their operations.[65] *Retainer search firms*—those that work on fee-paid assignments—are more popular among HR managers than are *contingency search firms*—those that receive a fee only if an employer hires the candidate suggested by the search firm. Contingency search firms are more aggressive and, because of their fee structure, at times they can be tempted to fill a position at any cost—even if the fit between the job and applicant is less than optimal.[66]

Educational institutions For entry-level openings, educational institutions are a good source of recruits. Counsellors, teachers, and university professors often provide recruiters with leads to desirable candidates. Many colleges and virtually all universities have placement assistance programs for current students. Thus, recruiters can use placement centres as a place to meet with potential recruits.

Studies indicate that students want campus recruiters to be well informed, honest, and skilled at communication.

> A 2004 survey of 20 000 Canadian college and university students show that today's students value opportunities for advancement and training and quality of colleagues over job security or initial salary (see Figure 5-11).[67]

Choosing the right person to recruit at a university is important. The job position and age of the recruiter may be important factors in creating a favourable impression on recruits,[68] if both suggest that the recruiter is in a position to influence hiring. In addition,

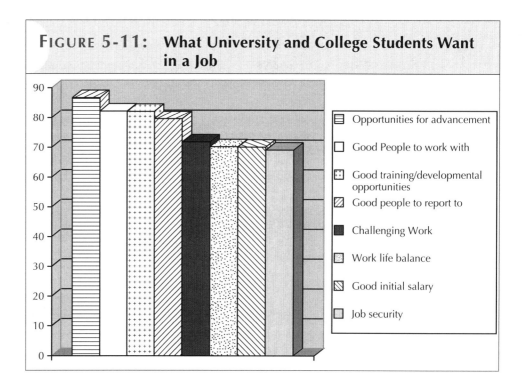

FIGURE 5-11:   **What University and College Students Want in a Job**

Legend:
- Opportunities for advancement
- Good People to work with
- Good training/developmental opportunities
- Good people to report to
- Challenging Work
- Work life balance
- Good initial salary
- Job security

the recruiter must also be able to plan and manage time and conduct valid interviews. A recruiter who wastes staff time to interview poorly qualified applicants, who is unable to weed out applicants who lack relevant experience, or who doesn't screen applicants during interview can end up selecting the wrong candidates. A person who can focus on the actual job duties and performance requirements is the best choice for avoiding these problems.[69]

Summer internships and co-op students

Many organizations find that summer internships significantly facilitate college and university recruitment efforts.

> These summer internships are more popular in large companies, such as Procter & Gamble and Aetna Life Insurance. However, even smaller organizations find that hiring students to complete summer projects helps them to identify qualified, motivated, and informed recruits.

Supervisors can evaluate summer students based on their success in completing their tasks. These interns are also exposed to the organization so that they have a clear idea of what to expect from the firm when they later join as full-time employees. Such "informed" recruits are less likely to leave the firm soon after they are hired.

In recent years, cooperative education has been gaining wide popularity in Canada. Under the co-op education program, students alternate study and work terms. Their work terms expose them to the realities of the work world. This also provides an excellent opportunity for the employer to assess the potential employee's ability and attitudes without incurring any significant costs.[70]

Professional associations

Often, professional associations can be a good source of job seekers. Many associations conduct placement activities to help both new and experienced professionals find jobs. Some have publications that accept classified advertisements. Professionals who belong to the appropriate associations are considered more likely to remain informed of the latest developments in their field, and so this channel of recruitment may lead to higher-quality applicants. Another advantage of this source of applicants is that it helps recruiters zero in on specialties, particularly in hard-to-fill technical areas.

> For example, many provincial human resource associations have been involved in matching employers with prospective candidates. Students who become members of these associations also get to meet practitioners, thus increasing their chances of finding a job in the human resource management field on graduation.

Advertising

Advertising can be classified into two broad groups: image advertising and job advertising. **Image advertising** refers to a firm's media events to make itself more visible to prospective employees and to create or improve own image in the minds of public. While at times image advertising focuses on filling immediate job vacancies, the primary goal is to improve organizational image and future recruitment capabilities. Image advertising can be particularly important if an organization is new, is in a highly competitive job market, or is trying to change its public image.

Image advertising: a firm's media events to make itself more visible to prospective employees and to create or improve its image in the minds of public

> In the early 1980s, Dow Chemical Company had to struggle with its public image as a "tough, arrogant, secretive, uncooperative, and insensitive" organization.[71] Unhappy with its public image, Dow made several changes, including pulling out of then-apartheid South Africa. A major strategy employed by the company to change public perception was a $60 million image advertising campaign, "Dow Lets You Do Great Things," in print and TV media. Dow also held open houses during this period. Only a few months after the ad campaign, public rating of the company had improved by six percentage points.[72]

Job advertisements, also called **want ads**, are typically posted in newspaper and trade and professional magazines. Job ads describe the job and its benefits, working conditions, and career potential, and provide information about the application procedure. Ads are an

Job advertisements or **want ads:** ads, often in a relevant newspaper or magazine, describing a job opening and application procedures

effective recruitment method because of their ability to reach a wide audience. For highly specialized recruits, ads may be placed in national or even international newspapers and professional journals.

> For example, recruiters in finance often advertise in Vancouver, Toronto, and Montreal newspapers because these cities are major banking centres. For recruiting highly qualified scientists and academic personnel, international advertising is common.

But want ads have some drawbacks. They may result in responses from thousands of job seekers, causing administrative challenges. Moreover, the ideal recruits are often already employed and are thus not even reading want ads. To avoid some of these problems, organizations use *blind ads*, which do not identify the employer. Blind ads direct applicants to send their resume to a postal box number. These ads allow the job opening to remain confidential, prevent countless telephone inquiries, and avoid the public relations problem of disappointed recruits.

Recruitment advertisements should be written from the viewpoint of the applicants and should thus reflect their motivations. Since the cost of most classified advertising is determined by the size of the advertisement, short blurbs briefly describing the job duties and minimum job qualifications are the norm. However, such traditional advertisements may be insufficient, particularly when recruiting people with hard-to-find skills or when labour markets are tight. Want ads must contain not only information about the job but also all relevant details of the job, the work setting, career potential and overall culture of the firm. The layout and design should be consistent with the message and reflect the image and character of the company and departments that are being represented.[73] Figure 5-12 lists some tips about designing want ads.

FIGURE 5-12:   Dos and Don'ts of Want Ads

DO:

- Understand your audience and use language they find comfortable.
- Include all relevant information about the job and the firm:
    - job title
    - job description
    - training offered
    - required qualifications, experience, competencies
    - career growth possibilities
    - location of the job
    - travel or other special requirements
    - salary, benefits, and other incentives
    - organizational strengths
- Sequence the content logically.
- Use an engaging style.
- Ensure that the ad stands out by using appropriate visual tension, balance, and colour contrast.
- Promote a favourable corporate image.

DON'T:

- Use jargon or language unfamiliar to the target audience.
- Use sexist, racist, or otherwise offensive language or terms.
- Violate any of the provisions of human rights legislation or other laws.
- Write copy longer than what is needed.
- Boast or make unsubstantiated claims.

Billboards and other media advertisements

Advertisements for recruits through other media—for example, billboards, television, and radio—are not very popular since the results rarely justify the expense. However, these approaches may be useful when unemployment is low and the target recruits are not likely to read want ads.

Because most readers travel by car, the amount of information that can be conveyed on a billboard is limited. Another limitation to this approach is that signs generally require considerable time to prepare. The decision to use a billboard is primarily driven by the type of job involved and the cost. However, if the job is one for which the firm is continuously recruiting, it may be worthwhile to have a billboard in visible locations.[74]

Transit advertising

Transit advertising involves placing posters in buses, commuter trains, and subway stations. Generally, these ads are only used by employers who have difficulty filling positions using traditional methods. Transit job advertising is relatively inexpensive. If it is placed in a specific geographic location (such as a particular bus stop), it allows an organization to target its advertising to a specific demographic or even ethnic group. If placed in a bus or train, a job advertisement can be seen by thousands of persons each week (or even day). In order to make it easy to respond, the organization should attach coupons that can be torn off, completed, and mailed.

Transit advertising: placing posters in buses, commuter trains, and subway stations

> One major Canadian hospital was able to attract a large number of applications from graduating nursing students by placing ads in buses serving major educational institutions. In another instance, a major U.S. airline was able to attract large number of minority applicants by placing ads along mass transit routes in immigrant neighbourhoods.[75]

Focus on Ethics

Recruitment activity includes situations that generate ethical dilemmas. Consider the following two situations and determine whether they are ethical. Rate them on a scale, from very unethical, somewhat unethical, unsure, to somewhat ethical or very ethical. Provide arguments for your position using the schema discussed in Chapter 1.

Upon graduation, you were hired as an assistant to a human resource manager in a medium-sized manufacturing firm in central Canada. Recently, your supervisor asked you to take care of all recruiting for the next few months. You have been doing a good job so far, and your supervisor is quite pleased with your work. But two situations have created major challenge for you:

1. One of your assembly units is located in a remote part of the country where it is hard to find employees locally. The unit requires three technical personnel urgently. No experience is required since the company will train the person for three months before sending him or her to the job location. You have visited a couple of technical colleges to do on-campus recruiting; however, when they are told of the location, most students show no further interest in the job. Recently, you were enjoying a beer with an old classmate who has since become a HR manager in another large company. After the preliminaries, you raised this problem to your friend and sought his advice. Your friend responded: "I don't see what the big problem is. You said that the recruit has to undergo three months training. Just tell him that you are looking for 'trainees' and that the job is transferable. Don't give all the details of the job location until the training is more or less over. Once the person has been with you for three months, it will be a lot easier to make him do what you want, since nobody wants to lose a job. Right?"

2. Your firm has been attempting to increase diversity in its workforce by hiring people belonging to different minority groups. Your success has been mixed. While many managers and supervisors to whom you talked are generally happy, you have been hearing a number of complaints from others about recruits from a particular minority community. According to your informants, these employees have consistently been "trouble makers," getting into loud arguments, verbal abuse, and even fistfights. Many of them were said to bring food that "stinks up the place," and they "dirty up washrooms by spilling water all over." During your meeting with your HR friend, you mentioned this problem. After listening to you, your friend commented: "Simple! You know that the members of this community can be identified from their names. Well, next time when applications come in, don't pass any of them to the managers. What is not known is not missed."

Human Resources and Social
Development:
www.hrsdc.gc.ca

Human Resources and Social Development
Human Resources and Social Development (HRSD) has over 300 service outlets and offers a variety of programs to employers and job applicants, including a job bank, electronic labour exchange, labour market information, and information about foreign workers. Some of the more useful tools for employers are listed below.

The Job Bank HRSD provides a comprehensive database of thousands of jobs and work opportunities available across Canada. When an employer has a job opening, the human resource department voluntarily notifies HRSD about the job and its requirements. Typically, the job opening information is then posted at HRSD's regional office(s) and Human Resource Centres. Here prospective employees can scan the job openings and discuss any vacancy with one of the counsellors available. The potential applicant can also look for jobs posted in the last 48 hours. There is also a separate section for jobs for students. Over 40 000 employers use the HRSD Internet site to advertise full-time, part-time, and summer job opportunities.[76]

Job Bank:
www.jobbank.gc.ca

Electronic Labour Exchange The Electronic Labour Exchange (ELE) is a computer-based recruitment tool that can match employer profiles with job seeker profiles. It relies on standard occupation checklists, with categories such as education, experience, and skills. The ELE uses information entered in the profile to automatically match job seekers to employers who are looking for candidates with the suitable skills for the job.

HRSD Electronic Labour
Exchange:
*http://srv601.hrdc-drhc.gc.ca/
JobMatching/common/
login.aspx
www.employers.jobbank.gc.ca/
common/login.asp?
LanguageCode=E*

Canada Work Infomation This bilingual directory provides fast and efficient links to information on jobs and recruiting, self-employment, workplace issues and supports, employment trends, and many occupations and careers. It covers topics such as resume writing, interview techniques, potential employment opportunities, and starting one's own business.

Job Futures The Job Futures website of HRSD offers information on the current and future demand for various occupations and job groupings.[77]

In summary, HRSD provides a virtually no-cost and effective recruitment source for employers. Most job vacancies posted in the HRSD are for white-collar, blue-collar, or technical employees, rather than managerial and professional persons.

HRSD Job Futures:
*www.jobfutures.ca/en/
home.shtml*

Labour organizations
When recruiters want people with trade skills, local labour organizations have rosters of those people who are looking for employment. For example, the local union of electricians keeps a list of electricians seeking jobs. A union hiring hall is a convenient channel for attracting large numbers of well-trained recruits for new projects.

Canadian Labour Congress:
www.clc-ctc.ca

Armed forces
Trained personnel leave the armed forces every day. Some veterans, such as those who have been trained as mechanics, welders, or pilots, have hard-to-find skills.

> For example, many technicians who maintain commercial jet airliners were first trained in the military.

Departing employees
Some of an organization's departing employees might gladly stay if they could rearrange their schedules or change the number of hours worked. Family responsibilities, health conditions, or other circumstances may lead a worker to quit when a transfer to a part-time job could retain valuable skills and training. Even if part-time work is not a solution, a temporary leave of absence may satisfy the employee and some future recruiting need of the employer. Sometimes, buy-backs are also worth looking. A *buy-back* occurs when an employee resigns to take another

job and the original employer outbids the new job offer. Buy-backs are not without problems, however. Offering a higher salary to some employees may result in others expecting similar raises. Employees may also reject a buy-back attempt because of the ethical issue raised by not reporting to jobs that they have already accepted.

Retired employees Mandatory retirement is becoming obsolete, and the average retirement age is rising in Canada. Despite this trend, there are large numbers of retirees willing to re-enter the workforce if the terms of employment and human resource policies are right. Too often, employers hold prejudices against and stereotypes about older workers, assuming them to be more expensive, lacking in fresh skills, and less adaptable and technologically savvy.[78] Such myths prevent employers from taking advantage of skilled workforce available.

The Internet The Internet is becoming a dominant recruiting tool due to a variety of reasons:

- The Internet is accessible 24 hours a day, seven days a week—without the limitations of a public library, an employment office, or even a newspaper ad. A recruit can access the Internet without even leaving the house.

- The Internet broadens the recruitment area to over a hundred countries without significantly increasing recruiting costs.

- By specifying the exact skills and competencies needed, Internet postings minimize the time needed to weed out unsuitable job candidates. Indeed, the applicants themselves may decide not to apply for unsuitable positions based on the information supplied.

- Internet postings enable the firm to identify a number of recruits faster.

- Internet postings are relatively inexpensive. Compared to the commissions paid to an executive search firm or the travel expenses of a campus recruiter, the cost of putting an ad on the Internet is minimal.

  By recruiting over the Internet, one company reported savings of $70 000 a day in paper costs related to recruiting, apart from $73 000 in annual savings in employee forms.[79]

More than 10% of American companies are already hiring a majority of their employees through the Internet.[80] Moreover, 88% of American HR professionals use Internet postings to find the right candidates, and 96% of American job seekers access online websites.[81] New recruitment software permits the recruiter to store, classify, and share resumes and other information in digital format, thus increasing the speed and overall value of information.[82]

Despite these advantages, much of Internet recruiting to date has focused on technical and information technology-related jobs and has been restricted to large organizations in IT industries. A large majority of Canadians—in some regions as high as 95%—still do not regularly use the Internet,[83] thus limiting its current recruitment effectiveness. However, Internet use is expected only to increase in the future.

To maximize the effectiveness of an Internet recruitment initiative, HR professionals should use the strategies shown in Figure 5-13.

Applicant tracking systems Some organizations have installed **applicant tracking systems (ATS)** that help store a large electronic file (or several inter-connected files) of all relevant attributes of potential candidates which can be readily accessed by key word search. Such systems not only broaden the recruitment pool but also improve the chances of a good match between the job requirements and applicant skills, thereby reducing the time and overall recruitment costs.[84]

Applicant tracking systems (ATS): a database of potential recruits that can match job requirements with applicant characteristics using key word searches and high-speed computers

> ## FIGURE 5-13:   Actions that Maximize Results from Internet Recruiting Efforts
>
> - Design the corporate webpage carefully[*] so that it conveys not only the recruiting message but also the overall culture and public image of the company.
> - Make your postings attractive. Online job postings should be visually exciting and interactive, as well as exhaustive. Since the website has to compete for attention, it is important that the website is eye-catching and easy to use.
> - Publish your web address on all public documents, including public relations notices and all other corporate communication devices.
> - Consider unconventional recruiting outlets, such as minority language newspapers, and include your website address in your ad.[#]
> - Make sure that the site is linked to all popular search engines, such as Yahoo and Google.
> - Ensure that the ad contains all key words likely to be used by recruits on search engines.[†]
> - List your ads on all major job bank and Internet recruiting sites, including the HRDC site. Allow career sites to send applicants to you,[‡] such as *www.workopolis.com, www.monsterboard.com, www.recruitersonline.com,* and *www.brassring.ca.*
> - Post the recruiting ads on Internet newsgroups. Virtually all are free. Since the newsgroups continuously update materials, you will need to re-insert your ad periodically. This also gives you an opportunity to revise the ad. Some of the popular newsgroups are "can.jobs," "ont.jobs," and "tor.jobs."
> - Target the recruiting websites in the province or territory (a) where you expect many of the recruits live or study, and (b) where the final job will be.
> - If national-level recruiting does not produce a satisfactory response, consider international recruiting. For New Zealand, go to *www.iconrec.co.nz.* For the U.K., go to *www.topjobs.co.uk.* For E-countries, go to *www.ecountries.com*
> - Use specialized websites aimed at different kinds of personnel. By advertising on specialized websites, you are likely to target specific markets.
>   For teachers: *www.recruitingteachers.org*
>   For fire and police personnel: *www.ifpra.com*
>   For engineers: *www.engineeringjobs.org*
>   For information technology personnel: *www.jobserve.com*
>
> Some of the other interesting websites with recruitment potential are Headhunter.net *(www.headhunter.net),* Career Magazine *(www.careermag.com),* and JobTrak *(www.jobtrak.com).*[§]

[*]Al Doran. (1997, Sept. 8). "The Site Is Up: Now How Do You Attract Job-Seekers?" *Canadian HR Reporter,* p. 9.
[#]Al Doran. (1997), op. cit.
[†]Gabriel Bouchard. (1998, Jan. 12). "A Panoply of Web Recruiting Ideas." *Canadian HR Reporter,* p. 4.
[‡]Debbie McGrath. (1997, Oct. 6). "Is Your Internet Recruiting Strategy Sending Qualified Candidates to Your Competitors?" *Canadian HR Reporter* (Guide to HR Technology), pp. G22-G23.
[§]Richard Nelson Bolles. (1997). *Job Hunting on the Internet.* Berkeley: Ten Speed Press.

When a manager submits a requisition for an opening, the recruiter simply matches the key requirements of the job with applicant characteristics. Thus, job requirements such as "needs significant accounting experience" and "should know Spanish" can immediately be matched with applicant characteristics.[85]

Several companies have found ATS highly beneficial. Consider this:

For one company, rapid growth and managing processes across 23 countries had meant that a paper-based staffing process was not meeting its needs in a timely and effective fashion. Hiring managers, recruiters, and HR staff were faxing, emailing, and literally hand-delivering resumes and offer letters. A new HR manager put the organization on a web-based ATS. By signing up on the new ATS, the company had 125 new employees up and running in 30 days![86]

Contingent, contract, and leased workers Contingent workers are useful when the work is of limited duration, so the firm can avoid fixed salary commitments. Employee leasing is a term used to reflect the hiring of employees for longer periods of time than contingent workers. These employees include the self-employed, temporary, or leased employees (those who work for an agency that has trained them and supplies these employees on a need basis), and independent contractors.[87] One reason leasing is popular is the cost. The employer pays a flat fee for the employees (and is not responsible for benefits). Contract and self-employed workers are often compensated on the basis of task completion and hence need less supervision. Often, they also require lower training costs.

A very large segment of the Canadian labour market is composed of contract workers. In many organizations, the proportion of the staff on contract is 7–10%. Information systems personnel are most likely to be on contract. Administration, finance, engineering, legal, and technical positions also use contract staff to some extent.[88]

Note that contract and leased employees may not always be committed to the goals and philosophy of the organization. In addition, because contingent employees are not part of an organization's regular workforce, they do not benefit from the statutory protections offered by various provincial employment laws.[89]

Alumni associations Another source of experienced employees is alumni associations of schools, colleges, and institutes.[90] These are particularly useful for hiring technical staff.

Direct mail solicitations Drawing upon marketing strategies, some firms have attempted direct mail recruiting with some success. This strategy allows an organization to target a specific segment of the population or a geographical area (using postal codes).

Some firms use door hangers, bargain shopper price lists, welcome wagons, and point-of-sale messages as their recruiting media as well.

Recruitment abroad More recently, several Canadian employers have looked abroad for securing skilled, hard-to-find employees.

Many high-tech and software companies today look to India as a major source of highly skilled programmers. Some of the software manufacturers have gone as far as locating their operations in Indian cities such as Bangalore and Chennai, while others have formed partnerships with Indian firms that periodically send staff to North America on a contract basis.

In recent years, Canada has been recruiting a large number of skilled workers from other countries. Foreign workers, especially from developing countries, may be less expensive in some instances than local professionals. With an aging domestic workforce and a predicted shortage of technical and highly skilled employees, foreign nationals may become an important source of our work force. However, relocation expenses to be paid can significantly add to the total cost in some instances. Firms hiring from abroad will need to train new recruits to adapt to local and organizational culture. The process of getting employment visas may also be time-consuming.

Information on hiring foreign workers:
www.hrsdc.gc.ca/asp/ gateway.asp?hr=en/epb/lmd/ fw/tempoffers.shtml&hs=hze

IMPLEMENTATION

Given the large number of choices available to the recruiter, which recruiting method should be used? In order to answer this question, the organization's recruitment objectives first must be clearly stated. Is the employer interested in filling the position quickly? Minimizing recruitment costs? Bringing more minorities into the workforce? Hiring individuals who will perform exceptionally well even without any training? Or who stay with the organization for at least a year? Or who will be satisfied with the position? As may be readily apparent, not all these objectives are mutually compatible. This means that it does not make much sense to think of one "best" recruitment method. Rather, in determining what method to use, employers must consider all job-related factors and their own resource constraints.

Once the organization has identified the recruitment method(s), it needs to implement these methods with speed and efficiency. For this reason, it must devise a proper system for managing applicants. It also has to draw up recruitment budgets and prepare schedules for campus visits or open houses and travel plans for the recruiter and the job applicants identified.

> "Hire for fit, train for skills," advises Sameera Sereda, a recruiting specialist in Calgary. According to Sereda, many recruiters simply focus on skills instead of on the fit with the company and its culture and goals. This also means that the recruiter has to go beyond likes and dislikes. "Most people are attracted to people like themselves ... but it does not mean that they're the best person," adds Sereda.[91] Other recruitment experts[92] advise companies to try not to focus too much on a wish list for each job; to look beyond job boards and use network and referrals; to have a sense of urgency about missing out on the best candidates; and to remember that some of the best job candidates may not be good at preparing resumes or handling interviews.

EVALUATING THE RECRUITMENT FUNCTION

Given the importance of human resources for successful implementation of corporate strategy, a firm should periodically evaluate its success in recruiting.[93] Typically, the recruitment process is expensive. Unless efforts are made to identify and control these costs, recruitment may not contribute to "bottom line" financial performance.[94] Recruitment costs can run as high as 50% of the yearly salary for professionals and managers; what is even more important, recruitment can reflect a firm's overall human resource strategy.[95] This means that the effectiveness of the recruiting function should be evaluated on an ongoing basis. Several assessment indices have been suggested in the past. The following four methods are the most popular.

1. COST PER HIRE

The dollar cost per person recruited is one possible measure of the effectiveness of the recruiting function. The costs should include not only the direct costs (e.g., recruiters' salaries, costs of advertisement, consultants' fees, and so on), but also apportioned costs and overheads (e.g., time of operating personnel, stationery, rent). Cost data collected from previous recruiting activities or industry averages could serve as useful benchmarks for comparison.

2. QUALITY OF HIRES AND COST

The performance, absenteeism, and motivation levels of employees recruited using different methods often show variation. The number and quality of resumes received gives an indication of the overall effectiveness of a recruitment method or source.

> Recruits selected through advertisements in professional journals and professional conventions may be qualitatively superior to walk-ins or recruits identified during campus visits.

3. Offers: Applicants Ratio

Even if a recruiting source brings in better-quality resumes, this may not result in more job offers. A better index is the ratio between the number of job offers and the total number of applicants for each recruitment method. In addition, the ratio of number of offers accepted to total number of job offers extended gives an indication of the overall effectiveness of the recruiting. However, the acceptance of a job offer is dependent on a number of extraneous variables, including the labour market situation, the compensation package offered by the organization and its competitors, the firm's location, and so on. So a low acceptance rate does not necessarily mean the recruitment method was weak.

4. Time Lapsed per Hire

The number of days, weeks, or months taken to fill a position provides yet another measure of recruitment effectiveness. Clearly, a firm that takes a week to fill a position when the industry average is 15 days is, in comparison, more efficient, whereas one that takes a month is wasting resources. Once again, several external and uncontrollable factors affect the time for recruiting; consequently, this index should be used in conjunction with other information.

Figure 5-14 shows some of the more popular measures used to evaluate the recruiting function. Note that a firm's human resource practices in other areas (e.g., selection, training) affect the outcomes on many of these indices.

> An online survey conducted by *Canadian HR Reporter* found that employee referrals were the most effective recruitment method, followed next by online job board and job posting on the company website. Newspaper advertisements were rated lower in effectiveness compared to the above methods. Job fairs were rated the lowest in overall effectiveness.[96]

Concurrent with recruitment, HR teams still need to identify selection tools for screening applicants. Once the pool of applicants has been found, the hiring process moves to the next stage—namely, selection. The next three chapters discuss in detail the various tools used for selecting job candidates from the applicant pool.

FIGURE 5-14: Popular Measures to Evaluate Recruitment Effectiveness

- Total number of applications received
- Total recruitment costs
- Cost per hire
- Cost per hire by method (or source)
- Time required to get applications
- Time elapsed before filling the vacancy
- Ratio of offers extended to number of applicants
- Performance rating of hires
- Turnover of hires
- Number of minority members attracted (if the firm actively promotes diversity)

Implications for Practice

1. Recruitment should be clearly linked to an organization's overall human resource strategy.

2. Understanding the motivations and job search strategies of applicants is critical for success of the recruiter.

3. Recruitment becomes more effective when the recruiter understands and attempts to match the abilities, aptitudes, and interests of the applicant with the job requirements

4. Determining recruitment objectives, organizational resources, and current strategies related to hiring

(e.g., internal vs. external) comes before choosing recruitment methods.

5. Different recruitment methods and sources have different strengths and weaknesses, especially for particular jobs.

6. A recruiter should be completely fair and ethical in all dealings.

7. Like all other human resource functions, the recruitment activity also needs to be evaluated for its degree of effectiveness and efficiency.

Key Terms for Review

Applicant tracking systems (ATS),   *p. 191*

Career,   *p. 165*

E→P Expectancy,   *p. 171*

Employee referrals,   *p. 184*

Equity theory,   *p. 172*

Ethnocentric organization,   *p. 180*

Expatriates,   *p. 180*

High-commitment strategy,   *p. 161*

Host country nationals (HCN),   *p. 180*

Hygiene factors,   *p. 170*

Image advertising,   *p. 187*

Image matching,   *p. 173*

Instrumentality,   *p. 171*

Job advertisements,   *p. 187*

Job fairs,   *p. 184*

Job posting,   *p. 182*

Learning theory,   *p. 171*

Low-commitment strategy,   *p. 161*

Monolithic organizations,   *p. 162*

Motivation factors,   *p. 170*

Multicultural organizations,   *p. 162*

Need for achievement,   *p. 171*

Need for affiliation,   *p. 171*

Need for power,   *p. 171*

Occupation,   *p. 165*

Open house,   *p. 184*

P→O Expectancy,   *p. 171*

Parent company nationals (PCN),   *p. 180*

Polycentric organization,   *p. 181*

Private employment agency,   *p. 185*

Professional search firms,   *p. 185*

Promote-from-within policies,   *p. 178*

Realistic job preview (RJP),   *p. 175*

Recruitment,   *p. 160*

Reinforcement theory,   *p. 171*

Requisition,   *p. 176*

Third country nationals (TCN),   *p. 180*

Transit advertising,   *p. 189*

Valence,   *p. 171*

Vocation,   *p. 165*

Vocational maturity,   *p. 168*

Walk-ins,   *p. 182*

Want ads,   *p. 187*

Write-ins,   *p. 182*

Discussion Questions

1. Discuss the link between an organization's culture and strategy and its recruitment activities. Is the link relevant for small businesses that lack formalized strategies?

2. Discuss a job search process you used on a past occasion. How does it compare to the steps discussed in this chapter?

3. Would the recruitment methods be different for two similarly-sized firms operating in different industries? Why or why not?

4. What approach to evaluating recruitment effectiveness would you recommend? Why?

Critical Thinking Questions

1. Your firm, a rapidly growing automobile tire and service company, has continually needed to hire qualified technicians. Because of the recent decline and downsizing of some auto manufacturers in the region, you have been receiving a large number of unsolicited applications (both walk-ins and write-ins). Although this has reduced the pressure on your recruiting efforts, closer examination of several resumes shows that the applicants do not have the required competencies. What should you do to attract highly qualified applicants without significantly increasing your recruitment costs?

2. In your own job search processes, how do you select employers? What criteria do you use to identify and shortlist them? Discuss your strategies in a group. Are there differences between your approach and those employed by others in the group? To the process discussed in this book? What are the implications of these differences?

3. You work as the human resource manager in a growing organization attempting to increase workforce diversity. For a recent job opening, one external and one internal candidate were in the final short list. Both are equally qualified, but the external candidate is from a minority group. Your organization is very keen to attract people from this group. If not selected for the position, the internal candidate is not expected to quit. But you feel that a decision to hire an outsider will reduce this employee's morale. The manager to whom the new employee will report has sought your advice on selecting the final candidate and will go with your choice. Whom would you recommend? Why?

4. Would the criteria you employ in evaluating recruitment effectiveness in the case of a school be different from that used in the case of a fast-food chain? Why?

Web Research

Examine the newspaper recruiting advertisements of three similar manufacturing organizations and three similar service organizations. Then go to their websites and examine their stated human resource and employee development policies.

1. Are there systematic differences in their stated HR strategies/policies (especially related to hiring) that can be attributed to their size, environments, or strategic differences?

2. What differences in required interpersonal competencies do you note across organizations in the same industry?

3. Do you observe any major differences in the interpersonal competencies between service and manufacturing organizations? What are they?

4. Are the statements in their print ads consistent with the message in their websites?

CASE INCIDENT

Expansion at Ontario Engineering Works

Ontario Engineering Works is considering a major expansion. Management expects the number of employees to increase by almost 30% in the next few years to meet the needs of expansion. The company has been keeping records of its experiences with recruiting methods in recent past. Figure A shows a summary of relevant data for the production and sales work force.

FIGURE A: Details of Past Recruitment Outcomes

	Walk-in	Write-in	HRSD	Advertisements	Employee referrals	Campus recruiting	Internet
Total number of applications							
Production	90	170	40	230	30	30	410
Sales	30	60	130	420	20	40	300
Total yield (%)*							
Production	9	17	4	23	3	3	41
Sales	3	6	13	42	2	4	30
Ratio (%) of acceptance to applications							
Production	30	40	20	50	50	60	8
Sales	30	80	25	50	40	50	12
Ratio (%) of acceptance to job offers							
Production	50	60	70	75	60	75	50
Sales	70	80	80	50	50	60	40
Cost of recruiting per person hired ($)							
Production	20	40	12	110	20	20	40
Sales	20	30	9	140	20	30	30
Employee turnover within a two-year period							
Production	14	15	10	12.5	4	7.5	20
Sales	10	5	7.5	15	9	14	18

*Yield denotes the percentage of total applications emerging from this method.

Question

1. *Make your recommendation on the best recruitment method(s) for each type of work force.*

CASE

Metro Police Department

Deputy Chief George MacKinnon knew that something had to be done—and soon!

He looked at the report containing the latest recruitment statistics Inspector Ken Claremont had left on his table earlier that morning. When Richard Tanner, the human resource director, suddenly took long-term leave of absence to be with his terminally ill wife, Claremont had stepped into the position. Claremont, an operational officer, had little prior training to manage human resources; but MacKinnon also knew that he had little choice in the matter, since the only other "free" officer was much more junior than Claremont. The result is that for the last five months, Claremont was basically learning on

the job. It also meant that he had to constantly devote some attention to HR issues—taking him away from his main job.

"Troubles never come in single," he murmured. Six months ago, his organization was accused of racial profiling on two separate occasions. About two months ago, there was also a complaint from one of the women officers of sexual harassment by her supervisor. The print and TV media had played up the incidents—causing him endless worries and distraction. Finally, when the harassment case went before the provincial human rights commission, the tribunal had decided in favour of the department, but not before admonishing it for poor representation of women and minorities in its workforce.

FIGURE 1: Metro Police Department's Recruitment Experience

Details	White Males	Women	African-Canadian	Aboriginal	Arab	South Asian & Chinese	Gay/ Lesbian*	Persons with Disabilities
Number who attended recruitment sessions held in high schools	43	100	15	5	4	50	3	2
Number who attended recruiting sessions in colleges and public events	100	150	40	15	6	20	22	8
% of attendees who later submitted applications	70	40	60	40	20	10	40	40
% of applicants who were found qualified after interview	37	20	15	25	50	75	30	50
Number of persons who accepted job offers	33	10	3	1	0	1	1	1
% of those offered a job who accepted it	90	50	60	50	-	20	33	25

*Estimates since the form did not ask for details.

Not that they had not put any effort into minority recruitment! During the last two years, the department had held information sessions at universities, colleges, community groups, and even high schools. Recruitment brochures have been widely distributed on all those occasions and left with HRSD, local churches, and events where young people were likely to attend. During the multicultural festival, the department had regularly managed booths. On MacKinnon's advice, Claremont had even arranged for an open house recently. But the only people who came to see them were a few winos and locals who were looking for free refreshments. In other recruitment meetings, a few people expressed interest in applying, at least initially, but this interest did not translate into final completed applications or job offers. Figure 1 shows the details of the department's minority recruitment efforts in the last two years.

Over those two years, the department managed to hire at least a few people in these minority groups (in all fifty officers were hired during the two year period)

Minority	Number hired
Women	10
African Canadians	3
Aboriginals	1
Chinese/South Asian	1
Gay/Lesbian	1
Persons with Disabilities	1

MacKinnon glanced at the new recruitment and final hiring figures—not a single promising minority recruit in this new list, he noted. While the department wanted to improve on the above record, it was doubtful whether the department would be able to even maintain this record this year. What is worse, the only senior African-Canadian officer in the force, John Kirk, was thinking of moving to the RCMP. While there were six African-Canadian officers in the department, only one had risen up the ranks. If that other officer also left, there would not be a single senior non-white officer, since all Asian and Aboriginal officers were recent recruits. MacKinnon had tried his best to keep Kirk in the department, but he seemed to have set his heart on moving to RCMP. "Well, what can't be avoided has to be endured," he told himself as he picked up the phone to call Claremont for a meeting.

Metro Police Department attempts to achieve it mission of "Leading, Protecting, and Serving the Metro Community" through deployment of 450 sworn officers and 60 civil staff. In its recruiting brochures, it underscores the opportunity provided to employees to "make a difference each day." To be a police officer, an applicant must meet the following minimum qualifications:

- 19 years of age by application deadline
- No criminal convictions for which a pardon has not been granted
- Canadian citizen or landed immigrant
- Grade 12 education with academic courses in English and Math
- Valid Class 5 driver's license
- No history of improper conduct or a poor employment, military, financial, or driving record

The recruits are asked to submit a variety of documentation to confirm the above and have to undergo a number of tests of their physical and mental abilities. For most positions, the department requires the following:

- Copy of birth certificate
- Copy of driver's license
- High School Diploma with transcript
- Valid Standard First Aid and CPR Level C
- Swimming certificate for Water Rescue for First Responders
- Typing Certificate (25 words per minute minimum speed) for most positions
- Proof of uncorrected vision not less than 20/60 in each eye, 20/40 in one eye and 20/100 in the other. Vision must be correctable to 20/20 and 20/25. Color vision must be normal.
- Three letters of reference with at least one from a current supervisor and at least one from an educational instructor

Apart from the patrolling role (with which the general public identifies policing), the police department includes a number of other investigative, administrative, and technical careers. Some of these require university and post-graduate qualifications. Despite its efforts at recruiting from minority groups, the workforce in Metro Police in all work categories was still primarily white male. Figure 2 shows the make up of its current workforce (only sworn officers), but the percentages are not vastly different in other job categories.

The majority of police work consists of general tasks. Once a person is hired, he or she participates in a rigorous training program to become an effective police officer. However, the applicants themselves bring many skills to the job. For example, good officers have strong observational and interpersonal skills; and despite the best training, weaknesses in these critical skills are hard to remove. Good officers also need good memory, since they have to be competely familiar with portions of the *Criminal Code*, the *Motor Vehicle Act*, other federal and provincial statutes, and the department regulations and procedures manual.

The salary and benefit package offered to police officers is competitive. New police officers receive a starting salary of about $40 000, with annual salary increases. A First Class Constable currently earns about $65 000. The pension benefits are quite generous, and officers can retire early from the force without reduction in pension. There are also opportunities to earn overtime and extra duty allowance above the regular salary. Accumulated overtime enables an officer to schedule extra days off.

The meeting with Claremont took the better part of an hour. In less than a half hour, MacKinnon had a meeting scheduled with the Mayor, who was anxiously awaiting "some major changes in the profile of the department workforce." *The Daily Sun* had already dubbed Metro Police as "White Male Buddy Club." If the results of current recruitment drive became public, that image was going to persist.

As always, Claremont had no new ideas to suggest. He was a good man, but not particularly creative in coming up with solutions. No, MacKinnon knew he would have to come up with a strategy of his own to attract more minorities into the force.

But, what? He asked himself as he reached for the fifth cup of coffee. His doctor had ordered him to stop drinking coffee. But today was going to be one of those difficult days...

Questions

1. *What initial conclusions can you make based on the data presented in the case?*

2. *What factors might explain the absence of an adequate number of minorities in the Metro Police Department?*

3. *What actions would you take now if you were MacKinnon? Would you suggest use of different recruitment efforts to target different minority groups? What kinds?*

FIGURE 2: Minorities in Metro Police Department (Sworn Officers Only)

Metro Region and Metro Police Dept.	Total	Women	African-Canadian	Aboriginal	Arab	Chinese and South Asian	Gay/ Lesbian	Persons with Disabilities
Metro Region	500 000	240 000	25 000	10 000	7500	7500	2500	55 000
Metro Police Department (Sworn Officers Only)	450	50	6	1	0	1	1	1

CHAPTER

6 APPLICANT SCREENING

"At the (screening) point where the most candidates are rejected, organizations are using either off-the-shelf or untested application forms, and asking people with no training to make significant decisions. The damage that this could do to your chances of landing the best recruits is clear."

Robert Wood and Tim Payne[1]

CHAPTER OBJECTIVES

After studying this chapter, you should be able to:

- List the steps in selection of employees

- Discuss the steps in screening candidates by telephone and the do's and don'ts of telephone interviews

- Describe the role of courtesy interviews

- List the items included in a typical job application form

- Describe the process of designing weighted application and bio-graphical blanks

- Discuss the advantages and limitations of computer-based screening

Canadian Youth Buddies (CYB), a large volunteer organization with branches in all major Canadian cities, is dedicated to enhancing the lives of children and youth with illnesses, disabilities, or life challenges by providing friendship, support, and encouragement in social, educational, and recreational activities. Over the years, the CYB had built up a reputation as a caring, professionally managed, but volunteer-driven organization. While volunteers (who are carefully selected for the purpose) drive many of its activities, CYB also employs hundreds of people. Given CYB's reputation, it attracts hundreds of applications for each job position advertised. But because of its clientele and reputation, CYB can afford to hire only the best.

During preliminary screening, the HR department carefully goes through each application form, quickly scanning for competencies it considers critical for success in the organization. In particular, candidates are initially sorted into two groups: those with volunteering experience, especially with youths or children, and those who do not. Only candidates from the second group who appear exceptionally promising are considered. Other information provided in their resumes on special training and skills are also considered at this screening stage. All recruits who pass the initial screening undergo a short telephone interview to clarify the quality of their prior experience and their training, career goals, and availability. Only about 30% of those interviewed over the telephone move to the next stage, where HR staff contact their references. During telephone conversations with the referees, HR staff ask specific behavioural questions about the applicants, and they remove about a third of the candidates from the list based on the responses. Those who remain on the active list are called for an on-site interview and are hired based on the results of the interview. For one job position, CYB had 570 applications, out of which less than 80 applications reached the second stage of the telephone interview.

The last chapter examined the importance of recruitment for strategic success and detailed methods that can attract high quality applicants. But effective recruiting can bring hundreds of applications. In addition, organizations such as Canadian Youth Buddies receive hundreds of applications because of their reputation. But high response in turn creates another challenge: how do you sift the most promising applicants from this large pool? How do you ensure that valuable time and resources are not devoted to processing job applications that show little potential? Robert Wood and Tim Payne state in the opening quote that not all organizations use valid or systematic approach to applicant screening. Yet, many organizations, such as CYB described in the opening vignette, have systematic approaches to screening candidates and identifying applicants who are promising employees.

Job application forms, resumes, reference checks, and interviews are the most commonly used screening tools. But HR departments can also screen initial recruit telephone and email inquiries against a set of job relevant criteria, and then encourage only those who match the criteria to send in a completed application. In general, through **initial screening**, you can better match applicants with the job requirements, so that only those applicants with greatest potential move into the next selection stage (see Figure 6-1).

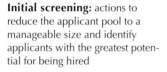

Initial screening: actions to reduce the applicant pool to a manageable size and identify applicants with the greatest potential for being hired

Job applicants who pass the initial screening are then typically assessed through employment tests and interviews. One study[2] found that half of the responding organizations in Canada used some form of employment or job aptitude tests in its recruitment process. In addition, virtually every organization uses a comprehensive interview of job applicants as part of the selection process. Recruiters sometimes also check the

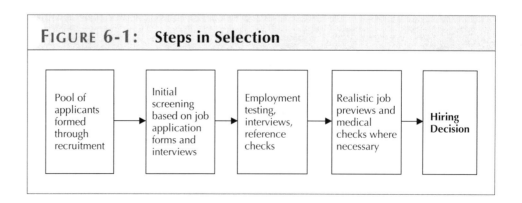

FIGURE 6-1: Steps in Selection

| Pool of applicants formed through recruitment | → | Initial screening based on job application forms and interviews | → | Employment testing, interviews, reference checks | → | Realistic job previews and medical checks where necessary | → | **Hiring Decision** |

applicant's background and medical history. Some organizations include realistic job preview as part of the selection process to ensure that the job meets the applicant's expectations. Finally, the recruitment team offers employment to the successful candidates.

However, not all organizations have such elaborate and systematic selection processes. Indeed, in many small organizations, the hiring decision is often based on a single interview with the owner or manager. Many small organizations omit steps that they believe fail to yield valid and useful information to predict job success or that involve costs that far exceed potential benefits.[3] But depending on the type of recruits, the selection process may show other variations.

> For instance, for internal applicants, steps such as verifying references and medical examination are irrelevant. On the other hand, in some industries, such as retail, where employers lose billions of dollars through employee theft, personal reference checks are very popular when hiring people from outside. Over 80% of Canadian retailers verify past performance through reference checks, while about 10% conduct honesty tests.[4]

In most organizations, a medical evaluation, if done at all, is carried out only after the hiring decision is made. Organizations must show that the medical evaluation is job-related. Physical examination can only be used to screen out applicants who are physically unable to carry out the job.

> For example, fire departments may reasonably ask firefighter applicants to demonstrate a certain level of physical fitness that would enable them to climb ladders, lug ten-centimeter water-filled hoses, or carry injured victims.[5]

This chapter introduces you to initial screening procedures. Initial screening involves actions aimed at reducing the applicant pool to a manageable size and identifying those applicants with greatest potential for hiring. Many techniques, such as telephone screening, preliminary interviews, and web-based aptitude or attitude questions are currently popular. The techniques used vary depending on the number of applications and the resources available for the organization in question.

> For example, Wal-Mart has a toll-free applicant pre-screening system. Cisco's website has a test that aims to match applicant aptitude with the organizational expectations. Several investment companies have computerized aptitude tests on their websites that applicants must complete before making a job application. Only candidates who receive a minimum score are asked to submit a formal job application.

APPLICANT SCREENING BY PHONE

Several employers use the phone to screen out applicants. In **telephone screening**, either the staffing specialist in the HR department or the hiring manager conducts a telephone interview with each applicant to assess the person's qualifications for the job and decide whether to place the candidate in the active applicant list. Regardless who does the screening, the following steps have to be completed.

Telephone screening: a brief telephone interview to assess the candidate's qualifications and decide whether the candidate should continue in the application process

1. PREPARE A LIST OF QUESTIONS

The list of interview questions should be directly related to the job position for which the candidate is being considered. Only questions on items critical for the job should be included for the purpose of the interview. More detailed questions should wait for the employment interview at a later stage in selection. The purpose of the screening questions is to find out whether the candidate possesses minimum requirements to warrant further attention.

The questions included should meet all the requirements of the *Canadian Human Rights Act* and provincial legislation.

For example, for a job which involves extensive travel or frequent relocations, asking a candidate whether (s)he has a spouse/children who might object to such frequent changes is illegal. Instead, you should mention the job requirement of frequent travel or relocation and ask the candidate whether he or she will face any difficulty in this regard.

Similarly, include no questions on applicant characteristics, especially age, gender, religion, disabilities, family status, and ethnicity, in the checklist.

2. MAKE ARRANGEMENTS FOR THE TELEPHONE SCREENING

The screening interview should be held at a time and in a place free from any distractions or interruptions. Schedule it at a reasonable time (e.g., not during lunch hours or in late evenings unless the candidate had requested it). In scheduling back-to-back telephone sessions, ensure that enough time is left between interviews for completing notes or other evaluation forms. If a recording of the telephone screening process is desired, make arrangements for this as well. Finally, the applicant must be informed about such arrangements and their consent obtained before the interview begins.

3. INTRODUCE THE PURPOSE OF THE TELEPHONE INTERVIEW

The interview should begin by briefly stating of the purpose of the interview and, if the time was not arranged in advance, verifying that this is a convenient time for an interview. If not, identify a mutually convenient alternate time for the purpose.

Focus on Ethics

You work as an assistant in a human resource department of a large manufacturing facility. The production process at the factory is mostly automated, but the process operators still have to be skilled and often must operate in a humid and noisy work environment. However, your company has a reputation as a good employer and pay-master; hence, you get a large number of applications for every open position, many of them unsolicited. You role is to manage employee records, especially those relating to benefits and pension; however, today you have an opportunity to observe the other five HR employees in action.

Their present decision dilemma relates to Joe, a recruiter working in your department. Joe, like you, reports to the human resource manager. During interactions with Joe both at work and outside, you have learned about his prejudice against members of two ethnic groups, Groups X and Y. Joe is in charge of preliminary screening of all applicants. During telephone screening, you overhear Joe discourage applicants from Groups X and Y by pointing out negative aspects of the work—often exaggerating some of the adverse working conditions. In contrast, when he is in conversation with other applicants, he focuses on the strengths of the company, especially the company's good pay and the potential for career progress. The result is that in the past two years, not one applicant from X and Y has moved to the second stage of the selection process.

You are troubled by the situation but are unsure what to do or whether you should take any action at all.

4. SHARE JOB INFORMATION

The interviewer should describe the job in enough detail so that the applicants can decide for themselves (1) whether they are really serious about applying, and (2) whether they are qualified. Sharing accurate job information frequently encourages the unqualified or marginally qualified applicant to voluntarily withdraw from the candidacy, thus reducing costs to both parties.[6] Information about salary ranges for the job and relevant information about organizational expectations and culture also result in voluntary withdrawal of candidates whose expectations do not match the organization's reality. Such screening can reduce employee disappointment and lower departure rates of newly hired candidates from the firm.

5. CREATE RAPPORT

The interviewer should make every effort to put the candidate at ease and use a positive, friendly tone. The responsibility is on the interviewer to establish a relaxed atmosphere. Without rapport, the interviewer may not get an accurate picture of the applicant's potential. The interview should begin with supportive, non-threatening questions and quickly move to the statement of the purpose of the interview. As much as possible, use open-ended questions to encourage dialogue. Avoid asking leading questions that direct the applicant to the desired response (e.g., "Do you think that you will like meeting people on the job?"). Do not interrupt the candidate while he or she is speaking.

6. SELL THE ORGANIZATION

Often the telephone interview is the applicant's first interaction with a member of the firm. But in some instances, it may be the only interaction he or she will ever have. This means that the interviewer's statements and tone may leave a lasting impression, with implications for the success of present and future recruitment and marketing efforts. The interviewer should make an effort to present the organization in a positive, realistic manner. Also, always treat the applicant with courtesy in a professional manner.

Figure 6-2 summarizes some of the dos and don'ts of telephone interviews.

FIGURE 6-2:   Dos and Don'ts of Telephone Screening

DO:

- Identify a time and place where you will not be distracted or interrupted.
- Prepare a list of questions that are job relevant.
- Listen!
- Ask specific questions to help you assess whether the candidate has key job competencies that warrant further consideration.
- Clearly state the purpose of the interview so that there are no misunderstandings or waste of time.
- Use a positive, friendly tone.
- Describe the job in detail so that the applicant can judge for himself/herself whether there is a good match.
- Explain the next step in the process to the candidate at the end of the interview.

FIGURE 6-2:   (*Continued*)

DON'T:

- Ask any questions that are illegal.
- Dominate the interview.
- Spend time thoroughly evaluating all relevant attributes. This can be done at later stages of selection.
- Tape the interview without asking permission from the applicant.
- Rush through interviews without making notes. You are bound to forget details of each interview after a lapse of time or a few interviews. Make notes immediately after each interview.
- Sound evaluative or critical of the applicant. Your goal is to get relevant information, not to pass judgment on someone's decisions or lifestyle.
- Oversell the organization. This may create future disappointment after hiring.

COURTESY INTERVIEW

Courtesy interview: a brief, non-rigorous interview with a walk-in applicant aimed at screening out obviously inappropriate candidates before they apply

Job applicants will generally make initial contact either in person, in writing, or more recently, through email. Sometimes applicants "walk in" to inquire about possible job vacancies. In these cases, the receptionist provides them with basic information on jobs available and hours of work. When the applicant is a "walk-in," a preliminary interview—typically with a representative of the human resource department, or the manager in the case of a very small firm—is often granted as a courtesy. This **courtesy interview**, as it is sometimes called, is not likely to be very rigorous and is aimed at screening out obvious "misfits" (e.g., someone who is not willing to work late evenings or the weekends but is interested in a salesperson's job with the firm requiring considerable hours during those periods); but rather, the goal is to talk generally about the position and the candidate's interest.

Courtesy interviews are an important part of good public relations by the firm, since information conveyed during these meetings can affect a firm's public perceptions and even marketing success in the long term. The professionalism displayed by the HR staff during this early encounter may have lasting implications for its future recruitment success. If the applicant looks promising after the interview, he or she is typically asked to complete a formal application form.

JOB APPLICATION FORMS

Job application form: standard document that collects information about applicants

A **job application form** collects information about recruits in a uniform written format and hence is an important part of recruitment efforts. Even when recruits volunteer detailed information about themselves, organizations still require them to fill out application forms, so that all information gathered is comparable. Each human resource department generally designs its own form. Nevertheless, certain features are common. Figure 6-3 provides a typical example of an application form and its major divisions.

NAME AND ADDRESS

Most application forms begin with a request for personal data, such as name, address, and telephone number. Requests for personal data, such as place of birth, marital status,

FIGURE 6-3: A Sample Job Application Form

The Great Lakes Electronics, Inc.
"An Equal-Opportunity Employer"
Application for Employment

Personal Data
Name
Address
Phone Number
email

Employment Status

Type of employment sought (Check all applicable)
Full-time ☐   Part-time ☐   Permanent ☐   Temporary ☐

Job or position sought _____ Responding to ad? Yes____ No ____

Date of availability, if hired: _____ (Day, Month, Year)

Approximate wages/salary desired $ _____ per month

Education and Skills
Circle the highest grade or years completed.
        9 10 11 12 13   1 2 3 4   1 2   1 2 3 4
        High School   University   Graduate   Doctoral or Post Graduate

Please provide the following information about your education.
(Include only vocational schools and colleges.)
1. School name
School address
Date of admission
Date of completion
Degree or Diploma Received

2. School name
School address
Date of admission
Date of completion
Degree or Diploma Received

3. School name
School address
Date of admission
Date of completion
Degree or Diploma Received

4. School name
School address
Date of admission
Date of completion
Degree or Diploma Received

Please attach additional sheets if needed. Additional sheets included? Yes ☐   No ☐

Please describe your work skills. Include machines, tools, equipment, and other abilities
you possess. Be specific.

Examples: General Skills: Institutional sales, direct marketing, compensation management,
benefits management. IT and Programming Skills: Oracle, Unix, Java, and so on.

General Skills	IT/Programming Skills

FIGURE 6-3: (*Continued*)

Work History

Beginning with your most recent or current employer, please provide the following information about each employer. If additional space is needed, please use an additional sheet.

Employer 1 _____
Dates of employment: From   To
Employer's address
Your job title
Supervisor's name
Job duties
Starting pay
Ending pay

Employer 2_____
Dates of employment: From   To
Employer's address
Your job title
Supervisor's name
Job duties
Starting pay
Ending pay

Employer 3 _____
Dates of employment: From   To
Employer's address
Your job title
Supervisor's name
Job duties
Starting pay
Ending pay

Employer 4_____
Dates of employment: From   To
Employer's address
Your job title
Supervisor's name
Job duties
Starting pay
Ending pay

Service in Canadian Armed Services

If you were a member of the Canadian Armed Forces, please provide the following information:
Branch of service
Rank at discharge
Dates of service (list beginning and ending dates)
Responsibilities
Type of discharge

Memberships, Awards, and Hobbies

1. List civic/professional/social organizations to which you have belonged.

2. List any awards you have received.

3. What are your hobbies?

> ## FIGURE 6-3: (Continued)
>
> **Please feel free to add any other information you think should be considered in evaluating your application.**
>
> **References**
>
> In the space provided, list the names of three referees whom we can contact to understand more about your work experience and capabilities. Please list the names of persons who can provide valid information about your work experience or skills. Ideally, these should be your past work supervisors or work peers who have come to know you well. In any event, the referees should not be members of your family.
>
> Name
> Address
>
> Name
> Address
>
> Name
> Address
>
> By my signature on this application:
> *a) I authorize the verification of the above information and any other necessary inquiries that may be needed to determine my suitability for employment.*
> *b) I affirm that the above information is true to the best of my knowledge.*
>
> **Applicant's Signature** _____   **Date** _____

number of dependents, sex, race, religion, or national origin, is illegal and can lead to charges of discrimination. The human resource department must be able to show that all questions it asks are job-related. Applications *may* solicit information about health, height, weight, handicaps that relate to the job, major illnesses, and claims for injuries, but only under limited circumstances. Here again, such questions may cause legal problems. Discriminating against handicapped individuals is prohibited under the *Canadian Human Rights Act*. The burden of proof that such questions are job-related falls on the employer.

EMPLOYMENT STATUS

Some questions on the application form concern the applicant's employment objective and availability. Included here are questions about the position sought, willingness to accept other positions, date available for work, salary or wages desired, and acceptability of part-time and full-time work schedules. This information helps a recruiter match the applicant's objective and the organization's needs.

EDUCATION AND SKILLS

The objective of the education and skills section of the application form is to uncover the job seeker's abilities. Traditionally, education has been a major criterion in evaluating job seekers, since education level implies certain cognitive abilities. But questions about specific skills are also used to judge prospective employees. More than any other part of the application form, the skills section reveals the suitability of a candidate for a particular job. In the sample job application form in Figure 6-3, Great Lakes Electronics wanted specific information on IT and computer programming skills because these skills were critical for the business. Broad or uncertain responses in this section eliminates the application from consideration. An example follows:

Junior Recruiter: Under "skills," the applicant wrote "can handle various office positions." Also, under "salary desired," the applicant wrote " the going rate or better." What should I do with this application?

Employment Manager: You are not a mindreader. Put that application in the inactive file and forget about it.

WORK HISTORY

Information about work history tells a recruiter whether the applicant is someone who hops from job to job or is likely to be a long-service employee. In addition, a quick review of the stated job titles, duties, responsibilities, and ending pay also shows whether the candidate is a potentially capable applicant. But if this information does not coincide with what an experienced recruiter expects to see, the candidate may have exaggerated some items.

MILITARY BACKGROUND

The military offers standardized training to all its employees and fosters an ability to function in a structured environment—something that is valued by many employers. For this reason, some application forms request information on military experience. Questions usually include rank at discharge, date of discharge, area of service, and type of discharge.

MEMBERSHIPS, AWARDS, AND HOBBIES

For many managerial and professional positions, off-the-job activities may make one candidate preferable over another. Memberships in civic, social, and professional organizations indicate the recruit's concern about community and career. Awards show recognition for noteworthy achievements. Hobbies may reinforce important job skills and indicate opportunities for further service to the company:

> When handed a pile of completed applications for the position of an investment advisor for a large financial institution, Kim Crawford, the firm's employment manager, sorted the completed applications into two piles. When asked what criteria were being used to sort the applications, she said, "I'm looking for golfers. Many of our big clients are found on Saturday afternoons at the golf course."

REFERENCES

In addition to references from peers and previous employers, applications may also ask for other "reference-like" information. But be aware that questions about the job seeker's credit history, criminal record, and family or friends who work for the organization are allowed only if the employer can justify their use (e.g., if the job involves sensitive information, cash, or other valuables). If these criteria disproportionately discriminate against a protected group, the employer could be exposed to the risk of possible litigation.

SIGNATURE LINE

Candidates are usually required to sign and date their applications to authorize the employer to check references and undertake any other necessary investigations. Another common provision of the signature line is a statement that the applicant affirms the information in the application to be true and accurate as far as is known. Although many people give this clause little thought, falsification of an application form is grounds for discharge in most organizations, as Clayton Barns of the City Fire Fighters found out:

> Clayton Barns lied about his age to get into the firefighter training program. As he neared retirement age, Jim was notified that he would have to retire in six months, instead of the thirty-six months as he had calculated. When Clayton protested, the lie he made several years before was exposed. Clayton was given the option of being terminated or taking early retirement at substantially reduced benefits.

Sometimes withholding vital information is the same as providing inaccurate information, as a top bureaucrat hired by the City of Waterloo found out:

> In 2004, the newly hired Chief Administrative Officer of the City of Waterloo was fired three weeks after hiring because he had not provided the employer with critical information relevant to the hiring decision. A forensic auditor examining the applicant's work history found that at his earlier work site, he had been involved in a situation where rules had been broken and he had had an important role in a $11.4 million project that went bad.[7]

The top three areas that tend to be exaggerated or hidden, especially for senior executives and managers, are

- reasons for leaving prior jobs
- results and accomplishments
- job responsibilities[8]

Information on compensation, education, and date of employment are also often fabricated, although less frequently.

WEIGHTED APPLICATION BLANKS (WABs)

The **weighted application blank (WAB)** or **form** allows the employer to predict an applicant's future job success from application blanks that have built in weights for information relating to an applicant's work-related and other personal details. WAB is actually a technique for scoring application forms, rather than a markedly different kind of application form. The procedure helps the employer identify which attributes (e.g., work experience or education) are most critical for successful job performance and helps incorporate that information into a mathematical model to predict future job success.

Weighted application blank (WAB) or **form:** application forms that include carefully developed questions with built-in, weighted answers to allow the employer to predict future job success

> In one firm, educational qualifications may be more critical for successful job performance than past work experience. The WAB prepared in this organization will give higher weights to education than years of past experience. In another firm, the situation may be quite the opposite: work experience is more critical than formal education for successful job performance. In this situation, the underlying mathematical model will give higher weight to work experience when compared to education.

The WAB is particularly useful in these employment situations:

- jobs in which large number of employees perform similar activities
- jobs in which the turnover rate is very high

Information on bio-data's predictive ability:
*www.radford.edu/
~applyhrm/2004/
MS%209_1_%20Dean.pdf*

- jobs for which it is expensive to conduct other forms of tests or interviews[9]

- jobs that are complex and require expensive and lengthy training programs[10]

- jobs where failure rates are high and unacceptable

- jobs for which adequate personal records are available to the employer[11]

- jobs for which large number of applications are submitted and applicant screening is complex and costly

The idea of the WAB originated over 110 years ago, when Thomas Peters of Washington Life Insurance Company of Atlanta suggested that one way to improve the selection of life insurance agents was for managers to "require all applicants to answer a list of standardized questions, such as the following: Present residence? Residences during the previous ten years?... Amount of unencumbered real estate? Occupation during previous ten years?"[12]

While WAB has been refined since then, most of the revisions have been made to the statistical procedures; but the idea itself remains close to Peters' original suggestions. The procedure aims to determine if individual items on an application form (such as educational qualifications or prior work experience) distinguish between successful and unsuccessful employees. Once identified, items related to job success are differentially weighted to reflect their degree of importance in predicting job performance and success. All future job applicants are then scored on these items, and then HR staff calculate the summated scores predicting their potential job success. These total scores are used for selection purposes. These total scores resemble a candidate's score on interviews or employment tests.

DEVELOPING WEIGHTED APPLICATION BLANKS

Developing a valid WAB requires great care and typically consists of nine steps (see Figure 6-4).

1. Identify performance criterion
First, identify a valid performance criterion, following steps detailed in Chapter 2 of this text. The WAB must be tailored to predict this performance criterion. Typical criteria include:

- Job tenure

- Quantity of performance

- Absenteeism

- Supervisory ratings of performance

- Trainability (or success in specific training programs)

- Rate of salary increase

As discussed in Chapter 3, the criterion chosen should be reliable, valid, and relevant for the organization and controllable by the employee. If the criterion is unreliable, its predictability will be low. In other words, the success of the entire process depends on the quality of the criterion measures. Consider this situation:

> In a large retail chain with hundreds of branches all over Canada, one branch manager was known among his employees for being "easy on them." During the annual performance reviews, he rarely gave anyone less than a 4 on a 5-point scale on most performance items. But his ratings did not match the actual job performance of his employees, since everyone was more or less guaranteed of a good rating and resultant salary raise.

For this company, a WAB, no matter how well developed, is unlikely to predict true job performance of the branch's employees since the criterion measure of performance (namely, supervisory ratings) is invalid.

FIGURE 6-4:   Steps in Developing WABs

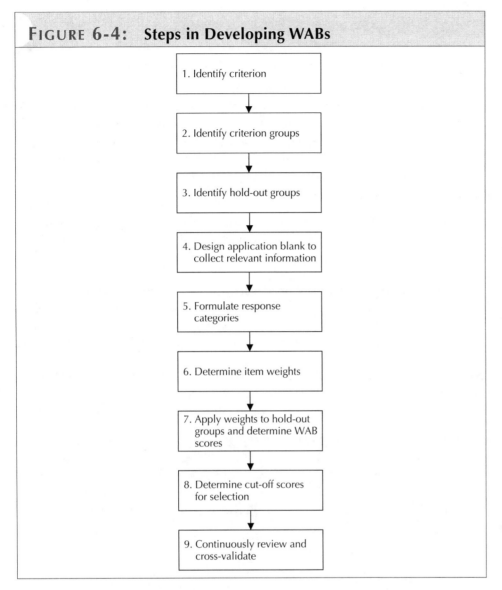

1. Identify criterion

2. Identify criterion groups

3. Identify hold-out groups

4. Design application blank to collect relevant information

5. Formulate response categories

6. Determine item weights

7. Apply weights to hold-out groups and determine WAB scores

8. Determine cut-off scores for selection

9. Continuously review and cross-validate

2. Identify criterion groups

The next step is to identify **criterion groups** or groups of current employees who can be considered "successful" and "unsuccessful" on the chosen criterion.

> Thus, if Great Lakes Electronics defines its criterion measure as job tenure, it might define a tenure of six months or less as "short tenure" (or "unsuccessful") and one year or more as "longer tenure" ("successful"). All employees will be classified into one of these two groups. Employees with tenure of six months or more but less than a year will not be included for the purpose of the study.

The exact cut-off numbers used for forming criterion groups depend on the organization's goals and present realities. For one firm, short tenure may be six months, while the same for another may be one year. Only after a thorough analysis of the organization's mission, realities, and environmental conditions, can definite conclusions be formed.

Ideally, one should have at least 150 employees in each group. Some writers recommend as high as 500 in each group to ensure high validity.[13]

3. Identify hold-out groups

Next, identify hold-out groups of employees. **Hold-out groups** are employee groups used to validate the weights. Ideally, these groups should be almost equal in size as the two criterion groups, but often practical realities necessitate somewhat smaller hold-out groups.

Criterion groups: groups of current employees who can be categorized as "successful" and "unsuccessful" on the chosen criterion

Hold-out group: a group of employees for whom predictor and criterion measures are available, but who were not involved in the earlier development of WAB; for this reason, they can be used to validate the WAB

Great Lakes Electronics had formed two criterion groups. Its short-tenure group had 200 employees, while its long-tenure had 220 employees. It randomly chose 50 employees from the short-tenure group and 55 employees from its long-tenure group to form hold-out groups. Its weighting groups now consisted of 150 (short-term) and 165 (long-term) employees.

An important consideration when forming the hold-out group is the notion of *randomization*. The employees selected to form the hold-out groups should be randomly selected from the larger group so that they do not show any systematic variation from the parent group. In other words, the hold-out group should have the same employee profile (e.g., age, gender, race, education, etc.) as the group which was used to identify the weights, which in turn, should be very similar to a firm's present and future applicants.

4. Design application blanks

Often the traditional application blanks will need to be modified to seek additional information needed to predict success on the chosen criterion. England[14] recommends including as many items as possible in the initial analysis, since many items may not differentiate between successful and unsuccessful criterion groups.

When asking for additional information, ensure that the questions do not violate provisions of the *Canadian Human Rights Act* or similar provincial legislation. The sole objective should be to identify items that are predictive of the criterion earlier identified. Some illustrative biographical information that have been found to be related to job tenure (the criterion used by Great Lakes Electronics) are shown in Figure 6-5. Note that the most obvious items in an application form are not necessarily the ones that distinguish the two criterion groups. Note also that the same question in the application form can be used to generate information on more than one criterion (e.g., types of jobs, tenure on the jobs).

5. Formulate item response categories

Next, code the items in the application blank so that they become useful for statistical analysis and prediction. This means creating response categories for each of the WAB items. For example, on the application blank, the original question may be "Give information about your education below." But to score this item as a WAB, it must be recoded into response categories, such as the following:

A. Less than high school

B. High school diploma

FIGURE 6-5: Illustrative Items Related to Job Tenure

- Size of home town
- Length of residence in previous addresses
- Number of times moved in the last 15 years
- Number of previous jobs
- Types of jobs held in the past
- Types of courses taken in school or college
- Tenure in previous jobs
- Distance between residence and employment location
- Length of time before available for a position
- Reason for leaving last job
- Whether the applicant gave previous supervisors as referees
- Applicant's evaluation of the previous supervisor or job
- Salary differentials between jobs held

C. Certificate or community college diploma beyond high school

D. University degree or higher

It is often necessary to reformulate every item for predicting job tenure into response categories. In some instances, the application form may have to be redesigned completely.

> In the past, Great Lakes Electronics had asked a single question on applicant's part-time work experience. A review of the tenure record of its employees indicated to the human resource manager that longer-term employees, by and large, had held part-time jobs in the electronic or home entertainment industry. In contrast, many shorter-term employees had worked in a variety of other industries, such as fast food and house painting. To investigate the matter further, the firm modified its application blanks so that all new applicants had to provide full details of the part-time jobs they held in the past, along with tenure information.

6. Determine item weights
For the WAB to be useful, employees in the "successful" and "unsuccessful" criterion groups should differ in their responses on one or more items. Where there are such differences, differential weights are attached to the item to indicate the item's importance in predicting success. In other words, **item weights** denote the relative importance of an item in a WAB for predicting success on the criterion.

Item weights: the relative importance of an item in a WAB for predicting success on the criterion

Establishing weights is a fairly complex process, often involving statistical techniques such as correlation, hierarchical and logistic regression, and discriminant analysis.[15] Some elementary notions of correlation and regression are discussed in Appendix 4A. But discussion of the more advanced topics in statistics is beyond the scope of this book. Some researchers have also formulated tables to help identify appropriate weights. While this chapter cannot explain the procedure for identifying exact weights, it can explain the *logic* behind the weighting process.

Consider the data provided in Figure 6-6. Assume that the firm is interested in reducing its absenteeism rate by hiring employees who share the profiles of employees with low absenteeism rates. Then assume that the human resource manager found a strong correlation between education levels and absenteeism rates (in particular, more

---

FIGURE 6-6: Assigning Weights to WAB Response Categories in Great Lakes Electronics

WAB Item and Response Categories	Employees with good attendance record (Col 1)	Employees with poor attendance record (Col 2)	Col 1 – Col 2 (Col 3)	Relative Weight *Method A* (Col 4)	Relative Weight *Method B* (Col 5)
Education Level					
A. Less than high school	60	40	20	0.2	60/60 = 1.00
B. High school diploma	65	35	30	0.3	65/60 = 1.08
C. Post secondary certificate or community college diploma	70	30	40	0.4	70/60 = 1.17
D. University degree or higher	80	20	60	0.6	80/60 = 1.33

Note: Fictitious data for illustration purposes only.

educated employees were absent less frequently). To simplify the calculations, it is assumed that there are 100 employees in each educational category. Of the 100, those with good attendance records in each educational group are shown in Column 1 of Figure 6-6.

To compute the difference between the group with good attendance and the group with poor attendance for employees with less than high school education, calculate the difference between figures in Columns 1 and 2: in this case, it is 20. The respective figures for the other education groups are 30, 40, and 60. One approach to assigning weights (we shall refer to this as Method A) recognizes these proportions and ensures that the relative weights are in the same ratio as the "success rates" for different groups. Note that the weights themselves may be quite different. What column 4 shows is the relative standing of the various response categories. This approach is popularly referred to as the *vertical percentage approach*.

In contrast, a *horizontal percentage approach* (Method B) uses the lowest response category on the criterion as its base and computes the relative weights. In Figure 6.6, the lowest success rate (or the lowest rate of "good attendance") was found in employees with less than high school education (60). So this number is used as a base for comparison purposes. If this education group is given a weight of 1.0, then the other education groups have to score higher relative to this number. For example, those with a high school diploma will get a relative weight of 1.08 ($1 \times 65/60$). The numbers for other education groups are also calculated in the same fashion. These are shown in column 5.

As mentioned, Figure 6.6 shows only relative weights; the precise weights must be calculated after taking into account the range of values and number of categories involved. If a weight of 2 is assigned for employees without a high school diploma under Method A, then the weights for employees with high school diplomas, post secondary certificates, and university degrees will be approximately 3, 4, and 6 respectively. Similar weights for other items (e.g., years of work experience, types of jobs held, types of courses taken, etc.) are identified to distinguish between employees who score high and those who score low on attendance record. However, before actually employing these weights for selection purposes, they have to be checked for their validity.

7. Apply weights to hold-out groups and determine WAB scores

With the weights identified, they are now applied to a group of employees other than the two groups to check for their validity. Avoid using the same group of employees for both identifying and validating the weights since this results in considerable bias and distortion and reduces the overall effectiveness of the WAB.

The best way to validate the weights is to try out the weights on *new* applicants. This process is analogous to the predictive validation process discussed in Chapter 4. In this approach, new applicants complete the WAB as well as all other traditional selection measures. They are hired on the basis of their scores on normal selection measures, without their WAB scores. After a reasonable time period, after which the employee's success or failure on the criterion measure (namely, attendance) can be validly measured, correlate the weights identified earlier on the WAB application form with the criterion measure. If employees who have better attendance record have higher WAB scores, then that is an indication that the weights have validity. This process of checking, referred to as *cross-validation*, is essential for establishing validity.

In practice, however, it may not be feasible to wait for such a lengthy validation process. To save time, the organization may end up using a variant of the concurrent validation model discussed in Chapter 4. In this approach, use the hold-out group identified in step 3 to check the validity of the weights.

In the case of Great Lakes Electronics the hold-out groups it formed by randomly selecting 50 employees from the short tenure group and 55 employees from its long tenure employees will be used for the cross-validation exercise.

However, the above approach suffers from many of the limitations of the concurrent validation discussed earlier. First, existing employees may systematically display behaviours or characteristics that are uncharacteristic of new entrants. Furthermore, the sample of the current workforce suffers from range restriction on criterion measures and other relevant attributes, since people with very poor attendance records may have already been terminated or voluntarily withdrawn from the firm's workforce.

If the weights have validity, one would expect employees in the hold-out group with a better attendance record to receive a high overall score. But if no relationship exists, then reexamine the process of identifying the WAB weights and identify new predictors.

An Item Scoring Procedure: *users.ugent.be/~flievens/ scoring.pdf*

8. Determine cut-off scores for selection Where the WAB is a good predictor of the criterion measure (e.g., good attendance), the employer can identify a cut-off score that separates the low- and high-criterion measure groups. Figure 6-7 illustrates cut-off scores. The WAB scores are shown on the x-axis, and the number of employees receiving each score is shown on the y-axis. Employees with poor attendance consistently receive low scores on this validated WAB while those with good attendance consistently receive high scores. Thus, a cut-off score of 6 can maximize the probability of the employee possessing a good attendance record. Note that if you set a score higher than 6, you are likely to reject applicants who will prove to be successful on our criterion measure. Similarly, a score lower than 6 means hiring some employees who are likely to have poor attendance. Other situational factors affect the

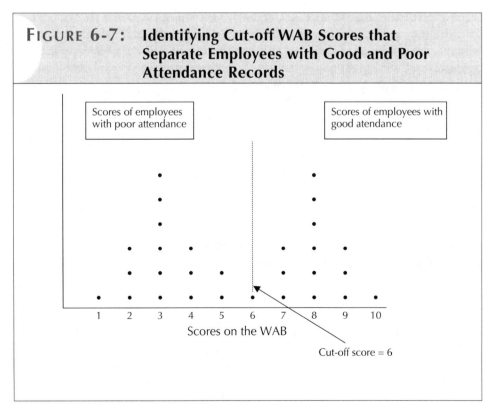

FIGURE 6-7: Identifying Cut-off WAB Scores that Separate Employees with Good and Poor Attendance Records

Scores of employees with poor attendance

Scores of employees with good atendance

Scores on the WAB

Cut-off score = 6

Note: Fictitious data for illustration purposes only.

choice of cut-off score. For example, in a tight labour market with few applicants, the employer may have to relax the cut-off score; but when there are abundant applications, the same employer may be able to use the original cut-off score to screen applicants.

9. Provide continuous review and cross validation Establishing validity of the WAB should not be a one-time exercise. Changes in applicant profile, production processes, and environmental and socio-economic variables affect both predictors and criterion measures. Hence, continuous review of the WAB weights and cut-off scores is necessary for maintaining its validity. Cross-validating it for new employee groups ensures its continued applicability, especially in times of major social or economic changes.

> Great Lakes Electronics had established a WAB that, among other things, used length of residence in previous addresses, number of times moved in the last 15 years, number of previous jobs, and types of jobs held in the past as predictors of job tenure. This was done at a time when over 85% of its workforce came from white, middle/lower economic classes. However, in the last five years, a large number of Asian immigrants and retired persons have sought employment in the company. These groups of employees had different backgrounds (e.g., many Asians complete their university studies before seeking full-time employment) and displayed qualitatively different behaviours (e.g., many retired persons would have held many more jobs than younger workers) from its past workforce. The company decided to ignore WAB score when hiring employees from these groups. As soon as it had a reasonable sample, it planned to conduct a cross validation for these groups.

USEFULNESS OF WABS

Weighted application blanks are popularly used in two stages of hiring:

1. As a screening device As an initial screening tool, WAB is particularly useful when testing and interviewing candidates is very expensive, or when the large size of applicant pool results in high administrative costs. When used as a preliminary screening tool, all applicants complete the WAB, and only the successful ones (based on existing cut-off scores) move to the next stage in selection.

> For example, in one study, where the objective was to identify the managerial potential of applicants, an earlier screening using a weighted application blank resulted in the removal of 62% of applicants. These same applicants failed to exhibit high potential in a separate assessment centre evaluation. In contrast, 83% of those who scored high on the WAB performed very well in the assessment centre exercise.[16] These results suggest that the WAB was relevant.

2. As an additional selection tool Many employers use WABs as a supplementary selection tool. They give the entire selection battery, such as employment tests, interviews, and WAB, to all applicants who reach the selection stage. The usefulness of the WAB depends on whether it enhances prediction of job success compared to other tools.

> One real estate company uses WAB along with job interviews and references to select its agents. While the interviews and references help the firm to assess some of the more obvious applicant characteristics, the WAB taps into some unique information related to the applicant's background and interests. For example, through validation studies, the company found that applicants who played active roles in student associations in schools and universities had higher success potential. The company's WAB also gave higher weights to golf and pool players, rather than tennis or basketball players, since the former games were more likely to expose the candidate to potential clients.

Whichever way it is used, a WAB has several advantages:

- Compared to employment tests or assessment centre procedures, WAB is much cheaper to administer. While the initial design and cross validation of the instrument takes time and resources (including possible hiring of consultants), once formulated, administration and scoring take little time and resources. There is also no additional cost in collecting the information from the job applicant.

- Job applicants do not find it threatening. Unlike tests and assessment centre evaluations, WAB does not induce any anxiety in the minds of the applicant. All applicants are used to completing job application forms, and the WAB gives no indication which answers are right or wrong.

- The logistics involved in administering WABs are far simpler than in the case of tests or interviews. Completing the form does not require the one-to-one interaction that interviews require. Nor does it require any special facilities (e.g., space).

But be aware of the potential limitations of WABs:

- The measure of success (that is, the criterion) used in developing WABs may change in relative importance over time.[17] For example, over time, attendance (the criterion we used in our example) may cease to be a major concern for the firm, especially if the new hires using WABs prove to be high scorers on this dimension. A WAB's ability to predict criterion can decay over time.[18] This means that a new WAB has to be developed to meet the emerging requirements of the organization.

- Current employees are used to validate a WAB. But new, younger hires may be systematically and qualitatively different from the present pool of employees.

- No single WAB will apply to all jobs in an organization. Unique characteristics of a job require that a WAB be developed for that job.

- The process of developing a WAB requires some degree of familiarity with statistical tools and analysis, which may be beyond the abilities of typical human resource practitioners.

- Changes in an organization's strategy, labour market conditions, or human resource policies may reduce the predictive power of the WAB.[19]

In summary, the WAB is a very useful tool, especially for organizations that receive large numbers of applications or that want to predict and control a critical job success factor. While the WAB is fairly versatile and economical, you still need to periodically validate it for continued relevance. In addition, you must ensure that none of the items used in the WAB violate human rights and other employment laws. When carefully developed and used, the WAB can provide a powerful additional tool that enhances the quality of the selection process.

> For example, in one study, a WAB was used to predict the performance of taxi drivers. While it separated successful from unsuccessful drivers, what was even more interesting was the fact that seven items included in the WAB significantly improved prediction over the company's selection tests assessing mental alertness and accident susceptibility. When cross-validated against 188 new drivers, the WAB rejected 60% of the poorest drivers.[20]

More recently, several researchers and employers have expanded on the WAB and applied it to biodata to create a new screening tool known as a Biographical Information Blank.

BIOGRAPHICAL INFORMATION BLANKS (BIBs)

Biographical information blank (BIB): a job-screening tool that uses information on work-related variables, personal interests, attitudes, values, and life experiences to predict job success

Biographical information blank (BIB) expands the notion of weighted application blank to include information on applicant's interests, values, and attitudes. In a BIB, information on work-related variables (e.g., educational background and work experience), personal interests (e.g., hobbies and use of leisure time), attitudes (e.g., attitude toward supervision), values (e.g., emphasis on materialism) and life experiences (e.g., early childhood events or behaviours) are collected and validated for their ability to predict job success, and the resulting weights are used to screen job applicants. Typically, the information is collected in a multiple-choice format to make coding and interpretation easier; but in some BIBs, the applicant may choose more than one response. Figure 6-8 illustrates different types of questions included in a BIB.

BIBs are based on the premise that in comparable contexts, the best predictor of future behaviour is past behaviour. Indeed, a number of studies have indicated that this is a reasonable assumption. For example, the best predictor of a student's college grade

---

FIGURE 6-8:   Sample Types of Questions in a BIB

1. Which of the following activities would you most *prefer* to engage in your leisure time? Check only one. Remember, you don't have to be good at it. The question refers to your preference. (*Single Choice—no underlying continuum*)

   ☐ Read a book

   ☐ Volunteer for some event or agency

   ☐ Play golf, tennis, or ping-pong

   ☐ Play basketball, hockey, volleyball, or soccer

   ☐ Watch a film

   ☐ Join a children's party and play with them

   ☐ Sketch a picture or play a song

2. Which of the following activities did you participate in when you were 18 years old? Check as many as relevant. (*Multiple choice—no underlying continuum*)

   ☐ Worked at a full-time job

   ☐ Started a small business

   ☐ Took courses in the evening

   ☐ Drove a car

   ☐ Traveled 500 kms or more on your own away from home

   ☐ Raised money for a local organization

3. In how many teams or workgroups would you have participated in the last year? (*Single choice—underlying continuum*)

   ☐ None

   ☐ 1

   ☐ 2–3

   ☐ 4–5

   ☐ 6–8

   ☐ More than 8

point average is the person's high school performance. Similarly, a person's childhood behaviours are good predictors of later job behaviours, as the following example illustrates:

> In one study, job applicants who as youth had built model airplanes that had been able to fly were found to be better students in flight training. What was even more interesting was the fact that this behaviour alone more accurately predicted success in the training program than the entire test battery employed for hiring trainee pilots. Apparently, the candidate's early experience with airplanes reflected a sustaining interest and ability in flying.[21]

TYPES OF BIOGRAPHICAL INFORMATION

There is no universal agreement on what should be included in the biographical data. In general, the questions pertain to a job applicant's personal backgrounds, life experiences, attitudes, and values. In many BIBs, questions relate these topics:

- **School performance:** achievements and academic attitudes
- **Drive:** motivation to succeed, to set high goals, and to attain them
- **Early family responsibility:** taking responsibility for family when very young
- **Family experience:** happy home and parental experience
- **Higher educational achievement:** post-secondary educational achievements
- **Career stability:** mid-life occupational stability
- **Leadership and group participation:** involvement in teams, groups, and other organized activities, and the roles played therein
- **Financial responsibility:** ability and experience handling finances, and financial status in general

Certainly, many of these dimensions are fairly stable. Many (e.g., group participation skills and drive) are also relevant for most jobs, although the degree of importance of each dimension may vary from one job to another. These differences mean that different weights may have to be given to each topic. Some of the other common items in BIBs are:

- Educational experiences (namely, the applicant's evaluation of his or her own experiences in high school and post-secondary institutions)
- Hobbies
- Use of leisure time
- Early work experience
- Attitude towards healthy living
- Own health
- Family relations
- Success in social, educational, or occupational pursuits
- Disappointments and learning from them
- Career aspirations
- Self-perceptions

The items included may be historical, current, or future-oriented; verifiable or unverifiable; specific or general; and actual or hypothetical in nature. Some sample items are shown in Figure 6-9.

FIGURE 6-9: Sample Items in BIBs

1. **The items can refer to the past, present, or future:**
   - How many jobs have you held in the past ten years? *[Past]*
   - What do you like/dislike most about your present job? *[Present]*
   - What kind of a job would you like to hold ten years from now? *[Future]*

2. **The items can be verifiable or unverifiable:**
   - What was your grade average in school? *[Verifiable]*
   - What was your favourite subject in school? *[Unverifiable]*

3. **The question may be specific or general:**
   - Did you play any group games in school, such as volleyball, basketball, hockey, or soccer? *[Specific]*
   - While in school, what was your favourite activity? *[General]*

4. **The question may pertain to some real or hypothetical situation:**
   - Did you work overtime in the last two weeks? *[Actual]*
   - If you were asked to work overtime continuously for a month, would that upset you? *[Hypothetical]*

Whatever the questions involved, the type of scale used to assess applicant responses can significantly affect their scoring and use in statistical analysis. Ideally, single-choice format questions with an underlying continuum should be used (see Figure 6-8), since this format facilitates scoring. However, practical realities may require the use of other forms of questions. In such instances, it may be necessary to develop special procedures for scoring.

ADVANTAGES OF USING BIOGRAPHICAL INFORMATION

As a screening or selection tool, biographical information has a number of advantages. Some of these were already discussed under WAB earlier. But here are some additional benefits specific to BIBs:

Improves understanding of performance Biodata items allow the recruiter to better understand the "why" behind effective performance. Typically, WAB items only help predict job success. BIB items offer a more elaborate explanation why some employees are better workers, and they detail employee motivational frameworks. Thus, in the long term, this knowledge helps managers understand what types of employees stay on a particular job, are more effective, and qualify for promotion to the next rank.

Prevents discrimination When carefully cross-validated, BIB contains only items that are valid predictors of job success. While in the initial stages, some of the items included in a BIB may raise controversy, successful cross-validation attempts ensures that the BIB is not culturally biased or unfair to specific groups. In general, biodata is among the most favourable of selection measures for women, minorities, and older job applicants, since these groups score as well on biodata questions as non-minority groups.

Provides validity without expense When carefully developed, biodata can be among the best predictors of job success. Yet the information is far cheaper to collect than that collected through copyrighted tests. Several studies have shown consistently high validity for BIBs, ranging from 0.30s to 0.40s.[22] For some occupations, such as sales, scientific and engineering, and clerical, the validities are higher: 0.46 to 0.52.[23]

Works well in a selection battery In general, biodata questionnaire scores show low correlation with scores in other skill and ability tests. This means that they tap into different dimensions of job performance. For this reason, including BIBs in a selection battery along with tests, interviews, and references will provide an employer with a broader understanding of the candidate.

Recognizes the principle of equipollence Personality tests assume that certain personality traits are critical for job success; however, as one researcher noted, biodata items recognize the principle of equipollence—that people with diametrically different personality traits may be equally effective in a job. Thus, past success, however achieved, can be effectively used to predict future job success.

Certainly, vastly different behaviours, strategies, and personalities can be successful in the same job. Depending on the situation, different behaviours may be appropriate:

> In a university classroom setting equally effective instructors use very different teaching methods. Some instructors primarily use lectures, while others use active learning strategies with continuous student participation. In the same way, successful salespersons exhibit widely different behaviours: some are "pushy" and aggressive, while others achieve the same results through a passive, soft-sell approach.

STEPS IN CONSTRUCTING BIBs

The steps involved in constructing BIBs are similar to those in the design of WABs or any other selection tool.

Step 1: Determine the need Because of the time and expense involved in designing a BIB, generally only jobs which require a relatively high degree of responsibility and impact on the organization ever need one. For lower-level jobs, a WAB will usually suffice. In general, BIBs are designed for managerial positions, although a number of other responsible positions, such as insurance agents, pharmaceutical scientists, research scientists and investment brokers, may also be appropriate.

Step 2: Conduct job analysis and identify criterion measure(s)
Job analysis is needed to identify reliable and valid criterion measures for the BIB. The relevant criterion varies from one organization to the next, and from one time period to the next. For this reason, take the time to identify it carefully. Here are some of the popular criteria:

- Tenure of the employee
- Quantity of performance
- Quality of performance
- Safety on the job
- Effectiveness ratings
- Potential for management development
- Overall creativity

- Number of new designs or products developed
- Potential for international assignments
- Client satisfaction measures

In the past, some researchers[24] have suggested using a broader approach to improve success at identifying appropriate criteria. Instead of choosing a single criterion or set of criteria, they advocate using Functional Job Analysis (FJA) to identify what a job incumbent does (that is, what procedures and processes are employed), and how a task is performed (that is, what kind of mental, physical, and interpersonal activities are involved in the job). (See Chapter 2 for details on FJA.)

> For an employee working with data, relevant activities may include comparing information, computing, analyzing, merging and compiling, synthesizing, and reporting. The skills needed for the tasks in each of these stages are quite distinct.

These differences mean that specific behaviours predictive of success in each activity may prove to be more useful. By combining FJA with literature searches, observation, record analysis, and expert surveys, salient dimensions of the job that need to be included in the BIB can be identified.

Step 3: Form tentative hypotheses

The next step is to formulate tentative hypotheses about predictors of job success. While this is a critical stage in the formulation of the BIB, no single action guarantees success in identifying relevant predictors. To improve the predictive ability of the items you select, consider the following:

- Reviews of research studies that appear in respected journals, such as *Journal of Applied Psychology, Journal of Consulting Psychology, Psychological Bulletin, Academy of Management,* and *Personnel Psychology*
- Surveys and consultations of experts in the area
- Past case studies on organizations or relevant job groups
- Observation of successful and unsuccessful job incumbents
- Use of creative alternative generation techniques, such as brainstorming, relational algorithm, and synectics

Once the tentative hypotheses about work success have been formulated, they need to be linked to early life experiences which are predictive of success. The following example illustrates the process:

> One study attempted to identify early life experiences associated with success in management consulting. A thorough analysis of consultants' jobs indicated that most successful consultants worked with top management and tended to develop as generalists focusing on general management and financial matters. Further analysis of consultant roles resulted in formulation of a hypothesis: successful consultants had backgrounds that provided them with considerable exposure to top management culture, which gave them expertise in dealing with managers. Once the researchers had formulated this hypothesis, they identified specific life history experiences relating to it. For example, applicants with parents who had high levels of education and held top management positions were thought to be more likely to be familiar with top management culture and thus more comfortable interacting with top managers. In addition, an applicant's prior association with a prestigious college or university could give these same skills. Similarly, military experience in the navy or air force was also considered indicative of exposure to top management culture.[25]

As the above example shows, forming tentative hypotheses about job success requires considerable expertise and judgment and should be done only after an exhaustive analysis of the factors affecting job performance.

Step 4: Identify potential biodata items

The hypotheses about job performance guide the identification of potential items to include in the BIB. Some past researchers have identified life history factors that may serve as the starting points in an effort to design a BIB:[26]

- Information relating to school and education
- Recreation and hobbies
- Self impressions
- Values, opinions, and preferences
- Habits and attitudes
- Parental home, childhood, teen years
- Personal attributes

Sometimes other items, such as attitudes toward money, human relations skills, and health, are included. When identifying items for the BIB, ensure that those you choose have some relevance for the job in question and follow these guidelines:[27]

- In general, the items should relate to past behaviour, experiences, or attitudes and values.
- As far as possible, ensure that the items are verifiable.
- Avoid questions of an intrusive nature (e.g., parental relationships), since many people find such questions offensive.
- Avoid items prohibited by the human rights legislation (e.g., questions about religion).
- All questions should contain options, such as a "not relevant" or "undecided" choice. Moreover, the choices offered should be equally attractive, lest the applicants be led to offer what they consider to be the socially desirable responses.

As far as possible, items should relate to first-hand impressions or recollections and measure unique, discrete events (e.g., the age when secured the first part-time job).

Step 5: Validate, score, and cross-validate

Once the items have been chosen, a panel of experts should carefully scrutinize them to eliminate biased, irrelevant, and objectionable material. Pretest the items on a small sample of relevant employees to reduce the number of items further, since the employees can let you know if they consider some of the remaining items ambiguous or objectionable.

Then administer the final list of items to a large and representative sample of job applicants and employees. While there is no ideal sample size, many studies have used samples of about 300 participants. Two authors[28] have suggested 500 people for dependable, generalizable findings.

The steps in validation are similar to those discussed under validation of the WAB. Delete items that show little variation between successful and unsuccessful job performance, that are potentially discriminatory, or that show no correlation with the criterion.

Score the BIB using manual weighting processes or statistical procedures. Like the WAB, the BIBs also have to be cross-validated.

CAUTIONS ABOUT USING BIBs

While BIBs have been found to be highly reliable and consistently valid, some cautions are in order. Studies have found that applicants' ideas about management skills may affect their responses, which reduces the validity of the score as a predictor of job success. Correlations with self-deception and impression management are very modest in most instances.[29] But informing the respondents that their answers are subject to independent verification may reduce the incidence of faking even further.

Another problem is indirect discrimination. While only job-relevant items are included in a BIB so that items themselves will not discriminate against any group, the relative weights attached to response categories could adversely affect a minority group.

> In one study, the BIB item "How were you referred for a job with us?" was found to discriminate against black applicants. The organization had attached a positive weight to those who applied because of current employee references. Since most black applicants did not have friends or acquaintances within the largely white firm who could refer them to the job, they consistently received lower scores on this question. The firm finally changed the weight attached to the question to avoid unintended discrimination against minority applicants.[30]

Changing weights for minority groups is one strategy to avoid potential, unintended discrimination. However, only continuous monitoring and cross-validation will bring such inequities to the attention of the decision-makers. This kind of monitoring requires considerable expertise and resource allocation, which may be beyond the capabilities of a typical employer, especially in a small organization.

In summary, BIBs are useful selection tools. Edwin Ghiselli's[31] classic review of the validity of aptitude tests revealed that when averaged over a number of occupations, biographical data was the most successful predictor of job success. Later studies[32] have also shown consistent validity coefficients for biographical data, often exceeding 0.30 (higher than most available tests). However, to reap their full benefits and to avoid potential discrimination against minority groups, BIBs must be designed and validated carefully, often with assistance from outside experts.

ELECTRONIC SCREENING OF APPLICATIONS

Many employers today are developing web applications that build an applicant profile through answers to a series of questions. Applicants must answer questions to get through the application, and in so doing, they help the employer decide whether to move the applicant to the next stage of selection.

Other employers prepare scannable application forms. A scannable application form is one that can be "read" by a computer equipped with Optical Character Recognition (OCR) hardware and software. The hardware scans text from paper into electronic format and then enters it into a database. Special software searches applicant resumes in the database for keywords, phrases, or qualifications desired by the firm. The software then creates a summary of the applicant profile and ranks it among other qualified candidates for the position. When well developed, **applicant tracking systems (ATS)** provide an organization with databases of potential candidates and facilitate good matches between job requirements and applicant characteristics. In addition, through ATS, employers are able to keep a large electronic file (or several inter-connected files) of all relevant attributes of potential candidates which can be readily accessed using key search words. ATS has become an initial employment screening tool among medium- to large-sized companies.

Scannable application forms offer numerous advantages for employers and job applicants:

- **Speed:** Electronic applicant screening speeds up the entire hiring process. This benefits both the employers and the job applicants, since it significantly reduces the processing and waiting time.

Applicant tracking systems (ATS): a database of potential recruits that can match job requirements with applicant characteristics though key word searches

- **Match between job requirements and applicant characteristics:** Employers can more easily find potential candidates by searching through their database and identifying those that match their needs.

- **Multiple jobs:** Resumes may be considered for current as well as future positions. An applicant may also get selected for a position that (s)he did not originally apply for, since the computer selects names on the basis of specific competencies and key words. If the database is used by the entire company, a resume may be considered for jobs in all departments in the company.

- **Avoid personal bias:** Unlike humans, computers hold no bias. Scanned resumes can reduce exclusion due to bias in the selection process.

- **Longevity of the application:** Most employers retain paper resumes for a set period of time (6 months to one year), rather than untill the time they fill a particular job position. But resumes that have been electronically scanned into a database can be retrieved, or "hit," at any time. With no additional effort from job applicants, these resumes may be seen by many additional people for months or years, depending on the organization's policy.

- **Lower overheads:** Human resource departments can be much smaller, and fewer staff are needed. Yet operating efficiency and speed can be greater.

But applications that are computer-scanned and preserved do have some limitations:

- The human discretion and judgment, a critical variable in many selection contexts, is all but eliminated from the initial screening process. Computers are machines devoid of capacity to respond to "grey areas." They follow simple decision rules to accept or reject applicants. As a result, some qualified applicants might not be considered if their application forms did not contain the same key words and phrases as the searcher.

- Resumes that have been in a database for a long period of time may become outdated and no longer reflect an applicant's current competencies or status.

- If the searcher pulls up information on salary and working conditions, this may reduce opportunities for the new recruit to negotiate.

- Machines do make errors, even if they do so less than humans.

A majority of medium- to large-sized companies are expected to use computers to process job applications in the foreseeable future.[33] This means that job applicants today have to be prepared to respond to such scannable application forms (or resumes, depending on the employer). An electronic application form is somewhat different from a paper resume and requires special considerations[34] (see Figure 6-10 for suggestions in preparing resumes).

FIGURE 6-10: Dos and Don'ts of Preparing Resumes for Electronic Screeners

DO:

- **Use standard resume format:** Use common headings, such as career objectives, education, work experience, as seen in resumes. These are also commonly used as search words by many employers.

- **Use white or very light-coloured paper:** When scanned, your writings will not be clear on dark-colored paper or paper with designs or linings.

- **Simplify:** Remove italic, bold, and other formatting in your resume, since scanners typically do not recognize these and are likely to get confused.

FIGURE 6-10: *(Continued)*

- **Use nouns:** Where possible, use nouns rather than verbs (e.g., accountant rather than accounting)
- **Be very specific:** Computer searches are by key words. If you know Java or C++, say so, rather than stating "knows computer languages." The same applies for skills you possess, awards you have received, and professional organizations to which you belong.
- **List degrees with specialization:** For example, do not simply say "undergraduate degree in commerce," but rather "B.Comm, Major: Finance."
- **List professional association memberships:** Include the exact names of professional associations in which you are a member. Beware of correct spelling, since computers do not make allowances for spelling errors!

DON'T:

- **Deviate from instructions:** If you do not follow the instructions on the form precisely, the computer will probably reject your application. The same can happen if you fold or staple an application against instructions.
- **Exaggerate:** Many programs have built-in checks to spot exaggeration. For example, if the years you mention under experience do not add up correctly, the computer is more likely than a staff member to catch the exaggeration.
- **Abbreviate:** Using excess abbreviations can result in confusion and rejection. However, standard, well-known abbreviations (e.g., MBA) are acceptable.
- **Be vague or general:** Avoid terms such as "a number of years of experience in cloth industry." Instead, write "seven years as textile designer" and "five years as factory superintendent."

Note: All the dos and don'ts that apply to resumes in general are also applicable to electronic submissions and scanned resumes.

Once the job applicant successfully clears initial screening, he or she enters the pool of applicants being seriously considered for the job position. The recruiters then use several selection tools, including tests and interviews, to select the best qualified candidates from this pool. The next two chapters discuss these steps in detail.

Implications for Practice

1. An organization's initial screening procedure should be well developed to match the applicant with job requirements. Good initial screening systems ensure that only qualified candidates progress to the next stage, while at the same time not unfairly rejecting any highly qualified applicants. In almost all organizations (except the very small ones where the volume of applications may be low) effective initial screening can save time and resources.

2. When conducting a telephone screening interview, ensure that the questions are simple and straightforward and directly related to the job position. Include only questions on information critical for the job. More detailed questions should wait until the interview.

3. Whether interviewing by telephone or in person, describe the job in enough detail so that the applicants can decide for themselves whether they are (1) really serious about applying and (2) adequately qualified.

4. Always make every effort to put the candidate at ease by using a positive, friendly tone. The burden is on the interviewer to establish a relaxed atmosphere.

5. The job application form should ask only for information permitted by the law, and it should collect information in a uniform manner.

6. Where cost-benefit analysis justifies the design of WAB or BIB, carry out a careful analysis of the job, the working conditions, and job success factors before identifying and validating items for the WAB or BIB instrument.

7. Develop WAB and BIB on as large a sample as possible, with a minimum of 300 application forms from persons hired and on whom criterion measures are available.

8. Cross-validate WAB and BIB using a different sample from the ones on which they were designed.

9. Continuously review WAB and BIB for relevance to applicant groups and job demands. A validity check every three or four years would meet the requirements in most situations.

10. Applicant tracking systems using computers can offer several advantages to an employer. However, the system should be periodically monitored to ensure currency and accuracy.

Key Terms for Review

Applicant tracking systems (ATS), *p. 226*

Biographical information blank (BIB), *p. 220*

Courtesy interview, *p. 206*

Criterion groups, *p. 213*

Hold-out group, *p. 213*

Initial screening, *p. 202*

Item weights, *p. 215*

Job application form, *p. 206*

Telephone screening, *p. 203*

Weighted application blank (WAB) or form, *p. 211*

Discussion Questions

1. What are the steps in the selection process? Would the process be different in large and small organizations?

2. If you were asked by your institution to help the admission office conduct a phone-a-thon to attract high school graduates, how would you structure your telephone interview to attract the best students?

3. What are courtesy interviews? Why would organizations spend time meeting with applicants who are unlikely to be hired?

4. List the items typically included in job application forms. Would the items included show variation across organizations?

5. What are weighted application blanks? How are they different from biographical blanks?

6. Would computer-based screening be applicable for all job positions? Why?

Critical Thinking Questions

1. Assume you were asked to be part of a committee formed to select the dean (or area head) of your institution. During the first meeting, you were asked for your input on the steps in the selection process. What suggestions would you give?

2. In the above example, assume that your committee decided to hire an executive search firm to identify potential candidates. The search firm has come up with a dozen names for the position. Because of time and resource constraints, only three candidates can be interviewed. To identify the best three, the chair of the search committee is planning to do a telephone interview with each candidate. She has asked you for your ideas on questions to include in the interview. What suggestions would you give to her?

3. A local small-business owner who runs a chain of popular eateries in the area has recently confided in you about a problem she currently faces and a possible course of action that she is contemplating. She tells you that on average she receives unsolicited resumes from 10–12 people who drop by her office. In the past, she has met with each applicant briefly, but now she finds that this practice is cutting into her time. In the future, she is thinking of placing a board in front of her office which reads, "No vacancy. Sorry, we have no job positions open." What advice would you give her?

4. Would the items in a job application form for a bank be different from the one for an auto dealership? Why or why not?

5. If you were asked to design a weighted application blank for the local police, what steps would you take?

6. Do you think that your educational institution should introduce computer-based screening for all student applicants to first-year programs? Why or why not?

Web Research

Using the Internet, collect job application forms for a bank, an insurance company, an airline, and a manufacturing unit. What is common on all these forms? What differences do you observe? How do you account for these differences?

CASE INCIDENT

Ontario Electronics Company Limited: Applicant Screening in Plant C

Note: This case continues from Chapter 1: Ontario Electronics Company Ltd. Review the case background in Chapter 1 before examining this case.

While in recent years, Ontario Electronics has done well financially, top management is unhappy with the productivity levels in some of the plants, especially Plant C. Tim Hutton, who was recently hired as a staffing analyst, reviewed the records and studied the situation for over a month. He also surveyed a representative sample of all workers in Plant C. A brief summary of Hutton's findings is provided in the case in Chapter 1 of the text. Based on the findings, the company made some changes in its human resource policies and introduced additional training at Plant C.

Shortly afterward, the management compared the performance of Plant C with two other comparable plants (in size and production volumes). Their findings are shown in Table A.

TABLE A:

Item	Plant C	Plant 1	Plant 2
Median performance appraisal ratings	4	5	6
Absenteeism rate (%)	7	5	4
Number of new product innovations in a two-year period	1	4	5
Employee turnover rate	10	5	3

Because of increasing demand for its products, OECL is currently planning to expand its capacity at Plant C. Initially, it will begin with a third shift, which will be followed by constructing a new facility near the old plant to increase capacity by another 25%. The new plant is expected to open in seven months. Meanwhile, the management is planning to hire an additional 30 full-time workers, 5 supervisors, and approximately 50 part-time workers. The management believes that the infusion of new people into the plant will help improve the situation and accelerate productivity growth. Already, the plant has begun to show some signs of improvement.

But because of tight local labour market conditions, many of the recruits may have to come from other parts of the country and even abroad (including the U.S., India, Taiwan, or Korea). Since putting all recruits through its selection battery will be expensive, the firm is considering some form of applicant screening. The company has a good reputation and typically gets 20–25 applications for each vacant position advertised. Of course, because of the specialized nature of the various positions, many of these applications do not qualify.

Questions

1. *What kind of screening procedure would you recommend?*

2. *Would your screening for supervisory personnel be any different from that for other employees? How*

CASE

Note: This case continues from Chapter 4: Kanata Food Distributors. Review the case background in Chapters 1, 2, 3, and 4 before examining this case.

Compared to other grocery stores, Kanata Food Distributor's Super K stores offer a limited range of products in family sizes at discount prices. The family-size products they do have are a relatively newer line (they were introduced as a competitive weapon against the in-roads made by large grocery warehouses of Costco, Loblaws and Metro). In addition, many of the newer Super K stores use an automated scanning system to prevent long line-ups at the checkout point. Approximately 30% of the total revenues for Kanata emerge from this line of business. One persistent problem facing the management has been the absenteeism rates of Super K employees. Since the profit margins on the products sold at Super K stores are low, maintaining high productivity levels (which includes eliminating absenteeism) is a high priority for the organization.

Recently, the management randomly chose three Super K stores and looked into their absenteeism pattern, especially among cashiers and other workers who work on the shop floor, including stocking, packing, and delivery. Table 1 summarizes the key findings, along with some information on the profile of the workers who were reviewed for the purpose. While most of the stores have a diverse workforce, the profiles of workers show some variation across stores because of their location. For example, in one store, which is located near two high schools, a large number of part-time employees are high school students.

Super K management is currently reviewing its hiring and other related human resource policies. It is embarking on a major expansion plan that will require the hiring of many new cashiers. Needless to state, the management would like to reduce absenteeism rates among new hires.

TABLE 1: Absenteeism Rates in Three Randomly Chosen Super K Stores

Period	Store 1	Store 2	Store 3
This Year			
First Quarter	13%	9%	10%
Second Quarter	11%	8%	8%
Third Quarter	10%	13%	9%
Last Quarter	17%	10%	10%
Last Year			
First Quarter	16%	12%	14%
Second Quarter	14%	10%	12%
Third Quarter	16%	16%	13%
Last Quarter	22%	12%	14%
Year Before			
First Quarter	19%	13%	15%
Second Quarter	17%	12%	14%
Third Quarter	17%	18%	15%
Last Quarter	23%	13%	15%
Workforce Characteristics			
Nature of workforce			
Full-time	63%	30%	49%
Part-time	37%	70%	51%
Median age	42 years	23 Years	49 years
Gender			
Men	38%	52%	47%
Women	62%	48%	53%
Education level			
Less than high school	30%	70%	25%
High school	65%	29%	67%
Post-secondary	5%	1%	8%

TABLE 1:   (Continued)

Median performance ratings (by supervisors) on a 10-point scale	7.25	6.0	6.75
Tenure of employees			
Less than 2 Years	30%	80%	33%
2 years or more	70%	20%	67%

Questions

1. Based on the material presented in the case, what conclusions can you form about Super K's recruitment processes?

2. What suggestions would you make to the company's management to improve its hiring outcome? Why?

*Case written by Professor Hari Das of Saint Mary's University, Halifax. All rights retained by the author, © 2005.

CHAPTER

7 USE OF TESTS IN SELECTION

"Executives and managers have found testing extremely valuable, particularly in tapping subtleties, that no other tool provides. With a growing trend as well for using psychological consultants in team building, stress management, and other organizational matters once applicants are already aboard, the likelihood of reverting back to pretesting era is nil."

Edward Hoffman[1]

CHAPTER OBJECTIVES

After studying this chapter, you should be able to:

- Describe the reasons for popularity of tests and the potential dangers when using them

- Discuss the popular types of tests available today

- Discuss steps to ensure proper use of selection tests

A large electronic appliances retail chain was concerned about its declining sales, especially since the arrival of low-price competitors such as Wal-Mart and Costco in several locations where the firm had once dominated. Initially, the firm attempted to meet the competition through price reduction and advertising. When those efforts did not achieve the intended results, it decided to hire more aggressive, customer-oriented sales staff. A new personality test with proven validity in similar work settings was included in the selection battery. However, until the new test was validated for its workforce, the management was hesitant to use it for hiring employees. Over the following ten months, it hired forty new sales assistants, most of them full-time and on commission basis. Each candidate completed the personality test as part of their application, although the test results were not used in the selection decision. Six months after they were hired, the human resource department compared the test scores against the performance of each new employee. The cut-off score suggested by the test maker was used to classify each employee into a "pass" or a "fail" category. By comparing the supervisory ratings of the employees over a three-month period, management discovered that those who had higher scores on the personality test had an average 12% lead over those with lower scores. What was even more striking was the difference in the commissions earned by the two groups. On average, the high scorers had earned 26% more commission than low scorers and had 38% higher sales volume. Encouraged by the results, the firm decided to employ the test in all future hiring decisions.

Not all organizations employing tests experience such positive results; however, more and more organizations are finding that valid employment tests can play an integral part of their selection battery, providing important insights into the job applicant's personality, values, and work ethic. No wonder the number of Canadian employers using employment tests has been steadily increasing. One study showed that personality tests are now commonly used to select middle management employees, and aptitude tests are common for white-collar nonprofessional jobs. Nearly 50% of employers use at least one paper-and-pencil test.[2]

POPULARITY OF TESTS

What makes employment tests popular? Both practitioners and researchers have identified a number of benefits associated with the use of employment tests.

STRENGTHS OF SELECTION TESTS

Employment tests have been found to be objective, valid, and versatile in several settings.

Objective assessment Well-designed tests provide a fair and objective basis for assessing an applicant's potential, since the assessor's bias, background, and perceptual inaccuracies do not influence the test scores. Interviews, reference checks, and other personal evaluation methods are vulnerable to the stereotypes, personal biases, and perceptual limitations of the evaluator.

> According to a survey by the Ivey School of Business in London, Ontario, most Canadian firms continue to use informal interviews and resumes for all types of positions; and in that process, they often fail to get the right person for the job. The interview is still the most common tool for selecting senior employees. A significant number of these new hires will have to be fired within the first three months to a year. "Technically, similar results could be achieved by flipping a coin or using a horoscope. This is very unfortunate, because with a little forethought and research, any organization could increase the overall quality of its people by 30% to 50%," notes John Eggers, a co-author of the study.[3]

In contrast, tests are administered under standardized conditions by trained staff. For example, the Canadian Psychological Association (CPA) provides Guidelines for Educational and Psychological Testing. Further, because of the objective nature of test scores, they can be more easily interpreted and combined with other predictors than reference letters or other personal evaluations.

High reliability and validity Well-designed tests have high reliability and proven validity, which facilitates interpretation of the scores. In addition, through procedures such as validity generalization (see Chapter 4), they can also be adapted to alternate settings.

Versatility Tests can be used both for recruiting purposes and for new hires after they have joined the organization. The Canadian Psychological Association notes that tests are particularly helpful for

Canadian Psychological Association:
www.cpa.ca

1. selecting individuals for an entry-level position,
2. making differential job assignments,
3. promoting individuals within an organization,
4. identifying employees with training potential, and
5. counselling and identifying individuals for specialized positions.

Hidden values and traits An applicant's core values, work-related attitudes, and stable personality traits are invisible. While reports of past experiences contained in resumes, work samples, and referee reports provide some valid information about an applicant's past and likely future behaviours, they can also be faked or misrepresented. In contrast, well-designed tests provide clues to an individual's core values and personality (see Figure 7-1). In some situations, tests uncover personality issues that may not come to light in any other way. Consider the following example:

> A large apartment complex was about to hire a couple as the new superintendents on the basis of their interview scores and references. But before handing over the keys to the apartment, the owners decided to administer a test that measured a variety of personality issues, including honesty. The test scores on honesty were very low. These scores prompted the owners to probe into their backgrounds. They discovered that the man had just been released from prison after serving time for armed robbery, and the woman was due to appear in the court on shoplifting charges![4]

WEAKNESSES OF SELECTION TESTS

Despite their popularity and usefulness, tests have some problems. But keep in mind that many of the problems are because of the improper *application* of the tests, rather than the tests themselves.

Tests with questionable reliability and validity This textbook has stressed the importance of reliability and validity of selection procedures and criteria (see

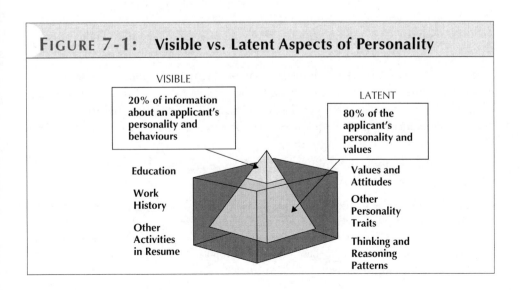

FIGURE 7-1:   Visible vs. Latent Aspects of Personality

VISIBLE

20% of information about an applicant's personality and behaviours

LATENT

80% of the applicant's personality and values

Education

Work History

Other Activities in Resume

Values and Attitudes

Other Personality Traits

Thinking and Reasoning Patterns

Chapter 4). Some employers believe that tests purchased from a reputable test publisher already have proven reliability and validity. However, not all tests have been tested.

> The Buros Institute of Mental Measurements, which reviewed more than 1000 commercially available tests published in recent years, concluded that over 22% of them did not have any reliability information; 7% had neither reliability nor validity data; and 28% did not report any normative data to help the user compare scores against a standard.[5]

The human resource manager should not assume that tests have proven reliability or validity until they have seen psychometric data pertaining to the tests. Reputable test publishers provide this information upfront and also continually review test results and norms for different population segments.

Misuse of tests

Misuse of tests A related problem is the use of tests for purposes for which they were not meant. Using the wrong test or using the right test in the wrong way means the employer wastes time and money, while very likely turning down the best candidates for the job.

> A case in point is the use of Myers-Brigg Type Indicator (MBTI,) which many recruiters use to screen applicants. But MBTI tests were not designed for applicant screening. "You'll probably find a lot of people who are tempted to use MBTI for a selection type of process. But it's not recommended to use that for personnel selection simply due to the way it works," according to Shawn Bakker, a chartered psychologist at Psychometrics Canada, an Edmonton-based firm that specializes in providing test measures for personnel selection.[6] MBTI won't help organizations evaluate candidates because it really only distinguishes between extroverts and introverts.

A personality test such as Myers-Briggs works better for other settings, such as organizations attempting to develop existing staff. It can help groups improve inter-member communication or help individuals identify their own strengths and weaknesses.[7] Problems arise when employers are unaware of the purpose of tests or testing procedures. For example, a good understanding of the typical content of tests is required to choose well from dozens of tests purporting to measure sales aptitude:

> Tests aimed at assessing potential for technical sales are different from those for retail operations. Similarly, a test for a sales manager should include leadership, employee management, and strategic planning abilities, while a test for a floor worker will not need to consider these traits to the same extent.

The onus is on the employer to ensure that only qualified persons interpret test results. Many reputable test publishers require buyers of tests to establish their credibility in administering and interpreting results before they agree to the sale.

Testing beyond bona fide job requirements

Testing beyond bona fide job requirements The onus is on the employer to show that the tests are measuring bona fide job requirements (BFJR). The knowledge, skills, abilities, or other competencies (KSAO) tested must be related to job performance criteria identified through job analysis. Tests should only be used to assess BFJR listed in job descriptions and specifications. Since job content changes over time, job analysis should be done continuously to reflect changes in tasks, technology, and job demands.

> In the 1960s, a supermarket cashier needed mathematical skills (such as adding, subtracting, and multiplying,) since calculators were relatively uncommon. However, in the 1970s and 1980s, this skill became relatively less important for that job. Today, with electronic scanners, mathematical skills have become even less important for cashiers. Thus, employment tests from the past would be completely inappropriate for hiring cashiers today.

Selection tests should "accurately assess the individual's performance or capacity to perform the essential components of the job in question, safely, efficiently and reliably."[8] However, many organizations fail to meet this requirement, making them vulnerable to litigation and loss of qualified job applicants. Note also that even where a requirement is bona fide, the employer still has the responsibility to make reasonable accommodation for differences in ability (see Chapter 3).

> A man was refused a technician's job because he failed a hearing test, which he had taken without his hearing aid. He asserted that he could perform the job using a hearing device. Medical advisers for the company claimed that the job required perfect normal hearing. After conciliation, the company agreed that with a hearing aid, the man would be able to do the job. The complaint was settled with the complainant being hired as a technician and paid damages of $750.

When testing applicants with disabilities, employers must make special efforts to ensure that the test is fair. They must accommodate people with disabilities by giving them a test that is as neutral to their disability as possible.

> For example, an employer administering an oral test to applicants for a programmer's job to test their knowledge of programming can offer to print a copy of the test to a partially deaf applicant. This is a reasonable accommodation because hearing is not as critical for the job.

Risk of unintended discrimination

Chapter 3 discussed how even systematic employment procedures can discriminate against specific groups unintentionally. When a test continuously rejects people of a particular race, sex, religion, or national origin or has any other *adverse effect* on a minority group, it violates the *Canadian Human Rights Act* and related provincial legislation. Many of the tests used in Canada were developed in the United States, so in some cases they are partially invalid, since they were developed for a different culture. Moreover, too often, tests fail to predict job performance.[9] A Toronto-based industrial psychologist has estimated that "only 3% of firms use properly validated selection tests."[10] If this estimate is correct, then human resources professionals need to increase their scrutiny of testing and its relationship to discrimination.

Even when tests have been validated, the type of validation used may render the test invalid for a particular culture. The following landmark case illustrates this point:

> The Albemarle Paper Company, a U.S. firm, gave several black workers a battery of tests that had not been validated. The workers sued Albemarle, so the company then implemented a validation study. But the study had several weaknesses, and the court ruled the tests invalid and discriminatory. The major problem was that Albemarle had used tests that had been validated for advanced jobs, not the entry-level positions to which tests were being applied, and then tried to validate them for entry-level positions after-the-fact. But to be useful and effective, tests must be validated on jobs to which tests are being applied. Furthermore, even if tests are valid for one cultural group (e.g., white workers), they cannot necessarily be applied fairly to another group (black workers). Tests must be validated for all the groups to whom the test applies.[11]

Human resource specialists should conduct their own studies to make sure a particular test is valid for its planned use. The HR specialist should also be aware of the variables surrounding a job applicant's performance on a specific test.

> For example, a multiple-choice aptitude test may discriminate against groups of applicants who have weak test-taking skills but have strong skills for the actual job. Test-taking anxiety levels may vary across applicant groups. Some studies indicate that females exhibit higher levels of stress over tests than males.[12]

Information on psychological tests and validity:
www.apa.org/science/ testing.html

Invasion of privacy During the hiring process, job applicants must reveal a lot of information about themselves. But no matter what selection tool is used, requesting information that is not job-related is unethical. All applicants have a right to privacy, and employers must recognize and respect this right. In this context, personality tests run the risk of invading an individual's privacy, especially if the tests inquire about topics that are personal in nature, such as core values, religious beliefs, or sexual practices. In addition, psychological tests should not be treated as medical tests by requiring information that might suggest a mental disorder or impairment. Further, HR departments must safeguard all information collected during selection. This information should be only released to personnel who have legitimate and professional interest in the job applicant.

> Many work settings have introduced workplace privacy policies. In several provinces, privacy is becoming an important issue. For example, municipal and provincial employees in Ontario have right to access and protect their own personal information, including information obtained through employment testing.

American Psychological Association information on testing:
www.apa.org/science/testing.html

Variety of tests:
www.queendom.com/tests/

TYPES OF TESTS

Figure 7-2 lists some of the currently popular employment tests. It shows the variety of tests available. However, each type of test has only limited usefulness. The exact purpose of a test, its design, its reliability and validity information, its administrative instructions, and its applications are recorded in the test manual, which staff should review thoroughly before administering a test. While a detailed discussion of each test is beyond the scope of this book, major types of tests are briefly discussed below.

FIGURE 7-2: Popular Employment Tests

1. KNOWLEDGE TESTS
Mathematical tests
Verbal ability tests
Minnesota Clerical Tests
Tests conducted by professional organizations (e.g., legal, accounting)

2. ABILITY AND APTITUDE TESTS
Differential Aptitude Tests (DAT)
Comprehensive Ability Battery (CAB)
General Aptitude Test Battery (GATB)
Otis-Lennon Mental Ability Test
Wechsler Adult Intelligence Scale
Wonderlic Personnel Test
Watson-Glaser Critical Thinking Appraisal
Stromberg Dexterity Test
O'Connor Tweezer Dexterity Test
Purdue Peg Board Test
Visual Skills Tests
Dynamometer Grip Strength Test
Ishihara Test for Color Blindness

3. VOCATIONAL INTEREST TESTS
Kuder Preference and Interest Scales
Strong Interest Inventory
Jackson Vocational Interest Inventory
Vocational Preference Inventory
Stanford-Binet Intelligence Scale

FIGURE 7-2:   (*Continued*)

4. LEADERSHIP AND EMOTIONAL INTELLIGENCE TESTS
Multifactor Leadership Questionnaire
Leadership Opinion Questionnaire
How to Supervise?
Multifactor Emotional Intelligence Scale (MEIS)
Emotional Competence Inventory (ECI)
Bar-On Emotional Quotient Inventory (EQI)
Miner Sentence Completion Scale
Work Profile Questionnaire—Emotional Intelligence

5. PERSONALITY TESTS
Sixteen Personality Factor Questionnaire (16PF)
Hogan Personality Inventory
Guilford-Zimmerman Temperament Survey
Jackson Personality Inventory
California Psychological Inventory
Work Profile Questionnaire
Handwriting Analysis
Minnesota Multiphasic Personality Inventory
Projective Techniques
Thematic Apperception Tests (TAT)

6. WORK SAMPLES AND SIMULATIONS
Work Samples
Assessment Centres

7. HONESTY/INTEGRITY TESTS
Reid Report
Stanton Survey
Hogan Personality Inventory—Reliability Scale
London House Personnel Selection Inventory
PDI Employment Inventory
Graphology/Lie Detector Tests

8. MEDICAL AND DRUG TESTS
Drug tests
Medical tests
Genetic screening

KNOWLEDGE TESTS

Job knowledge tests attempt to assess the degree to which job applicants are knowledgeable about concepts, issues, or procedures essential for successful job performance. Typically, job knowledge tests or trade tests consist of a series of "key" questions that differentiate the truly skilled and experienced applicants from those who are less knowledgeable or from "trade bluffers."[13] Although these tests may be written or oral, they are typically written. There are two important uses of job knowledge tests: (1) to check an applicant's claims about their knowledge, and (2) to assess the job knowledge of present employees being considered for promotion or transfer. Other knowledge tests summarize an applicant's knowledge in a specific area. Figure 7-3 shows an example of a knowledge test.

These tests are generally highly reliable because they measure only information and knowledge, with validities that average 0.45 against job performance. These tests can be particularly helpful when recruiters must select candidates for highly complex jobs.[14]

Job knowledge tests: examine the degree to which job applicants are knowledgeable about concepts, issues, or procedures essential for successful job performance

---

FIGURE 7-3:   A Knowledge Test for Elementary Concepts in Physics

1. A fundamental unit is a

   A) Joule.
   B) metre.
   C) Hertz.
   D) Gauss.
   E) Newton.

2. A _____ is a unit for measuring frequency.

   A) Joule
   B) metre
   C) Hertz
   D) Gauss
   E) Newton

3. Two unequal masses falling freely from the same point above would experience the same

   A) acceleration.
   B) change in mass.
   C) decrease in potential energy.
   D) increase in kinetic energy.
   E) increase in momentum.

4. The internal energy of water is determined by

   A) phase.
   B) mass.
   C) temperature.
   D) A and B above.
   E) A, B, and C.

Answers: 1B, 2C, 3A, 4E

Arithmetic tests for an accountant, a "bar exam" for lawyers, a tax law test for a tax specialist, and a weather test for a pilot are all examples of knowledge tests.

However, care must be taken to ensure that the knowledge being tested is needed to perform the job. Consider the following example:

> An Ontario trucking company once gave all its applicants an extensive reading test. However, because the drivers received their instructions orally and were shown on a map where to go, the reading test had no relationship to job performance; it did not distinguish good drivers from bad ones. It only distinguished between those who could read English well and those who could not.[15]

Practical intelligence: the practical ability to accomplish tasks and solve problems successfully, rather than professed or theoretical knowledge

Some researchers[16] have argued that "practical intelligence"—the ability to get things done without help from others—is critical for job success. In a sense, **practical intelligence** is the difference between professed or theoretical knowledge and the practical knowledge to get a job done. This is considered akin to "organizational smarts," the ability to influence others, minimize resistance, and get things done. Unfortunately, available research evidence[17] does not provide much support for practical intelligence as a predictor of job success. Thus, while this remains an interesting and intriguing notion, further operationalization and testing of this construct is needed before using it for employment purposes.

Focus on Ethics

Recently, you became an assistant to the human resources manager at a grocery chain employing approximately 300 people. The HR Department consists of three employees, including yourself, all of whom report to the HR manager. So far, you have liked the way the system works here—that is, until this week.

Your boss is currently on leave and will not be back for nearly three weeks. When she left, she asked you to "take care of the ship," since the other two employees were tied up with other projects. This week, you have to make two decisions, both of which appear difficult.

1. Elizabeth Bean, the mother of your schoolmate, Bob, recently applied for a position in the company. She did well in the employment test and interview and had relevant work experience, so she was offered employment in the company, subject to passing a ten-item honesty test. Two critical questions in the test are "I know a dishonest individual" and "A number of teenagers whom I know have shoplifted." In the test's scoring scheme, a "yes" answer to either one of these questions results in loss of several points. Ms. Bean had said "yes" to both questions, which resulted in a failing score. But yesterday you remembered an event that happened over ten years ago: Bob and a couple of his other friends had once been caught shoplifting. Although it was treated as a minor offence at that time

and Bob was let go (Bob is currently working as an assistant in a law firm), his mother had apparently remembered that incident and truthfully reported it during the test. You have known Ms. Bean for over 12 years now, and she has always impressed you by her high ethical standards, such as the time she returned a wallet containing $300 to a person who had left it behind in a church. What should you do now on the matter of hiring Ms. Bean?

2. Your firm's employment test is scored on a 0–60 scale, where the optimal score for successful candidates for the cashier's position is in the 30–40 range. The test measures general cognitive ability and variety-seeking behaviour (e.g., curiosity, originality). The norms for the test were fixed with a sample of 4000 cashiers. Although the same test is used for hiring for all positions, the cut-off scores are different for different jobs (e.g., you scored 55 when you took the test). Both management and the test makers believe that candidates with high scores will get bored with routine jobs and leave. Recently, your neighbour, Mack, told you that he is planning to apply for a cashier's position in your firm. Mack is a very bright young man, and you would really like him to join your firm. However, you suspect that he will top the test, and on that ground would probably get rejected. Should you advise Mack not to do "too well" in the test, which he is scheduled to write tomorrow?

VOCATIONAL INTEREST TESTS

Vocational interest tests show how a person's interest pattern compares with successful job incumbents. They indicate the occupations or areas of work where a person is most likely to be interested and to find most satisfying. The underlying assumption is that people do well at and remain in a job that they enjoy.

A variety of vocational interest inventories are currently available. Chapter 5 discusses some of the more popular vocational and career planning theories and models. Using these theories, researchers have designed vocational interest inventories and tests (see Figure 7-2). Of these, the Strong's Vocational Interest Blank has been very popular with many employers and recruiters. But note that these inventories, including Strong's, are more useful in predicting job stability than they are in predicting job success.[18] Even though interest may define the direction of effort, it does not guarantee success. Hence these tests should not be confused with aptitude or ability tests.

Be aware that most of these tests are susceptible to faking. Applicants may try to put their best foot forward by giving answers that they think the employer wants to hear.[19] For this reason, these measures are more appropriate for counselling employees than for making hiring decisions.

Vocational interest tests: tests of a person's interest patterns compared with successful job incumbents, thereby indicating the occupations or areas of work where a person is most likely to be successful

ABILITY AND APTITUDE TESTS

Ability tests: tests that measure a person's mental, mechanical, physical, and clerical abilities

Aptitude tests: tests that measure a person's natural inclination or quickness to learn and understand job or trade processes

Ability tests measure an individual's mental, mechanical, physical (e.g., psycho-motor coordination), and clerical abilities. In contrast, **aptitude tests** measure an individual's innate ability to learn and understand processes. However, researchers[20] indicate that this distinction is arbitrary. Both ability and aptitude tests measure the individual's lifetime accumulation of learning from all sources, including informal learning experiences. Both types of test measure "what a person has learned up to the time he or she takes the test. No test can truly measure future capacity to learn,"[21] since almost all these tests involve measurement of some actual behaviour, whether writing answers or giving verbal responses.

Finger dexterity, eye-hand coordination, and psycho-motor coordination are some examples of abilities tested with ability tests.

Skills: proficiencies at specific tasks, based on past learning, experience, and aptitude

Closely related to abilities and aptitudes, but still distinct from them, are skills. **Skills** refer to the degree of proficiency in a specific task, based on past learning, experience, and aptitude. Skills tests range from typing tests to architectural drafting tests. While partially determined by past training, skills are still influenced by other factors.

Thus, two keyboard operators may have same level of ability at typing, yet one of them may possess vastly superior typing skills.

The construct validity of aptitude tests has received increased attention, and the results are positive. But construct validation in employment settings is still rare.[22] Most validation studies focus on specific criteria, such as absenteeism, tenure, and quality consciousness. Often supervisory ratings, rather than objective indices, are employed to validate the tests.

Over the years, more than 50 distinct human abilities have been identified.[23] These are classified into four major groups: cognitive, psycho-motor, sensory/perceptual, and physical.

Cognitive abilities: general intellectual abilities, such as verbal and numerical abilities, problem solving, reasoning, ordering, logical evaluation, and information processing

Cognitive abilities

Cognitive abilities are related to general intellectual abilities, such as verbal and numerical abilities, problem solving, reasoning, ordering, logical evaluation, and information processing. These abilities primarily reflect an individual's capacity to mentally manipulate words, figures, symbols, numbers, and logical order.

For example, The Wonderlic Personnel Test, first developed in 1938, is a popular 50-item test that assesses vocabulary, syllogisms, arithmetic reasoning, analogies, spatial relations, and perceptual skills. The parallel-form reliability for the test ranges from 0.82 to 0.94. Because of its strong psychometric properties, this test is often included in selection programs.[24]

FIGURE 7-4:   Abilities Assessed by Popular Mental Ability Tests

Verbal comprehension
Semantic relations
Conceptual classification
Logical ordering
Logical evaluation
Intuitive reasoning
General reasoning
Numerical mastery
Spatial orientation
Figural classification

FIGURE 7-5: A Sample Verbal and Quantitative Reasoning Ability Test

Verbal Reasoning	Quantitative Reasoning
1. Circle the word that best explains the meaning of the word in capitals. ACQUIESCE A) drench B) assent C) yield D) dispute E) accumulate 2. Circle the word pair that expresses the same relationship as the pair in capital letters. FOOTPRINTS: EFFACE A) gulley : widen B) target : omit C) record : obliterate D) represent : hope E) laud : success 3. The word "thwart" means A) waive B) foil C) vacillate D) relinquish E) satiate	4. What number divided by 4/5 is equal to 3/8 of 96? A) 36 B) 45 C) 96 D) 12 E) 81 5. If 3 = 0, 4 = 4, 5 = 8, 6 = 12, then 7 = ? A) 7 B) 14 C) 16 D) 18 E) 20 6. If a decorative cloth costs $12 per square metre, how much will it cost to buy a piece that will decorate an area that is 9 metres long and 12 metres wide? A) $144 B) $108 C) $252 D) $1296 E) $129.60
Answers: 1B, 2C, 3B	**Answers:** 4B, 5C, 6D

The target abilities measured by popular mental ability tests are shown in Figure 7-4. But keep in mind that these abilities are all quite distinct; mental ability tests do not all measure the same abilities and cannot simply be substituted one for another. For example, a test that assesses verbal and quantitative reasoning is shown in Figure 7-5.

More recently, general mental ability (usually referred to as "g" or GMA) has become a very popular idea. **General mental ability** refers to the underlying factor that determines most mental abilities, such as verbal and mathematical reasoning, manipulation of symbols and information, and logical reasoning. This factor is believed to promote learning, problem solving, and communication. As indicative of a person's "brain power," GMA has been found to predict a new employee's performance during job training and general job performance.[25] The relationship between GMA and job performance holds for most types of jobs, especially those that require high levels of reasoning, such as managerial and professional occupations. With validity coefficients of 0.50, GMA tests are among the most valid tests.[26] But note that mental ability tests do not measure work attitudes, dependability, or interpersonal skills.[27] Mental ability tests may also adversely impact against minority groups and hence should be implemented with care. Cognitive ability tests are generally paper-and-pencil tests (or more recently, computer interactive tests).

General mental ability ("g"): underlying intelligence factor that explains most mental abilities (verbal and mathematical reasoning, manipulation of symbols and information, and logical reasoning) and supports effective learning, problem solving, and communications

Developed at the Bow Valley College in Calgary, the test of Workplace Essential Skills (known by the acronym TOWES) assesses three essential worker skills: text reading, document use, and numeracy. Candidates assume the role of a worker who must process information embedded in an authentic workplace document—forms, labels, safety information and so on—and use that information to complete a task and solve a problem.[28]

Psycho-motor abilities

Psycho-motor abilities reflect a person's ability to control muscle movements, including finger dexterity, arm-hand steadiness, multi-limb coordination, response time, and overall manual dexterity. "Finger dexterity" refers to the ability to make precise, coordinated movements with the fingertips, such as required by a watchmaker or computer repairperson. "Manual dexterity" involves coordinated movements of hands and arms, while "wrist finger speed" refers to the ability to make wrist-flexing and finger movements rapidly.[29]

Unlike cognitive ability tests, these are rarely paper and pencil tests. In psycho-motor tests, the applicant performs standardized tasks using a specialized piece of equipment.

> For example, the Purdue Pegboard Test, which measures finger dexterity, requires the person to insert as many pegs as possible into a pegboard in a predetermined time period. Similarly, the test which measures gross arm movement speed requires the applicant to strike a wired metal stylus at targets of varying sizes see through ten metal-lined holes in a wooden board.

By their very nature, psycho-motor tests are actual performance tests and assess skills that are closely related to actual job performance. Most of them have high validity in predicting future job performance.

> A driving license is given after a "road test," which evaluates the driver's eye-hand-foot coordination and ability to respond to stimuli. The admission tests in many Canadian dental schools include tests for finger and manual dexterity.

Because of their high face-validity, many employers assume that these tests are valid. However, these tests can still result in unintended discrimination against specific applicant groups.

Sensory/perceptual abilities

Sensory and perceptual abilities refer to a person's vision, hearing, and sensory capabilities. Tests designed to assess these abilities focus on vision and colour discrimination, speech recognition, and hearing.

> Most people are familiar with the Snellen Chart used by optometrists for assessing vision. Similar tests using sophisticated equipment are available for testing auditory and tactile abilities of individuals. Pilots have to be tested for specific standards in vision.

More advanced sensory/perceptual ability tests (several of which are commercially available) focus on figure/object recognition and learning, cognition, motor control, and physical disabilities. Subtests examine visual-motor speed, position in space, eye-hand coordination, copying spatial relations, figure-ground distinction, visual closure, and form constancy. Most of these tests require specialized equipment.

Careful identification of the standards required for the job should precede interpretation of the tests. Unless the standards required are bona fide job requirements, the organization may expose itself to possible litigation.

A more recent development is the use of computer-interactive performance tests. The advent of computers has opened up new possibilities for measuring perceptual-motor skills (e.g., reaction time and control precision), perceptual speed, and spatial visualization. Computers can also measure human capabilities not measurable by printed tests:

> For instance, through simulation, computer-interactive tests can measure an applicant's abilities in time sharing, concentration, and working under time pressures. A life insurance company presents fact-based scenarios to job applicants using a computer. The candidates' reactions to the scenarios, both mental (e.g., comprehension, coding, calculation) and motor (e.g. keying speed, accuracy) are assessed while the job candidate processes claims on the computer screen.[30]

Physical abilities Researchers have identified physical abilities that predict job performance. While there are many interpretations, **physical abilities** generally refer to muscular strength, cardiovascular endurance, and movement quality.

Physical abilities: an individual's muscular strength, cardiovascular endurance, and movement quality

- *Muscular strength* refers to the ability to apply or resist force through muscular contraction, which in turn relates to an individual's muscular power, tension, and endurance.

- *Cardiovascular endurance* reflects the capacity to sustain muscular activity over an extended period of time.

- *Movement quality* measures an individual's flexibility, balance, and muscular integration.

Research on physical abilities has shown significant validities for physical ability tests for many trades and occupations. Examples include army enlists (0.87), pipeline workers (0.63), and electrical workers (0.53). For jobs such as firefighters, police officers, construction workers, utility repair personnel, established minimum physical abilities are common.[31]

Research evidence from the U.S. indicates that workers are three times more likely to be injured while performing jobs for which they have not demonstrated the required capabilities. On other hand, physical ability tests often adversely impact on women and other minority groups. The example of the women firefighters in Chapter 3 illustrates how setting minimum physical standards that are not bona fide job requirements can result in discrimination charges.

Faced with this dilemma, some employers have opted for medical and physical fitness exams to provide a measure of physical ability. However, this is no substitute for physical ability tests and cannot predict the applicant's ability to perform a task safely For example, a medical test typically assesses whether an applicant has a healthy cardiovascular system, not whether the applicant has cardiovascular endurance in a specific activity for a set period of time—unless, of course, a physical ability test is included as a part of such an examination.

Other employers have attempted to prescribe *physical standards* as a way to overcome the problem. Thus, rather than measuring a person's strength, they prescribe specific heights and weights, assuming that people who fall within a range of height and weight have the required physical abilities. But these requirements don't necessarily correlate with specific abilities. Physical standards can also adversely discriminate against applicant groups who possess the required abilities but not the standards.

For example, Asian Canadians on average are shorter than Caucasian or African Canadians. Establishing minimum height requirements could preclude many qualified Asians from being hired.

Thus, physical ability requirements must be set only after a thorough job analysis. They should reflect bona fide job requirements. Even when such standards are prescribed, the employer has to make reasonable accommodation to ensure that no minority group is adversely affected.

LEADERSHIP AND EMOTIONAL INTELLIGENCE TESTS

Currently, there are over 8000 books on leadership in print; yet there is no agreement on the attributes of the ideal leader. Effective leaders can have vastly different leadership styles; nor does a single leadership style seem successful in all settings. For this reason, accurately assessing the leadership potential of applicants is very difficult. In general, several dimensions of effective leadership[32] are assessed:

- Vision and the ability to think in big-picture terms rather than in minute details
- Optimism and excitement about purpose
- Ability to value subordinates and others for their unique talents and to inspire them to the common cause
- Integrity
- Ability to provide clear directives and feedback
- Ability to facilitate action and removal of obstacles
- Commitment to the cause and hard work

Many devices for assessing leadership have become popular. The 45-item Multifactor Leadership Questionnaire[33] assesses six dimensions of leadership: intellectual stimulation, contingent reward, management by exception, charisma, laissez-faire, and individualized consideration. It has so far generated over 200 studies worldwide and has been used by many large banks, community action agencies, oil companies, and the army.

Another widely used measure is the Leadership Practices Inventory (LPI), which assesses five dimensions of leadership: challenging the process, inspiring a shared vision, enabling others to act, modelling the way, and encouraging. The 30-item LPI has become very popular, especially in corporate training programs on leadership, because it is easy to administer.

Over the past decade, emotional intelligence has become a popular buzzword in the media and in industry. David Goleman, who popularized this concept, uses the term **emotional intelligence (EQ)** to refer to a set of abilities including self control, zeal, impulse control, and delayed gratification, so that one can regulate one's mood and hope and persist in the face of frustration. More recent researchers have defined it differently. For example, two researchers[34] have identified the following seven competencies associated with the construct:

- *Self awareness*: the awareness of one's feelings and ability to recognize and manage these.
- *Motivation*: the drive and energy to achieve results, balance short- and long-term goals, and deal with challenge and rejection
- *Influence*: the ability to persuade others to change their view points
- *Emotional resilience*: the ability to perform well and consistently in a range of situations and under pressure
- *Interpersonal sensitivity*: the awareness of the needs and feelings of others and ability to use this awareness effectively when dealing with others
- *Decisiveness*: the ability to use insight and arrive at a decision when faced with ambiguous information
- *Conscientiousness*: the ability to display commitment to a course of action and to act consistently and ethically.

But emotional intelligence has its critics. There is also an on-going debate about the distinctiveness of the construct of emotional intelligence and whether it is identical to existing personality traits.[35] Furthermore, the available measures of EQ appear to have questionable predictive validity. Given these problems, it may be premature to employ this construct in selection decisions.

But in general, leadership tests are becoming more innovative. Computers have facilitated the capture the complex and dynamic dimensions of leadership. Video shows

Multifactor Leadership Questionnaire
www.mindgarden.com/ products/mlq.htm

Emotional intelligence (EQ): psycho-emotional abilities, including self control, zeal, impulse control, and delayed gratification, which regulate mood and help the person persist in the face of frustration

movement and depicts richer and more detailed behavioural incidents.[36] By capturing more detailed and accurate information, newer tests can increase the fidelity with which leadership ability is measured.

> A program called AccuVision shows the job applicant videotaped job situations likely to be encountered on the job. The applicant selects a behavioural option in response to the situation. The response is entered in the computer and scored according to predetermined criteria.[37]

High-tech tests have other advantages. Watching a video-based test also exposes candidates to the types of decisions they will have to make on the job and the types of activities they will encounter. Video-based tests can also be administered to groups of candidates at the same time, thus reducing the costs. Moreover, even though developing reliable and valid tests that can be administered on the computer may involve higher start-up costs, research indicates that improved reliability of such interactive tests makes them worthwhile.[38]

PERSONALITY TESTS

While there is no single agreed-upon definition of **personality characteristics**, they can be broadly described to include combinations of thoughts, feelings, and behaviours that shape the way a person responds to the environment. Personality traits are latent potentials in the individual; understanding what triggers them helps managers understand the role of personality in shaping behaviour at work place.[39] Some personality characteristics seem intuitively more important for certain jobs.

> For example, jobs such as receptionists, customer service personnel, college and school instructors, and sales staff include interacting with people. Interpersonal skills may be critical for success in such jobs. On the other hand, jobs such as computer programmer, architect, and designer require ability to do abstract thinking and conceptualizing. On the other hand, astronauts, airline pilots, and air traffic controllers need to have a high ability to tolerate uncertainty and to manage stress.

Studies indicate that personality variables are useful in predicting job performance.

> For example, successful managers have been found to score high on characteristics such as drive, energy, self-confidence, social adjustment, and emotional stability.[40]

Some traits, such as conscientiousness, have been found to be predictive of job success across jobs, while other traits are correlated with specific criteria or specific occupation. For example, extroversion correlates with job success in sales and management jobs; openness to experience and agreeableness have shown some promise as predictors of job performance in other settings.[41]

> For example, the CEOs of several large and successful firms, such as Southwest Airlines, Heinz, and Rubbermaid, have been reported to often work 80 to 90 hours a week.[42] Measures of conscientiousness have been shown to be inversely related to absenteeism.[43]

But there are over 18 000 traits identified so far,[44] so organizations cannot measure them all! Researchers have attempted to reduce this to a manageable number. For example, Raymond B.Cattell[45] used correlational analysis to identify 16 traits for use in recruitment and selection. More recently, the "Big Five Personality Factors" (namely, extroversion, emotional stability, agreeableness, openness to experience, and conscientiousness) have been identified as a set of human traits with meaning in the workplace:[46]

- *Extroversion*: sociable, gregarious, assertive, talkative, and active
- *Emotional stability*: being generally unemotional, tending not to be tense, nervous, excitable, insecure, apprehensive, or easily upset

Personality characteristics: thoughts, feelings, traits, and behaviours that combine distinctly and uniquely in each individual and shape the way that person responds to his or her environment

Information on personality tests: *www.2h.com/ personality-tests.html*

- *Agreeableness*: flexible, courteous, trusting, good-natured, forgiving, cooperative, and tolerant
- *Openness to experience*: curious, imaginative, original, broadminded, cultured, and artistically sensitive
- *Conscientiousness*: organized, responsible, planning, dependable, persevering, and achievement-focused

These traits have shown considerable promise in predicting performance, with typical validities ranging from 0.20 to 0.30, depending on the job under consideration.[47] Conscientiousness predicts managerial performance at 0.22 on average, with 0.23 for sales and 0.20 for other professions. Corrected mean validity is 0.18 for managers for extroversion.[48] Research suggests that the Big Five dimensions can predict at least one aspect of performance with accuracy.

An online version of the Big Five Personality Test: *www.outofservice.com/ bigfive/*

> Extroversion predicts job performance in jobs involving social interactions such as sales; agreeableness and emotional Stability shapes success in jobs involving interpersonal interactions. Openness to experience has been found to be related to success in training programs.[49]

Some personality characteristics and cognitive abilities may be a useful part of a HR manager's arsenal of selection tools.[50] However, as in the case of all other tests, continuous validation must be done to ensure that the test does not discriminate against any specific groups.

WORK SAMPLES AND SIMULATIONS

Work samples and simulations: test situations that require applicants to demonstrate job performance behaviours under controlled conditions that approximate those in the real workplace

Work samples and simulations require the job applicant to demonstrate behaviours related to job performance under controlled conditions that approximate those found in the real workplace. Two major tools are used in this context: work sample tests and simulations and assessment centres.

Work sample tests and simulations

Work sample tests include key tasks representative of the real job. However, the candidate is not asked to perform the real job itself for a variety of reasons, including cost, safety, and disruption to the workplace. Work samples include both psycho-motor and verbal behaviours associated with the job.

> For example, a work sample test given to an applicant for a clerical position in an accounting office may ask the candidate to complete some important forms (e.g., expenditure logs or tax forms), formulate a budget, word-process a letter, and respond to a telephone message.

Not every aspect of the job is included in the work sample test—just the most critical ones for job success. The test should be carried out under standardized conditions, using uniform instructions for all applicants. The test may be done either at the real work place or a specially designed location. Wherever it is done, recognize that the test scores provide only an estimate of future job performance. In the real work place, other situational factors can affect performance.

The difference between work samples and simulations is in their closeness to real life work setting. Simulations are particularly useful when the job involved is very complex or there is a possibility of considerable disruption or danger.

> Computer-assisted flight simulators are popular in the aviation industry for safety reasons. These simulators replicate many of the real life events and work conditions; however, they are still quite different from the challenges the person faces in the cockpit.

Assessment centres A popular procedure for identifying managerial potential is the assessment centre (AC).[51] **Assessment centres** use several methods of assessment, including paper-and-pencil tests, job simulations, in-basket exercises, projective tests, interviews, personality inventories, and/or leaderless group discussions to measure intellectual ability, work and career orientation, leadership, and managerial potential of the applicants (see Figure 7-6). Leaderless group discussions, role-playing, and in-basket exercises typically focus on assessing an applicant's administrative skill.

> Currently, Assessment Centres are popular at Alcan, Nortel, Ontario Hydro, Weyerhaeuser Canada, and Steinberg Ltd.[52] Ford Motor, General Motors, and Canadian Forces are some large employers who routinely AC for selecting employees for senior positions. Assessment Centres are increasing in popularity in several municipal, provincial, and federal government units as well. For example, the Public Service Commission of Canada uses it to select candidates for senior managerial positions. Currently, over 20 000 organizations in North America use AC.

Assessment centres do more than simply test applicants. Through the use of multiple assessment techniques and multiple assessors (or panel judges), ACs are able to predict a candidate's future job behaviour and managerial potential. The assessment process itself may vary in length from a few hours to several days, depending on an organization's needs and objectives. A typical AC evaluation for a first-level supervisory job lasts one to two days. In recent years, the AC technique has become increasingly popular for nonsupervisory and skilled labour as well. Whatever format and objective is used, all ACs share some common features:

- All use multiple tools to assess the competencies and/or potential of the participants.
- Behaviours and competencies are directly related to the KSAOs for the job under consideration.

Assessment centres: several methods of assessment, including paper-and-pencil tests, job simulations, in-basket exercises, projective tests, interviews, personality inventories, and/or leaderless group discussions, to measure intellectual ability, work and career orientation, leadership and managerial potential

---

FIGURE 7-6:   Tools Used in Assessment Centres

Assessment Centres typically use a variety of tools. The more popular ones are:

- **Tests**: Aptitude, ability, and personality tests are used to provide insight into the participant's skill set, attitudes, and general personality characteristics.
- **Projective Techniques**: Open-ended tools such as inkblots, pictures, and sentence completion tests allow respondents to project their own interpretations; and in that process, they disclose their hidden personality and values. A similar tool is the *thematic apperception test* (TAT), in which participants tell stories about each of the 19 cards depicting people in ambiguous situations.
- **Role play**: Role play exercises replicating job requirements help identify the competencies of the applicant.
- **In-baskets**: The participants are assigned a role and have to deal with the items in the in-basket as they feel the role demands. In-baskets are usually time-limited exercises. The participant's decisions are evaluated using a standardized scoring key.
- **Job Simulation**: Job simulations reveal candidate abilities and behaviours in key job duties.
- **Observation**: Trained observers assess the applicant's behaviours and overt actions during the assessment centre exercises, including their time management skills.
- **Interviews**: In-depth interviews form an essential part of many assessment centres. These interviews usually assess both job competencies and future potential.
- **Analytical Exercises**: In some assessment centres, written exercises with scenarios and data are given to participants. Participants are required to present their own analysis of the situation, along with solutions to the problems.
- **Team Exercises**: Team activities and exercises can assess the participant's ability to work with others. These activities may have to be completed by the entire group or by individuals. Some assessment centres used games with Lego or Survival Exercises.

- Sufficient job-related tasks/simulations are used to assess these KSAOs.
- Several assessors, usually diverse in age, gender, and other key attributes, including functional specialty, assess the participants.
- Predetermined criteria, scoring keys, and assessment procedures are used to evaluate participant's decisions or solutions.
- A summary report of the participant's KSAOs and observed behaviours are provided at the end of the assessment.

Research studies evaluating the validity of the assessment centre technique have reported positive conclusions, indicating a median 0.40 correlation coefficient between AC ratings and criteria such as career progress, salary advances, supervisor ratings, and evaluations of potential progress.[53] This has led to a phenomenal growth in the number of organizations using the AC technique.

HONESTY AND INTEGRITY TESTS

Employee theft and misuse of company property has become an increasing concern for many Canadian employers.

> Theft and misuse of company property costs for Canadian retailers are estimated at over $2.3 billion a year. The average amount stolen by employees now stands at over $450 and more than three times as much is lost through theft by customers. One U.S. study places the amount of workplace theft in America at $40 billion annually. Over 6% of job applicants may be involved in thefts in previous jobs; many others commit felonies or minor crimes. It is estimated that crime increases retail prices by approximately 15%.[54]

Employee theft statistics have prompted several employers to test the integrity of job applicants. Honesty tests are also of great interest to employers for another reason: if the candidate is not honest in the job application form and interview, much of the information collected to assess the applicant's suitability for the position is useless. This means that the wrong applicants are hired, and organizational productivity suffers.

A number of methods have been developed to help employers assess the integrity level of new hires. But all are controversial. The methods currently in vogue include graphic response tests, paper-and-pencil tests, credit report checks, and voice stress analyzers. The first two, which are also the more popular methods, will be discussed here.

Graphic response tests Graphic response tests seek information about applicants in ways that cannot be distorted easily. The polygraph (or lie detector) is the most common. It measures physiological changes as a person responds to questions. When people tell lies, their conscience usually causes involuntary physiological reactions detectable by the polygraph. At $30 to $60 per test, it is more economical than a detailed background check on applicants. In the United States, almost one-half of all retail firms are reported to use polygraph tests, although many legislatures, including the U.S. Congress, have banned polygraph testing from pre-employment screening procedures.

In addition to ethical and public relations considerations, there are serious questions about the ability of most lie detector operators to administer and interpret the results validly.[55] Although the general public often believes in the ability of polygraphs to detect lies, the empirical evidence supporting this has been scant. Only a few jurisdictions in North America have any licensing requirements for polygraph operators. This means that the interpretations are suspect.

In Ontario, the use of lie-detector tests for the purpose of employment is prohibited under the *Employment Standards Act*. Employers desiring to use this test should check its legality in other provinces.[56]

Paper-and-pencil honesty tests

As polygraph tests draw criticisms about their accuracy and appropriateness, paper-and-pencil tests are being used to assess attitudes about honesty and presumably on-the-job behaviours.[57] They are easy to administer, inexpensive (typically available at less than $20 per administration), and compared to polygraphs, relatively free of controversy. For example, one test can measure tendencies toward cheating, deceiving, and stealing.[58] Most paper-and-pencil honesty tests fall into one of two categories:

- **Overt tests** that ask direct questions about past thefts or attitudes toward dishonest behaviours. A test, such as the Reid Report, asks direct questions about an individual's attitude toward theft.

- **Covert measures** are included as parts of other tests, where the person taking the test is not aware of the true objective of the employer. For example, the Reliability Scale of Hogan Personality Inventory measures a person's honesty and reliability, although the person taking the test does not recognize this. Personality-oriented integrity tests do not ask direct questions about theft or other dishonest behaviours, but measure the reliability and social conformity of employees and make inferences about their honesty from these scores.

Overt tests are more susceptible to faking than covert tests. Despite this, even overt honesty tests have been found to be useful. When confronted by direct questions, many individuals are likely to openly admit dishonest behaviours. A review of a dozen paper-and-pencil integrity tests found potential validity for some tests.[59] Other comprehensive analyses of honesty and integrity tests also reveal that they have some degree of validity in predicting disruptive behaviours, such as theft, disciplinary problems, and absenteeism.[60]

> For example, the London House Personnel Selection Inventory (PSI) significantly predicts employees who end up being caught stealing. The PSI, which resulted from over 15 years of research by psychologists, criminologists, and legal experts, is reported to have a reliability of over 0.90. It also has convergent validity with polygraph scores, anonymous admissions of theft by the applicants, and results of quasi-experiments using the same respondents.[61]

In other instances, the predictive validity and usefulness have been impressive:

> Stanton Survey, an honesty test developed by Pinkerton Services Group, was tested for its validity using 4665 applicants. Of these, 50% were given the Stanton Survey, and the other 50% were not. Of the applicants, 37% of those not tested were later dismissed for theft, while only 22.6% of those tested with Stanton Survey were dismissed for the same reason. The number of policy violators in the untested group was 10.4% compared to 1.5% in the tested group. The average loss from the untested group was approximately $208 higher compared to the tested group.[62]

Yet honesty tests present human resource specialists with an inherent dilemma. On the one hand, these methods seem to offer additional screening techniques to identify applicants who are unlikely to be productive and reliable. On the other hand, such tests are subject to errors.[63] When they are inaccurate, needless discrimination results. Available evidence indicates that honesty tests result in false-positives—that is, they may screen out applicants who are inherently honest but who are categorized as dishonest using the test scores.

Overt tests: honesty tests that ask direct questions about past thefts and attitudes toward dishonest behaviour

Covert measures: test questions with hidden objectives blended into a larger test

In the past, a major grocery chain in Atlantic Canada received considerable unfavourable publicity for its use of integrity tests. After serving the company for six years, an employee took a year off to look after her family. During the period, the firm had introduced mandatory honesty tests for all its employees. Under the new policy, only those who passed the test were offered employment in the company. When reapplying for a position in the company, she had to take the test, which she failed, even though she had had an impeccable work record and no criminal record whatsoever (not even a parking ticket !). The firm refused to rehire the employee.

Many applicants and employees consider these tests to be an invasion of their privacy. There are also other administrative problems with many honesty tests where the testing agencies do not provide detailed scoring keys or benchmarks. Despite these problems, honesty tests have become popular, especially in the retail industry.

MEDICAL AND DRUG TESTS

Medical and drug tests focus on the applicant's physical and mental fitness to perform the job safely and at the required levels.

Medical tests In several organizations, a medical evaluation of the applicant is an integral part of the selection process. Normally, the evaluation is a health checklist that asks the applicant to indicate health and accident information. The questionnaire is sometimes supplemented with a physical examination by a company nurse or physician. The medical evaluation is particularly valued by employers when:

• unhealthy or physically unfit employees can cause a significant cost or safety hazard;

• provincial or local health regulations or officials require these tests, particularly in food-handling operations, where communicable diseases are a danger;

• the job entails considerable stress;

• the job involved is dangerous (e.g., deep-sea fishing or space travel).

Many employers have done away with medical tests because of the costs involved. Also, if an organization rejects an applicant based on a medical test, charges of discrimination under the *Canadian Human Rights Act* or related provincial legislation will likely result. A congenital health condition may be considered a disability, and failure to hire may be seen as discrimination against the qualified applicant.

To avoid discrimination, job applicants should not be asked to undergo any medical tests until after a job offer. Once a decision has been made to offer the applicant a job, the offer can be made conditional on the applicant passing a medical exam. To meet legal requirements, the organization must require the exam for all entering employees who are doing the same job. Medical examinations should be conducted only if the job requires a clearly determined level of physical effort or other abilities (e.g., ability to climb poles). But at this stage, an applicant can be rejected only if reasonable accommodations cannot be made to allow the person to perform the job.

For example, imposing a particular standard of vision or audition may be questioned by applicants who can reach the necessary level with glasses or hearing aids. Similarly, height restriction for telephone installers on the grounds that short persons cannot get ladders from the truck would be discriminatory. Instead, organizations can provide stools for workers to stand on while removing ladders.[64]

The expertise with which the medical evidence is interpreted will also determine the strength of the employer's case in the event of a legal action by a rejected job applicant. Consider this example:

> Tony Kearsley applied for a position as a firefighter with the city of St. Catharines. He was accepted, conditional upon passing a medial examination. But the medical examination revealed that he had atrial fibrillation (a mild heart condition). The medical practitioner, a general practitioner, refused to pass him, claiming that it increased the risk of a stroke by 1 to 5% a year. In addition, the medical examiner felt that Mr. Kearsley's condition could result in the heart not being able to pump sufficient blood to his organs during the extreme rigours of firefighting. But other experts whom the complainant consulted had advised him that it was a benign condition that would not interfere with his ability to do the job. During the appeal, the Ontario Human Rights Commission called in a medical expert in the area of atrial fibrillation, who testified that the increase in probability of a stroke for someone of Kearsley's age was inconsequential and possibly 0.2% per year. The expert also testified that there was no increased risk of heart failure in someone like Kearsley, who was otherwise in good health. The Board asked the City to hire Kearsley within 75 days and pay him damages for the salary he lost until that date.[65]

In summary, to avoid possible allegations of discrimination, medical examinations should be conducted only when they are absolutely necessary. Here are guidelines for conducting medical examination provided by Ontario Human Rights Commission:[66]

- Only qualified professionals should conduct medical testing and competent laboratories analyze the results.

- Where medical testing is appropriate, the employer should notify job applicants of this requirement at the time an offer of employment is made.

- There should be objective, rational justification for the test. There should be an objective basis to believe that the degree, nature, scope, and probability of risk caused by a medical condition will adversely affect the safety of co-workers or the public.

- Procedures should be instituted for the physician to review the test results with the employee concerned.

- All health assessment information should remain exclusively with the examining physician, not in the employee's personnel file.

Drug tests The use of drugs such as marijuana and cocaine by employees on the job as well as outside the workplace has been on the increase. A survey[67] of nearly 14 000 Canadians aged 15 or over found that the use of alcohol and illicit drugs is increasing. Consider these statistics:

Information on drug addiction in Canada: *www.ccsa.ca/CCSA/EN/Resear ch/Research_Activities/ CanadianAddictionSurvey.htm*

- 79.3% of Canadians consume alcohol; only 38.7% of those who drink are light, infrequent drinkers (fewer than five drinks when drinking, less than once a week).

- Overall, 44.5% of Canadians report using cannabis at least once in their lifetime, and 14.1% report using in the previous 12-month period.

- Almost 70% of those between 18 and 24 have used cannabis at least once.

- Self-reported rates of illicit drug use increased from 28.5% in 1994 to 45.0% in 2004.

Illegal drug use increases early mortality rates, accidents, theft, and poor job performance. Moreover, if the drug user's performance impacts customers or fellow employees, lawsuits can follow.

A large majority (86%) of CEOs of Canadian organizations who responded to a survey considered substance abuse a serious or a very serious problem. A similar survey in the

United States estimated a figure of US$26 billion annually in higher health-care costs and lost productivity due to illicit drug use.[68]

This situation has prompted a growing number of Canadian employers to include drug testing in their selection process.

> Workplace substance abuse is estimated to cost Canadian employers $2.6 billion annually.[69] Although drug abuse among workers in Canada is still quite moderate compared to that in the United States, it warrants serious attention, especially in major centers such as Toronto, Vancouver, and Montreal.

In the United States, more than two-thirds of large employers test job applicants for drug abuse.

> In the United States, the U.S. Department of Labor estimates that drug use in the workplace costs employers $75 to $100 billion annually in lost time, accidents, health care, and workers' compensation costs. Sixty-five per cent of all accidents on the job are directly related to drugs or alcohol.[70] Concern about employee drug use has spurred IBM, American Airlines, and many other organizations to require all job applicants to pass a urinalysis test for marijuana and cocaine. Typically, drug screening is done either before or immediately after the hiring decision. These organizations seek to avoid the economic and legal risks associated with drug users.

Through the analysis of urine or blood samples, laboratories are able to screen for the presence of drugs. In the past, some Canadian employers have required their employees to undergo drug tests.

> CN Rail introduced a drug screening test for its blue-collar workers as early as in mid-1980s.[71] The Toronto Dominion Bank, Imperial Oil Limited, the Federal Transport Department, and the Winnipeg police force and transportation industry (under federal jurisdiction) are among organizations that introduced early drug testing.[72]

TD Bank's drug testing policy resulted in a landmark court case, which defined the parameters for drug testing in this country. Executives of Toronto Dominion Bank, defending a policy that required all new and returning employees to undergo urinalysis within 48 hours of accepting an employment offer, argued that drug users are more likely to associate with criminal elements and are therefore more susceptible to criminal influence that might lead to blackmail and perhaps theft. TD's aim was to address the potential impact of drugs on health and work performance of the employees and to preserve the safety of funds and employees.[73] But the Canadian Civil Liberties Association called for an outright ban on employee drug tests, saying no person should "be required to share urine with a stranger" as a condition of employment.[74] It pointed out that drug tests are not completely reliable indicators of safe performance: at best, they show only that an employee may have used a particular drug at some point in the past, perhaps several weeks before.[75] The Association lost,[76] though the court did find mandatory urinalysis intrusive. Then in 1998, in a 2-1 decision, the Federal Court of Appeal found the bank's anti-drug program discriminatory. Justice F. Joseph Macdonald held that the bank's policy resulted in indirect discrimination against drug-dependent employees. While the bank's rule of three positive tests leading to dismissal applied to both new and returning employees, "the rule directly impacts more negatively on a protected class of individuals under the Canadian Human Rights Act—drug dependent users."[77]

This means that today an employer must delicately balance the individual rights of the employee against risk of liability and lack of safety at the workplace. To meet the Canadian Human Rights Commission policy on drug testing, the following conditions have to be met:

- Without any demonstrable relationship to job performance, drug and alcohol testing has been found to be a violation of employee rights. In the normal course of events, drug testing is not justified for positions where safety is not a concern.

- Drug testing is permissible if safety is of fundamental importance and the employer can demonstrate that there are no alternate, cost-effective methods to assure that employees are not incapacitated on the job.

- Pre-employment testing should be undertaken only after a firm job offer has been made.

- If an employee tests positive, the organization must make all efforts to accommodate him or her. It should refer the employee to an employee assistance program or a substance abuse professional to discover the extent of drug dependence. If found not to be substance-dependent, the employee should return to the position; if found to be dependent, the employee should be referred to rehabilitation.

- If rehabilitation is successful, the employee should be returned to the former position.

All the cautions listed for ability, personality, and medical tests also apply to drug tests. A relationship or rational connection between the drug or alcohol testing and job performance is an important component of any lawful drug- or alcohol-testing policy.[78] More recently, there has been an increasing interest in drug tests in many Canadian provinces. Alberta is a good example:

> Drug testing is a hot issue in Alberta. It is being driven in large part, by oil and gas firms that are spending billions of dollars on massive oil sands projects, where even a minor employee error can be very expensive. Considerable debate centers around pre-employment testing, random testing and reasonable grounds for testing, and there is pressure on the provincial government to clearly lay out what is permissible and what is not. At the same time, Alberta's Bill C-45, nicknamed the "corporate killing" law, also puts pressure on employers to pay greater attention to worker safety, since employers can be held liable for returning workers back to work if their performance endangers themselves and others.[79]

Because most drug tests do not yield accurate data on current impairment or usage level and because some may be unreliable, even the pursuit of a productive, safe workplace may not justify universal, mandatory drug testing. More recently, simple tests that measure impairment of manual dexterity and eye-hand coordination have been developed with considerable promise for identifying impaired employees.[80] The arrival of more such tests may help firms achieve their objectives while safeguarding employee dignity and privacy.

USING TESTS PROPERLY

Besides the specific cautions associated with individual tests, human resource specialists should realize that testing is not always feasible. Even when an organization can develop or buy tests, the cost may not be justifiable for jobs that have low selection ratios or that are seldom filled.

> For many specialized positions, especially senior technical or professional jobs, the selection ratio may be very small. At the same time, the number of job openings even in a relatively long period may be small. In such circumstances, elaborate tests may be impractical. For this reason, organizations use other predictors to assess candidate potential. In limited circumstances, work sample tests may also be useful. For example, the hiring of faculty in many business schools in this country is based on work history, interviews, references, and an oral presentation in a classroom setting—similar to a work sample.

Indeed, in some situations, other tools may be more cost effective than employment tests. Consider the following experience of Macy's, the large U.S. retailer:

> Macy's Department Stores screens out approximately 5% of potential hires through background checks. These background checks often indicate that a candidate has previously

stolen from another Macy's or Federated department store. In one instance, an employee at Macy's was incorrectly hired because the background check was not conducted appropriately. This single hire resulted in more than $1 million worth of lost revenue due to theft and subsequent legal and security fees. The employee would never have been hired if the background check had been conducted correctly.[81]

The following guidelines are likely to enhance the validity and cost-effectiveness of the testing procedure.

1. BE CLEAR ABOUT YOUR CRITERIA

The first step in selecting a test is to determine the current performance criteria and the expected level of performance.

> For instance, if customer service is the most critical aspect of the job performance, the selection tool should help the firm predict sociability, persistence, and energy level, rather than examining analytical skills or conformity. If theft is the most important issue, then you should consider assessment tools specifically designed to identify and eliminate candidates who are likely to steal. Even an attribute such as "communication skills" may mean very different things for different positions, even within the same organization. A publications editor may need strong writing and editing abilities as well as close attention to detail, whereas a public relations or customer service representative in the same firm needs to think clearly under pressure and be able to articulate vocally and with clarity. Different assessment tools are needed to validly measure these different communication skills.

Employment tests are only one of several techniques used in the selection process, because they are limited to factors that can be tested and validated easily. Other items not measurable by testing may be equally important. With a combination of selection tools, an employer can get a well-rounded view of the candidate. One rule of thumb often used is that pre-employment testing should comprise no more than one-third of the total selection process.[82] Figure 7-7 provides broad guidelines showing the effectiveness of popular selection tools for testing specific criteria. Note that the table is only a general guide and will require modifications to meet the unique needs of a situation.

2. USE TESTS EARLY ON

Organizations must be flexible about using tests. Tests do not need to be the first or last step in the selection process. Human resource experts should use them when they are appropriate. However, consider the comments of an experienced human resource manager of a large chain of grocery stores:

> "Many human resource managers in other industries use testing only after other steps in the selection process. In the grocery business, you must test first. Why waste time interviewing a grocery clerk who doesn't know that three for 88 cents is 30 cents apiece? Besides, when we take applications on Tuesdays, we may have 300 of them. Interviews would take 75 hours a week, and my staff consists of a clerk and myself. But through testing, we can test the entire group in an hour. Then we interview only those who score well."[83]

Generally, organizations should test early in the process, so that if the individual's scores raise questions, you have a method of following up on those questions.

FIGURE 7-7: Matching Performance Criteria to Popular Selection Tools

Performance Criteria	Selection Tools						
	Application Blank/WAB/BIB	Structured Interview	Reference Checks/Background Checks	Ability, Aptitude Tests	Personality Tests, Leadership Inventories	Integrity and Drug Tests	Work Samples, Simulation
Tenure	●	●	●	●	●		
Absenteeism	●		●		●	●	
Customer Service	●	●	●	●	●		●
Specialist Knowledge	●						●
Deviant Behaviour (e.g., theft)	●		●			●	
Physical Performance			●				●
Problem Solving, Leadership		●	●	●	●		●

3. USE ONLY VALIDATED TESTS

Ensure that the tests used have predictive or concurrent validity. Both validity methods relate test scores to some criterion, usually performance. The higher the correlation between test scores and the criterion, the more effective the test is. Empirical validation approaches are generally preferred because they are less subjective than rational methods. Regardless of which approach is used, testing experts advise separate validation studies for different subgroups, such as women and minorities.[84] Otherwise, over time, the test may result in systemic discrimination against specific, protected groups.

> Available evidence on the validation of various selection tests by Canadian organizations portrays a disappointing picture. In a 1999 survey of 202 Canadian organizations, 73% indicated they did not validate any of their selection methods, including interviews. Indeed, many respondents did not even know the meaning of the various types of validity.[85] This means that many Canadian organizations are not using as effective a selection process as they could or should.

Not all types of tests are equally valid. Figure 7-8 summarizes the validities of major tests. As the figure shows, work samples, cognitive ability tests, and job knowledge tests offer the greatest promise in the employment context.

When selecting commercial tests off-the-shelf, consider the following:

• Unless the decision is very simple, create a formal team to oversee the implementation of assessment tools. This team could determine assessment tool requirements,

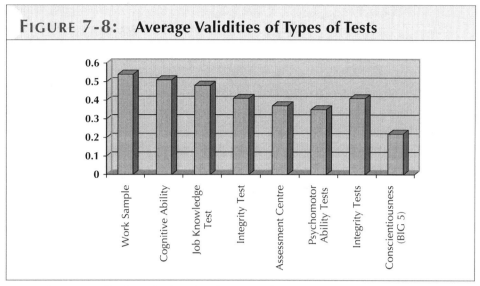

FIGURE 7-8: Average Validities of Types of Tests

Source: Chart prepared by the author based on data reported in a number of past research studies including the following: F.L. Schmidt and J.E. Hunter. (1998). "The Validity and Utility of Selection Methods in Personnel Psychology: Practical and Theoretical Implications of 85 Years of Research Findings." *Psychological Bulletin, 124,* pp. 267–74; Robert Tett and Dawn Burnett. (2003). "A Personality Trait-Based Interactionist Model of Job Performance." *Journal of Applied Psychology, 88,* 3, pp. 500–517; Robert Gatewood and Hubert Field. (2001). *Human Resource Selection.* Mason, OH: South-Western/Thomson.

research and gather information from vendors, and implementat the decisions. The team should include representatives from the major stakeholder groups affected by the new tools.[86]

- The team or HR staff should collect information on all aspects of tests (including its reliability, validity, differential validity for subgroups, and norms for various groups). Vendors of tests have summaries of validity data available for prospective clients. This data will provide evidence of the tool's performance on jobs similar to those in your organization. Look for "hard numbers" linked to criteria, such as supervisor ratings, tenure, and absenteeism.

- Reject tests outright if they do not have sound psychometric data.

- Examine independent evaluations of the test, especially those published in reputable journals and well-designed studies

- Examine the organization's capabilities to administer and interpret scores correctly.

- Administer the test following procedures described in the testing manual.

4. CHECK FOR ADVERSE IMPACT

As already mentioned in this chapter and in Chapter 3, organizations must continually monitor tests and testing processes to ensure that they actually predict high-performers, rather than creating an adverse impact. Tests perceived to be unfair need special consideration and review.

> In one study, American job applicants were asked to rate selection tools for their effectiveness and fairness. Work samples, interviews, and resumes had the highest perceived effectiveness and fairness. Honesty tests and personality tests scored the lowest among selection tools. Graphology (or handwriting tests) had the lowest ratings.[87]

Keep in mind that employers have an obligation to make reasonable accommodation during test administration and interpretation of the scores for people with disabilities of weak test-taking skills.

5. RESPECT THE PRIVACY AND DIGNITY OF APPLICANTS

Job applicants must be told why they are being tested and how the process will take place. They are entitled to feedback on the test results and on the decisions based on those test results. The information should be provided in non-technical language in the context of the test's purpose.

There is no justification for collecting non-job-related data from applicants. The employer also has a duty to protect the privacy of the applicant. Data collected should not be made available to anyone not professionally connected to the hiring decision.

The following chapter looks at two other major tools used during selection, namely, interviews and reference checks.

Implications for Practice

1. Employment tests are a versatile, objective, and valid method for measuring applicant abilities and potential. They also help assess hidden traits, values, and motivations. Where feasible, include tests in the selection battery, so that the recruiter receives a comprehensive evaluation of the applicant competencies.

2. Despite their popularity and usefulness, tests and testing are not without problems. Although many of the problems are due to the improper *use* of the tests, rather than to the tests themselves, always ensure that tests do not unfairly discriminate against any person or group.

3. Choose tests only after a thorough job analysis and understanding of the job requirements.

4. When purchasing tests from commercial vendors, follow the guidelines outlined in this chapter.

5. Continually monitor test results and the testing process to ensure that they do not unintentionally discriminate against any protected group.

6. While testing, take steps to protect the privacy and dignity of the applicants.

Key Terms for Review

Ability tests, *p. 242*

Aptitude tests, *p. 242*

Assessment centres, *p. 249*

Cognitive abilities, *p. 242*

Covert measures, *p. 251*

Emotional intelligence (EQ), *p. 246*

General mental ability ("g"), *p. 243*

Job knowledge tests, *p. 239*

Overt tests, *p. 251*

Personality characteristics, *p. 247*

Physical abilities, *p. 245*

Practical intelligence, *p. 240*

Psycho-motor coordination, *p. 244*

Skills, *p. 242*

Vocational interest tests, *p. 241*

Work samples and simulations, *p. 248*

Discussion Questions

1. Many employers use tests. What factors have led to the popularity of tests? In your opinion, is this a good trend?

2. How do you select the right type of test for a particular job?

3. If you were the Assistant to the Human Resource Manager in a medium-sized supermarket chain, what tests would be useful in selecting cashiers in the chain? Assuming that you are going to purchase a test from a vendor, what actions would you take?

Critical Thinking Questions

1. You are being interviewed for the position of Assistant to the Human Resource Manager in a medium-sized autoparts manufacturing firm that employs about 180 mostly blue-collar staff full time and another 200 part time. During the job interview, the interviewer says she is skeptical about employment tests, stating that in a "ten-minute, face-to-face meeting with candidates" she can adequately judge their potential. She concluded that "all this fuss about employment testing is unnecessary." Then she asks for your opinion. What response might you give her?

2. If you were to identify tests for salespeople working in an auto dealership, what tests would you choose? Would these be the same as the tests you would choose for customer representatives working in a financial services agency? Why or why not?

3. You are currently working as the assistant to the Human Resource Manager in a brewery. Of late, the absenteeism rate at the brewery has been rising. Your boss feels that better hiring practices, including use of tests, is called for and asks you to look into the situation. What would you do?

Web Research

Collect information about one type of test offered by *at least* two different testing agencies or publishers. What psychometric data about the tests is available from the test publishers? What information is lacking? Which test package seems more complete?

CASE INCIDENT
Ontario Electronics: Complaints about Hiring and Promotion

Note: This case continues from Chapter 6: Ontario Electronics Company Ltd. Review the case background in Chapters 1 and 6 before examining this case.

OECL is somewhat unhappy with the productivity levels in Plant C (see case in Chapter 6). The management has decided to focus on this plant to improve work procedures and productivity.

Tim Hutton, the Staffing Analyst, has studied the situation for over one month. He also talked informally to a representative sample of workers in Plant C. Some of the incidents narrated to Hutton are listed below:

- Four months ago, Melissa Steele had complained to the Plant Manager that her supervisor had discriminated against her on the basis of disability by denying her job opportunities. Although she had done well in the written ability test and had good scores in a work sample test, she was not selected for the new position in the quality control section because the supervisor perceived her to be drug-dependent. Ms. Steele agrees that she had had a drug problem two years previously but she has been drug-free since then. The new position paid nearly 35% more than her present salary, and she was very upset. She claimed that she had not used drugs during the last eighteen months. Although she had worked in the quality control position for two weeks on a temporary basis, she was not considered for the competition because she had not been drug-free for a sufficient period of time. The Plant Manager has not taken any action about the complaint until this point. During a meeting, Steele told Hutton that she is planning to go to the Human Rights Commission.

- Mina Ghosh told Hutton that her supervisor threatened to terminate her employment if she did not accept a job which involved considerable travel for most days in the month. Although the new job pays better than her present job, Ghosh cited family reasons for refusing the job. The mother of two young children, she had recently undergone surgery. In addition, since her husband was posted overseas, she needed to leave the children with her parents when she was working, despite her father's heart condition. The supervisor told Hutton that Ghosh received the highest score in the ability test, and he was simply following the internal HR policies on hiring, promotion, and transfer. In any case, as supervisor, he had the authority to assign people to jobs he deemed best. In his mind, he was simply assigning the best person for the job.

- Mary Rudder, an employee in the purchasing section, is angry with her supervisor. Rudder was recently denied the position of Assistant to the Purchase Officer. She believes that it was because she is a woman. The supervisor told Hutton that the decision had nothing to do with her gender. In his words, "Ms. Rudder had mediocre scores on the ability test, and that was that." When Hutton communicated this to Rudder, she responded, "Who is he kidding? The person he selected had just three points higher than me in the test. He is also two years junior to

me. Do you think that three lousy points on that dumb test more than compensates for two years of my work here?"

Questions

1. *What are the issues relevant to selection and testing in these situations?*
2. *What should Hutton do in each situation?*
3. *Do any of these events reveal other problematic issues at Plant C?*

CASE
Kanata Food Distributors: Selecting New Product Idea Originators*

Note: This case continues from Chapter 6: Kanata Food Distributors. Review the case background in Chapters 1, 2, 3, 4, and 6 before examining this case.

About eight years ago, Kanata Food Distributes started offering major brand-name grocery items, baked products, prepared foods and, more recently, premium quality meals. Today, approximately 30% of the total revenues for the firm come from this line of business: about 50% comes from ninety 24-7 Stores. (See case in Chapter 3 for more background.)

Kanata believes that changes are occurring in this sector which will have major impact on the future operations and the firm's employment policy. Several of these changes are discussed in cases at the end of Chapters 1 and 3. The firm is also embarking on a major expansion into the lucrative low-fat, healthy-food market. All its grocery stores, 24-7 stores, and pastry food outlets will soon offer new low-fat, company-brand products.

Currently, the firm is planning to hire five officers in the middle management level to oversee identification of feasible new products and shepherd them into the market. The position was tentatively called "Product Idea Originators." Management felt that apart from sound technical knowledge, the new hires should also possess emotional intelligence (EQ) to influence and get along with people. Given these requirements, management believed

that an Emotional Intelligence test should be administered in the hiring process.

A Scarborough-based consultant with whom the firm had dealings about a year before was contracted to help choose a test. After three weeks of searching, the consultant identified a test that appeared to measure the following five key dimensions of EQ:

- *Self awareness* (SA): the awareness of one's feelings and ability to recognize and manage these.
- *Enthusiasm* (E): the drive and energy to achieve results
- *Emotional resilience* (ER): the ability to perform well and consistently in a range of situations and under pressure
- *Interpersonal sensitivity* (IS): the awareness of the needs and feelings of others and ability to use this awareness effectively when dealing with others
- *Decisiveness* (D): the ability to make decisions under pressure and with limited information; the applicant's commitment to a goal

*Case written by Professor Hari Das of Saint Mary's University, Halifax. All rights retained by the author, © 2005.

TABLE 1:

Applicant	SA	E	ER	IS	D	Total score (Max=100)	Gender	Minority member or not
1	14	14	12	14	15	69	M	NO
2	14	15	11	14	16	70	M	NO
3	15	16	12	15	15	73	M	NO
4	15	16	13	17	12	73	F	NO
5	16	15	11	16	11	69	F	YES
6	14	14	12	16	12	68	M	YES
7	15	15	10	13	15	68	M	NO
8	14	14	12	14	16	70	M	NO
9	15	14	11	12	17	69	M	NO
10	15	15	13	14	12	69	M	YES
11	16	15	12	15	11	69	F	YES
12	15	16	11	15	12	69	F	NO
13	14	15	12	16	12	69	F	NO
14	15	14	12	16	12	69	M	YES
15	14	15	12	13	15	69	M	NO
16	15	15	13	13	16	72	M	NO
17	14	16	12	17	10	69	F	YES
18	16	15	12	14	15	72	M	NO
19	14	15	13	15	14	71	M	NO
20	15	15	11	16	15	72	M	NO
21	14	15	11	14	16	70	M	NO
22	15	14	12	15	17	73	M	NO

The test was administered to the 22 applicants who passed preliminary screening. Table 1 indicates their scores on the above five dimensions, along with their total scores and some relevant demographic information. Each dimension is scored out of 20.

Since the median total score was 69, the consultant suggested that this be used as the cut-off score. Based on this decision rule, the ten applicants who received a score higher than 69 were called for a final interview.

Questions

1. *Evaluate the approach taken by the firm to hire the new personnel.*

2. *Based on these test results, what recommendations would you make to the management? Why?*

CHAPTER

"Traditional interviewing methods do not work well to identify competencies. Numerous studies have shown that unstructured, nonbehavioural selection interviews have little power to predict who will do a good job."

Lyle M. Spencer and Signe M. Spencer[1]

CHAPTER OBJECTIVES

After studying this chapter, you should be able to:

- Discuss the validity and usefulness of interviews in assessing various job-related constructs

- Describe the situational factors that influence the validity of interviews

- Discuss the usefulness of various types of interviews

- Describe how to conduct valid interviews

- Outline actions to enhance the usefulness and validity of reference checks

In a recent merger, Metro Transportation Company (MTC) and Rural City Transport (RCT) joined forces to form Eastern Canadian Transfers Limited (ECTL). The newly formed ECTL had set high goals for itself, including expanding its services to seven new regions and additional client groups. To implement its expansion plans, ECTL decided to hire seven new Regional Managers. Initially, most of the hiring would be done through internal transfers and promotions, since such a strategy would provide continuity to the existing practices and also improve employee morale. Four senior managers, two from MTC and RCT, interviewed all 22 internal applicants. For the purpose of the interviews, the managers brought their own list of interview questions and scored the candidates on their criteria using a ten-point scale.

At the end of interviews, they calculated the total score for each candidate, compared scores, and chose those with the highest total scores for the positions.

But the interview process did not have the desired beneficial effects. In fact, it created several new problems. Of the 13 MTC employees who were interviewed for the position, only two received uniformly high scores, while only a single candidate from the pool of nine RCT applicants was considered adequate by all four interviewers. But further examination of the interview results showed interesting patterns. The MTC interviewers tended to favour MTC employees, while the RCT interviewers scored RCT employees twice as high as MTC applicants with similar qualifications and backgrounds. Moreover, the interviewers had different ideas about the relative importance of each attribute for the job. While MTC interviewers argued that higher weights should be given to work experience, especially in a metropolitan setting, the RCT interviewers were more inclined to give higher weight to formal qualifications and potential. The MTC interviewers were also likely to give greater weight to personal appearance and demeanour, while the RCT managers gave higher weight to friendliness and past record for on-time delivery. Unable to agree on uniform criteria or their relative importance, the team decided to fill only three positions.

As soon as the names of the three new hires were announced, a number of interviewees complained about unfairness of the interview process. Some complained about the lack of interest shown by interviewers from the opposite unit. Others questioned the relevance of some of the interview questions. Three of the applicants who were not selected for the position left ECTL for a competitor.

The management was taken aback by the unexpected outcomes. It then hired a local management consultant, who suggested an immediate, in-depth job analysis of the new regional manager's position to identify the job responsibilities, specifications, and KSAs. Before a new round of hiring would begin, all interviewers would agree on the selection criteria and interview questions. The consultant was also going to train the managers in interviewing techniques before the actual selection process began.

As the above incident illustrates, weak job interviews can cause considerable damage to an organization. Not only do they result in a poor fit between the capabilities of the person hired and the job requirements, but they also cause high-quality applicants to quit. In internal hiring scenarios like this one, it can also cause employee dissatisfaction and poor employee morale, in addition to potential legal issues.

Employment interview: a formal, in-depth dialogue between an applicant and one or more interviewers who, based on the candidate's interview performance, make judgments about the applicant's fit to the requirements of the job

Despite such risks, employment interviews (or in-depth interviews or selection interviews as they are also known) are the most widely used selection technique. The **employment interview** is a formal, in-depth conversation conducted between a job applicant and one or more interviewers who, based on the candidate's interview performance, make judgments about the applicant's fit with the open position. The interviewer seeks to answer two broad questions: Can the applicant do the job? How does the applicant compare with others who are applying for the job? The employment interview is distinct from the screening interview discussed in Chapter 6. The screening interview assesses the job applicant on *general characteristics* and eliminates obvious misfits from further consideration. In contract, the employment interview focuses on the *specific job-related knowledge, skills and abilities* (KSAs).

The popularity of employment interviews attests to their flexibility and usefulness. Interview formats can be adapted to hire unskilled, skilled, technical, managerial, and staff employees. They are suitable for small and large organizations. Unlike psychological tests and assessment centre technique, they require little additional equipment, few resources, and no experts. Compared to several other selection tools, the standard interview also possesses some unique strengths:

- *It assesses the match between the applicant's personality and organizational culture*: Besides assessing a candidate's ability to perform well on the job, an employer also wants to match the person's personality with that of the team he or she will have to work with. An interview provides an opportunity to assess personality and personal fit with the organizational culture.

- *It sells the firm and aids future recruitment efforts*: An interview provides the firm with an opportunity to sell a job to a candidate. In high-demand areas, such as engineering, electronics, and business administration, "selling" the company to top candidates assumes great importance. The dissemination of information through interviews facilitates current recruitment and leaves a lasting impression in the minds of many applicants, even if they are not chosen for the position. Typically, interviewers highlight the employment policies, compensation, flexible work arrangements, career opportunities and overall quality of work life to convince top applicants to choose the firm.

- *It can improve public image*: An interview is a public relations tool. Interviewees are potential consumers, clients, and voters. Their perception of fair treatment could have important consequences for the firm's marketing and success.

- *It facilitates two-way interaction*: In a well-conducted interview, interviewers learn about the applicant while the applicant learns about the employer. An interview offers the organization an opportunity to answer the candidate's questions regarding the job, career opportunities, and company policies. Most other selection tools (e.g., tests or reference checks) do not offer opportunities for two-way interaction.

No wonder interviews are among the most popular selection tools among employers. However, interviews do have shortcomings. The most noticeable flaw is their varying reliability and validity. When not properly executed (as in the opening vignette), they not only fail to select the right candidates but also cause problems for an organization.

This chapter prepares you to conduct effective interviews. Here, we discuss the usefulness and validity of interviews and the steps needed to enhance interview validity. The chapter also provides guidelines on conducting reference checks on applicants.

While a large number of factors affect interview outcomes, most can be grouped under three headings: focus of the interview and the constructs measured during the interview; situational factors affecting interviews; and the type of interviews employed (see Figure 8-1).

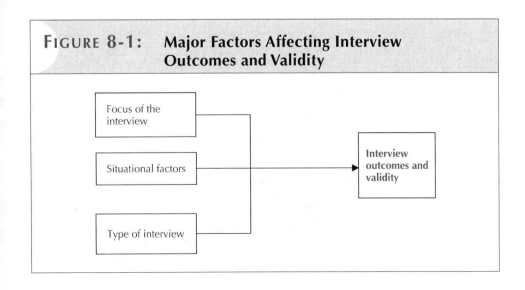

FIGURE 8-1: Major Factors Affecting Interview Outcomes and Validity

FOCUS OF INTERVIEWS

One advantage of interviews is that the data gatherer and interpreter (namely, the interviewer) is a human being who understands the organization and the job.[2] Many practitioners believe that this makes employment interviews particularly helpful in assessing the applicant-organization fit, because the interviewer meets the applicant face-to-face and forms an overall impression.

Interviews measure some constructs better than they do others. For example, interviews are particularly helpful for assessing constructs directly related to job content or knowledge and to social relations on the job. Yet they generally can't assess an applicant's personality dimensions or hidden values. This means that even among the best planned and executed interviews, validities vary, depending on the constructs being assessed. What popular constructs do interviews measure, and how reliable are they at predicting future job performance?

Although interview reliability and validity has been well researched, much less is known about the constructs that are assessable through employment interviews.[3] Researchers have suggested that interviews can assess cognitive ability,[4] motivation,[5] social skills,[6] and person-organization fit.[7] However, the extent to which most of these constructs are accurately assessed in interviews remains unclear.[8] The only item that has been examined empirically to any significant extent is cognitive ability: research indicates that on average, cognitive ability represents less than 20% of the variance in interview ratings.[9] An interview's capacity to assess other constructs depends on its structure. Results from structured interviews, in which questions and their sequence are predetermined, have been found to be qualitatively different from those from unstructured or free-flowing interviews.[10]

In general, interviews seem to tap into job relevant attributes (see Figure 8-2). But the ability of interviews to validly assess knowledge, skills, and job relevant attitudes (KSAs) varies.

JOB KNOWLEDGE, SKILLS, AND CAPABILITIES

Interviewers often try to use interviews to assess job-related knowledge, capabilities, and skills. One review found that this group of skills accounted for more than 25% of all

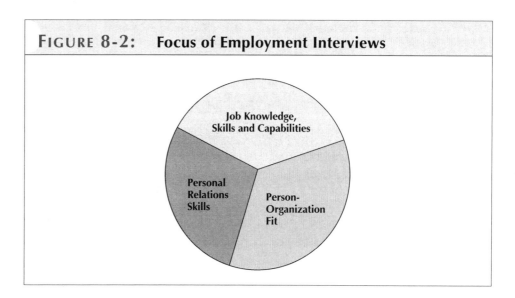

FIGURE 8-2:   Focus of Employment Interviews

the characteristics rated during an interview.[11] This group can be divided into two sub groups: knowledge and skills directly related to the job under consideration; and general mental capabilities of the applicants.

Job knowledge and skills

When interviewing for job knowledge and skills, the interviewer attempts to find out whether the applicant knows specific information relevant for job performance.

> In a police organization, officers seeking promotion to the rank of sergeant are asked interview questions about appropriate procedures for dealing with drunk driving, suspected theft, youth crime, and aggravated assault. The applicant's knowledge of the procedural differences in each case is noted and used in the selection decision.

Job knowledge and skill questions are perhaps the most straightforward questions in the interview, since the basic knowledge to perform the task has inherent face and content validity. However, when the number of job knowledge questions is large and the answers are to be short and routine, a written test may be preferable to an interview.[12] If the job involves manipulating complex instruments, stimuli, or information, simulation or other assessment tools may be more valid than interview responses. Job knowledge questions may be appropriate when the applicant has serious reading or writing deficiencies,[13] such that written tests may not validly assess true job knowledge. Interviews are also useful devices for eliciting additional information about an applicant's education, training, and background, especially if the job application form is brief. In addition, job knowledge and skill questions are particularly valid for advisory and consulting jobs that involve verbalization of highly complex concepts, as well as for technical information jobs and positions requiring oral presentations of knowledge.

> A large management consulting firm processes all its applicants for consultant's position through a series of interviews each lasting one to three hours. During these interviews (some of which are panel interviews with multiple interviewers present), the focus is on assessing an applicant's ability to systematically break a complex problem down into manageable parts. During the interviews, the interviewees work with complex problem scenarios, make chains of causal connections among facts, and offer solutions based on the synthesis of information presented.

Since a management consultant must be able to analyze information, understand interdependencies and their implications for problems on hand, and cohesively present observed relationships and own solutions to a client, the interview process attempts to assess these skills. Since there is a very close match between the actual job requirements and what is being assessed during the interview, the validity is also increased.

> Asking applicants for a position of a project manager in a construction firm about the principles of logistic planning or PERT/CPM techniques may have inherent validity; however, asking the same applicants about the programming features of a word processor may not.

Always pay careful attention to the choice of interview questions to ensure that they validly measure relevant job knowledge. In general, questions should not focus on material easily learned on the job or in a training program once the candidate is hired.

Validity of job knowledge and skills questions

In general, questions on job knowledge and skills have shown acceptable validity. In one review of six studies involving 2600 interviewees, job knowledge and skills had a mean validity of 0.23 in predicting job performance. When the figure was corrected for range restriction in the interview and measurement error in performance ratings, the validity rose to 0.42, thus representing over 16% of the variation in performance. Note that these values reflect the mean validity across different types of jobs; for this reason, they raise the question that the same construct may have different validity coefficients for different types of jobs. In general, structured interviews with predetermined lists of questions based on job analysis data produce higher validities. Develop new interview questions carefully so that they validly assess capabilities and knowledge. Question development is discussed later in this chapter.

Mental capabilities Many interviewers attempt to measure mental capabilities through interviews, such as general intelligence, applied mental skills, creativity, and innovation. They want to know how well applicants can assimilate, process, and synthesize information.

Validity of mental capability questions Early studies suggested that ratings of mental ability were good predictors of performance;[14] however, more recent research casts doubts on this idea.[15] In one recent review,[16] interview ratings of mental ability did not correlate strongly with job performance. Interviewer ratings of general intelligence had correlations ranging from 0.04 to 0.22 with a mean correlation of 0.13, while applied mental skills had a range of 0.08 to 0.22 with a mean rating of 0.15. Even when the correlation was corrected for range restriction in the interview and measurement error in performance evaluation, these figures did not appreciably increase. The highest mean corrected validities were observed for ratings of creativity (0.58); however, this figure was based on only four studies, thus casting doubts about its generalizability to other work settings.[17] Furthermore, interviewer ratings of general intelligence do not tend to have strong relationship with actual mental ability.

PERSONAL RELATIONS SKILLS

Many interviewers assign great importance to skills or characteristics considered important for successful personal interaction, especially in short-term initial meetings. Included here are basic personality traits and tendencies, applied social skills such as communication skills, and job-related physical attributes, such as demeanour.

Basic personality tendencies Interviewers are interested in personality traits, such as extroversion, conscientiousness, agreeableness, openness to experience, and emotional stability. *Conscientiousness* is the single most commonly rated trait in interviews.[18] The underlying focus is the Big Five personality traits (see p. 247) under different labels. For example, in an interview, *extroversion* may be called *assertiveness, energy, positive outlook,* or *energy,* and *conscientiousness* as *reliability, willingness to work hard, integrity, ethics,* and *persistence.* Other personality traits, such as *self-reliance, independence, empathy,* and *maturity,* are also popular items in interviews.

Validity of personality tendency questions Of all the personality traits assessed in interviews, *agreeableness* and *emotional stability* seem most promising in their ability to predict job performance. A recent review of interview procedures[19] found that the mean validity coefficient for *agreeableness* was 0.28. When corrected for range restriction and reliability of performance ratings, this rose to 0.51. The uncorrected and corrected validities for emotional stability were 0.26 and 0.47 respectively. Mean uncorrected validities for ratings of other traits ranged from a low of 0.08 to a high of 0.18. Yet despite the importance given to the construct *conscientiousness* in interviews, its predictive validity has not been found to be high (0.18); even after correcting for range restriction and reliability, this validity did rise beyond 0.33.

Applied social skills Applied social skills, such as communication skills (e.g., oral communication, voice and speech, listening skills), interpersonal skills (e.g., social sensitivity, tact, ability to empathize and create rapport), leadership, and persuasion-negotiation skills, are considered very important by many interviewers.

Validity of applied social skills questions Studies have found that interview ratings of leadership skills and interpersonal skills have respective mean validity correlations of 0.26 and 0.21 with performance. The corrected correlations for the same constructs were 0.47 and 0.39. Interview ratings of communication and persuasion skills have not shown great promise, with validities typically 0.13 or 0.14.[20]

Physical attributes

Many interviews look for job-related physical attributes during an interview, such as agility, physical ability, stamina, and even physical appearance and attractiveness. In assessing such attributes, the onus is on the interviewers to show that they do not violate the provisions of the human rights legislation and the Charter of Rights.

Validity of physical attribute assessments These attributes do not have high validity. Studies have shown a correlation of –0.18 to 0.15 for physical attributes to actual job performance.[21]

PERSON–ORGANIZATION FIT

Often, interviewers look for a fit between the applicant and the organization. For this reason, they focus on the applicant's general values, attitudes, career goals, and interests.

Values and attitudes

An applicant's core values relate to quality, appreciation for diversity, customer focus, as well as work-related attitudes, such as pride in the organization, work commitment, and willingness to be a good organizational citizen. "Organizational citizenship" is perhaps the most difficult attribute to assess in any valid fashion, since it is a complex construct consisting of several dimensions,[22] such as work habits, multi-tasking skills, helpfulness to co-workers, tolerance of temporary impositions, ability to make timely and constructive comments, foresight, proactive behaviours, and high motivation and drive. Several of these dimensions are difficult to assess, since the applicant's answer to a question such as "Would you be occasionally willing to work overtime if needed?" is unverifiable. The interviewee will simply provide the desired answers. This means that the interview questions have to be carefully formulated.

> Procter & Gamble has an innovative approach to form judgments about job applicants on five factors deemed critical for job success in the company: working well with others, stamina and agility, willingness to work hard, learning the work, and initiative. The interviewers ask the applicant to describe experiences from either a work or nonwork setting that illustrate each of the five factors. For example, for the item, "working well with others," the interviewers may say, "Describe a situation in which you had to work closely with a small group to complete a project." Later, in two follow-up interviews, interviewers probe the responses to these questions in depth, with each interviewer independently rating the applicant on a seven-point scale for each of the five factors.[23]

Validity of questions on values consistent with organizational priorities Ratings of organizational fit have shown considerable promise. One past review which looked at ratings of over 900 applicants showed that the average validity correlation for ratings of organizational fit was 0.27 (which rose to 0.49 when corrected for range restriction and poor reliability of performance ratings).[24]

Career goals and interests

The job applicant's career and occupational interests and goals are of interest to the interviewer because they help predict future contribution to and tenure in the organization. Included here are commitment to a career, job interests, hobbies, and extracurricular activities.

Validity of career goal questions Interviews have not shown great potential to validly assess career goals and interests, possibly because of the "impression management" efforts by the applicant. Often, interviewees simply say what they believe interviewers want to hear. A review looking at over 900 applicants showed that the average validity coefficient for this construct was 0.13. Even after correcting for measurement errors, it did not rise substantially (0.24).[25]

In general, while interviews are very versatile and useful, they have some inherent limitations. Research indicates that they are best suited for assessing job knowledge, applied social skills, and general work attitudes (see Figure 8-3). But they do not adequately assess personality traits or mental abilities. Often, the way a construct is defined affects how well it adapts to an interview.

> For example, flight attendants on short-duration flights require the ability to effectively interact with passengers. However, because the flights are short, these are typically non-recurrent interactions. The behaviours and social skills needed for such a short interaction can be assessed in an interview. However, if these competencies are defined as "friendliness" or "professionalism," the interviewers may find them harder to validly assess in an interview.

Other selection tools, such as personality tests, are more appropriate when the objective is to assess innate traits and hidden values. In addition, the interview's ability to predict future job performance depends on the overall interview structure. However, interview validity depends on other factors as well. The following section looks at some of the external factors that affect interview reliability and validity.

SITUATIONAL FACTORS AFFECTING INTERVIEW VALIDITY

Situational factors that affect interview outcomes can be divided into four groups: interview questions, interviewer characteristics, applicant characteristics, and scoring and weighting.

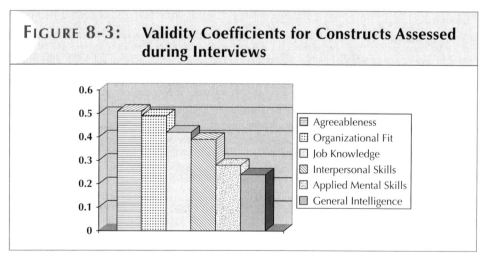

FIGURE 8-3:   Validity Coefficients for Constructs Assessed during Interviews

Legend:
- Agreeableness
- Organizational Fit
- Job Knowledge
- Interpersonal Skills
- Applied Mental Skills
- General Intelligence

Sources: Chart prepared by the author based on data presented in Allen I. Huffcut, James M. Conway, Philip L. Roth and Nancy J. Stone. (2001). "Identification and Meta-Analytic Assessment of Psychological Constructs Measured In Employment Interviews." *Journal of Applied Psychology, 86,* 5, pp. 902-906; and Richard A. Postuma, Frederick P. Morgerson, and Michael A. Campion. (2002). "Beyond Employment Interview Validity: A Comprehensive Narrative Review of Recent Research and Trends over Time." *Personnel Psychology*, pp. 38–46.

INTERVIEW QUESTIONS

The nature of the questions used affect the reliability and validity of interviews. If the questions are not related to job requirements or future job performance, validity suffers. If the questions used are not consistent among interviewers, the responses cannot be properly compared, resulting in lowered reliability and usefulness. To ensure high reliability and validity, all interviewers should use same questions.

> One American study found that less than one third of companies surveyed used a structured interview format with a predetermined set of questions.[26] The situation in Canada is likely to be quite similar, especially in organizations where interviews are conducted by untrained people. An online survey conducted by *Canadian HR Reporter* elicited responses from 166 readers, a large majority of whom claimed to use behavioural interviews.[27] However, these findings cannot be generalized to managers who do not have any HR training and who are not subscribers to the publication.

Another study reviewed over 51 000 interview ratings and concluded that structured interviews, where the constructs, the interview questions and their order of presentation and scoring were predetermined, exhibited high validity at 0.62. However, in unstructured interviews, the validity dropped to 0.31.[28] Later studies have also shown validities in the range of 0.41 to 0.49 for structured interviews.[29] Unstructured interviews are more likely to result in errors:

- Interviewer stereotypes and halo effect (see Figure 8-5) are more likely.
- Interviewers tend to remember best the first and last job applicants.
- Unfavourable information provided by the applicant has a greater influence on the interviewer evaluation than favourable information.
- Interviewers make a decision to hire or not hire before completing the entire interview.

The exact nature of questions depends on the job itself and the type of interview employed. Emerging evidence indicates that general questions which require the interviewer to make inferences reduce reliability and validity.

> Thus, a question such as "Have you taken any courses in human resource management?" is not very useful when hiring personnel, since this requires the interviewer to make inferences about the applicant or ask further questions to clarify the person's job knowledge. If the applicant states that he or she has taken four courses, the interviewer would need to follow-up with questions about the nature of the courses, the grades received, etc. Even then, there is no guarantee that the applicant possesses specific job knowledge. Not all courses are the same, nor do identical grades from different instructors reflect the same level of knowledge. The interviewer still has to make inferences about the applicant's job knowledge. Instead, a question such as "What are the steps in conducting a behavioural description interview for sales people?" requires much less inference on the part of the interviewer and directly assesses the candidate's job knowledge.

Canadian law prohibits the use of questions considered discriminatory. Figure 8-4 lists sample permissible and illegal interview questions.

INTERVIEWER CHARACTERISTICS

Interviewer-related factors and interviewer behaviours can affect interview outcomes. The more important ones are discussed below.

FIGURE 8-4:   Permissible Questions Under Canadian Law

Item	Not permissible to ask for:	Acceptable to ask for:
Address	Address outside Canada	Current or recent address and duration of stay
Age	Birth certificates, baptism record, or about age in general	Ask applicants if they are eligible to work under Canadian laws regarding age restrictions.
Sex	Details about pregnancy, family plans; no separate application forms for men and women allowed.	Ask whether the person can meet work schedule requirements.
Family status	Number of children or childcare arrangements	Ask whether the applicant can work various shifts, meet required work hours, and where relevant, overtime.
Origin	Details of birthplace, nationality of ancestors, ethnicity, etc.	Simply ask whether the applicant is legally entitled to work in Canada.
Religion	Details of religious affiliation, church or temple membership, frequency of church attendance, etc.	Explain the required work shift and hours and ask whether they pose any problem for the applicant.
Disability	Listing of disabilities or health problems, including mental health or emotional problems; questions on psychiatric care, whether the applicant drinks or uses drugs; whether applicant has received workers' compensation	Ask if applicant has any condition that could affect ability to do the job. Ask if the applicant has any condition that has a bearing on selection decision.
Conviction	Whether the applicant has ever been convicted or arrested; whether the applicant has a criminal record	Ask if applicant is eligible for bonding if that is a job requirement; ask if the applicant has committed a crime for which a pardon has not been granted.
Race, colour	Any question about race or colour including colour of eyes, skin, hair, etc. It is illegal to ask for a photograph to be attached to applications or sent to the interviewer before interview.	No questions are allowed.
Languages	Mother tongue, where language skills obtained	Ask if the applicant has the required language proficiency for the job.

Pre-interview impressions: evaluations of the applicant formed by the interviewer based on information available before the interview begins

Pre-interview impressions

Pre-interview impressions refer to applicant evaluations formed on the basis of information available to an interviewer before the interview begins. Research indicates that interviewers often make pre-interview judgments, and these judgments can influence interview ratings.[30] Thus, interviewers sometimes conduct interviews based on pre-interview impressions of the applicant.[31] Moreover, the relationship between between pre-interview ratings and post-interview ratings is stronger than the relationship between pre-interview screening decisions and post-interview ratings. In effect, interviewers are also susceptible to **confirmatory bias**, in which interviewers seek information that supports or confirms viewpoints they already hold. Favourable pre-interview impressions result in extra time spent recruiting the applicant, attributing favourable interview performance to internal (applicant-related) causes, and attributing unfavourable performances to external causes.[32] Interviewers with positive first impressions of applicants (based on test scores and applicant blank information) also approach the interview more positively, with behaviours oriented towards extending a job offer and "selling" the organization and the job.[33]

Research[34] indicates that interviewer **knowledge structures**, or beliefs about the job requirements and applicant characteristics, also influence their interview behaviour. These knowledge structures include stereotypes, categorizations of people, and hypotheses about personality traits as they relate to physical appearance, behaviour, social relationships, and personal origins. Interviewers make impressions about the job applicant in these categories and then compare the applicant against either an ideal candidate or another applicants.[35]

> Thus, if an interviewer has a prevailing belief that the job under consideration is a "male" job, men and women are likely to be treated differently, even if they possess similar qualifications and experience.[36]

Early studies indicated that interviewer stereotypes and perceptions of an "ideal" candidate biased their evaluation of applicants.[37] More recent research[38] "lends further support to the idea that individual recruiters may have conceptions about the ideal candidate that carry across organizations. The limited experimental evidence suggests that for some jobs and interviews, sex-related **stereotypes** may be related to interviewer cognitive schema."[39] The emerging evidence also indicates that these stereotypes affect the interviewer's thought processes, rather than their final decision on whom to hire.[40] But legal constraints and anti-discrimination legislation may end up preventing interviewers from giving much weight to their stereotypes.

Some common interviewer mistakes (summarized in Figure 8-5) lower the effectiveness of the interview. When the applicant is judged according to the **halo effect** or other personal biases, applicants are accepted or rejected for reasons that have no bearing on future job performance. Likewise, **leading questions** and **interview domination** do not allow the interviewer to learn of the applicant's potential. Often the final employment decision is based on a guess, with little or no substantiation. All these interview errors reduce the validity and reliability of the interview, while wasting organizational resources and the applicant's time.

Attribution of causes

Interview ratings are susceptible to first impressions: that is, the interviewer's initial impressions affect the way he or she conducts the interview.[41] The interviewer's first response to the applicant's behaviour at the beginning of the interview is to attribute it to personality traits.[42] Then, during the course of the interview, the interviewer may adjust this attribution to include situational factors, such as nervousness. But the interviewer's prejudices and preconceptions guide the way he or she processes and uses all this information.

> Thus, high grades in university or high school may be interpreted by one interviewer as reflective of applicant's intelligence or perseverance while another may interpret them as indicative of grade inflation. The exact interpretation depends on the interviewer's prior beliefs about the candidate and evidence collected during the interview up to that point.

Confirmatory bias: tendency to seek information that supports or confirms viewpoints a person already holds

Knowledge structures: beliefs (often erroneous) about what the job requires and who the applicant is

Stereotypes: preconceived and long-held ideas about specific groups, which negatively affect their interview ratings

Halo effect: an error in which positive, limited information about an applicant biases the interviewer to believe other characteristics are also positive

Leading questions: questions that "telegraph" the desired answer to the applicant because of weak wording

Interviewer domination: interviewer use of the interview to brag about their own successes, oversell the firm, or carry on a social conversation, instead of collecting job-relevant information from the applicant

---

FIGURE 8-5:   Common Interviewer Mistakes

Halo Effect: occurs when interviewers use limited information about an applicant, which biases their evaluation of the person's other characteristics. In other words, some information about the applicant erroneously dominates interviewer's thought and decision process and distorts the overall evaluation of the candidate.

Examples:

1. An applicant who has a firm handshake is considered a leading candidate even before the interview begins.
2. An applicant who dresses conservatively is considered as dull and not creative and mentally rejected for a position which calls for innovation.

Stereotypes: result when an interviewer subconsciously harbours prejudices about specific groups, which negatively affect their interview ratings.

Examples:

1. "Accountants are not outgoing or humorous people."
2. "Asians are not good for public relations jobs."

Leading questions: imply the desired answer to the applicant. By the very framing of the question, the interviewer tells the applicant what answer is desired.

Examples:

1. "Do you think you will like this job which involves regularly meeting people?"
2. "Do you think that a firm should be socially responsible?"

Interviewer domination: occurs when interviewers use the interview to brag about their own successes, oversell the firm, or carry on a social conversation instead of collecting job-relevant information from the applicant.

Cognitive complexity: a dimension of intelligence that reflects the ability to deal with complex social phenomena

Evidence suggests that an interviewer's **cognitive complexity** (the type of intelligence that reflects the ability to deal with complex social phenomena) also affects how the interviewer processes information and attributes cause and effect during and interview.[43] Interviewers with higher levels of general mental ability may be able to interpret complex social behaviours more accurately. Few controlled studies have examined the impact of these variables on interview outcomes. Hence, until further research is available, interviewers should simply be aware of the influence of their biases and first impressions.

Similarity to applicants

If an interviewer's attitudes and demographics are similar to those of the applicant, the interviewer will tend to inflate the interview ratings. Unstructured interviews are especially susceptible to interviewer biases. However, the relationship is not simple in all cases. For example, research suggests that female interviewers tend to report better interview experiences with female applicants and rate females more favourably than males, while male interviewers do not report differences in reactions to male and female applicants.[44] In the same way, race affects interview ratings but not always in the same way. In racially balanced interview panels, interviewers tend to rate same-race applicants higher than other-race applicants; however, on panels dominated by black interviewers, no biases were observable.[45] As one large review of the interview literature concluded, these differences may be more than a simple matter of demographic similarity between the applicant and the interviewer; instead, they may be more closely related to underlying factors, such as attitudes and values.[46] However, biases such as these are far less pronounced in structured interviews with clear job requirements.[47]

Experience and training While one would expect a significant relationship between interviewer experience and training and interview outcomes, few studies have systematically examined this topic; hence, the conclusions are very tentative. The few studies that exist found that higher interviewer experience leads to lower ratings of applicants.[48] Moreover, if the interviewer's experience is related to greater cognitive complexity, then it is often associated with more valid ratings.[49] Recently, interviewer training has become very popular. One outcome of this training has been increased use of structured interviews, for which there is well-researched validity.[50] The superiority of structured interviews is discussed in a later section.

APPLICANT CHARACTERISTICS

A number of applicant characteristics, including appearance, demographic characteristics, personality, nonverbal behaviours, and skills in impression management, have been found to be related to interview outcomes.

Appearance An applicant's physical attractiveness, clothing, and weight seem to influence interview outcomes.[51] While much of the research evidence is based on studies using college students, available data suggest that unattractive, poorly dressed applicants get negative ratings. Even the colour of the clothing may have some bearing on interviewer evaluations of the applicant:

> One controlled experiment[52] found that female applicants wearing masculine-styled attire (e.g., dark blue suit) were judged to be more forceful, self-reliant, dynamic, aggressive, and decisive than those wearing more feminine-styled clothing (e.g., a beige dress). Similarly, applicants who were perceived as obese received lower ratings than those with normal weight—in several cases, accounting for 35% of the variance in hiring decisions.[53]

Demographic characteristics Research shows that the effect of demographic characteristics on interview outcomes is somewhat small and inconsistent. Human rights laws have substantially reduced overt discrimination on the basis of gender, race, age, and disability; however, at an unconscious level, several of these variables can still play a role in the interview outcomes.

> An early study[54] indicated that female applicants generally receive lower ratings than their male counterparts; however, later studies have not supported this finding. In addition, managers were found to prefer older workers for low-status jobs, although they exhibited no differential age preferences for high-status jobs.[55]

Personality and non-verbal behaviours Current evidence indicates that personality characteristics, such as extraversion, conscientiousness, and need for achievement, are modestly related to applicant performance in an interview.[56] But keep in mind that many of these studies were done in research settings; in an actual job situation, applicants may fake social behaviours they believe are desirable for the job. In general, job requirements tend to define which personality traits are important for the job, and interviews tend to weight these heavily in an interview.

> For example, when hiring for a job that involves considerable teamwork, interviewers are likely to pay special attention to a candidate's behaviours and statements reflecting the trait of agreeableness rather than need for achievement.

The candidate's nonverbal behaviours can also affect interview outcomes. Visual cues, such as physical attractiveness, eye contact, smiling, and hand gestures, as well as speech patterns, such as variability in pitch and loudness, and number and duration of pauses, also affect ratings.[57]

Women applicants may use more head-nodding and smiling and are more likely to alter their nonverbal behaviour in response to the friendliness of the interviewer. Men typically use more gestures. Behaviours that reflect greater assertiveness are considered more masculine and are rated higher. Unassertive women applicants are rated lower and receive shorter interviews.[58]

Impression management:
attempts by applicants to create a favourable impression by monitoring and responding to interviewer reactions

Impression management **Impression management** tactics, or attempts by job applicants to create a favourable impression by monitoring and responding to interviewer reactions, have been shown to have an impact on interview outcomes.[59] A skilled interviewee can monitor clues about the interviewer's behaviours and interests and quickly adapt to the situation, guiding the conversation toward positive topics, using faked nonverbal behaviours, and thereby impressing the interviewer.

Thus, a job applicant who observes a golf club or fishing rod in the interviewer's office may guide the conversation toward golfing or fishing, expressing high interest and subtly reinforcing the interviewer's self image as a good golfer or fisher through verbal statements or body language. At the end of the interview, the interviewer is left with a general good feeling about the candidate, who usually receives a higher rating.

In these situations, instead of hiring the *best-qualified and best-suited* candidate, the interviewer often ends up hiring the candidate whom he or she *liked best.*

Scoring and Weighting Interview Information

An early study concluded that negative information about the applicant tends to be weighted more heavily than positive information, and that the order of presentation of negative and positive information during the interview can affect interviewer judgments.[60] Even experienced interviewers give more weight to negative information than to positive information when making decisions. For example, if an interviewer is making judgments about an applicant's tenure potential, negative information plays a more influential role than positive information.[61]

In summary, situational factors including interviewer and interviewee characteristics affect interview outcomes. But these biases can be reduced by using structured and behavioural interviews. The next section describes the strengths and weaknesses of interview options.

TYPES OF INTERVIEWS

Interviews are commonly conducted between the interviewer and the applicant on a one-to-one basis. However, panel and group interviews are sometimes used.

In a **panel interview,** two or more interviewers interview the candidate(s) simultaneously. This allows all interviewers to evaluate the individual(s) on the same questions and answers. Since the interviewers observe and hear the same things, they are likely to reach similar conclusions. Hence, reliability is improved. A variation is a **group interview,** in which one interviewer interviews two or more applicants together. Group interviews save time, especially for busy executives, and permit instant comparison of applicant answers. But, as Figure 8-6 shows, one-on-one interviews are more popular with Canadian managers than panel or group interviews.

Panel interview: an interview in which two or more interviewers interview the candidate(s) simultaneously

Group interview: an interview in which two or more applicants are interviewed at the same time by one interviewer

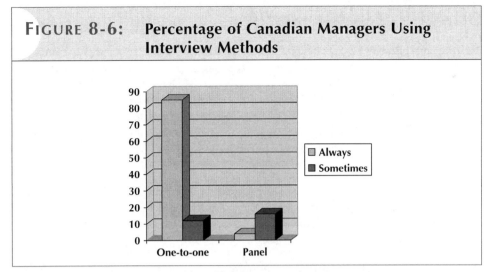

FIGURE 8-6:   Percentage of Canadian Managers Using Interview Methods

Source: Chart created by the author based on results of a survey by *Canadian HR Reporter* in April, 2005, reported by Todd Humber, "Recruitment is not getting any better," *Canadian HR Reporter*, May 23, 2005, Page R-2.

UNSTRUCTURED INTERVIEWS

Unstructured interviews allow the interviewer to develop questions as the interview proceeds and to develop topics as they arise. Thus, interviewers can ask any question that they please. The choice of questions is determined completely by the interviewer. The end result resembles a friendly conversation. Unfortunately, the unstructured method lacks the reliability of a structured interview because each applicant is asked a different series of questions. Even worse, this approach may overlook key areas of the applicant's skills or background. It is also more vulnerable to several of the interviewer errors noted earlier, as well as to the applicant's impression management tactics. For these reasons, unstructured interviews are not recommended. However, they continue to be very popular, especially with untrained interviewers.

> **Unstructured interviews:** interviews during which the interviewer develops questions as the interview proceeds and discusses topics as they arise

STRUCTURED INTERVIEWS

Structured interviews rely on a predetermined set of questions. The recruitment team develops the questions before the interview begins and asks the same questions for every applicant. This approach improves the reliability of the interview process. However, it does not allow the interviewer to follow up on interesting or unusual responses. The end result is an interview that seems quite mechanical to all concerned. The rigid format may even convey a lack of interest to applicants who are used to more flexible interviews.

> **Structured interviews:** interviews based on predetermined sets of questions

In **mixed interviews**, interviewers typically use a blend of structured and unstructured questions. The structured questions provide a base of information that allows comparisons between candidates. But the unstructured questions make the interview more conversational and permit greater in-depth investigation of specific topics. This technique provides more insights into the unique differences between applicants. Mixed interviews are popular with community college and university recruiters.

> **Mixed interviews:** interviews during which interviewers use both structured and unstructured questions

SITUATIONAL INTERVIEWS

Situational interviews: interviews in which specific activities and behaviours representative of a job are identified and then used to form questions that ask applicants how they would behave in a situation

In **situational interviews**, specific activities and behaviours representative of a job are identified and then used to form questions that ask applicants how they would behave in a situation. Preparing for situational interviews involves the following steps:[62]

1. Thoroughly analyze the job to identify specific, representative activities.

2. Identify critical incidents. A critical incident is work behaviour by previous employees that represent particularly good or bad job performance. Typically, several critical incidents are collected for a single job.

    > For example, a critical incident for a college instructor may describe how a previous instructor who discovered that several students were not doing well in the course offered to teach supplementary classes on evenings and Sundays for no additional reward.

3. The collected incidents are sorted into groups of similar behaviours, called *behavioural dimensions*. Retain only those behaviours that can be reliably sorted into behavioural dimensions.

    > A behavioural dimension for a college instructor might be "in-class teaching style." Examples of dimensions for other jobs are "customer service," "technical knowledge," and "concern for quality."

4. Choose a small but representative number of incidents from each dimension, in consultation with supervisors and other knowledge experts. The exact number of incidents chosen will depend on the critical nature of the dimension and the available interview time.

5. Rephrase the incidents as questions ending with "What would you do?" followed by multiple behavioural options. Select behavioural options based on actual employee behaviours in the past or responses received in other interviews.

6. Score the candidate's answers using a five-point scale. Establish the value for each behaviour in consultation with job supervisors and other area experts. Retain only those answers that everyone agrees are "low," "average," or "high" for job success.

7. Don't allow the job applicant to see the answers or the scale. Then rate the applicant's answers on a predetermined continuum. If the behavioural responses have been carefully prepared, the applicant's responses will tend to be very similar to the answers on the scoring sheet. If not, then the interviewer simply chooses the closest answer.

8. Determine a total score for the applicant by summing up the scores for the individual items. Alternatively, a series of separate scores can be generated by treating each dimension score independently.

Figure 8-7 provides an illustration of the situational interview questions and scoring scales for the position of a college instructor.

Situational interviews such as the above are believed to be highly job-related, reliable and valid,[63] because they reflect the applicant's behavioural intentions and the critical behaviours needed for the job.[64] Some studies have found higher reliability and validity in situational and behavioural description interviews than in traditional, unstructured interviews.[65] For example, one study reported interrater reliability estimates ranging from 0.76 to 0.87.[66] An early study that examined several situational interview validity coefficients (with a sample exceeding 900) reported an average validity of 0.50 in predicting later job performance.[67] In addition to the absolute level of predictive validity, the situational interview has also been shown to be relatively superior to some

---

FIGURE 8-7: Illustrative Situational Interview Questions and Scoring Scales for a College Instructor

A) *A guest speaker was making a presentation about the invisible obstacles facing women managers. When the speaker was half-way through her speech, one of the male students walked out of the class. What do you do?*

1 (low)	I would stop him and tell him that it is impolite to leave while the speaker is making a presentation
3 (average)	I would ignore the event. It could very well be that he had some emergency to attend to.
5 (high)	I would meet with him outside the class later, and ask him why he left the class. I would advise him to avoid similar behaviours in future. In a later class, without mentioning any names, I would state the need for polite behaviours especially when guests are present.

B) *To your surprise and dismay, you find that more than half the students in your class have failed the first midterm of your course. You had thought of this as a fairly good class and were expecting them to do well. What do you do now?*

1 (low)	I would ignore the event, hoping that the students will catch up.
3 (average)	I would make my expectations clear and tell the students in a friendly but firm tone that they have to exert more effort to do well in the course.
5 (high)	I would find out from the students what went wrong and which concepts they found hard. I would then go over the concepts again until they understood them. If required, I would hold special classes.

Note: The scoring schema will not be available to the interviewee.

---

other interview forms. One study examining 143 validity coefficients found that the average validity for situational interviews was 0.50, higher than all other job-related interview styles (0.39).[68]

BEHAVIOURAL DESCRIPTION INTERVIEWS

Behavioural description interviews[69] are similar to situational interviews in many respects. Like situational interviews, **behavioural description interviews** are based on the principle that the best predictor of people's future behaviour is their past behaviour in a similar circumstance and focus on assessing applicants on important behavioural dimensions of the job. But the focus is on typical performance dimensions. The behavioural dimensions identified (see above under situational interview) can describe either maximum or typical performance of an individual. Maximum performance dimensions usually deal with knowledge and technical expertise. Typical performance dimensions deal with interpersonal skills, time management, organization skills, and courteous and punctual behaviour. The behavioural description interview recognizes that the typical performance dimensions are easier to assess during an interview.

> Thus, in the case of a university professor, a behavioural description interview would deal with performance dimensions such as ability to plan courses and deliver them, ability to deal with students and coworkers, and contributions to the profession and community. More complex dimensions, such as fundamental research contributions and knowledge of specific statistical programs or research designs, are better assessed using other evaluation tools.

Behavioural description interviews: interviews that assess an applicant on typical performance dimensions of the job by focusing on the applicant's past behaviour in similar situations

Behavioural description interviews focus on the applicant's most recent but most enduring work-related behaviour. The steps involved in designing behavioural interview questions are similar to situational interviews:

1. Identify critical incidents and associated questions for each *typical* performance dimension. If how much the applicant *knows* or *can do* is critical to job performance, the dimension tends toward maximum performance.[70]

2. Form each question to include appropriate follow-up questions. The main question identifies a particular incident or instance from the applicant's past. The follow-up questions seek to find out the exact behaviours of the applicant in that situation.

3. Distinguish between questions appropriate for applicants with prior work experience related to the job in question and those without such experience. The latter type of question focuses on the same performance dimension in a more general way.

> For example, to an applicant for the position of a college instructor who already possesses teaching experience, the question might look like this: "Tell me about the most difficult student you have had in the last year and how you handled him or her." For an applicant with no experience, an equivalent question might be something like this: "All of us during our work or other activities occasionally come across difficult people. Tell me about an instance where you came across a difficult individual and how you handled the situation."

4. Score each behavioural dimension separately. After the interview, look at the notes (or go over the recording) and place the candidate into one of the five groups, where each group represents 20% of the applicants. Figure 8-8 illustrates interview questions and scoring format.

5. In some instances, the dimensions might have to be weighted differentially before computing a total score. But weighting is not advised unless the dimensions are markedly different in importance.

Like situational interviews, studies have produced encouraging validity coefficients for behavioural description interviews: in the range of 0.50 to 0.57.[71] One comparative study of behavioural and situational interviews showed that the behaviour-type interview was better able to predict performance than the situational interview.[72]

Other variations of structured interviews exist. For example, in a **comprehensive structured interview**,[73] situational interview questions are combined with questions about job knowledge, job performance, and worker characteristics or worker willingness. The result is a highly structured interview. Similarly, **Job Content Method**[74] focuses on developing structured interview questions that relate to a small number of KSAs covering personal relations, good citizenship, and job knowledge. Regardless of the label, structured interviews focus on enhancing reliability and validity through consistent interview practices. In the aggregate, the available evidence indicates that this form of interview may currently offer the best results among interview techniques. No wonder that more Canadian managers are opting for these types of interviews.

> A survey of 202 Canadian organizations indicates that structured and behavioural description interviews are gaining popularity[75] (see Figure 8-9). In another survey of managers carried out in 2005, over 90% of the respondents reported that they conduct behavioural interviews. Over 60% reported using panel interviews.[76]

However, especially in small firms, untrained interviewers make a large portion of hiring decisions, and they are more likely to use unstructured interviews.

Comprehensive structured interview: an interview in which situational questions are combined with questions about job knowledge, job performance, and worker willingness

Job Content Method develops structured interview questions that relate to a smaller number of KSAs covering personal relations, good citizenship, and job knowledge

FIGURE 8-8: **Illustrative Behavioural Description Interview Questions and Scoring for the Position of a College Instructor**

A) In this profession, one occasionally comes across a difficult student. Tell me about a difficult student whom you had in the last 12 months.

Follow-up questions:

1. Why do you consider him/her difficult?
2. What exactly did (s)he do?
3. What was the impact of his or her behaviour on you, others, and the class?
4. What did you do or say?
5. Were you successful in resolving the event? How do you know?
6. What did you learn from this? Would your behaviour be different in the future?

B) Tell me about a time when you helped a student in understanding a difficult concept.

Follow-up questions:

1. What was the concept?
2. How did you know that the student was having problems with it?
3. What did you do or say that helped?
4. How did you know that you were successful?
5. What will you do in future to ensure that students are following you?

The following is a sample schema for rating the interviewees (not seen by the interviewee).

Interview Performance Rating

	1	2	3	4	5
Dimension	**Bottom 20%**	**Next 20%**	**Middle 20%**	**Next 20%**	**Top 20%**
1. In-class teaching style				X	
2. Student counselling		X			
....					
....					
10. Collegial nature and good peer relations					X

Total Score: 4 + 2 +.................+ 5 = **38 or 76%** [= (38/50) × 100]

COMPUTER-ASSISTED INTERVIEWING

Technology is changing how organizations recruit and select in ways that could not have been imagined a few years ago. Videoconference interviews, videophone interviews, and computerized interviews are becoming increasingly popular because they reduce the time and travel costs associated with personal interviews. While automated hiring technologies are still in their infancy, one can envision a future where the hiring cycle time is reduced by 90% because recruiters can call up information about a potential hire on their computer screens. Nike is one example of a company that has begun to use computer-assisted interviewing:

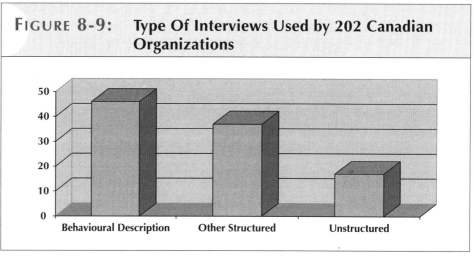

FIGURE 8-9:   **Type Of Interviews Used by 202 Canadian Organizations**

Source: Chart prepared by the author based on the statistics reported in Sean Way and James Thacker. (1999, Oct-Nov.). "Selection Practices: Where are Canadian Organizations?" *HR Professional,* pp. 33–37.

Recently, Nike used Interactive Voice Response Technology (IVR) to interview the 6000 applicants for 250 job positions. Applicants responded to eight questions over the telephone, and more than half of them were immediately screened for lack of retail experience or non-availability during desired work-hours. The remainder had a computer-assisted interview at the store, followed by a personal interview. Using computer-assisted interviews helped the firm not only to fill positions faster but also to reduce employee turnover by 21% in two years.[77]

While computer-assisted interviews may make the interviews uniform (thus potentially increasing their reliability), some managers feel uncomfortable with the in-depth electronic profiling typical of these interviews. Moreover, while long-distance interviews can be valid predictors of job performance,[78] some interviewers find the lack of personal contact unsatisfying or even unpleasant. This approach may also exclude persons who do not give responses in the desired range, even though they have skills the firm needs. Unlike machines, human interviewers can pick up additional valuable information and cues and use judgment when processing them. Finally, electronic profiling may end up selecting persons who all have the same personality traits; in this way, diversity, which can be a company's strength, may be lost.

Recently, more sophisticated approaches have been used to collect information from applicants while simultaneously reducing costs. These approaches include hiring companies to produce videos of applicants to send to employers, streaming video attachments sent by email, and third-party website hosts and recruitment links.

A video resume hosting company: *www.marketyourself.ca*

CONDUCTING VALID INTERVIEWS

Regardless of the method used, all effective employment interviews require careful planning and execution at five distinct stages.[79] These stages are listed in Figure 8-10 and are discussed below.

STAGE 1: INTERVIEWER PREPARATION

Obviously, before the interview begins, the interviewer needs to prepare. The preparation focuses on four areas: (1) defining the scope of the interview, (2) interviewer

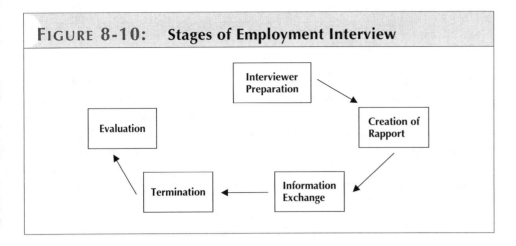

FIGURE 8-10: **Stages of Employment Interview**

training, (3) developing interview questions, and (4) becoming familiar with the applicant's resume.

Defining the scope of the interview

Interviews become ineffective when they try accomplish too many objectives. Often, interviews are required to attract high-calibre potential employees, do public relations for the firm, and select the best employee from the pool of recruits. However, "the purposes and the data for public relations, recruitment and, selection are simply not the same."[80] Hence, the recruitment and selection functions should be kept separate, so that the employment interview can be used exclusively to assess key KSAs. Answers to the following questions can help define the KSAs and the scope of the interview:

- What is the purpose of the job?
- What tasks must be carried out? What responsibilities are associated with the job?
- What are the success criteria for this job? How will we distinguish between a good employee and a poor one?
- What knowledge, skills, competencies, and other work habits are associated with successful and outstanding job performance?

Some of the actions to promote a good impression and do public relations for the firm may be very subtle, such as non-verbal behaviors (see Stage 2 on p. 284).

Interviewer training

Interviewers should be trained prior to conducting employment interviews. The training should focus on (1) receiving information, (2) evaluating information, and (3) monitoring and regulating interviewer behaviour during interviews.[81]

Receiving information Interviewers should be trained in (1) establishing rapport with the interviewee, (2) reducing their anxiety levels, (3) accurately interpreting information, (4) making notes, and (5) minimizing the effect of their own behaviour and expectations on what the applicant says. They should also learn to be culturally sensitive so that they do not misinterpret nonverbal cues and form wrong conclusions about candidates from different cultural groups.

> For example, many Asians avoid looking someone straight into the eye, since it is considered impolite in their culture. Moreover, many cultures do not value the "strong handshake" that Canadians consider as a sign of integrity.

Interviewers should be trained to avoid scoring such nonverbal behaviours and to prevent such behaviours from influencing their decisions.

Evaluating information The interviewer should learn about stereotypes, halo effects, similar-to-me effects, and first impressions errors. They should be trained to identify candidates who engage in impression management tactics. The training should also focus on how to weight and score interview information to come out with a total score.

Information on preparation for an interview:
www.interviewcoach.com

Monitoring and regulating interviewer behaviours Interviewers should be made aware of their own stereotypes, biases, and behaviours that can make job candidates uncomfortable during the interview. Interviewers should also be trained (1) to link interview questions tightly to job analysis results, (2) to use a variety of questions, (3) to ask the same questions of each candidate, and (4) to base rating scales for scoring answers on examples and illustrations.[82] Interviewers should also be familiar with human rights legislation, as well as techniques to elicit maximum information while maintaining a friendly atmosphere.[83]

Developing interview questions
Since all forms of structured interviews have been shown to be superior to unstructured interviews, with higher reliability and validity, interviewers need to develop a list of uniform questions before the interview. The questions they develop depend in part on the type of interview to be used (Figures 8-7 and 8-8 show sample questions for situational and behavioural description interviews). In all cases, follow these guidelines:

- Formulate a set of questions for each KSA to be measured during an interview
- Use multiple questions for each KSA to increase reliability. Depending on a single question may save time, but it can result in poor reliability and lower predictive validity.
- Identify a clear scoring format for each question before the interview begins.
- Clearly link the weighting of the performance dimensions measured to prior job analysis results.

Also consider what questions the applicant is likely to ask. You may have to explain job duties, performance standards, pay, benefits, and other areas of interest. Be prepared to answer any questions on these matters.

Reviewing the applicant's details
Another task the interviewer should undertake before the interview is to review available information about the applicant. Some research affirms the benefit of looking at the resume and application form prior to the interview;[84] however, subsequent research has not always supported these findings. Indeed, an interviewer's pre-interview impressions about a candidate may affect behaviours during the interview and post-interview evaluations. As a result, provide only those details relating to the KSAs to be covered during the interview to the interviewer; the interviewer can then save interview time and focus on important points. Familiarity with the applicant's background will also help the interviewer identify incomplete or contradictory statements on the application form. Details such as employment gaps and irregular career pattern may be red flags to an interviewer, who can then clarify them during the interview. While reviewing job application forms, bear in mind that some of the best candidates may not be skilled at preparing eye-catching resumes. The reverse is also true: someone with a well-designed and attractive resume is not guaranteed to be a great employee. Avoid prejudging the applicant's potential.

STAGE 2: CREATION OF RAPPORT

The interviewer should greet candidates with a warm smile, show them into the office, make small talk, and reduce nervousness. It is the interviewer's responsibility to establish a relaxed rapport with the recruit. Without this rapport, the interviewer may not be able to validly assess the applicant's potential. Rapport is aided by beginning the interview on time and starting with neutral questions such as, "Did you have any problem finding the office?" Through positive body language, such as a smile, a friendly handshake, a relaxed posture, and a clean desk, the interviewer can communicate without words and maintain rapport throughout the interview session. Maintaining rapport is important not only to put the candidate at ease but also to create an overall positive image about the organization.

> "Treat the interview process as an opportunity to market your company," says Tim Collins, President of StaffLink Solutions in Toronto. "You are the front-line of communication. There's a tremendous PR opportunity. You are not going to hire every person you interview. But if they have a positive experience, that will affect 5, 10, 20 other people."[85]

STAGE 3: INFORMATION EXCHANGE

The heart of the interview process is the exchange of information. Depending on the type of interview being used, the interviewer may pose situational or behavioural questions. In all interviews, the focus is on learning as much as possible about the KSAs being assessed. Questions that begin with *How, What, Why, Compare, Describe, Expand,* and *Could you tell me more about* are likely to solicit open responses, while questions that can be answered with a simple *yes* or *no* do not give the interviewer much insight.[86] As already noted, asking specific behavioural description questions that assess an applicant's knowledge, skill, ability, and other characteristics (such as work-shift availability, personality characteristics) significantly add to the validity of the information collected. Some of the guidelines for asking questions are given in Figure 8-11.

STAGE 4: TERMINATION

As the list of questions nears an end, the interviewer must draw the session to a close. Here again, nonverbal communication is useful. Sitting erect, turning toward the door, or glancing at a watch all cue the applicant that the interview is almost over. Some interviewers terminate the interview by asking, "Do you have any final questions?" Then the interviewer informs the applicant about the next step in the recruitment process, which may be to wait for a call or letter. If the interviewer is likely to contact referees or call the applicant back for a second interview, mention this at this time.

FIGURE 8-11:   Guidelines for Asking Questions

- Ask each question in turn without omitting any.
- Do not rush the candidate. Indicate to him or her that he has enough time to reflect and respond.
- After asking a question, try to remain quiet for several seconds to give the applicant a chance to think. During the period when the applicant is reflecting, the interviewers can update notes or look down to reduce tension.
- Rephrase or repeat a question if it was not clear to the applicant.
- If after rephrasing the applicant still has difficulty responding to the question, tell him/her that you will come back to it later and move on.
- Broaden or make the question specific depending on the applicant's background.
- In all instances, reassure the applicant that it is normal to take time to respond.

Focus on Ethics

You recently joined Ontario Textiles Corporation, a medium-sized textile manufacturer located near Sudbury, Ontario, as Assistant to the Human Resource Manager. On your arrival, you noted that the company has policies and systematic procedures covering most HR activities. But recently you came across two situations that were not covered. To complicate matters, the Human Resource Manager is on holiday and away from the country. Prior to departure, she had asked you to "look after all recruitment and selection matters" in her absence.

1. Among the seven candidates considered for the post of Work Supervisor in Plant B, Ann Smith was the top choice of two out of the three interviewers. Another candidate, Brad Long, was equally qualified for the position, and he was the choice of the third member of the interview committee. But Len Kaiser, the Plant Manager (to whom the Work Supervisor would report) prefers Ann. One of the requirements for the position is that depending on work demands, the hired candidate must be willing to work in any of the three shifts in the company. During the interview, all candidates were apprised of this requirement.

   Earlier today, Mark Gammon, a long-term employee of the company and Ann's neighbour, mentioned to you that Ann is four months pregnant. You believe that if Len learns about this pregnancy, he will switch in favour of Brad Long. It is also possible that with a new baby, Ann might be unwilling to take night shifts in the future. Indeed, had Len known about Ann's condition it is very doubtful

whether he would have seriously considered Ann, although it is illegal to discriminate against someone on this ground.

2. Martha Furnishings Ltd (MFL), a large interior furnishing firm in Vancouver, B.C., is about to hire one of your long-term employees, Ken Wood, for the position of Office Manager. MFL's human resource manager has scheduled a telephone interview with you seeking more information about Ken. When you went through Ken's records, you found that he was a highly conscientious and punctual employee who exhibited a commitment to high-quality work. Ken's performance appraisal records also show that he had maintained excellent relations with his peers and clients. However, there was one black spot in his record. Against the company rules, Ken was running a small business from his home. When discovered, Ken disbanded the formal business, but was reported to still be running the business in a more informal fashion. You also heard through the grapevine that Ken had "borrowed" some money from the company funds to finance his operations, but when discovered, he repaid the "loan" to the company. There is no mention of any of these incidents in his employee records; but given these incidents, it is unlikely that Ken would be rehired by your company if he were to apply for the job in future. If you mention his activities to the new employer, Ken is unlikely to get the job.

What will you do in each case? Defend your choice in light of the material discussed in Chapter 1 and compare your answers to those of other students.

Finally, the interview should end by thanking the applicant for coming to the interview and escorting him or her to the door.

STAGE 5: EVALUATION

Immediately after the interview ends, the interviewer should record specific answers and general questions. Figures 8-8 and 8-9 show scoring procedures for situational and behavioural interviews.

REFERENCE CHECKS IN SELECTION

Is the applicant a good, reliable worker? What are the work habits of the applicant? Is he or she punctual, dependable, cooperative, and adaptable? To answer questions like these, employment specialists use references.

A recent survey showed that 84% of companies have had to fire people for reasons that could have been discovered by proper reference checks. More than 93% of the respondents said they had found exaggerations on resumes, and 86% had found outright misrepresentations.[87] One large U.S. company that routinely conducts reference checks (and had conducted 2.6 million background checks in 2001 alone) found that 44% of applicants lied about their work histories, 41% lied about their education, and 23% falsified credentials or services.[88]

Yet many professionals have a very skeptical attitude toward references. As the following incident illustrates, previous employers are not always candid about the employees, especially with negative information:

> John Adams had already impressed his interviewers a few minutes after the interview began. The position was that of a store manager in a large building supplies chain. His ready wit, ability to think on the spot, and keen mind appealed to the interviewers. Equally attractive was what his previous employers had to say about him. One of the referees called him a young dynamo because of his drive and enthusiasm; another commented on John's ability to "come out with totally creative ideas" and his "methodical approach to problems." John Adams was hired for the position by the firm and did perform true to these statements— for the first three months. But by sheer accident one day, a colleague noted a shortfall in the cash register. Investigation revealed that Adams had been systematically stealing money from his employer. Even worse, he had a history of embezzling accounts with his three previous employers. One of the previous employers later admitted being aware of a couple of incidents where Adams had received kickbacks from vendors. But none of the referees had mentioned of these concerns in their letters.[89]

Lack of candor in reference letters is due to several reasons. In the United States, employers are legally required to show reference letters to applicants, which results in decreased honesty. Moreover, in order to get rid of bad employees, some employers willingly write inflated letters. Others are just reluctant to pass judgment on a fellow human being in writing. Many employers are also afraid of the legal repercussions of giving poor reference. This means that you should:

- receive written permission from the applicant to conduct a reference check;

- get confirmation in writing from the applicant that the referees have been given permission to be contacted; and

- immediately identify yourself when contacting the referees and provide assurances that all information provided will be treated with confidentiality. You should also develop a *confidentiality policy document* to send to referees before contacting them.

One reason that outcomes from reference checks are poor is that many managers do not seek the right information or ask the right questions. But their ability to gather relevant information seems to be improving.

> In a 2005 Canadian survey of managers, 92% of respondents reported that during background checks, they focused on previous employment history. At least 50% also checked academic qualifications and criminal record. Only about 10% checked credit ratings.[90]

Figure 8-12 suggests ways to effectively conduct reference checks.

Many employers now prefer telephone checks to letters of reference (see Figure 8-13). Besides providing a faster response, often at lower cost, telephone inquiries have the advantage of directness: voice inflections or hesitation at blunt questions can tip you off to underlying problems. In practice, however, only a small proportion of all reference checks seek negative information. Most reference checks are used to verify application information and gather additional data. For some positions, employers also require **background checks**, typically performed by professional agencies, to validate the information in an applicant's resume, certificates, accreditation claims, and past achievements. For sensitive government or private industry jobs, police or security services, and high profile positions, field investigations are also common. **Field investigations** are

Background checks: validation of the information in an applicant's resume, certificates, accreditation claims, and other past achievements, usually done by an outside agency

Field investigations: professional investigation which includes interviews with former employers, employees and coworkers, as well as police records, credit checks, court records, criminal activities, media reports, and other matters relevant to the job and mentioned during the job interview

---

FIGURE 8-12:   Suggestions for Conducting Reference Checks

Use credible sources only: Former work supervisors are typically the most useful sources. Former subordinates, peers, and supervisors may also offer insights into other dimensions of an applicant's past performance, although you should recognize that they may not have access to performance records. Letters from acquaintances and friends are not useful for predicting future job success.

Take careful notes: If you are collecting information in person or over the telephone, ensure that the notes you take are accurate and validated by the source. Avoid making any negative or discriminatory statements during the conversation, since they could be used by an unsuccessful applicant as evidence of unfair hiring practices.

Use the telephone: Referees are more likely to be honest over the telephone rather than in a formal letter.

Seek information on job-related behaviours: Ask for information about specific behaviours, such as punctuality and absenteeism, rather than about personality traits, such as ambition, which are hard to reliably assess. Ask questions such as:

- *In what capacity did you know the applicant and how long?*
- *How well did (s)he get along with peers, supervisors, clients, etc.?*
- *How is this person's behaviour in a group setting?*
- *Did the person have attendance problems? Was (s)he usually punctual? Was (s)he willing to take on extra responsibilites if necessary?*
- *Would you re-hire the employee?*
- *Why did the person quit?*
- *On a scale of 1 to 10, where 10 is your best employee and 1 is your weakest employee, where would you rate this person?*
- *If you were to divide your workforce into five groups—bottom 20%, next 20%, middle 20%, next 20% and top 20%—where would this employee fit?*

Listen for phrases with hidden meanings: Most referees do not blatantly lie; they simply don't tell the whole truth. A person who is described as "deeply committed to family and friends" may be someone who is unwilling to work beyond five o' clock; an "individualist" may be an individual who cannot work with others.

Source: Adapted and expanded on Hari Das and Mallika Das. (1988, June-July). "But He Had Excellent References: Refining the Reference Letter." *The Human Resource*, pp. 15–16. Reprinted by permission of the authors.

performed by professional agencies and include interviews with former employers, employees, and co-workers, as well as police records, credit checks, court records, criminal activities, media reports, and other matters relevant to the job and mentioned during the job interview. Background checks have become increasingly popular as employers become more focused on ethical standards.

FIGURE 8-13:   Reference Checks used by 202 Canadian Organizations

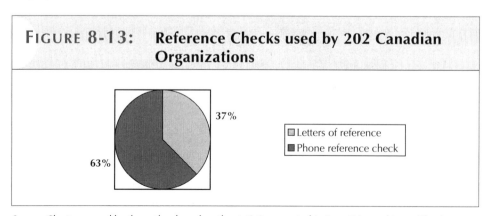

37%

63%

☐ Letters of reference
■ Phone reference check

Source: Chart prepared by the author based on the statistics reported in Sean Way and James Thacker. (1999, Oct-Nov.). "Selection Practices: Where are Canadian Organizations?" *HR Professional*, p.35.

Pinkerton Security and Investigation Services screens more than a million job applicants each year.[91]

Organizations conduct reference checks as one of the final steps in reviewing an applicant's qualifications and suitability for the position. The hiring manager or an HR specialist typically conducts the reference check. Often, they seek little more than confirmation of prior employment. In some cases, the referees provide only basic information to protect themselves (e.g., simply stating that a person worked for them in the past in a certain capacity during specific dates). This lack of candor has caused some human resource specialists to omit the reference check step entirely from the selection process. But keep in mind that reference letters are no substitute for other selection tools, such as valid application blanks, tests, and interviews. Where used, reference checks should focus on job-related behaviours noticed by the referee.[92]

However, reference and background checks can play an important role for some jobs. Consider these facts:

> According to the Retail Council of Canada, internal theft accounts for 48% of retail losses—more than $1 billion annually.[93] Moreover, a study by Infocheck showed that reference checks raised a red flag for 35% of job applicants—and those applicants had already gone through several rounds of interviews. Of this sample, 7.5% had criminal records, 25% were classified as poor performers by their references, 27% had fabricated their educational credentials, and 19% had been fired from their previous employment.[9]

Once the information on various predictors (such as tests, interviews, and reference checks) is collected, it must be combined in order to make a final decision on a job applicant. This final step in selection is discussed in the next chapter

Implications for Practice

1. Restrict the scope of the interview so that it focuses on information about applicant's job knowledge, sociability, and general work habits.

2. Always use structured interviews, such as behavioural description or situational interviews, or a variant of these two styles.

3. Limit the interviewer's access to pre-interview data, since providing too much information about the applicant's ability (as in test scores) or other background may bias the interviewers. However, you do need to provide the interview with key details about the applicant's KSAs.

4. Design the interview questions carefully so that they directly relate to the job analysis. To enhance reliability, assess each KSA with several questions.

5. Train the interviewers so that they are very familar with the activities in each of the five interview stages.

6. Develop the scoring key for the interview before the interview begins.

7. Check the interview records periodically to determine the validity of your interview methods.

8. Perform reference checks with previous employers (and others, in some instances) to find out more about an applicant's work habits. Avoid using reference checks to discover complex personality traits or deep-rooted values.

9. Follow the suggestions in this chapter for more effective reference checks.

Key Terms for Review

Discussion Questions

1. What kind of constructs can interviews measure most effectively? Why?

2. What situational factors influence interview outcomes? Cite two variables that you have personally experienced (as either an interviewer or an interviewee) which had an impact on interview outcomes.

3. Describe an interview that you underwent recently. What type of an interview was it (structured, unstructured, behavioural, etc.)? What improvements could you now suggest to the interviewers, based on information in this chapter?

4. Describe the five stages of interviewing.

5. If you had to do a reference check for a new hire in the human resource department, how would you do it?

Critical Thinking Questions

1. Ideas and Images, a software development firm with six employees, was the brainchild of Mark Tanner, a computer graphics artist who dropped out of college to start the business. The firm, though small by industry standards, has grown rapidly, mainly because of its reputation for innovative products. Mark is now planning to enter the field of live-action 3-D graphics, for which he must attract a highly skilled, innovative programmer who has not only technical skills but also creative abilities including visualization, imagery, and graphic editing skills. Mark is planning to interview four of the thirty-two applicants, based on the details they wrote in the firm's standard application form. His hiring decision will be based entirely on the impressions he gets during the interview. While talking to you about the company, he sought your opinion on his hiring plans. What advice would you give to him?

2. You are the student representative on the Dean selection committee. Over the next several weeks, the committee will interview ten candidates for the position. Based on information in this chapter, what suggestions would you make to the committee to ensure high validity for your interviews?

3. What kind of an interview would you recommend to select the Dean (see Question 2)? Why?

4. If you were to conduct interviews to select (a) cashiers in a fast food restaurant and (b) architects for a large construction company, would the interviews be different? If so, then how?

5. If you were to do reference checks for the applicant for the architect's position (see Question 4), how would you do it?

Web Research

Visit the websites of three medium-sized to large firms, each from a different industry, and note their hiring policies and preliminary screening criteria/process. For maximum variation, select some high tech and some traditional industries. What commonalities do you see? What differences are apparent?

CASE INCIDENT

Atlantic Builders Inc.

Atlantic Builders Incorporated (ABI) is a construction company with its head office in Saint John, N.B., and offices in four other major Atlantic Canadian cities. Bob McDonald began the company in his garage forty years ago, and through hard work and vision, he built a company that today employs nearly 200 full-time employees, including 30 construction engineers and nine architects. Bob also believed in introducing systems and procedures and in focusing on results. According to policy, the firm hired employees using three predictors: biographical application blanks, aptitude test, and a three-member panel interview. The firm routinely employed a large number of part-timers and subcontracts several of their activities to other units to reduce fixed overheads. Bob then retired, and Bob's son, Mark, has since become the new CEO. Compared to Bob, Mark has a more easy-going style of management, a factor that has been a constant irritant for Sharifa Carson, the firm's human resource manager, who began her job at ABI four years before Bob took over.

A few weeks ago, while Sharifa was away on leave, Mark's cousin, Etienne, who heads the Fredericton office of ABI, brought his 18-year-old daughter Susan to the human resource department and told Sharifa's assistant that Susan would start working at ABI. Two days later, when Sharifa returned to work, she was surprised at and dismayed that Susan was dumped at her office without going through any selection procedures; but she also did not want to make a big issue out of it. She found a desk and office for Susan and gave her some simple paperwork. Since Susan did not have any skills relevant to ABI's business, it was difficult to meaningfully engage her. Susan spent most of her time talking to the architects and construction engineers, often to the chagrin of everyone concerned. The only exception was Craig Chu, a 26-year-old engineer, who had taken an interest in her. Rumours said that Craig and Susan were dating each other. In any event, they were found to be spending considerable time together at the office.

Many other assistants in the office began complaining that Susan was not doing anything to earn her salary. In addition, many engineers complained to Sharifa about the constant interruption to their work and about Craig's declining work efforts.

Questions

1. *What is the underlying problem in this situation? What issues are relevant in analyzing the situation?*

2. *What options are open to Sharifa? What should she do now? Why?*

CASE

*Kanata Food Distributors—Selecting a Super K Manager**

Note: This case continues from Chapter 7: Kanata Food Distributors. Review the case background in Chapters 1, 2, 3, 4, 6, and 7 before examining this case.

One persistent problem facing Kanata Food Distributors has been the absenteeism rates of Super K employees. Since the margins on the products sold in Super K are low, maintaining high productivity levels (which also includes eliminating absenteeism) is a high priority for the organization. To complicate matters, five of the present Super K store managers are leaving the firm, either through retirement or for personal reasons. The company is also embarking on a major expansion plan that will require the hiring of dozens of new cashiers.

Questions

1. *Based on the material presented in the case (see Chapters 1, 2, 3, 4, 6, and 7) and your familiarity with the industry, what KSAs are appropriate for store managers?*

2. *Assume that the firm is planning to use interviews as part of its hiring process. What kind of interviews would you suggest? Why?*

3. *Develop an interview checklist for hiring managers, including a scoring key.*

---

*Case written by Professor Hari Das of Saint Mary's University, Halifax. All rights retained by the author, © 2005

CHAPTER

"Establishing satisfactory cutoff scores is one of the most complicated and controversial issues in the area of personnel selection. ... Although a variety of approaches for determining cutoff scores have been introduced in the area of educational measurement... little work has been done in the personnel management or industrial psychology domains. In addition, most of the previously proposed methods are applicable to normative data or content validity studies rather than to criterion-related validity studies"

Scott L. Martin and Nambury S. Raju[1]

CHAPTER OBJECTIVES

After studying this chapter, you should be able to:

- Discuss different ways to combining predictors
- Create a process for establishing cut-off scores
- Discuss the steps to take once the selection decision has been made

A large hotel chain was planning to open a new resort-casino employing 1300 full-time staff in a few months' time. The firm began trying to fill eleven major types of jobs. In preparation, several months earlier, it had advertised in newspapers and other media. Job seekers could log onto the company's website, apply for the positions, and track their progress online. Applicants could also mail in their applications or submit them in person. All applications were entered into a central electronic file. Once the initial recruitment was over, a computer screened all 6100 applications, reducing the number of qualified applicants to about 5200. Then the remaining applicants took a general ability test, which they could do either on the web or in person on certain days. These test scores eliminated another 3200 applicants. The firm then interviewed the remaining candidates. After a panel interview, successful candidates went on to a supplementary on-location interview with their immediate boss and members of the human resource department. This was followed by reference, security, and credit checks (for some positions). The successful hires then participated in job training and orientation programs. By the time the resort opened a few weeks later, all employees were competely familiar with their job duties.

Large scale hiring such as in the opening vignette, where 6100 applications had to be matched with eleven job types, can be challenging indeed! Fortunately, high-speed computers can facilitate screening (see Chapter 6). In addition, tests can help achieve better fit between job applicants and job requirements (see Chapter 7). As well, structured interviews (see Chapter 8) result in more accurate assessment of applicant skills and better matches between KSAs and job requirements.

In the opening vignette, minimum cut-off test scores in tests helped the hotel reduce the size of the applicant pool by over 3000 applicants. This is an example of a minimum hurdle rule. But it is not the only way to use predictor scores to make selection decisions. This chapter will introduce you to several other approaches to combining predictor scores. It will also explain the steps to take after successful applicants have been identified.

APPROACHES TO COMBINING PREDICTOR SCORES

Two major decisions have to be made when combining predictor scores: (1) whether to use an objective or subjective approach and (2) what weight or importance to assign to different predictors.

SUBJECTIVE VS. OBJECTIVE APPROACHES

When collecting information on predictors and using them to make selection decisions, an organization has to choose between objective and subjective approaches,[2] both in information collection and decision making (see Figure 9-1).

Subjective predictors are items such as interview scores (in which data was collected through human perception and judgment). In contrast, *objective* information can be found in test scores. Subjective/objective differences affect data interpretation as well. Statistical techniques (such as regression equations and statistical formulae) are examples of objective methods for combining predictor scores, whereas subjective human judgment or inference can combine the same data and make selection decisions. Four major methods of collecting and combining information show the range between subjective and objective perspectives:[3] the pure judgmental approach, the trait ratings approach, the profile interpretation approach, and the pure statistical approach (see Figure 9-1).

FIGURE 9-1: Approaches to Collecting and Utilizing Information on Predictors

Method of Collecting Information on Predictors	Method of Combining Predictor Scores	
	Subjective	*Objective*
Subjective	Purely Judgmental	Trait Ratings
Objective	Profile Interpretation	Purely Statistical

Source: Adapted from Bernard M. Bass and Gerald V. Barrett. (1981). *People, Work and Organizations,* 2nd edition. Boston: Allyn & Bacon, p. 392; Jack Sawyer. (1966). "Measurement and Prediction: Clinical and Statistical." *Psychological Bulletin, 66,* pp. 178–200.

Pure judgmental approach:
predictors are selected and used
based exclusively on the judgments of the decision maker or
a group of experts

Pure judgmental approach

When using a **pure judgmental approach**, a deci-
sion maker selects and uses predictors based on his or her own judgments or those of
a group of experts. The decision maker forms an overall judgment of the job applicant based on interview results and his or her intuitive awareness of the organization's
performance expectations and standards.

> For example, a recruiter may select a salesperson simply on the basis of his or her judg-
> ment of the applicant's performance during the interview. He or she does not make formal
> assessments or keep records of the performance of applicants on a set of predictors. Based
> on his or her own experience with good and poor salespersons in the past, the recruiter
> intuitively rates job applicants and makes a selection.

In the pure judgmental approach, decision makers base their decisions on gut feelings
that would be hard to justify in the event of legal or human rights complaints. Despite
this drawback, many small, owner-managed firms continue to use purely judgmental
methods of identifying and combining predictors.

Trait ratings: the recruiter enters
judgmental data (such as interviews and application blanks)
into a mathematical formula to
calculate a total score for each
candidate

Trait ratings approach

When using **trait ratings**, decision makers rate job
applicants based on judgmental data, such as interviews and application blanks,
which they then enter into mathematical formulas to calculate a total score for each
candidate.

> When interviewing salespeople, an organization might decide to use trait ratings. Using a
> ten-point scale, three managers interview all job applicants, and a referee gives an additional
> rating. Assume that the organization decides to give 75% weight to interview scores and
> 25% weight to referee ratings. If an applicant receives three interview ratings of 7, 9, and 8
> (or an average rating of 8), and if the referee has rated the applicant as 10, the total score for
> the applicant will be $(8 \times 0.75) + (10 \times 0.25) = 8.50$.

In the trait rating method, firms select applicants based on their total score. Once the
information is collected and entered into the formula, the decision is almost automatic.

**Profile interpretation
approach:** a recruiter collects
objective data about applicants
but judges and interprets the data
without statistical or mathematical
tools

Profile interpretation approach

When using **profile interpretation approach**,
organizations collect objective data, but combine them judgmentally without using
statistical or mathematical tools. The decision maker reviews all objectively collected
information but makes an overall evaluation of the applicant's suitability for the
position.

> In the salespeople example, assume that each job applicant is asked to take two tests: a
> cognitive ability test and a test which measures Sales Aptitude, both rated on a 100-point
> scale. Further assume that three candidates who take the tests receive the following scores:
>
> > Candidate A: Cognitive Ability= 50, Sales Aptitude= 80
> > Candidate B: Cognitive Ability= 80, Sales Aptitude= 40
> > Candidate C: Cognitive Ability= 70, Sales Aptitude= 70
>
> The decision maker who looks at the above data will choose Candidate A if he believes
> that Sales Aptitude scores are the most critical in predicting future
> performance.

Note that another decision maker looking at the same data might come to a different
conclusion: if that decision maker believed that cognitive ability is more important
than aptitude, he or she would choose Candidate B. Similarly, if a decision maker
believed that both are equally important and that a high score on one dimension does
not compensate for a low score on another, then he or she would choose Candidate C.
Thus, the judgmental nature of the decision causes confusion and potential problems.
Some of these problems are discussed in a later section in this chapter.

Statistical approaches When using a **statistical approach** for making selection decisions, decision makers collect relatively large amounts of information on predictors and combine them mechanically using mathematical formulas to come to a decision.

Statistical approach: decision makers collect large amounts of data and combine them mechanically to come to a decision

> For example, a recruiter would ask all job applicants for the salesperson's position to take the two objective tests (typically using a computer). The firm would have predetermined the relative weights of the two tests. The recruiter would then only receive a printout of the total score of each job applicant. For instance, if the relative weights for Cognitive Ability and Sales Aptitude are 60 and 40 respectively, then the total score for the three candidates would be A=62, B=64 and C=70.

The above basic approaches—pure judgmental, trait rating, profile interpretation, and statistical—have a few variations. For example, both objective and subjective data can be collected and *combined judgmentally*. This approach, called the *judgmental composite approach* by some writers, is popular in many organizations:

> In the salespeople example, the manager would look at the test scores, interview scores, and data gleaned from biographical blanks, and make a judgmental decision about an applicant.

Objective and subjective data can also be combined mechanically using computers or mathematical formulae (called the *mechanical composite* approach). Assessment centres used for managerial development and promotion decisions often use a mechanical composite approach to combine predictor scores

> In the salespeople example, the interview scores, reference ratings, and test scores would have predetermined weights, and the recruiter would combine them all using a formula.

WHICH APPROACH TO USE?

Research has consistently found that statistical and mechanical composite approaches are always either equal or superior to other methods.[4] Why do more objective approaches such as these two methods generate better results? The six factors that make them more reliable and efficient are discussed below.

1. Limits on cognitive capacity
Nobel laureate Herbert A. Simon[5] pointed out that even the best decision makers have obvious constraints on their computational capabilities. Simon's **bounded rationality model** suggests that the finite cognitive capacity of decision makers, the severe environmental constraints operating on them (such as lack of adequate time and the presence of organizational policies), and the high uncertainty associated with future events make it impossible to order preferences perfectly. No decision maker is aware of all alternatives open to him or her or all the consequences of each alternative. Thus, the behaviour of decision makers is inherently limited.

Bounded rationality model: theory that perfect decisions are impossible because of the finite cognitive capacity of decision makers, the severe environmental constraints operating on them, and the high uncertainty associated with future events

> A manager is trying to select one out of 200 applications for a job with seven key dimensions. Since she is using four predictors, each containing seven major items, she has to critically assess, synthesize, and process 5600 combination pieces of information—something that is beyond the capabilities of most managers, especially when operating under severe time constraints.

2. Insensitivity to sample size
Because people tend to ignore the importance of sample size in determining accuracy, they jump to conclusions based on small samples.

> Many decision makers form stereotypes about applicants. They base their stereotypes on prior experiences with a small number of other candidates.

3. Assigning weights
To accurately predict employee suitability, decision makers have to depend on the accuracy of the weights assigned to predictor scores. But assigning weights in a precise manner is difficult,[6] especially for large numbers of predictors and large numbers of applicants.

Illusory correlation: the tendency to overestimate the probability of two events occurring together if these events have occurred together in the past

4. Illusory correlation
Because of **illusory correlation**, people tend to overestimate the probability that two events will occur together if they have found that these events occurred together in the past.

> Thus, a manager might form an erroneous theory about job behaviours based on his own experience. Many employers believe that "those who eat quickly are energetic workers" or those who walk sprightly are more energetic and determined.[7]

Decision makers form these implicit managerial theories based on their past experience, not on sound job analysis or real job duties. Even if the manager's past experience were true at that time, this is no assurance that the same ideas are still relevant.

5. Personal biases
Interviewer biases were listed in Chapter 7. But there are additional decision biases. For example, people often believe that events they can easily recall from memory occur (or occurred) more frequently than events they recall less easily. In all types of biases, gut feelings receive more weight than established criteria, attributes, and procedures.

As Simon pointed out, optimal decisions are almost never made except by chance. Decision makers typically reduce the complexity and ambiguity they face by constructing a simplified model of reality. In their models, they take into account only a limited number of factors and consider and evaluate only a limited range of consequences. They typically choose the first course of action whose outcome is satisfactory, and they stop searching for alternatives as soon as they find a workable model. This behaviour is known as *satisficing* ("satisfy" plus "suffice"), rather than maximizing or optimizing. But satisficing generates decisions that can be mutually inconsistent, especially when the decisions are complex and ambiguous.

> In a selection process, bias and satisficing may translate into settling for the first satisfactory applicant. Efforts to find out more about other promising candidates may be rejected as a waste of time.

6. Continuous revision of the model
Whenever additional data on applicants becomes available, decision makers can use statistical programs to automatically update the decision models. These efforts allow the organization to improve its decision-making model and adapt it to changing environmental conditions.[8]

But many managers rely on models developed early in their careers and never change them, resulting in increasing (rather than decreasing) numbers of hiring errors throughout their careers. Although research evidence supports the superiority of mechanical and statistical approaches, many managers are averse to using them, primarily because they know little about them. Often managers feel threatened if asked to use statistical decision rules rather than their own simple judgment. This means that the human resource specialist has the added challenge of "selling" these tools to managers.

ASSIGNING WEIGHTS TO PREDICTORS

Consider how one brokerage firm used predictors when selecting customer service personnel:

> A brokerage firm requires all applicants to take an aptitude test, which is available on its website. Only those who receive above the cut-off score proceed to the next stage, namely,

completing an application form, which is then screened by the computer using specific criteria. Candidates who pass this screening go through a battery of three tests, which are scored mechanically. The top 20% of the candidates are invited for a panel interview. Interviewer scores are summated, and the top ten candidates for each job position are called for a second interview. For those who are successful, referees' comments (usually, at least two) are gathered and combined. The candidate with the top combined score is usually considered for the position.

You can combine predictor scores in several ways. The above example shows a sequential approach: an applicant has to meet certain minimum standards on each predictor before he or she moves to the next predictor. However, this is only one of the available choices. Five popular approaches are briefly discussed below.

1. Multiple regression

In **multiple regression**, predictor scores are regressed against the criterion scores to develop a regression equation that predicts the criterion. Regression weights indicate the relative importance of each predictor in determining the final score. The predicted criterion scores of applicants becomes a guideline for the selection decision.[9] Consider the following example:

> Saskatoon Office Supplies (SOS) identified three predictors for their sales staff, namely, a general cognitive ability test ($x1$), a sales aptitude test ($x2$,) and scores in an interview ($x3$). Each predictor has a maximum score of 100. Based on validation studies, SOS developed a regression equation that shows differential weights for each predictor when predicting job performance (y) as follows:
>
> $$y \text{ (predicted)} = 10 + 2x1 + 3x2 + 1x3.$$
>
> (where the intercept value of the regression line is 10, and $x1$, $x2$ and $x3$ are scores in the cognitive ability test, sales aptitude test, and interview respectively)

Four job applicants, Ann, Barry, Chan and Darlene, received the scores shown in Figure 9-2. Using the regression equation, SOS managers could easily calculate the predicted scores for the four applicants: Ann = 420, Barry = 415, Chan = 440 and Darlene = 415. Based on total scores, Chan would be ranked the highest, followed by Ann, and then Barry and Darlene.

This example highlights two important caveats of regression equations. First, even candidates having different scores on the various predictors can come out with identical predicted job performance (like Barry and Darlene). Second, a high score on one predictor may compensate a low score on another. For example, compared to Barry, Ann had lower scores on the cognitive ability test, yet ended up with a higher total score.

Multiple regression: predictor scores are regressed against the criterion scores to develop a regression equation that predicts the criterion. The regression weights indicate the relative importance of each predictor in determining the final score

FIGURE 9-2: Scores Received by Four Job Applicants in Saskatoon Office Supplies

Applicant	Cognitive Ability Test	Sales Aptitude Test	Interview Score	Predicted Job Performance
Ann	70	70	60	420
Barry	80	65	50	415
Chan	50	80	90	440
Darlene	70	55	100	415
Regression Weights	2	3	1	—

Thus, predictors are assumed to be additive and to compensate for one another (that is, performing well on one predictor compensates for a relatively poorer performance on the other).[10] Hence, multiple regression is best used when a trade-off among predictor scores does not affect overall job performance.

The above example uses linear multiple regression: that is, the predictors are assumed to be linearly related to the criterion; in other words, for every unit increase or decrease in the value of the predictor, there is the same incremental increase or decrease in the value of the criterion score. But nonlinear relationships are possible. In Figure 9-3, Graph A shows that for every increase in the value of the predictor, the predicted value of the criterion increases linearly. In Graph B, the rate of increase is not constant across the various values of the predictor. In Graph C, a low and high value of the predictor is associated with a low value of the criterion; but a medium value is associated with a high criterion score. Yet multiple regression is a flexible approach that can be modified to handle such nonlinear relationships.

Regression equations can also be designed for related jobs using the same predictors but with different weights and different predictors. However, proper use of these equations requires some knowledge of statistical methods and assumptions—something that may be beyond the capabilities of many decision makers.

2. Multiple cut-offs

In the **multiple cut-off approach,** cut-off scores are set for each predictor so that each applicant is evaluated on a pass-fail basis. Applicants are rejected if any one of their predictor scores falls below a set minimum score.

Multiple cut-off approach: sets cut-off scores for every predictor and rejects all applicants who score below the cut-off on any predictor

> Assume that Saskatoon Office Supplies had set a cut-off score of 60 for the two tests and 50 for interview score. In this case, only Ann and Barry will qualify. The applicant pool would have been reduced by 50%, since two out of the four candidates would have been rejected by the cut-off decision.

The multiple cut-off approach has a few advantages. First, it narrows the applicant pool to a much smaller size. In addition, managers find this approach easy to understand.[11] Hence, the acceptance of this approach is high. However, this method assumes a nonlinear relationship between the predictors that may not be supported by the data. A deficiency in one predictor cannot be compensated by superior performance on another. In the absence of strong evidence supporting such an assumption, the organization may reject a number of applicants who are actually qualified to do the job. This can, in turn, result in poor public relations and possible legal challenges.

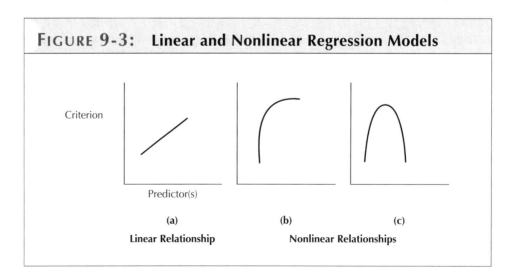

FIGURE 9-3:   Linear and Nonlinear Regression Models

Criterion

Predictor(s)

(a)
Linear Relationship

(b)   (c)
Nonlinear Relationships

In our example, Chan would be rejected, even though under the multiple regression model, he had the highest total score for potential performance. Similarly, Darlene would be rejected, although she scored 100% in the interview.

A multiple cut-off approach is most defensible when minimum abilities are essential for job performance.

For example, eyesight, colour vision, strength, and speed of movement are required for several jobs in police forces, fire departments, and armed forces. Minimum requirements for these ability requirements may be justified in such situations.[12]

3. Multiple hurdle approach

In the **multiple hurdle approach**, applicants must submit to and pass several predictors sequentially and are not permitted to proceed until they have satisfactory scores at each level.

> If Saskatoon Office Supplies were employing a multiple hurdle model, it would first administer a general ability test to all its applicants. Only those who were successful would proceed to the sales aptitude test. The, only those successful at the aptitude test would be interviewed. As a result, Chan might never be tested for sales aptitude, just as Darlene might never be called for the interview.

The multiple hurdle approach, like the multiple cut-off approach, assumes that a minimum level of performance on each predictor is necessary. Thus, a high level of performance on one predictor cannot compensate for a deficiency in another one. The essential difference here is that predictor information is collected sequentially. In this way, the organization can save time and money by eliminating some applicants before they perform all the tests and interviews. However, this can also result in underestimation of the validity of subsequent predictors, since only those who qualify in earlier predictors form the sample for the remaining predictors. Another disadvantage is the amount of time involved in passing applicants through sequential predictors.

> For some job positions, such as highly skilled trades people and computer software programmers, where there is a huge demand for qualified applicants, sequential administration of predictors can result in loss of potential candidates. An organization might lose good applicants even before they reach the final stages of hiring.

The multiple hurdle approach is particularly relevant to organizations which put newly hired employees through long and expensive training programs.[13] It is also helpful when an organization uses expensive predictors (e.g., an expensive assessment centre evaluation, or inviting job applicants from abroad). But by placing expensive predictors toward the end of the selection process, the firm can screen out less desirable candidates first and save considerable resources.

4. Combination approach

The **combination approach** uses a combination of the multiple cut-off and regression approaches to select job candidates. Here, all job applicants are assessed on all predictors. An applicant with any predictor score below the set minimum is rejected, as in the multiple cut-off method. But the decision maker then uses the multiple regression approach to calculate the total predicted scores of remaining applicants. Applicants are rank ordered on the basis of their predicted criterion scores.

> In Saskatoon Office Supplies, if a minimum score of 55 on each predictor is needed, then only Ann and Darlene would proceed to the final list. But since Ann's total score is higher than Darlene's, Ann would be selected for the position.

The combination method takes advantage of the strengths of both methods. It assumes that a minimal level of performance on each predictor is vital for job performance;

Multiple hurdle approach: applicants must pass each predictor in sequence

Combination approach: combines the multiple cut-off and regression approaches to select job candidates

but beyond this level, the predictors are compensatory—that is, a relatively low score on one can be made up by superior performance on the other. One disadvantage of this method is expense: the combination approach is more costly to administer than the multiple hurdle approach, since it does not significantly reduce the applicant pool.

5. Profile matching

Profile matching: predictor scores of current, successful employees are used to generate an ideal profile, to which all applicant scores are compared

In **profile matching**, an organization assesses current, successful employees with several predictors. It averages their scores on each predictor to generate an overall profile of scores necessary for successful job performance. A recruiter then measures job applicants on these predictors and compares their score profiles to the ideal profile. Job applicants whose profiles are most similar to the ideal profile are selected.

Statistical procedures are used to define profile similarity. Two popular approaches[14] are outlined here.

Distance approach

Distance approach: computes the differences between the applicant's score and the ideal profile on each predictor and then squares and sums these differences

When using the **distance approach** to profile matching, an organization computes the differences between the applicant's score and the ideal profile on each predictor and then squares and sums these differences (see Figure 9-4). The larger the difference, the weaker the match.

> For example, assume that Saskatoon Office Supplies had found that superior employees scored an average of 80 in the cognitive ability test, 75 on the sales aptitude test, and 80 on the job interview. These are the "ideal" scores. The recruiter computes the differences between each applicant's score and these ideal scores, then squares and sums that difference. The candidate with the lowest score (in this case, Ann) will be selected (see Figure 9-3).

The problem with the distance approach is that it does not discriminate between positive and negative deviations.

> Thus, Darlene, who scored 100 in the interview, would have the same difference score on this predictor as Ann, who scored 60.

Correlation approach

Correlation approach: calculating the correlation between applicant predictor scores and the ideal predictor scores

A second approach, namely, the **correlation approach** to profile matching, involves calculating the correlation between applicant predictor scores and ideal scores. The higher the correlation, the better the match.

> Among the four applicants, Darlene's scores reflect the highest correlation with the ideal score; hence, she would be selected.

FIGURE 9-4: Use of Distance Approach in Profile Matching

Applicant	Cognitive Ability Test	Sales Aptitude Test	Interview Score	Total Distance Score
"Ideal Employee" score	80	75	80	—
Ann	70	70	60	$(70–80)^2 + (70–75)^2 + (60–80)^2 = 525$
Barry	80	65	50	$(80–80)^2 + (65–75)^2 + (50–80)^2 = 1000$
Chan	50	80	90	$(50–80)^2 + (80–75)^2 + (90–80)^2 = 1025$
Darlene	70	55	100	$(70–80)^2 + (55–75)^2 + (100–80)^2 = 900$

Many writers and practitioners recommend profile matching as a way to avoid establishing arbitrary cut-off scores.[15] Some[16] have recommended using the distance approach because it considers profile level, dispersion, and shape, whereas the correlation approach considers only profile shape. Whatever the approach, profile matching assumes that the composite profile of the successful employee is significantly different from that of the unsuccessful employee. It is an appropriate method when there is clearly a best type of employee for the job.

But there are some subtle disadvantages. For example, non-ideal employees could score higher as well as lower than the ideal employee, which would affect the scoring of applicants; but this assumption may not be valid in all settings. Furthermore, "ideal employees" have only average scores on some attributes, whereas higher scores on those attributes might in fact have made those ideal employees even better.

Restriction of range is also a problem, since truly poor performers are often hard to find (they may have been fired or not hired initially). Only continuous empirical validation of the predictors can support the use of profiles, since with changes in technology and job demands, the "ideal profile" may not remain consistent. For this reason, in many situations, a multiple regression model may be a better alternative to profile matching.

ESTABLISHING CUT-OFF SCORES

Whatever the approach for combining predictors, an organization still has to identify cut-off scores for each predictor. This task has to be done carefully, since too-high and too-low cut-off scores result in undesirable consequences.

Figure 9-5 is a schematic of the decision-making process. The horizontal line in the diagram represents a dividing line. Those above the line are high performers on the criterion measure and considered "successful" recruits by the employer. Those below the line are considered unsuccessful or poor performers. The vertical line represents the

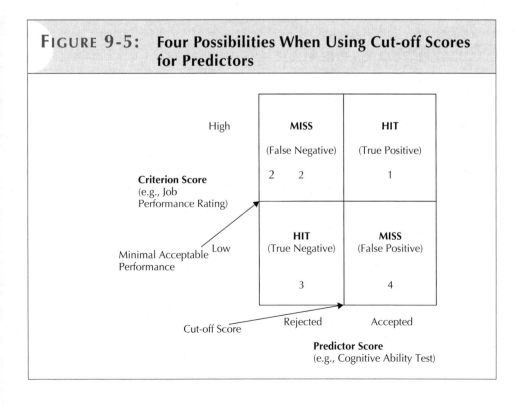

FIGURE 9-5: Four Possibilities When Using Cut-off Scores for Predictors

cutting point on the predictor. Applicants who scored at or above the cut-off score are hired; those who score below the line would be rejected. Using both horizontal and vertical lines, we can identify four quadrants. All applicants fall into one of these quadrants.

True positive: applicants for whom success is predicted (based on high predictor scores) and who would be successful on the job

False negative: applicants for whom success was not predicted (based on low predictor scores), but who would have been successful if hired

True negative: applicants for whom success was not predicted (based on low predictor scores) and who would not be successful on the job

False positive: applications for whom success was predicted (based on high predictor scores), but who would not have been successful if hired

- *Quadrant 1* (True positive) represents those applicants who scored well on the predictor (e.g., test), for whom success is predicted, and who were indeed successful on the job.

- *Quadrant 2* (False negative) represents those applicants who did not score well, for whom success was not predicted (based on their predictor scores), but who would be successful on the job if hired.

- *Quadrant 3* (True negative) represents those applicants who did not score well, for whom success was not predicted (based on their predictor scores), and who would not do well if hired.

- *Quadrant 4* (False positive) represents those who scored well, for whom success was predicted, but who would not succeed on the job if hired.

Since the objective is to hire people who will do well on the job and to reject those who will not, candidates who fall into quadrants 1 and 2 are the right choices. However, false negatives and false positives in applicant predictors cause concern. If the predictor is not valid or if the cut-off scores are incorrect, large numbers of applicants could fall into these categories.

False negative results are particularly worrisome when a predictor unfairly rejects large numbers of qualified applicants, especially from minority groups. Once an organization determines the cut-off score, people who score below that line may never move through the remaining selection steps (especially when a multiple hurdle model is used), thus resulting in unintended and systemic discrimination. False negative errors are also very costly in terms of personnel and competitive edge, since a competitor may hire highly qualified applicants rejected by the firm. The situation is made all the more complex by the fact that the employer may not even be aware of the lost opportunities.

Single Predictor Case

When the selection is based on a single predictor, establishing a cut-off score is relatively easy. Thorndike[17] suggested the following approach, which many practitioners and researchers have been found to be satisfactory:

1. Estimate the number of positions to be filled in a specified future period. In general, use a two- to three-year period, since a lot can change beyond that period. In the case of rapidly changing jobs, a shorter time horizon may be more appropriate.

2. Estimate the number of applications expected during that time period.

3. Estimate the expected distribution of applicant scores on the single predictor chosen.

4. Determine the cut-off score based on the percentage of applicants needed to fill the vacancies and the *standard error of measurement*, which estimates the magnitude of the error in a test score (see Appendix 4A).

   For example, if a firm expects to have 20 job openings and 200 applications over the next two years, then the selection ratio is 0.10 (i.e., 20/200) or 10%. Because 90% of the applicants will be rejected, the cut-off score is usually set at the 90th percentile of the local norms (that is, norms based on the organization's past experience), minus one standard error of measurement.

MULTIPLE PREDICTOR CASE

When an organization uses more than one predictor, it must establish cut-off scores for each one. One popular method for setting these cut-off scores, the Angoff Method,[18] follows three steps:

1. Using expert advice, rate all test items for their difficulty. In estimating the level of difficulty, consider the proportion of *minimally acceptable applicants* who would answer each question correctly. The focus is not on outstanding or even average job applicants, but rather on the minimally acceptable applicants. (The second column in Figure 9-6 shows the proportion of minimally acceptable applicants who would answer the particular test item correctly.)

2. Add these proportions together to identify the raw (or unmodified) cut-off score.

3. Use the standard error of the test to adjust the reliability of the measure. Deduct one standard error of measurement from the above figure to identify the adjusted cut-off score.

FAIRNESS IN SELECTION

As emphasized throughout this book, no selection tool is perfectly valid. Typical validities for various predictors range from 0.3 to 0.6. The risk of false negatives and false

FIGURE 9-6: The Angoff Method for Identifying Cut-off Scores

Test Item Number	Proportion of Applicants Answering the Item Correctly
1	.80
2	.50
3	.90
4	.45
5	.55
6	.80
7	.70
8	.90
9	.30
10	.60
11	.65
12	.55
13	.85
14	.75
15	.80
16	.70
17	.90
18	.40
19	.50
20	.70
	Sum = 13.30

Raw Cut-off Score	= 13.30
Adjusted cut-off score with a standard error measurement of 2.2	= Raw cut-off score *minus* standard error measurement = 13.30–2.2 **= 11.10**

positives persists all the time. Moreover, if a test is differentially valid for several employee groups, the risk of under- and over-prediction is magnified.

Figure 9-7 illustrates this phenomenon. The diagram shows the test scores and job performance ratings of two groups of employees (A and B). Their average performance ratings are equal, but their test scores differ. Based on the shape of the scatter diagram, Group A will have higher test validity than B. Group A shape is oval, whereas the Group B shape is closer to a circle, which indicates that Group B persons with low or high scores on the test will display similar job performance. These two groups will have different regression lines, and, if the test is used for prediction purposes, Group A would almost always be under-predicted. If any one particular cut-off score was employed, many Group A employees would be rejected, since their average test score is below that of Group B employees. Thus, selection test bias against Group A employees is a certain possibility. However, many Group B employees who got higher scores will in fact be *poorer* performers than members of Group A.

In general, compute cut-off scores with great care. Not only should they not unfairly discriminate against any particular group, but they should also be perceived as "fair" by all concerned (see Chapter 3). To ensure perceived fairness, an organization must continually assess the impact of selection procedures on certain groups and take timely corrective actions. The ethical and administrative standards employed must be of the highest order. Only trained professionals should interpret the selection outcomes, especially the test results, and set cut-off scores, and only after careful analysis of the results. Here are some approaches to enhance perceived fairness.

Top-down selection approach: an organization rank-orders applicant scores from highest to lowest and offers jobs moving from the top down, until all job positions are filled

Apply banding In a **top-down selection approach**, an organization rank-orders applicant scores from highest to lowest and offers jobs moving from the top down, until all job positions are filled. If an applicant turns down the job offer, the person with the next-highest score is offered the job.[19] Ranking applicants by their predictor (or total) scores assumes that there is a linear relationship between predictor and criterion scores, so that a person with a high score will perform better on the job than another who has a lower score. As long as this assumption is valid, top-down selection may be ideal for maximizing future job performance.

But one problem with the top-down approach is that it can adversely impact minority groups, especially when mental ability tests are used. Traditionally, mainstream populations tend to score higher on these tests than immigrant or non-mainstream

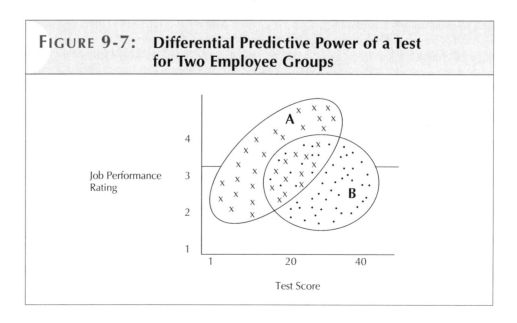

FIGURE 9-7:   **Differential Predictive Power of a Test for Two Employee Groups**

populations because of subtle cultural biases in the tests (such as linguistic and idiomatic usages). Thus, the top-down approach can result in disproportionately greater hiring of members of the dominant culture group. To overcome this problem, **race norming**, or ranking applicants on the predictor scores within their relevant race group, has been suggested. In race norming, Caucasians would be ranked relative to other Caucasians, Asians relative to other Asians, and so on. The top-ranking Caucasian and other race candidates would then be selected, followed by second-ranking Caucasian and other race candidates, and so on, until all job positions were filled. While race norming is illegal in the United States,[20] it is not banned in Canada, although public reaction to this approach has not been very positive.

> In a bid to attract more women into its workforce, a Canadian fire department attempted to establish differential cut-off scores for male and female applicants. But the public outcry was so strong against the approach that it finally abandoned the initiative.

A better solution may be **banding**, or classifying job applicants into different groups (or bands) based on equivalent ranges of scores, after taking measurement errors into consideration. Since predictors are rarely perfectly reliable (see Chapter 4), organizations must use standard error of measurement to adjust for errors in measurement. From this, they establish a range of scores they consider equal. Bands around a given score are calculated as plus or minus 1.96 times the standard error of measurement. The value of 1.96 refers to the Z value for 95% confidence level. (For details on Z or standard normal distribution, see Appendix 4A.)

BAND WIDTH = Upper bound: OBSERVED SCORE + [1.96 × SEM]

Lower bound: OBSERVED SCORE − [1.96 × SEM]

(where SEM is the standard error of measurement)

For example, if the highest observed score on an instrument is 82, and the standard error of measurement of the same instrument is 2.98, it can be statistically established that the scores ranging from 76.15 to 82 are not significantly different and the differences could have been caused simply by the poor reliability of the measuring instrument. This is also true of the upper scores. The difference between scores of 82 and 87.84 are also not statistically significant, although this is not relevant for our case, since no one received a higher score than 82.

There are different approaches to establishing and using bands. **Fixed bands** begin with the top score and consider all applicants who belong to that band before moving on to the next-highest band. Fixed bands use the top score attained as the starting point. The top score minus the bandwidth (in our above example, 2.98 × 1.96 or 5.84) shows the lower boundary for that band. Figure 9-8 shows the scores received by members of majority and minority community members. Assume that the top score in the test was 82. Then the first bandwidth extends from 82 minus 5.84, or up to 76 (after rounding off). Note that there is no need to go above 82, since that was the top score in the test. The next band boundary will be 76 minus 5.84, or 70; the third band would be 69 to 63; and so on. The scores of 18 persons who fall into these three bands are shown in the figure.

Now, assume that the organization is hiring only one candidate at this time. The firm would be justified in hiring the minority applicant who received the score of 80, although this was not the top score. When we account for the measurement error, the differences between 82, 81, and 80 are not statistically significant. If, however, the firm were to hire two candidates, the second candidate would have to come from the two other applicants in the same band. If it were hiring four candidates, it would take the first three candidates in the first band and one of the minority candidates from the second band. In this way, the organization can meet its employment equity objectives without changing cut-off scores.

A sliding band approach extends this notion even further. In a **sliding band**, not every applicant in one band needs to be selected before considering applicants in the

Race norming: ranking applicants based on predictor scores within their relevant race group

Banding: classifying job applicants into different bands based on equivalent ranges of scores, after taking measurement errors into consideration

Fixed bands: the recruiter begins with the top band and considers all applicants in that band before moving on to the next band

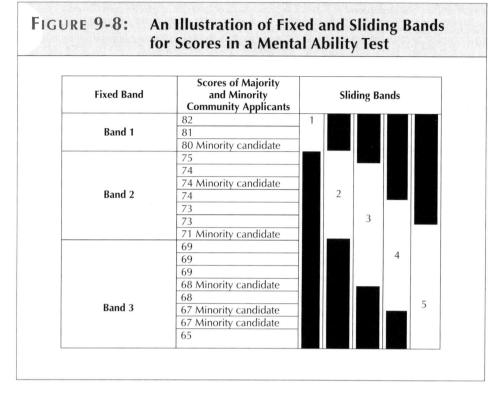

FIGURE 9-8:   An Illustration of Fixed and Sliding Bands for Scores in a Mental Ability Test

Fixed Band	Scores of Majority and Minority Community Applicants	Sliding Bands
Band 1	82	
	81	
	80 Minority candidate	
Band 2	75	
	74	
	74 Minority candidate	
	74	
	73	
	73	
	71 Minority candidate	
Band 3	69	
	69	
	69	
	68 Minority candidate	
	68	
	67 Minority candidate	
	67 Minority candidate	
	65	

Sliding band: based on fixed bands, but for which not every applicant in one band needs to be selected before considering applicants in the next band

immediately adjacent band. In our example, if there is only one job position, the minority candidate (with a score of 80) would be hired to meet employment equity objectives.[21] If there is a second position, the top scorer in that band, namely, the majority community candidate who received the score of 82, would also be selected. If the organization were to hire three, it would move on to the next band, where it would select the minority candidates receiving the scores of 74 and 71. But if enough people are hired that the highest-scoring majority candidate in this band is selected (namely, the one with the score 75), then the organization would move to the next band, with the upper bandwidth of 74 and the lower bandwidth of 68 (that is, 74 minus 5.84, rounded off to the next whole number) and so on. Figure 9-8 also shows what sliding bands look like.

The sliding band approach has several advantages. First, it provides a larger pool of applicants to choose from than a fixed band and can result in a larger number of successful minority applicants. It can also reduce the adverse impact of selection procedures on specific groups. Of course, the number of minority applicants chosen depends on a variety of factors, such as the distribution of scores of minority members and the proportion of the total applicant pool who belong to minority groups. While banding is legal in Canada, organizations need to explain the principle underlying the approach to gain acceptance from employees and unions. There is also some evidence that banding, which deviates from top-down hiring, may result in the decrease in the overall performance of the group hired.

Use predictors supported by validity generalization studies
As detailed in Chapter 4, validity generalization studies help an organization apply validity information accumulated about one set of jobs to other similar jobs. If the job is one for which widely accepted validity generalization data are available, then these data can provide both validity and a perception of fairness. But generalized data assume that there are no organizational effects on validity: the same predictor is relevant across organizations for similar jobs.[22] Generalized data also help justify the use of some tests (e.g., mental ability tests), especially if the jobs are complex.[23]

Focus on Ethics

You work as the Assistant Human Resource Manager in a large manufacturing firm that has historically had low representation from a particular minority community. While 15% of the local labour market is this minority group, your organization has historically employed less than 1%. Last year, your firm decided to hire more people from this group. To match the labour market participation rate, you would need to hire 20 persons from this group in the near future. For this year, management had established a quota of hiring three persons from this group. It has already achieved this target. Of the four persons hired so far this year, three were from this group.

Your firm uses three predictors for hiring: biographical blanks, a cognitive ability test, and a panel interview. Only persons who successfully complete one step move onto the next stage of selection. The cut-off score for the cognitive test is 70, and the test has a standard error of 3. This means that scores between 67 and 73 are statistically equivalent.

Your present decision problem concerns minority-group Applicant M, who received a score of 69 in the cognitive ability test. There were three others ahead of him—all from the majority community and all with higher test scores (72, 71, and 71 respectively).

Here is the dilemma: Based on the test score, you are supposed to recommend only three names to the panel for interviews. But you feel that you should recommend Applicant M as one of the three, dropping the majority candidate who received 71 from the list, to further the organization's goals to achieve employment equity. On the other hand, you feel that the majority community members deserve a "break," since you have already hired your quota of minority candidates for this year.

You have to make the decision today.

Use systematic approaches To increase perceptions of fairness, managers and others involved in selection decisions should participate in all stages of data collection and analysis. All concerned should collaborate to assess the nature of job performance, the predictors, and the assessment of psychometric properties. But decision makers trained in the specific procedures (e.g., interviewing) should have the role of combining the scores and making the final decisions, rather than line managers who might base decisions on intuition or gut feelings.[24]

Research studies and organizational experience indicate that systematic decision-making procedures, such as the ones listed in this chapter, enhance the quality of the final selection decisions. While developing complex, formal systems may be difficult for small organizations, they can still use ideas from this chapter. Haphazard combinations of predictors and gut feelings reduce the effectiveness of the selection and adversely affect the perceived fairness of the system.

Keep procedures transparent Increasing the transparency of the selection procedures enhances perceived fairness. Policies guiding the use of predictors should be written.[25] Moreover, accurate records of each phase of selection should be available for examination, and rejected candidates should be handled courteously. A written policy statement designating who makes final decisions will prevent controversies and confusion.[26]

Audit selection procedures periodically Like any other organizational system, selection procedures also are subject to attrition. New types of jobs and new technology make existing predictors or cut-off scores obsolete. Only a periodical audit can keep the selection system current. The steps in auditing selection systems are detailed in Chapter 11.

OFFER OF EMPLOYMENT AND FOLLOW-UP

Realistic job preview(RJP): allowing candidates to see the type of work, equipment, and working conditions of the job in the real work setting before offering a job

Increasingly, many organizations are including a realistic job preview as part of the selection process to expose the new hires to the actual job setting. A **realistic job preview (RJP)** allows the potential employee to understand the job setting before deciding to accept the job. It often includes seeing the type of work, the equipment, and the working conditions.

Realistic job previews serve many purposes. First, if candidates have unmet expectations about a job, often they can become dissatisfied after being hired. The realistic job preview helps prevent job dissatisfaction by giving the newcomer insight into the job.

Recently hired employees who have had a realistic job preview are less likely to be shocked by the job or the job setting on the first day they report to work.[27] As two past writers noted:

> The RJP functions very much like a medical vaccination. ... The typical medical vaccination injects one with a small, weakened dose of germs, so that one's body can develop a natural resistance to that disease. The RJP functions similarly by presenting job candidates with a small dose of "organizational reality." And, like the medical vaccination, the RJP is probably much less effective after a person has already entered a new organization.[28]

Research has shown that in nine out of ten cases, employee turnover is higher when job previews are not used.[29]

> In one mental health care facility, the human resource department used to "warn" potential employees about the unpleasant aspects of a job. When dealing with some patients, employees might be subjected to verbal or physical abuse. Employees were also told that the work was often repetitive and closely supervised. Realistic job previews (RJP) were found to decrease turnover rates at this institution; but it had no effect on job performance.

The disadvantage of RJP is that more candidates may refuse to accept job offers when the working conditions do not appear appealing. However, in the long term, this may be less costly than high turnover.

Once an organization has identified successful applicants and allowed them to assess the working conditions, it should present them with offers of employment. But before sending appointment letters, it should ensure that the terms of employment are within labour guidelines defined by federal and provincial labour legislation. In addition, all required departments and officials should review the terms of the offer. In many organizations, managers in compensation, finance, and human resource departments along with the immediate boss, all expect to see the conditions of employment before the actual hiring. Senior appointments may require approvals from higher levels, sometimes at the Board level.

For applicants who were rejected, the recruiter should send a courteous message promptly. The message should reflect respect for the candidate and appreciation for their efforts. The letter should also state whether the organization plans to keep their applications on file for future job openings.

Most organizations initially extend a verbal offer to the applicant with a broad overview of the terms of the employment. Sometimes, an organization has to negotiate terms with the applicant; and if unsuccessful, it has to make an offer to an alternate applicant. In these situations, "selling" the organization during the interview is important.

Formal offer package: written offer of employment that contains all conditions of employment

If the terms are acceptable to the candidate, the organization sends a **formal offer package** containing all conditions of employment. Some of the common provisions in employment offers are shown in Figure 9-9. Almost invariably, the offer is accompanied by a job acceptance form (unless the applicant is asked to sign a duplicate copy of the

---

FIGURE 9-9:   Common Provisions in Employment Offers

- Name of the applicant and address
- Job title
- Instructions on how to respond to the offer
- Full time or part time; hours if part-time
- Benefits offered as part of the employment
- Conditions of union membership (if close-shop provisions exist)
- Conditions governing the appointment (e.g., medical exam, drug test, or security check)
- Probationary period
- Other terms of employment, especially relating to the performance review process, travel or shift requirements, termination, etc.
- Company privacy policy
- Confidentiality and non-disclosure clauses

---

offer and return), as well as documents covering company benefits policy, performance review process, and other forms needed for reporting results of tests. For specific types of jobs, the successful applicant may also need to take additional medical, physical fitness, or drug tests. As already detailed in Chapters 3 and 7, these additional tests have to be bona fide job requirements. Should the applicant fail a required test, the organization should notify him or her immediately, and then make an offer to the second candidate on the list.

Formal employment contracts offer protection to both employers and employees. Despite this protection, many employers do not use them.[30] One reason is the "honeymoon mentality" that exists when an employee is hired: the last thing the employer wants to think about is the possibility of terminating the employee. As a result, they do not make up an employment contract, which legally protects the organization in case the new employee does not work out. Moreover, many employees, especially those in low-level jobs, do not want a contract, since they find that they are better protected by common law than by restrictions contained in a contract.[31]

But employers are beginning to recognize the importance of employment contracts covering all major contingencies. Employment contracts have to be carefully planned and worded. The following are special considerations for an employment contract:[32]

- *Explicitly state what the probationary period is*: Many employers believe that all new employees are automatically subject to a probationary period. This is not the case. Three months is a common probationary period in many provincial employment standards legislation, during which time the employee is not entitled to termination pay. However, an organization can make this period longer or shorter. The employment contract should explicitly state the length of the probationary period.

- *Explicitly state the beginning date of employment*: In today's work setting, many employees move from job to job frequently (sometimes returning to the same employer). Thus, the organization needs to explicitly state the beginning date of employment, so that it does not have to compensate the employee for time served elsewhere.

- *Get the employment contract signed before the employee begins work*: In law, a contract is enforceable only if the employee receives a *consideration*, or something in exchange for agreeing to be bound by the terms of the contract. In the employment context, the employer offers the consideration of a job offer in return for the employee's promise to perform the job duties as detailed in employment contract. However, if the employee has already begun work before signing the contract, there is no consideration passed on to the employee. Depending on the circumstances, such a contract may become unenforceable, especially if no fresh consideration was offered to the employee.

- *State the procedures for termination of employment*: Details relating to termination, dismissal procedures, and notice should be included in the contract. The dismissal provisions should meet minimal employment standards in the province and explicitly state the compensation the employee would be entitled to. For example, would the employee receive bonus or incentive pay for the period of notice? Would short- or long-term disability policies apply to the employee?

- *Include necessary but not overly restrictive covenants*: Some employment contracts include restrictive covenants, such as technical confidentiality agreements, non-solicitation of clients, suppliers and employees, and non-compete clauses.[33] When including such covenants, ensure that they are not overly restrictive, or they will be struck down by a court. As one legal expert pointed out, "If you have drafted your non-compete clause overly broad in terms of geographic area or time, the court won't rewrite it for you. They'll simply strike it out."[34]

Information on employment contracts:

www.employmentlawtoday. com/loginArea/guestview.asp? articleid=181

www.blakes.com/english/ publications/leb/ employmentcontracts.asp

When the organization has received written acceptance of the offer and contract, and the applicant has successfully completed any required pre-employment tests, the organization sends a welcome letter describing orientation programs, as well as an employee handbook. Key information specific to the terms of the employment (such as starting date and location) are mentioned in the welcoming letter.

On the specific date when the new employee reports for work, the on-boarding process begins. This process is detailed in the next chapter.

Implications for Practice

1. Avoid using gut feelings when combining scores on predictors. Systematic and logic-driven cut-off procedures generate greater accuracy and greater perceptions of fairness.

2. While a number of alternate decision rules and mathematical procedures are available for combining predictors, each approach has limitations. Keep these limitations in mind when selecting a particular method.

3. While a top-down selection approach is likely to generate maximum performance among applicants, employment equity considerations may require banding or other approaches. In such instances, bands should be established carefully and systematically.

4. To improve perceived fairness about selection procedures, follow the suggestions made in this chapter.

5. Audit selection systems periodically to enhance their effectiveness and perceived fairness.

6. Once the selection decision has been made, inform the new hire of the follow-up procedures in a timely and courteous fashion.

7. Always treat the rejected applicants with courtesy and dignity.

8. Always plan and word employment contracts carefully to ensure they meet all legal requirements.

Key Terms for Review

Banding, *p. 305*

Bounded rationality model, *p. 295*

Combination approach, *p. 299*

Correlation approach, *p. 300*

Distance approach, *p. 300*

False negative, *p. 302*

False positive, *p. 302*

Fixed bands, *p. 305*

Formal offer package, *p. 308*

Illusory correlation, *p. 296*

Multiple cut-off approach, *p. 298*

Multiple hurdle approach, *p. 299*

Multiple regression, *p. 297*

Profile interpretation approach, *p. 294*

Profile matching, *p. 300*

Pure judgmental approach, *p. 294*

Discussion Questions

1. If your organization were using two predictors, namely, application blanks and one-on-one interviews, what approach would you use to combine the information from the two predictors? What if your organization is a call centre that hires forty-five employees each month and uses a computerized sales aptitude test and a performance test as two major predictors?

2. What should you consider when establishing cut-off scores?

3. Discuss the steps to take once you have made the selection decision for hiring a new admin assistant for your department.

Critical Thinking Questions

1. You are being interviewed for the position of Assistant to the Human Resource Manager in a medium-sized firm where individual managers do most of the hiring. The role of the human resource department is mainly to place want ads and arrange interviews for the managers. The managers make decisions based on a single interview and a review of the application blank. During the job interview, the human resource manager asks you how you would improve the system and what your specific actions would be. What answer would you give?

2. As part of improving the selection procedure, your organization has recently introduced a new cognitive ability test. How will you determine a suitable cut-off score for the test?

3. When you were accepted to college or university, what kind of "admission package" and what information did you receive? How could this admissions package be improved?

Web Research

Conduct a search of at least five MBA programs in this country, two from large universities and three from medium and small universities. Make a note of their admission criteria and requirements, including stated cut-off scores for standardized admission tests (e.g., GMAT or TOEFL). What similarities and differences do you see among the business schools?

CASE INCIDENT

Selection at Cosmos Limited

Cosmos Limited, a rapidly expanding furniture chain whose major customers are businesses, introduced a new sales aptitude test for hiring its sales staff. In an attempt to validate the test, it classified 100 newly hired employees into two groups five months after hiring: those who were rated "successful" by their supervisors based on their sales volume, and those who were considered "unsuccessful." Based on the distribution of the test scores, the firm also identified a future cut-off score for hiring salespeople. Figure A shows how the hundred employees fell into the quadrants. The figures in parentheses in each quadrant show the number of minority employees in each group.

Questions

1. *What conclusions can you form from the data presented?*

2. *What advice would you give to the firm's management?*

FIGURE A: Scores and Performance Ratings of 100 Employees

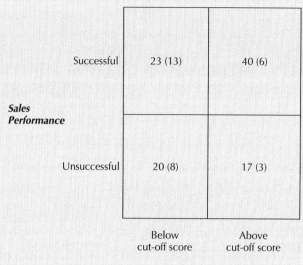

Sales Performance

Successful   23 (13)   40 (6)

Unsuccessful   20 (8)   17 (3)

Below   Above
cut-off score   cut-off score

Sales Aptitude Test

CASE

Kanata Food Distributors: Assessing the New Assessment Centre*

Note: This case continues from Chapter 8: Kanata Food Distributors. Review the case background in Chapters 1, 2, 3, 4, 6, 7, and 8 before examining this case.

Kanata Food Distributors has embarked on a rapid expansion plan which requires a significant number of additional management staff. For the purpose of developing management potential of its employees, the firm began a new Management Development and Assessment Centre in Scarborough, Ontario. Supervisors from several units were requested to recommend employees for training and development. At the new centre, the first batch of 30 employees were put through a battery of tests and training procedures including the following:

General Cognitive Ability Test (COGSC): A general cognitive ability test that is rated on a 0–100 scale. Studies with the scale outside Canada (mostly in Europe and southern United States) have shown the average score on this test to be 68, with a standard deviation of 11.

Interviewing Score (INTVW): A structured interview designed by a local consultant for assessing the

decision-making potential of the employee (scored on a 0–100 scale). Since this is a new assessment tool, validity information is not available. However, prior administration of the tool, especially in automobile companies, had indicated average scores of 71, with a standard deviation of 6.

Leadership Aptitude Inventory (LEAD): An established leadership aptitude inventory that is scored on a 0–100 scale. Prior administration in Canada, especially in the banking and food industry, has shown average scores of 73, with a standard deviation of 7.

In-Basket Exercise Score (INBSKT): An in-basket designed for food industry management which has shown high criterion validity elsewhere. The average scores on this measure in other administrations were 62–67 (depending on management level and industry). The standard deviation has typically been 10.

*Case written by Professor Hari Das of Saint Mary's University, Halifax. All rights retained by the author, © 2005.

The supervisor's rating of each candidate during the past year (SUPR) along with the final assessment centre rating (ACTR) are shown in the table (see Table 1). Both are rated on a ten-point scale, with 10 being "outstanding." Figure 1 also provides some additional demographic information about the trainees. A "1" under STATUS indicates that the employee is from a minority group.

Questions

1. What conclusions can you form from the above information?

2. What is your assessment of the company's efforts at management development?

3. What suggestions would you make to the management?

TABLE 1: Scores Received by 30 Employees at the Assessment Centre along with their Supervisory Ratings.

NAME	COGSC	INTVW	LEAD	INBSKT	SUPR	ACTR	STATUS	AGE
Atkins	80.00	70.00	80.00	70.00	9.00	8.00	2.00	35.00
Appleby	80.00	65.00	80.00	70.00	7.00	8.00	2.00	40.00
Bluming	80.00	70.00	78.00	75.00	10.00	8.00	2.00	30.00
Badekar	70.00	55.00	75.00	60.00	6.00	7.00	1.00	44.00
Chan	60.00	55.00	70.00	55.00	5.00	6.00	1.00	48.00
Chung	50.00	45.00	60.00	48.00	6.00	5.00	1.00	46.00
Christie	78.00	60.00	80.00	70.00	7.00	8.00	2.00	39.00
Dumont	68.00	70.00	70.00	60.00	8.00	7.00	2.00	32.00
Dar	58.00	55.00	60.00	55.00	6.00	6.00	1.00	45.00
David	86.00	70.00	84.00	80.00	10.00	9.00	2.00	33.00
Elliott	68.00	80.00	70.00	60.00	8.00	7.00	2.00	32.00
Eskatoni	65.00	45.00	70.00	55.00	6.00	7.00	1.00	40.00
Fatima	78.00	55.00	75.00	70.00	6.00	8.00	1.00	45.00
Ferguson	68.00	55.00	72.00	67.00	9.00	7.00	1.00	39.00
Gregg	87.00	80.00	88.00	78.00	8.00	9.00	2.00	31.00
Hudson	58.00	70.00	60.00	55.00	6.00	6.00	2.00	50.00
Iver	45.00	65.00	60.00	45.00	6.00	5.00	2.00	50.00
Johns	58.00	70.00	65.00	50.00	7.00	6.00	2.00	45.00
Klemp	75.00	65.00	75.00	76.00	6.00	8.00	2.00	50.00
Kinsy	78.00	80.00	75.00	77.00	9.00	8.00	2.00	37.00
Lyla	68.00	55.00	70.00	66.00	6.00	7.00	1.00	48.00
Limery	68.00	70.00	70.00	65.00	7.00	7.00	2.00	42.00
Living	78.00	55.00	75.00	64.00	7.00	8.00	2.00	38.00
Mathis	68.00	60.00	70.00	65.00	6.00	7.00	2.00	42.00
Munro	65.00	60.00	68.00	68.00	6.00	7.00	2.00	45.00
Marle	68.00	70.00	67.00	66.00	7.00	7.00	2.00	42.00
Nimo	65.00	55.00	66.00	65.00	6.00	7.00	2.00	40.00
Nair	58.00	65.00	60.00	55.00	5.00	6.00	1.00	50.00
Raine	55.00	70.00	60.00	55.00	5.00	6.00	2.00	45.00
Stock	82.00	55.00	80.00	88.00	10.00	9.00	2.00	30.00

CHAPTER

10 DEPLOYMENT, DEVELOPMENT, AND TERMINATION OF HUMAN RESOURCES

"To make the connection between people and profits, organizations are going to have to think a little differently and manage a lot differently than many of their competitors ... When you look at your work force, do you see the source of your organization's sustained success and your people as the only thing that differentiates you from your competition? Or do you, like so many, see people as labour costs to be reduced or eliminated; implicit contracts for careers and job security as constraints to be negated; and mutual trust and respect as luxuries not affordable under current competitive conditions, to be replaced by some optimal compensation and incentive arrangements that attempt to make trust unnecessary? How we look at things affect how they look and what we do."

Jeffery Pfeffer[1]

CHAPTER OBJECTIVES

After studying this chapter, you should be able to:

- Describe the deployment of and on-boarding procedures for new employees
- Discuss the employer's role in employee career development
- Describe the special considerations for staffing international operations
- Discuss the steps for dismissing an employee

Condoleeza Lewis was hired by National Electronics to be part of their client services division. On a Thursday, she arrived at her new employer's office five minutes ahead of the appointed time. However, no one was there to greet her, even after the appointed time had expired. Ten minutes later, her new boss arrived at the site, greeted her, and showed her into her new office. He gave her an Employee Handbook and asked her to read it until he had some free time to meet with her. Over two hours later, he returned with a stack of files and asked her to take care of them. He provided no instructions or guidelines on how to handle files. As he left her, he told her that he had to go to the field office for a day-long meeting. Neither at the break nor at lunchtime was there anyone to show her around or to help her find the cafeteria or other facilities. Finally, she approached a co-worker to seek direction on the files. Unfortunately, the coworker was not familiar with the files and could not be of much help to her.

The next day, rumours were spreading that Condoleeza, an African-Canadian, had been hired for employment equity purposes and "did not know her job." Condoleeza's boss was still away. During the next week, she tried to get more information about her job duties and prospects from the human resource department. She also tried to meet a few other managers on her own, but most were "busy in meetings" most of the time, and the few whom she did meet with could not give her any valuable information. Frustrated, she quit her job on the sixth day.

Soon Condoleeza was hired by the firm's competitor. There she received a day-long orientation to the organization, her coworkers, and her job, and learned about her job duties. Her boss escorted her around the offices of all key executives and introduced them to her. Two weeks later, the human resource manager sat with her to inquire into her experiences and clarify queries. Condoleeza was so pleased with her new job and colleagues that she spent long hours at the office, often putting in unpaid overtime. Indeed, next year, she was nominated as one of the top two customer service representatives.

Condoleeza's experience at National Electronics is not unusual. In an effort to cut costs and time, many employers do not pay adequate attention to employee orientation and other on-boarding procedures. They fail to recognize that the early experiences of a new hire have a lasting influence on work behaviour, productivity, and work attitudes. Frustrated new employees leave the organization, causing significant additional hiring costs and lost time. Even if the employee does not leave the firm, early experiences have a lasting influence on their motivation and perceptions of what the organization values.

This chapter introduces you to the important topic of deployment of human resources. It describes the steps for bringing newly hired employees up to speed and preparing them for future responsibilities. It also looks at the special challenges of hiring for international operations. Finally, it describes how to terminate an employee.

DEPLOYMENT PROCEDURES

Deployment refers to activities aimed at placing newly hired employees in their job positions so that they quickly learn to execute their job responsibilities. Deployment includes orientation to the position and the organization, socialization to familiarize the new employees with the firm and its culture, and allocation of job duties. In effect, deployment begins when selection ends. Figure 10-1 summarizes the key deployment activities discussed in this chapter.

Deployment: activities aimed at placing newly hired employees in their job positions so that they quickly learn to execute their job responsibilities

BEFORE ARRIVAL

Written information sent to the new hire serves three purposes: (1) to clarify the terms of the appointment, (2) to persuade the hire to accept the offer, and (3) to facilitate speedy arrival at the worksite by ensuring all necessary clearance. Simultaneously, management must let the current employees know about the new hires. Three distinct but interrelated activities take place at this stage: documentation, identification, and communication.

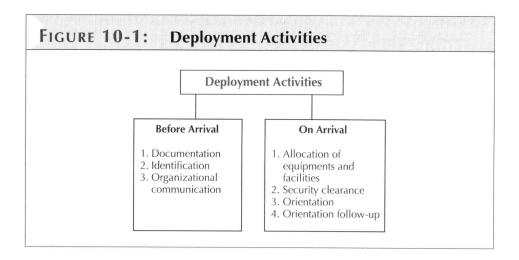

FIGURE 10-1:   Deployment Activities

Documentation As mentioned in Chapter 9, once an organization has made its selection decisions, it sends the candidates formal job offers along with all relevant supporting information. At a minimum, the documentation must include details about the job offer, instructions on how to respond to the offer, and conditions governing the job offer (especially medical exams and probationary status). Management must ensure that all forms and documents related to the hire are signed before the start date, then consolidated and saved in a new file for the employee.

When hiring workers from abroad, an organization must also send documents for securing work permits and visas. Note that every foreign worker who does not belong to the exempt categories needs a work permit to take employment in Canada. The following occupations do not need work permits:[2]

- foreign government officials, representatives, and their family members
- professional and semi-professional coaches, athletes, and referees
- North American media crew
- public speakers
- clergy
- convention organizers
- civil aviation inspectors
- crew members of vessels of foreign ownership
- accident inspectors

In addition, workers covered by international agreements (such as the North American Free Trade Agreement, the Canada-Chile Free Trade Agreement, and the General Agreement of Trade in Services) also are exempt. In cases where an organization has to apply for permits, it must also obtain a labour market opinion confirmation from HRSD prior to qualifying for the permit. Applying for a labour market opinion confirmation can be a time-consuming exercise, since the employer often has to advertise the position for a minimum of two to three weeks in national newspapers, then interview potential candidates and keep detailed records, before being allowed to complete an application for hiring a foreign worker.[3]

Identification The new employee has to be assigned identification numbers necessary to access organizational systems and services. While the details are normally provided to the employee after arrival, arrangements have to be made before that date and the information kept ready for these numbers:

- employee number
- employee ID, if separate from the above number
- information necessary for payroll forms (e.g., TD1 and Social Insurance Number), HRIS, benefits, and pension
- security cards for entry into office and facilities
- computer ID and system access number

Organizational communication The organization must inform all concerned departments and employees about the impending arrival of the new hire. It has to make plans for office space, security clearance, and safety orientation. If the employer offers benefits such as free meals or transportation, these departments have to know about the new employee.

ON ARRIVAL

Allocation of equipment and facilities On arrival, the supervisor has to direct the new employees to the assigned office space and introduce them to all facilities and equipment. He or she also has to make arrangements with the information technology department to assign email addresses.

Security clearance The supervisor should now present the employees with security and access cards that will allow them to access to all space and equipment. In many organizations, card allocation is part of the general orientation

Results of a survey on how organizations conduct orientation: *www.thetrainingclinic.com/ orientation/ orient%20survey.htm*

Orientation Even the most qualified and competent new hire requires initial training to familiarize them with the organizational culture and the job duties. Sometimes the gap between a new employee's abilities and the job's demands may be substantial. As Figure 10-2 illustrates, orientation supplements the new worker's abilities to bring them up to speed. Although orientation is time-consuming and expensive, it reduces employee turnover and helps new employees become productive sooner.

Effective orientation programs familiarize new employees with their roles, the organization, and other employees. Unless new hires perceive that the organization welcomes them and tries to make them comfortable, they are unlikely to stay.[4] If properly done, orientation can result in several beneficial outcomes discussed below.

Articles on orientation and new employee training: *www.articles911.com/ Human_Resources/Orientation*

Reduce errors and save time Orientation gives employees a clear idea of expectations, which in turn results in fewer mistakes.[5] For some jobs, duties and job expectations

Focus on Ethics

You work for a highly innovative medium-sized electronics firm as a software engineer. A large competitor of the firm offers you almost double the salary for doing more or less the same work in their company. While the competitor has so far not made any explicit demands, you understand from others working in the firm that the job offer is usually contingent on your giving away inside company information about the old employer. If at a later date you refuse to give such information, your career with the new employer may be in jeopardy. While you have not signed any non-compete or confidentiality agreement with your present employer, you are uncomfortable about divulging their secrets to the new employer, since you feel loyal to the firm. However, because of family responsibilities, you need the additional money.

What should you do?

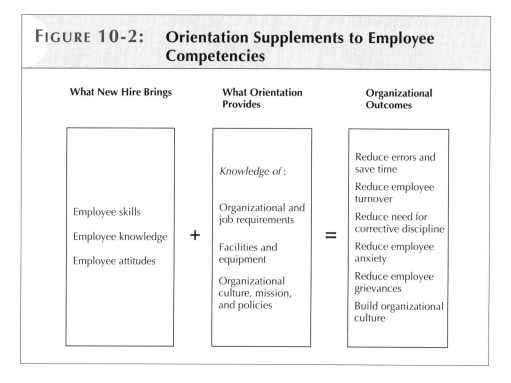

FIGURE 10-2: Orientation Supplements to Employee Competencies

What New Hire Brings		What Orientation Provides		Organizational Outcomes
Employee skills Employee knowledge Employee attitudes	**+**	*Knowledge of :* Organizational and job requirements Facilities and equipment Organizational culture, mission, and policies	**=**	Reduce errors and save time Reduce employee turnover Reduce need for corrective discipline Reduce employee anxiety Reduce employee grievances Build organizational culture

are clear. However, for most jobs, there are no clear-cut lists of "desirable" behaviours or job outcomes. Effective orientation is absolutely necessary to communicate to employees what the organization expects of them and what they can expect in return. Furthermore, new employees are usually less efficient than experienced employees. This slow productivity combined with other orientation costs (e.g., supervisor's time and attention) makes start-up costs for new employees significant. However, in the long run, a good start saves the organization time and money later.

Reduce employee turnover The probability that an employee will quit the organization is highest during their first few months of employment. If the gap between a new hire's expectations and the reality of the job is too large, that employee will take action.

> For a major Canadian bank, the annual turnover averages 5% of its work force. While at first glance this looks reasonable, the size of the bank's work force warrants action to reduce it. For example, with a workforce of over 30 000, this means that nearly 1500 employees leave the bank in a year. With thousands of employees leaving each year, the costs of turnover can quickly escalate into the millions of dollars.

When experienced, long-service employees quit, the loss to the organization can be incalculable, because they take knowledge and skills away with them.[6] But effective orientation can lower turnover. Most new employees would like to know "what it takes to get ahead in this organization." In the absence of orientation responding to such questions, they may have to find answers to their questions informally through the grapevine. Unfortunately, there is no guarantee that they will find the right answers.

Reduce need for corrective discipline Communicating policies and regulations to new employees early reduces undesirable behaviour and deviation from established policies. An effective orientation program clarifies the rights and duties of employees, outlines disciplinary requirements, and spells out the consequences of deviating from the prescribed path.

Reduce employee anxiety On arrival, new employees experience stress caused by unfamiliar surroundings and expectations. Organizations can considerably reduce this stress by communicating with new employees openly, clarifying roles, and familiarizing them with organizational objectives. This in turn helps employees pick up speed.

Reduce employee grievances Grievances often result from ambiguous job expectations and unclear responsibilities. An effective orientation program specifies both, thereby reducing the possibility and frequency of employee grievances.

Build organizational culture through socialization **Organizational culture** is the distinctive patterns of behaviour and underlying values, beliefs, meanings, and knowledge shared by organizational members. Culture is learned and shared by the members of an organization and has a compelling influence on their behaviours. Many organizations have been able to increase their strategic success by creating and communicating distinct cultural values to their members. Home Depot is a good example.

> Home Depot is known for its strong organizational culture. For example, its culture places overriding importance on customer satisfaction. The company is often willing to spend hundreds of additional dollars to ensure customer satisfaction. Home Depot's well-communicated values help employees choose actions in line with company objectives without going through extra channels.

Thus, early socialization helps a new employee understand and adopt the culture of the organization.[7] **Socialization** is the continuing process through which employees understand and accept the values, norms, and beliefs of the organization. While most professions and formal education programs prepare a candidate for a specific job, it is the early interactions within an organization that cement these values and relevant job attitudes. Formal programs, such as orientation, training, and job rotation, and informal interactions with one's boss and co-workers, teach the new hire about what the organization values and rewards. Day-to-day interactions, conditioning, and reinforcement result in new values, attitudes, and behaviours. Through orientation, the recruit is transformed from an outsider into a full-fledged member of the organization.

In summary, an effective orientation program helps new hires understand the social, technical, and cultural aspects of the workplace. Orientation programs speed up the socialization process and benefit both the employee and the organization.

Content of orientation programs Most organizations conduct orientation on an individual basis, although group orientation programs can occur when several employees are hired at the same time.

Most orientation programs introduce new employees to their jobs, colleagues, and the organization's policies. Figure 10-3 lists the topics typically covered during orientation. Typically, the orientation discusses organizational issues that new employees need to be aware of. It often includes a film or slide show describing the history, products, services, and policies of the organization. Unless they have already received one in the mail, new employees also receive an **employee handbook** that explains key benefits, policies, and general information about the company. Supervisors introduce the new employee to co-workers and other relevant personnel. Introductions are usually followed by a tour of the facilities and an explanation of the job, its objectives, and related information. Human resource experts may also discuss various benefits and human resource policies as part of the program.

In some organizations, the orientation program may take half a day to a whole day. For some jobs, it can be done in a couple of hours or less.

> A Canadian study[8] showed that roughly 10% of orientations lasted one hour, but 51% took a day or longer. The same study reported that more than two-thirds of firms conducted the orientation immediately after the employee reported to work.

Organizational culture: the distinctive patterns of behaviour and underlying values, beliefs, meanings, and knowledge shared by organizational members

Socialization: the continuing process through which employees understand and accept the values, norms, and beliefs of the organization

Employee handbook: book explaining key benefits, policies, and general information about the company

FIGURE 10-3:   Content of Orientation Programs

About the Organization	About the Job	About Other People	About Employee Benefits and Future
• History of the organization • Product line or services • Goals and key strategies • Organization structure • Company strategy, policies, and rules • Names and titles of key managers • Facilities and layout • Corporate culture and values	• Overview of job and how it relates to other jobs • Job location • Job tasks, objectives, accountabilities • Safety standards and procedures • Emergency procedures • Rest breaks	Introductions to • Supervisor • Co-workers • HR department staff • Union representative • Employee counsellor • Trainers • Senior management (in some instances)	• Pay scales and pay days • Vacation and holidays • Retirement benefits • Insurance benefits • Medical and health benefits • Employer provided services • Potential career growth patterns • Training and education benefits • Counselling

Buddy system: a senior worker shows the new hire around and orients him or her to the systems and people

For employers that hire workers only occasionally and in small numbers, there may be no formal orientation program. Instead, they use a **buddy system,** where the employee is introduced to a senior worker who shows the new person around. These highly informal arrangements are also used by some large companies. But while useful, such informal efforts are no substitute for formal orientation programs and hence should not be the sole method of socializing employees. Indeed, informal orientation may give the new employee inadequate and conflicting information. Studies have shown that well prepared, formal orientation programs add value. One study[9] revealed that employees attending the orientation programs were significantly better socialized on three of six socialization measures than employees who did not attend orientation. Employees attending orientation programs also had significantly higher levels of organizational commitment than non-participants.

Orientation is important for all new employees, regardless whether they are managerial, clerical, or technical; but ensuring the new managers are effective in the new setting and culture can be challenging:

> A 2003 survey of 826 HR directors indicated that 40% of all new leaders, including those promoted and hired from outside an organization, fail to meet the expectations of management. Two major reasons given for this failure were the new manager's inability to build effective relationships with peers and subordinates (82%) and his or her lack of internal political skills (50%). These issues highlight the importance of assimilating new managers successfully so that they can respond to the existing culture.[10]

Thus, orientation of new managers must expose them to the organizational realities and inform them "how things get done around here," including information on the following:[11]

• How do people get things done? Do they rely on chain of command or informal networks?

• How does the boss's boss make decisions?

- Are top-level managers accessible?

- Does the organization have primarily a short-term or long-term orientation?

- Are people rewarded for thinking outside the box?

- How are differences of opinion dealt with?

- What are some stories, myths, and folklores in the organization?

Orientation follow-up Orientation should not be a one-shot event. Often, the new employee is overwhelmed when expected to absorb too much information in a short time. Also, later on, after reading the manuals and forms, the recruit may have new questions. The human resource department should make an effort to follow-up on new employees and answer their ongoing questions. Ideally, orientation follow-up should occur one week and one month after the start date. One human resource consultant recommends seeking feedback from new hires after one, three, and six months.[12]

FACILITATING CAREER GROWTH OF EMPLOYEES

As the opening quote to this chapter showed, enlightened and effective employers respect their employees and show sustained commitment to their welfare. Today's knowledge economy makes employees the most valuable part of organizational resources. In turn, this means that the organization has to constantly develop employee capabilities and potential, create settings where employees continuously learn, and develop creative solutions to emerging challenges.

Facilitating an employee's career growth requires:

1. preparing them for greater challenges through employee development;

2. assisting them in career planning; and

3. fostering a culture that encourages learning and development.

DEVELOPMENTAL ACTIVITIES

Training focuses on teachings skills needed for effective performance of current jobs. Development, in contrast, focuses on developing employee potential for future challenges and responsibilities. Developmental strategies can be categorized in three broad groups:[13] cognitive, behavioural, and situational strategies.

Cognitive training Cognitive training focuses on deepening employee thoughts and ideas through new knowledge or process changes. Cognitive training is part of an organization's ongoing information-sharing process: continually evolving and changing internal roles and communication patterns to adapt to environmental demands. Cognitive development seems to promote constant learning and upgrading. Yet it is one of the least effective methods for bringing about behavioural changes, since cognitive training methods (lectures, seminars, and academic education) are relatively passive. Thus, while cognitive training may enhance overall knowledge, it does little to change an employee's values or behaviours.

Cognitive training: deepening employee thoughts and ideas through new knowledge and process changes (e.g., lectures, seminars, and academic education)

Behavioural approaches to training Behavioural approaches, as the term suggests, focus primarily on changing employee behaviours through experiential exercises such as behaviour modelling, role play, and team-building games. The goal is to help the employee understand and display desirable behaviours. Behavioural objectives can

Behavioural approaches: changing employee behaviours through experiential exercises (e.g., behaviour modelling, role play, and team-building exercises)

include employing an appropriate management style for the situation, positively interacting with customers, managing conflict with others, and communicating effectively internally and externally. Some of the more popular tools used for behavioural changes are:

- *behaviour modeling.*[14] A manager acts as the "model" displaying the desired behaviours vividly and consistently. The trainee learns to imitate the model and is reinforced whenever the desired behaviour is achieved.

- *role play.* The trainee assumes the role of someone else involved in a situation to get insight into the problem.

- *sensitivity training.* Intensive training sessions help employees become aware of the impact of their own behaviour on others and prepare them for more effective interactions with culturally diverse people.[15]

- *team building.*[16] Team members diagnose group processes and devise solutions to problems.

- *coaching.* Establishes an ongoing professional relationship between an expert and the trainee, who learns desired behaviours or skills through ongoing and specific advice.

- *mentoring.* The employee establishes a close relationship with a boss or another experienced employee (and usually someone with more seniority or authority), who takes a personal interest in the employee's career.[17]

In general, the behavioural approach has greater impact on shaping employee behaviours and skills than cognitive training.

Situational approach to training

Also referred to as "environmental strategies," the **situational approach** focuses on exposing the trainee to a variety of different settings and contexts ("situations") that help the employee learn new skills, attitudes, and values. Like the behavioural approach, it focuses on shaping employee behaviours and related attitudes. Some popular situational approaches include the following.

- *Job rotation* exposes employees to different work settings. It is very useful[18] for developing managerial skills, since it sensitizes managers to different problems and priorities. In Japan, management trainees are sometimes rotated through several departments for two years or more before they are assigned a specific job responsibility. This in turn helps them incorporate whole-organization priorities into their decisions.

- *Temporary assignments* allow employees to gain valuable experience outside their regular jobs. For example, an employee in the production department may be asked to work with a product design committee to help develop a marketable product.

- *Employee exchange programs* are used by Bell Canada, IBM, Xerox, and the federal government of Canada. The organization "hires" a loaned employee for an extended period of time, such as a year. Both the hosts and the guests learn valuable lessons through such exchange programs.

- *Matrix management structures* expand the traditional functional structure to make more effective use of employee capabilities. Often, a limited number of skilled employees has to be apportioned among competing priorities throughout the organization, not just in the employee's own department. However, in that process, the employee learns new skills. Many universities employ a matrix structure to make the best use of scarce faculty by assigning them to teach in different programs. Professors formally report to the chairs of their respective functional department; but for

Situational approach: exposing the employee to different settings and contexts to teach the employee new skills, attitudes, and values (e.g., job rotation, employee exchanges)

instructional purposes, they also report to the director of the program in which they are teaching. Such multiple roles help faculty members understand the needs of different programs and student groups.

But the situational approach, while effective and beneficial to all concerned, is also the most difficult to implement, since it disrupts the day-to-day working of the organization. For this reason, only organizations with long-term vision and a clear commitment to employee development have been successful with these approaches.

ASSISTANCE IN CAREER PLANNING

In an individualist society such as Canada, most people believe that career development is an employee's responsibility. However, it is in an organization's interest to assist them in reaching their dreams. For example, a frustrated employee may move to another employer; alternatively, a competent employee may simply be unaware of opportunities in the organization and work at below his or her true ability levels.

Human resource departments can encourage career planning in two major ways: through career information and through counselling.

Career information Human resource departments can increase employee awareness of potential careers within the organization through educational techniques. For example, presentations, memoranda, and position papers from senior executives can stimulate employee interest at low cost to the employer. Workshops and seminars on career planning can increase employee interest by helping the employee set career goals, identify career paths, and uncover specific career development activities. These educational activities may be supplemented by print or audiovisual information on career planning.

Career counselling Many progressive employers offer career counselling services. The counsellor may simply be a mentor who provides information about job opportunities and required competencies; it may be a professional counsellor with training in career and aptitude test administration (see Chapter 7). The steps in career choice discussed in Chapter 5 are also followed through in career counselling sessions.

In addition, the notion of **360-degree career development** is gaining popularity. This approach takes a holistic view of employee career development, focusing on attracting, identifying, assessing, developing, and promoting employees.[19]

360-degree career development: a holistic view of employee career development, focusing on attracting, identifying, assessing, developing, and promoting employees

FOSTERING A LEARNING ENVIRONMENT

According to one researcher, a **learning organization** continually encourages employees to grow and learn together and nurtures new and expansive patterns of thinking.[20] In such settings, members of the organization see processes and events in their entirety, recognize interrelationships and patterns of change, and infer associations and connections. Employees are encouraged to continually clarify and deepen personal visions and see reality objectively. The mental models of how and why things work the way they do are continually tested and revised so that true learning takes place.

Consider the difference between North American and Japanese organizations:

In North America, the people who spend the most time learning about quality are shop floor employees, who typically spend five days learning about statistical process control. Their bosses get the three-day course, and the CEOs get a two-hour briefing. In contrast, Japanese organizations do exactly the opposite: the CEOs get the most training, and the shop floor employees get the least. The symbolic significance of the Japanese model is that their leaders are learners.[21]

Learning organization: encourages employees to grow and learn together and nurtures new, expansive patterns of thinking

A policy for continuous learning at the treasury board: *www.tbs-sct.gc.ca/ pubs_pol/hrpubs/tb_856/pclpsc -pacfpc1_e.asp*

In learning organizations, shared vision binds the employees at all levels around a common identity and sense of destiny. With a genuine organizational vision, people take on tasks because they want to, not because they have to. Figure 10-4 illustrates some key characteristics of an organization that fosters a learning culture.

Structure and systems *Learning* means disorganizing what employees already know to accommodate new information. It means creating exceptions to existing systems and procedures. In contrast, *organizing* means reducing variety and streamlining information. Thus, in a sense, organizing and learning are essentially antithetical processes.[22] So if learning is to become a way of life, then the organization must consciously reward it. Learning organizations incorporate appropriate internal rewards and procedures to encourage experimentation, ownership of actions, and learning. For example, "knowledge-based pay" and "skill-based pay" are becoming increasingly popular in organizations that give priority to learning.

> In organizations including General Foods, Polaroid, and Mars, "pay for skill" has generally been accompanied by positive outcomes.[23]

Simultaneously, these organizations remove existing disincentives to learning. They replace the traditional practice of using supervisor-led performance appraisals to determine pay raises with employee shares in profits and stock ownership plans.

> One organization pays all its employees a 10% bonus for meeting company goals. Employees also receive $500 for each new idea adopted. One employee received $7500 for generating creative solutions.[24]

Information sharing If employees are to make appropriate decisions, they must have valid information. In learning organizations, this type of information sharing reaches extraordinary levels. Reports, meetings, financial statements, newsletters, email, voice-mail, intranets, and broadcasts are used to facilitate information transmission.

> One firm routinely feeds the results of customer surveys to all employees, along with the company performance on 100 key operational dimensions.[25]

Empowerment Learning organizations give decision-making power to their employees to a much higher level than other firms. In some organizations, virtually all decisions are made by teams of employees.

> As an example of extremely high empowerment, one organization expects employees to behave and make decisions as if they were owners. Employees receive all relevant information

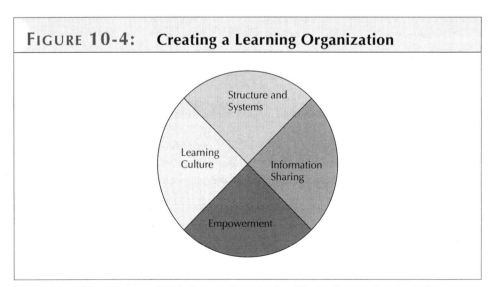

FIGURE 10-4:   **Creating a Learning Organization**

Source: Adapted from Hari Das. (1998). *Strategic Organizational Design.* Toronto: Prentice-Hall, p. 482.

and are trusted to make appropriate decisions.[26] In another firm, top management does not set budgets. Instead, teams of employees discuss needs for the next period, decide what is appropriate, and create feasible budgets. Sometimes, decisions involve the purchase of equipment worth over $1 million.[27]

Establishing a learning culture Organizations that value learning attempt to establish a learning culture. A learning organization recognizes that learning can take place in interactions with customers, suppliers, other employees, in new assignments and in task forces; and that formal training and development programs are not the only ways to learn. In a learning organization, everyone is engaged in identifying and resolving problems and in experimenting to improve performance. Leaders in a learning organization try to create a shared vision of the organizational mission. If the vision is clear, employees can be allowed to identify and solve problems on their own.

Learning includes more than simply accounting, marketing, and engineering principles. It enhances each employee's skills as well as the organization's capability to try new things. Often, employees acquire their new knowledge from engaging in independent action and experimentation, rather than from books or training sessions.

> An example of such independent action would be a store clerk taking the initiative to use a new computer program to track customer demands and change reordering procedures to better meet customer needs.

To become a learning organization, a firm must also encourage "unlearning." Unlearning needs to start with the top management and include every worker. Successful learning organizations assume that everyone is capable of learning and creates a rewarding, supportive environment. Further, task assignments and promotions are also planned bearing the learning agenda in mind. When employees are hired, their ability to learn is rated more highly than their ability to do the present job.

> A past president of Pepsi emphasized hiring learners. According to him, the best way to start is to hire a group of proven managers without having any particular jobs in mind for them. As job openings emerge, they can be slotted into them; meanwhile, the company has access to the skills of proficient managers who are not overly influenced by the internal culture and past ways of doing things.[28]

In summary, progressive employers ensure the continuous development of the employees and take active interest in their personal career development. Employees respond with positive work attitudes and behaviour.

> In 1997, Molson Breweries opened the Molson Personal Learning and Development Centre in Etobicoke, Ontario. The objective was to help employees sharpen and broaden the skill sets needed for their jobs and beyond. As Lloyd Livingstone, brewing training specialist and coordinator for the development of the Learning Centre, put it: "It really is a fun place; to look around and see these guys excited about learning, it really makes you feel excited too." Employees are offered a combination of mandatory training and personal career development. Training methods include Personal Learning Maps (a competency-based learning plan for each employee), a database of courses sorted by skills, a platform for launching multimedia training, and an administration program that allows managers to track employee progress and add new skills and courses to the system. The system encourages interaction between employees and managers, and even senior executives participate.[29]

STAFFING INTERNATIONAL OPERATIONS

As discussed in Chapters 3 and 5, staffing international operations raises additional challenges: determining the source of recruits (expatriates, host country nationals, or third country nationals), meeting additional governmental regulations (e.g., work permits, security and supplementary medical clearance), and differential reward systems (see Figure 10-5). For firms branching out internationally for the first time, the issues can seem daunting. The organization must extensively research local hiring practices, the availability of skilled labour, and local employment regulations.[30]

> For example, advance research is critical for expansions into China. In order to operate successfuly, the China-based office must develop relationships with government officials and local entrepreneurs. Often relationships must build for years before a company becomes successful in a new venture.[31] Moreover, upon arrival in China, a new employee has to go to a police station immediately and apply for a registration certificate. The employee also needs to complete several forms to get a work permit and residence license.[32] Cultural differences are important and subtle. The Chinese use much more indirect language than Canadians, who tend to communicate very directly. They also focus more than Canadians on hierarchy of authority, long-time orientation, and collectivistic values.

This means that expatriate staff need cross-cultural competencies, as well as an ability to survive and succeed in a foreign setting (see Figure 10-6). However, to validly assess these attributes, an organization requires special testing tools.

RECRUITMENT

The two sources of potential applicants for openings are current employees and new hires. Reassigning current employees offers an opportunity for career development, in addition to filling a job opening.

> Several large companies such as Procter and Gamble and Gillette move executives around the world.

Although an international assignment often looks attractive to first-time applicants, career, family, language, and cultural considerations may prevent experienced candidates from applying. Dual-career families, children, and assignments to developing countries are often significant barriers to recruitment. To overcome these barriers, organizations should consider other sources of recruits, as illustrated by Colgate-Palmolive:

> In the past, Colgate-Palmolive's senior management recognized difficulties securing top executive talent for its international operations. Since international business is critical to the company's overall success, management decided to re-examine its recruitment practices. As a result, Colgate developed a new strategy of recruiting students from reputed undergraduate and

---

FIGURE 10-5: Typical Supplementary Benefits Offered to Expatriate Staff

Overseas Premium: Additional salary offered to compensate for the inconvenience of living abroad. Typically, this ranges from 10% to 20% of base salary.

Moving Allowance: Cost of transportation of expatriate, family, and their goods to the new location and accommodation until they are settled in the new place (e.g., hotel and meals).

Home Leave: Transportation for expatriate and family to visit home, along with time off.

Housing allowance: Provision of house free of rent or at a concessional rate.

Cost of Living Allowance: Supplementary allowance to allow the expatriate to maintain the same living standards as at home.

Education Allowance: Reimbursement of expatriate's children's tuition fees in a school that provides them with a quality of education that is equivalent to that in Canada.

FIGURE 10-6:   Some Important Skills for Expatriate Employees*

Cultural Adaptability: Ability to understand and adapt to local cultural norms and practices without losing track of one's objectives or standards.

Multidimensional Perspective: Ability to recognize the multiple dimensions of a problem and the interrelationship of variables affecting it. The capacity to conceptualize and resolve a problem from multi-functional, multi-product, multi-country, and multi-cultural levels.

Resourcefulness: Ability to adapt one's own solutions, actions, and practices to the needs of the situation and incorporate political, cultural, technological, and other constraints when identifying and implementing solutions to problems.

Negotiation skills: Ability to conduct strategic business negotiations in a multicultural and political environment. Ability to understand the motivations of the "other side" and respond to them to arrive at solutions that are satisfactory to both parties.

Decision-Making and Leadership Skills: Ability to make decisions under severe time and resource constraints; capacity to develop innovative solutions and to inspire subordinates, teams, and others toward those solutions.

---

* For example, see Rosalie Tung. (1981, Spring). "Selection and Training of Personnel for Overseas Assignments." *Columbia Journal of World Business, 16*, 1: 68-78; Allan Bird and Roger Dunbar. (1991, Spring). "Getting the Job Done Over There: Expatriate Productivity." *National Productivity Review, 10*, 2: 145-156; Michael Schell and Charlene Solomon. (1997). *Capitalizing on the Global Work-Force.* Chicago: Irwin Professional Publishing; Terence Brake, Danielle Walker, and Thomas Walker. (1995). *Doing Business Internationally: The Guide to Cross Cultural Success.* Princeton, NJ: Training Management Corporation.

MBA programs whose experience, education, and language skills demonstrated their commitment to an international career.[33]

Many of the recruiting approaches discussed in Chapter 5 can be adapted for overseas recruitment. Of course, the organization must keep in mind the local cultural values and customs. In developing countries, recruiting skilled employees can sometimes pose a major challenge because of economic and social conditions, such as a low literacy rate.

SELECTION

To select the right person to fill an international opening means considering more than just technical or managerial ability. Global managers have to be very versatile, aware of global issues, sensitive to cultural challenges, and capable of managing decentralized operations and making in-roads into the new social milieu.[34] Here are some personal qualities of successful expatriates:[35]

- cultural self-awareness
- curiosity about other cultures
- tolerance for ambiguous situations
- acceptance of differences in cultural values
- ability to develop relationships with people
- willingness to expand definition of success

As Figure 10-6 shows, the expatriate employee needs unique skills and competencies to survive and succeed in a foreign setting. The person's ability to manage a diverse workforce and adapt to the company and country culture are critical. The person selected should be mature and emotionally stable, while possessing all relevant managerial and technical competencies.

> Research indicates that one in four (and often more) expatriate managers fail in their new job assignments, costing their employers US$40 000 to $250 000.[36]

The manager's inability to adapt to new settings, the spouse's inability to adapt to the new surroundings, family-related problems, and any mismatch between manager personality and new work culture are key factors in expatriate manager failure.[37] For women managers, working in foreign cultures where women have historically had low status may pose special problems, although host country nationals often view female expatriates first as foreigners and second as women.

While prior experience living and working abroad are among the best predictors of future success, such evidence may not always be available. An organization will need additional hiring predictors, such as tests, in-baskets, and situational interviews. Tests measuring attitudes and characteristics necessary for work in foreign settings and others measuring ability to learn foreign languages are currently available. Hiring third-country nationals can be particularly challenging due to language and cultural differences. To overcome some of these challenges, many firms use **transnational teams** composed of employees from several countries working together on projects that span several countries. Such teams are vital for carrying out assignments that one manager cannot do alone. These teams of experts can transcend existing organizational structure, transfer technology and other resources from one region or country to another, respond to new challenges, and make fast decisions.

Transnational teams: teams of employees from several countries work together on projects that span several countries

ORIENTATION AND TRAINING

Orientation for expatriate employee should cover geography, politics, culture, and procedures, as well as the people whom the new job incumbent will encounter in the new position. International orientations may begin weeks or even months before an assignment begins and may last for weeks afterward. Although predeparture orientation is common, an on-site orientation after arrival is also often necessary to help the new job incumbent to settle into the role. Details of culture, language, local customs, social attitudes toward time and punctuality, power, teamwork, use of titles, social taboos, and degree of formality in interaction with the local population are integral components of such an orientation.

Language Training the expatriate employee to speak the native language is a priority. While English is almost universally accepted for international business, there are positions or geographical areas where knowledge of local language is a must. Even if English is the primary language of use in the new location, it still may show systematic variations depending on the country:

> In England, to "table" a topic at a meeting means to discuss it now; in Canada, it means to postpone discussion of a subject. The "elevator" is a "lift" in several countries, just as "gum" is "glue." The trunk of a car is a "dickey" in India, a word that denotes a male organ in New Zealand.

Cultural norms Different societies show consistent and marked differences on several cultural dimensions.

> For example, Canadians are "individualistic:" they prefer a social framework in which individuals are supposed to take care of themselves and their immediate families only. But in many Asian and South American cultures, people are "collectivist:" they value a tightly

knit social framework in which individuals take care of their relatives, clan, or members of their group in exchange for unquestioning loyalty.

North Americans score high on achievement, assertiveness, and material success; while Nordic countries such as Sweden or Finland value relationships, modesty, caring for the weak, and quality of life. Lack of understanding of such differences can make the expatriate employee ineffective when dealing with others abroad.

The success of an expatriate employee abroad also depends on the degree to which the person's family feels comfortable in the new location. Often career success is closely related to success in managing personal and family life abroad.[38] Recognizing this, many employers also invite the employee's spouse to participate in orientation and training sessions:

> An integral part of the orientation in a firm with multinational operations is a two-week language and culture orientation course, which spouses attend. The orientation often includes a visit from an employee or spouse who has served in the location. Apart from the personal touch, repatriated families are likely to have keen insights about a particular location and its culture.[39]

In summary, the hiring and placement of expatriates requires careful consideration of many variables. Departing employees need to be trained in the local language, cultural norms of the host country, and personal and family life management in the new location. The expatriates should be able to make a basic attitudinal shift away from monocultural assumptions that value conformity to organizational rules and be open to alternate lifestyles and multiple paths leading to the same goal.

TERMINATING EMPLOYEES

Despite the best human resource planning, selection, and training procedures, employers often have to layoff or terminate employees. There are two types of employee separations: voluntary separations and involuntary separations. **Voluntary separations** occur when the employee leaves the firm for personal or professional reasons. In contrast, **involuntary separations** are caused when the management initiates the termination of an employee for economic or other reasons. Typical examples include layoffs, downsizing, and dismissals. **Termination**, or permanent separation of the employee from the organization (also referred to as being fired, discharged, separated, or dismissed), has to be done as humanely as possible and only as a last resort. Human resource managers often provide advice to line managers on alternatives to termination; and in those instances where it is unavoidable, they advise managers how to develop appropriate security measures to protect corporate assets while preserving the dignity of the terminated employee. In all instances, care should be taken to avoid **wrongful dismissal**, that is, dismissal without just cause or reasonable notice of termination.

Termination should occur only for just cause and only with adequate warning. The offending employee or poor performer should be warned in clear and unequivocal terms that failure to improve behaviour will result in discipline (including possible discharge). Figure 10-7 illustrates a policy of **progressive discipline**, where repeated offences are accompanied by stronger penalties and finally discharge. Managers must also clearly indicate in writing the nature of the problem and the impact of the offender's behaviour on organizational performance, success, or stature in the larger society.

Voluntary separations: the employee leaves the firm for personal or professional reasons

Involuntary separations: management initiates the termination of an employee for economic or other reasons

Termination: permanent separation of the employee from the organization

Wrongful dismissal: dismissal without just cause or reasonable notice of termination

Progressive discipline: a sequence of increasing penalties for repeated offences

FIGURE 10-7:	Illustration of a Progressive Discipline System
First violation:	Verbal reprimand and counselling by the supervisor
Second violation:	Written reprimand, counselling, and a record in the file
Third violation:	One or two day suspension from work (depending on the gravity of offence)
Fourth violation:	Suspension for one week or longer
Fifth violation:	Discharge for cause

TERMINATION PROCEDURES

Managers should handle involuntary separations carefully and follow these steps (see also Figure 10-8):[40]

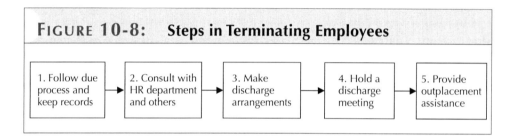

FIGURE 10-8:   Steps in Terminating Employees

1. Follow due process and keep records → 2. Consult with HR department and others → 3. Make discharge arrangements → 4. Hold a discharge meeting → 5. Provide outplacement assistance

Due process: a system of consistent rules and procedures through which employees can respond to the charges against them

1. Follow due process and keep records Due process is a system of consistent rules and procedures where employees are provided with an opportunity to respond to the charges against them. Managers should always follow due process in terminations. Moreover, they must keep sufficient documentation to support all charges against employees. They should only resort to dismissal for just cause after all avenues for corrective action and change in employee behaviour have been explored. Past court decisions indicate that just cause may include the following:[41]

- violation of a fundamental term of the employment contract (e.g., stealing) or making false statements or omitting essential facts in the employment application

- endangering health and safety of others

- illegal conduct

- insubordination

- serious misconduct in the workplace or a persistent misconduct of a more minor nature that remains uncorrected

- persistent and deliberate poor job performance despite warning, training, feedback, and provision of appropriate working conditions

Employers are responsible for showing that they have given adequate warnings to the erring employee and appropriate training, time, and feedback to improve performance.[42] In the case of long-term employees, a one-time behaviour, even a refusal to attend to work, may not constitute just cause for dismissal, as the following case showed:

> Timothy Minott had worked for O' Shanter Development Company for eleven years. Until his dismissal, the employer did not have any complaints about Minott or his performance. But one day, Minott refused to show up for work and was given a two-day disciplinary

Articles on handling "difficult" employees:
www.hr-guide.com

Articles on disciplinary practices:
www.p-management.com/articles/2008.htm

suspension without pay. A misunderstanding about the date on which the suspension was to be served led to a heated exchange between Minott and his supervisor, at the end of which Minott was terminated. The judge of Minott's wrongful dismissal case concluded that Minott was honestly confused about the dates on which his suspension was to have been served, and his failure to return to work on the date his employer expected him was not just cause for termination. In a later decision, an appeal court judge stated that given the long record of loyal service by the employee and the fact that he was not given any warning by the employer that his job was in jeopardy, even a willful refusal to attend work for one day did not constitute just cause.[43]

Dismissal of unionized employees should conform to the provisions of the collective agreement signed between the management and the union. Some employee behaviours that may qualify for dismissal are listed in Figure 10-9. If just cause does not exist, an employer is expected to give reasonable notice to the employee whose services are being terminated. All Canadian provinces have employment standards legislation that require minimum periods of notice (usually termed "reasonable notice") to employees terminated without cause. Past court decisions indicate that reasonable notice should reflect employee's age, length of service, salary, occupational status, and labour market conditions.

FIGURE 10-9: Situations When Dismissal May Be Appropriate

- Theft of company property
- Vandalism of company property
- Falsification of employment application
- Consumption of illegal drugs or alcohol at work
- Fraud, theft, and falsification of company records
- Unauthorized release of confidential information
- Receipt of bribes, gifts, or rewards for offering a service that undermines the organization's interests and solely focuses on personal gain
- Abandoning the job or not showing up for work for an extended period (usually, a week) without offering an explanation or receiving a leave of absence from management
- Endangering the health and safety of self and others
- Other illegal conduct, such as drug trafficking

Source: Adapted from Hari Das, *Performance Management*, 2003, p. 263. Pearson Education. Reprinted with permission of Pearson Education Canada.

2. Consultations with all concerned
Normally, the human resource department approves all terminations of employee services. In any event, terminations should conform to organizational policies and provisions of collective agreements where they exist. When terminating senior employees, managers may need approval from the Board or other higher levels. Sometimes legal council is also necessary before making a decision on terminating an employee.

3. Making discharge arrangements
Managers should take care of all relevant security measures (e.g., invalidating employee passwords to accounts and phone, releasing office and parking space held by the employee) before the termination meeting. If the employee's history indicates potential for an emotional outburst or violence, precautionary security arrangements may be required. Some of the "dos and don'ts" in the context of terminating an employee are listed in Figure 10-10.

4. Termination meeting
Always hold the termination meeting in the presence of another manager (preferably the human resource manager) as a witness in a private and neutral location. The termination meeting should cover all termination-related

---

FIGURE 10-10:   Dos and Don'ts When Terminating
                  Employees

DO:

- Review the decision to terminate very carefully, looking at all possible repercussions, including legal repercussions.
- Consult the human resource department and/or legal counsel before undertaking the decision.
- Inform your own boss about the decision to terminate the employee (to avoid possible complications when the employee appeals to higher management).
- Plan to hold the termination meeting in the presence of a manager, preferably some one from the human resource department.
- Invalidate the employee's passwords and access words to the systems before the termination meeting.
- Make security arrangements if the employee's past behaviour gives reason to believe that a violent outburst is possible.
- Get straight to the point, rather than beating around the bush or trying to rationalize the decision. Explain the context as concisely as possible and state the termination decision at the beginning of the script.*
- Make detailed notes of the discussion either during or immediately following the meeting.
- Clearly identify the reason for termination.
- Provide the employee a copy of the termination letter and an opportunity to read it thoroughly.
- Where feasible, identify positive aspects of the termination, highlighting how this will help the employee to get a fresh start or find a solution to his or her problems.
- Ensure that the employee has received at least the minimum notice and/or severance pay required by the provincial employment standards legislation.
- Give the name of a contact person for future questions.
- Ensure that all company property and employee identification cards have been returned by the employee.
- Thank the employee for something that you can mention with honesty.
- Invite the career transition consultant into the room before the meeting ends and make introductions.*

DON'T:

- Terminate the employee in public.
- Terminate the employee on special days (important holidays, employee's birthday, or anniversary day). In general, do not terminate on a Friday since it is difficult to connect with advisers and access support over the weekend.
- Engage in a lengthy debate with the employee over the decision to terminate.
- Respond to threats by the employee to go to a lawyer or to the union.
- Go to a termination meeting without a letter for the employee, reiterating the facts and explaining the support being offered.*
- Get angry or threaten the employee even if the employee is angry. Anger is a natural response for people who receive a termination order.

* Margaret Watters. (2003, Oct. 20). "The right and wrong way to deliver bad news." *Canadian HR Reporter*, p. 11 and 15.
Source: Adapted from Hari Das, *Performance Management*, 2003, p. 264. Pearson Education. Reprinted with permission of Pearson Education Canada.

issues before the employee leaves the location. It also offers an opportunity to return employee's back pay, benefits, and other properties and provide him or her with information about his or her record of employment. The notice and severance pay offered to the employee should at a minimum meet the standards established by the provincial employment standards. A checklist of key items to consider in the wake of termination is shown in Figure 10-11. Figure 10-12 provides an illustration of the notice and severance policies for one large manufacturing organization.

A landmark Supreme Court decision in 1997 (*Wallace v United Grain Growers*), underscored the importance of good faith and fair dealing in terminating employees. Similar cases have upheld this principle. For example, wrongly accusing an employee of theft and communicating this accusation to potential employers of a dismissed employee is not acceptable (*Trask v Terra Nova Motors Ltd*). Similarly, *Dunning v Royal Bank* pointed out that the employer has a duty to communicate the termination decision in a timely and transparent manner.[44]

FIGURE 10-11:   Checklist of Items to Consider at Termination

Employee Name:

Job Title:

Employee Identification Number:

Last working day:

Reason for Termination:

Were all the following items discussed with the employee?

Item		Comments if any (especially if box not checked)
Severance Pay	☐	
Pick-up of last pay cheque	☐	
Pay in lieu of vacation	☐	
Company pension plan	☐	
Unemployment Insurance	☐	
Group insurance	☐	
Other benefits/allowances	☐	
Stock ownership	☐	
Company life insurance	☐	
Profit sharing pay outs/bonus	☐	
Patent obligations/trade secrets	☐	
Advances outstanding from employee	☐	
Mail pick-up	☐	

Did the employee return all the following items?

Item	Yes	No	Comments
Door keys or sensor cards	☐	☐	
ID cards/badges	☐	☐	
Car keys	☐	☐	
Computer/accessories	☐	☐	
Cellular phone	☐	☐	
Credit cards	☐	☐	
Uniforms (if applicable)	☐	☐	
Office records/files	☐	☐	
Locker keys	☐	☐	

Name of the person preparing this sheet: _____   Date: _____

Source: Adapted from Hari Das, *Performance Management*, 2003, p. 265. Pearson Education. Reprinted with permission of Pearson Education Canada.

FIGURE 10-12:	**Termination Notice and Severance Pay Policies of One Large Manufacturer**	
Length of Service	**Notice**	**Severance Pay Offered**
Up to 3 months (probationary period)	1 day	None
3 months to 4 years	1 week's notice per year of service	None
5 years to 8 years	1 week's notice per year of service	1 week's pay per year of service
Over 8 years	8 weeks	26 weeks' pay

Source: Adapted from Hari Das, *Performance Management*, 2003, p. 265. Pearson Education. Reprinted with permission of Pearson Education Canada.

5. Outplacement assistance Increasingly, many progressive employers offer **outplacement** services, which help terminated employees find new jobs in other firms. These efforts may include providing office space, secretarial service, photocopying machines, long-distance phone calls, counselling, and referral services. More specifically, the human resource department can offer its expertise in the following ways:

- providing advice on how and where to look for a job
- offering assistance in updating resumes
- offering advice on skills and qualification gaps
- recommending counsellors for overcoming post-termination stress and trauma
- contacting outplacement agencies which can help the employee find alternate employment (with employee consent)

> **Outplacement:** services to help terminated employees find new jobs in other firms

For voluntary separations, an exit interview is important. **Exit interviews** provide useful insights into the strengths and weaknesses of the firm, with a particular focus on human resource practices and areas needing improvement. Since departing employees are more likely to provide honest assessments of working conditions, their feedback can help introduce additional supervisory training, improve working conditions, and revise recruitment and compensation policies. A sample exit interview form is shown in Figure 10-13.

> **Exit interviews:** meeting with the departing employee that provides insights into the strengths and weaknesses of the firm, with a particular focus on human resource practices and areas needing improvement

A 2004 survey of 2800 Canadian employees[45] found that a good benefits package was a key factor in employee decisions to quit a job, with 49% saying that a good benefits package would make them stay with their current job. Moreover, of those who had quit jobs, 25% reported that they'd done so for a better benefits package, 26% said it was due to lack of career growth potential, and 36% said it was because they believed they could get a better salary elsewhere

To conclude, rules for termination must be reasonable and consistently employed. Reasonableness of these rules is measured against these criteria:[46]

- The rules must be consistent with the provisions of the collective agreement between the firm and its union.
- The rules must be clear and unequivocal.
- The rules must be brought to the attention of the employee affected before the company acts on it.
- The employee concerned must have been notified that a breach of the rule could result in his or her discharge if the rule is used as a foundation for discharge.
- The rules should have been consistently enforced by the company since the time they were formulated.

FIGURE 10-13:   A Sample Exit Interview Form

Kanata Electronics
Exit Interview Form

Employee's Name _____   Date Hired   _____
Interviewed by   _____   Date Leaving _____
Supervisor   _____   Department   _____

1. What is your reason for leaving our firm?
2. What could we have done to keep you here?
3. Would you recommend Kanata Electronics to your friends as a place to work? Why?
4. Did you find the new job or did the employer reach you?
5. Are there things we could have done to make your job more fulfilling?
6. What are the things you liked about your job here? What things did you dislike?
7. What are some of your suggestions to make Kanata Electronics a better place to work?
8. What is your evaluation of the following? Use a scale of "poor," "fair," "good," "very good," and "excellent." (Note: ask for qualitative comments in each case)

   a) How we made you feel welcome when you joined us:
   b) How you were treated by your supervisor:
   c) How you were treated by your peers:
   d) Your working conditions:
   e) The salary we offer:
   f) The benefits we offer:
   g) The career opportunities our firm offers:
   h) The sense of accomplishment your work gave you:
   i) The opportunities to expand your skills and knowledge:

THANKS FOR YOUR CONTRIBUTIONS IN THE PAST. WE WISH YOU ALL THE BEST IN YOUR NEW POSITION!

The last provision is very important, since a firm must treat all its employees consistently. It also demonstrates the importance of keeping clear records of each employee offence and the way it was handled. One court case[47] underscores the importance of consistent management action in the case of discipline:

> MacMillan Bloedel dismissed an employee after the person was discovered smoking marijuana at work. The arbitrator recognized the employer's argument that this was a very serious offence. The employee involved had also known about the employer's commitment to a drug-free work setting. However, the union pointed out that the employer's past practice had been to suspend employees for 30 days for this offence. The arbitrator held that the employer has an obligation to serve notice of an intention to change its approach to a workplace rule, including the punishment involved. The employee was reinstated, and a 30-day suspension was substituted for the dismissal.

Even well-managed systems and practices may need to be adjusted to keep up with changing workforces and societal expectations. The next chapter deals with reviewing the staffing system to maintain its currency and effectiveness.

Implications for Practice

1. The information sent to the new hire should clarify the terms of the appointment and facilitate job acceptance and speedy arrival at work site by ensuring all necessary clearance.

2. Even the most qualified and competent new hire will require orientation and some initial training to familiarize them with the organizational culture and job duties. Hence, a sound and formal orientation program is important for all organizations.

3. Socialization is the continuing process through which an employee understands and accepts the values, norms, and beliefs held by others in the organization.

Because socialization shapes employee work habits, organizations should plan to communicate the values and mission of the organization to new hires.

4. Continuous employee development is a high priority in today's knowledge economy. Employers can choose strategies from cognitive, behavioural, and situational approaches.

5. Selecting employees to fill international openings requires great care, since expatriates have to be versatile, globally aware, culturally sensitive, and capable of managing decentralized operations and making in-roads into the new social milieu.

6. Organizations terminating employees must do so as humanely as possible and only as a last resort. In all instances, employers must follow due process and carry out the termination in a systematic manner.

7. For voluntary separations, employers should schedule exit interviews so that the organization can improve its internal procedures and working conditions.

8. For terminations, organizations should offer the departing employee outplacement assistance.

Key Terms for Review

360-degree career development,   *p. 323*

Behavioural approaches,   *p. 321*

Buddy system,   *p. 320*

Cognitive training,   *p. 321*

Deployment,   *p. 315*

Due process,   *p. 330*

Employee handbook,   *p. 319*

Exit interviews,   *p. 334*

Involuntary separations,   *p. 329*

Learning organization,   *p. 323*

Organizational culture,   *p. 319*

Outplacement,   *p. 334*

Progressive discipline,   *p. 329*

Situational approach,   *p. 322*

Socialization,   *p. 319*

Termination,   *p. 329*

Transnational teams,   *p. 328*

Voluntary separations,   *p. 329*

Wrongful dismissal,   *p. 329*

Discussion Questions

1. Discuss the orientation procedure that your college or university offered on your arrival. Did it include all the steps recommended in this chapter? What improvements would you recommend?

2. In an individualist society such as Canada, why should employers be concerned about the career development of their employees?

3. What factors should organizations consider when staffing international operations?

4. Discuss the steps in the event the organization has to terminate an employee.

Critical Thinking Questions

1. You were recently hired as the human resource manager in a small organization employing eighteen full-time employees and a few part-timers. Your company has been growing quite fast in the last few years; however, because the operations are seasonal, the company has been mainly using part-time employees. On arrival, you find that the part-timers receive very little orientation before they are put to work. When you mentioned this to a few supervisors, their typical response was: "We make sure that only the right folks are hired. If you hire the right person, you don't need a whole lot of showing around." What would your response be?

2. After graduation, you joined a large firm as a management trainee. Your goal is to one day become a senior executive of this company. What type of information would you need, and what

career development programs would you develop for yourself? (You may want to refer back to material in Chapter 5 on career choice and development.)

3. Your company is planning to expand operations abroad. Would the characteristics you require of the new employees be different if you were planning to initially place them in Boston? Would your answer be different if you were looking for people who would have to be located in Bangalore, India?

4. Michel Smith, a supervisor in the manufacturing plant of the company where you work as the human resource manager, caught Jim Moore drinking liquor during lunch break on company premises. Michel wants to fire Jim to make him an example for others. What advice would you give to Michel?

Web Research

Search the web for cases on employee dismissal in two different countries. Collect at least ten cases covering two different countries. What new insights due they provide? Do you note any differences across countries?

CASE INCIDENT

Highland Tastes*

Steve McDonald, the manager of Highland Tastes, was at his wits end. He had just finished talking to Michael, one of the waiters at Highland Tastes, the small restaurant that he managed. "It's always one thing or the other with Michael. I wish I had never hired him!" thought Steve. "For now, I'll ask Cindy to take the birthday cake over to Table 6." But he knew he had to find a solution to this problem.

Highland Tastes is a family-owned restaurant located in Sydney, N.S. It had been started twenty years ago by Steve's father, Russell McDonald. It had taken a while for Russell to get his restaurant on a firm footing, but now it was a thriving business. Steve took over from his father just two years ago.

Two months ago, he had hired Michael as a waiter. Michael is a Jehovah's Witness. As a Jehovah's Witness, he does not believe in celebrating birthdays. One of the customers at Table 6 was celebrating his birthday, and as was the custom at Highland Tastes, a small complementary birthday cake was to be served to the customer. So Steve, not knowing about Michael's beliefs, had taken out a chocolate birthday cake and had handed it over to Michael. Michael had said very politely "I can take the cake over, but I will not wish the customer Happy Birthday."

Steve had been shocked. "Why not?" he had asked Michael. Michael responded that it was against his religious beliefs.

"I am not asking you to sing Happy Birthday," Steve had argued. But Michael had been adamant. That's when Steve had decided to ask Cindy to take the cake over to the table.

This was not the first time that Michael's religious beliefs had caused friction in the workplace. One month previously, at Christmas time, all the employees had gathered together to put up a Christmas tree and decorate the dining room. Michael, who was on duty, had been asked to pitch in. He had refused because his religious beliefs did not permit him to celebrate Christmas. Some of the other employees had been really upset at his refusal to join in. Thomas, one of the other waiters, had almost come to blows with Michael over the issue. Steve had stepped in and calmed Thomas down. While he had found it hard to accept Michael's behaviour, he had told Thomas and the other employees that no one should be forced to participate in a religious custom. "After all, Thomas," Steve had said, "you wouldn't like it if you were forced to participate in a Hindu or Muslim festival, would you?" Thomas had backed off; but Steve knew that tension remained between Michael and the others ever since.

"Not participating in Christmas—I can understand that", thought Steve. "But this is different. It has nothing to do with any particular religion. It is just a friendly gesture. Why can't he be flexible? After all, he is from the area and knew birthday celebrations were a tradition at this restaurant. He should have told me," thought Steve. But at the same time, he also knew that Michael was a good worker. He was pleasant and friendly, and customers seemed to like him. He was willing to work odd shifts and never complained when he had work on a long weekend. "I wonder what will come up next," thought Steve. "Maybe I should fire him."

Questions

1. *Would refusing to wish a customer "Happy Birthday" constitute valid grounds for dismissal?*

2. *What would you do if you were in Steve's position? Why?*

3. *Could this situation have been avoided? How?*

*This case was prepared by Mallika Das of Department of Business Administration and Tourism and Hospitality Management, Mount Saint Vincent University, as a basis for class discussion. Case reproduced with the permission of the author.

CASE

Kanata Food Distributors: Managing Employee Relations*

Note: This case continues from Chapter 9: Kanata Food Distributors. Review the case background in Chapters 1, 2, 3, 4, 5, 6, 7, 8, and 9 before examining this case.

Kanata Food Distributors has embarked on a rapid expansion plan which requires a significant number of additional management staff (see previous chapters for more background). A few senior supervisors and employees were promoted to fill the new managerial and supervisory positions. However, this has also brought in a few new challenges. Some of the employees who were not promoted seemed disgruntled; and there were rumours that at least a few were planning to leave. Moreover, some of the new managers and supervisors have had problems making timely and correct decisions. Coincidentally, this has also been the time when a number of new employee-related and disciplinary problems have cropped up. Many supervisors have routinely approached the human resource manager seeking advice on these problems, causing a major strain on the HR staff, who have to handle these problems along with their routine duties. Here are samples of the problems reaching the human resource department in the recent past (for which decisions have not yet been made):

- An employee hired nine months ago as an assistant to the purchasing officer had indicated in her resume that she held a bachelor's degree in nutrition. However, recently, it has come to the attention of the supervisor that she had in fact, dropped out of the university after her second year. He wants to fire her but is unsure whether he can.

- An employee hired last year to the firm's transport section had indicated during a job interview that he had six years of work experience in a previous courier company. However, he had only really worked for five years and had been earning a thousand dollars less per year than he had claimed. When confronted, he claimed that he had forgotten the exact details, since he had not been employed for the last four years, during which time he had been volunteering in Africa. The supervisor feels that the person lied and deserved to be fired.

- One of the supervisors in the financial services department took a file home for the weekend. The file contained sensitive details about the company's market share, financial strategies, and budgets. Unfortunately, the employee lost the file while travelling in the rapid transit system. The manager wants to take disciplinary action against him, since the company policy does not allow anyone to remove company property from the premises, including records. Further, if the documents fall into the hands of the competition, they could cause considerable damage to the firm's success. The employee claims that in the past, other supervisors have taken files home to work on them and that this behaviour does not constitute "theft."

- Three employees in the baking division have been caught colluding and "writing-off" stale cakes and pastries. However, instead of throwing them away, they have been selling them to a corner store for a fraction of the retail price. The amount involved came to about $400 a month. When asked, the employees commented, "You are going to throw the darn things away! What if we give them to someone who can sell them?"

The human resource manager is away, and her assistant is not quite sure what advice to give to the various supervisors involved at this time.

Questions

1. *What is your evaluation of each situation described above? What recommendations would you make and why?*

2. *Would you make any other recommendations to the company? What? Elaborate the steps involved.*

*Case written by Professor Hari Das of Saint Mary's University, Halifax. All rights retained by the author, © 2005.

PART 4

EVALUATION OF THE STAFFING FUNCTION

Staffing systems, no matter how effective and valid, have to be periodically reviewed to ensure their continued relevance to emerging realities. The needs of user departments have to be monitored on an on-going basis to ensure client satisfaction. The final part of this book looks at the important task of auditing a staffing department and its activities in order to review and enhance the department's overall effectiveness.

11 STAFFING AUDIT AND SYSTEM IMPROVEMENT

> *"Several studies...[report] that a strong correlation exists between improved human resources management and a company's financial performance. With so much at stake, why is it that an investment decision about human assets still generally receive much less scrutiny than one about capital? I believe an important factor has been the comparative lack of measurement techniques for assessing the effectiveness and results of human resources interventions."*

Larry Morden[1]

CHAPTER OBJECTIVES

After studying this chapter, you should be able to:

- Discuss the importance of auditing staffing functions

- Outline the steps in a staffing audit

- Discuss approaches to auditing and the methods used for data collection

- Discuss the contents of the staffing audit report

- Discuss the characteristics of a self-renewing organization

Fred is the manager of a fast food franchise located two blocks from an inner-city high school with predominantly disadvantaged youngsters. Sales to students comprise a large part of his sales. Fred's primary source of labour is students. Consequently, many of Fred's hires need confidence-building and extra training because they are young and from disadvantaged homes. The extra training time drives up his labour costs. The high-school customers come in throughout the day and litter the eating area. Maintaining a clean restaurant is difficult without driving away his main source of business. Despite his best efforts, Fred gets marked down on "cleanliness" in every standardized appraisal of the franchise. At night, the roughness of the neighbourhood necessitates a security guard to walk and monitor the premises. While this helps the business, it also drives up overhead "costs"—another dimension on which Fred is being evaluated by the franchise. Fred invariably gets the lowest pay increase each year.[2]

Consider Fred's dilemma: to get higher performance ratings, he has to keep the premises cleaner and overheads lower; however, doing just that will cut into his overall performance and success. If he hires his workers from other segments of the society, his training costs may come down. Relocating to another place may obviate the need for a full-time security guard, but it will also adversely affect his revenues. The very actions that help him score high ratings on some performance dimensions may actually spell disaster in the longer term.

It is not unusual to see such inconsistencies and contradictions even in well-designed staffing systems. Only continuous review and reassessment of the system can help reduce or eliminate such inconsistencies. This chapter discusses the various to tools for reviewing the staffing system. But first, we must examine factors that make reviews essential.

WHY AUDIT A STAFFING SYSTEM?

Staffing system audit: formal report evaluating all human resource activities, systems, and procedures connected with staffing

A **staffing system audit** evaluates all human resource activities, systems, and procedures connected with staffing. It gives feedback about the staffing function to human resource specialists while simultaneously informing line managers about the organizational and employee impact of their staffing-related decisions. An examination of staffing practices may uncover better ways for the HR department to contribute to organizational and employee objectives. If the evaluation is done properly, it can also build support between staffing personnel and operating managers. Consider the following example:

Kim Chan: (Plant Manager)	I thought that as staffing specialists, you'd know the best way to plan and monitor human resources. Why the audit, then?
Matteo Galetti: (Staffing specialist)	We realize that there is always room for improvement. In fact, the reason we are doing this review is to check our methods and learn how we can better serve managers like yourself.
Kim Chan:	What do you hope to discover? I thought with all those monthly and quarterly reports about absenteeism and turnover, you already have all the necessary information.
Matteo Galetti:	First, we want to see if our present selection procedures are being followed. We need uniformity in job analysis, human resource planning, selection, and deployment practices. If there is no uniformity, employees may perceive inequity, which can cause poor morale and performance. If there is inconsistency in the practices, we want to find out why. Maybe managers and employees don't understand our procedures. Or maybe our methods aren't practical and should be changed. Second, we are checking to ensure compliance with laws such as human rights, safety, and others. This audit is not a 'witch hunt.' We are simply trying to improve our performance.

As the above dialogue indicates, several benefits result from a staffing audit. Figure 11-1 lists the major ones. An audit reminds managers like Kim of the contribution made by staffing function. It also creates a more professional image of the larger human resource department among managers and human resource specialists.

Indeed, a number of internal and external factors make frequent staffing reviews necessary. Four of these are discussed below:

FIGURE 11-1:   **Benefits of a Staffing Audit**

- Helps align staffing practices with the strategic success of the larger organization
- Provides specific, verifiable data on contributions of the staffing system
- Improves the professional image of the staffing function and HR department
- Clarifies duties and responsibilities of staffing specialists
- Stimulates uniformity of hiring and deployment practices
- Finds critical staffing problems
- Ensures timely compliance with legal requirements
- Reduces human resource costs through more effective procedures
- Helps redesign jobs to maximize efficiency and employee satisfaction and eliminate redundant job specifications

---

1. ENVIRONMENTAL CHANGES

All organizations and their parts are influenced by changes in their environment. The staffing function is no exception. Changes in technology, the legal system, economy, and society profoundly affect staffing practices.

An organization's decision to install sophisticated computer systems or automate some of its activities means that the qualifications of employees hired in the future would need to be different from those of employees already hired. Moreover, new employment laws mean modifying job specifications and hiring criteria. Finally, changes in the demographic and ethnic composition of the surrounding community may require new hiring predictors.

2. ORGANIZATIONAL ENTROPY

Almost all systems have entropic tendencies. **Entropy** is the tendency of a system to run down over time. In the absence of continuous vigilance and follow-up, communications break down, employees make mistakes, and systems and rules take on too much importance. **Organizational atrophy** results when organizations lose muscle tone, and their internal operating systems break down.[3] A principal cause of atrophy is the "success breeds failure syndrome." Past successes often make organizations feel invincible, and they stop adapting to customers, employees, and the public. They start applying standard procedures and policies indiscriminately, even when novel responses are called for, thus reducing their effectiveness. Unless systems are continuously monitored, they ultimately break down or slowly die away.

Entropy: the tendency of a system to run down over time

Organizational atrophy: the tendency of organizations to lose muscle tone and of internal operating systems to break down

3. STRATEGIC, STRUCTURAL, OR TACTICAL CHANGES

To respond to economic turbulence, most organizations adapt by changing their strategic or tactical plans. Some firms also have to restructure their organization or activities. Whatever the response, any change in strategy, structure, or tactics affect the roles, required competencies, and behaviours of employees, which in turn necessitates the identification of new performance criteria and hiring practices.

For example, a decision to change strategy from cost leadership to differentiation has profound implications on new hiring. Under a cost leadership, employees need only a narrow range of skills; whereas in a differentiation strategy, they need to be highly skilled. If the strategy changes, the type of employees hired by the firm in future will change as well.

FIGURE 11-2:	Indices of Human Resource Management Effectiveness in Canadian Organizations	
Index	**Organizations Across Canada (Except Atlantic Canada) (n = 650)**	**Organizations in Four Atlantic Provinces (n = 1277)**
Productivity	4.38	4.38
Employee satisfaction	4.02	4.21
Employee commitment	4.33	4.38
Grievance rate	2.02	1.90
Absenteeism	2.68	2.28
Turnover	1.99	2.11
Employee quality of life	4.15	4.16

Note: All items are measured on a scale of 1 = *very low*; 6 = *very high*.
Source: Terry Wagar. (1993, October). *Human Resource Management and Labour Relations: A Study of Canadian Organizations.* Halifax: Saint Mary's University, pp. 10-13.

In addition, if a firm decides to move towards a team-based structure, its leadership behaviours will have to change, as well as its hiring criteria for leaders, so that all leaders in the new structure will be able to inspire team members.

4. DEMOGRAPHIC CHANGES

The workforce composition in most organizations continually changes. The percentage of women, minorities, and the physically challenged in the workforce is increasing, requiring new hiring and deployment practices. The level of education of workers is also on the rise, with associated increases in workplace expectations. Consider this example:

> The high percentage of knowledge workers in most organizations necessitates changes in performance criteria for supervisory personnel. The old notion of leaders being directive, "take-charge" individuals is no longer valid for many modern firms. Instead, today's leaders have to inspire employees and act as catalysts to bring out the best in individual workers and teams. This means that organizations must assess supervisor applicants for their ability to inspire and direct, rather than to control and command.

Staffing audits may also highlight areas where current human resource management functions in a firm excel and where they are weak. Comparing in-house practices with industry benchmarks and similar organizations can provide insights into the effectiveness of staffing practices. Figure 11-2 summarizes the results of two large-scale research studies that collected indices of human resource management effectiveness in Canadian organizations. Indices such as these not only provide benchmarks for comparison purposes but also help initiate improvements in selection practices.

STEPS IN A STAFFING AUDIT

A staffing audit involves four major steps:

1. Defining the scope of the audit
2. Choosing the research approach

FIGURE 11-3:   An Overview of the Staffing Audit Process

SCOPE →	APPROACH →	COLLECTION →	REPORTING
1. Alignment with corporate strategy	1. Comparative	1. Interviews	1. Strategic
		2. Surveys	
2. Systems and Structure	2. Compliance	3. Field experiments	2. Operational
		4. Company records	
3. Impact on performance	3. Objective-based	5. External information	

Source: Adapted from Hari Das, *Performance Management*, 2003, p. 276. Pearson Education. Reprinted with permission of Pearson Education Canada.

3.   Identifying the data collection method

4.   Preparing the data analysis, evaluation, and report

Figure 11-3 shows these steps, which are discussed in detail below.

SCOPE OF THE STAFFING AUDIT

The scope of an audit extends beyond the staffing department's actions. The department does not operate in isolation. Its success depends on how well it performs and how well its programs are carried out by others in the organization. Consider how supervisors in one firm reduced the effectiveness of their staffing process:

> To assess the promotion potential of employees, Calgary Petroleum Company used a behaviourally anchored rating scale that had high predictive validity. Supervisors were expected to spend at least one hour rating and counselling employees on ways to improve performance in the future. To become a work supervisor, an employee needed a minimum of three years of performance improvement. However, in practice, this rarely occurred. Most supervisors spent less than twenty minutes on the activity, with the result that employees received very little feedback on their performance. Employee performance showed no consistent improvement over time, which disqualified many of them for promotion. Many employees blamed the rating scale and promotion appraisal procedure for their lack of promotions.

An audit uncovered the problems with the program and led to additional training for supervisors in employee appraisal and counselling. If the audit had not uncovered this problem, employee dissatisfaction might have grown worse.

As the above example illustrates, "people problems" are seldom confined to the staffing department or even the larger human resource department. Over time, staffing audits have expanded such that they transcend the concerns of a single department and its operating managers. In practice, the scope of the audit typically focuses on alignment among corporate strategy, staffing systems and structure, and performance outcomes.

Alignment with the corporate strategy While staffing specialists do not set corporate strategy, they strongly determine its success. If the calibre and behaviours of hires are not aligned with corporate strategy, a firm's competitiveness is reduced. Whether the company stresses superior marketing (McCain Foods), service (Maritime Life), innovation (Nortel), or low-cost operations (Canadian Tire), staffing is affected. More specifically, the following staffing issues need to be examined in detail:

- Are the hiring and promotion criteria consistent with corporate strategy?

- Do the performance criteria and standards align with the firm's strategy and competitive advantage?

- Is the staffing system supportive of excellence?

- Are supervisors competent in hiring hew employees and assessing current employees validly to further corporate goals?

- Are the firm's internal human resource deployment practices supportive of the organizational strategy?

Although the HR department may lack the necessary resources to do a thorough audit the corporate strategy and its fit with the external environment, it must still do so. Staffing professionals must audit the department's policies and practices against the firm's strategic plans.

Articles on strategy, mission, and HR systems:
www.chrs.net

An organization that employed a low-cost strategy employed students and other part-time workers, often offering little more than minimum wages. But eventually, the firm changed its strategy in favour of growth through aggressive acquisitions. Yet several managers continued the old practice of hiring low-wage employees, even though the firm's new rapid-growth strategy required highly skilled, longer-term employees. An audit revealed high turnover and low morale among employees who did not have adequate skills to meet the new work demands. Based on the audit results, the organization implemented a new training program to upgrade the skill levels of employees. The hiring policy was also revised to focus on permanent, highly skilled employees who could easily fit into a growing organization.

Audit of staffing systems and structure

Audits should logically begin with a review of the staffing department's work. Figure 11-4 lists some of the questions to consider. As Figure 11-4 shows, an audit should focus on three areas: planning, execution, and control. These three areas of the audit supplement and integrate with one another. As such, no single area should be overemphasized in the audit. In general, an audit touches on every topic discussed in this book.

Admittedly, an audit of every activity is time-consuming. The criteria used to evaluate specific staffing functions, such as recruiting and selection, are discussed in earlier

Articles on staffing systems and human resource performance:
www.p-management.com
www.hr-guide.com

FIGURE 11-4: **Sample Questions to Assess Staffing System and Structure**

Planning

- What are the specific objectives of the staffing department? What criteria (e.g., employee turnover, employee performance, and costs) will be used to assess its contribution to the larger organization?
- How systematic is human resource planning? How appropriate is the planning process, given the firm's strategy and environments? How responsive is the process to changes?
- Who is responsible for its execution? What are the expected outcomes of each position?
- How do individual objectives reflect and support organizational strategies? How well integrated are these objectives amongst themselves?

Execution

- What policies and procedures seem to support the execution of the staffing plans? How appropriate are the recruitment, selection, orientation, and deployment procedures?
- Are the systems and procedures mutually consistent? Are the action plans reasonable and attainable?
- How reliable and valid are the staffing procedures? Are the predictors and criteria reviewed frequently for their continued relevance?
- Do all employees know what is expected of them? How does the department ensure that they do?

chapters. Because these criteria are both numerous and interrelated, large organizations use sampling techniques to identify tasks and positions to audit in each time period. Some large organizations also have full-time audit teams similar to those who conduct financial audits. These teams are especially useful when the human resource department is decentralized into regional or field offices. Through audits, the organization can maintain consistency in its practices.

Audit of managerial compliance An audit also reviews how well managers comply with staffing policies and procedures. If managers ignore policies or violate employee relations laws, the audit will uncover these errors so that timely corrective action can be taken.

> A woman was denied a job in a large, diversified firm because her husband was already employed in the same branch of the firm. After a complaint to the human resource department, the staffing officer intervened and asked the hiring manager for an explanation. The manager was under the impression that the company had a policy of not hiring relatives of existing staff. The staffing department explained to him that neither a formal policy nor past practices in the firm supported such a position. Further, such an action could be criticized for discriminating against a person on the basis of marital status. When a new vacancy emerged in the unit within a few weeks, the manager hired the woman for the position.

Besides assuring compliance, the audit can improve the staffing department's image and contribution to the company. Operating managers may gain a higher respect for the department when an audit seeks their views. If the comments of managers lead to action, these managers will regard the HR department as responsive to their needs and effective in achieving organizational objectives. Consider how one staffing department improved its image and effectiveness:

> When an audit team conducted several interviews with divisional managers of a large food processing unit with three processing plants, they discovered a pattern in the comments. Most managers believed that the staffing department was communicating the need for valid job interviews; however, the staffing department made no effort to train the managers to conduct interviews. The result was that many newly hired employees did not have adequate skills to carry out their duties. Further, although the firm was committed to diversity, the proportion of visible minorities and physically challenged employees in the workforce was still very small. The managers felt that an organization-wide training program in conducting effective interviews would better equip the supervisors and section managers to hire employees. In her next budget, the manager of the staffing department sought funds for a two-day workshop on interviewing for all junior managers. Later feedback indicated that the divisional managers appreciated the department's responsiveness. What is more, within a year, the quality of new hires increased, as indicated by their productivity and work quality levels. In a few years, the proportion of visible minorities and physically challenged employees in the firm's workforce had also shown a remarkable increase.

Audit of performance As mentioned in Chapter 1, an effective staffing department helps the firm achieve its mission by introducing methods to attract and utilize valuable human capital. These methods should result in benefits to both employees and the larger organization, preparing the firm for the global economy, rapidly changing technology, and a diverse workforce.

For auditing the performance of individual employees and teams, organizations can use the methods discussed in Chapter 2. For auditing organizational performance, a team must examine major issues, such as profitability and productivity gain, as well as less tangible outcomes (see Figure 2-3 on page 36 for popular organizational goals and sample measures for each). Figure 11-5 shows sample measures to assess the performance of a hamburger chain. Note that several of these measures have a direct relationship to the effectiveness of staffing function.

FIGURE 11-5:   Sample Measures to Assess the Performance of a Fast Food Hamburger Chain

Inputs
- Quality of raw materials used
- Qualifications and competence levels of employees hired
- Selection ratio (i.e., number of applications for each job vacancy) for various jobs
- Sophistication of the kitchen equipment used
- Cost of raising capital when needed

Processes
- Productivity levels
- Number of hamburgers/other products which don't meet quality standards
- Employee absenteeism rates
- Employee turnover
- Input:output (or efficiency) ratio for products and processes
- Time taken to produce products

Outputs
- Profitability
- Market share
- Number of new products introduced
- Employee satisfaction and morale
- Number of new socially responsive initiatives
- Innovation; ability to adapt to new challenges

RESEARCH APPROACHES TO AUDITS

A staffing audit may be done using a variety of research approaches. Sometimes the "research" is little more than an informal investigation or fact-finding effort. At other times, the approach may be advanced, relying on sophisticated research designs and statistics.[4] Whether informal or rigorous, the research seeks contributions from the organization. The three most common research approaches are the comparative approach, the compliance approach, and the objective-based approach. Figure 11-6 summarizes the benchmarks in each approach.[5]

Comparative approach:
comparing results with those of another division or with the staffing department

Comparative approach
Perhaps the simplest form of research is the **comparative approach**. It uses the staffing department or function in another firm as a model. The audit team then compares its results or procedures with those of the other organization. This approach is often used to compare the results of specific staffing activities or programs and their relation to costs, selection ratio, qualifications of hires, absence, turnover, and salary data. This approach also makes sense when a new selection or recruiting procedure is being tried for the first time.

> For example, when Alberta Gas Exploration Ltd introduced a diversity training program for its supervisors to encourage hiring of visible minorities, it copied major features of a long-running similar program at another local firm. Later, an audit compared the results of the two programs, which helped Alberta Gas to remove bugs from its training program.

Sometimes, the opinions of an outside expert may help evaluate the department or one of its programs. Standards set by a consultant or by published research findings serve as benchmarks for the audit team.

FIGURE 11-6: Popular Benchmarks in Staffing Audits

Approach	Typical Benchmarks Used
Comparative Approach	1. Comparable firm's performance
	2. General industry standards
	3. Judgements of an expert
	4. Company historical data
	5. Other external standards if available
Compliance Approach	1. Legal requirements
	2. Company policies and rules
	3. Company ethical code
	4. Minimum regulations in the industry (e.g., criteria imposed by safety standards)
Objectives-based Approach	1. System or HR Department objectives
	2. Strategic goals of the firm

For example, a well-respected professor in human resource management with considerable practical experience was invited by Nova Scotia Food Processors to evaluate its employee staffing systems and practices. After a detailed review, the professor concluded that the job specifications and hiring criteria for several jobs, especially in the firm's new automated plant, were outdated. Improvements in the interview procedures were also suggested. A comparison of supervisory attitudes and performance levels of new hires before and after the change showed that the firm had benefited by these changes.

Another approach is to develop statistical measures of performance based on the company's existing information system. For example, research into the company's records on productivity, wastage, and absenteeism and turnover rates can indicate how well the staffing department meets key corporate objectives. Figure 11-7 lists some useful indicators for evaluating the effectiveness of key staffing functions. Organizations using this statistical approach usually supplement it with comparisons to external information, which they gather from other firms and express as ratios:

> Nova Scotia Food Processors, which has a workforce of 300 employees, had to hire 45 employees on average each year to replace those who quit. The firm recognized that its turnover rate of 15% was significantly higher than the industry. Analysis of company records also indicated that the quit rates had increased in the last two years, while the firm had been changing its recruitment sources. Based on the findings, the management decided to investigate this increase. Meanwhile, management expanded its sources of recruits so that it could find new employees.

Setting performance standards and evaluating performance pose special challenges in small businesses, since many do not have elaborate staffing systems. The day-to-day activities of managing and improving employee performance assume great importance. To maintain high employee productivity, reviews of staffing processes must happen almost continuously. The comparative approach to a staffing audit is particularly helpful in small businesses. Managers must assess the effectiveness of current staffing procedures by looking at concrete indicators, as well as by observing employee behaviours. Some questions to ask in this context include the following:

- What is the selection ratio of our unit compared to similar firms?

- Do we get high-calibre applicants, or are most of the applicants mediocre?

FIGURE 11-7:   Indices for Measuring Staffing System Effectiveness

Recruitment

- Total number of applications received from each recruitment source within a set time period
- Time required to get applications
- Time elapsed before filling job positions
- Costs per person hired
- Ratio of number of job offers to job applications

Selection

- Selection ratio
- Productivity records of new hires (for all selection methods used)
- Supervisory satisfaction with performance of new hires
- Training costs of newer employees over time and in different selection methods
- Turnover rates for new hires
- Absenteeism rates for new hires
- Job satisfaction/morale measures of new hires
- Costs of selection procedures per position and over time

Orientation

- Reactions of new employees about orientation program
- Measures of satisfaction of new hires (organizational, job, etc.)
- Turnover rates of new hires
- Absenteeism rates of new hires
- Productivity rates of new hires and the time taken to reach normal performance

Control

- What systems currently exist to ensure proper execution of plans? What records, information, and procedures are used for this purpose?
- Who is responsible for monitoring the execution of these plans? Does the person have enough authority, information, and resources to do the job well?
- What plan of action exists to monitor deviations and take corrective actions? How timely and effective are the corrective actions?

- Are our employees capable of taking up new challenges? Are they promotable to more responsible positions?

- How do employee turnover figures of our firm compare to those of similar firms? To the industry in general?

- How does our current absenteeism rate compare to the industry and to our own past records?

- What are employee attitudes towards their jobs? Are improvements needed?

- Do we have to spend a lot of resources to train entry-level workers to do their jobs satisfactorily?

- How expensive is our recruitment and selection system? Compared to other similar firms? Compared to past years?

- Do our new employees make a lot of mistakes? How long do they take to reach acceptable performance levels for quantity and quality?

- Are our employees innovative? Do they come up with new ideas to improve our firm's effectiveness?

- How do our compensation levels compare with the industry? Do we have to offer a significant premium to attract high calibre employees? Why?

Compliance approach
The **compliance approach** reviews past recruitment, hiring, and deployment practices to determine if those actions followed company policies and legal requirements. Often the audit team reviews a sample of job descriptions, specifications, and employment tests, interviews, promotions, appraisals, discipline forms, and past statistics. The purpose of the review is to ensure that field offices and operating managers comply with internal rules and legal regulations:

> An internal audit of the interview process used at Nova Scotia Food Processors revealed that the department managers followed the correct procedures. But the audit team noticed that the interview records kept by many lower-level work supervisors had comments written in the margins referring to personal data that were not supposed to be asked about, such as marital status, ages of children, and race-related matters. Because the audit noticed this discriminatory practice, lower-level managers were informed of the laws governing interviews and instructed to not ask questions that were discriminatory in nature.

For global organizations, uniform human resource policies and practices throughout world operations may be desirable, but they may also be hard to achieve. Different countries and cultures value different attributes in their employees. Geographical and cultural distances pose severe communication problems for expatriate managers in hiring, job specifications, and recruitment and selection practices. In addition, the differing legal frameworks in each country mean that the same practice are not acceptable everywhere. Thus, staffing practices must first comply with local laws, as well as home-office human resource policies and ethical codes.

Compliance approach: reviewing past practices to determine if those actions followed company policies and legal requirements

Objectives-based approach
The **objectives-based approach** compares specific objectives with actual achievements to identify appropriate corrective actions.[6]

> For example, supervisors may set a goal of reducing staffing costs or improving employee productivity. Then these objectives can be compared against actual achievements. The audit would evaluate the trends in this area.

No single audit approach works for all situations. More commonly, audit teams use several strategies, depending on the specific staffing activities under evaluation. Whatever the approach, audit teams involve managers in developing relevant criteria for evaluating staffing functions.

Objectives-based approach: comparing specific objectives with actual achievements to identify appropriate corrective actions

RESEARCH DESIGN AND DATA COLLECTION METHODS

For all audits, audit teams must collect data about staffing system and activities. Typically, they will need several data collection tools or sources, since each tool or source provides only one type of information. Popular data collection tools include interviews, surveys, experiments, company records, and external information.

Interviews
Interviews, or face-to-face meetings with employees and managers, collect information based on a list of questions (usually called an "interview schedule"). Comments from managers and employees help the audit team find areas needing improvement. When the criticisms are valid, the audit team recommends changes. But when the criticisms are invalid, the HR department may have to educate the organization about the procedures being questioned:

Interviews: face-to-face meetings with employees and managers to collect information based on a list of questions (often called an "interview schedule")

> Linda McDonald served as a member of an audit team at Canadian Electronics Ltd., a medium-sized manufacturer and distributor of electronics, computer software, and

telecommunications equipment, which was quickly expanding into foreign markets. She interviewed several managers, who complained that the frequent updating of job descriptions and specifications was a problem. They said that this task took away time from other important activities. Linda understood their concerns. She explained that the unique nature of the industry coupled with the fast growth of the firm necessitated frequent hiring and training of staff. Unless job duties and specifications were clearly identified, the training may not be properly carried out; wrong hiring may in fact result in greater loss of time and inefficiency for various departments than updating job descriptions. Although many managers still disliked the situation, the audit interview helped them understand the need for the frequent changes.

Interviews are helpful in assessing a firm's internal culture. Such cultural audits aim to gauge the prevailing organizational culture and the way it is revealed to members. While in-depth interviews can provide useful information, note that culture is often invisible, even to close observers; and hence audit teams must assess it using tools and significant samples over a relatively long period of time.

Sometimes, instead of individual interviews, an audit teams uses group or team interviews and focus groups. In a **focus group** of eight to twelve knowledgeable employees, an unbiased discussion leader guides unstructured and free-flowing discussion about staffing-related matters. After the initial warm-up, when members introduce themselves, the discussion leader (usually called the "moderator") sets the ground rules for the discussion and introduces the topic. Usually focus groups last from one to two hours. A typical approach is to have the group talk about staffing activities in the company and the specific strategies or methods used by the department in achieving organizational goals. From this discussion, the discussion leader may direct the group to talk about how they feel about the staffing practices and then move on to a discussion of what changes and improvements they would like to see. The focus group session at Windsor Family Credit Union follows this general pattern:

> Windsor Family Credit Union, located in Windsor, Ontario, employs 115 full-time and part-time employees. Getting the best people and retaining them is a top human resource concern in the organization. In order to achieve this goal, the management attempts to understand the core employee values and priorities and respond to them in a timely fashion. For this reason, the organization conducts focus groups with employees within 18 months of their arrival. They also organize a CEO-advisory committee, a group of 12 employees who have breakfast once every quarter with the president to discuss issues of importance.[7]

In most focus groups, the moderator intervenes in group discussion only to introduce topics of importance that may not have come up spontaneously, to move on when a topic has been exhausted, or to bring the discussion back to the area of interest when it has wandered into irrelevant areas. These discussions are usually taped so that the moderator can concentrate on keeping the discussion on track without fear of losing important information. To be effective, moderators must blend into the group and be accepted as members, rather than as directors who asks questions that others are expected to answer.

Surveys

Surveys Many companies supplement interviews with surveys. A **survey** gathers information from a sample of persons through a questionnaire. Surveys can be done through office mail, Canada Post, telephone, fax, or more recently, the Internet. Unlike interviews, which are time-consuming, costly, and limited to only a few people, surveys offer a broader, more accurate picture of employee perceptions. Mail questionnaires can reach a geographically dispersed sample simultaneously at a relatively low cost. For this reason, surveys are particularly attractive to large organizations operating across the country or across nations. Respondents can fill out questionnaires at their convenience, thus increasing the probability of response. Also, the anonymity offered by questionnaires may result in more candid answers than face-to-face interviews, especially if the survey includes any sensitive or socially undesirable information. Telephone and Internet surveys can improve the speed of data collection significantly. They are also extremely cheap compared to interviews.

Focus group: an unstructured discussion of staffing-related issues, by eight to twelve knowledgeable employees guided by a moderator

Survey: information gathered from a sample of persons through a questionnaire

Information on employee surveys:
www.hr-guide.com

Surveys can be several pages long and cover information on several staffing-related topics. However, to be effective, a survey does not need to be long. Sometimes, even a short survey of newly hired employees, such as the one shown in Figure 11-8, may capture important aspects of staffing. Naturally, when more information is needed, questionnaires are longer. When longer questionnaires are used, the answers are grouped into areas of analysis to find out where employee attitudes are high or low. The survey results may also be compared across departments, to other similar firms, to past survey findings, or to corporate objectives. Further analysis may identify problems with specific supervisors, employee subgroups or job positions.

George Brown College of Applied Arts and Technology, which has three campuses in Ontario and employs 1100 full-time employees, uses student surveys to gauge the effectiveness of faculty selection function. Between 2003 and 2005, the college had to hire about 400 people, mostly to replace retiring employees. Through annual student satisfaction surveys, the college assesses the quality of instruction they receive, which in turn indicates the college's success in hiring qualified faculty.[8]

Surveys give valuable feedback about changes needed to staffing procedures. Trends in the responses suggest whether specific challenges are becoming more or less important to employees.

FIGURE 11-8: A Short Survey of New-Employee Attitudes on Staffing Procedures

Welcome to Maple Leaf Grocers! We are delighted to have you as part of our team. As you may have already noted, we try to continuously improve our HR systems and procedures. For this reason, we would like to know what you think of our staffing activities. Please indicate the degree of your agreement or disagreement with each statement by checking the appropriate boxes. Do not omit any item. Do not write your name or other identifying information anywhere on this form. Please return the completed form to the Staffing Department, or drop it in the box kept outside the Human Resources Department WITHIN ONE WEEK. Thank you!

	Strongly Agree	Agree	Undecided	Disagree	Strongly Disagree
1. The job description in the recruitment ad accurately reflected the duties I was hired to carryout on a day-to-day basis.					
2. All the personnel with whom I interacted during the hiring process were courteous.					
3. The questions in employment tests were clear and unambiguous.					
4. During the job interview, the interviewer made efforts to ease my tension.					
5. The orientation procedures helped me understand organizational policies and procedures.					
6. My supervisor actively helped me ease into my duties and get to know my colleagues.					
7. Overall, I believe that the hiring procedures in this firm are fair to everyone.					

Any additional comments:

_____

_____

_____

Gender: **Age:**   Under 40   Over 40

Date: _____

Experiments

Experimentation is yet another powerful tool available to an audit team. In an **experiment**, conditions are controlled so that one or more variables can be manipulated in order to test a hypothesis. The ideal research design is a field experiment that allows the staffing department to compare an experimental and a control group under realistic conditions.

> For example, the department may implement a training program in interviewing techniques for half of a division's supervisors. This half is the experimental group. The control group is the supervisors who do not receive training. The organization later compares the quality of hires by both groups. If the experimental group has significantly better employees, this is evidence that the training program was effective.

Experiments provide maximum control over variables and help the staffing department separate the effects of extraneous factors on an outcome. For example, the length of training and type of training (e.g., lecture versus role play) can be manipulated to identify the ideal training procedure. However, experimentation does have several drawbacks. Many managers are reluctant to experiment with only some workers because of morale problems and potential dissatisfaction among those who were not selected. Similarly, those involved may feel manipulated. In addition, the long-term results of the experiment may be confounded by changes in the work environment or simply by the two groups talking with each other about the experiment. Experiments that require control over several variables may also require the presence of a highly qualified researcher, which adds to the expense. However, experiments provide useful cause-effect testing where they are practicable.

Company records

Interviews or surveys do not reveal all problems; nor does the staffing department generally use these more expensive forms of data collection when the data is already available within the organization. The **use of company records** involves systematic and in-depth analysis of the company records and operating results to identify patterns and possibilities for improving staffing practices. Some problems can only be found by studying records, such as compliance with company procedures and laws. The records normally reviewed by an audit team are listed in Figure 11-9 and discussed in the following paragraphs.

1. *Productivity records.* Production records, absenteeism patterns, scrap rates, and wastage all provide clues about prevailing productivity levels and trends. In addition, statistics on absenteeism patterns and turnover figures may provide the human resource department with important clues about more serious underlying problems,[9] especially those related to recruitment, selection, and orientation.

2. *Employee files and records.* Employee files can provide information on turnover and absenteeism patterns, career progress for certain employee groups, and information on the effectiveness of hiring, deployment, and career counselling programs.

3. *Performance evaluation records.* Performance evaluation records may provide valuable insights into the relative effectiveness of internal and external recruiting policies and specific employee training programs. Sometimes, the analysis may also give clues on the appropriateness of performance measures.

4. *Safety records.* Safety and health records may reveal violations of provisions of the *Canada Labour Code* or other provincial safety and health regulations. The number of employees who have made claims on workmen's compensation plans, classified by job, employee category, and time periods; the number of safety violations observed; and number of complaints from employees about workplace safety are all important indicators of problems.[10] Identifying these problems helps the firm streamline its recruitment and selection procedures.

FIGURE 11-9: Sample Company Records Used for Staffing Audit

1. **Productivity records**
   - Cost of production of different products, components, or processes
   - Wastage and scrap rates for various processes and plants
   - Absenteeism figures categorized by plant, section, time period, and employee group
   - Employee turnover figures categorized by plant, section, time period, and employee group

2. **Employee files and records**
   - Turnover and absenteeism records classified by age, gender, and department
   - Comparison of the above across time, department, and industry data on file
   - Career progression patterns of specific groups of employees (e.g., visible minorities, women)
   - Accuracy, completeness, and currency of information obtained through random inspections
   - Number, types, and patterns of disciplinary and interpersonal problems

3. **Performance evaluation records**
   - Performance of employees hired using different selection procedures
   - Performance evaluation of internally promoted candidates by their supervisors
   - Performance of new hires classified by source of recruits

4. **Safety records**
   - Statistics on accidents classified by plant, section, and process. Comparisons of these statistics with previous years and similar plants in the industry to find patterns
   - Statistics on accidents before and after specific safety training programs
   - Number of employees who have made claims on worker's compensation plans, classified by job, employee category, and time period
   - Number of complaints from employees or unions about working conditions and workplace safety

5. **Legal compliance records**
   - Firm's compliance with all labour laws, as evidenced by job specifications, hiring criteria, and disciplinary procedures
   - Number and patterns of sexual or other discrimination charges
   - Employment equity goals of the firm versus actual achievements
   - Patterns in grievances (e.g., arising from specific contract clauses or supervisors)

5. *Legal compliance records (4).* Although several large companies employ one or more persons to monitor the company's compliance with laws, an audit can further check on compliance. The audit team usually concentrates its attention on hiring criteria, workforce composition (especially the number of women, visible minorities, and physically challenged), employee satisfaction records (especially those relating to equity), and disciplinary and dismissal procedures. If patterns are detected, the organization needs to identify the underlying causes and start corrective actions.

External information Research into internal attitudes and records may uncover unfavourable trends. But outside comparisons also give the staffing department a perspective against which it can judge the firm's activities. Some information is available readily, while other data may be difficult to find. Most external information is available from the publications of Statistics Canada, Industry Canada, and Human Resources and Social Development.

For example, audit teams can benchmark workplace absenteeism using Statistics Canada figures (available since 1977). They can also compare past figures and industry, occupational,

Statistics Canada Website:
www.statcan.ca

HRSD website:
www.hrsdc.gc.ca

Focus on Ethics

You are the Director of Human Resources in a medium-sized firm about to hire an assistant in your department, who will be reporting to your deputy manager. Martha Brewster, your neighbour for 20 years, indicated to you that her daughter has applied for the position in your firm and it will be nice if "you could look into it." You have always liked Martha, and she has been very helpful to your family, especially when your children were young. She has also been a very kind neighbour and family friend who helped your spouse and children while you were abroad for 20 months on deputation. You looked at Martha's daughter's background. While she meets the minimum job requirements, there are at least two other candidates who are more qualified and a much better fit for the job. Moreover, one of the other candidates is known to your subordinates, who would wonder why she was not hired. However, you are convinced that with encouragement, Martha's daughter would perform the job competently.

What action should you take?

Society for Human Resource Management:
www.shrm.org

Canadian Council of HR Associations:
www.chrpcanada.com

McMaster University HR Web:
http://hr.mcmaster.ca

provincial, and demographic patterns (e.g., age and gender). Such comparisons may indicate changes the organization can make to recruitment and hiring procedures to reduce the problem.

These agencies regularly publish information about employee turnover rates and severity and frequency rates of accidents.[11] Industry associations and boards of trade usually make available to members specialized data, such as turnover rates, absenteeism rates, standard wage rates, growth rates, standardized job descriptions, accident rates, and benefit costs. In addition, consultants and university research bureaus may be able to provide other needed information through research. Published reports of surveys on topics such as absenteeism can often provide important insights to the audit team.[12]

THE AUDIT REPORT

Audit report: a comprehensive description of staffing activities, including recommendations for maintaining effective practices and improving ineffective practices

An **audit report** is a comprehensive description of staffing activities, which includes recommendations for both maintaining effective practices and improving ineffective practices. Balanced audit reports include both good and bad practices, which encourages the organization to accept the recommendations.

The audit report should look at both strategic and operational improvements in performance.

- *Strategic* actions often require fundamental changes in the way the firm defines effective performance, hires new employees, and assesses their performance. For example, an organization's strategic shift require fundamental changes in the way it defines, measures, and rewards performance (see also Chapter 1).

- Such fundamental changes may not always be necessary. But even when they are not, *operational* improvements to fine-tune staffing systems may be required.

The audit report should highlight these necessary changes by classifying them into two types of actions: actions to be carried out by line managers, and actions to be carried out by the staffing department. For line managers, the report summarizes staffing objectives, responsibilities, and duties. Examples of duties include setting performance standards, hiring employees, and assessing their performance. The report also identifies "people problems" and highlights violations of policies and employment laws. Finally, it reveals poor management practices along with recommendations.

The staffing department should review the audit report, paying particular attention to the following:

- attitudes of managers and employees toward the staffing department services;
- the audit team's opinion on the department's objectives and its methods of achieving them;
- problems in the context of staffing and their implications; and
- strategies for making needed changes, including identification of a clear, time-bound action plan.

With the information contained in the audit report, the staffing department can take a broad view of their functions. Instead of solving problems haphazardly, the staffing manager can focus on those areas that have the greatest potential for improving the department's contribution to the firm. The department can also study emerging trends and take corrective action while the problems are still minor. By promptly responding to the problems of operating managers, the department can also earn support from them.

Perhaps most important, the audit serves as a map for future efforts and a reference point for future audits. With knowledge of the department's present performance, the manager can make long-range plans to upgrade crucial activities. These plans identify new goals for the department.[13] And these goals serve as standards—standards that future audit teams will use to evaluate the firm's staffing activities. Ultimately, it is how effectively the organization prepares itself for the future that will spell its success, or even the very survival.

Implications for Practice

1. Periodic audits of staffing functions assess the overall usefulness and value-adding function of staffing and to provide feedback about how well managers are meeting their staffing duties.

2. Certain internal and external factors can necessitate more frequent reviews of and modifications to staffing practices. Organizations that operate in turbulent environments face growth or re-structure challenges, or undergo other major strategic initiatives are likely to need extra audits of their staffing systems and procedures.

3. The scope of a staffing audit should go beyond the function or department and should focus on alignment with corporate strategy, structure, and performance outcomes.

4. The research approach used should recognize the goals and resources of the firm and can range from an informal investigation or fact-finding effort to rigorous designs that test one or more hypotheses. Depending on the objectives and resource constraints, an organization can use the comparative, compliance, or objective-based audit methods (or a combination of these).

5. Regardless of the research approach, an organization should use several data collection tools to gauge effectiveness of staffing systems, since each tool provides only limited insight. Popular data collection tools and sources include interviews, surveys, experiments, company records, and external information.

6. To make the audit information useful and directive, the audit team should compile it into a comprehensive report with recommendations for maintaining effective practices and for improving ineffective practices. Recognizing both good and bad practices is more balanced and encourages acceptance of the report. The audit report should also look at both strategic and operational improvements in performance.

Key Terms for Review

Audit report, *p. 354*

Comparative approach, *p. 346*

Compliance approach, *p. 349*

Entropy, *p. 341*

Experiment, *p. 352*

Focus group, *p. 350*

Interviews, *p. 349*

Objectives-based approach, *p. 349*

Organizational atrophy, *p. 341*

Staffing system audit, *p. 340*

Survey, *p. 350*

Use of company records, *p. 352*

Discussion Questions

1. Do you think that a staffing audit is important for all types of organizations? Are larger organizations more likely than small organizations to need the audit?

2. If you were asked to evaluate the staffing system of an organization, what steps would you take?

3. Are surveys a better tool for staffing audits than interviews and company records? Why or why not?

4. What typical areas should a staffing audit report focus on?

Critical Thinking Questions

1. Your college or university has hired you to look into the selection procedures for its support staff. What criteria would you employ? What questions would you ask?

2. You have been hired as a consultant to evaluate and improve the performance of assembly unit in a garment factory that employs mostly immigrant workers who only speak Mandarin or Punjabi. How would you go about your task of setting performance standards and hiring criteria?

3. "Interviews make the respondents shy, and surveys make them lie," noted a manager who was disillusioned with the lack of candor by respondents. Do you agree? What steps can you take to ensure that the data you collect represents the reality?

4. If you were to write an audit report for the garment factory in Question 2 above, what sections should the report have?

Web Research

Collect absenteeism and employee turnover rates from any two industries over the last eight years. What patterns do you see? What are the implications for individual organizations operating in this industry? Are recommendations to reduce these rates likely to be different for smaller and larger firms operating in the same industry?

CASE INCIDENT

Hiring at Pacific Canadian College

Amy Meadowbrook, Chairperson of the Department of Business Administration in Pacific Canadian College (PCC), had always been aware of the challenges of hiring faculty. But even she did not realize that it would be this formidable.

Located in British Columbia, PCC has a student body of 2200, of which 70% are women. The college began operations with just 105 students over 80 years ago and has grown rapidly in size and stature. Today it is recognized as a major center for women's studies, including disciplines such as dietetics, dramatic arts, hospitality, finance, business, and botanical science. PCC's largest department is Business Administration, which employs 19 full-time faculty and 8 part-time faculty and accounts for 600 students. The present incident relates to the hiring of an instructor in this department.

While 70% of the student body in the Department of Business Administration are women, only 30% of the full-time faculty in the same department are female. Moreover, only 40% of the part-time faculty in the department are female. The Collective Agreement between the faculty union and the management states that "not withstanding the 'no discrimination' clause in an earlier article, the university's policy of preferred hiring of women is to continue." Despite such actions, the gender ratio in the faculty has not changed significantly in recent years.

Two other universities, University A and University D, operate near PCC. University A has undergraduate, graduate, and doctoral programs in business, while University D, which is larger than A, has only undergraduate and MBA programs in business. Despite the higher stature and larger size of these universities, PCC has been able to attract high-calibre students to its program because of its small-school atmosphere and friendly faculty.

Recently, two teaching positions in PCC's Department of Business Administration have become vacant. One is a tenure-track, full-time position, for which a completed or nearly completed doctoral degree in business and prior teaching experience in the discipline are key requirements. PCC has always valued research and in recent years has denied tenure and/or promotions to professors who had no academic publications. The second vacancy is a non-tenure track (or terminal) teaching position lasting up to two years, for which a Master's degree in business with "significant relevant experience" is required. The positions were advertised in the news bulletins of the Canadian Association of University Teachers and a local newspaper. A staffing committee consisting of two male and one female faculty was formed to evaluate the applicant pool and make recommendations to the department and the dean of the department.

Past practice in the university and the department was for the staffing committee to identify the three best applicants for each position and invite them for a campus interview. During the interview, each applicant would be expected to make an oral presentation on one of their research topics. The presentation would be open to anyone in the university, including students. Once the campus visits were over, the department would meet as a whole and deliberate on the applicants. The best candidate for each position would be identified on the basis of a secret ballot. The proceedings of the Department were maintained as confidential.

Both the open job positions involved teaching human resource management courses with particular focus on diversity management. Given that there were only 42 applicants to choose from, Jack Yateman, the Chair of the Staffing Committee, decided that only three candidates would be invited for campus interviews for both positions combined. Miu Diang, the female member of the committee, objected to this idea, pointing out that there were several adequately qualified persons in the recruitment pool who met the requirements and "appeared promising." Since several were local candidates, PCC would not have to pay for their travel and lodging during campus visits. However, Norman Kelly, the third member and a past chair of the Department of Business Administration, supported Yateman's decision that inviting many applicants for the interview was a "waste of resources and time." Both Yateman and Kelly felt that the top candidate should be offered the tenure track position and the runner-up the two-year terminal position.

The three candidates interviewed were Brad Bentely, Eleanor Kateman, and Joan Vandersam. Their qualifications are summarized in Table A:

TABLE A:

Characteristic	Brad Bentley	Eleanor Kateman	Joan Vandersam
Education	MBA and MPA (Master of Public Administration). Three months ago, he was enrolled in a long-distance PhD program at a relatively unknown American university. Will take at least five years for completion of the degree program.	MBA. Has completed all coursework and comprehensive examinations for PhD degree at University A and is one year away from getting her PhD degree.	MSc in Applied Psychology from University A, where she is also currently enrolled in the PhD program. She has completed all coursework and comprehensive examinations and is ten months away from getting her PhD degree.
Teaching experience	Taught human resource management, organizational behaviour, introduction to management, business strategy, marketing, and managing diversity courses for the past 10 years at PCC, University A, and University D. In PCC he worked as a non-tenure-track instructor, while in University A and D he taught as a part-time instructor.	Taught human resource management, organizational behaviour, organizational theory, introduction to business, and business strategy for 6 years part-time at PCC, University A, and University D.	Taught human resource management, organizational behaviour, psychology, and business strategy courses at University A for 2 years.
Student evaluations of teaching effectiveness	On 20 course evaluations, average rating is 4.4 with a standard deviation of 1.6.	On 22 course evaluations, average rating is 4.6 with a standard deviation of 1.4.	On 9 course evaluations, average rating is 4.0 with a standard deviation of 1.3.
Research productivity	No journal articles; has presented two papers at regional conferences.	Two journal articles including one in the highly respected *Academy of Management Executive* and six papers presented at regional, national, and international conferences, some of which are highly respected in the field.	One article in a respected journal and eight papers at regional, national, and international conferences, some of which are highly respected in the field

TABLE A: (Continued)

Characteristic	Brad Bentley	Eleanor Kateman	Joan Vandersam
Work experience	Worked as a management consultant and trainer for 14 years. Most of the consulting work involved small business problems relating to employee relations.	Was a senior manager in a telecom company for 16 years before changing careers. Has some consulting experience, especially in the areas of human resource management and diversity training.	Has no full-time work experience but has worked most summers in organizations focusing on worker safety, employee counselling, and mental health.

The three candidates were interviewed by all department faculty and made formal presentations on their research. Kateman and Vandersam presented key findings from their research related to their doctoral dissertation, while Bentley made a presentation on a general business topic. Afterward, the selection committee met again. The ratings of the candidates by the three members based on their evaluation of teaching, research, and relevant work experience are shown in Table B.

TABLE B:

	Bentley	Kateman	Vandersam
Diang	3	1	2
Kelly	1	2	3
Yateman	1	3	2

The Department of Business Administration faculty met as a group and discussed the three candidates. The members felt that Vandersam had less teaching experience than both Bentley and Kateman, who had taught a wide range of courses. Some members felt that since Bentley had taught a wider variety of courses and had greater teaching experience, he should be offered a position; but most women faculty disagreed with this. In their minds, Kateman had also taught several courses and had as good if not better student evaluations. Some members expressed concerns over the fact that Vandersam did not have an MBA, which could limit her ability to teach certain business courses, although this concern was not universal. Indeed three members (two males) stated that they preferred having a colleague with a different background, since this would add a "fresh approach" to the teaching of business courses. By and large, the members of the Department felt that "Kateman and Vandersam were superior on this criterion" although three male faculty members (Yateman and two untenured faculty) did not agree.

After three meetings lasting two hours each, the decision on the top candidate for the position was put to vote. The results were:

Total number of faculty voted =17 (Men = 10 Women = 7)

Total votes received by each candidate:
Bentley = 11 (Men = 10; Women = 1)

Kateman = 6 (All six who voted were women)

Amy Meadowbrook is now in the process of writing a letter to the Dean and the Academic Vice President of the college summarizing the results of the deliberations of the department. She knows she will have a difficult time summarizing the often-conflicting evaluations of the candidates. The task is made more difficult by the fact that in the previous year, when Bentley had applied for a similar position and had been recommended for that position, the Academic Vice President had summarily rejected his candidature on the grounds that he lacked qualifications for the position. Since then, Bentley had joined a PhD program; but it was debatable whether this alone would suffice.

"How should I 'sell' Bentley to the AVP?" wondered Meadowbrook as she reached for her seventh cup of coffee of the day. Her doctor had advised her against coffee, but she also realized that it was going to be one of those difficult days where she will need caffeine to keep her going.

Questions

1. *What is your assessment of the situation? What factors seem to be at work here?*

2. *What improvements, if any, can you recommend to the hiring procedures at PCC?*

CASE

Shop and Save Supermarket: Views on Staffing Systems

Shop and Save Supermarket (SSS) is a regional grocery chain with 45 supermarkets spread all over Eastern Canada. The firm, which began as a mom-and-pop store in Halifax 25 years ago, eventually grew to employ 480 full-time employees and 2300 part-time employees,* and with annual revenues of $2.4 billion. Historically, the firm took pride in its informal, family atmosphere with few systems and procedures for most human resource matters. For example, the firm does not have rigid job descriptions or specifications, nor any systematic job evaluation schemes. Jane Werther, who joined the firm eight months ago as its Human Resource Manager, has been developing systems and procedures, especially relating to staffing. She has also introduced a formal orientation program and has encouraged work supervisors and department heads to counsel their subordinates on matters relating to career progress within the company.

In an effort to gauge the views of managers, supervisors, and staff, the human resource department identified 60 full-time and 100 part-time employees for interviews. The details of the sample are shown in Table 1. Werther and three other persons (a full-time assistant in the department and two graduate students hired part time for this purpose) interviewed all the employees over a month. An interview schedule was prepared. The questions used for the survey and the average responses for each question by different groups of employees are shown in Table 2.

---

*The number of part-time employees varies from time to time. The total number refers to the date on which the survey began.

TABLE 1: Sample Used for Interviews

	Total number	Number interviewed
Cashiers		
Full-time		
Men	20	10
Women	146	16
Part-time		
Men	117	11
Women	1310	17
Other employees		
Full-time		
Men	50	2
Women	40	2
Part-time		
Men	330	32
Women	530	40
Supervisors		
Men	140	20
Women	16	3
Managers		
Men	60	5
Women	8	2
Total		
Full-time	480	60
Part-time	2287	100
GRAND TOTAL	**2767**	**160**

TABLE 2:　Interview Questions and Average Scores for Various Groups of Employees

(**Note:** *The participants were asked to respond to each question using a five-point scale. For all questions, the higher the score, the more positive the response. Some of the questions were considered irrelevant for the management group and hence were not used.*)

	Cashiers				Other				Supervisors		Managers	
	Full-time		Part-time		Full-time		Part-time					
	M	F	M	F	M	F	M	F	M	F	M	F
Hiring Procedures												
1. Based on your experience, do you think that the hiring procedures are fair?	3.7	3.1	3.1	2.8	3.8	3.2	3.4	2.9	4.1	3.9	4.5	4.3
2. Are the hiring criteria appropriate?	3.9	3.7	3.8	3.6	3.9	3.4	3.5	3.2	4.3	4.0	4.6	4.0
3. Do you believe that the best person for the job is always hired?	3.8	3.0	3.2	3.0	3.8	2.8	3.4	3.0	4.2	4.0	4.5	4.2
4. Are the criteria communicated to job applicants?	3.9	3.6	3.5	3.3	3.8	3.3	3.2	3.0	4.2	3.8	4.2	3.9
Deployment												
5. Are the employee transfer and promotion policies appropriate?	4.2	3.8	4.0	3.4	3.2	3.0	2.8	2.6	3.5	3.2	4.4	3.8
6. Are the rewards for your job fair and equitable?	4.0	3.6	3.8	3.2	3.0	2.8	2.7	2.5	3.4	3.1	4.2	3.6
Orientation and Initial Training												
7. Did the orientation program prepare you for your job?	4.1	3.7	3.8	3.4	3.2	3.2	3.2	3.1	3.2	3.0	n/a	n/a
8. Did the initial training help you learn about your tasks clearly?	3.5	3.3	3.2	3.1	3.0	2.9	2.9	2.7	3.7	3.4	n/a	n/a
Counseling												
9. Does your supervisor show genuine concern for you?	4.1	3.7	3.8	3.4	3.2	3.2	3.2	3.1	3.2	3.0	n/a	n/a
10. Does your supervisor provide useful advice for your career advancement?	3.5	3.3	3.2	3.1	3.0	2.9	2.9	2.7	3.7	3.4	n/a	n/a
Overall												
11. Overall, do you feel that you have a future in this firm?	3.9	3.8	3.5	3.4	3.3	3.3	3.0	2.8	3.9	3.5	4.6	4.4
12. Overall, are the HR department and staffing procedures effective?	4.4	4.3	4.3	4.2	4.2	4.1	4.2	4.4	4.3	4.4	4.6	4.3

QUESTIONS

1. *What is your overall evaluation of the audit? What improvements, if any, would you recommend for future audits?*

2. *Based on the current findings, what conclusions would you form? What recommendations would you make to the human resource department? To the top management?*

REQUIRED PROFESSIONAL CAPABILITIES—ENTRY-LEVEL RPCS

STAFFING

Identifies potential sources of qualified candidates

- external market sources
- internal demographics
- recruitment techniques
- relevant legislation
- common and statutory law (e.g., employment standards, labour relations)
- relevant legislation (e.g., human rights, employment equity, pay equity)
- recruiting sources and techniques

Implements and monitors processes for attracting qualified candidates

- job markets
- provider sources
- recruitment techniques/ethics
- relevant legislation
- communication tools and techniques
- common and statutory law (e.g., employment standards, labour relations)
- relevant legislation (e.g., human rights, employment equity, pay equity)
- recruiting sources and techniques
- communication theories and techniques

Evaluates recruiting effectiveness

- assessment tools
- benchmarking techniques
- company plans and programs
- communication tools
- statistical analysis
- recruiting sources and techniques
- research methods and designs (including measurement of HR)
- validity and reliability (conceptual definitions and assessment techniques)
- measurement tools and their limitations
- statistical analyses and evaluation
- statistical and practical significance
- validation of selection and training decisions and measures

Analyzes position requirements to establish selection criteria

- human rights legislation
- employment equity legislation
- employment law
- statistical analysis methodology
- recruitment practices
- relevant legislation (e.g., human rights, employment equity, pay equity)
- methods of job analysis
- recruiting sources and techniques
- selection concepts, assessments, and techniques (e.g., interviews, tests, and other widely used selection procedures)
- statistical analyses and evaluation

Establishes screening and assessment procedures

- assessment tools
- human rights legislation
- employment legislation
- corporate policies
- recruitment practices
- common and statutory law (e.g., employment standards, labour relations)
- relevant legislation (e.g., human rights, employment equity, pay equity)
- validity and reliability (conceptual definitions and assessment techniques)
- validation of selection and training decisions and measures
- recruiting sources and techniques
- selection concepts, assessments, and techniques (e.g., interviews, tests, and other widely used selection procedures)

Establishes appointment procedures

- human rights legislation
- employment legislation
- past practices of the organization
- best practices of staffing appointment procedures
- relevant legislation (e.g., human rights, employment equity, pay equity)
- selection concepts, assessments, and techniques (e.g., interviews, tests, and other widely used selection procedures)

Develops orientation policies and procedures for new employees

- employment legislation
- company procedures and practices
- HR practices
- external market conditions
- common and statutory law (e.g., employment standards, labour relations)
- relevant legislation (e.g., human rights, employment equity, pay equity)
- basic orientation and career development needs of new employees

Develops deployment procedures (e.g. transfers, secondments, and reassignments)

- service providers
- employment law
- collective agreements
- human rights legislation
- relevant legislation (e.g., human rights, employment equity, pay equity)
- selection concepts, assessments, and techniques (e.g., interviews, tests, and other widely used selection procedures)
- methods of matching skills and people

Implements deployment procedures ensuring necessary compensation and benefit changes, and education plans are addressed

- job market conditions
- service providers
- employment law
- collective agreements
- human rights legislation
- relevant legislation (e.g., human rights, employment equity, pay equity)
- selection concepts, assessments, and techniques (e.g., interviews, tests, and other widely used selection procedures)
- administration of the collective agreement
- legal context of labour relations
- career and succession planning and management

REQUIRED PROFESSIONAL CAPABILITIES—RPCS FOR EXPERIENCED PROFESSIONALS

STAFFING

- identifies the organization's HR needs
- identifies potential sources of qualified candidates
- selects candidates and negotiates terms and conditions of employment
- if necessary, develops employment contract with successful candidate(s)
- evaluates screening, selection and orientation processes, and outcomes at the organizational level
- advises clients on matters of sub-standard performance, discipline, and ultimately, termination
- advises clients on alternatives to terminations
- develops procedures for the defensible termination of employees in circumstances where termination is determined to be the only course of action
- develops appropriate security strategies to protect corporate assets while preserving the dignity of terminated employees
- participates in the termination process by preparing termination notices, conducting exit interviews, and arranging outplacement services

Source: Canadian Council of Human Resources Associations. **http://www.cchra-ccarh.ca/parc/en/ section_3/ss_3/333e.asp.** Reproduced with the permission of the Canadian Council of Human Resources Associations.

ENDNOTES

Chapter 1

1. Lyle Spencer and Signe Spencer. (1993). *Competence at Work*. New York: John Wiley, p. 239.

2. J.E. Hunter and F.L. Schmidt. (1982). "Fitting People to Jobs: The Impact of Personnel Selection on National Productivity," In M.D. Dunnette and E.A.Fleishman (eds). *Human Performance and Productivity: Human Capability Assessment*. Hillsdale, NJ: Erlbaum, pp. 233–292.

3. For a discussion, see R.D. Gatewood and H.S. Feild. (2001). *Human Resource Selection*, 5th edition. Mason, OH: South Western, pp. 208–210. For an alternative estimate model, see W. Cascio. (1993). "Assessing the Utility of Selection Devices." In Schmitt and W.C.Borman (eds). *Personnel Selection in Organizations*. San Francisco: Jossey-Bass, pp. 318–320.

4. See http://www.gib.ca/ retrieved on March 11, 2005. Also see J. Masters. (1986, April). "Brave New Breweries." *Canadian Business*, 59, 4, pp. 56–63.

5. See http://www.haley.on.ca/haley.html retrieved on March 11, 2005. Also see P. O. Connor. (1981, Dec. 2). "Haley Moves into High Gear." *Canadian Business*, 54, pp. 39–48.

6. L.L. Baird, I. Meshoulam, and G. DeGive. (1983). "Meshing Human Resource Planning with Strategic Business Planning: A Model Approach." *Personnel*, 60, 5, pp. 14–25.

7. O. Lundy and M. Cowling. (1996). *Strategic Human Resource Management*. London: Routledge, pp. 84–85.

8. Peter Bamberger and Ilan Meshoulam. (2000). *Human Resource Strategy*. Thousand Oaks, CA: Sage Publications, p. 25.

9. See http://www.geappliances.ca/corporate/profile.jsp retrieved on March 12, 2005. Also see Andrew Campbell. (1985, February). "Turning Workers into Risk Takers." *Canadian Business*, p. 109.

10. "Canada: A Special Report." (1999, June 28). *Time*, p. 41.

11. Bruce Little and Marian Stinson. (2001, Feb. 22). "Canada Reports String of Trade Records." *The Globe and Mail* [Toronto], p. B1, B10.

12. Madelaine Drohan. (2003, Dec. 15). "We are No.2 and Falling." *The Globe and Mail* [Toronto], p. A15.

13. H. Bredrup. (1995). "Background for Performance Management." In A. Rolstadas (ed). *Performance Management: A Business Process Benchmarking Approach*. London: Chapman and Hall, p. 61.

14. OECD study figures reported in *The Globe and Mail*, October 3, 2005, p. B6.

15. Bruce Little. (2001, Feb. 15). "U.S. Pulls Ahead in Productivity." *The Globe and Mail* [Toronto], p. B3.

16. Anne Golden. (2002, Nov. 13). "If We Snooze, We Lose." *The Globe and Mail* [Toronto], p. A15. Barrie McKenna. (2002, Nov. 13). "Canada Sinks to Eighth Place in Competitiveness Ranking." *The Globe and Mail*, pp. B1/9.

17. "Canada Edging Up in Ability to Compete, WEF Says." (2005, Sept. 29). *The Globe and Mail* [Toronto], p. B7.

18. See http://www.newswire.ca/en/releases/archive/September2005/28/c4870.html.

19. Report by Canadian Manufacturers and Exporters quoted in "Canada Rates Last in Survey of G7 Countries." (2001, Aug. 1). *The Globe and Mail*, p. B1.

20. John McCallum. (2000, May). "Will Canada Matter in 2020?" *Royal Bank Current Analysis*, Royal Bank of Canada Economics Department, p. 5.

21. Jeffrey Simpson. (2002, Oct. 1). "Dull Maybe, But Productivity's Our Future." *The Globe and Mail* [Toronto], p.A15.

22. David Dodge. (2005, April 25). "Canada's Competitiveness Depends on Developing Youth, Retaining Older Workers." *Canadian HR Reporter*, p. 19.

23. "The Path to Unlocking Employee Knowledge." (1999, Oct. 25). *The Globe and Mail* [Toronto], p.M1.

24. "The Industries that Will Define the Decade." (1997, April 21). *The Globe and Mail*, p.A6

25. "The Accenture High Performance Workforce Study 2002/2003." (2003, March). *Accenture Magazine*.

26. See http://www.watsonwyatt.com/surveys/hci/ retrieved on March 13, 2005.

27. Results of the 2005 Global Human Capital Study reported in: Susan Singh. (2005, June 6). "Globalization Puts Focus on HR." *Canadian HR Reporter*, p. 1, 15.

28. Ross Laver. (1997, Feb. 24). "Kids, Bosses and Work." *Maclean's*, p. 38.

29. See http://www.literacy.ca/litand/1.htm.

30. R.T. Evers. (1993, Fall). "Making the Match: How Ontario's Employers Can Help Graduates Develop Exactly the Right Skills Portfolios They'll Need as Tomorrow's Corporate Managers." *Challenges*, pp. 8–9.

31. Results of International Adult Literacy Survey reported on http://www.nald.ca/nts/ialsreps/high2.htm February 10, 1998. See also Morton Ritts. (1986, May). "What if Johnny Still Can't Read." *Canadian Business*, pp. 54–57, 124.

32. R.T. Evers. (1993, Fall). "Making the Match: How Ontario's Employers Can Help Graduates Develop Exactly the Right Skills Portfolios They'll Need as Tomorrow's Corporate Managers." *Challenges*, pp. 8–9.

33. "Poor Showing on Tests behind Math Change." (2004, Nov. 26). *The Chronicle-Herald*, p. A3.

34. Shannon Martin. (2005, July 18). "Firms Pursuing the Business Case for Essential Skills." *Canadian HR Reporter*, p. 11.

35. John Porter. (1965). *The Vertical Mosaic: An Analysis of Social Class and Power in Canada*. Toronto: University of Toronto Press, 1965. See also V.V. Murray. (1974). "Canadian Cultural Values and Personnel Administration." In Harish Jain (ed). *Contemporary Issues in Canadian Personnel Administration*. Scarborough, ON: Prentice-Hall.

36. Statistics Canada figures, quoted by Jill Mahoney (2005, March 23). "Visible Majority by 2017." *The Globe and Mail*, pp. A1, A7.

37. "Face of Canada Changes." (1997, Nov. 5). *The Globe and Mail*, p. A1.

38. "No Longer a Two-Language Nation." (1997, Dec. 3). *The Mail Star*, p. A19.

39. *Canadian HR Reporter*, December 18, 2000, p. 6.

40. Gordon Nixon. (2005, July 18). "The Immigrant Imperative: Why Canada Can't Afford to Continue to Waste the Skills of Newcomers." *Canadian HR Reporter*, p. 19.

41. David Brown. (2005, Jan. 31). "Ottawa Asks Why Skilled Immigrants Drive Cabs." *Canadian HR Reporter*, p. 1, 5.

42. "Poll: Prejudice Still with Us." (2005, March 21). *The Chronicle Herald, 57, 67,* p. A1, A2.

43. Rukhsana Khan. (2003, Dec. 23). "This is Our Home Too." *The Globe and Mail,* p. A13.

44. Jane Armstrong. (2002, March 15). "Canada is 30 Millon, But Will That Last?" *The Globe and Mail,* p. A1.

45. "Labour Shortage Woes Loom, Research Says." (2005, Sept. 29). *The Globe and Mail,* p. B7.

46. Statistics Canada. *Fertility in Canada: From Baby Boom to Baby Bust.* Ottawa: Catalogue 91–524XPE, April 3, 1989.

47. "Labour Shortage Woes Loom, Research Says." (2005, Sept. 29). *The Globe and Mail,* p. B7.

48. J. Dumas. (1995). "Greying of the Workforce: Report on a Symposium." *Perspectives on Labour and Income, 7,* 1:34. Ottawa: Statistics Canada, 75–001E.

49. Steve Nyce and Sylvester Schieber. (2002). *The Decade of the Employee: The Workforce Challenges Facing the Developed Economies of the World over the Next Ten Years.* Retrieved March 13, 2005 from http://www.watsonwyatt.com/surveys/hci/.

50. For a good exposition of the differences between two age groups, please see Claire Raines and Jim Hunt. (2000). *The X-ers and the Boomers.* Berkeley, CA: Crisp Publications, pp. 32–39.

51. Barbarra Kofman and Kailin Eckler. (2005, April 25). "They are Your Future: Attracting and Retaining Generation Y." *Canadian HR Reporter,* p. 7.

52. Lauren Keating. (2000, May). "The In Crowds." *Shopping Center World, 29,* 5, pp. 160–165.

53. Joyce M. Wolburg and James Pokrywczynski. (2001, Sept/Oct). "A Psychographic Analysis of Generation Y College Students." *Journal of Advertising Research, 41,* 5, pp. 33–52.

54. Michael Adams and Christine de Panafieu. (2003, June 16). "God is Dead? Whatever." *The Globe and Mail,* p. A8.

55. Carol Verret. (n.d.). "Generation Y: Motivating and Training a New Generation of Employees." Retrieved March 27, 2005 from **http://www.hotel-online.com/Trends/Carolverret/ GenerationY_Nov2000.html.**

56. Robert Trigaux. (2003, Dec. 15). "Generation Y Needs New Business Model." *Seattle Post-Intelligencer.* Retrieved March 27, 2005 from http://seattlepi.nwsource.com/business/ 152415_tunein15.html.

57. Professor Richard Woodward of University of Calgary quoted by McMurdy. (1993, Jan. 4). "Falling Expectations." *Maclean's,* p. 36.

58. Simon Tuck. (1999, May 1). "Internet Milestone Set as 50% Connected in Canada." *The Globe and Mail,* p. B1.

59. "Working from Home Cuts Employee Stress, Study Finds." (1994, Nov. 16). *The Globe and Mail,* p. B19.

60. Stephen Jackson. (1998, Sept. 7). "All of HR Reaps Benefits from Performance-Based Job Descriptions." *Canadian HR Reporter,* p. 12.

61. Peter F. Drucker. (1973). *Management: Tasks, Responsibilities and Practice.* New York: Harper and Row, Chapter 7.

62. L. Smircich. (1983). "Concepts of Culture and Organizational Analysis." *Administrative Science Quarterly, 28,* pp. 339–58; L. Smircich. (1983). "Organizations as Shared Meanings." In L. R. Pondy, P. J. Frost, G. Morgan and T. C. Dandridge (eds). *Organizational Symbolism.* Greenwich, CT: Jai Press, pp. 55–68; V. Sathe. (1985). *Culture and Related Corporate Realities.* Homewood, IL: Irwin, pp. 9–25.

63. Hari Das. (1998). *Strategic Organizational Design.* Scarborough, ON: Prentice-Hall, pp. 324–329.

64. See **http://www.sierrasystems.com/SSG/About+Us/.**

65. D'Arcy Jenish. (2001, Nov. 5). "Ten that Made the Grade." *Maclean's,* p. 50. See also Richard Yerema. (2000). *Canada's Top 100 Employers.* Toronto: Mediacorp Canada Inc., pp. 244–246.

66. Peter Bamberger and Ilan Meshoulam. (2000). *Human Resource Strategy.* Thousand Oaks, CA: Sage Publications, p. 24.

67. Hari Das. (1998). *Strategic Organizational Design.* Scarborough, ON: Prentice-Hall, p. 204.

68. Adapted from H.F. Schwind, H. Das, and T. Wagar. (2005). *Canadian Human Resource Management,* 7th edition. Toronto: McGraw-Hill Ryerson, p. 27.

69. D.P. Lepak and S.A. Snell. (1999). "The Strategic Management of Human Capital: Determinants and Implications of Different Relationships." *Academy of Management Review, 24,* 1, pp. 1–18.

70. Peter Bamberger and Ian Meshoulam. (2000). *Human Resource Strategy.* Thousand Oaks, CA: Sage Publications, p. 57.

71. For example, see D.P. Lepak and S.A. Snell. (1999). "The Strategic Management of Human Capital: Determinants and Implications of Different Relationships." *Academy of Management Review, 24,* 1, pp. 1–18; D. Organ. (1988). *Organizational Citizenship Behaviour.* Lexington, MA: D.C. Heath; Peter Bamberger and Ilan Meshoulam. (2000). *Human Resource Strategy.* Thousand Oaks, CA: Sage Publications; L. Dyer and G.W. Holder. (1988). "A Strategic Perspective of Human Resources Management." In L. Dyer and G.W. Holder (eds). *Human Resources Management: Evolving Roles and Responsibilities.* Washington, DC: American Society for Personnel Administration, pp. 1–45; D. Organ. (1988). *Organizational Citizenship Behaviour.* Lexington, MA: D.C. Heath; P. Osterman. (1987). "Choice of Employment Systems in Internal Labour Markets." *Industrial Relations, 26,* 1, pp. 48–63; P. Osterman. (1995). "Work/Family Programs and the Employment Relationship." *Administrative Science Quarterly, 40,* pp. 681–700; P.M. Swiercz. (1995). "Research Update: Strategic HRM." *Human Resource Planning, 18,* 3, pp. 53–62.

72. J. Arthur. (1994). "Effects of Human Resource Systems on Manufacturing Performance and Turnover," *Academy of Management Journal, 37,* pp. 670–687.

73. J.P. MacDuffie. (1995). "Human Resource Bundles and Manufacturing Performance: Organizational Logic and Flexible Production Systems in the World of Auto Industry." *Industrial and Labor Relations Review, 48,* pp. 197–221.

74. P. Osterman. (1987). "Choice of Employment Systems in Internal Labour Markets." *Industrial Relations, 26,* 1, pp. 48–63; P. Osterman. (1995). "Work/Family Programs and the Employment Relationship." *Administrative Science Quarterly, 40,* pp. 681–700; Peter Bamberger and Ilan Meshoulam. (2000). *Human Resource Strategy,* Thousand Oaks, CA: Sage Publications, p. 61.

75. P. Osterman. (1987). "Choice of Employment Systems in Internal Labour Markets." *Industrial Relations, 26,* 1, pp. 48–63; P. Osterman. (1995). "Work/Family Programs and the Employment Relationship." *Administrative Science Quarterly, 40,* pp. 681–700.

76. Peter Bamberger and Ilan Meshoulam. (2000). *Human Resource Strategy.* Thousand Oaks, CA: Sage Publications, p. 61.

77. Peter Bamberger and Ilan Meshoulam. (2000), p. 61.

78. R.E. Miles and C.C. Snow. (1984). "Designing Strategic Human Resource Systems." *Organizational Dynamics, 13,* 1, pp. 36–52.

79. Richard Mirabile. (1997, August). "Everything You Wanted to Know About Competency Modeling." *Training and Development,* pp. 73–77.

80. Patricia A. McLagan. (1997, May). "Competencies: The Next Generation," *Training and Development,* p. 41.

81. Shona McKay. (2001, February). "The Best 35 Companies to Work for in Canada." *Report on Business Magazine,* p. 61.

82. Joe Chidley and Andrew Wahl. (1999, March 12). "The New Worker's Paradise." *Canadian Business,* pp. 37–38.

83. Arthur Young, Wayne Brockbank, and Dave Ulrich. (1994). "Lower Cost, Higher Value: Human Resource Function in Transformation." *Human Resource Planning, 17,* 3, pp. 10–12.

84. Timothy Appleby and Michael Den Tandt. (2003, Dec. 19). "Airport Workers Corrupted by Easy Money, Lax Screening." *The Globe and Mail,* p. A1; A11.

85. Alan Barratt and Dimitri Georgides. (1995). "The Synolic Approach to Human Resource Development." *Executive Development, 8,* 2, pp. 29–32.

Chapter 2

1. Subhir Chowdhury. (2000). "Towards the Future of Management." In Subhir Chowdhury (ed). *Management 21C.* Harlow, UK: Pearson Education, pp. 10–11.

2. M.L. Blum and J.C. Naylor. (1968). *Industrial Psychology, Its Theoretical and Social Foundations* (Revised edition). New York: Harper & Row.

3. H.F. Schwind, H. Das, and T. Wagar. (2002). *Canadian Human Resource Management* 6th edition. Toronto: McGraw-Hill Ryerson, pp. 415–416.

4. Robert Kaplan and David Norton. (1996, Jan–Feb.). "Using the Balanced Score Card as a Strategic Management System." *Harvard Business Review.*

5. For example, see D. Whetten, K. Cameron, and M. Woods. (1994). *Developing Management Skills for Europe.* London: Harper Collins.

6. E.L. Thorndike. (1949). *Personnel Selection: Test and Measurement Techniques.* New York: Wiley.

7. J.P. Campbell, J.J. McHenry, and L.L. Wise. (1990). "Modeling Job Performance in a Population of Jobs." *Personnel Psychology, 43,* pp. 313–333.

8. C.H. Rush. (1953). "A Factorial Study of Sales Criteria." *Personnel Psychology, 6,* pp. 9–24.

9. E.A. Fleishman and G.N. Ornstein. (1960). "An Analysis of Pilot Flying Performance in Terms of Component Abilities." *Journal of Applied Psychology, 44,* pp. 146–155.

10. E.E. Ghiselli and M. Haire. (1960). "The Validation of Selection Tests in the Light of Dynamic Nature of Criteria." *Personnel Psychology, 13,* pp. 225–231.

11. Adapted from F.A. Kingsbury. (1933). "Psychological Tests for Executives." *Personnel, 9,* 121–133.

12. J. Schneider and J.O. Mitchel. (1980). "Functions of Life Insurance Agency Managers and Relationships with Agency Characteristics and Managerial Tenure." *Personnel Psychology, 33,* pp. 795–808.

13. H.F. Schwind, H. Das, and T. Wagar. (2002). *Canadian Human Resource Management,* 6th edition, Toronto: McGraw-Hill Ryerson.

14. For example, see Susan Greenberg and Raymond Bello. (1992, July). "Re-Write Job Descriptions: Focus on Functions." *HR Focus, 69,* p.10.; Michael Brannick, Joan Brannick, and Edward Levine. (1992). "Job Analysis, Personnel Selection and the ADA." *Human Resource Management Review, 2,* 3, pp. 171–182.

15. William Wooten. (1993). "Using Knowledge, Skill and Ability (KSA) Data to Identify Career Planning Opportunities: An Application of Job Analysis to Internal Manpower Planning." *Public Personnel Administrator, 22,* 4, pp. 551–563.

16. Sidney Fine. (1973). *Functional Job Analysis Scales: A Desk Aid.* Kalamazoo, MI: Upjohn Institute for Employment Research.

17. Howard Olson, Sidney Fine, David Myers, and Margarette Jennings. (1981, Summer). "The Use of Functional Analysis in Establishing Performance for Heavy Equipment Operators." *Personnel Psychology,* p. 354.

18. Purdue Research Foundation. (1989). *Position Analysis Questionnaire.* West Lafayette, IN: 47907.

19. Wayne Cascio. (1991). *Applied Psychology in Personnel Management,* 4th edition. Englewood Cliffs, NJ: Prentice-Hall, p. 207.

20. Paul Sparks. (1982). "Job Analysis." In K. Rowland and G. Ferris (eds). *Personnel Management.* Boston: Allyn & Bacon; Edward L. Levine, Ronald A. Ash, H. Hall, and Frank Sistrunk. (1983). "Evaluation of Job Analysis Methods by Experienced Job Analysts." *Academy of Management Journal, 26,* 2, pp. 339–48; E.J. McCormick. (1979). *Job Analysis: Methods and Applications.* New York: AMACOM; Luis R. Gomez-Mejia, Ronald C. Page, and Walter W. Tornow. (1982). "A Comparison of the Practical Utility of Traditional, Statistical and Hybrid Job Evaluation Approaches." *Academy of Management Journal, 25,* 4, pp. 790–809; Ronald A. Ash and Edward Levine. (1980, Nov.-Dec.). "A Framework for Evaluating Job Analysis Methods." *Personnel,* pp. 53–59.

21. M.J. Martinko. (1988). "Observing the Work." In S. Gael (ed). *The Job Analysis Handbook for Business, Industry and Government, 1.* New York: Wiley, pp. 419–431.

22. Hari Das, Peter J. Frost, and J. Thad Barnowe. (1979, January). "Behaviourally Anchored Scales for Assessing Behavioural Science Teaching." *Canadian Journal of Behavioural Science, 11,* 1, pp. 79–88; Tom Janz. (1981). "Estimating the Standard Deviation of Job Performance: A Behavioural Approach." *Administrative Sciences Association of Canada (Organizational Behaviour Division) Meeting Proceedings, 2,* Part 5, pp. 70–78.

23. Brigid Hayes. (2005, July 18). "Canadian Organizations Move to Develop Workplace Literacy and Numerical Skills." *Canadian HR Reporter,* p. 7, 10.

24. Richard Swanson. (1996). *Analysis for Improving Performance.* San Francisco: Berrett-Koehler Publishers, p. 100.

25. Richard Mirabile. (1997, August). "Everything You Wanted to Know About Competency Modeling." *Training and Development,* pp. 73–77.

26. Patricia A. McLagan. (1997, May). "Competencies: The Next Generation." *Training and Development,* p. 41.

27. Jean-Pascal Souque. (1996). *Focus on Competencies,* Report No. 177–96. Ottawa: The Conference Board of Canada, p. 18.

28. F.M. Lopez. (1988). "Threshold Traits Analysis System." In S. Gael (ed). *The Job Analysis Handbook for Business, Industry and Government,* Vol. 1. New York: Wiley, pp. 880–901.

29. E.A. Fleishman and M.D. Mumford. (1988). "Ability Requirement Scales." In S. Gael (ed). *The Job Analysis Handbook for Business, Industry and Government,* Vol. 1. New York: Wiley, pp. 917–935; E.A. Fleishman and M.K. Quaintance. (1984). *Taxonomies of Human Performance: The Description of Human Tasks.* Orlando, FL: Academic Press.

30. E.S. Primoff and L.D. Eyde. (1988). "Job Element Analysis." In S. Gael (ed). *The Job Analysis Handbook for Business, Industry and Government,* Vol. 1. New York: Wiley, pp. 807–824.

31. Brian Orr. (1997, April 21). "The Challenge of Benchmarking HR Performance." *Canadian HR Reporter*, p. 6.

32. Results of the report *Building the Future: An Integrated Strategy for Nursing Human Resources in Canada* and a survey by Rebecca Hagey of the University of Toronto, reported in Uyen Vu. (2005, June 6). "Nursing Needs Mending: Reports." *Canadian HR Reporter*, p. 1, 3.

33. Jeffrey Pfeffer. (1998). *The Human Equation*. Boston: Harvard Business School Press, p. 143.

34. R.M. Guion. (1965). *Personnel Testing*. New York: McGraw-Hill, p. 96.

35. Wayne Cascio. (1998). *Applied Psychology in Human Resource Management*. NJ: Prentice Hall, p. 69.

36. Luis Gomez-Mejia, David Balkin, Robert Cardy, and David Dimick. (2000). *Managing Human Resources*. Scarborough, ON: Prentice Hall, p. 209.

37. H.F. Schwind, H. Das, and T. Wagar. (2005). *Canadian Human Resource Management: A Strategic Approach*, 7th edition. Toronto: McGraw-Hill Ryerson, p. 110.

38. A.L. Delbecq, A.H. Van de Ven, and D.H. Gustafson. (1975). "Group Techniques for Progress Planning: A Guide to Nominal and Delphi Process." Glenview, IL: Scott, Foresman; J.M. Bartwrek and J.K. Muringhan. (1984). "The Nominal Group Technique: Expanding the Basic Procedure and Underlying Assumptions." *Group and Organizational Studies*, 9, pp. 417–32.

39. James W. Walker. (1976, June). "Human Resource Planning: Managerial Concerns and Practices." *Business Horizons*, pp. 56–57. See also George S. Odiorne. (1986, December). "The Crystal Ball of HR Strategy." *Personnel Administrator*, pp. 103–106; John A. Byrne and Alison L. Cowan. (1986, Sept. 22). "Should Companies Groom New Leaders Or Buy Them?" *Business Week*, pp. 94–96.

40. R. Meehan and B.S. Ahmed. (1990). "Forecasting Human Resource Requirements: A Demand Model." *Human Resource Planning*, 13, 4, pp. 297–307.

41. John Hooper and R.F. Catalanello. (1981). "Markov Analysis Applied to Forecasting Technical Personnel." *Human Resource Planning*, 4, pp. 41–47.

42. Richard J. Niehaus. (1980). "Human Resource Planning Flow Models." *Human Resource Planning*, 3, pp. 177–187.

43. P.F. Buller and W.R. Maki. (1981). "A Case History of a Manpower Planning Model." *Human Resource Planning*, 4, 3, pp. 129–37.

44. Brian Parker and David Caine. (1996). "Holonic Modelling: Human Resource Planning and the Two Faces of Janus." *International Journal of Manpower*, 17, 8, pp. 30–45.

Chapter 3

1. Fiorella Callocchia and Joan Bolland. (2003). *Best Practices: Recruitment and Selection*. Toronto: Thomson/Carswell, p. 41.

2. *Andrews v. Department of Transport*. (1994). Ottawa: Canadian Human Rights Commission.

3. "Minority Lawyers Get Boost." (2000, Sept. 7). *The Mail Star*, p. A1.

4. "Disabled at Pizza Hut." (1989, September). *Business Month*, p. 16.

5. "Human Rights and the Canadian Human Rights Commission." (1999). Brochure published by the Canadian Human Rights Commission, Catalogue Number H21-35/1999.

6. David Brown. (2005, April 25) "Still Too Few Visible Minorities in Federal Public Service: Report." *Canadian HR Reporter*, p. 2.

7. "'Culture Fit' Feels like Racism to Many Visible Minorities." (2004, Oct. 11). *Canadian HR Reporter*, p. 2.

8. See http://www.chrc-ccdp.ca/pdf/AR_2004_RA_en.pdf retrieved on August 1, 2005.

9. Theo Anne Opie. (2005, April–May). "The Secret Garden." *HR Professional*, pp. 18–25.

10. *Ontario Human Rights Commission et. al v. the Borough of Etobicoke*. (1982). Canadian Human Rights Commisssion, D/783/6894–1982.

11. *Annual Report of the Canadian Human Rights Commission*. (1999), pp. 6–7.

12. *Annual Report of the CHRC*. (1999), pp. 6–7.

13. Jon Kesselman. (2004, Aug. 21). "Why Wasn't Mandatory Retirement Retired Long Ago?" *The Globe and Mail*, p. A-13.

14. Uyen Vu. (2005, July 18). "End of Mandatory Retirement the Start of Work for HR." *Canadian HR Reporter*, p. 1, 6.

15. See http://www.hrsdc.gc.ca/asp/gateway.asp?hr=en/mb/accommodation/accommodpage.shtml&hs=wzp.

16. "Accommodating Employees' Religious Beliefs." (1990). *The Worklife Report*, 7, 5. Kingston, ON: IR Research Services, p. 8. See also *Annual Report of the Canadian Human Rights Commission*. (1991), p. 63.

17. Mallika Das. (1997). "Workforce 2000: Diversity in the Workplace." In *Managing Diversity: Gender and Other Issues*, Third Edition. Halifax, NS: Open Learning Program, Mount Saint Vincent University, p. 4. See also A.V. Subbarao. (1994)."Managing Workforce Diversity in Canada: Problems and Prospects." *Working Paper 94-25*. Ottawa: University of Ottawa.

18. See http://www.hrsdc.gc.ca/en/lp/lo/lswe/we/information/what.shtml.

19. See http://www.hrsdc.gc.ca/en/lp/lo/lswe/we/publications/mr/myths_realities.shtml#myth1/.

20. H. Schwind, H. Das, and T. Wagar. (2005). *Canadian Human Resource Management*, 7th edition. Toronto: McGraw-Hill Ryerson, p. 189.

21. See http://www.hrsdc.gc.ca/en/lp/lo/lswe/we/information/what.shtml.

22. See http://www.hrsdc.gc.ca/en/lp/lo/lswe/we/information/what.shtml.

23. H. Schwind, H. Das, and T. Wagar. (2005). *Canadian Human Resource Management*, 7th edition. Toronto: McGraw-Hill Ryerson, p. 193.

24. Shenaz Modi. (2005, April–May). "Employment Equity." *HR Professional*, p. 26.

25. Shenaz Modi. (2005, April–May), p. 26.

26. Fiorella Callocchia and Joan Bolland. (2003). *Best Practices: Recruitment and Selection*. Toronto: Thompson/Carswell, p. 41.

27. Simmons da Silva and Sinton. "Employee or Independent Contractor?" Retrieved November 2002 from http://www.lawcan.com/articles/business/art-biz-employee_ind_part1.html. See also Selene McLeod. (2002, April). Consulting and Independent Contractors. " *The Quill*. Southwestern Ontario Chapter of the Society for Technical Communication. Retrieved from http://www.stc.waterloo.on.ca/publications/april02quill.pdf.

28. Susan N. Houseman. (1999, August). "Flexible Staffing Arrangements. A Report on Temporary Help." *futurework*. Retrieved from http://www.dol.gov/ dol/asp/public/futurework/conference/staffing/exec_s.htm.

29. David Brown. (2004, Nov. 8). "Labour Law Reform Urged." *Canadian HR Reporter*, pp. 1–4.

30. Fiorella Callocchia and Joan Bolland. (2003). *Best Practices: Recruitment and Selection*. Toronto: Thompson/Carswell, p. 4–5.

31. See **http://campus.golservices.gc.ca/view_lesson.jsp?courseId=21&lessonId=31.**

32. See **http://campus.golservices.gc.ca/view_lesson.jsp?courseId=21&lessonId=31.**

33. A.R. Vining, D.C. McPhillips, and A.E. Boardman. (1986). "Use of Statistical Evidence in Employment Discrimination Litigation." *The Canadian Bar Review*, 64, pp. 660–702. See also Victor Catano, Steven Cronshaw, Willi Wiesner, Rick Hackett, and Laura Methot. (2001). *Recruitment and Selection in Canada*, 2nd edition. Toronto: Nelson/Thomson Learning, p. 45.

34. Uyen Vu. (2004, Nov. 8). "FedEx Holds Managers Accountable for Diversity." *Canadian HR Reporter*, p. 3.

35. Anne Marie Francesco and Barry Allen Gold. (2005). *International Organizational Behaviour*, 2nd edition. Upper Saddle River, NJ: Pearson/Prentice Hall, pp. 76–77.

36. Uyen Vu. (2005, Aug. 15). "Labour Code Review Wide Open." *Canadian HR Reporter*, p. 1.

37. David Brown. (2004, Nov. 8). "Labour Law Reform Urged." *Canadian HR Reporter*, p. 1.

38. H. Schwind, H. Das, and T. Wagar. (2005). *Canadian Human Resource Management*, 7th edition. Toronto: McGraw-Hill Ryerson, p. 195.

Chapter 4

1. James N. Baron and David M. Kreps. (1999). *Strategic Human Resources*. New York: John Wiley, p. 218.

2. Canadian Human Rights Commission. (2001). *Race, Colour, National or Ethnic Origin: Anti discrimination Casebook*. Minister of Public Works and Government Services, Catalogue Number HR21–56–2001, pp. 12–13. Reproduced with the permission of the Ministry of Public Works and Government Services, 2005.

3. See Robert M.Guion. (1965). *Personnel Testing*. New York: McGraw-Hill, pp. 28–29; and Edwin E. Ghiselli. (1964). *Theory of Psychological Measurement*. Bombay: Tata McGraw-Hill, Chapter 8.

4. Robert M. Guion. (1965). *Personnel Testing*. New York: McGraw Hill, p. 28

5. Robert Gatewood and Hubert Feild. (2001). *Human Resource Selection*, 5th edition, Toronto: South Western/Thomson Learning, p. 117.

6. Robert M. Guion. (1965). *Personnel Testing*. New York: McGraw-Hill, p. 30.

7. "Recruitment Problems HR Faces." (2005, June 6). *Canadian HR Reporter*, p. 20. See also "Report on Recruitment and Staffing." (2005, May 23). *Canadian HR Reporter*, p. 3.

8. Norman Trainor. (1998, Nov. 26). "Using Measurement to Predict Performance." *Canadian HR Reporter*, p. 7.

9. Martin Dewey. (1981, Feb. 7). "Employers Take a Hard Look at the Validity and Value of Psychological Screening." *The Globe and Mail* [Toronto], p. B1.

10. James Leduinka and Lyle F. Schoenfeldt. (1978, Spring). "Legal Development in Employment Testing: Albermarle and Beyond." *Personnel Psychology*, pp. 1–13.

11. Robert M. Guion. (1965). *Personnel Testing*, New York: McGraw-Hill, p. 31

12. Robert M. Guion. (1965), p. 40.

13. Robert Gatewood and Hubert Feild. (2001). *Human Resource Selection*, 5th edition. Toronto: South Western/Thomson Learning, p. 124.

14. Robert M. Guion. (1965). *Personnel Testing*. New York: McGraw Hill, p. 40.

15. For example, see Robert M. Guion. (1965). *Personnel Testing*, New York: McGraw Hill, p. 40.

16. Mary J. Allen and Wendy M. Yen. (1979). *Introduction to Measurement Theory*. Monterey, CA: Brooks/Cole, p. 77.

17. Robert Gatewood and Hubert Feild. (2001). *Human Resource Selection*, 5th edition, Toronto: South Western/Thomson Learning, p. 128.

18. Edwin E. Ghiselli. (1964). *Theory of Psychological Measurement*. New York: McGraw-Hill, TMH Edition, p. 280.

19. Rulon, P.J. (1939). "A Simplified Procedure for Determining the Reliability of a Test by Split Halves." *Harvard Educational Review*, 9, pp. 99–103; Robert M. Guion. (1965). *Personnel Testing*. New York: McGraw Hill, pp. 42–43.

20. Robert M. Guion. (1965). *Personnel Testing*. New York: McGraw-Hill, p. 42.

21. Robert M. Guion. (1965), p. 43. See also David Magnusson. (1966). *Test Theory*. Reading, MA: Addison-Wesley, pp. 73–74.

22. G.F. Kuder and M.W. Richardson. (1937). "The Theory of Estimation of Test Reliability." *Psychometrika*, 2, pp. 151–160

23. Lee J. Cronbach. (1951). "Coefficient Alpha and the Internal Structure of Tests." *Psychometrika*, 16, pp. 297–334.

24. Frank B. Womer. (1968). *Basic Concepts in Testing*. Boston: Houghton Mifflin, p. 41.

25. Maurice G. Kendall and Alan Stuart. (1977). *The Advanced Theory of Statistics*, 4th edition. London: Griffin.

26. Cohen, J. (1960). "A Coefficient of Agreement for Nominal Scales." *Educational and Psychological Measurement*, 20, pp. 37–46.

27. Keith Miller. (1980). *Principles of Everyday Behaviour*, 2nd edition. Monterey, CA: Brooks/Cole.

28. Wayne Cascio. (1998). *Applied Psychology in Human Resource Management*, 5th edition. Upper Saddle River, NJ: Prentice Hall, p. 94.

29. Wayne Cascio. (1998), p. 94.

30. Alexander G. Wesman. (1952). *Reliability and Confidence*. Test Service Bulletin No 44. New York: The Psychological Corporation, p. 3.

31. Jum C. Nunnally. (1967). *Psychometric Theory*. New York: McGraw-Hill, p. 226

32. Truman Kelly. (1927). *Interpretations of Educational Measurements*. Yonkers, NY: World Book.

33. Lewis R. Aiken. (1988). *Psychological Testing and Assessment*, 2nd edition. Boston: Allyn & Bacon, p. 100; Elliot A. Weiner and Barbara J. Stewart. (1984). *Assessing Individuals*. Boston: Little, Brown, p. 69.

34. Robert M. Guion. (1965). *Personnel Testing*. New York: McGraw Hill, pp. 40–44.

35. Edwin E. Ghiselli. (1964). *Theory of Psychological Measurement*. New York: McGraw-Hill, TMH Edition, p. 288.

36. Robert Gatewood and Hubert Feild. (2001). *Human Resource Selection*, 5th edition. Toronto: South Western/Thomson Learning, p. 148.

37. Edwin E. Ghiselli. (1964). *Theory of Psychological Measurement*. New York: McGraw-Hill, TMH Edition, p. 288

38. Robert M. Guion. (1965). *Personnel Testing*. New York: McGraw-Hill, p. 123.

39. Robert Gatewood and Hubert Feild. (2001). *Human Resource Selection*, 5th edition. Toronto: South Western/Thomson Learning, p. 162.

40. Robert M. Guion and C.J. Cranny. (1982). "A Note on Concurrent and Predictive Validity Designs: A Critical Re-Analysis." *Journal of Applied Psychology*, 67, p. 240; Frank Landy. (1985). *Psychology of Work Behaviour*. Homewood, Illinois: Dorsey Press, p. 65.

41. Robert M. Guion. (1965). *Personnel Testing*. New York: McGraw-Hill, pp. 165–168

42. Philippe Cattin. (1980). "Estimation of the Predictive Power of a Regression Model." *Journal of Applied Psychology*, 65, pp. 407–414; Kevin Murphy. (1984). "Cost-Benefit Considerations in Choosing Among Cross Validation Methods." *Personnel Psychology*, 37, pp. 15–22.

43. Robert Gatewood and Hubert Feild. (2001). *Human Resource Selection*, 5th edition. Toronto: South Western/Thomson Learning, p. 171.

44. Robert Gatewood and Hubert Feild. (2001), p. 171.

45. Charles Huling, R.A. Henry, and S.L. Noon. (1990). "Adding a Dimension: Time as a Factor in the Generalizability of Predictive Relationships." *Psychological Bulletin*, 107, pp. 28–340.

46. E.E. Ghiselli and M. Haire. (1960). "The Validation of Selection Tests in the Light of the Dynamic Character of Criteria." *Personnel Psychology*, 13, pp. 225–232.

47. Robert M. Guion. (1965). *Personnel Testing*. New York: McGraw-Hill, pp. 125–126.

48. E.E. Jennings. (1953). "The Motivation Factor in Testing Supervisors." *Journal of Applied Psychology*, 37, pp. 168–169.

49. Robert M. Guion. (1965). *Personnel Testing*. New York: McGraw-Hill, p. 128.

50. Neal Schmitt, Richard Z. Gooding, Raymond A. Noe, and Michael Kirsch. (1984). "Meta-analyses of Validity Studies Published Between 1964 and 1982 and the Investigation of Study Characteristics." *Personnel Psychology*, 37, pp. 407–422.

51. D.S. Ones, C. Viswesvaran, and F.I. Schmidt. (1993). "Comprehensive Meta-Analysis of Integrity Test Validities: Findings and Implications for Personnel Selection Theories of Job Performance." *Journal of Applied Psychology*, 78, pp. 679–703. See also R.P. Tett, D.N. Jackson, and M. Rothstein. (1991). "Personality Measures as Predictors of Job Performance: A Meta-Analytic Review." *Personnel Psychology*, 44, pp. 703–742.

52. Robert M. Guion. (1965). *Personnel Testing*. New York: McGraw-Hill, p. 170.

53. Elmer Lemke and William Wiersma. (1976). *Principles of Psychological Measurement*. Chicago: Rand McNally, p. 110.

54. Ebel, R.L. (1977). "Prediction? Validation? Construct Validity?" *Personnel Psychology*, 30, pp. 55–63.

55. Samuel B. Green and Thomas Stutzman. (1986). "An Evaluation of Methods to Select Respondents to Structured Job Analysis Questionnaires." *Personnel Psychology*, 39, pp. 543–564. See also Samuel B. Green and John G. Veres. (1988). "Evaluation of an Index to Detect Inaccurate Respondents to a Task Analysis Inventory." Auburn AL: Department of Psychology, Auburn University.

56. Douglas Pine. (1995). "Assessing the Validity of Job Ratings: An Empirical Study of False Reporting in Task Inventories." *Public Personnel Management*, 24, pp. 451–460. Also see Samuel B. Green and Thomas Stutzman. (1986). "An Evaluation of Methods to Select Respondents to Structured Job Analysis Questionnaires." *Personnel Psychology*, 39, pp. 543–564.

57. Richard Barrett. (1998). *Challenging the Myths of Fair Employment Practice*. Westport, CT: Quorum Books, pp. 62–76.

58. Robert Gatewood and Hubert Feild. (2001). *Human Resource Selection*, 5th edition. Toronto: South Western/Thomson Learning, p.176.

59. Irwin L. Goldstein, Sheldon Zedeck, and Benjamin Schneider. (1993). "An Exploration of the Job Analysis-Content Validity Process." In Neal Schmitt and Walter C. Borman (eds). *Personnel Selection in Organizations*. San Francisco: Jossey Bass, pp. 7–10.

60. Irwin L. Goldstein, Sheldon Zedeck, and Benjamin Schneider. (1993), pp. 7–10.

61. Robert M. Guion. (1965). *Personnel Testing*. New York: McGraw-Hill, p. 124.

62. S. Adams. (1950). "Does Face Validity Exist?" *Educational and Psychological Measurement*, 10, pp. 320–328.

63. Robert M. Guion. (1965). *Personnel Testing*. New York: McGraw-Hill, p.125.

64. Benjamin Schneider and Neal Schmitt. (1986). *Staffing Organizations*. Glenview, IL: Scott, Foresman and Company, p. 249.

65. Benjamin Schneider. (1976). *Staffing Organizations*. Santa Monica, CA: Good Year Publishing Company, p. 130.

66. M.D. Dunnette. (1973). "Performance Equals Ability and What?" *Department of Psychology, Technical Report #4009*. Minneapolis: University of Minnesota.

67. R.R. Grooms and N.S. Endler. (1960). "The Effect of Anxiety on Academic Achievement." *Journal of Educational Psychology*, 51, pp. 229–304.

68. Marvin D. Dunnette. (1966). *Personnel Selection and Placement*. Belmont, CA: Brooks/Cole Publishing Company, p. 140.

Appendix 4A

1. Appendix prepared by Dr. Hari Das of Sobey's School of Business, Saint Mary's University, Halifax. All rights reserved by the author, © 2005.

2. John T. Roscoe. (1969). *Fundamentals of Research Statistics*. New York: Holt, Rinehart and Winston, Inc., p. 7.

3. Elmer Lemke and William Wiersma. (1976). *Principles of Psychological Measurement*. Chicago: Rand McNally Publishing, p. 17.

4. Roger Pfaffenberger and James Patterson. (1987). *Statistical Methods*, Third edition. Homewood, Illinois: Irwin, p. 275.

5. Elmer Lemke and William Wiersma. (1976). *Principles of Psychological Measurement*. Chicago: Rand McNally Publishing, p. 29.

Chapter 5

1. Peter Cappelli. (1999). *The New Deal at Work*. Boston: Harvard Business School Press, p. 17.

2. Peter Cappelli. (1999), p. 5.

3. Dave Ulrich. (1997). *Human Resource Champions*. Boston: Harvard Business School Press, p. 13.

4. C.C. Snow and S.A. Snell. (1993). "Staffing Strategy." In N. Schmitt, W.C. Borman, and Associates. *Personnel Selection in Organizations*. San Francisco: Jossey Bass, pp. 448–480.

5. For example, see Barry A. Macy and Hiroaki Izumi. (1993). "Organizational Change, Design, and Work Innovation: A Meta-Analysis of 131 North American Field Studies, 1961–1991." In W.A. Passmore and R.W. Woodman (eds.). *Research in Organizational Change and Development*, 7.

Greenwich, CT: Jai Press, pp. 235–313; John E. Delery and D. Harold Doty. (1996). "Modes of Theorizing in Strategic Human Resource Management: Tests of Universalistic, Contingency and Configurational Performance Predictions." *Academy of Management Journal*, 39, pp. 821–826.

6. Dwight L. Gertz and Joao P.A. Bapista. (1995). *Grow to be Great*. New York: Free Press.

7. John Leopold, Lynetter Harris, and Tony Watson. (2005). *The Strategic Managing of Human Resources*. Harlow, UK: Prentice-Hall, pp. 27–32.

8. Jeffrey Pfeffer. (1998). *The Human Equation*. Boston: Harvard Business School Press, p.11.

9. Jeffrey Pfeffer. (1998), p. 14.

10. T. Cox, Jr. (1993). *Cultural Diversity in Organizations: Theory, Research and Practice*. San Francisco: Berrett-Koehler.

11. Statistics Canada figures reported in the *The Globe and Mail* [Toronto], April 19, 2005, p. A5.

12. Results of a 2004 Statistics Canada survey reported in *The Globe and Mail* [Toronto], April 19, 2005, p. A5.

13. T. Cox, Jr. (1991, May). "The Multicultural Organization." *Academy of Management Executive*, pp. 34–47.

14. For example, see J.A. Bellizzi and R.W. Hasty. (2000). "The Effects of Hiring Decisions on the Level of Discipline Used in Response to Poor Performance." *Management Decision, 38*, 3, pp. 154–159.

15. John MacDuffie and Thomas Kochan. (1995). "Do US Firms Invest Less in Human Resources? Training in the World Auto Industry." *Industrial Relations, 34*, p. 156.

16. John MacDuffie. (1995). "Human Resource Bundles and Manufacturing Performance: Organizational Logic and Flexible Production Systems in the World Auto Industry." *Industrial and Labour Relations Review, 48*, pp. 211–212.

17. Jeffrey B. Arthur. (1995). "Effects of Human Resource Systems on Manufacturing Performance and Turnover." *Academy of Management Journal, 37*, p. 676.

18. Casey Ichniowski. (1992). "Human Resource Practices and Productive Labour-Management Relations." In David Lewin, Olivia Mitchell, and Peter Sherer (eds.). *Research Frontiers in Industrial Relations and Human Resources*. Madison, WI: Industrial Relations Research Association, pp. 239–271.

19. D.E. Super and M.J. Bohn. (1970). *Occupational Psychology*. Belmont, CA: Wadsworth.

20. Rosenberg, M. (1957). *Occupation and Values*. Glencoe, IL: Free Press. See also J.C. Flanagan and W.W. Cooley. (1966). *Project Talent: One Year Follow-Up Studies*. Pittsburgh: University of Pittsburgh Press.

21. Benjamin Schneider. (1976). *Staffing Organizations*. Santa Monica, CA: Goodyear Publishing, pp. 78–80.

22. Benjamin Schneider. (1976), p. 77. See also A.P. Garbin and F.L. Bates. (1966). "Occupational Prestige and Its Correlates: A Re-Examination." *Social Forces, 44*, pp. 295–302.

23. D.L. Shappell, L.G. Hall, and R.B. Tarrier. (1971). "Perceptions of the World of Work: Inner City versus the Suburbia." *Journal of Counselling Psychology, 18*, pp. 55–59

24. W.H. Sewell and A.M. Orenstein. (1965). "Community of Residence and Occupational Choice." *American Journal of Sociology, 70*, pp. 551–563.

25. Benjamin Schneider. (1976). *Staffing Organizations*. Santa Monica, CA: Goodyear Publishing, p. 80.

26. Benjamin Schneider. (1976), p. 80.

27. Samuel Osipow. (1968). *Theories of Career Development*. New York: Appleton-Century-Crofts, p. 41.

28. Stephen Weinrach. (1984). "Determinants of Vocational Choice: Holland's Theory." In Duane Brown, Linda Brooks, and Associates. *Career Choice and Development*. San Francisco: Jossey-Bass Publishers, pp. 61–93.

29. D.J. Prediger. (1981). "A Note on the Self-Directed Search Validity for Females." *Vocational Guidance Quarterly*, 30, 2, pp. 117–129. See also D.J. Prediger. (1982). "Do SDS Scores Really Help Females? A Reply to Holland." *Vocational Guidance Quarterly*, 30, 3, pp. 198–199.

30. Stephen Weinrach. (1984). "Determinants of Vocational Choice: Holland's Theory." In Duane Brown, Linda Brooks, and Associates. *Career Choice and Development*, San Francisco: Jossey-Bass Publishers, p. 76.

31. Andy Shaw. (2005, May 23). "Cities Come to HR Aid." *Canadian HR Reporter*, p. 1, 11.

32. Benjamin Schneider and Neal Schmitt. (1986). *Staffing Organizations*, 2nd edition. Glenview, IL: Scott, Foresman and Company, p. 155.

33. P.M. Blau, et al. (1956). "Occupational Choice: A Conceptual Framework." *Industrial and Labour Relations Review, 9*, pp. 531–543; W.H. Mobley. (1982). *Employee Turnover: Causes, Consequences and Control*. Reading, MA: Addison-Wesley.

34. Benjamin Schneider and Neal Schmitt. (1986). *Staffing Organizations*, 2nd edition. Glenview, IL: Scott, Foresman and Company, p. 155.

35. David Brown. (2005, June 20). "TD Gives Employees Tool to Chart Career Paths." *Canadian HR Reporter*, p. 11, 13.

36. A.W. Astin. (1966). "Effect of Different College Environments on the Vocational Choices of High Aptitude Students." *Journal of Counselling Psychology*, 12, pp. 28–34.

37. Benjamin Schneider. (1976). *Staffing Organizations*. Santa Monica, CA: Good Year Publishing, p. 90.

38. For example, see C.R. Tatro and A.P. Garbin. (1973). "The Industrial Prestige Hierarchy." *Journal of Vocational Behaviour*, 3, pp. 383–391.

39. V.R. Tom. (1971). "The Role of Personality and Organizational Images in the Recruitment Process." *Organizational Behaviour and Human Performance*, 6, pp. 573–591.

40. J.P. Wanous and A. Colella. (1989). "Organizational Entry Research: Current Status and Future Directions." In K.M. Rowland and G.R. Ferris (eds.). *Research in Personnel and Human Resource Management*, 7. Greenwich, CT: Jai Press, pp. 59–120.

41. F. Trompenaars. (1994). *Riding the Waves of Culture: Understanding Diversity in Global Business*. New York: Irwin.

42. James Breaugh. (1992). *Recruitment: Science and Practice*. Boston: PWS-Kent Publishing Company, pp. 67–77.

43. P.O. Soelberg. (1967). Unprogrammed Decision Making. *Industrial Management Review*, 8, pp. 19–29.

44. *Discussion Paper No. 156*. (1980). Ottawa: Economic Council of Canada.

45. M. Magnus. (1985). "Recruitment Ads at Work." *Personnel Journal*, 4, p. 64.

46. Paula Popovich and John Wanous. (1982, October). "The Realistic Job Preview as a Persuasive Communication." *Academy of Management Review*, p. 571.

47. M.R. Buckley, et al. (1998). "Investigating Newcomer Expectations and Job-Related Outcomes." *Journal of Applied Psychology*, 83, pp. 452–461.

48. Eve Lazarus. (2005, June–July). "Once Upon a Time." *HR Professional*, pp. 26–27.

49. "Recruitment Problems HR Faces." (2005, June 6). *Canadian HR Reporter*, p. 20. See also "Report on Recruitment and Staffing." (2005, May 23). *Canadian HR Reporter*.

50. George Raine, President of Montana HR Consultants, Personal communication, May 7, 2005.

51. Lisa Butler. (1999, May 3). "Corporate Culture Can Be Your Key to Success on the Hiring Front." *Canadian HR Reporter*, p. 22.

52. "What Benefits are Companies Offering Now?" (2000, June). *HR Focus*, 77, 6, p. 5.

53. Jeff Holloway. (2004, November) "Recruiting on Principle: Selling a Company's Values." *Canadian HR Reporter*, p. 7.

54. M.B. Teagarden, et al. (1995). "The Best Practices Learning Curve: Human Resource Practices in Mexico's Maquiladora Industry." In O. Shenkar (ed.). *Global Perspectives of Human Resource Management*. Upper Saddle River, NJ: Prentice Hall.

55. Uyen Vu. (2005, April 25). "Ottawa Cops Pursuing Diversity." *Canadian HR Reporter*, p. 1, 5.

56. James Breaugh. (1992). *Recruitment: Science and Practice*. Boston: PWS-Kent Publishing, p. 277.

57. L.S. Kleiman and K.J. Clark. (1984). "An Effective Job Posting System." *Personnel Journal*, 63, pp. 20–25.

58. "E-mail Is Now the Preferred Way to Receive Resumes." (2000, July). *HR Focus*, 77, 7, p. 8.

59. Larry Stevens. (1993, April). "Resume Scanning Simplifies Tracking." *Personnel Journal*, 72, 4, pp. 77–79.

60. Alan Halcrow. (1988, November). "Employees Are Your Best Recruiters." *Personnel Journal*, pp. 42–48.

61. Joey Goodings. (1999, Feb. 22). "Job Fairs: It's a Jungle Out There." *Canadian HR Reporter*, p. G–11.

62. S. Drake. (1992). "Temporaries Are Here to Stay." *Human Resource Executive*, 6, 2, pp. 27–30.

63. Al Doran. (1997, Jan. 13). "Popularity of Recruiting on the Internet Up." *Canadian HR Reporter*, p. 8.

64. V. Catano, et al. (1997). *Recruitment and Selection in Canada*. Toronto: ITP Nelson, p. 263.

65. Ben V. Luden. (1992, May). "HR vs. Executive Search." *Personnel Journal*, pp. 104–110.

66. Al Doran. (1997, Jan. 13). "Popularity of Recruiting on the Internet Up." *Canadian HR Reporter*, p. 8.

67. From *Learning to Work*. (Spring 2004). An online survey of students from Canadian universities and colleges commissioned by nine of Canada's largest employers and conducted in by D-Code and Brainstorm Consulting. Results reported in *Canadian HR Reporter* (April 25, 2005), p. 9

68. Madalyn Freund and Patricia Somers. (1979, April). "Ethics in College Recruiting: Views from the Front Lines," *Personnel Administrator*, pp. 30–33. Joe Thomas. (1980, January). "College Recruitment: How to Use Student Perceptions of Business." *Personnel Journal*, pp. 44–46. Donald P. Rogers and Michael Z. Sincoff. (1978, Autumn). "Favorable Impression Characteristics of the Recruitment Interviewer." *Personnel Psychology*, pp. 495–504.

69. Stephen Jackson. (1999, Jan. 25). "Performance Based Selection Nets Top Performers." *Canadian HR Reporter*, p. 6.

70. Nathan Laurie and Mark Laurie. (2000, Jan. 17). "No Holds Barred in Fight for Students to Fill Internship Programs." *Canadian HR Reporter*, p. 15.

71. J. Bussey. (1987, Jan. 10). "Dow Chemical Tries to Shed Tough Image and Court the Public." *Wall Street Journal*, p. 29.

72. James Breaugh. (1992). *Recruitment: Science and Practice*. Boston: PWS-Kent Publishing Company, p. 281.

73. James Breaugh. (1992), p. 294.

74. James Breaugh. (1992), p. 294.

75. S.L. Bem. (1981). *Bem Sex Role Inventory: Manual*. Palo Alto, CA: Consulting Psychologists Press.

76. *Government of Canada Services for You, Catalogue No. PF4–2/2000*. (2000). Ottawa: Ministry of Public Works and Government Services.

77. See also *Job Futures: World of Work*. Applied Research Branch, HRDC, Hull, Quebec K1A 0J2, National edition, Undated (Distributed in January 2003).

78. Graham Lowe. (2004, Nov. 18). "Revamp HR Policies to Retain Older Worker." *Canadian HR Reporter*, p. 17.

79. Al Doran. (1997, Jan. 13). "Popularity of Recruiting on the Internet Up." *Canadian HR Reporter*, p. 8.

80. Sherwood Ross. (2001, March 21). "Job Hunt Moves on Line." *The Globe and Mail* [Toronto], p. B16.

81. See http://www.shrm.org.

82. Yves Lermusiaux. (1999, April 5). "Recruiting Effectively over the Internet." *Canadian HR Reporter*, p. 2.

83. Mark Swartz, (1997, June 2). "Jobs Are Online: What About Job Seekers?" *Canadian HR Reporter*, p. 21.

84. Al Doran. (1999, Feb. 8). "Paper Resumes Out, Electronic Resume Creation In." *Canadian HR Reporter*, p. 9.

85. Peg Anthony. (1990, April). "Track Applicants, Track Costs." *Personnel Journal*, pp. 75–81. See also William C. Delone. (1993, April). "Telephone Job Posting Cuts Costs." *Personnel Journal*, 72, 4, pp. 115–18.

86. Matt Robinson. (2004, Oct. 11). "Applicant Tracking Tools Evolve with Technology." *Canadian HR Reporter*, p. 16.

87. J. Ross. (1991, February). "Effective Ways to Hire Contingent Personnel." *HR Magazine*, pp. 52–54.

88. Chris Knight. (1996, Oct. 21). "Contractors Become Fixture in Workplace." *Canadian HR Reporter*, p. 14.

89. Roger Smithies and Leslie Steeves. (1998, Jan. 12). "Define Contractor Relationships with Care." *Canadian HR Reporter*, p. 12.

90. T. Lee. (1991, June 11). "Alumni Go Back to Schools to Hunt Jobs." *Wall Street Journal*, p. B1. See also C.D. Fyock. (1991). "Ways to Recruit Top Talent." *HR Magazine*, 36, 7, pp. 33–35.

91. Sameera Sereda, quoted by Ann MacCaulay. (2005, June 6). "Don't Let Processes Get in the Way of a Good Hire, and Other Lessons." *Canadian HR Reporter*, p. 17.

92. Ann MacCaulay. (2005, June 6). "Don't Let Processes Get in the Way of a Good Hire, and Other Lessons." *Canadian HR Reporter*, p. 20.

93. Seyed-Mahmoud Aghazadeh. (1999). "Human Resource Management: Issues and Challenges in the New Millennium." *Management Research News*, 22, 12, pp. 19–32.

94. Ian Clark. (1999). "Corporate Human Resources and 'Bottom-line' Financial Performance." *Personnel Review*, 28, 4, pp. 290–306.

95. Robert Sibson. (1975, Feb. 14). "The High Cost of Hiring." *Nation's Business*, pp. 85–88; J. Scott Lord (1987, April). "How Recruitment Efforts Can Elevate Credibility." *Personnel Journal*, 66, 4.

96. Todd Humber. (2005, May 23). "Recruitment Isn't Getting any Easier." Recruitment and Staffing, Special supplement to *Canadian HR Reporter*, p. R2.

Chapter 6

1. Robert Wood and Tim Payne. (1998). *Competency Based Recruitment and Selection*. Chichester, UK: Wiley, p. 74.

2. James W. Thacker and R. Julian Cattaneo. (1993, March). *Survey of Personnel Practices in Canadian Organizations: A Report to Respondents*. Working Paper W92–04, Faculty of Business Administration, University of Windsor.

3. Andrew Templer, Julian Cattaneo, David De Cenzo, and Stephen Robbins. (1999). *Human Resource Management*. Toronto: John Wiley & Sons, p. 179.

4. Sharon Lebrun. (1997, May 5). "Retailers lose $3 Million a Day to Employees." *Canadian HR Reporter*, pp. 1–2.

5. Andrew Templer, Julian Cattaneo, David De Cenzo, and Stephen Robbins. (1999). *Human Resource Management*. Toronto: John Wiley & Sons, p. 182.

6. Andrew Templer, Julian Cattaneo, David De Cenzo, and Stephen Robbins. (1999). *Human Resource Management*. Toronto: John Wiley & Sons, p. 179.

7. David Brown. (2004, Oct. 11). "Waterloo Forced to Fire Top Bureaucrat Weeks after Hiring." *Canadian HR Reporter*, p. 3.

8. "Most Common Executive Embellishments." (2004, Oct. 11). *Canadian HR Reporter*, p. 3.

9. George England. (1971). *Development and Use of Weighted Application Blanks*. Minneapolis: Industrial Relations Centre, University of Minnesota, p. 63.

10. Robert Gatewood and Hubert Feild. (2001). *Human Resource Selection*, 5th edition. Mason, OH: South-Western, p. 472.

11. N. Friedman and Ernest J. McCormick. (1952). "A Study of Personal Data as Predictors of the Job Behaviour of Telephone Operators." *Proceedings of the Indiana Academy of Science*, 62, pp. 293–294.

12. From Leonard W. Ferguson. (1961). "The Development of Industrial Psychology." In Byron H. Gilmer (ed). *Industrial Psychology*, pp. 18–37.

13. Michael G. Aamodt and Walter L. Pierce. (1987). "Comparison of the Rare Response and Vertical Percent Methods for Scoring the Biographical Information Blank." *Educational and Psychological Measurement*, 47, p. 506; Steven H. Brown. (1994). "Validating Biodata." In Garnett S. Stokes, Michael Mumford, and Williams A. Owens (eds.). *Biodata Handabook*, Palo Alto, CA: CPP Books, p. 208.

14. George England. (1971). *Development and Use of Weighted Application Blanks*. Minneapolis: Industrial Relations Centre, University of Minnesota, pp. 60–68.

15. George England. (1971). *Development and Use of Weighted Application Blanks*. Minneapolis: Industrial Relations Centre, University of Minnesota, pp. 60–63; William B. Lecznar and John T. Dailey. (1950). "Keying Biographical Inventories in Classification Test Batteries." *American Psychologist*, 5, p. 279; Michael P. Malone. (1978). *Predictive Efficiency and Discriminatory Impact of Verifiable Biographical Data as a Function of Data Analysis Procedure*. Doctoral dissertation, University of Minnesota, Minneapolis.

16. Marilyn K. Quaintance. (1981). *Development of a Weighted Application Blank to Predict Managerial Assessment Center Performance*. Doctoral Dissertation, George Washington University, Washington, D.C.

17. George England. (1971). *Development and Use of Weighted Application Blanks*. Minneapolis: Industrial Relations Centre, University of Minnesota, pp. 64–68.

18. Marvin D. Dunnette, Wayne K. Kirchner, James R. Erickson, and Paul A. Banas. (1960). "Predicting Turnover among Female Office Workers." *Personnel Administration*, 23, pp. 45–50. See also Paul Wernimont. (1962). "Re-evaluation of a Weighted Application Blank for Office Personnel." *Journal of Applied Psychology*, 46, pp. 417–419.

19. Darrell E. Roach. (1971). "Double Cross Validation of a Weighted Application Blank over Time." *Journal of Applied Psychology*, 55, pp. 157–160.

20. Morris Viteles. (1932). *Industrial Psychology*. New York: Norton.

21. Edward Cureton. (1965). "Comment" In Edwin R. Henry, *Use of Autobiographical Data as Psychological Predictors*, Greensboro, NC: The Richardson Foundation, 1965, p. 13.

22. For example, see W.A. Owens. (1976). "Background Data." In M.D. Dunnette (ed). *Handbook of Industrial Psychology*. New York: Rand-McNally; Lyle Schoenfeldt. (1999). "From Dust Bowl Empiricism to Rational Constructs in Biographical Data." *Human Resource Management Review*, 9, 2, pp. 147–167.

23. R.R. Reilly and G.T. Chao. (1982). "Validity and Rairness of Some Alternative Employee Selection Procedures." *Personnel Psychology*, 35, pp. 1–62.

24. Sidney Fine and Steven Cronshaw. (1994). "The Role of Job Analysis in Establishing the Validity of Biodata." In Garnett S. Stokes, Michael D. Mumford, and William Owns (eds.). *Biodata Handbook*. Palo Alto, CA: CPP Books, pp. 39–64.

25. John B. Miner. (1971). "Success in Management Consulting and the Concept of Eliteness Motivation." *Academy of Management Journal*, 14, pp. 367–378.

26. For a detailed list, see James R. Glennon, Lewis E. Albright, and William A. Owens. (1966). *A Catalog of Life History Items*. Greensboro, NC: The Richardson Foundation. See also William A. Owens and Edwin R. Henry. (1966). *Biographical Data in Industrial Psychology: A Review and Evaluation*. Greensboro, NC: The Richardson Foundation; Terrence Mitchell. (1994). "The Utility of Biodata." In Garnett S. Stokes, Michael D. Mumford, and William Owns (eds.). *Biodata Handbook*. Palo Alto, CA: CPP Books, pp. 492–493.

27. Michael D. Mumford and William A. Owens. (1987). "Methodology Review: Principles, Procedures and Findings in the Application of Background Data Measures." *Applied Psychological Measurement*, 11, p. 2–10. See also Robert Gatewood and Hubert Feild. (2001). *Human Resource Selection*, 5th edition. Mason, OH: South-Western, p. 494.

28. Robert Gatewood and Hubert Feild. (2001). *Human Resource Selection*, 5th edition, Mason, OH: South-Western, p. 495.

29. For example, see Frederick L. Oswald, et al. (2004). "Developing a Biodata Measure and Situational Judgment Inventory as Predictors of College Student Performance." *Journal of Applied Psychology*, 89, 2, pp. 187–207.

30. Laurence Siegel and Irving Lane. (1969). *Personnel and Organizational Psychology*, Homewood, IL: Irwin.

31. Edwin Ghiselli. (1966). *The Validity of Occupational Aptitude Tests*. New York: Wiley.

32. For example, see James J. Asher. (1979). "The Biographical Item: Can It Be Improved?" *Personnel Psychology*, 25, p. 759.

33. Joyce Lain Kennedy and Thomas J. Morrow. (1994). *The Electronic Resume Revolution*. New York: Wiley and Sons.

34. For other suggestions on the matter, see Joyce Lain Kennedy and Thomas J. Morrow. (1994). *The Electronic Resume Revolution*. New York: Wiley and Sons; Joyce Lain Kennedy and Thomas J. Morrow. (1994). *The Electronic Job Search Revolution*. New York: Wiley and Sons.

Chapter 7

1. Edward Hoffman. (2002). *Psychological Testing at Work*. New York: McGraw Hill, p. 2.

2. J.W. Thacker and R.J. Cattaneo. (1987). *Survey of Personnel Practices in Canadian Organizations*. Working Paper No.

87–03. Windsor: University of Windsor, Faculty of Business Administration.

3.   Laura Cassiani. (2001, March 26). "Employers Gambling When It Comes to Hiring: Survey: A Quarter of New Hires are Underperforming." *Canadian HR Reporter*, p. 6

4.   John Towler. (2005, July 18). "Test Before You Hire." *Canadian HR Reporter*, p. 2.

5.   Robert Gatewood and Hubert Feild. (2001). *Human Resource Selection*, 5th edition. Mason, OH: South-Western/Thomson Learning, p. 155.

6.   Todd Humber. (2004, May 17). "Psychometric Testing Often Misused in Recruitment." *Canadian HR Reporter*, p. 3.

7.   Todd Humber. (2004, May 17), p. 3

8.   Canadian Human Rights Commission. (1985). *Bona Fide Occupational Requirement and Bona Fide Justification: Interim Policies and Explanatory Notes*. Ottawa, p. 11.

9.   Norman Trainor. (1998, Nov. 16). "Using Measurement to Predict Performance." *Canadian HR Reporter*, p. 7.

10. Martin Dewey. (1981, Feb. 7). "Employers Take a Hard Look at the Validity and Value of Psychological Screening." *The Globe and Mail* [Toronto], p. B1.

11. James Leduinka and Lyle F. Schoenfeldt. (1978, Spring). "Legal Development in Employment Testing: Albermarle and Beyond." *Personnel Psychology*, pp. 1–13.

12. Julie McCarthy and Richard Goffin. (2000). "Test Taking Anxiety in a Selection Context: The Moderating Role of Applicant Gender." *ASAC-IFSAM 2000 Conference Human Resource Division Proceedings*, 21, 9, pp. 69–77.

13. Dale Yoder and Herbert Heneman. (1979). *ASPA Handbook of Personnel and Industrial Relations*. Washington, DC: The Bureau of National Affairs, pp. 4.140–4.141.

14. D.A. Dye, M. Reck, and M.A. McDaniel. (1993). "The Validity of Job Knowledge Measures." *International Journal of Selection and Assessment*, 1, pp. 153–157.

15. H.F. Schwind, H. Das, and T. Wagar. (2005). *Canadian Human Resource Management*, 7th edition. Toronto: McGraw-Hill Ryerson, p. 261.

16. For example, see R.J. Sternberg, R.K. Wagner, W.M. Williams, and J.A. Horvath. (1995). "Testing Common Sense." *American Psychologist*, 50, pp. 912–927.

17. For example, see R.E. Lobsenz. (1999). "Do Measures of Tacit Knowledge Assess Psychological Phenomena Distinct from General Ability, Personality, and Social Knowledge?" *Dissertation Abstracts International*: *Section B-The Sciences and Engineering*, 59: p. 05147.

18. Dale Yoder and Herbert Heneman. (1979). *ASPA Handbook of Personnel and Industrial Relations*. Washington, DC: The Bureau of National Affairs, pp. 4.142.

19. Dale Yoder and Herbert Heneman. (1979), pp. 4.142.

20. Robert Gatewood and Hubert Feild. (2001). *Human Resource Selection*, 5th edition. Mason, OH: South-Western/Thomson Learning, p. 568.

21. Robert Gatewood and Hubert Feild. (2001), pp. 568–9

22. Neal Schmitt and Benjamin Schneider. (1990). *Organizational Entry*. Greenwich, CN: Jai Press, p. 137.

23. For more information, see Edwin A. Fleishman. (1992). *Physical Abilities Analysis Manual*, revised edition. Palo Alto, CA: Consulting Psychologists Press, 1992; Edwin A. Fleishman and Michael D. Mumford. (1988). "Ability Requirement Scales." In Sidney Gael (ed.). *Job Analysis Handbook for Business, Industry and Government*, 2. New York: Wiley;

E. Fleishman and M.K. Quaintance. (1984). *Taxonomies of Human Performance: The Description of Human Tasks*. Orlando, FL: Academic Press.

24. John Foley. (1972). "Review of the Wonderlic Personal Test." In Oscar K. Boros (ed.). *The Seventh Mental Measurements Year Book*. Highland Park, NJ: Gryphon Press, pp. 401–403.

25. M.J. Ree and T.R. Carretta. (1998). "General Cognitive Ability and Occupational Performance." In C.L. Cooper and I.T. Robertson (eds.). *International Review of Industrial and Organizational Psychology*, 13. London: John Wiley, pp. 159–184.

26. L. Gottfredson. (1997). "Why G Matters: The Complexity of Everyday Life." *Intelligence*, 24, pp. 79–132. See also L. Gottfredson. (1986). "Societal Consequences of the G Factor in Employment." *Journal of Vocational Behaviour*, 29, pp. 379–411.

27. Joseph Abraham and John Morrison. (2005). "Mental Ability Testing." Retrieved from **http://www.ppicentral.com/Pdf/ ability.pdf** on August 10, 2005.

28. Conrad Murphy. (2005, July 18). "Assessing Essential Skills to Recruit and Train." *Canadian HR Reporter*, p. 11.

29. Dale Yoder and Herbert Heneman. (1979). *ASPA Handbook of Personnel and Industrial Relations*. Washington, DC: The Bureau of National Affairs, pp. 4.140– 4.140.

30. S. Sillup. (1992, May). "Applicant Screening Cuts Turnover Costs." *Personnel Journal*, pp. 115–16.

31. E.A. Fleishman and M.D. Mumford. (1988). "Ability Requirement Scales." In Sidney Gael (ed.). *Job Analysis Handbook for Business, Industry and Government*, 2. New York: Wiley.

32. Edward Hoffman. (2002). *Psychological Testing at Work*. New York: McGraw Hill, p. 143.

33. See Bernard Bass and Bruce Avolio. (1995). *MLQ Multifactor Leadership Questionnaire*. Redwood City, CA: Mind Garden.

34. Victor Dulewicz and Malcolm Higgs. (1999). "Can Emotional Intelligence be Measured and Developed?" *Leadership and Organization Development Journal*, 20, 5, pp. 242–252.

35. For example, see L. Polednik and E. Greig. (2000). "Personality and Emotional Intelligence." *The British Journal of Administrative Management*, 19, pp. 9–12.

36. H.F. Schwind, H. Das, and T. Wagar. (2005). *Canadian Human Resource Management*, 7th edition. Toronto: McGraw-Hill Ryerson, p. 266.

37. Electronic Selection Systems Corporation, AccuVision. (1992). *Assessment Technology for Today, Tomorrow and Beyond*. Maitland, FL: Electronic Selection Systems, Inc.

38. For example, see R.C. Overton, H.J. Harms, L.R. Taylor, and M.J. Zickar (1997). "Adapting to Adaptive Testing." *Personnel Psychology*, 50, pp. 171–185.

39. R.P. Tett and H.A. Gutterman. (2000). "Situation Trait Relevance, Trait Expression and Cross-Situational Consistency." *Journal of Research in Personality*, 34, pp. 397–423.

40. Glen Grimsley and Hilton Jarrett. (1975). "The Relation of Past Managerial Achievement to Test Measures Obtained in the Employment Situation: Methodology and Results II." *Personnel Psychology*, 28, pp. 215–231.

41. P.T. Costa, Jr. (1996). "Work and Personality: Using the NEO-PI-R in Industrial/Organizational Psychology." *Applied Psychology: An International Review*, 45, pp. 225–41.

42. L. Smith. (1994, Nov. 28). "Stamina: Who Has It, Why You Need It and How You Can Get It." *Fortune*, p. 31.

43. Ian Gellatly and P. Gregory Irving. (1999). "The Moderating Role of Perceived Autonomy on Personality-Performance Relations within a Public Sector Organization." In Gerard Seijts (ed.). *ASAC 1999 (Human Resource Division) Proceedings*, 20, 9, pp. 49–58.

44. Richard Lanyon and Leonard Goodstein. (1982). *Personality Assessment*, 2nd edition. New York: Wiley, p. 28.

45. Raymond B. Cattell. (1965). *The Scientific Analysis of Personality*. Baltimore: Penguin Books.

46. See Robert T. Hogan. (1995). "Personality and Personality Measurement." In Marvin Dunnett and Leatta Hough (eds.). *The Handbook of Industrial and Organizational Psychology*, 2. Palo Alto, CA: Consulting Psychologists Press, pp. 873–919.

47. For example, see S. Adler. (1996). "Personality and Work Behaviour: Exploring the Linkages." *Applied Psychology: An International Review*, pp. 207–224.

48. Robert Tett and Dawn Burnett. (2003). "A Personality Trait-Based Interactionist Model of Job Performance." *Journal of Applied Psychology*, 88, 3, pp. 500–517.

49. For example, see M.K. Mount, M.R. Barrick, and G.L. Stewart. (1998). "Five Factor Model of Personality and Performance in Jobs Involving Interpersonal Interactions." *Human Performance*, 11, pp. 145–165.

50. Simon Taggar. (2000). "Personality, Cognitive Ability and Behaviour: The Antecedents of Effective Autonomous Work Teams." In Joanne Dick (ed.). *ASAC-IFSAM 2000 Conference Human Resource Division Proceedings*, 21, 9, pp. 59–66.

51. Robert Wood and Tim Payne. (1998). *Competency Based Recruitment and Selection*. Chichester, UK: Wiley, pp. 153–169.

52. H.F. Schwind, H. Das, and T. Wagar. (2005). *Canadian Human Resource Management*, 7th edition. Toronto: McGraw-Hill Ryerson, p. 265.

53. H.F. Schwind, H. Das, and T. Wagar. (2005), p. 266.

54. "Should You Tell All?" (1990, May 27). *Parade Magazine*, p. 5.

55. D.T. Lykken (1985, Sept.). "The Case Against the Polygraph in Employment Screening." *Personnel Administrator*, pp. 59–65.

56. "Workplace Privacy." (1994). *Ontario Commissioner's Report, Worklife Report*, 9, 3, pp. 8–9.

57. Paul Sackett and James Warek. (1996). "New Developments in the Use of Measures of Honesty, Integrity, Conscientiousness, Dependability, Trustworthiness, and Reliability for Personnel Selection." *Personal Psychology*, 49, pp. 787–829. See also Robert M. Madigan, K. Dow Scott, Diana L. Deadrick, and J.A. Stoddard. (1986, September). "Employment Testing: The U.S. Job Service is Spearheading a Revolution." *Personnel Administrator*, pp. 102–12.

58. Adelheid Nicol and Sampo Paunonen. (1998). "Workplace Honesty: The Development of a New Measure." In Caroline Weber (ed.). *ASAC 1998 (Human Resources Divison) Proceedings*, 19, 9, pp. 31–42.

59. P.R. Sackett and M.M. Harris. (1984). "Honesty Testing for Personnel Selection: A Review and a Critique." *Personnel Psychology*, 37, pp. 221–45.

60. D.S. Ones, C. Visweswaran, and F.L. Schmidt. (1993, August). "Comprehensive Meta Analysis of Integrity Test Validities: Findings and Implications for Personnel Selection and Theories of Job Performance." *Journal of Applied Psychology*, 78, pp. 679–703. See also P.R. Sackett, L.R. Burris, and C. Callahan. (1989, Autumn). "Integrity Testing for Personal Selection: An Update." *Personnel Psychology*, 42, pp. 91–529.

61. Dennis S. Joy. (1991). "Basic Psychometric Properties of a Pre-employment Honesty Test: Reliability, Validity and Fairness." In John W. Jones (ed.). *Pre-employment Honesty Testing*. New York: Quorum Books, pp. 65–88.

62. See http://www.bsgcorp.com/journal/journal.html, December 25, 2000.

63. H.F. Schwind, H. Das, and T. Wagar. (2005). *Canadian Human Resource Management*, 7th edition. Toronto: McGraw-Hill Ryerson, p. 268.

64. H.F. Schwind, H. Das, and T. Wagar. (2005), p. 273.

65. *Kearsley v. City of St. Catharines*. (2002, April 2). Board of Inquiry decision 02-005. Ontario Human Rights Tribunal. http://www.hrto.ca/english/decisions/2002. © Queen's Printer for Ontario, 2002. Reprinted with permission.

66. *Human Rights at Work*. (1999). Ontario Human Rights Commission, Approved by Commission on September 22, 1999, pp. 58–60. See also http://www.obrc.on.ca.

67. Health Canada. (2004, November). *Canadian Addiction Survey Highlights*, pp. 6–14.

68. B.L. Thompson. (1990, November). "A Surprising Ally in the Drug Wars." *Training*, pp. 11–17.

69. Ted Thaler. (1990, Oct. 24). "Substance Abuse Costing Employers Estimated $2.6-B." *Canadian HR Reporter*, p. 1.

70. Jane Easter Bahls. (1998, February). "Drugs in the Workplace." *HR Magazine*. Retrieved from www.shrm.org/hrmagazine.

71. C. Languedoc. (1987, April 13). "Battle Lines Forming over Worker Drug Test." *The Financial Post*, pp. 1, 4.

72. "Imperial Oil to Test Staff for Drugs" (1991, Oct. 5). *The Globe and Mail* [Toronto], p. B1. See also "Mandatory Drug Testing Attracts Controversy." (1991, April 9). *Canadian Employment Law Today*, pp. 635–46.

73. Jeffrey Miller. (1998, Sept. 21). "Drug Testing Dealt a Blow by Federal Court" *Canadian HR Reporter*, p. 5.

74. Virginia Galt. (1992, Feb. 22). "Total Ban Sought on Drug Testing by Employers." *The Globe and Mail* [Toronto]. p. 6.

75. *Canadian Human Rights Commission Annual Report 1993*. (1994). Ottawa: Ministry of Supply and Services Canada, pp. 35–36.

76. "The Case Against Drug Testing." (1994, Aug. 19). *The Globe and Mail* [Toronto]. p. A18.

77. Jeffrey Miller. (1998), p. 5.

78. *Human Rights at Work* (1999). Ontario Human Rights Commission. Retrieved from http://www.obrc.on.ca.

79. "The Changing Legal Landscape." (2005, Jan. 31). Report on Employment Law, Supplement to *Canadian HR Reporter*, p. R11.

80. "Catch-22: Under Imperial Oil's Revamped Drug Policy." (1994, Nov-Dec). *Journal of the Addiction Research Foundation*, 22, 6, p. 12.

81. Statistics provided by Brian Fuller, formerly a director of security administration for Macy's Department Stores, quoted from http://www.workforce.com/archive/feature/23/37/23/index.php.

82. Charles Handler and Steven Hunt. (2002, December). "Picking the Right Assessment Tools." *Workforce Online*. Retrieved from http://www.workforce.com/archive/feature/23/37/23/index.php.

83. H.F. Schwind, H. Das, and T. Wagar. (2005). *Canadian Human Resource Management*, 7th edition. Toronto: McGraw-Hill Ryerson, p. 268.

84. For an example, see William G. Doerner and Terry Nowell. (1999). "The Reliability of the Behavioural-Personnel Assessment Device (B-PAD) in Selecting Police Recruits." *Policing*, 22, 3, pp. 343–352.

85. Sean Way and James Thacker. (1999, Oct-Nov). "Selection Practices: Where are Canadian Organizations?" *HR Professional*, p. 35.

86. Charles Handler and Steven Hunt. (2002, December). "Choosing the Right Assessment Vendor." *Workforce Online*. Retrieved on August 12, 2005 from **http://www.workforce.com/archive/feature/23/37/23/index.php.**

87. D.D. Steiner and S.W. Gilliland. (1996). "Fairness Reactions to Personnel Selection Techniques in France and the United States." *Journal of Applied Psychology, 81*, pp. 131–141.

Chapter 8

1. Lyle M. Spencer and Signe M. Spencer. (1993). *Competence at Work*. New York: John Wiley & Sons, p. 114.

2. Robert D. Gatewood and Hubert S. Feild. (2001). *Human Resource Selection, 5th* edition. Mason, OH: South Western/Thompson Learning, p. 526.

3. F.L. Schmidt and M. Rader. (1999). "Exploring the Boundary Conditions for Interview Validity: Meta-Analytic Validity Findings for a New Interview Type." *Personnel Psychology, 52*, pp. 445–464.

4. M.A. Campion, E.D. Purcell, and B.K. Brown. (1988). "Structured Interviewing: Raising the Psychometric Properties of the Employment Interview." *Personnel Psychology, 41*, pp. 25–42.

5. L. Ulrich and D. Trumbo. (1965). "The Selection Interview since 1949." *Psychological Bulletin, 63*, pp. 100–116.

6. R.D. Arvey and J.E. Campion. (1982). "The Employment Interview: A Summary and Review of Recent Research." *Personnel Psychology, 35*, pp. 281–322.

7. M.M. Harris. (1999). "What is Being Measured?" In R.W. Eder and M.M. Harris (eds.). *The Employment Interview Handbook*. Thousand Oaks, CA: Sage, pp. 143–157.

8. Allen I. Huffcut, James M. Conway, Philip L. Roth, and Nancy J. Stone. (2001). "Identification and Meta-Analytic Assessment of Psychological Constructs Measured In Employment Interviews." *Journal of Applied Psychology, 86, 5,* pp. 897–913.

9. A. Huffcut, P. Roth, and M. McDaniel. (1996). A Meta Analytic Investigation of Cognitive Ability in Employment Interview Evaluations: Moderating Characteristics and Implications for Incremental Validity. *Journal of Applied Psychology, 81*, pp. 459–473.

10. Allen I. Huffcut, James M. Conway, Philip L. Roth, and Nancy J. Stone. (2001). "Identification and Meta-Analytic Assessment of Psychological Constructs Measured In Employment Interviews." *Journal of Applied Psychology, 86, 5,* p. 905.

11. Allen I. Huffcut, James M. Conway, Philip L. Roth, and Nancy J. Stone. (2001), p. 908.

12. Robert D. Gatewood and Hubert S. Feild. (2001). *Human Resource Selection, 5th* edition. Mason, OH: South Western/Thompson Learning, p. 525.

13. Robert D. Gatewood and Hubert S. Feild. (2001), p. 525.

14. J.E. Hunter and R.F. Hunter. (1984). "Validity and Utility of Alternate Predictors of Job Performance." *Psychological Bulletin, 96*, pp. 72–98.

15. For a good review, see Richard A. Postuma, Frederick P. Morgerson, and Michael A. Campion. (2002). "Beyond Employment Interview Validity: A Comprehensive Narrative Review of Recent Research and Trends over Time." *Personnel Psychology, 55*, pp. 1–81.

16. Allen I. Huffcut, James M. Conway, Philip L. Roth, and Nancy J. Stone. (2001). "Identification and Meta-Analytic Assessment of Psychological Constructs Measured In Employment Interviews." *Journal of Applied Psychology, 86, 5,* p. 909.

17. Allen I. Huffcut, James M. Conway, Philip L. Roth, and Nancy J. Stone. (2001), p. 903.

18. Allen I. Huffcut, James M. Conway, Philip L. Roth, and Nancy J. Stone. (2001), p. 908.

19. Allen I. Huffcut, James M. Conway, Philip L. Roth, and Nancy J. Stone. (2001), p. 906.

20. Allen I. Huffcut, James M. Conway, Philip L. Roth, and Nancy J. Stone. (2001), p. 906.

21. Allen I. Huffcut, James M. Conway, Philip L. Roth, and Nancy J. Stone. (2001), p. 906.

22. David Grove. (1981). "A Behavioural Consistency Approach to Decision Making in Employment Selection." *Personnel Psychology, 34*, pp. 55–64.

23. David Grove. (1981), pp. 55–64.

24. Allen I. Huffcut, James M. Conway, Philip L. Roth, and Nancy J. Stone. (2001), p. 906.

25. Allen I. Huffcut, James M. Conway, Philip L. Roth, and Nancy J. Stone. (2001), p. 906.

26. The Bureau of National Affairs. (1994). *Recruiting and Selection Procedures*. PPF Survey No. 146.

27. Todd Humber. (2005, May 23). "Recruitment Isn't Getting any Easier." Report on Recruitment and Staffing, Supplement to *Canadian HR Reporter*, p. R2.

28. Willi H. Weisner and Steven F. Cronshaw. (1988). "A Meta-Analytic Investigation of the Impact of Interview Format and Degree of Structure on the Validity of Employment Interview." *Journal of Occupational Psychology, 61*, pp. 275–290.

29. Cynthica Searcy, Patty Nio Woods, Robert Gatewood, and Charles E. Lance. (1993). *The Structured Interview: A Meta-Analytic Search for Moderators*. Paper presented at the Society of Industrial and Organizational Psychology, 1993; Michael A. McDaniel, Deborah L. Whetzel, Frank L. Schmidt, and Steven D. Maurer. (1994). "The Validity of Employment Interview: A Comprehensive Review and Meta Analysis." *Journal of Applied Psychology, 79*, pp. 599–616.

30. Richard A. Postuma, Frederick P. Morgerson, and Michael A. Campion. (2002). "Beyond Employment Interview Validity: A Comprehensive Narrative Review of Recent Research and Trends over Time." *Personnel Psychology, 55*, p. 18.

31. Thomas W. Dougherty, Daniel B. Turban, and John C. Callender. (1994). "Confirming First Impressions in the Employment Interview: A Field Study of Interview Behaviour." *Journal of Applied Psychology, 79*, pp. 659–665.

32. A.P. Philips and R.L. Dipboye. (1989). "Correlational Tests of Predictions from a Process Model of the Interview." *Journal of Applied Psychology, 74*, pp. 41–52.

33. T.W. Dougherty, D.B. Turban, and J.C. Callender. (1994). "Confirming First Impressions in the Employment Interview: A Field Study of Interview Behaviour." *Journal of Applied Psychology, 79*, p. 665.

34. Robert L. Dipboye. (1992). *Selection Interviews: Process, Perspectives*, Cincinnati: South-Western. See also George Dreher and Paul Sackett. (1983). *Perspective on Employee Staffing and Selection*. Homewood, IL: Richard D. Irwin.

35. Robert D. Gatewood and Hubert S. Feild. (2001). *Human Resource Selection, 5th* edition. Mason, OH: South Western/Thompson Learning, p. 536.

36. James E. Campion and Richard D. Arvey. (1989). "Unfair Discrimination in the Interview." In R.W. Eder and G.R. Ferris (ed.). *The Employment Interviews*. Newbury Park, CA: Sage.

37. N. Schmitt. (1976). "Social and Situational Determinants of Interview Decisions: Implications for the Employment Interview." *Personnel Psychology*, 29, pp. 79–101.

38. C.L. Adkins, C.J. Russell, and J.D. Werbel. (1994). "Judgments of Fit in Selection Process: The Role of Work Value Congruence." *Personnel Psychology*, 47, pp. 605–623.

39. Richard A. Postuma, Frederick P. Morgerson, and Michael A. Campion. (2002). "Beyond Employment Interview Validity: A Comprehensive Narrative Review of Recent Research and Trends over Time." *Personnel Psychology*, 55, p. 35.

40. Richard A. Postuma, Frederick P. Morgerson, and Michael A. Campion. (2002), p. 35.

41. Thomas W. Dougherty, Daniel B. Turban, and John C. Callender. (1994). "Confirming First Impressions in the Employment Interview: A Field Study of Interview Behaviour." *Journal of Applied Psychology*, 79, pp. 659–665.

42. Robert D. Gatewood and Hubert S. Feild. (2001). *Human Resource Selection,* 5th edition. Mason, OH: South Western/Thompson Learning, p. 536.

43. Richard A. Postuma, Frederick P. Morgerson, and Michael A. Campion. (2002). "Beyond Employment Interview Validity: A Comprehensive Narrative Review of Recent Research and Trends over Time." *Personnel Psychology*, 55, p. 37.

44. Laura Graves and Gary Powell. (1996). "Sex Similarity, Quality of the Employment Interview and Recruiters's Evaluation of Actual Applicants." *Journal of Occupational and Organizational Psychology*, 69, pp. 243–261.

45. Amelia Prewett-Livingston, Hubert S. Feild, John G. Veres, and Philip M. Lewis. (1996). "Effects of Race on Interview Ratings in a Situational Panel Interview." *Journal of Applied Psychology*, 81, pp. 178–186.

46. Richard A. Postuma, Frederick P. Morgerson, and Michael A. Campion. (2002). "Beyond Employment Interview Validity: A Comprehensive Narrative Review of Recent Research and Trends over Time." *Personnel Psychology*, 55, p. 25.

47. A. Dalessio and A.S. Imada. (1984). "Relationship between Interview Selection Decisions and Perceptions of Applicant Similarity to an Ideal Employment and Self: A Field Study." *Human Relations*, 37, pp. 67–80.

48. A. Furnam and E. Burbeck. (1989). "Employment Interview Outcomes as a Function of Interviewers' Experience." *Perceptual and Motor Skills*, 69, pp. 395–402.

49. L.M. Graves. (1993). "Sources of Individual Differences in Interview Effectiveness: A Model and Implications for Future Research." *Journal of Organizational Behaviour*, 14, pp. 349–370.

50. M.A. Campion, D.K. Palmer, and J.E. Campion. (1997). "A Review of Structure in the Selection Interview." *Personnel Psychology*, 50, pp. 655–702.

51. Richard A. Postuma, Frederick P. Morgerson, and Michael A. Campion. (2002). "Beyond Employment Interview Validity: A Comprehensive Narrative Review of Recent Research and Trends over Time." *Personnel Psychology*, 55, p. 22.

52. S.M. Forsythe. (1990). "Effects of Applicants' Clothing on Interviewer's Decisions to Hire." *Journal of Applied Social Psychology*, 20, pp. 1579–1595.

53. R. Pingitore, B.L. Dugoni, R.S. Tindale, and B. Spring. (1994). "Bias Against Overweight Job Applicants in a Simulated Employment Interview." *Journal of Applied Psychology*, 79, pp. 909–917.

54. R.D. Arvey and J.E. Campion. (1982). "The Employment Interview: A Summary and Review of Recent Research." *Personnel Psychology*, 35, pp. 281–322.

55. M.S. Singer and C. Sewell. (1989). "Applicant Age and Selection Interview Decisions: Effect of Information Exposure on Age Discrimination in Personnel Selection." *Personnel Psychology*, 42, pp. 135–154.

56. Richard A. Postuma, Frederick P. Morgerson, and Michael A. Campion. (2002), p. 31.

57. T. DeGroot and S.J. Motowidlo. (1999). "Why Visual and Vocal Interview Cues Can Affect Interviewers' Judgments and Predict Job Performance." *Journal of Applied Psychology*, 84, pp. 986–993.

58. C.B. Johnson. (1990). "Bias in the Selection Interview: Self or Other Directed?" Doctoral dissertation, Kansas State University, 1989. *Dissertation Abstracts International*, 50, p. 5912.

59. C.K. Stevens and A.L. Kristof. (1995). "Making the Right Impression: A Field Study of Applicant Impression Management during Job Interviews." *Journal of Applied Psychology*, 80, pp. 587–606.

60. N. Schmitt. (1976). "Social and Situational Determinants of Interview Decisions: Implications for the Employment Interview." *Personnel Psychology*, 29, pp. 79–101.

61. K.S. Morton. (1994). "A Schema Model of Dispositional Attribution in the Employment Selection Process." Doctoral dissertation, University of California, Santa Barbara. *Dissertation Abstracts International*, 49, p. 2927.

62. Gary P. Latham, Lise M. Saari, Elliott D. Pursell, and Michael A. Campion. (1980). "The Situational Interview." *Journal of Applied Psychology, 65*, pp. 422–427.

63. For example, see Jeff A. Weekley and Joseph A. Gier. (1987). "Reliability and Validity of the Situational Interview for a Sales Position." *Journal of Applied Psychology, 3,* pp. 484–487; Gary P. Latham and Lise M. Saari. (1984). "Do People Do What They Say? Further Studies on the Situational Interview." *Journal of Applied Psychology, 4,* pp. 569–573.

64. Stephen Maurer. (1997). "The Potential of Situational Interview: Existing Research and Unresolved Issues." *Human Resource Management Review, 7,* 2, pp. 185–201.

65. Tom Janz. (1989). "The Patterned Behavioural Description Interview: The Best Prophet of the Future is the Past." In Eder and Ferris (eds.). *The Employment Interview,* Newberry Park, CA: 1989. pp. 158–68; C. Orpen. (1985). "Patterned Behavioural Description Interview Versus Unstructured Interviews: A Comparative Validity Study." *Journal of Applied Psychology, 70,* pp. 774–76; J. (1988). "Comparing the Use and Validity of Opinions Versus Behavioural Descriptions in the Employment Interview." Unpublished manuscript, University of Calgary; G.P. Latham and B.J. Finnegam. (1987). "The Practicality of the Situational Interview." Paper presented at the Academy of Management meeting, New Orleans.

66. Michael Harris. (1989). "Reconsidering the Employment Interview: A Review of Recent Literature and Suggestions for Future Research." *Personnel Psychology*, 42, pp. 691–726.

67. M.A. McDaniel, D.L. Whetzel, F.L. Schmidt, and S.D. Maurer. (1994). "The Validity of Employment Interviews: A Comprehensive Review and Meta Analysis." *Journal of Applied Psychology*, 79, pp. 599–616.

68. Ibid.

69. Tom Janz. (1982). "Initial Comparisons of Patterned Behaviour Description Interviews versus Unstructured Interviews." *Journal of Applied Psychology*, 67, pp. 577–580. See also Tom Janz, Lowell Hellervik, and David C. Gilmore. (1986). *Behavioural Description Interviewing.* Boston: Allyn & Bacon.

70. Tom Janz. (1982). "Initial Comparisons of Patterned Behaviour Description Interviews versus Unstructured Interviews." *Journal of Applied Psychology*, 67, pp. 577–580. See also Tom Janz, Lowell Hellervik, and David C. Gilmore. (1986). *Behavioural Description Interviewing*. Boston: Allyn & Bacon

71. M.A. McDaniel, D.L. Whetzel, F.L. Schmidt, and S.D. Maurer. (1994), op. cit. See also A.I. Huffcutt and W. Arthur, Jr. (1994). "Hunter and Hunter Revisited: Interview Validity for Entry Level Jobs." *Journal of Applied Psychology*, 22, pp. 184–190.

72. Michael A. Campion, James E. Campion, and Peter J. Hudson. (1994). "Structured Interviewing: A Note on the Incremental Validity and Alternate Question Types." *Journal of Applied Psychology*, 79, pp. 998–1102.

73. M.A. Campion, E.D. Pursell, and B.K. Brown. (1988). "Structured Interviewing: Raising the Psychometric Properties of the Employment Interview." *Personnel Psychology*, 41, pp. 25–42; M.M. Harris. (1989). "Reconsidering the Employment Interview: A Review of Recent Literature and Suggestions for Future Research." *Personnel Psychology*, 42, pp. 691–726.

74. Robert D. Gatewood and Hubert S. Field. (2001). *Human Resource Selection*, 5th edition, Mason, OH: South Western/Thompson Learning, p. 544.

75. Sean Way and James Thacker. (1999, Oct-Nov.). "Selection Practices: Where are Canadian Organizations?" *HR Professional*, pp. 33–37.

76. Todd Humber. (2005, May 23). "Recruiting Isn't Getting any Easier." Report on Recruitment & Staffing Supplement to *Canadian HR Reporter*, p. R2.

77. Linda Thornburg. (1998, February). "Computer Assisted Interviewing Shortens Hiring Cycle." *HR Magazine*, pp. 1–5.

78. F.L. Schmidt and M. Rader. (1999). "Exploring the Boundary Conditions for Interview Validity: Meta-Analytic Validity Findings for a New Interview Type." *Personnel Psychology*, 52, pp. 445–464.

79. H.F. Schwind, H. Das, and T.F. Wagar. (2005). *Canadian Human Resource Management: A Strategic Approach*, 7th edition. Toronto: McGraw-Hill Ryerson, pp. 284–288.

80. Robert D. Gatewood and Hubert S. Feild. (2001). *Human Resource Selection*, 5th edition. Mason, OH: South Western/Thompson Learning, p. 550.

81. Robert D. Gatewood and Hubert S. Feild. (2001), pp. 560–1.

82. Wayne Cascio. (1998). *Applied Psychology in Human Resource Management*, 5th edition. Upper Saddle River, NJ: Prentice-Hall, p. 199.

83. Stephen Jackson. (1997, June 16). "Interviewers Need to Be Taught, Not Told, How to Hire the Best." *Canadian HR Reporter*, p. 8.

84. D.H. Tucker and P.M. Rowe. (1977). "Consulting the Application Form Prior to the Interview: An Essential Step in the Selection Process." *Journal of Applied Psychology*, 62.

85. Tim Collins, as quoted by Ann Macaulay. (2005, June 6). "Don't Let Processes Get in the Way of a Good Hire, and Other Lessons." *Canadian HR Reporter*.

86. Michael H. Frisch. (1981). *Coaching and Counselling Handbook*. New York: Resource Dynamics.

87. Lesley Young. (1999, Jan. 25). "Reference Checking Skills Sorely Lacking." *Canadian HR Reporter*, p. 1.

88. Pamela Babcock. (2003, October). "Spotting Lies." *HR Magazine*, 48, 10, p. 46.

89. Hari Das and Mallika Das. (1988). "But He Had Excellent References: Refining the Reference Letter." *The Human Resource*, pp. 15–16.

90. Todd Humber. (2005, May 23). "Recruiting Isn't Getting any Easier." Report on Recruitment & Staffing Supplement to *Canadian HR Reporter*, p. R2.

91. Bob Smith. (1993, September). "The Evolution of Pinkerton." *Management Review*, 82, p. 56.

92. Stephen Jackson. (1997, April 21). "Objective Descriptions, Not Opinions, Should Be Aim of Reference Checks." *Canadian HR Reporter*, p. 10.

93. Statistics quoted by Vincent Tsang. (2005, May 23). "No More Excuses." Report on Recruitment and Staffing, Supplement to *Canadian HR Reporter*, p. R5.

94. Vincent Tsang. (2005), p. R5, R7.

Chapter 9

1. Scott L. Martin and Nambury S. Raju. (1992). "Determining Cutoff Scores that Optimize Utility: A Recognition of Recruiting Costs." *Journal of Applied Psychology*, 77, 1, p. 15.

2. Jack Sawyer. (1966). "Measurement and Prediction: Clinical and Statistical." *Psychological Bulletin*, 66, pp. 178–200. Also see Bernard M. Bass and Gerald V. Barrett. (1981). *People, Work and Organizations*, 2nd edition. Boston: Allyn & Bacon, p. 392.

3. Jack Sawyer. (1966). "Measurement and Prediction: Clinical and Statistical." *Psychological Bulletin*, 66, pp. 178–200.

4. Jack Sawyer. (1966). "Measurement and Prediction: Clinical and Statistical." *Psychological Bulletin*, 66, pp. 178–200; Paul Meehl. (1986). "Causes and Effects of My Disturbing Little Book." *Journal of Personality Assessment*, 50, pp. 370–375; Benjamin Kleinmutz. (1990). "Why We Still Use our Heads Instead of Formulas: Toward an Integrative Approach." *Psychological Bulletin*, 107, pp. 296–310.

5. H. A. Simon. (1947). *Administrative Behavior: A Study of Decision Making Processes in Administrative Organizations*. New York: MacMillan; H.A. Simon. (1955). "A Behavioral Model of Rational Choice." *Quarterly Journal of Economics*, 64, pp. 99–110; H.A. Simon. (1956). "Rational Choice and the Structure of the Environment." *Psychological Review*, 63, pp. 129–38.

6. Bernard M. Bass and Gerald V. Barrett. (1981). *People, Work and Organizations*, 2nd edition. Boston: Allyn & Bacon, pp. 397–398.

7. Victor Catano, Steven Cronshaw, Willi Wiesner, Rick Hackett, and Laura Methot. (2001). *Recruitment and Selection in Canada*, 2nd edition. Toronto: Nelson/Thomson Learning, p. 438.

8. Bernard M. Bass and Gerald V. Barrett. (1981). *People, Work and Organizations*, 2nd edition. Boston: Allyn & Bacon, pp. 397–398.

9. Wayne F. Cascio. (1991). *Applied Psychology in Personnel Management*, 4th edition. Englewood Cliffs, NJ: Prentice Hall, pp. 285–287; Milton L. Blum and James C. Naylor. (1969). *Industrial Psychology: Its Theoretical and Social Foundations*. New York: Harper & Row, pp. 67–70.

10. Milton L. Blum and James C. Naylor. (1969). *Industrial Psychology: Its Theoretical and Social Foundations*. New York: Harper & Row, pp. 67–70.

11. Cynthia D. Fisher, Lyle F. Schoenfeldt, and James B. Shaw. (1990). *Human Resource Management*. Boston: Houghton Mifflin, p. 231.

12. Neal Schmitt and Richard Klimosky. (1991). *Research Methods in Human Resource Management*. Cincinnati: South Western, p. 302.

13. R. R. Reilly and W.R. Manese. (1979). "The Validation of a Minicourse for Telephone Company Switching Technicians." *Personnel Psychology, 32*, pp. 83–90.

14. Milton L. Blum and James C. Naylor. (1969). *Industrial Psychology: Its Theoretical and Social Foundations*. New York: Harper & Row, pp. 67–70.

15. For example, see, J.C. Nunnally. (1978). *Psychometric Theory*, 2nd edition. New York: McGraw-Hill, pp. 435–440; Milton L. Blum and James C. Naylor. (1969). *Industrial Psychology: Its Theoretical and Social Foundations*. New York: Harper & Row, pp. 67–70.

16. For example, see J.C. Nunnally. (1978). *Psychometric Theory*, 2nd edition. New York: McGraw-Hill, pp. 438–440

17. Robert L. Thorndike. (1949). *Personnel Selection: Test and Measurement Techniques*. New York: Wiley.

18. William H. Angoff. (1971). "Scales, Norms and Equivalent Scores." In Robert L. Thorndike (ed.). *Educational Measurement*. Washington, DC: American Council on Education, pp. 508–600.

19. Robert Gatewood and Hubert Field. (2001). *Human Resource Selection*, 5th edition. Toronto: South Western/Thomson Learning, p. 250

20. Section 106 of the 1991 Civil Rights Act prohibits hiring on the basis of race, among other things.

21. For instance, see Paul R. Sackett and Steffanie L. Wilk. (1994). "Within-Group Norming and Other Forms of Score Adjustment in Preemployment Testing." *American Psychologist, 49*, p. 938.

22. Frank L. Schmidt and John E. Hunter. (1980). "The Future of Criterion-Related Validity." *Personnel Psychology, 33*, pp. 41–60.

23. Frank L. Schmidt and John E. Hunter. (1998). "The Validity and Utility of Selection Methods in Personnel Psychology: Practical and Theoretical Implications of 85 years of Research Findings." *Psychological Bulletin, 124*, pp. 262–275.

24. Robert Gatewood and Hubert Feild. (2001). *Human Resource Selection*, 5th edition. Toronto: South Western/Thomson Learning, p. 262.

25. Robert M. Guion. (1965). *Personnel Testing*. New York: McGraw Hill, p. 494.

26. Robert M. Guion. (1965), p. 494.

27. Stephen Jackson. (1997, March 24). "Give Job Applicants the Whole Truth." *Canadian HR Reporter*, p. 9.

28. Paula Popovich and John P. Wanous. (1982, October). "The Realistic Job Preview as a Persuasive Communication." *Academy of Management Review*, p. 571.

29. H.F. Schwind, H. Das, and T. Wagner. (2005). *Canadian Human Resource Management: A Strategic Approach*, 7th edition. Toronto: McGraw-Hill Ryerson, p. 272.

30. "Employers Understand Value of Employees." (2005, Jan. 31). Report on Employment Law, supplement to *Canadian HR Reporter*, p. R3.

31. "Employers Understand Value of Employees." (2005, Jan.31), p. R3.

32. David Whitten. (2005, June 20). "Steering Clear of Contract Landmines." *Canadian HR Reporter*, pp. 5–6.

33. "Employers Understand Value of Employees." (2005, Jan. 31), p. R3.

34. Colin Gibson, a partner in Harris and Company, a Vancouver law firm, as quoted by Todd Humber. (2005, June 20). "Protecting the Most Valuable Asset." *Canadian HR Reporter*, p. 7.

Chapter 10

1. Jefferey Pfeffer. (1998). *Human Equation*. Boston: Harvard Business School Press, p. xviii–xix.

2. Sergio Karas (2005, Jan. 31). "Getting Foreign Workers into Canada." Report on Employment Law, supplement to *Canadian HR Reporter*, p. R10.

3. Sergio Karas. (2005, Jan. 31), p. R10.

4. Uyen Vu. (2005, April 25). "Ottawa Cops Pursuing Diversity." *Canadian HR Reporter*, p. 1, 5.

5. Bill Pomfret. (1999, Jan. 25). "Sound Employee Orientation Program Boosts Productivity and Safety." *Canadian HR Reporter*, p. 17.

6. Edward Lowe. (2002, July). "Understanding the Cost of Employee Turnover." *Perspectives*. Retrieved from **http://peerspectives.org**.

7. "Orientation: A Healthy Start to Training." (2002, Nov. 18). *Canadian HR Reporter*, p. G8.

8. Steven L. McShane and Trudy Baal. (1984, December). *Employee Socialization Practices on Canada's West Coast: A Management Report*. Burnaby, BC: Faculty of Business Administration, Simon Fraser University.

9. Howard J. Klein and Natasha A. Weaver. (2000, Spring). "The Effectiveness of an Organizational-Level Orientation Training Program in the Socialization of New Hires." *Personnel Psychology, 53*, 1, pp. 44–62.

10. Donna Van Alstine. (2005, Sept. 12). "Looking for Fit or Fit to Lead?" *Canadian HR Reporter*, p. 18.

11. Donna Van Alstine. (2005, Sept. 12), p. 18.

12. John Sullivan. (2001, Aug. 13). "A Manager's Guide to Orientation." Retrieved from **http://www.erexchange.com**.

13. Kenneth N. Wexley and Gary P. Latham. (1991). *Developing and Training Human Resources in Organizations*, 2nd edition. New York: HarperCollins.

14. Pescuric and W.C. Byham. (1996, July). "The New Look of Behavior Modeling." *Training & Development*, pp. 24–30; H.P. Sims and C.C. Manz. (1982, January). "Modeling Influences on Employee Behavior." *Personnel Journal*, pp. 58–65.

15. T.G. Cummings and C.G. Worley. (1993). *Organization Development and Change*, 5th edition. Minneapolis/St. Paul: West Publishing, pp. 198–201.

16. T.G. Cummings and C.G. Worley. (1993). *Organization Development and Change*, p. 168.

17. Suzan Butyn. (2003, Jan. 27). "Mentoring Your Way to Improved Retention." *Canadian HR Reporter*, pp. 13–15.

18. See Dan MacLeod and Eric Kennedy. (1993). *Job Rotation System*. Retrieved from **http://www.danmacleod.com/Articles/job.htm**.

19. Nikola Menalo. (2000, July 28). "The 360-Degree of Career Development." *ComputerWorld Canada*, p. 37.

20. Peter M. Senge. (1990). *The Fifth Discipline: The Art and Practices of the Learning Organization*. New York: Doubleday/Currency.

21. Interview with Peter Senge, by Patricia A. Galagan. (1991, October). *Training and Development Journal*, pp. 37–44.

22. Karl Weick and Frances Westley. (1996). "Organizational Learning: Affirming an Oxymoron." In Stewart Clegg, Cynthia Hardy, and Walter Nord (eds.). *Handbook of Organization Studies*. London: Sage, p. 440.

23. Michael McGill and John Slocum. (1994). *The Smarter Organization*. New York: John Wiley, p. 159.

24. L. Rhodes and P. Amend. (1986, August). "The Turnaround." *Inc*, pp. 42–48.

25. John Case. (1992, March) "The Change Masters." *Inc*, pp. 58–70.

26. Jack Stack. (1992, June). "The Great Game of Business." *Inc*, pp. 53–66.

27. John Case. (1992, March). "The Change Masters." *Inc*, pp. 58–70; E. Pearson. (1987, July-Aug.). "Muscle-Build the Organization." *Harvard Business Review*, pp. 49–55.

28. A.E. Pearson. (1987). "Muscle-Build the Organization." *Harvard Business Review* July–August, pp. 49–55.

29. Jamie Harrison. (1998, Jan. 26). "Molson Opens Learning Centre." *Canadian HR Reporter*, pp. 1–2. See also Norman L. Trainor. (1998, Jan. 26). "Defining the Learning Organization." *Canadian HR Reporter*, p. 9.

30. Gail Reinhart. (200, March 14). "Preparing for Global Expansion: A Primer." *Canadian HR Reporter*, p. 14.

31. Gail Reinhart. (2005, March 14), p. 14.

32. Uyen Vu. (2005, Sept. 26). "Doing Business in China has Everything to Do with People." *Canadian HR Reporter*, p. 5.

33. Paul Brocklyn. (1989, March). "Developing the International Executive." *Personnel*, p. 44.

34. Peter Blunt. (1990, June). "Recent Developments in Human Resource Management: The Good, the Bad and the Ugly." *International Journal of Human Resource Management*, pp. 45–59; Sheila Rothwell. (1993, Summer). "Leadership Development and International HRM." *Manager Update*, No. 4, pp. 20–32.

35. Linda Grobovksy. (1998, Nov. 16). "Relocating Employees in a Global Workforce." *Canadian HR Reporter*, pp. 16–17.

36. For example, see Gary Hogan and Jane Goodson. (1990, January). "The Key to Expatriate Success." *Training and Development Journal*, 44, 1, pp. 50–52; Raymond Stone. (1991). "Expatriate Selection and Failure." *Human Resource Planning*, 14, 1, pp. 9–18; Allan Bird and Roger Dunbar. (1991, Spring). "Getting the Job Done over There: Improving Expatriate Productivity." *National Productivity Review*, 10, 2, pp. 145–156.

37. Raymond Stone. (1991). "Expatriate Selection and Failure." *Human Resource Planning*, 14, 1, pp. 9–18; Rosalie Tung. (1981, Spring). "Selection and Training of Personnel for Overseas Assignments." *Columbia Journal of World Business*, 16, 1, pp. 68–78.

38. Edward Dunbar and Allan Katcher. (1990, September). "Preparing Managers for Foreign Assignments." *Training and Development Journal*, 44, 9, pp. 45–47; Paul Sullivan. (1991, September). "Training's Role in Global Business." *Executive Excellence*, No. 9, pp. 9–10.

39. See Paul Brocklyn (1989, March). "Developing the International Executive." *Personnel*, p. 46. See also Nancy Napier and Richard Peterson. (1991, March). "Expatriate Re-Entry: What do Repatriates Have to Say?" *Human Resource Planning*, pp. 19–28.

40. Material in this section is adapted from Hari Das. (2003). *Performance Management*. Toronto: Pearson Education, pp. 262–265.

41. For example, see H.F. Schwind, H. Das, and T. Wagar. (2002). *Canadian Human Resource Management*. Toronto: McGraw-Hill Ryerson Limited, pp. 516–519; Rights Management Consultants (1999). *Best Practices: Termination*. Scarborough, ON: Carswell, p. 4–4.

42. *Canadian Employment Law Today*. (1991, June 26). Toronto: MPL Communications Inc., pp. 685–86; Howard Levitt. (1992). *The Law of Dismissal in Canada*, 2nd edition. Aurora, ON: Canada Law Book.

43. Ontario Court of Appeal decision on January 9, 1999; 168 D.L.R. (4th) 270.

44. Todd Humber. (2005, May 23). "Recruiting Isn't Getting any Easier." Report on Recruitment and Staffing, supplement to *Canadian HR Reporter*, p. R2.

45. Emma Harrington. (2004, Nov. 22). "What to Pitch to Employees." *Canadian HR Reporter*, p. 7.

46. *Lumber & Sawmill Workers Union, Local 2537 and KVP Co.* (1965). 16 L.A.C., 73, Ontario-Robinson, p. 85.

47. *Macmillan Bloedel Ltd and C.E.P. Local 76.* (1997). 65 L.A.C., 4th 240 (B.C.).

Chapter 11

1. Larry Morden. (1998). "Measuring Human Resources Effectiveness." In Margaret Butteriss (ed.). *Re-inventing HR*. Toronto: John Wiley & Sons, p. 95.

2. Tom Coens and Mary Jenkins. (2000). *Abolishing Performance Appraisals*. San Francisco: Berrett-Koehler Publishers, p. 49.

3. D. A. Whetten. (1980). "Sources, Responses and Effects of Organizational Decline." In J.R.Kimberly, R.H.Miles, et al. (eds.). *The Organizational Life Cycle*. San Francisco: Jossey Bass, p. 355.

4. Fred Luthans and Terry L. Maris. (1979, October). "Evaluating Personnel Programs through the Reversal Technique." *Personnel Journal*, pp. 692–97.

5. George Odiorne. (1972). "Evaluating the Personnel Program." In Joseph Famularo (ed.). *Handbook of Modern Personnel Administration*. New York: McGraw-Hill. See also Walter Mahler. (1979). "Auditing PAIR" in Dale Yoder and Herbert Hengman (eds.). *ASPA Handbook of Personnel and Industrial Relations*. Washington DC: The Bureau of National Affairs, pp. 2–91 to 2–108; and P. Vytenis and P. Kuraitis (1981, November). "The Personnel Audit." *Personnel Administrator*, pp. 29–34.

6. George Odiorne. (1972). pp. 13–39.

7. "Gauging HR's Contribution." (2005, May 23). *Canadian HR Reporter*, p. 5.

8. "Gauging HR's Contribution." (2005, May 23), p. 5.

9. Nora Spinks. (1997, March 24). "The Absence of Absence in the Changing Workplace." *Canadian HR Reporter*, pp. 19–20.

10. For example, see Russ Kisby. (1997, Oct. 20). "The ROI of Healthy Workplaces." *Canadian HR Reporter*, p. 31.

11. Brian Orr. (1997, April 21). "The Challenge of Benchmarking HR Performance." *Canadian HR Reporter*, p. 6.

12. For example, see Ian Cunningham and Philip James. (2000). "Absence and Return to Work: Towards a Research Agenda." *Personnel Review*, 29, 1, pp. 33–47.

13. For example, see Linda Alker and David McHugh. (2000). "Human Resource Maintenance." *Journal of Managerial Psychology*, 15, 4, pp. 303–323.

INDEX